Bangladesh

the Bradt Travel Guide

Mikey Leung   Belinda Meggitt

www.bradtguides.com

Bradt Travel Guides Ltd, UK
The Globe Pequot Press Inc, USA

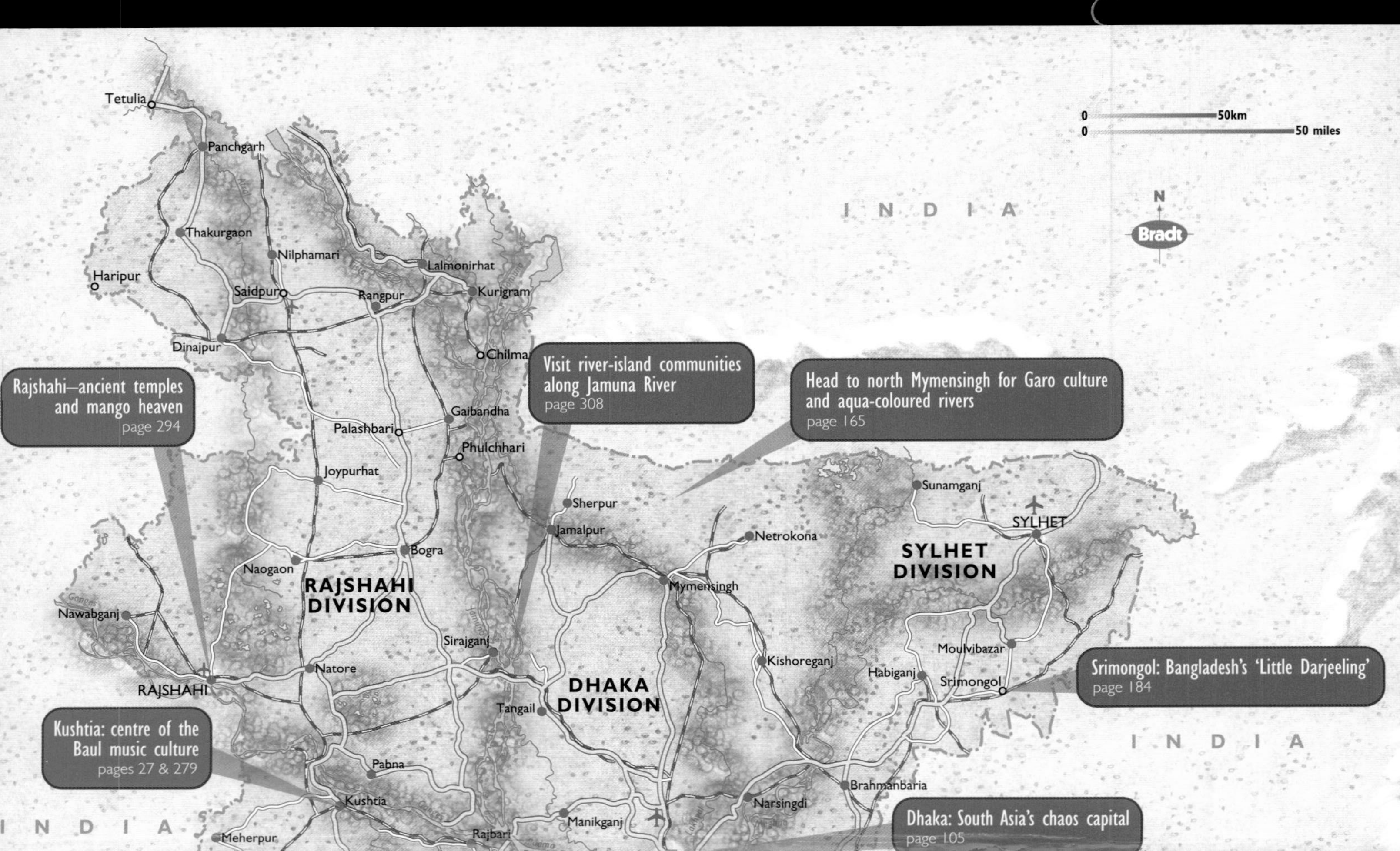

INDIA
N
Bradt
0 50km
0 50 miles
Tetulia
Panchgarh
Haripur
Thakurgaon
Nilphamari
Saidpur
Rangpur
Lalmonirhat
Kurigram
Dinajpur
Chilma
Gaibandha
Palashbari
Phulchhari
Joypurhat
Bogra
Naogaon
RAJSHAHI DIVISION
Nawabganj
RAJSHAHI
Natore
Sirajganj
Pabna
Kushtia
Meherpur
Rajbari
Manikganj
Tangail
DHAKA DIVISION
Sherpur
Jamalpur
Mymensingh
Netrokona
Kishoreganj
Narsingdi
Brahmanbaria
Sunamganj
SYLHET
SYLHET DIVISION
Moulvibazar
Habiganj
Srimongol
Rajshahi–ancient temples and mango heaven
page 294
Visit river-island communities along Jamuna River
page 308
Head to north Mymensingh for Garo culture and aqua-coloured rivers
page 165
Srimongol: Bangladesh's 'Little Darjeeling'
page 184
Kushtia: centre of the Baul music culture
pages 27 & 279
Dhaka: South Asia's chaos capital
page 105

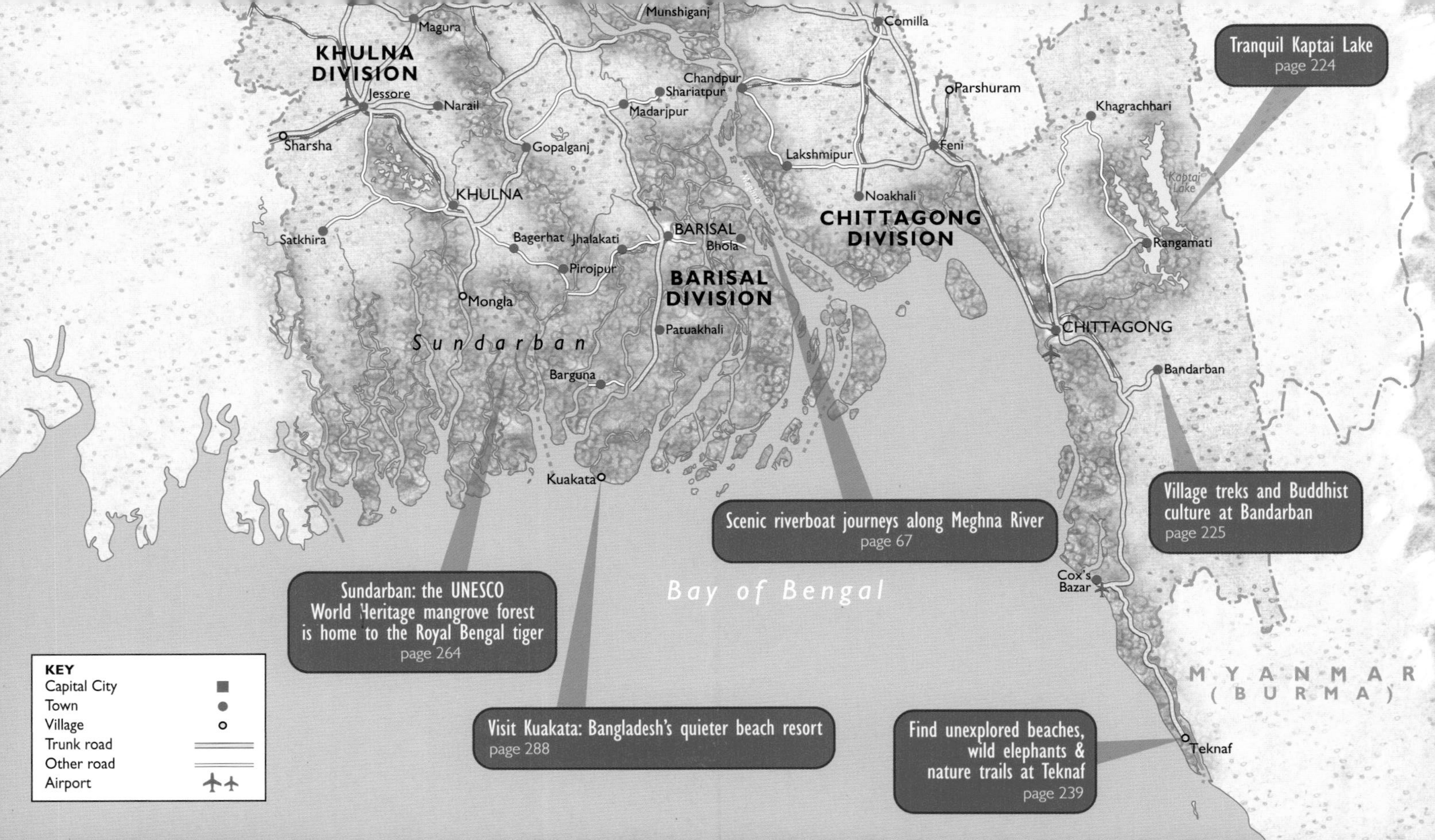

Tranquil Kaptai Lake
page 224
Village treks and Buddhist culture at Bandarban
page 225
Scenic riverboat journeys along Meghna River
page 67
Sundarban: the UNESCO World Heritage mangrove forest is home to the Royal Bengal tiger
page 264
Visit Kuakata: Bangladesh's quieter beach resort
page 288
Find unexplored beaches, wild elephants & nature trails at Teknaf
page 239
KHULNA DIVISION
BARISAL DIVISION
CHITTAGONG DIVISION
MYANMAR (BURMA)
Bay of Bengal
Sundarban
Munshiganj
Magura
Comilla
Jessore
Narail
Sharsha
Chandpur
Shariatpur
Madarjpur
Parshuram
Khagrachhari
Gopalganj
Feni
Lakshmipur
Kaptai Lake
KHULNA
Noakhali
Satkhira
Bagerhat
Jhalakati
BARISAL
Bhola
Rangamati
Pirojpur
Mongla
Patuakhali
CHITTAGONG
Bandarban
Barguna
Meghna
Kuakata
Cox's Bazar
Teknaf
KEY
Capital City
Town
Village
Trunk road
Other road
Airport

Bangladesh Don't miss...

Sundarban The UNESCO World Heritage mangrove forest is home to the Royal Bengal tiger

(TA/FLPA) page 264

Majestic rivers Explore the heart of the world's second-largest river delta

(BM) page 3

Srimongol
Bangladesh's 'Little Darjeeling' is carpeted with tea plantations and perfect for cycle journeys (BM) page 184

Chittagong Hill Tracts
Bangladesh's least-explored region is home to a wide variety of ethnic groups (BM) page 216

People
Fantastic photo opportunities of people everywhere in the country (BM) page 18

left Rickshaw rush hour, Dhaka (BM) pages 26–7

below Fancy a traditional razor-blade shave? Pop into one of Dhaka's side-street barbers (BM)

bottom Quench your thirst in a local tea stall, Dhaka (BM)

right **Hotch-potch homes: city life is often cramped and busy, especially in Old Dhaka's renowned Shakhari Bazaar** (BM) pages 142–3

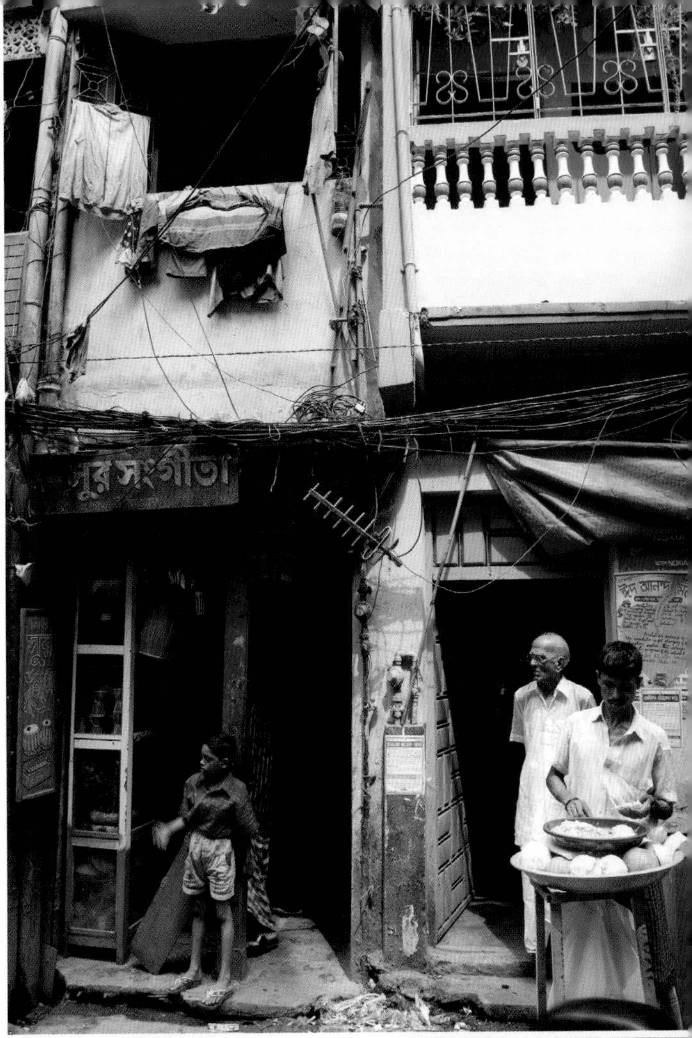

below **Local boys make the most of the monsoon season** (ML) page 4

above **Street beggar** (BM) page 65

top left **Hindu worshipper. He holds a *lingam*, the symbol of worship to the Hindu God Shiva** (BM) page 22

left **Gypsy painting traditional designs on to her face** (BM)

below **Weddings are always an elaborate affair: a Hindu bride waits for her husband-to-be, Chittagong** (BM) page 199

AUTHORS

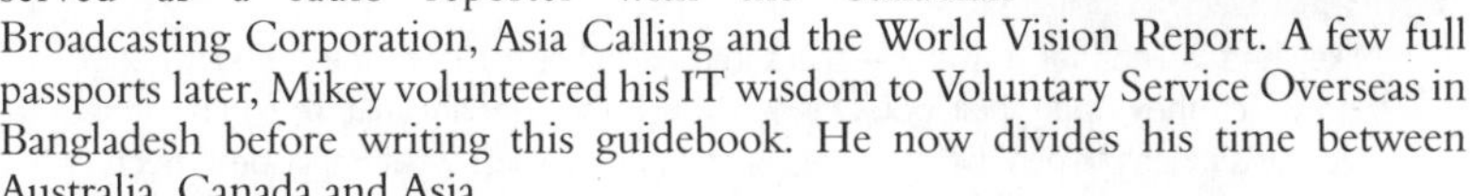

Mikey Leung has enjoyed a careening career track that barely runs on the rails. Since completing degrees in anthropology and ecology, he's worked in too many fields to name, although tour leader, freelance journalist and information technology specialist top the list. A former tour leader with Intrepid Travel, he spent 2.5 years leading trips throughout Asia and pursuing rather unhealthy addictions to spicy food and foreign languages (Chinese, Thai and now Bengali). After turning to the pen, he wrote for various in-flight and business magazines including *CNN Traveller*, and served as a radio reporter with the Canadian Broadcasting Corporation, Asia Calling and the World Vision Report. A few full passports later, Mikey volunteered his IT wisdom to Voluntary Service Overseas in Bangladesh before writing this guidebook. He now divides his time between Australia, Canada and Asia.

Belinda Meggitt is an Australian physiotherapist and nutritionist who originally came to Bangladesh as an Australian Youth Ambassador for Development. While training local therapists in the art of easing disabilities, she discovered an extraordinary passion for photographing Bangladesh and the realities its people face. After spending a year volunteering in a remote village near Chittagong, Belinda turned her focus on travel and helped author this guide. She's now exploring Australia's Top End and works in the field of indigenous health.

AUTHORS' STORY

While some people question the need for a guide in a country with so few foreign tourists, this simple fact is what makes the need for a new guide so great. This is doubly true for Bangladesh, whose world reputation takes regular beatings in the foreign press when it makes the headlines for catastrophe. To all those who doubt, we now ask you to seek the reality behind the veil, to notice the colour hidden in the corners, and to search the beauty hidden inside this friendly region of south Asia whose people may be short on space and material wealth, but who possess hearts of infinite kindness.

To be frank, researching this guide was a right pain in the backside. Without a reliable central information source for anything, almost everything needed to be cross-referenced and double-checked. Bangladesh and 'information society' are rarely written in the same sentence. This is compounded by the fact that things change so quickly in the country, especially the main cities. But by looking deeper and staying for as long as you possibly can (as a volunteer, aid worker, expatriate or businessperson), a real picture emerges of a vibrant and diverse country whose secrets are waiting to be discovered below the surface. We hope this guide helps you in that search.

PUBLISHER'S FOREWORD

Adrian Phillips

The first Bradt travel guide was written in 1974 by George and Hilary Bradt on a river barge floating down a tributary of the Amazon. In the 1980s and '90s the focus shifted away from hiking to broader-based guides covering new destinations – usually the first to be published about these places. In the 21st century Bradt continues to publish such ground-breaking guides, as well as others to established holiday destinations, incorporating in-depth information on culture and natural history alongside the nuts and bolts of where to stay and what to see.

Bradt authors support responsible travel, and provide advice not only on minimum impact but also on how to give something back through local charities. In this way a true synergy is achieved between the traveller and local communities.

* * *

Mikey and Belinda tell it as it is – that's immediately clear from the Authors' Story with which they open their book, and in which they declare that 'researching this guide was a right pain in the backside'. Such honesty is just what Bangladesh needs. Mikey and Belinda set out to look beyond the 'veil' – the images of flooding and poverty that invariably attach themselves to this country – and search out the beauty and kindness that also typify Bangladesh. We hope they help to change the world's perception, and encourage travellers to explore a colourful and diverse nation.

First edition published September 2009. Reprinted September 2010.

Bradt Travel Guides Ltd, 23 High Street, Chalfont St Peter, Bucks SL9 9QE, England
www.bradtguides.com

Published in the USA by The Globe Pequot Press Inc, PO Box 480, Guilford, Connecticut 06437-0480

Editorial Project Manager: Emma Thomson

British Library Cataloguing in Publication Data

A catalogue record for this book is available from the British Library

ISBN-13: 978 1 84162 293 4

Photographs Belinda Meggitt (BM), Mikey Leung (ML), Shehzad Noorani/Still Pictures (SN/SP), Theo Allofs/FLPA (TA/FLPA), Elisabeth Fahrni Mansur & Rubaiyat Mansur Mowgli, Bangladesh Cetacean Diversity Project/WCS (E&RMansur/BCDP).
Front cover Young man in a rickshaw in the rain, Jessore (SN/SP)
Back cover Bengal tiger (TA/FLPA), Rickshaw driver, Dhaka (BM)
Title page Parbatipur girl, CHT (BM), Rice paddies, CHT (BM), Painted truck (BM)
Maps Dave Priestley

Typeset from the authors' disk by Wakewing, High Wycombe
Production managed by Jellyfish Print Solutions and manufactured in India

Acknowledgements

A project like this is made up on the strength of those who have supported it. Below are just a few of the notables. We'd like to thank Mahmud and Sujan at MAP Photography for helping us with every random photography question conceivable. Elisabeth Fahrni Mansur and Hasan Mansur for trip logistics, text cross-checking and for the endless offers of support. Lindy Hogan and Asaduzzaman Kanan for checking out and proofing.

Midori Courtice for her box text contribution. Taimur Islam and Homaira Zaman of the Urban Study Group for their continuous efforts to preserve Old Dhaka's history and buildings. Ashley Wheaton for moral and proofing support. Kristin Boekhoff for being a friend to us both. Maya and Jewel at Green House Bed and Breakfast for welcoming us like family. Rick Symington for encouraging that ridiculous motorbike journey from Nepal to Dhaka and making it possible by taking some of our stuff with him. The crew at Voluntary Service Overseas (VSO) deserve thanks for starting off Mikey's Bangladesh adventures on the right foot, and the crew at the AYAD Programme for helping out Bel, especially Badrul. Chris Greenwood and Adam Barlow of the Sundarban Tiger Project for their info. Kate Meehan and Rebecca Knowles of the Asian University for Women for their info and for their amazing mission. Parker Mah, Stine Bang and James Elms for various text contributions and feedback. Didar and crew at Bangladesh Ecotours for showing us another wonderful side of the Chittagong Hill Tracts, Hasan Shahid and Hasan Zahid at Petro Aviation for their hospitality. Alexandra Tyers for proofreading assistance. Sajid Chowdhury for crowd control at various points. Andrew Morris for being so inspiring about Bangladesh through his writings. Steve Micetic for the brotherly and crocodile support. Isaac Sairs for taking two-wheeled travel to another level and sharing that. Razu of Classic Tours for random requests and help. Kamran Nazim Chowdhury of Nazimgarh Resort for hosting our visit and showing us his turf. Lakshmikanta Singh of Ethnic Community Development Organisation for doing what he does and sharing his work. Denis and Carmella Rayen of Cherrapunjee Holiday Resort for being such gracious hosts. Tuli Dewan and Moung Thowai Ching of Green Hill for helping us get around Rangamati with ease. Wilm van Bekkum and Sarah Barnett for long nights of guitar, drinks and power outages. The entire gang at VSO Bangladesh, but especially our friends Mahtabul Hakim, Marufa Sultana and Mohammed Saifullah. Monica Gray, Tania Cass, Maeve Hall, Lucinda Garrido, Mike Mangano for various hits of friendship along the journey. Charlie in Bandarban for tolerating so much questioning about the hill tracts situation. Jessica Ayers for her climate change expertise. Mark and Cassie Dummett for being colleagues and fans. Heidi Eisenhauer for information and spiritual support. David Nazmul Azam of Rupantar Ecotourism for being a steady foundation of ecotourism in Sundarban. Farhad and Farida Akhter of UBINIG. Ric Goodman, Kate Conroy, David Panetta and Lucy Cooper of the Char Livelihoods Programme. Jason Cons for shining a light into Bangladesh's most hidden corners in the enclaves. Siddiqua Khanam for her red tape scissors. Yousuf for the amazing views from his cockpit. Fred, Cate and Zachary for being like friends and family. Tarmie for incredible and unstoppable Chittagong hospitality – thank you for being such a great friend to us both. Lysanna for insider info on the CHT. No doubt we have missed countless others, but to all of you who pitched in with chairs, beds or amazing meals – thank you. To the editorial team at Bradt Travel Guides, especially Emma Thomson, Helen Calderon, David Priestley and Deborah Gerrard for their patient expertise in seeing this guide through all its birthing pains. And finally, to all the millions of Bangladeshis who pointed us in the right (and sometimes wrong) direction during the research path.

DEDICATION

Mikey dedicates this book to his parents who have finally accepted his addiction to travel.

Belinda dedicates the book to her family for supporting her decision to live in Bangladesh, and especially to Sal, who risked insanity to join her on parts of the journey.

FEEDBACK REQUEST

Please help us to keep this book up to date and make the next edition even better by sending comments and suggestions to: Bangladesh updates, Bradt Travel Guides, 23 High Street, Chalfont St Peter, Bucks SL9 9QE or send us an email at info@bradtguides.com. Alternatively, you can check for updates at www.bangladeshtraveller.com and contact the authors by email directly at joybangla.info@gmail.com.

Contents

LIST OF MAPS

Introduction

If Bangladesh were a person, she would be a youthful teenager, full of life and energy but with a decidedly emotional temperament to which wisdom or logic could not be easily applied. You would regard her as full of potential and while she seems eager to learn, a scarcity of sensible role models and life opportunities has limited her capacities, thus you couldn't yet be sure who she would be in her adult future. You would watch her struggle vigorously in all that she did, and despite the fact you might conclude that the cards are stacked against her, you could never fault her spirit or her resilience, not for a second.

To witness this resilience amongst Bangladeshi people is the single most striking and memorable feature of a visit to the country. Against a long list of challenges – poverty, political pandering, natural calamities and now climate change – millions of Bangladeshis have but one possession and almost nothing else: the strength of their spirit and their willingness to carry on. Thankfully, unlike the country's early days of uncertainty, there are more and more encouraging signs of maturity nowadays, despite distinct growing pains. Of the eight United Nations-defined Millennium Development Goals (poverty elimination targets), Bangladesh is widely acknowledged to be 'on track' for meeting half of them, although a burgeoning population and a rather incomprehensible political system blunts these extraordinary achievements.

Demographic and political acne aside, travellers will discover Bangladesh's true beauty lies well outside its crowded and polluted cities. In a country beset by water, river journeys offer the most memorable way to see and experience a place that is more than 50% underwater during the rainy season. Interestingly, these are also the same areas that may be lost to the sea in a climate change scenario, with some companies being bold enough to offer 'global warming tours', and with all the current media attention these might very well become popular one day.

Visitors will also find a rather surprising amount of cultural diversity behind Bangladesh's persona, as Bengal has long been a meeting place of Arab traders, Arakanese raiders, Mughal masters and dozens of ethnically unique indigenous groups, most of whom share more similarities with southeast Asia than India. The Chittagong Hill Tracts, with its geographical and ethnic wealth, is the focal point of this diversity but remains the country's best-kept secret. While Islam permeates the nation's affairs, attitudes towards the religion are in fact much more liberal. Significant populations of Hindus, Buddhists and Christians reside within Bangladesh's borders. One of the country's founding cornerstones lay in having a political identity that remained separate from a religious one.

The 'sights' in Bangladesh don't compare to those of its neighbours, but that's not really what a journey to the country's many temples, mosques and monasteries is all about. Compared to the 'been there, done that' travelling mentality of many global nomads, it is both refreshing and compelling to know that one can still have honest and real experiences in a country that remains so unexplored and unknown to foreign tourism. While this could be considered both a blessing (Bangladesh's utterly sincere generosity is often surprising to India-hardened travellers) and a curse (luxuries are few and far between), travellers will certainly leave knowing that if they've survived in Bangladesh, there are few other places where they'd feel out of their depth. Furthermore, those who decide to engage with Bangladesh on a deeper level (ie: as volunteers, development workers or business people) will often be rewarded with even greater opportunities to see the story behind the horrible headlines Bangladesh often produces.

Last but not least, no introduction would be complete without reference to Bangladeshi hospitality, which is best experienced in the countryside or in the homes of local friends. Each Bangladeshi considers it both a pleasure and a duty to be of service to a foreign guest, and will often offer visitors far more than they can sometimes themselves afford, and with nearly unstoppable enthusiasm. This hospitality is so generous that most notions of Western kindness do seem paltry in comparison. The best thing you can do is accept such hospitality graciously and repay the favour in whatever way you feel capable and in whatever timeframe you see fit; certainly, printing and sending photographs back to your hosts would be the absolute least you could do. But do be aware that some visitors, having been so impacted by the level of poverty and lack of opportunities, have decided to set up entire slum schools or countryside hospitals funded entirely on donations. Or write travel guidebooks.

Above all, it will be that resilient teenager spirit that leaves the longest lasting impression. It's in the eyes of the cyclone victims who smile in the midst of a relief operation; it's in the happiness of the street children who you discover are still children at heart despite enraging conditions; it's the survivor spirit living inside the widowed woman who attends NGO training to improve her lot and says that she can inspire other women to do the same. To meet this young and youthful spirit up close is to understand the nature of the human spirit.

Part One

GENERAL INFORMATION

BANGLADESH AT A GLANCE

Location East India, south Asia
Neighbouring countries India, Myanmar, Bhutan, Nepal
Size 143,998km^2
Population 155.99 million (2009 est)
Population density 1,045 per km^2
Climate Tropical: mild winter (October to March); hot, humid summer (March to June); humid, warm rainy monsoon (June to October)
Status Republic
Life expectancy 62 (male), 63 (female)
Capital Dhaka, 12.29 million (2008 est)
Other main towns Chittagong, Sylhet, Rajshahi, Khulna, Barisal, Jessore, Bogra, Rangpur
Economy Agriculture, garment manufacturing, shrimp farming
GDP US$208.3 billion (purchasing power parity)
Languages Bangla (official language); English widely spoken
Religion Muslim majority (90%); Hindu (9%); Buddhists, Christians
Currency Taka
Exchange rate US$1=Tk68.8; £1=Tk112.7; €1=Tk96.1 (June 2009)
International telephone code +880
Time GMT +6 all year round
Electrical voltage 220V; 50Hz frequency
Weights and measures Metric
National Animal Sundarban Tiger
National fish Hilsha
National fruit Jackfruit
Regular public holidays 21 February (International Mother Language Day); 26 March (Independence Day); 14 April (Bangla New Year); 1 May (Labour Day); 16 December (Victory Day; Bijoy Dibosh); 25 December (Christmas)
Public holidays with varying dates Late September 2009 (Eid-ul Fitr or end of Ramadan); late November 2009 (Eid-ul Adha); May (Buddha Purnima); September (Janmasthami; Hindu); October (Durga Puja; Hindu)
Government Structure Parliamentary republic
Country flag Red disc – located just left of centre – on bottle green background disc

1

Background Information

GEOGRAPHY

If you ever wanted to experience the living reality of the idiom 'when it rains, it pours', Bangladesh is the place to be. During the yearly south Asian monsoon, almost all the water collected by the Himalayas in Nepal, north/northeast India and Bhutan transits through Bangladesh on its journey to the Bay of Bengal, depositing life-giving minerals to the soil all along the Ganges Delta, the largest river delta in the world. It is here that the mountains literally crumble to the sea. This has resulted in Bangladesh's flatland alluvial topography, which is the defining characteristic of the country except in the hilly regions of the southeast and northeast. The mighty Ganges and Brahmaputra rivers are called the Padma and the Jamuna in Bangladesh, and both of these massive rivers join several other smaller tributaries to eventually become the Lower Meghna, forming the great Gangetic Delta. At its widest point near Bhola Island, the river stretches to a yawning 12km-wide breadth on its final leg towards the sea. Seen from a boat, the distinctions between land, river, ocean and sky become decidedly uncertain.

As the rivers have gradually shaped and reshaped this land, they have shaped the destinies of its people. It would be a mistake to picture the historic locations of Bangladesh's rivers according to current maps. For instance, the Brahmaputra used to flow east of Dhaka's present location before a major flood caused it to change course over a 30-year span during the mid-18th century. Simultaneously, the Ganges has also undergone similar changes, as it used to flow through West Bengal via the Hooghly River (today much smaller than it used to be).

Nowhere is this destiny more uncertain than in the country's two disaster-prone areas. Firstly, the coast bordering the Bay of Bengal is vulnerable to tidal surges from cyclones. Secondly, the country's *char* areas, or river islands, are also extremely prone to seasonal flooding. These islands lie mostly in the northern reaches of the Jamuna River of Rajshahi Division; many inhabited islands are destroyed and reformed each year by flooding. Despite the fact most of the islands are little more than infertile sandbars, poverty forces millions of people to live on them under the risk that their houses could be swept away each year.

In the Lower Meghna region, another area of exposure lies directly adjacent to the Bay of Bengal. Here, two processes of land loss and land accretion happen simultaneously. While the Meghna tears away strips of land beneath the villages each year, its decreasing speed causes it to deposit massive amounts of Himalayan silt into the bay, forming new land that becomes populated almost immediately despite the fact that the precious land doesn't become fully fertile for years. Some geologists even claim that Bangladesh is 'gaining landmass', putting the supposed doomsday scenario of climate change into question.

Where the land ends, the Bay of Bengal begins. Most of the sea adjacent to Bangladesh is quite shallow, a result of sedimentation from the region's mighty rivers. About 50km off the coast from the Sundarbans Forest is a deep undersea canyon known as the 'Swatch-of-No-Ground', where the sea floor drops to a depth of over 1,200m at some points. The swatch transports nutrient-rich sediments from the continental shelf to the deep-sea alluvial fan making up the bay. The abundance of these nutrients results in a relatively abundant population of cetaceans at the swatch.

In terms of forest cover, Bangladesh's natural places are sadly few and far between. While the world's largest mangrove forest at Sundarban remains protected, many of Bangladesh's other national parks have not fared so well. Thankfully, with increasing stability and economic development, conservation programmes are finally starting to get off the ground.

As you start travelling eastward, Bangladesh's geographic portrait takes on a new perspective. While most of the country lies at or just above sea level, the flat landscape gives way to low undulating hills in the Chittagong Hill Tracts and the hilly regions of Sylhet, some of which climb to 1,000m above sea level. This landscape is the result of the Indian tectonic plate pushing up against the Asian landmass, the same phenomenon that has resulted in the creation of the Himalayas. Visits to this area offer an experience of the true diversity that Bangladesh possesses, both geographically and culturally.

Finally, the region's last major significant geographical feature is a massive 120km-long strip of beach lining the internal eastern coastline of Bangladesh, said to be the longest natural beach in the world (at 254km, Brazil's Cassino Beach is longer, but according to the *Guinness Book of World Records*, it is partly manmade). Starting at Cox's Bazaar, the white sand stretches all the way down to the Teknaf Peninsula, poking up again briefly at the coral reef island of St Martin's. Most of this beach lies undeveloped except at Cox's Bazaar, where native mangrove forests have long been replaced by jungles of hotels.

CLIMATE

If you come from a temperate climate you might be surprised to discover that despite the fact peak temperature varies between 20°C and 40°C, Bangladeshis recognise no fewer than six seasons over their landscape. Mostly these can be grouped into three smaller seasons. In the winter months of late October to February, conditions are comfortable and dry, with temperatures staying somewhere between 15°C and 25°C, except in December and January, when cold spells grip the land and impenetrable fogs linger well into the morning. From March to May, the heat and humidity build to a point where nearly everything is sweating and hot, and temperatures climb sometimes upwards to a stifling 40°C. Finally, everyone breathes a sigh of relief when the rain bladder breaks and the monsoonal rains reduce temperatures to a more tolerable level through the months of June to September. Each season has a brief transitional period, giving rise to the reason Bangladeshis name six seasons.

Almost all of the country's rainfall comes during June to September, as northerly winds blow moisture up from the Bay of Bengal into the mountain wall that is the Himalayas. As the moisture accumulates, the skies eventually belch out their water over Bangladesh and the surrounding regions. Like many other areas that experience monsoonal rain, it seldom rains all day every day. But there can be spells where it drizzles for an entire week, and nearly everything becomes sodden, even if it's inside and well out of the rain.

On the matter of natural disasters, Bangladeshis are both particularly prone but also partially adapted. In a normal year, a great degree of Bangladesh is flooded, leaving rich alluvial soils from which to grow next year's harvests. However, in an abnormal year such as 2007, when two floods and a cyclone struck within a period of six months, you wonder how it is possible for millions of people to cope in such

CYCLONES AND BANGLADESH

On 15 November 2007, Cyclone Sidr made landfall near Sundarban in southwest Bangladesh. With winds of up to 240kmph and tidal surges varying between 8ft and 12ft, it was actually somewhat surprising to hear that this time around, only 3,447 deaths were officially recorded, although some aid agencies put that number closer to 10,000. Unbelievably, these low casualty figures are in fact a sign that Bangladesh's cyclone preparedness has improved over the years. When Cyclone Bhola devastated then East Pakistan in 1970 there were an estimated 300,000–500,000 deaths. In 1991, a cyclone of similar magnitude struck Chittagong's shores, causing an estimated 140,000–200,000 deaths as well as millions of dollars of damage. Seen comparatively, a 95% decrease in the death toll over the last major cyclone seems like a major accomplishment.

The decreased casualties are largely the result of a much improved cyclone forecast and warning system (which in some cases consists of a man riding a rickshaw blasting out the warning over a battery-powered loudspeaker), plus a wide network of cyclone shelters which double as schools during sunnier days. Cyclone Sidr will not be the last cyclone to strike Bangladesh's shores, and thankfully there is evidence that preparedness is better than it used to be. Nevertheless, two years after the disaster, you wonder where the US$550 million in relief commitments has gone.

extraordinary circumstances. As the winds make their transition from north to south, the conditions for cyclones are created during the months of May–June and October–November (see box above).

CLIMATE CHANGE When the Intergovernmental Panel on Climate Change released its fourth assessment report in 2007, it marked a major landmark in the debate over global warming. The report seemed to leave little doubt that our planet was warming; the potential disastrous effects would be felt across the world and the media presented these stories with a new sense of urgency not seen in previous years. It seemed poignant that in Bangladesh, 2007 also marked an extraordinary year when it faced two bouts of severe flooding over August and September and a devastating cyclone in November, just weeks before negotiators from around the world were to gather at the United Nations Framework Convention on Climate Change meeting in Bali. It was an extraordinary year and the global spotlight focused even more tightly on Bangladesh because of these disasters. It seemed that, in addition to its already immense climatic challenges, Bangladesh would also become the 'ground zero' of climate change.

Climate change effects manifest themselves in a variety of ways in Bangladesh, but to understand this story we must first visit the snow-capped peaks of the Himalayas. Water from these mountains gathers in both the Brahmaputra and Ganges river systems across India and these combine to form the Meghna in Bangladesh. Under a global warming scenario, the water from snowmelt increases, causing exponentially greater flooding in the plains below. Similarly, some scientists have observed that while the absolute rainfall over south Asia has not increased in the past few decades, there have been greater incidences of shorter, more intense monsoonal rains. As a result, flooding occurs every year in Bangladesh to varying degrees, but in some years it is far more widespread than others. Similarly, and definitely more devastating, are the cyclones that sweep up from the Bay of Bengal into Bangladesh, India and Myanmar. With winds breaching 200kmph, these events are most deadly when they whip up a tidal surge that pounds the low-lying coastal areas.

All of these effects have enormous, nearly indefinable social, environmental and economic impacts on the country, unfortunate because in the bigger picture, Bangladesh's contribution to the effects of global warming are negligible at best and while its capacity to cope with increased disasters has improved, it remains tenuous. The most frequently presented statistic is that if the sea level rises just 1m, 20 million people will be displaced in Bangladesh. For a country of this size, already so densely populated, you can't help but wonder how the people are going to cope. Currently, the effects of increased salinity in coastal areas and severe flooding on the major rivers are already keenly felt by Bangladeshi people. In some areas, the effects of river erosion cause thousands of people to be displaced every year.

HISTORY

To see the Bangladesh of today against its glorious history, it is both enlightening and depressing to imagine that Bengal used to occupy such a place of glory and power in the subcontinent. During the 16th century, its wealth supported the Mughal Empire, and at its zenith in the mid-18th century, Bengal's cotton and silk textiles were in demand worldwide with Dutch, Portuguese, British and French traders landing on its shores. However, the late colonial period marked a substantial change as the British proved themselves successful at draining Bengal of its wealth and destroying its cotton industry. Despite its past triumphs, 1943 proved to be the watershed year in this demise, when a terrible famine gripped the people, leaving an estimated three to five million dead from starvation, a tragedy from which modern Bangladesh has yet to fully recover. To understand such atmospheric heights and catastrophic falls, let us start from the beginning.

ANCIENT BENGAL Early archaeological evidence, while scant, does indicate the presence of an ancient society composed of Dravidian, Mongoloid and Vedic people living along the banks of the lower Ganges River, one that pre-dated the Aryan invasion of 2000–1500BC. As these invaders spread from the west to the east they brought with them the first signs of civilisation, such as language (Sanskrit), religion (Hinduism) and social organisation (caste). The invasion culminated in the Magadha Empire, the first major empire of the subcontinent, which maintained a capital at Patna on the Ganges River. The invaders also maintained a sense of division between themselves and the people, and rarely intermarried. This tradition persists to this day. You will notice that Bangladesh's educated, upper-class individuals have a lighter skin colour and fairer complexions, distinct from the darker-skinned features of the lower-middle class and villagers.

Although the lower classes of Bengal were incorporated into the cultural milieu of the Aryans, this melding of cultures went both ways. While Hindu caste structure was applied to the masses, there was also a love of nature, a faith in the elements and a sense of gentleness that was incorporated into the ruling religion. Thus it can be said that the Bangladeshi love for the rivers and the land, today most poignantly expressed in the musings of poet Lalon Shah, comes from somewhere very deep and ancient in the soul of Bangladeshis.

THE BUDDHIST ERA In nearby Bihar, the support of Buddhism by the Maurya and Gupta empires brought about a series of changes across Bengal (ranging from 321BC to AD550). Most local people did not philosophically identify with the ruling religion, and because of its concept of caste they would be forever doomed to be the 'feet' of a Hindu kingdom. Thus it was that Buddha's philosophy of peace and self-enlightenment took hold amongst the people of Bengal, and attracted a great number of converts. After several centuries, the faith developed three major strongholds in modern-day Bangladesh: the city ruins at Mahasthan; the largest Buddhist temple ruins in the world at Paharpur; and a series of temples amongst the Moinamoti ruins of Comilla. The religion had such a presence here that monks came from as far away as China and southeast Asia to study Buddhism, with some of Bengal's earliest traveller accounts coming from Chinese travellers to the region. These included monks Fa Xien and Xuen Zhang, with the latter coming in the 7th century AD. The Pala dynasty, which reigned from the 8th to the 12th century, marked the last period of the dominance of Buddhism on the subcontinent.

The heritage of this period still lives today amongst the people, according to some scholars. The tradition of giving, the gentleness and charity to all people is still very much present in the modern-day villagers, regardless of their religion. It is perhaps from this period that Bangladeshis inherited their extraordinary kindness and generosity, especially the kindness shown towards foreign guests.

HINDUISM RETURNS As Buddhism reached its zenith in the 6th and 7th centuries, there were already signs that Hinduism was to make a resurgence, based on reforms happening amongst the foremost minds of its practitioners. The source of this growth was in southern India, where along with the power of the Sena dynasty came new strands of Hindu belief that eventually converted whole monasteries to Hinduism. As a result, Buddhism was pushed to the corners of Bengal, damaged but never destroyed.

The Sena dynasty was not necessarily a cohesive one inside Bengal, with most of the territory being broken into a series of smaller kingdoms marked by geographical separation. It was also during this time that the notion of a 'greater Bangladesh' emerged, one that encompassed the Bengali-speaking people of Orissa, Bihar and regions of today's northeastern India. But before any such notions could seriously take hold, Muslim warriors arrived from the northwest.

MUGHAL REIGN Islam took its first steps in south Asia when Mahmud of Ghazni crossed the Khyber Pass following the historic routes used by previous invaders. Though Mahmud won territory via military victory, it was the characteristics inherent in the religion that paved the way for its dominance in Bengal. By professing the tenets of sympathy, empathy and a sense of one-ness, Islam won the hearts and minds of south Asia with its soft power, eventually reaching Bengal by 1200.

Using promises of an afterlife for obeying Islamic tenets, huge conversions in the region followed, but the reasons for its development into two distinct regions of south Asia (ie: Pakistan and East Bengal) remain unclear. Perhaps the religion found converts among the farming settlements of Bengal because they were also the lowest in the food chain of the Hindu caste hierarchy. Another theory is tied to the monastic life of Buddhism, one that shared some of the austere discipline required of Muslims. Some argue that the military class of the Hindus felt more ties to the orderly practices of Islam and thus converted.

For whatever reason, Islam's dominance was cemented in Bengal by the 13th century, achieved through a network of Sufi saints (whose *mazars*, or tombs, are scattered around the country). The region flourished with wealth under Mughal command. Several achievements pepper the history of this time, including a unity of India that included Bengal, plus the creation of the Grand Trunk Road linking Delhi to Dhaka, with smaller extensions to Sonargaon. The region even enjoyed a surplus with its trading partners and became so wealthy that when the British managed to take control over it in 1757, its wealth eventually supported their conquest of India.

THE BRITISH IN BENGAL Europeans began landing on south Asia's shores during the 16th century in an attempt to circumvent trading middlemen throughout central Asia. Other than establishing the region's first foreign trading ports, the Portuguese managed to earn themselves reputations as fierce marauders but they never became anything more substantial than that. They were soon followed by Dutch, English and French traders, who fought wars with one another all over the subcontinent for positions of trading power. By the 17th century, the British East India Company had gained the upper hand in this conflict and had established a growing trading port in Calcutta. Despite the disintegration of the Mughal Empire through the early part of the 18th century, strong leadership in Bengal kept it economically powerful, further strengthened by its European trading connections.

The story of what happened next is well known. The last nawab (Mughal landowner or ruler) of Bengal was a young, antagonistic but intelligent man named Siraj-uh-Daulah. Upon ascension to the throne in 1756, one of his first military moves was to oust the English from Calcutta in a surprise defeat. Those not lucky enough to escape were imprisoned in an underground prison cell, famously called the 'Black Hole of Calcutta', in which several suffocated, although the exact story is not known. The following year, the English regrouped under the leadership of Robert Clive, retook Calcutta and eventually defeated Siraj at the 1757 Battle of Plassey. Despite being terribly outnumbered, Clive won a victory on the day with the collusion of Siraj's closest general Mir Zafar and the successful execution of brilliant military strategy. After the victory, the first lots of Bengal's wealth were transported to Calcutta on English boats.

At this point, there are some notable differences between Bengali and English historians. While the former argue that the company's imperialistic designs over India were present from the beginning, the latter state that the company's ascension to an empire was motivated by money and little else. According to journalist James Novak, in his passionately written documentary book *Bangladesh: Reflections on the Water*, it was not until eight years after the historic Battle of Plassey, during which Britain acquired control of the Bengal treasury, did the London shareholders of the East India Company even conceive that the company could rule the subcontinent.

Regardless of historical viewpoint, there began a great exodus of Bengal's wealth to English shores, in the form of direct payments between the nawab and the heads of the company, as well as preferential trade policies that further bled the wealth away. After Clive's final departure from India in 1760, English merchants stepped up their trading offensive with impunity over the locals, silencing any opposition with force. Some pockets of resistance were found among the remains of the nawab but never could the opposition become a cohesive enough force to withstand the English assault. Eventually the haemorrhage led to such heights and Bengal was in such disarray that when a famine struck in 1770, some historians say that over one-third – perhaps ten million – of Bengal's peasantry starved.

Surprisingly, the resilience of early Bengal demonstrated itself shortly after this catastrophic event. When Warren Hastings took over control of the company in 1770, he represented a change in the company's policies. Surely, control over Bengal was bent purely towards economic conquest with an iron fist, but Hastings was also a passionate Orientalist, who spoke Bengali, Hindustani and Persian. During his reign he reinstated regular governance and created education institutions that would later gain prominence in British India. Under the next governor, Lord Cornwallis, a new taxation system was introduced which regulated the flow of income from Bengal and into British hands. And so the wealth of Bengal became the platform by which the company captured control over India.

The economic gains and pains were many in this period. While the British created an elaborate railway system that functions to this day, it also destroyed

Bengal's cotton industry, which under Mughal rule had enjoyed worldwide importance. By creating unfair duties in favour of English traders, there was no way that Bengal's producers could compete and British-made goods flooded the market. The fall was so catastrophic that the former metropolis at Dhaka, once the centre of Mughal trading and weaving, was slowly fading into the jungle.

BENGAL RENAISSANCE The 19th century marked a turning point and an eventual resurgence of the Indian identity. With the influence of Western ideas, liberalism, science and education, democracy, art and also literature, the latter part of the century witnessed what is referred to as the Bengal Renaissance. The period produced some of the most well-known Bengali intellectuals, including Rabindranath Tagore. Unfortunately, most of these achievements centred on the Hindu intellectual class that resided in West Bengal. The Muslims of the eastern, agricultural heart of Bengal had remained insular, perhaps still stung over the loss of the Mughal Empire.

As the Hindu intellectual class began to gain power, agitation for independence forced the British to look for partners amidst Bengal's eastern region. In this part of the empire, the Muslims had been quietly becoming a majority right underneath the noses of the British Raj and their network of Hindu *zamindars* (landlord tax collectors) throughout the country. As the British now found themselves in charge of a massive, almost ungovernable area, they decided to partition Bengal along religious lines in 1905, an event that precipitated the eventual independence of India. The decision was protested across Bengal and eventually annulled six years later.

The British never forgot this humiliating reversal, and soon decided to relocate the capital to New Delhi in 1912, using much of Bengal's wealth to build it. As the centre of power shifted away from Kolkata, the region became a forgotten backwater of the colonial empire. After 150 years of British rule, the pauperisation and robbery of Bengal was so complete that when the massive famine of 1943 struck, Bangladesh's present-day image of poverty and need was created and lingers to this day.

INDEPENDENCE Despite the reversal of the 1905 partition, the seeds for an independent Muslim nation were sown. This set the stage for the following decades of Hindu–Muslim rivalries across India, and eventually the emergence of modern Bangladesh. As the movement for independence gathered steam across India, British control over the subcontinent was weakened by both world wars, and eventually its power began to disintegrate, despite the violence it used to try and quell revolts in India.

As partition became inevitable, it was evident that there was no way to create an independent India in which the two faiths could live together under one roof. This was especially apparent in Bengal, where transgressions between Hindus and Muslims erupted in communal violence and murderous reprisals. It was so bad that Gandhi himself spent several months in the year preceding his assassination walking barefoot between villages in Noakhali, the scene of some of the worst Hindu–Muslim violence. Unfortunately his efforts were in vain. When the British eventually handed over control of India, they had divided it into two countries. In Bengal, they had used the lines similar to the 1905 partition and thus East Pakistan was created on 15 August 1947.

EAST PAKISTAN Looking back six decades, it is hard to imagine how one country could exist, cleaved apart by the wedge of India and farther still in terms of identity. The Muslims of East Pakistan shared the same language, ethnicity and culture as the Hindus of West Bengal, and yet after partition they were to be ruled by their Muslim brethren in Karachi, 1,700km away. In a sense the region was destined to become a country one day and it was only a matter of time. Longings for independence had already begun in the early part of the 20th century when the region suffered through its first partition, in 1905, only to be hewn back together again with its subsequent annulment in 1911. But after the creation of India and Pakistan as a result of the British departure in 1947, this longing would eventually take shape again in the form of the Language Movement in the 1950s.

Certainly, the West Pakistanis encouraged this independence with their early assertions of authority over the new state. One of their earliest blunders was to name Urdu as the national language of Pakistan, opening the door for separatist protest based on language, which the future leaders of the independence movement were obviously keen to exploit. The 1960s also saw the deaths of Huseyn Shaheed Suhrawardy and Fazlul Huq, marking the end of a generation of leaders who had fought for an independent Muslim state separate from India. In their place came the Awami League leaders who would redefine the Indian independence movement into that of a Bangladeshi one.

Foremost among these leaders was the high-flying Sheikh Mujib Rahman, whose blend of militant politics and widespread emotional appeal eventually defined the political future of the not-yet-in-existence country of Bangladesh. From his early days the sheikh was a people's politician, who, Gandhi-like, walked from village to village praying at mosques, sweating in rice paddies and crying at funerals. While he was never credited for his intellectual prowess, he was an extraordinarily vigorous organiser of others who could whip up nationalist sentiment – he was in tune with the hearts of his people. Without ever uttering the word 'independence', he was able to create a movement that massed political pressure from below.

The movement reached its height in 1970 when the Pakistani government called an election and the Awami League won; the sheikh was to become the prime minister of the whole of Pakistan. At this point, the West Pakistan administration made its second major blunder when it denied the sheikh's demands for more autonomy and disbanded the first session of parliament. On 8 March 1971, he all but called for independence at a massive rally at the Ramna race course, and on 25 March he was arrested, shortly after telling news reporters that an agreement was near. The next night, a then young army major named Zia Rahman rallied his troops and captured the Chittagong radio station. In the name of Sheikh Mujib, he officially declared the independence of Bangladesh.

Amidst the jubilant cries of enthusiasm, a volcano of hostilities erupted when the Pakistani army began indiscriminately killing students at Dhaka University, as well as shelling Hindu neighbourhoods. And thus began the bloody birth of Bangladesh.

LIBERATION WAR After the initial conflict broke out, a new government was formed in exile on the Indian border, and the freedom fighters, taking the title Mukti Bahini, began a guerrilla war. Although the fighters were never a cohesive force that could actually stop the Pakistani rampage, they instead served to harass them at every turn. The fighters were also aided by small pockets of anonymous resistance that remained hidden among the general populace and achieved small victories, including cutting Dhaka's power in a daring raid.

Many harrowing accounts also exist on the atrocities committed during the war, and most of it was focused towards the Hindu villages and neighbourhoods of the country. 'Operation Searchlight' was designed by the Pakistani army to systematically root out subversive forces, but in reality it was a killing and raping spree conducted against anyone they deemed was assisting the freedom effort. As a result, a great exodus occurred over the nine-month war, as an estimated ten million refugees poured over the Indian border to escape the bloodbath.

Although the Indians implicitly assisted the freedom fighters with training and arms, it would not be until December 1971 when they brought the full force of their army to bear. After the Pakistani army ran a pre-emptive strike over Indian territory on 3 December, war was declared and the Indians moved to liberate the country, needing only two weeks to complete the task. The Pakistani army, in a last cowardly move, rounded up 250 of their most hated intellectuals and journalists on 12 December and killed them indiscriminately, dumping their bodies in a killing field on the outskirts of Dhaka. By 14 December, the war was over, and a historic surrender signed at Dhaka's Ramna race course, in the same place from which the sheikh had held his historic rally.

Estimates of the number of people killed vary from 300,000 to three million, though the true number probably lies closer to one million. In the context of 20th-century genocides, that number may not be large but it was the particular brutality of these murders that still stirs deep injustice in the minds of Bangladeshis, even to the present day. Today, most of the war's murderers and their collaborators remain untried, including General Tikka Khan, whom locals refer to as the 'Butcher of Bengal'. Khan died in 2002 and was given a state burial in Pakistan. Other war criminals still remain closer to home, and used to occupy positions of political power.

At the conclusion of the war, Sheikh Mujib was released from prison and returned to Bangladesh, where he took the reins of the newly created Bangladesh.

EARLY DAYS OF BANGLADESH While Sheikh Mujib had characterised the independence movement and served to catalyse its ideals, he would turn out to be a terrible statesman and politician. His methods of gaining power through the use of *gomastas*, or mafia, would become a political tradition that still carries on to this day. When the aid dollar arrived from international quarters for recovery, much of it was siphoned off into his officials' pockets, including that of his own son. Finally, his choice of political advisers was based on loyalty – to himself, that is – and not other ideas such as merit or intelligence. His mismanagement culminated in a 1974 famine and gave secularism a bad name. Discontent had risen to such a point that when the sheikh was assassinated in August 1975 in his own home, there was only a quiet grieving around Bangladesh. People seemed to be relieved from the corruption and insecurity of Sheikh Mujib's clumsy rule, but disappointed that the people's politician had met such a sorry end. His entire family was also murdered with him, except two daughters, Sheikh Hasina and Sheikh Rehana, who were out of the country at the time.

Following a coup and a counter-coup among army generals, it fell to the other major figure in Bangladesh's liberation to restore stability: Major Zia. A prominent fighter in the war, Zia was largely respected for his soldierly attitude and ability to articulate ideas. These ideas were to move Bangladesh forward during the years Zia was in charge. After taking over leadership of the country in 1978 and successfully winning an election under the mantle of the Bangladesh National Party, he restored the constitution and set the nation on its secular course, although he violently quelled a lot of internal rebellion to achieve that. He also looked outside for ways to assist his country, and more donor money came in under his reign.

It is worth backtracking to describe internal problems that plague Bangladesh to this day, issues that Zia tried to solve, but whose ghosts still linger. After inheriting a broken country from the sheikh and a fragmented chain of command in the army, Zia was faced with the difficult task of sorting out who had been responsible for what in the Liberation War. There were some amidst his ranks who had not supported the rebellion and in fact even sided with the Pakistanis, perhaps out of fear, perhaps not. Some of these collaborators were even known murderers. Zia executed some of these criminals and pardoned others, and so today a number of these individuals still roam freely within Bangladesh society. This is the source of a great deal of controversy and results in the corresponding cries for justice every year during the 16 December Victory Day celebrations.

Despite Zia's efforts to make the army subservient to the political government, the same violent means that Zia had used eventually swallowed him as well. He was assassinated in Chittagong in May 1981 by an ambitious general.

ERSHAD AND POLITICAL GOVERNMENT Soon after Zia's assassination, the constitution dictated that the vice-president assume power. However it was not long before the military stepped in once again via a bloodless coup, this time propagated by General Hossain Mohammad Ershad. Bangladesh's latest leader differed from his predecessors in the sense that he was bred from a newer generation of individuals, those who had tasted money and power and craved only more of it. Ershad was more known for his exploits among women and he was rumoured to spend more time on the golf course than in governance. He was also extremely conflict averse, so much so that as his reign came to an end in the face of a series of political strikes he was taken down without much of a fight, his authority flickering out like a dying light bulb. Despite these criticisms, the stability endowed by Ershad's rule paved the way for some economic progress.

Eventually the country returned to a political government once again, and in 1991, the Bangladesh National Party (BNP), led by Zia Rahman's widow, Khaleda Zia, came to power in an election. Her government would be the first political government to last more than a couple of years and instituted a few notable reforms, including the introduction of free and compulsory education within the country and beginning the construction of the Jamuna Bridge. Her government would nevertheless become mired in controversy over by-elections in 1994 that led to a total boycott of parliament by all opposition parties.

Order would not be restored until after two – yes, two – 1996 elections were held that left the Awami League (AL) in charge of the country, with Sheikh Hasina at its head. While in charge, the AL signed a peace treaty with rebel forces inside the Chittagong Hill Tracts, as well as an agreement with India over the Farakka Barrage, which was rerouting Ganges water and keeping it inside India. Hasina eventually became the country's first prime minister to complete a full five-year term without being assassinated, jailed or deposed from power.

The BNP then returned to power at the election in 2001 and oversaw a difficult period in Bangladesh because of terrorism, including an August 2005 incident that had 500 improvised explosives go off almost simultaneously across Bangladesh. There was also an attempt made on Sheikh Hasina's life in 2004, when grenades rained down on a party rally and killed 21 people, including some or her closest aides. Security personnel rushed her into a bulletproof vehicle and she was fortunate to escape with hearing loss her only injury.

CARETAKER GOVERNMENT Despite the entrance of political leadership, it became evident that the governance style of Bangladesh had not yet changed as the country fell to the bottom of Transparency International's rankings as the most corrupt country in the world, a position it occupied for four successive years between 2001 and 2004. Despite some extraordinary economic achievements in the face of such adversities, the country remained politically immature, and during the run-up to the 2007 election, it became apparent that the rivalries between the two parties would be a contest to the death. As the Awami League had called a non-stop *hartal*, or political strike, to press home demands for a fair election, it seemed that the election process was speeding towards a brick wall.

On 11 January 2007, everything went quiet when President Iajuddin Ahmed declared a state of emergency and the army took over control of security once again, making it the fourth or fifth time (it's easy to lose count) that the army had ruled over Bangladesh. The election, scheduled to occur only 11 days later, was postponed.

The army then installed a technocrat civilian government while it controlled things behind the scenes, and promised to hold elections two years later. They also attempted to put their house in order by starting an anti-corruption drive that netted both former prime ministers and several members of their families, jailing them on charges of extortion. After a protracted battle at the courts, both prime ministers were granted bail on medical grounds and as preparations for an election in 2008 went ahead, it appeared that only incremental gains had been made in the political landscape of Bangladesh.

Despite the lack of change in the political parties, the election went ahead on 29 December 2008 under conditions that international and local observers declared both 'free and fair'. Sheikh Hasina's Awami League won by a landslide, claiming 230 seats, with its allies grabbing another 32 more. It was a result which the BNP could not deny, although they did claim 'vote rigging' in what was obviously a face-saving measure. During campaigning, some very big promises were made that reflected a change in how the country would be governed. The first big test came on 25 February 2009, when low-ranking troops at the Bangladesh Rifles headquarters began murdering their officers (the Rifles are Bangladesh's paramilitary force responsible for border security). When the shooting stopped, over 60 had been killed and buried in mass graves or nearby sewer drains. While the massacre was widely acknowledged to be an attempt to destabilise Bangladesh's already fragile government, its perpetrators were still unknown as this book went to press. Heading into the future, it is hoped that the Awami League will successfully redefine the political landscape by moving away from the patterns that have defined Bangladesh's dysfunctional politics for so long.

GOVERNMENT AND POLITICS

After so much blood was shed in the creation of Bangladesh, it is now promising to see that after almost four decades, the young political system has advanced and evolved, as its latest leaders have at least managed to finish their political terms without being assassinated. Indeed, the governance system of the country still has a long way to go.

Although the constitution has mandated a parliamentary democracy in Bangladesh, rarely has this lofty ideal reflected ground realities. Elected governments of the last two decades have not resulted in responsive political institutions or substantial welfare for most people. Instead, most politicians and their families have profited from the political power imbued to them by election. The cause of this largely goes back to the founding of the nation and its first leaders. Under Mujib, Zia and Ershad, political power was gathered more and more into the hands of the executive officers who at first represented military interests; surprisingly these early leaders spent a great deal of time shaping the constitution to legitimise their rule. Today, the judiciary and legislature lack the power to effectively curb executive decisions and hence the system of checks and balances normally inherent in a parliamentary democracy do not function very well in Bangladesh.

There are two major political parties in Bangladesh: the Awami League (AL), and the Bangladesh National Party (BNP). The former, led by Sheikh Mujib's surviving daughter Sheikh Hasina, is known to be the more left-wing party of the two and governed Bangladesh from 1996 to 2001. Opposite them is the BNP, headed by Zia Rahman's widow Begum Khaleda Zia, the party favouring increased economic liberalisation and possessing more religious overtones, given its alliance with the Islamist Jamaat-e-Islami Party. The BNP has had three terms in government, from 1991 to 1996, a brief few months in 1996, and a final term from 2001 to 2006. Although the point can be made that Bangladesh has had two former prime ministers who are women, it needs to be understood that this situation is simply the result of politics based on dynastic traditions, and not a merit-based system. Women otherwise remain virtually invisible in Bangladeshi politics.

The influence of Islam on politics is also a source of contention within the governance structure of Bangladesh. Although the country was founded on secular ideals, Islam did and still does remain very close to the heart of many Bangladeshis, and although the majority of people supported Sheikh Mujib during the East Pakistan period, his early policies of Bangladesh seemed to cut Islam out of the country's identity entirely, a move that aggrieved the historical memories of those who believed the Hindus were attempting the same thing in pre-partition India. As a result, Islamic framework was reintroduced into the constitution during the reign of Zia, although the document also specified the rights of all people regardless of race, religion, creed or gender should be protected – perhaps another lofty ideal that has yet to reflect the country's ground reality. Today most people believe that political and religious identities should remain separate, although there is a vocal minority, in the form of the Jamaat-e-Islami Party, which believes Bangladesh should once again become what they call a 'democratic Islamic state'.

Now let us return to the lack of a functioning democracy, a fact that became very apparent in the recent explosions within the minefield that is Bangladeshi politics. During November 2006, just before the BNP was to hand over power to a caretaker administration to manage the election, the Awami League asserted that the former government had rigged the election commission with its own staff. Without other avenues for discussion or debate, the AL used its favourite weapon, the country-choking political strike, or *hartal*, to press for its demands. Soon the conflict escalated and by November 2006, goons from both parties were busy killing each other in the streets in a 'winner-take-all' style contest, again a result of the fact that power in Bangladesh remains so absolute and there was so much at stake.

Put more simply, the winners of such political confrontations would normally spend their political terms bullying the opposition and reversing its former policies, while the loser would have no recourse except to call more *hartals* to press for its demands. On 11 January 2007, the security situation deteriorated in the face of such severe strikes that the country was suffocating itself. Eventually, President Iajuddin Ahmed stepped aside for the army to take control, an event known locally as '1/11' among political watchers. On the promise of creating a drive to clean up corruption and create a new voters' list (the earlier one had about ten million fake names), the military-backed caretaker government delayed elections for two years and declared a permanent 'state of emergency', which served to curb civil liberties in the face of the drive.

On first glance, Bangladesh's political system might seem incomprehensible to outsiders, but given the historical backdrop of the country's birth, the presence of severe growing pains is hardly surprising. After the AL's landslide victory in the parliamentary elections of late 2008, there was a wave of optimism and hope that swept the nation, signifying the potential for significant change in the way Bangladeshi politics is run, but most political observers are not holding their breath.

Perhaps the biggest losers in this political circus are those who remain outside the tent as millions of Bangladeshi people do not seem to have any tie to their political masters and the great majority live in positively medieval conditions, especially those who migrate to the cities in search of work but end up in terrible slums. As many development practitioners are quick to point out, stronger governance would definitely help improve the lot of Bangladeshi people. But such a utopian vision remains, at best, a few decades away.

ECONOMY

Since the inception of Bangladesh, the country has received approximately US$40 billion in foreign aid. Today it's pleasing to acknowledge that economic progress is being made and things are heading in a good direction, despite some unfathomable hindrances and political mismanagement.

In the early days, the country in fact shunned foreign money under the direction of Mujib, and then nationalised a great deal of its industries under his socialist whims, a burden that future political leaders had to painfully shed, with one notable example being the death of Bangladesh's jute industry in the last decade. Zia, on the other hand, used foreign money to incite economic growth, including the introduction of new infrastructure to aid the process. On balance, foreign aid dependence is now slowly decreasing and Bangladesh's development initiatives have met with mixed successes.

Encouraging signs, in the form of 6% GDP growth and the US$11 billion per year garment industry, have resulted in some real gains, with mostly women being employed in the ready-made garment trade. Bangladesh is also fortunate to benefit from substantial natural gas reserves in its northeast as well as potential deposits in the Bay of Bengal, which has resulted in a changeover to the use of compressed natural gas, or CNG, and reduced the country's dependence on petrol. Finally, the country also benefits from a seaport at Chittagong, which is where most of the garments are shipped *en route* to destinations in Europe or North America.

Nevertheless the cards seem stacked against Bangladesh and it remains aid-dependent, especially when natural disasters such as cyclones and severe floods strike, a phenomenon that will continue to dog Bangladesh's growth. It also faces serious challenges with respect to underemployment and a lack of innovation within its main agricultural industries. With the advent of climate change concerns and the potential risk to create even larger populations of displaced migrants, it seems that Bangladesh might begin looking towards its people – probably its greatest natural resource – as a source of future potential economic growth.

Remittances from Bangladeshis abroad are already growing from year to year, as almost US$5 billion was sent in the 2005–06 financial year. Most of these workers head to the Middle East or other neighbouring Muslim countries to benefit from employment opportunities abroad. Significant quantities of remittances also come from the US and the UK. Visitors to Kuala Lumpur International Airport will quickly notice that most of the service staff are from Bangladesh. Back at home, long lines of potential migrant workers are often seen outside the country's immigration and passport offices.

Unfortunately, this 'brain drain' effect is directly noticeable in Bangladesh. Despite the strong cultural ties to the motherland, the country's best and brightest minds are often found abroad, with most of them saying that given the corruption, instability and lack of opportunity in their country, they prefer to stay out. This lack of leadership and human capital inside Bangladesh could be another factor in describing why the country has yet to reach its full economic potential.

THE BANGLADESH GARMENT INDUSTRY

When the Multi-Fibre Agreement was instituted and extended during the last few decades of the 20th century, it mandated that the production of labour-intensive garments continue to be moved from developed to developing countries, a move that opened the window for Bangladesh to make real economic gains through this industry. As a result a number of garment producers looked to Bangladesh to set up and maintain production factories using the pool of cheap labour available in the country. In recent years, the industry has expanded to represent a major source of income for Bangladeshi manufacturers: in 2007, the industry made US$11 billion from its work.

Many of the factories have professional management and production practices, offering daycare, medical expenses and training facilities to its employees, the great majority of whom are women. But such exemplary provisions for workers are the exception rather than the norm. In many cases, labourers work on shifts of up to 12, 14 or even 16 hours if there is a deadline to be met. Monthly salaries range between Tk1,500 and Tk2,000 per month, which according to some NGOs and labour unions, isn't enough to even eat properly.

At other factories there has been a blatant disregard for safety requirements, which has resulted in the death of dozens of workers. The most disastrous of these incidents was the building collapse of the Spectrum Sweaters factory in Savar in April 2005, which resulted in the death of 64 workers and 74 injuries. The building was constructed on former marshland and was originally meant to be four floors, but had been later expanded to eight; workers who expressed concern over cracks in the walls a few days before the incident were told to go back to work.

In their defence, factory owners also claim that bureaucratic obstacles prevent them from doing more for their workers, as there are something like 19 licences required to own, build and run a garment factory, and the interest rates on loans are very high to create economic growth. They say that the competitiveness of the Bangladesh garment industry needs to be improved, so that even more economic growth opportunities can come to the country and the industry can be expanded.

In 2005 and 2006, these issues came to a head and protests broke out at garment factories in and around Dhaka, with several workers taking to the streets in a destructive rampage; some even destroyed their own factories. Labour representatives and NGOs who have pressed for improved conditions in the industry have a single loud and clear demand to increase salaries to a subsistence level of Tk3,000 per month, a move that garment factory owners say is impossible given their financial restrictions and potential returns. Over the last few years the industry has struggled to reform and now that the protectionism offered by the Multi-Fibre Agreement has expired, the future of Bangladesh's garment industries remains unclear.

DEVELOPMENT

Development and the evolution of its concepts have long been tied to the fate and history of modern Bangladesh. Any discussion of its effects will be laced with opinions on whether the aid enterprise – and the billions of dollars associated with it – have been effective in improving the conditions of Bangladesh's millions.

On one hand, 1971 saw a broken, war-battered country with a massive population and no resources or infrastructure to speak of. The government had not yet stabilised, and the billions of aid dollars that poured in surely did land in the pockets of corrupt officials. Almost four decades later, as foreign aid since 1971 tops approximately US$40 billion, some stark realities remain: fully one-third of Bangladesh's people still live on less than US$1 per day. Discovering that Bangladesh reached rock bottom as the most corrupt country in the world (according to Transparency International's rankings between 2001 and 2004), you will experience a sort of rage at the injustice of human greed and its corrosive effects so visible in Bangladesh. Looking out from the regal offices, massive apartments and four-star hotels of Gulshan into the heart of the Korail slum, a hotchpotch village of tin shacks and bamboo stilts, it's hard to understand where all that money has gone.

On the other hand, while it might be easy to tar the aid agencies and paint the institutions as corrupt, the development enterprise itself and its good intentions should never be forgotten. Historically, aid in Bangladesh did not function according to principles of efficiency and profit and its early practitioners, Bangladeshi or foreign, may have been great humanitarians but not necessarily efficient managers. This is especially true of the Structural Adjustment Programs established by institutions such as the Asian Development Bank and the World Bank, which have had limited success in achieving the intended economic and social outcomes. These projects are certainly based on noble and broad ideas but they have also lacked connection to the ground realities, with many ending up falling by the wayside. But that's the nature of the beast in Bangladesh. Any multi-million dollar aid programme, to be applied in a country with weak governance institutions and aging infrastructure, is bound to have difficulties and inefficiencies. These are obstacles that need to be overcome with time and

GRAMEEN BANK AND MICROCREDIT

Naturally, no story of poverty alleviation is complete without referring to Dr Mohammad Yunus and his Grameen Bank, now household names worldwide after he won the Nobel Peace Prize in late 2006 for inventing microcredit and earning himself the title of 'Banker to the Poor'. After winning the prize, the reaction among people was ecstatic, and his smiling face was rather hard to escape – enormous posters hung from buildings around town and major corporations bought full-page advertisements congratulating him. The rest of the world is no less taken with him and if you ever have the chance to meet the silver-haired celebrity, you'll be surprised at his soft spoken but inspirational words whose accent isn't quite Bangladeshi, but not quite American either.

Microcredit works on the basis that because the poor lack access to institutional credit, they are unable to work themselves out of poverty. With access to minuscule loans ranging between US$20 and US$200, they might be able to buy some implement, tool or technology they might not otherwise be able to afford and use it to create tiny businesses. In addition to its central lending programme, Grameen has also set up a network of businesses around its work. The earliest of these programmes was the 'mobile-phone ladies' who, with the help of a small loan from Grameen, became the owners of a phone kiosk where villagers could call other villagers over the mobile network. But since mobile-phone ownership became so popular in Bangladesh (there are now over 30 million subscribers), this flagship business has subsided and Grameen has moved into other businesses, including Grameen Shakti, which provides small solar panels to villagers, and Grameen Danone, which operates a yoghurt factory in Bogra.

Grameen offers internships out of its Dhaka office, which are actually more like exposure tours, according to those who have participated in them. See www.grameen-info.org for more information.

BRAC, THE WORLD'S LARGEST NGO

It is hardly surprising that one of the world's poorest countries could have spawned what has become the world's largest non-government organisation. With over 120,000 staff worldwide, the Bangladesh Rural Advancement Committee (BRAC) now has offices in Tanzania, Uganda and Afghanistan, and smaller operations in about a dozen other countries.

The organisation began shortly after the founding of Bangladesh in 1971, when it assisted refugees returning from India to be resettled in the homeland. Today the organisation is almost entirely self-financed with donations now comprising only 20% of its revenues. From the outset, BRAC recognised that women would be the catalysts of development in Bangladesh and focused its development activities on them, while also maintaining a staff ratio balanced in favour of women. Visitors will probably come across one of BRAC's most successful businesses when they shop at Aarong, a handicrafts, textiles and housewares chain store that supplies the wealthier households in Dhaka with excellent products.

BRAC also offers internships and research partnerships. The advice from previous interns and scholars is that you should leave your expectations at home. Visit www.brac.net for more information.

experience and those who criticise aid from the comforts of Western countries should really spend a day in the shoes of a Bangladeshi development worker and truly understand what the development enterprise is about and the passionate hearts of the people who work in it.

Thankfully, the practice of philanthropy has evolved in recent years, and new development approaches do employ more stringent checks and balances on the implementing agencies, as well as increased rigour in practices of monitoring and evaluation. Bangladesh has also managed to shed some of its aid dependence over the decades and it has maintained a healthy economic growth rate over the past ten years. Truly, any long-term development that occurs within the country has to come from within.

PEOPLE

Bangladesh's people are at once its best resource and its most bothersome burden, as the population has skyrocketed over its short history. When Bangladesh was East Bengal in 1905, there were an estimated 29 million people living within its borders, a number which increased to 44 million just 50 years later when the region became East Pakistan. By 1981, the census reported a population of 81 million, and since then that number has almost doubled. Today, estimates range between 151 million and 155 million people, resulting in a population density of over 1,050 souls per km^2. This makes Bangladesh the most densely populated nation in the world (excluding several city-states like Hong Kong, Singapore or Monaco), and it feels like that when dozens of people crowd to have a gander at the strange foreigner visiting their village. Current projections estimate that by 2080, the population of Bangladesh could be 250 million.

Another major characteristic of this population is that it is extremely young: more than one-third of its population are teenagers or younger. Speaking of teenagers, a likely cause for the situation is the widespread practice of early marriage in rural families, with females bearing the brunt of this population increase. Statisticians note that most females are married by 18 years of age, and by the time they're 20, more than half of them have had children, disrupting their future education and personal development potential. Additionally, a large number of mothers are malnourished before giving birth, resulting in high rates of infant and maternal mortality.

The burden of disability is shouldered by women in Bangladesh. Believed by some to be a 'curse of Allah's will', people with disabilities are often confined to their homes or pawned on the streets as beggars. It is estimated at least 10% of the population suffers from some form of disability, predominantly the result of diseases, malnutrition, congenital defects, accidents or injury. Although there is a shift towards inclusive education and the provision of health services for people with disabilities, many are still left behind in their homes to be cared for by their mothers or grandmothers.

Despite these grim appearances, Bangladesh has made headway with immunisation programmes and health treatments. Polio was essentially eradicated in 2000; although there was one case in 2006, it was met by a stringent polio vaccination drive to prevent an outbreak – a feat India has not yet achieved. Similarly Bangladesh has led the field in its treatment of cholera and its introduction of rehydration salts to prevent dehydration and ultimately death. High fevers during pregnancy are also a major cause of disabilities.

RACE AND DIVERSITY Racially speaking, Bengal's earliest inhabitants were the Dravidian tribespeople, overwhelmingly agricultural and darker skinned than the Aryan invaders who began populating Bengal between 2000BC and 1500BC. The racial balance again changed when the Muslims from the west began moving in during the 12th century, and people from all over the Islamic world landed on Bengal's shores. Finally, the region has also experienced racial influxes from the Tibeto-Burmese stock, which accounts for why the indigenous people of the Chittagong Hill Tracts and northeastern hill areas tend to resemble people from southeast Asia.

Cultural diversity within the population is hard to notice at first, but on second glance you can unearth a plethora of heterogeneity spread around the country. The Chittagong Hill Tracts hold the greatest array of these cultures, with its roughly one million people dispersed over 11 different ethnicities. The Chakma people, having long controlled the trade routes between the Arakan and Chittagong, seem to be the best integrated of these ethnicities. Other groups such as the Mru have deliberately tried to limit all foreign influence on their way of life. Pockets of different ethnicities are also found on the fringes of the country.

The hilly regions of the Sylhet Division are home to Khasi, Manipuri and Tripura people who are spread around villages near Srimongol, Maulvi Bazaar and Sylhet. The area bordering India, north of Mymensingh, holds about 200,000 Garo people, and that's just on the Bangladeshi side of the border. This ethnicity, having long had missionaries living in their midst, is primarily Christian. Towards the northwest other, smaller groups of ethnic people can be found, including the Santal and Urao people, who also have populations in West Bengal.

Development among the ethnic groups of Bangladesh is an often discussed topic in the country, especially having now passed the tenth anniversary of the signing of the Chittagong Hill Tracts Peace Accord in December 2007. Despite the recognition of ethnicities in the constitution and the signing of the peace accord, most of Bangladesh's ethnic groups lag far behind the mainstream in terms of development, economic and education indicators. Whether this is a result of deliberate negligence or a lack of resources is debatable, but the fact remains that these groups live on the fringes of society and are vulnerable to policy decisions that favour the mainstream Bengali people in the country and the resulting abuses of power.

MIGRATION Without the benefit of enough natural resources, many Bangladeshis now look to migration as a source for potential employment. This takes place on many levels, ranging from the farmer who leaves his Rangpur home to become a rickshaw wallah in Dhaka for a few months of the year, to the semi-educated individuals who become labourers in outside countries such as Malaysia, Saudi Arabia, Kuwait or the United Arab Emirates. Bangladeshis are now found all over the globe doing labour jobs that wealthier countries would sooner pass off.

Urban migration has resulted in severe population pressure, especially in the larger, crowded cities like Dhaka or Chittagong. In both cities, people are often found squeezed into every little nook and cranny and even spill out onto the streets. Most of the poorest people end up in slums under sanitary and living conditions that are far worse than their home villages, and yet they persist here because of the opportunities to earn an income that simply don't exist in their home towns.

One of the most well-known migrations is *monga* season in Bangladesh, which is the name for a seasonal famine period that happens twice a year. Once the crops are planted in the poorest regions of Rajshahi Division, usually around the areas of Kurigram and Gaibandha, there is no more work to be done locally until harvest time a few months later. Many rural migrants move to the city to take temporary labour jobs such as rickshaw wallahs or opportunistic day labourers. They are easily spotted around the streets of the capital every morning: men – sometimes even women – with shovels in hand and baskets perched on their heads, wait by the road to be hired into one of the many construction sites in cities.

On any given day the airport is also the scene of similar mass migrations. Dozens of men, sometimes outfitted in colourful overalls and toting small suitcases are seen preparing for travel to the Middle East or Malaysia as labourers. These migrants tend to be well off in the bigger picture, and often have to pay thousands of taka in upfront fees to immigration agents who control the opportunities to work abroad. In 2007, studies estimate that Bangladesh sent 800,000 migrants abroad for contractual labour jobs, second only to the Philippines.

Finally, it is worth noting that there is actually a body of 'migrants' who come to Bangladesh to escape something worse, and unsurprisingly these come entirely from Myanmar. The Rohingya refugees, who are estimated to be a population of 100,000 to 200,000 in Bangladesh, are Myanmarese Muslims who face severe persecution back home. Some have managed to integrate to some degree in the general population, but another 27,000 live in refugee camps in the Teknaf district of Cox's Bazaar.

LANGUAGE

With almost 200 million speakers, Bangla is the sixth most widely spoken language worldwide. Although it is a derivative of Sanskrit and therefore has its closest ties to Hindi, today's modern Bangla also incorporates a mishmash of influences that represent the region's history. The script is written from left to right and top to bottom, and thus reads the same as English. Linguists note three major periods in the evolution of the language, with the majority of its modern forms being derived during the 15th–18th centuries. Until the 18th century, there were simply no attempts to document the grammar of Bangla.

In Bangladesh, the largest influence over the language comes from Islam, using words that came along with the Arabs who were the first foreign traders in the country. As a result, incorporation of phrases such as *salaam aleikum* (God be with you) and Muslim names (Mohammed or Khaleda) demonstrate the language ties to the religion. In West Bengal however, words more appropriate to Hinduism are used, such as *nomoshkar* (greetings).

With the advent of the colonial period in the 19th century, the influence of English on Bangla began, with British law, language and culture making their presence felt all over the subcontinent but especially in Bengal, given the close nature of the relationship between the two regions and the fact that the East India Company's headquarters were located in Kolkata. Today this influence is apparent in the adoption of many transliterated English words – hospital is pronounced '*hosh-pit-al*' along with other more archaic words which you'll inevitably hear spoken during your visit. Modern speakers, especially members of the chic younger generation, freely admit that they speak 'Banglish', Bangla that is peppered with a range of accented English words.

Language and identity are closely related in Bangladesh. The foundations of the country's independence movement lay in the language movement of the 1950s, which was seeded in 1948 when the government declared that Urdu and only Urdu would be the state language of the newly created country, causing uproar in East Pakistan. The movement's earliest martyrs are recognised each year on Ekushey (Bangla for 21), when 12 students from Dhaka University were killed on 21 February 1952, during language protests. The Shahid Minar Statue, seen on the Tk2 banknote and located on the Dhaka University campus, commemorates this seminal event in the formation of Bangladesh. After several more years of Bangladeshi politicians stirring up nationalist sentiments via this issue, the central government relented and declared Bengali a second national language in 1956. Historians largely acknowledge that this turn of events only emboldened the nationalist sentiments and their leading politicians. During the liberation war the phrase '*Joy Bangla*' was used to proclaim independence from Pakistan, as opposed to the more Urdu-based phrase '*Bangladesh Zindabad*'.

Learning Bangla as a tourist is not entirely necessary as you will find many people who speak English or at least enough of it to do basic transactions and take directions. Whenever you are seriously stuck there is usually someone around who can translate for you. This is especially helpful when tangling with the country's jungle-like bureaucracy. But given the language's extraordinary history and its link to cultural identity, you will find many more doors and opportunities opening for you if you take the time to learn the basics and get over the shyness of cultural interaction. There is a particular habit among Bangladeshis to speak Bangla between each other even when a foreigner is present or sometimes in the middle of a business meeting. This should not be taken as rude, as the interrelatedness of language and identity in Bangladesh cannot be overemphasised.

The hardest stumbling blocks are grammar and verb conjugation in Bangla. Sentences use a subject–object–verb construction (ie: I books read) instead of the subject–verb–object (ie: I read books) structure used in English. Verbs need to be adjusted based on tense but thankfully there is one catch-all verb, *kora*, which means 'to do', and is used in many situations. Learning the alphabet is difficult at first but not impossible as signage written in both English and Bangla provides plenty of practice as you wade through traffic.

Taking a short language class when you arrive is helpful, especially if you will be staying for a period anywhere longer than three months, which will allow you to start getting an ear for the language and mastering its sounds. See the Language Schools listings in the Dhaka chapter for recommendations on learning Bangla during your visit (see page 137) and further reading (page 345) for language guides.

RELIGION

Islam is the overwhelmingly dominant religion in Bangladesh, but over its history Bengal has played host to Hinduism and Buddhism as well. Christianity, the smallest of the four religions, is mainly a result of missionaries who arrived in the British period and the Portuguese who came centuries earlier. Worldwide, Bangladesh has the fourth largest population of Muslims in the world, behind Indonesia, Pakistan and India.

While the constitution of Bangladesh mandates religious freedom, you may discover yourself bound to a religion you don't necessarily follow in practice, as a common question that Bangladeshis have is about your religion. Whatever your orientation is, it is best to pick one of the major religions and stick to it as atheism is a concept not well understood in the country.

ISLAM Although Arab traders had been landing on Bangladesh's shores for centuries, Bangladesh's mainstream religion only took hold with the arrival of Muslim invaders from the west in the early 13th century. One of the earliest movements occurred around the arrival of Muslim saint Hazrat Shah Jalal, who was one of the first to convert the Hindus and Buddhists to Islam *en masse*. Today his mausoleum, or *mazar* as it is known in Bangla, is one of Sylhet's chief tourism attractions for domestic tourists. Thousands of visitors come almost every weekend to pay homage at the shrine.

Sufism is another movement within Islam that is also largely credited for the mass conversions not only in Bengal but also across south Asia. The movement is perhaps more aligned with the Bangladeshi spirit, in the sense that it promotes a sense of personal devotion to Allah that isn't necessarily bound within the ritualistic observance of Islam. This is in opposition to the Ulama-based approach, which favours the implementation of Sharia laws under the direction of the Koran.

The most major religious event in Bangladesh after Eid-ul Fitr is the Bishwas Ijtema congregation, a massive gathering that occurs around February of each year in Tongi, one of Dhaka's northern suburbs. In 2007, a record-breaking three million attendees arrived, making it the second largest gathering of Muslims after the Hajj.

Under the 2001 census, Muslims comprise almost 90% of the religious makeup of Bangladesh. The great majority of these are Sunni Muslims.

HINDUISM Hinduism in Bangladesh shares many similar cultural features to the kind practised in West Bengal, as the entire region used to be one nation before Bengal was cleaved into two parts. In the cities and towns of Bangladesh, its Hindu neighbourhoods tend to stand out in terms of visible culture; the colourful cosmos of Hindu deities stands in direct contrast to the more austere Muslim existence. Throughout the countryside are a number of Hindu temples, mostly attached to or very close to extensive *rajbaris*, or palaces. Former owners of these palaces used to form the administrative class of the British Empire in Bengal, and judging by the size of these palatial homes there is little doubt that their owners used to live well, before they were chased away or evicted during Bangladesh's recent conflicts.

Sadly, the story of Hinduism in Bangladesh is one of decline. In the early days of the British Empire, the Hindu people of Bengal were often given better access to important administrative positions and better opportunities for education. Thus developed a Hindu intelligentsia that began to threaten and agitate for independence from Britain in the late 19th century. In reaction, the British tried to inflame Muslim–Hindu rivalries in a bid to weaken their opponents. An especially poignant blow was the first partition of Bengal in 1905, which would be the precursor of so much Hindu–Muslim violence in the century to come. Leading up to the partition of India in 1947, the Hindus faced even greater violence and subjugation, with mass riots and murders based on religion occurring on a regular basis. In 1971, the Hindu population was specifically targeted for attack by the Pakistani army across Bangladesh, and sometimes, summarily executed.

All of this racially motivated violence has resulted in a decline of the Hindu population in Bangladesh, estimated to be 28% in 1941 but dropping to 10% in 2001. Despite the enshrining of minority rights in the constitution of Bangladesh and a general attitude of tolerance towards other religions among the greater population, some violence has occurred as a result of the changing political landscape. Bangladesh's Awami League Party, having had some previous ties to India and its foundation in secular principles, tends to count more Hindu people among its ranks.

BUDDHISM From the birth of Buddha in the 6th century BC until its decline in the 12th century, Bengal was a stronghold of Buddhism, in fact one of the last places the religion could be found in India. Its spread is largely credited to the patronage of successive kingdoms or dynasties during the early years, especially King Asoka, whose reign over the modern-day areas of West Bengal and Bihar allowed the religion to take root and flourish to such a degree that pilgrims came from as far away as China to visit the birthplace of the religion. Fa Xien and Xuen Zhang were two monks who wrote that they saw great monasteries and several active Buddhist institutions all along the banks of the middle and lower Ganges.

The religious practice grew especially under the rule of the Pala dynasty in the 8th century, the period which many of the ruins come from across historical Bengal. During the dynasty's later years the religion reached the southeastern areas of Bengal, including the present-day Chittagong Hill Tracts, where today the Theravada form of the faith, similar to that of Myanmar and Thailand, is still practised.

The arrival of the Muslims denotes the end of this period, and after suffering much destruction, many of the monks left for the higher climates of Nepal and Tibet.

CHRISTIANITY The history of Christianity in Bangladesh begins with the arrival of the Portuguese traders in the early 16th century. Their first trading posts in Bengal were naturally located at Chittagong, but they also maintained posts near present-day Kolkata and in Goa. When Dhaka became the capital of Bengal, the Portuguese and Armenians were the first Christians in the city and a few churches still stand as testament to their presence.

When the English arrived, they brought Christianity to new heights in Bengal. Missionary William Carey translated and printed the Bible in Bangla, and by doing so helped develop some of the first printing technology in Bengal. Although the population of Christians remains small in Bangladesh, many of the development initiatives of these early missionaries have left a legacy of scattered pockets of Christianity around the country. Perhaps the largest of these groups is among the Garo people in the Mymensingh district who mostly live close to the Indian border. They are estimated to be 200,000 strong, with an even larger contingent in India. Travelling Christians will find Christmas and Easter fantastic times to visit the Garo areas of the north.

EDUCATION

Viewed through the lens of the education Millennium Development Goals (MDG), Bangladesh is doing very well compared with some other countries. As government literature is quick to point out, Bangladesh is on track in promoting gender equality and empowering women, the third MDG. As it stands there are now equal ratios of girls to boys in primary and secondary education, and this will hopefully produce a newer generation of better-educated women. The 2007 opening of the Asian University for Women in Chittagong is also a hopeful sign. But as soon as you proceed into the upper echelons of society, you find that women are still excluded from political roles and are not as literate. Khaleda Zia and Sheikh Hasina attained their roles because of the dynastic nature of Bangladeshi politics, not because of any merits they won within the country's young political system. In terms of achieving universal primary education, the second MDG, Bangladesh has also been successful, but its government still battles the rural cultural practice of pulling children out of school to work at home and in the fields, especially girls.

Unfortunately, the nation's public higher education institutions have suffered from severe politicisation among its faculty and students. A case in point is at Dhaka University: at its inception in the early 19th century, its earliest administrators wanted to create a lighthouse of learning inside the educationally bereft eastern half of Bengal, to parallel the successes of the institutions of Calcutta. But by the time of partition, the campus had become a crucible of unrest that began with the language movement of the 1950s. As a result, the campuses have remained a source of anarchy over the last decade. As if to take a page from Mao's *Little Red Book*, students at the universities have become the pawns of the country's political panderings, and most of the wealthy class send their students to private institutions or abroad for higher education, if they can afford it.

THE ASIAN UNIVERSITY FOR WOMEN

Located in Chittagong, Bangladesh, the Asian University for Women (AUW) is based on the firm belief that education – especially higher education – provides a critical pathway to leadership development, economic progress, and social and political equity. The AUW will educate promising young women from diverse cultural, religious, ethnic and socio-economic backgrounds from across south and southeast Asia and the Middle East – with a particular emphasis on the inclusion of women from poor, rural and refugee populations. The university will enable its students to become skilled and innovative professionals, service-oriented leaders and promoters of tolerance and understanding.

Locating the AUW in Bangladesh affirms the university's dedication to the region. The country's history of state- and private-sector commitment to advancing education, as well as its secular political culture and a number of notable NGOs, such as BRAC and institutions like the Grameen Bank, are affirmations of the AUW's mission. The government of Bangladesh has been strongly supportive of the AUW vision since its inception – granting 100+ acres of land to the AUW, while also providing the university with a far-reaching and empowering charter, ensuring academic freedom and institutional autonomy which is critical to its success in the region.

With a population of approximately four million, Chittagong is the second largest city in Bangladesh, and serves as an international hub in the region – located 264km southeast of the nation's capital, Dhaka, it is well connected by air, road and rail. Historically, Chittagong has proven itself to be a principal centre for cultural, social, and commercial exchange between south Asia and the outside world. The university will capitalise on that history by joining both local women and its talented, all-female student body with the international community.

Students are recruited from countries throughout Asia, with the first undergraduate class heralding from Cambodia, Nepal, India, Pakistan, Sri Lanka and Bangladesh. With an

CULTURE

What Bangladeshis admittedly lack in terms of material wealth, they certainly make up for in artistic tradition. There are plenty of opportunities for the visitor to engage with both the historic art of Bangladesh and its more modern practitioners.

ARCHITECTURE As Bengal has had so many influences on its people and culture, so too have its artists and artisans. Remnants of ancient Bengal's art still remain scattered throughout the country today, in the form of the many ancient monuments that reveal a vibrant and diverse history. Each archaeological site possesses a religious and cultural history that is not often visible from the monuments themselves, especially the terracotta art that decorates some of the nation's most famous Buddhist and Hindu temples. Unfortunately, the lack of stone in a sandy delta with a punishing tropical climate means that many of these old buildings have not been able to stand the test of time. Worse yet, the historically important buildings are also not well maintained owing to a lack of resources as restoration work on old buildings is extremely expensive and detailed. Nevertheless, they are still interesting places to visit, because of the exciting rural journeys required to find such places – discovering these far-flung temples is an adventure in itself!

The earliest buildings derive from the Buddhist cultures that inhabited the area, and the great Buddhist monuments at Paharpur, Mahasthan (both near Bogra) and Moinamoti (near Comilla) stand as a testament to the former prominence of the religion. While most of the Buddhist monuments derive from the 4th to 8th

international faculty and established relationships with renowned, global-minded institutions such as Aalborg University, Denmark, and Stanford University, USA, the AUW has laid the groundwork in pioneering changes for women's education worldwide.

THE ACCESS ACADEMY Beginning with its 2009 academic year, the Access Academy (AA), the AUW's innovative year-long college preparatory programme, will admit only first-generation university attendees. After successful completion of the rigorous, all-English academy programme, students will enrol in the AUW under full scholarship. The academy's inaugural class, which began its studies in March 2008, has already demonstrated a great capacity for leadership, citizenship and English fluency. Current students were recruited from Cambodia, Nepal, India, Pakistan, Sri Lanka and Bangladesh, and are lively, enthusiastic and well aware of the challenges that face both themselves and their home countries. They provide endless hope and inspiration to the faculty that works with them on a daily basis in intimate classroom settings (the Access Academy and the Asian University for Women maintain a 1:13 teacher-to-student ratio). The Access Academy faculty was identified, recruited and trained by WorldTeach, a non-profit organisation affiliated with the Center for International Development at Harvard University.

HOW TO GET INVOLVED The AUW and the Access Academy welcome the support of the global community through both monetary donations and the mobilisation of a global network of volunteers. The AUW has partnered with WorldTeach to identify, recruit and train Access Academy teachers, who have all been drawn to the AUW because of its mission and unique students. For AUW volunteer and gift opportunities, ☎ +1 617 914 0500 or visit www.asian-university.org. For Academy teaching opportunities, please visit the WorldTeach website www.worldteach.org.

centuries, the 12th to 13th centuries saw a few Hindu monuments take prominence, including the well-known Kantanagar Temple in Dinajpur.

But when the Muslims came, everything changed. Their monuments, with their stout, fortress-like appearance, spoke of a more austere vision of the world and its people. The best example, the Shait Gumbad Mosque, lies at Bagerhat near Khulna. Later examples include the mosques in Dhaka, notably Khan Mohammad Mridha's Mosque, the Lalbagh Fort and the Sat Gumbad Mosque.

The advent of the British brought about another style of construction. A network of Hindu *zamindars* (feudal landlords), were used by the British to administer taxation and local affairs throughout the Bengal countryside (Rabindranath Tagore (see *Literature* below) was himself one of these *zamindars*). With the funds from their coffers, the Hindu landlords constructed massive palaces, known as *rajbaris*. They employed a Renaissance style marked by Corinthian, Ionic and even Doric columns, and huge, wide frontages that resemble some well-known European buildings. The best examples include the Natore Rajbari and the nearby Dighapatia Palace, plus the Awal Manzil in Sonargaon's Painam Nagar.

Finally, Bangladesh's modernist traditions are expressed in Dhaka's most noteworthy buildings. For example, the National Assembly building in Dhaka is definitely the country's most impressive structure, far more impressive than any replica of the Taj Mahal could be (yes, Bangladesh has a replica Taj Mahal near Sonargaon). Designed by American architect Louis Khan, the monolithic structure is easily one of his masterpieces. The imposing Baitul Mukarram Mosque, located at the central meeting point of New and Old Dhaka, is also representative of Bangladesh's concept of modern Islam. By not using a traditional dome in its construction, the architecture represents a significant break from typical mosque forms.

LITERATURE While the poetry and visual art of Rabindranath Tagore is largely associated with the intellectual traditions of Kolkata, his influence over all of Bengal can also be keenly felt in Bangladesh. Tagore largely described the humanity of the people as well as his love for the land. This is why his writings remain appealing to Bengali people who, regardless of religion, share this love of nature. Tagore received the Nobel Prize in Literature in 1913, as his verse, short stories, novels and poetry were already receiving worldwide acclaim. Poetry, particularly that of 'rebel poet' Kazi Nazrul Islam and modernist poet Jibananda Das, is also commonplace among Bangladeshi people, who are keen to recite these poems at special occasions or to stir up nationalist sentiment, as Sheikh Mujib Rahman did during his campaign for Bangladeshi independence.

FOLK ART Clay utensils, terracotta plaques and handpainted artwork display a folk art tradition that is very distinctive of Bengali art, as is weaving. During the 7th century, the textiles of Bengal were making their way to Europe. Known as muslin cloth, the material had a kind of fineness that is hard to discover today in modern Bangladesh. The most extravagant of these cloths is the *jamdani*, which in historical times was produced by imperial commission. Needlework, in the form of *nakshikantha*, is now a cottage industry in Bangladesh, mostly produced by village women. Used as a trousseau, or household cloth, the art depicts local history and myths. These cloths can be purchased in handicraft stores in Dhaka.

RICKSHAW ART 'Moving graffiti' is perhaps the best way to describe the art attached to Bangladesh's colourful rickshaw brigades, but if you ask an urbanite what they think of rickshaws, you might get an upturned nose in return. While most of these human-powered, highly decorated machines have disappeared with rising fortunes in other places, they still number in the hundreds of thousands in Dhaka. For the foreign visitor, these rickshaws and their drivers add character and colour to a city that would otherwise have a lot of acne to hide. But for locals, the traffic-impeding rickshaws and their drivers are themselves the nuisance that they would rather do without, especially as they park their vehicles directly on city streets at no cost whatsoever.

Nevertheless, the machines persist in Dhaka and on designs that have scarcely evolved in previous decades. At least, unlike Kolkata's hand-pulled rickshaws, the cycle version present in Bangladesh is more efficient, albeit only slightly so. The art adorning them has also barely changed, although the number of artists who are talented in creating the hand-painted plates is in decline as screen-printed versions are faster and cheaper to produce. The rickshaw plate (the lower section on the back) often depicts popular scenes, including bloody tableaux from the Liberation War or the pink pouts of Dhallywood stars. At one point in the 1970s, the scenes became so lewd that certain drawings were totally banned by the Dhaka city authorities, only to return a few years later. Stick around long enough and you might find yourself the owner of a rickshaw (and an accompanying wallah) too.

MUSIC AND DANCE In the remote villages and towns of Bengal, many people still remain illiterate and uneducated, and so the tradition of folk music and song in Bangladesh is ironically still quite strong. Village folk music is rich with the tradition of Bengal's history, and without the use of a text to transmit it, many villagers are still seen to gather around during special festivals or gatherings to listen to folk songs. Often these are accompanied with a harmonium (wooden accordion), a pair of *tablas* (Bengali drums) and an *ektara* (one-stringed instrument).

The Bauls of Bangladesh Perhaps Bangladesh might be a strange place to find a population of long-haired, pot-smoking bards, but that's not so far off when it comes to describing certain aspects of the Baul people. They are in fact a mystic-religious cult whose origins date back to the very roots of Bangladesh. With their beliefs in humanism, existentialism and a love for the land professed in song, many Bangladeshi people, especially intellectuals, identify with the Baul people philosophically, if not materially.

The patron saint of the Baul people is Fokir Lalon Shah, who was born to a Hindu family in Kushtia in southwest Bangladesh. Although there have been conflicting accounts written about his life, it is acknowledged that after being cast out from his family by religious edict, Lalon adopted several of the casteless tenets that would define the future movement. His medium for communicating these ideas was song; proponents of the philosophy say Lalon was able to take its most difficult concepts and make them widely understandable through music. Today there are two yearly festivals held in Kushtia, entitled Lalon Utsab, celebrating both his birth (February) and death (October). The celebration attracts thousands of people each year.

NATURAL HISTORY AND CONSERVATION

For a country this size, Bangladesh has been endowed with an extraordinary amount of natural wealth and abundance. While its floods do cause serious calamities to its people, the waters are also the source of rich Himalayan mineral deposits and without the yearly flooding, soil that already bears a heavy agricultural load would never replenish itself.

Imagine that several thousand years ago, one of the world's most densely populated countries was simply a swathe of wide jungle, where tigers, elephants and spotted deer roamed free. In ancient and medieval Bengal, forests of the area easily met the needs of local communities and forest cover remained stable. But during the Mughal period this changed. As increasingly large settlements were granted to local landlords under Mughal rule, many local people became subservient to them and were forced to generate payment revenue from cultivated lands, and thus a long process of forest denigration began. Bangladesh's forests fared no better under the country's colonial period with many being converted to meet the shipbuilding demands of the Royal Navy. During the period of East Pakistan, 'commercially invaluable' forests were cleared for more valuable species such as teak, with further losses occurring during the civil unrest of the Liberation War. It would not be until the 1980s when the first donor-funded protection programmes began, and met with mixed success.

Today, only 3% of the country's natural forests remain, down from 5% in the 1990s. Naturally, Sundarban is the most famous and well-recognised sanctuary in Bangladesh, and thankfully its borders haven't changed much in the last 125 years, as it attained 'Reserve Forest' status way back in 1876. Only the 10,000km^2 tract at Sundarban still holds Royal Bengal tigers in their natural habitat, and is one of the few truly wild reserves left on the subcontinent (the forest is shared between India and Bangladesh: 6,000km^2 lies in Bangladesh). Besides being the home of the tigers (see box *Tiger conservation efforts in the Sundarbans* opposite), the forest is also home to spotted deer, Irrawaddy dolphins and estuarine crocodiles. As the world's largest mangrove forest, it is also now a World Heritage Site. In 2008, scientists determined that Bangladesh has a population of over 6,000 Irrawaddy river dolphins, previously thought to be nearly extinct. The discovery makes Bangladesh the home of the largest sub-population of Irrawaddy dolphins in the world.

In a 'normal' conservation approach, it would be reasonable to assume that the government-appointed stewards of such natural wealth would be interested in protecting it, especially the kind of diversity offered by a country as rich in flora and fauna as tropical Bangladesh. But when the Chief Conservator of Forests, Md Osman Gani, was arrested in 2007 under the caretaker government's anti-corruption drive, Tk10,000,000 of cash – or roughly US$150,000 – was found stuffed into pillowcases, mattresses and rice bins. Further investigation revealed four times that amount in liquid assets scattered around his home. Endemic corruption and a traditional view of forests as 'money in the form of timber', according to one local journalist, has resulted in the steady decline of other less-known forests around the country, especially at Madhabpur and in the Chittagong Hill Tracts.

Perhaps this is understandable given the nature of the country's population size and its corresponding lack of abundance of natural resources – survival priorities, people always say. But the short-term gain and greed will eventually rob future generations of the benefits of nature, and that's why conservation efforts are important now and should not remain a 'luxury of a developed nations'. Fortunately, there are now some recent programmes that show encouraging signs. Ecotourism, like a seedling, is slowly taking root and there are a few organisations promoting the concept in their business; surely these are the operators who deserve more promotion and tourism business in the country's embryonic tourism industry.

Some lesser-known forests have become the focus of conservation efforts under a USAID-funded project entitled the Nishorgo Support Program, which has set up pilot ecotourism projects in Bangladesh's endangered natural areas, including local guides from the areas and basic but comfortable eco-cottages. The most well-

TIGER CONSERVATION EFFORTS IN THE SUNDARBANS

Chris Greenwood, Sundarbans Tiger Project

It was always known that tigers roamed the Sundarbans mangroves, but exactly how many nobody knew. The dense swampland makes counting an already elusive animal a difficult task, but more information was desperately needed to understand if this was indeed a large population in order to gain the support needed for its conservation. And so, the Sundarbans Tiger Project was born, a Bangladesh Forest Department-based initiative which started life as a research project trying to gather population information and shed light on the needs of the tiger in this unique environment. The findings have shown that the Bangladesh forest is home to somewhere between 300 and 500 tigers, a globally important population given the endangered status of the tiger worldwide. There is now a real need for conservation, one that requires a full-scale conservation effort to ensure the future for the Sundarbans tiger.

Only a few decades ago, tigers were seen as pests and rewards were given to hunters to kill them. Since the 1960s, there has been a massive change in attitudes towards conservation across the globe, including within the Bangladesh Forest Department. They initiated the Sundarbans Tiger Project together with international partners, and of note most recently was the development of a national Tiger Action Plan, demonstrating the Forest Department's continued commitment to forging a future for tigers. This plan is a policy-level document that outlines the objectives for conserving this magnificent animal in its own right and also as guardian of the important services provided by the Sundarbans forest to the nation. The plan identifies three key threats to tigers in the Sundarbans: loss of forest home; poaching of prey; and direct loss of the tigers through poaching and retribution killing by communities in response to man-eating and livestock loss.

The Sundarbans Tiger Project, together with other in-country partners is now busy expanding its activities to build a holistic conservation programme to deal with the threats outlined by the action plan. The task is an enormous and complex one, requiring a full team and broad spectrum of initiatives: research and monitoring, forest protection and law enforcement, policy and wildlife management, and education and awareness. Across all of these requirements is the need to work together with the local communities surrounding the forest who rely on it to survive.

A tough challenge for the programme is to engage the support of these local communities. It is difficult to discuss the importance of tigers with people who suffer the most as a result of tiger–human conflict, and whose priority is to win their daily battle against poverty. However, their support is fundamental to the long-term success of tiger-conservation efforts, and the team is working with the communities to find joint solutions, and to raise awareness as to the importance of tigers as a symbol of the health of the forest upon which we all depend.

The Save the Tiger Fund and the US Fish and Wildlife Service (USFWS) funded the inception of the project and initial studies carried out by the Forest Department with researchers from the University of Minnesota. The project also received support from the Disney Wildlife Conservation Fund, the BBC and private donors. The USFWS have been a continued support, and support from within Bangladesh has also grown, including from the Guide Tours Ltd, Synopsis and Banglalink. Recently the project has become affiliated with the Zoological Society of London which is helping to raise the profile of the Sundarbans tigers.

known project is at the Lawacherra National Park in Srimongol, where a tiny population of Hoolock gibbons manages to persist despite serious habitation threat. This tree-dwelling ape lives in the canopies of several rainforests around Bangladesh, with its highest concentration at Lawacherra. Another site lies just a few hours from Cox's Bazaar at the Teknaf Game Reserve, where wild Asian elephants are often seen roaming in the forest. The region would also be attractive for the fact it has some stunning beach vistas but lacks the hotel developments that currently crowd Cox's Bazaar. Visitors are encouraged to check out the Nishorgo website (*www.nishorgo.org*) to learn more.

Last but not least are Bangladesh's wetland areas, named *haors* in Bangla, which are important for two distinct reasons. Ecologically speaking, thousands of migratory birds use these regions as pitstops on their way to warmer climes and a visit during the winter season would prove to be a birdwatcher's paradise. Economically, the wetlands are also a significant source of fish. The wetlands are largely concentrated around the northwestern parts of the Sylhet Division, with the largest of these called the Hakaluki Haor in the Maulvi Bazaar district.

2

Practical Information

WHEN TO VISIT

If you benefit from being able to choose exactly when to visit Bangladesh, then go in November or December, when the humid and heavy heat of summer finally begins to ebb away. The skies are blue, the air is clear and the sunsets spectacular, although the clear skies mean that you won't see those dramatic monsoon clouds splayed across the landscape. At this time Bangladesh is busy but not frantic, moods are relaxed and congenial. The temperature is most favourable for travel, and air conditioning is no longer required in the evenings.

Late December to March brings even cooler temperatures and mild weather. While Bangladeshis are busy dressing up in hats and scarves preparing for what looks like impending sub-zero temperatures, visitors from temperate climes might also find the humid cold chillier than they expected, even if the actual temperature highs, say 20–25°C or 59–77°F, might not seem that cold. Sadly, the occasional cold wave does kill poor people in the country's remote regions, mostly because of a lack of warm clothing. Bangladesh's muddy soils, once so full of floodwater, eventually drain and dry out during these months, leaving cracked earth and drought conditions in some places. While it is still very pleasant to travel at this time, the lush nature of the land is diminished without the life-giving rains of the monsoon. Low temperatures can also result in foggy conditions, adding some interesting qualities to rural photographs, but sometimes delaying inbound flights as well. Birders will find this is the best time of year to see many flying migrants taking their winter homes, or passing through on their way to southern destinations.

If November is the best month, April and May are the worst. A nearly intolerable heat pervades everything, to the point where air conditioners can no longer hold it back and inconsistent power supply makes everyone dream of the upcoming downpours. The lack of rain also means that a thick layer of dust coats everything, especially in Dhaka, where the air is already rather leaden with pollutants.

When the first rains of June come, everyone breathes a sigh of relief and the land explodes with life. Contrary to popular expectation it does not rain all day every day; in fact it usually only rains in the afternoons. Temperatures are still hot, but the time just after a cooling shower is absolute bliss. Local street children literally dance with glee in the streets when it rains.

Travel during this season can be hit and miss. On one hand the rivers can be quite beautiful, especially when cumulus monsoon clouds form pluming chimneys over the landscape, their pan-flat bottoms mirroring the horizon. The forests and hills also come alive with the watery onslaught, their green hues a real contrast to the brown days of a few months previous. This is a fantastic, if slightly less safe time to see Bangladesh from the rivers (unpredictable weather can cause problems on launches, but this is no less dangerous than taking a bus on a

Bangladeshi highway). Northeast Bangladesh is also fantastic during this season, as the tea pickers come out during the late monsoon, and rivers flowing from the Khasia and Garo hills are in full spate. India-bound travellers or Bangladesh-based expatriates should include Meghalaya on their itineraries at this time of year. With over 12,000mm of rain annually, the village of Cherrapunjee regained the title of the wettest place on earth in 2007 (see *Chapter 5, Cherrapunjee*, page 181 for more information).

On the other hand, it's hard to make travel plans as the weather can be unpredictable at best, and frustrating at worst, so if you do decide you'd like to experience the monsoon from its wettest country, don't try to make too many hard and fast schedules – go with the flow, literally.

August and September are the typical flood seasons in Bangladesh, although a late deluge can sometimes cause problems all the way into October. During these late monsoon months, the weather is inconsistent and moody, dropping drenching downpours in some places but staying completely dry just a few kilometres away. Temperatures are still toasty, but by this time the country's hottest days have mostly passed. The rivers and wetlands are at their fullest in this season, and great big swathes of Bangladesh go underwater as far as the eye can see, giving the impression of being on the ocean instead of actually being on the land. Seen from the air, this phenomenon is most remarkable, as only the villages and embankments lying on high ground remain immune to the encroaching waters.

In short, any time of year is good to visit Bangladesh, but older or more comfort-seeking travellers would be best choosing the winter season, whereas adventurers might just think that dealing with a flood could be fun.

Finally, there is another way to look at the question of when to go that doesn't depend on the weather: that's to experience some of Bangladesh's many festivals and celebrations, which provide excellent and colourful photographic opportunities from a country whose celebrations have yet to be seen by the world eye.

Highlights include the mass exodus at Eid and the colourful Durga Puja celebration soon after. Otherwise Christmas among Bangladesh's Christians proves to be a good time with plenty of hard local drinks to be had. Finally, Bengali New Year (14 April) can be celebrated anywhere in Bangladesh but the best place to take it in is in the Chittagong Hill Tracts where celebrations during Boiju get rowdy and entertaining. Each of these options is best used if you live in the country and have some sort of personal connection in the place you wish to visit, although that's not entirely necessary as those who show up with an open mind will have no issues finding friends with whom to have a good time. Check the festival calendar in *Public holidays and festivals*, page 77, for more information.

HIGHLIGHTS

Bangladesh rarely makes any 'top ten' lists worldwide, but an often asked question comes more along the following lines: 'Since I'm in Bangladesh, what are the top ten things I should see?' Here's a suggestion list to get you started.

PEOPLE Above anything else, it is the people of Bangladesh who stand out as a highlight of this country, a definite positive when considering that the *desh* is one of the most heavily populated nations on earth. Your first impressions will no doubt centre on the unstoppable curiosity and unrelenting enthusiasm of the Bangladeshi people, followed by subsequent insights into their never-ending hospitality and graciousness towards foreign guests. Long after you've left it will be their kindnesses you will keep with you, as well as memories of interactions you had with a people who themselves crave real interaction with the outside world –

an opportunity so seldom few of them ever get to see with their own eyes. Bring your camera, and upon returning home you will see that it is overflowing with images of people.

SUNDARBAN Bangladesh's most pristine wilderness is a true oasis, where relaxing boat journeys can be had amongst peace and quiet – something quite rare in this populous nation. As the largest tract of mangroves in the world, it's also home to a significant wildlife population of spotted deer and man-eating Royal Bengal tigers.

CHITTAGONG HILL TRACTS This scenic destination offers hilly scenery, indigenous culture, hard drinks and serene Buddhist monasteries. It's also a geographic and cultural standout from the flat existence of the plains below. At Bandarban, there are plenty of unexplored trekking opportunities including the remote journey to one of Bangladesh's highest places, Kewkradang. At Rangamati, boating on Kaptai Lake is a peaceful way to pass time and relax.

SRIMONGOL The hills of this area are especially good both during and shortly after the monsoon. Cycle amongst tea plantations that carpet the landscape, and walk in rainforests that are alive with life (and leeches!). A tiny population of Hoolock gibbons remains in the Lawacherra Rainforest, desperately in need of conservation.

RIVERS Any river journey is an adventure in the country's aquatic arteries; these lead directly into Bangladesh's heart and soul. There are so many ways to do this: budget travellers can crash out on boat decks *en route* to Bangladesh's coastal south (air-conditioned cabins are also available on some boats), while luxury seekers can be served brie on a historic Bangladeshi sailing boat. The rocket paddlewheel lies somewhere in the middle and can act as a gateway to or away from Sundarban. Bangladesh is also home to the world's largest population of Irrawaddy river dolphins, with a population of 5,800 spread along the coast and especially concentrated in Sundarban. There are also Ganges river dolphins along the major rivers and finless porpoises and Indo-Pacific humpback dolphins who call the Bay of Bengal home.

BEACH As the longest natural beach in the world, Cox's Bazaar is often touted as Bangladesh's beach paradise. But the town itself, with its crowded conditions and rampant development, can be quite a letdown. Outside the town is a different story, however. While it's not easy to find a truly isolated, private piece of white sand, there are plenty of quiet areas awaiting intrepid travellers who travel southward along the length of the beach. St Martin's Island has also shared a similar fate with Cox's, but if you venture away from the main touristed areas, the real spirit of this beach remains. Visitors who would rather skip the Cox's experience entirely will find an excellent beach at Kuakata, although in a few years' time this place might soon resemble its bigger cousin. Finally, Bangladesh becomes home to a number of river beaches during the dry season (November to March), in which the water levels run low and these are easily as good as being on a beach by the coast. The best water for such river beaches comes from the Khasi Hills in the northern parts of Sylhet Division, in the areas that lie directly alongside the border with India.

RAINFORESTS Bangladesh's forests have been slowly decimated over the years, much to the dismay of conservationists and those who know that habitat quality is the key ingredient for the survival of endangered species. Aside from Sundarban, two national parks stand out as highlights: Lawacharra is easily combined with a visit to Srimongol (see above). Located at the southeastern tip of Bangladesh, the

Teknaf Game Reserve is one of Bangladesh's last remaining pristine rainforests and also holds a population of wild Asian elephants. There is also a newly established network of walking trails at both parks to get visitors into the forest and experiencing nature.

CHARS These river islands are spread amongst the basins of the country's major river systems. Scenic and serene, the *chars* are not easy places to reach as they can only be accessed by boat. But the stories of the people who live there, often the poorest of Bangladesh's poor, are extraordinary. As the islands are vulnerable to yearly flooding, they shift constantly, causing the inhabitants to move perhaps a dozen times or more in one lifetime. No government services exist, there are no roads and there is no electricity, which means that millions of inhabitants who live on the *chars* remain in positively medieval conditions. Serious adventurers might want to find their way to these unique and isolated places to see people who still remain on the very edges of existence. Kurigram, in the northeastern reaches of the Rajshahi Division, is the best place to visit the islands.

INDIGENOUS CULTURE Aside from the diversity found in the Chittagong Hill Tracts, budding anthropologists will find more diversity than they expected in other parts of Bangladesh. There are several groups of tribal people living on the fringes of Sylhet Division, including pockets of Tripuran, Manipuri and Khasi people. In the northern reaches of the Dhaka Division, Garo people populate the areas directly below the hills. Visiting these unique cultures gives visitors another take on the hospitality offered by the people of Bangladesh, and the opportunity to get a hard drink in this outwardly conservative nation.

RURAL BEAUTY Visitors from northern climates will find nothing more pleasant than the simple, verdant nature of the villages and towns of Bangladesh, most of which are pleasantly shaded under palm and coconut trees, and populated with villagers of an earnest and friendly demeanour. The real soul of the country lies here, far from the crowded cities of Dhaka and Chittagong. Rajshahi Division, especially in its western and northwestern corners, offers these experiences in abundance. May brings what is known locally as 'honey month', where several kinds of fruits become ripe for harvest, especially the magical mangoes.

PHOTOGRAPHY In a country full of colour, life, sound and vibrancy, photographers will find no shortage of material to work with, whether they be extraordinary river landscapes or dozens of beautiful faces, all of whom are rather eager to be photographed. Life spills out onto the streets, and rarely is Bangladesh tucked away behind curtains or swept under carpets. Visitors will find themselves able to see directly into the lives of local people, especially in the cities, who seem just as curious as they look back.

SUGGESTED ITINERARIES

THREE DAYS Take your first day exploring Old Dhaka, experiencing the frenetic energy offered by the historic capital. The second day can be spent doing a day trip out of the city: Savar or Sonargaon would be good, although a boat trip would be best – contact one of the local tour operators (see *Chapter 3*, *Tour operators*, page 118) to see if you can join a trip that's already been arranged. Finally, spend your last day like a Dhaka urbanite by checking out some of Bangladesh's many handicrafts or textile shops, some of which do business under free-trade banners. See pages 83 and 137, for more information.

ONE WEEK With a bit more time in your itinerary you have a range of options which would probably depend on what time of year you visit. If it's the winter season, a visit to Sundarban is a must, and will take four days at least, including transport to/from Dhaka and more if you opt to take the rocket. If it's the monsoon season, especially the months of July, August or September, Sylhet Division is the place to visit, as the lush nature of Bangladesh comes to life here amidst the tea plantations and the rainforests of the region. Finally, if indigenous culture is your bag, then one week is just enough time to visit the Chittagong Hill Tracts (CHT), which is good any time of year but especially during Bengali New Year in April. Another potential option is to combine a quick visit to the beach at Cox's Bazaar and stop in for a few days to the CHT.

15 DAYS With two weeks in hand, it is possible to visit the highlights of Bangladesh without rushing through it all. Start with a few days in the Sundarbans, followed by a cross-country journey to the CHT, and end with a stop into Srimongol. Dhaka can be done on either end of this trip. The day train from Chittagong to Srimongol (or vice versa) is a memorable and manageable journey that provides good vistas into the rural scenery of Bangladesh. Also, the land route from Sundarban to Chittagong can be accomplished via a long train or bus ride via Dhaka, but new flight services can take passengers directly from Jessore (the nearest airport to Sundarban) to Chittagong, which is the gateway to the CHT.

ONE MONTH A month is the ideal length of time to experience all that Bangladesh has to offer, with time to stop and/or volunteer if it so suits you. The above 15-day itinerary could be used, and then depending on your preference you could add some beach time at Cox's Bazaar or more time in the CHT. The extra time would also allow for a jaunt into Rajshahi Division, including Rajshahi, Bogra and Rangpur. This would offer the opportunity to add in quick stops to the archaeological highlights of 'Golden Bengal', and some time to check out the *char* areas highlighted above.

INDIA Visitors who combine a visit to Bangladesh on their India itineraries will instantly find that the sincerity and hospitality of the Bangladeshi people comes across as quite a surprise compared with the hustle and efficiency of the Indian tourism industry. If Darjeeling is the final destination, then cutting a track through western Bangladesh via Dhaka would give a good taste of the country's rural climes and could be done comfortably in about a week. If northeast India is on your itinerary, then two–three weeks would be enough to cross the eastern half of Bangladesh on your way to the Dawkhi/Tamabil border in Sylhet Division (a good reason to get a multiple-entry India visa!). If visiting during the monsoon season, then a visit to the 'wettest place on earth' at Cherrapunjee, Meghalaya, is a must.

TOURIST INFORMATION

Bangladesh's national tourism organisation is called the Bangladesh Parjatan Corporation, or *Parjatan*, meaning tourism, for short. The organisation's old Dhaka headquarters were recently demolished to make way for a road and its new address had yet to be decided. This was probably for the better as the organisation was largely ineffective and its materials well out of date. Travellers might find the services of a tour operator more efficient and helpful in the search for information and guidance when considering a journey to Bangladesh.

TOUR OPERATORS

UK

Exodus UK Grange Mills, Weir Rd, London SW12 0NE; ☎ +44 (0)208 675 5550; e sales@exodus.co.uk; www.exodus.co.uk. Offers a Darjeeling/Sikkim & northwest Bangladesh itinerary.
Explore UK Nelson Hse, 55 Victoria Rd, Farnborough, Hampshire GU14 7PA; ☎ +44 (0)845 013 1537; e hello@explore.co.uk; www.explore.co.uk. Also offers a package tour covering northwest Bangladesh, Darjeeling, Sikkim & Bhutan.
Saddle Skedaddle 110 Ouseburn Bldg, Albion Row, East Quayside, Newcastle upon Tyne NE6 1LL; ☎ +44 (0)191 265 1110; e info@skedaddle.co.uk; www.traidcraft-tours.co.uk. Offers specialised handicraft tours to Bangladesh with UBINIG, a Bangladeshi NGO with fantastic local knowledge.
Undiscovered Destinations Saville Exchange, Howard St, North Shields NE30 1SE; ☎ +44 (0)191 296 2674, 206 4038; e info@undiscovered-destinations.com; www.bangladesh-undiscovered.com. An operator with specialist knowledge of Bangladesh. The owner definitely has a special soft spot for the country.

EUROPE

Grace Tours Sankt Peders Stræde 28, 1453 København, Denmark; ☎ +45 33 117 117; e mail@gracetours.com; www.gracetours.com. Operates tours on an on-demand basis, for individual travellers. Resources are mostly in Danish, but do speak English if you call.
Thurgau Travel Rathausstrasse 5, 8570 Weinfelden, Switzerland; ☎ +41 71 626 55 00; e info@thurgautravel.ch; www.thurgautravel.ch. Specialises in private boat journeys in Bangladesh.

USA/CANADA

Asian Pacific Adventures 6065 Calvin Av, Tarzana, CA 91356, USA; ☎ +1 818 881 2745, +1 800 825 1680 (inside US, toll free); e info@asianpacificadventures.com; www.asianpacificadventures.com
Experience Bangladesh Austin, TX, USA; ☎ +1 512 263 0653; e contact@experiencebangladesh.com; www.experiencebangladesh.com. Unique perspective on tour operations to Bangladesh. Focuses mainly on tourism for poverty-alleviation purposes.
GAP Adventures 19 Charlotte St, Toronto ON, M5V 2H5, Canada; ☎ 1 800 708 7761 (in North America); +1 416 260 0999 (outside North America & UK); +1 246 426 2246 (agents outside North America & UK); +44 (0)870 999 0144 (UK); +1 888 800 4100 (USA); www.gapadventures.com. Package tours to Bangladesh, includes the highlights & professional logistical management.
Remote Lands 6th Flr, 845 Third Ave, New York, NY 10022; ☎ +1 646 415 8092; e info@remotelands.com. Luxury boutique operator offering specialised & highly organised individual tours to Bangladesh. All-inclusive tours generally start at US$750/day, including expert guides, drivers, internal flights, meals, hotels & activities.

AUSTRALIA

Intrepid Travel 11 Spring St, Fitzroy, Victoria 3065; ☎ +61 3 9473 2626, 9473 2673; e generalinfo@intrepidtravel.com; www.intrepidtravel.com. Offers packages covering the highlights of Bangladesh.

RED TAPE

VISAS AND ENTRY REQUIREMENTS All foreign visitors to Bangladesh require a visa. To be frank, getting a Bangladesh visa can be a pain in the backside, so let this process be your first lesson in the patience you will inevitably cultivate during your stay in Bangladesh. Because of a lack of information on visa regulations, procedures and the simple fact that not that many tourists or visitors come to Bangladesh (streamlined application processes are an innovation yet to be discovered in the country), you should apply for your visa as early as possible. Also note that each Bangladesh consular office applies the rules and regulations slightly differently, so if you're ever in doubt, call the relevant office and ask for directions or check the relevant websites (none of which are particularly well organised or even functional) to get yourself as informed as possible. Now that your expectations are set appropriately low, here are some directions to help ease the process.

Tourist visas are the easiest to obtain. Depending on the office you're dealing with, they can be issued for periods of up to two months (Australians can get six months), and whatever the length of your stay it is suggested that you apply for the maximum amount of time permitted, or at least specify a date that is a few days earlier than your expected arrival and at least a few days later than your expected departure. Most consular offices will request a letter of invitation along with the visa; this could be a letter from the tour operator or the contact that you may be visiting. Otherwise any manufactured letter that explains the purpose of your visit should satisfy the Bangladeshi bureaucratic urge for paper consumption. Other consular offices might request a hotel booking, air ticket confirmation or a signed invitation letter from Bangladesh. If such a letter is required, asking around on Lonely Planet's Thorn Tree forum will usually help you locate someone who can prepare such a letter on your behalf. Generally, building a 'paperwork' case for your visit to Bangladesh is what you should do, and the more paper you have to support the application, the more impressive it appears. The higher up the status of the letterhead (diplomatic or aid agencies rate very high), the better. A few travel advisories also specify that you should have an onward ticket to present on arrival, but immigration staff rarely request to see such paperwork.

Business visas are a slightly different story. They can be issued for periods up to six months, and require a letter introducing your company along with a letter from your proposed business partner clearly stating the purpose of your visit.

Visa fees vary from nationality to nationality as Bangladesh practises a reciprocal fee system. Whatever visa fee is charged to Bangladesh nationals when they apply is same rate charged to foreign visa applications. You can check the fee schedule on the immigration website (*www.dip.gov.bd*). Some common visa fees are: £40/52/75 for single-/double-/multiple-entry visas for UK nationals; US$131 for US nationals, regardless of length or number of entries; CAD$80/158 for single-/multiple-entry visas for Canadian nationals; and AUD$150 for single-/double-/multiple-entry visas for Australian nationals (in the case of Australia, all visa types are the same price so it may be best to apply for a multiple entry visa for the longest period permissible by the high commission).

Applying in India Applying for a tourist visa in India before your visit to Bangladesh is possible, but not desirable. Your best bet is again to get it before even setting foot in the subcontinent. The Kolkata visa office has an especially nasty reputation, and so if you need to apply for your tourist visa here make sure you also bring your patience, good humour and at least two or three extra days for interviews/ questions/problems. Also, applying for anything other than a tourist visa can cause difficulties and elicit many questions, most of which you should take in a friendly manner but also be firm about your needs. The Delhi office is also prone to application difficulties, although the travellers who are patient and aware of the bureaucracy seem to get through here with fewer problems. Should you be all the way out in Agartala, it is also possible to get tourist visas here for 15 days without difficulties; should you require a longer period you'll need to lock down an interview with officials to explain your cause. Also, keep in mind that holidays in Bangladesh differ from those in India, so if you're planning to apply anytime around Eid-ul Fitr (August–October), be prepared for extra delays. Come prepared with at least three passport-sized photographs and photocopies of your passport and onward flight arrangements, if any.

Long-term visa issues Employment and NGO visas are where things begin to get a bit more complicated, but your employer in Bangladesh should help you with obtaining the necessary paperwork. Most of the advice that follows is for those who have to do the applications themselves, such as consultants, freelancers or long-term volunteers.

Applying for the first visa is best done from your home country, as there tend to be more restrictions on visa applications for nationals from elsewhere (ie: when a Canadian national tries to apply for an NGO visa in China, it can cause a fair amount of confusion among consular officials). Americans tend to get better visas than other nationalities. In Australia, you are unlikely to get more than a six-month visa, unless you are associated with an Australian government aid programme.

If you obtain a visa that expires during your stay, begin the process for visa extension as soon as you are settled in Bangladesh. Security clearances and work permits are required for most visa extensions and these can take months and many painful hours wasted at various government offices. Bangladesh's visa office makes snails seem speedy, although believe it or not, things improved under the 2007–08 caretaker administration. Your host organisation should also assist with the visa extension process, but do be wary as they can sometimes be as clueless as you (reassurances of 'no problem, no problem' are often a warning sign in this regard). If your visa does expire you will have to pay a fine, a rate variable depending on your work and host organisation. You will also require an exit visa to leave Bangladesh and this can likewise take months to obtain.

If you find yourself in a real bind with visa issues (ie: lacking the correct paperwork and with less than a month to go until your visa expires), the least stressful but definitely most expensive option is to leave Bangladesh and apply for a new visa from outside. The bureaucratic chaos of Bangladesh apparently can't be escaped within the subcontinent, so consider heading to Thailand, Malaysia or Singapore for such a visa run as these offices tend to be far more generous with their visas. Also, this process can be complicated by a few other factors, such as whether you still have a valid Bangladeshi visa in your passport, which in some cases should have expired first. Finally, it is apparently impossible to change the visa type after your arrival, so do try to apply for the correct visa before your first arrival in the country, which will hopefully save you time and energy as you try to navigate Bangladesh's extraordinary bureaucracy.

Once you do have the correct paperwork in place, the immigration office will be able to extend your visa for the period of your work permit. Bribing at any consular or immigration office is not recommended – it may work, according to some of those who have tried otherwise, but it may also jeopardise your chances and does little for the global stance against corruption. It helps to carry around extra photocopies of your passport and passport-sized photos when dealing with these issues.

Landing permit As of 22 March 2008, the majority of nationals from Western countries (US, Canada, UK, Europe, Australia) could obtain a 'Landing Permit on Arrival' if you arrive in Dhaka with no visa, and while it may not be checked, you should also carry printed proof of your onward travel arrangements. With US$50, you can simply buy this landing permit when you arrive at Zia International Airport, and you should be granted a 15-day stay, which you can overstay for a few days, or even a couple of weeks and pay the Tk200 per day overstay fee. The permit would normally be issued to visitors hailing from most Western countries, especially when they arrive from a country with no resident Bangladeshi mission.

However, please note that this could change at any time and without warning – such are the vagaries of the Bangladesh immigration system. The rules surrounding this landing permit are not published anywhere and there is a general sense that officials do not want this system to be too widely known by visiting guests. Although for short-term tourist arrivals coming from a country that is not their home country, this is the best choice. The airport immigration telephone number at Zia International Airport is +880 2 891 4226, and if you speak Bangla or know a Bangla speaker you will be able to get up-to-the-minute details.

Whether or not you use the Landing Permit on Arrival system depends on whether or not you are the traveller who is willing to accept some degree of risk while you travel. Naturally, the safest option is to obtain a visa in your home country first, but if, for some circumstance of time and/or money you don't get the visa, and you don't need to stay in Bangladesh for longer than 15 days, a landing permit would certainly be easier than other potential bureaucratic speed bumps you could encounter at a Bangladeshi high commission or embassy abroad.

Finally, the Landing Permit on Arrival system should only be used if you also plan to depart from Zia International Airport, and not overland to India. Indian immigration officials will not recognise the landing permit and may refuse to issue a visa in Dhaka. Even if you already have an Indian visa, border officials may not permit you to cross with only a landing permit.

Given the multitude of complexities surrounding the landing permit, it is naturally best to obtain the necessary visa before your arrival in Bangladesh.

Visa extensions Visa processing is handled at the Department of Immigration and Passports (*Passport Bhaban, E7 Agargaon, Sher-e-Bangla Nagar, www.dip.gov.bd; visa drop-off* ⌚ *10.00–13.00 and pickup* ⌚ *14.00–16.00*). While affairs have become slightly more orderly at this aging office, do bring a sense of patience along with your necessary paperwork. If you have any friends at all in the government, having them place a phone call to the department will help speed up your visit immensely as you can be ushered in the 'back door' using your connections. Nonetheless, such connections will not help you if you don't have the right paperwork ready.

Landing permits and transit visas are non-extendable. Tourist visas can be extended for up to 30 days. A starting point of reference should be the department's website, where you will find a link at the bottom left under 'Visa Policy' where all the requirements for each visa are listed. Also, there is a link provided for the necessary 'Visa Fees' on the left sidebar and the 'Visa Form' on the right. Here's a checklist that you should prepare first:

- Passport photocopy
- Visa page photocopy
- Photocopy of the page containing your entry stamp
- One passport photo
- Visa fee (depends on nationality: UK US$65 for single entry, US$168 for multiple; US US$131 for single/multiple; Canada Tk3,300 for single or Tk6,600 for multiple)
- While it depends on the visa required, most require a letter from your employer and security clearance from the Ministry of Home Affairs. NGO visas require a work permit from the NGO bureau. Keep your original paperwork and make photocopies for processing – paperwork being 'lost' is an infrequent but not unheard of occurrence.

Indian visa It is possible to get an Indian visa in Dhaka and Chittagong, although the High Commission of India website (see page 40) advises foreign applicants, *other than those residing in Bangladesh*, to normally obtain a visa from the Indian mission located in their country of origin or residence. Thus, it is prudent to bring a covering letter indicating that you are a resident of Bangladesh or are employed with a local organisation (regardless of what your actual status is).

Using the normal process, the Dhaka office (*Indian Visa Application Centre, Hse 12, Rd 137, Gulshan 1, ☎ 02 989 3006; f 02 986 3229; e info@ivacbd.com; www.ivacbd.com; ⌚ 11.00–12.00 for application/pickup*) will grant six-month multiple-entry visas (Tk3,575 for most nationals, Tk3,300 for US nationals) to India although the length of visa does depend on the mood of the consular officials on the day of application. In addition, they sometimes request an extra Tk230 fee to send a clearance letter to Delhi. The whole process normally takes four working days. The Dhaka visa office is less unfriendly than the Chittagong visa office, and sometimes they have been known to give female applicants more trouble than men.

You will need to take the following paperwork and be prepared to fetch more at the consular officer's whim:

- Completed visa application form – available at the Indian high commission or online
- Your passport
- A photocopy of the headshot page of your passport as well as a photocopy of your Bangladesh visa
- Two passport photos
- Letter from your employer stating your reason for being in Bangladesh, your job, and your reason for travel to India
- Visa fee – check the website for the latest fees

E EMBASSIES AND HIGH COMMISSIONS

ABROAD

Australia 21 Culgoa Circuit, O'Malley, Canberra, ACT 2606; ☎ +61 2 6290 0511, 6290 0522, 6290 0533; e bdoot.canberra@cyberone.com.au; www.bangladoot-canberra.org

Belgium 29–31 Rue Jacques Jordaens, 1000 Brussels; ☎ +32 2 640 5500; e bdootbrussels@skynet.be, trade@bangladeshembassy.be; www.bangladeshembassy.be

Bhutan Plt HIG-3, Upper Chubachu, Thimphu; ☎ +975 2 322 539; e bdoot@druknet.bt

Canada Suite 302, 275 Bank St, Ottawa, ON, K2P 2L6; ☎ +1 613 236 0138, 236 0139; e info@bdhc.org, bangla@rogers.com; www.bdhc.org; A fire at the high commission in 2008 caused the office to be shifted to a temporary location. See website for the latest.

China 42 Guang Hua Lu, Beijing 100600; ☎ +86 10 6532 2521, 6532 3706; e bdemb@public3.bta.net.cn; www.bangladeshembassy.com.cn

France 39 rue Erlanger, 75016 Paris; ☎ +33 1 46 51 90 33, 46 51 98 30; e banglacom@free.fr, bdootpar@club-internet.fr, hoc_par@club-internet.fr

Germany Dovestrasse 1, 10587 Berlin; ☎ +49 3039 8975–0; e info@bangladeshembassy.de; www.bangladeshembassy.de

Hong Kong Ste 3807, China Resources Bldg, 26 Harbour Rd, Wanchai; ☎ +852 2827 4278, 2827 4279; e bangladt@netvigator.com

Indonesia Jalan Situbondo, No 12, Menteng, Jakarta; ☎ +62 21 314 690, 310 2705

India EP-39, Dr S Radha Krishna Marg, Chanakyapuri, New Delhi 110021; ☎ +91 11 2412 1389–94; e highcommissionba@eth.net; www.bhcdelhi.org; 9 Circus Av, Kolkata 700017; ☎ +91 33 2247 5208, 2247 5209; Bangladesh Visa Office, Colonel Chowmuhoni, Agartala 79901; ☎ +91 381 232 4807

Italy 14 Via Antonio Bertoloni, Rome 00197; ☎ +39 6 808 3595, 807 8541

Japan 4-15-15 Meguro, Meguro-Ku, Tokyo 153-0063; ☎ +81 3 5704 0216–8; e bdootjp@bdembjp.com; www.bdembjp.com

Malaysia No 204-1, Jalan Ampang, 50450 Kuala Lumpur; ☎ +60 3 242 3271, 242 2505

Myanmar 56 Kaba Aye Pagoda Rd, Yangon; ☎ +95 1 51174

Nepal Maharajganj, Ring Rd, Kathmandu; ☎ +977 1 414 943, 414 265

Netherlands Wassenaarseweg 39, 2596 CG, The Hague; ☎ +31 70 328 3722

Pakistan Hse 1, St 5, F-6/3, Islamabad; ☎ +92 51 2279 267; e bdhcisb@sat.net.pk
Singapore 91 Bencoolen St, No 06–01, Sunshine Plaza, Singapore 189652; ☎ +65 6255 0075; e bdoot@singnet.com.sg; www.bangladesh.org.sg
Spain 2nd Fl-D, C/Diego de Lieon-69, 28006 Madrid; ☎ +34 1 401 9932, 401 7149
Sweden Anderstorpsvägen 12 (1 Tr), 171 54 Solna, Stockholm; ☎ +46 8 730 5850; e banijya@bangladeshembassy.se
Thailand 727 Sukhumvit Soi 55 (Thonglor), Bangkok 10110; ☎ +66 2 392 9437–8; e bdoot@samart.co.th; 95 Huay Kaew Rd, T Suthep, A Muang, Chiang Mai 50200; ☎ +66 5 321 2373-4
UK 28 Queen's Gate, London SW7 5JA; ☎ 020 7584 0081; e attache@bhclondon.org.uk (consular information), info@bhclondon.org.uk (general information); www.bhclondon.org.uk; 3rd Flr, Cedar Hse, 2 Fairfield St, Manchester M1 3GF; ☎ 0161 236 4853; visas should be taken from London office.
USA 3510, International Dr NW, Washington DC 20008; ☎ +1 202 244 0183; e bdootwash@bangladoot.org; www.bangladoot.org; Suite 502, 211 East 43rd St, New York, NY 10017; ☎ +1 212 599 6767, 599 6850, 599 1874; e contact@bdcgny.org; www.bdcgny.org; Suite 605, 4201 Wilshire Bd, Los Angeles, CA 90010; ☎ +1 323 932 0100; e bcgla@earthlink.net
Vietnam 7th Fl, Daeha Business Ctr, 360 Kim Ma St, Hanoi; ☎ +84 4 771 6625, 771 7829; e bdoothn@netnam.org.vn

IN BANGLADESH

Afghanistan Hse 2A, Rd 24, Gulshan 1; ☎ 02 989 5994; e afghanembassydhaka@yahoo.com
Australia 184 Gulshan Av, Gulshan 2; ☎ 02 881 3101–5; e dima-dhaka@dfat.gov.au; www.bangladesh.embassy.gov.au/
Austria Safura Tower, 5th Flr, 20 Kemal Ataturk Av, Banani; ☎ 02 989 4329; e austriancon@quasemgroup.com
Bhutan Hse 12, Rd 107, Gulshan 2; ☎ 02 882 6863, 882 7160
Canada Hse 16A, Rd 48, Gulshan 2; ☎ 02 988 7091, 988 7097; e dhaka@international.gc.ca; www.bangladesh.gc.ca
China Plot 2–4, Rd 3, Blk 1, Baridhara; ☎ 02 882 4862, 882 4164; e chinaemb@bdmail.net; www.bd.chineseembassy.org
Denmark Hse 1, Rd 51, Gulshan 2; ☎ 02 882 1799; e dacamb@um.dk; www.ambdhaka.um.dk
European Economic Commission Hse 7, Rd 84, Gulshan 2; ☎ 02 882 4730; www.eudelbangladesh.org
France Hse 18, Rd 108, Gulshan 2; ☎ 02 881 3811–14; e webmestre.dacca-amba@diplomatie.gouv.fr; www.ambafrance-bd.org
Germany 178 Gulshan Av; ☎ 02 885 3521–24; e aadhaka@optimaxbd.net; www.dhaka.diplo.de
India Hse 2, Rd 142, Gulshan 1 (the best place for locally based foreigners to line up an Indian visa); ☎ 02 988 9339, 988 8789–91; e hoc@hcidhaka.org; www.hcidhaka.org; Hse 2, B-2, Rd 1, Khulshi, Chittagong; ☎ 031 654148; e ahcindia@spnetctg.com; www.ahcictg.org; Hse 284/2, Housing Estate, Sopura Uposhahar, Rajshahi; ☎ 0721 774841
Indonesia Hse 14 Rd 53, Gulshan 2; ☎ 02 988 1640–41; e indhaka@bangla.net; www.jakarta-dhaka.com
Italy Hse 2/3, Rd 74/79, Gulshan 2; ☎ 02 882 2781; e ambdhaka@dominox.com
Iraq Hse 8, Rd 59, Gulshan 2; ☎ 02 882 3277
Japan Hse 5–7, Dutabash Rd, Baridhara; ☎ 02 881 0087; e information@embjp.accesstel.net; www.bd.emb-japan.go.jp
Malaysia Hse 19, Rd 6, Baridhara; ☎ 02 882 7759-60; e mwdhaka@citech-bd.com; www.kln.gov.my/perwakilan/dhaka
Myanmar Hse 3, Rd 84, Gulshan 2; ☎ 02 989 6373; e mynembdk@siriusbroadband.com, mynembdk@siriusbb.com
Nepal United Nations Rd, Rd 2, Baridhara; ☎ 02 860 1790; e eondhaka@dbn-bd.net
Netherlands Hse 49, Rd 90, Gulshan 2; ☎ 02 882 2715–18; e dha@minbuza.nl; www.netherlandsembassydhaka.org
Norway Hse 9, Rd 111, Gulshan 2; ☎ 02 882 3065, 881 0563; e emb.dhaka@mfa.no; www.norway.org.bd
Pakistan Hse 2, Rd 71, Gulshan 2; ☎ 02 882 5388–9
Singapore Hse 15, Rd 68/A, Gulshan 2; ☎ 02 988 0404, 988 0337; e singcon_dha@sgmfa.gov.sg; www.mfa.gov.sg/dhaka
Sri Lanka Hse 15, Rd 50, Gulshan 2; ☎ 02 882 2790, 881 0779
Sweden Hse 1, Rd 51, Gulshan 2; ☎ 02 883 3144–7; e ambassaden.dhaka@sida.se; www.swedenabroad.com/dhaka
Thailand Hse 14, Rd 11, Baridhara; ☎ 01 881 2795–6, 8813260–1; e thaidac@mfa.go.th; www.thaidac.com
Turkey Hse 7, Rd 2, Baridhara, ☎ 02 882 2198
UK United Nations Rd, Baridhara; ☎ 02 882 2705–9; e dhaka.consular@fco.gov.uk; www.ukinbangladesh.fco.gov.uk

USA Madani Av, Baridhara, ☎ 02 885 5500; www.dhaka.usembassy.gov

Vietnam Hse 7, Rd 104, Gulshan 2; ☎ 02 885 4051, 885 4052; e vietnam@citech-bd.com; www.vietnamembassy-bangladesh.org

GETTING THERE AND AWAY

BY AIR Because Bangladesh doesn't receive a lot of air traffic, the country lacks competition among major carriers. As a result, the connections that do exist tend to be rather expensive due to a lack of critical mass and only one discount airline flies to Bangladesh (Air Asia recently added a Kuala Lumpur–Dhaka flight). While this may change with the entrance of several new local airlines, it may be a few years yet before the connections and their prices improve.

For the time being, however, there are at least daily services from other major cities of Asia, including Bangkok, Kuala Lumpur, Kunming, Singapore, Kolkata, Delhi and Kathmandu. Hong Kong is serviced five days a week. Flights to Mumbai and Karachi have less frequency than other south Asian cities. Almost all flights route through Dhaka, although you can arrive into Chittagong via Kolkata.

Further abroad, connections to the Middle East, particularly Dubai, Doha and Bahrain, are good. From Europe, London is the only direct transport link for Bangladesh, and you might be better off transiting via India if you're coming to/from other European countries. For the rest of Asia and for western North America, transiting via Hong Kong, Bangkok, Malaysia or Singapore seems best.

Biman Bangladesh is the country's national carrier. With frequent delays and a rather poor reputation, the airline's bloated expenses became an issue in 2007 when major changes were made under the caretaker administration. As it stands, the aging but mostly well-maintained fleet operates to the major cities named above, albeit with somewhat erratic schedules. If you can't find your airline of choice, do consider Biman in your flight plans as you simply won't have much other choice.

Flights from the UK/Europe The one place where Biman seems to offer competitive pricing is on the London–Dhaka route, where there is a substantial market for non-resident Bangladeshis returning to their villages and hometowns during the holidays or to see family. Although the flights might be crowded, departures are rarely on time and the passengers particularly unruly, the fares are the best for those on a budget.

Your other choices are via Emirates, Qatar Airways and Gulf Air. Emirates, Gulf Air and Qatar Airways offer daily flights to/from Dhaka with connections to other major cities in Europe and North America.

Biman Bangladesh 17 Conduit St, London W1R 9TD; ☎ 0207 629 0252, 629 0161; e bimanlondon@easynet.co.uk; www.bimanair.co.uk

British Airways London; ☎ 0844 493 0787 (general enquiries, reservations); www.britishairways.com; ⏲ 06.00–20.00 daily. Recently ceased flights to Dhaka, it is unknown whether they will begin again.

Emirates Airlines 1st Fl, Gloucester Pk, 95 Cromwell Rd, London SW7 4DL; ☎ 0844 800 2777; e ekuk@emirates.com; www.emirates.com; ⏲ 09.00–17.30 Mon–Fri, 09.00–15.30 Sat

Gulf Air Zone C, Terminal 3, London Heathrow Airport, Hounslow TW6 1NU; ☎ 0844 493 1717; e london.goldenfalcon@gulfair.com; www.gulfair.com; ⏲ 10.00–17.00 daily

Kuwait Airways www.kuwait-airways.com

Qatar Airways 1 Cluny Mews, West Kensington, London SW5 9EG; ☎ 0870 389 8090; www.qatarairways.com

Flights from North America Bangladesh lies on the opposite side of the planet from North America, and thus travellers from the eastern side will find easier connections through Europe or the Middle East (see *Flights from the UK/Europe*

above), whereas travellers from the west coast might find slightly better fares and shorter travelling times transiting through southeast Asia. Hong Kong seems to be the most civil place to break the journey, as Bangkok, Singapore and Malaysia involve long-haul flights of between 18 and 20 hours. The decision as to which way to go will probably depend on flight specials.

Air Canada www.aircanada.com
Air China www.airchina.com
American Airlines www.aa.com
Cathay Pacific www.cathaypacific.com
United Airlines www.united.com
Virgin Atlantic www.virgin-atlantic.com

Flights from southeast Asia/east Asia The following providers can usually accept bookings online with a credit card but in the hunt for the best price you should also talk with your local travel agent to see what kind of deals they can get.

Air Asia (Kuala Lumpur) www.airasia.com. At the time of publication, this budget carrier had recently started flights on the Kuala Lumpur–Dhaka route, making it the cheapest gateway from southeast Asia.
China Eastern (Kunming) www.ce-air.com. Cannot purchase tickets online; check with your travel agent.
Dragonair (Hong Kong) www.dragonair.com
Malaysian Airlines (Kuala Lumpur) www.malaysiaairlines.com
Singapore Airlines www.singaporeairlines.com
Thai Airways (Bangkok, flies to Chittagong) www.thaiair.com

Flights from south Asia As with all things south Asian, electronic communication is not yet up to par. The following websites tend to be incorrect, and their corresponding flight schedules inaccurate. In most cases the schedules are currently in a state of flux anyway, and if you do want a ticket from these airlines outside Bangladesh you'll need to purchase it through your local travel agent. For the latest information call the local offices.

Air India Express (Mumbai, Kolkata & international) www.airindiaexpress.in
Best Airways (Kuala Lumpur, Bangkok & domestic) www.bestairbd.com
GMG Airlines (Kolkata, Delhi, Kuala Lumpur & domestic) www.gmgairlines.com
Jet Airways (Delhi, Kolkata & international) www.jetairways.com
United Airways (Kolkata & domestic) www.uabdl.com

Recommended ticket agencies/carriers

UK

Flight Centre Australia: ☎ 133 133; Canada: ☎ 877 967 5302; New Zealand: ☎ 0800 24 35 44; South Africa: ☎ 0860 400 727; UK, ☎ 0870 499 0040; USA, ☎ 866 967 5351; www.flightcentre.com. Multi-national flight bookings, head office in Brisbane & over 1,500 branches worldwide.
STA Travel Main branches: Australia: ☎ 1300 733 035, www.statravel.com.au; Canada: ☎ 888 427 5639, www.statravel.ca; New Zealand: ☎ 0508 782 872, www.statravel.co.nz; South Africa: ☎ 0861 781 781, www.statravel.co.za; UK: ☎ 08701 630 026, www.statravel.co.uk; USA: ☎ 800 781 4040, www.statravel.com. The world's largest student travel agency.
Travel Bag ☎ 0800 082 5000; www.travelbag.co.uk
Trailfinders www.trailfinders.com. The UK's leading independent travel company.
Undiscovered Destinations www.bangladesh-undiscovered.com. A specialist on Bangladesh.

USA

Air Brokers International ☎ 800 883 3273; www.airbrokers.com. Specialises in round-the-world airfares.
Experience Bangladesh www.experiencebangladesh.com. Texas-based tour operator focusing primarily on study & exposure tours of Bangladesh. Can assist with flight arrangements.
Gateway Travel ☎ 800 423 4898; www.gatewaytrvl.com. Agents with a personalised touch.

Departure taxes Taxes are already included in the ticket price when departing by air. However, some land borders request that you pay a Tk300 departure tax at a nearby bank branch before departure (see individual crossing information as not all of them require a departure tax).

LAND ROUTES Bangladesh is almost wholly surrounded by India and while there has been talk over the years of a road connecting the region to China via Myanmar, no political will has yet to materialise on this front.

Major crossings into India are at Benapol/Petrapol, Burimari/Chengrabandha, Tamabil/Dawkhi and Akhuara/Agartala. They are major in the sense that they are well used by travellers and have regular transit services between Dhaka and the next major city, and also have facilities for vehicular traffic, should you be wishing to drive into Bangladesh with your own vehicle (a *carnet* is required; see page 69 for further details).

There are also a series of smaller crossings that would otherwise be inconvenient given the lack of regular public transport to/from these crossings. However, if you're the adventurous kind of traveller with a motorcycle, and you don't have the necessary paperwork to cross then you may find a friendly border official willing to let you pass without a *carnet*. These smaller crossings exist all along the border with India, but some known crossings are at Hili/Balurghat, Birol/Radhikapur, or Godagari/Lalgola and Malda/Gaur (all within Rajshahi Division).

Benapol/Petrapol (*06.00–18.30 daily*) Many travellers cross here either into or out of Bangladesh. Previously a 'change of route permit' was required if entering Bangladesh by air and exiting by land, but this is no longer the case. The border is open every day, but the least busy time is in the middle of the day, from about 11.00. For detailed directions about making the crossing, see *Chapter* 7, page 278.

Burimari/Chengrabandha (*07.30–17.30*) This crossing, located at the very northern tip of Rajshahi Division, is used to access Siliguri, from where you can travel to Bhutan, Darjeeling, Sikkim or Nepal. Like all the other borders, facilities here are basic. There is one unremarkable hotel at the BRTC bus office in Burimari, nothing more than a room with some beds, should you arrive late after the border has closed. Otherwise you will find some other basic and cheap options at nearby Patgram 12km away, or better yet you can stay at the well-serviced RDRS Guesthouse in Lalmonirhat (*Saptibari, Patgram Rd; 0591 61378; e rdrslal@tistaonline.com; dbl/AC $$–$$$*), 90km from Burimari. Crossing usually takes a couple of hours, especially if it's early in the morning and there are a fair number of other people in the queue.

When heading into Bangladesh, get enough taka from the money exchangers on the Indian side of the border, as there is none on the Bangladeshi side, and the nearest ATM is in Rangpur, over 100km away. Unlike the other borders there doesn't seem to be a departure tax levied on foreigners at Burimari, although if this does change it should be Tk300 like the other borders.

There is a daily Dhaka–Siliguri overnight bus service operated by Shyamoli Paribahan (*02 836 0241; duration: 15hrs; Tk1,300*). Tickets can be purchased at any Shyamoli Paribahan office, but the departure originates at Kamlapur Railway Station at 21.00 and passes through Gabtali Bus Station a half-hour later on its way out of Dhaka. Otherwise, you can reach Patgram from Rangpur (and vice versa) by bus, and from Patgram you can catch a smaller public bus to the border, as long as it's well before dusk. Once across the border you can pick up a local bus to Siliguri. If there doesn't seem to be a direct bus available, make for Jalpaiguri first where you can then change buses if need be.

From Siliguri, the same service to Dhaka operates from an office attached to the Central Plaza Hotel (*Hill Cart Rd, Pradham Nagar; ☎ +91 353 251 6119; located within rickshaw distance of main bus station; non-AC dbl Rs650*). Departing at 14.00, the ride takes a similar 15 hours and costs Rs700. If your plan is to stop in northwest Bangladesh first, your best bet is to take a bus from Siliguri to Jalpaiguri, and then catch onward transport to Chengrabandha. From there, if it's not too late, you can try to make for Lalmonirhat or Rangpur by local bus.

Tamabil/Dawkhi (*⊕ 09.00–18.00 daily*) This crossing is perhaps the best and least busy of all the road border crossings to India, and definitely the most scenic of the four road crossings. Tamabil is easily accessible from Sylhet via public bus (2.5hrs; Tk50) or even a privately hired taxi (Tk600) or baby taxi (Tk400, depending on your bargaining skills). At this crossing they do ask for the Tk300 departure tax, which must be paid for at the Sonali Bank (*⊕ 09.00–16.00*) at Jaintiapur (13km from Tamabil) first before coming to the border. Do leave as early as possible from Sylhet as the last bus to Shillong leaves by 13.00. Otherwise there are plenty of eager taxi drivers waiting to take you, but the costs will be quite high (Rs1,300–1,800). For Cherrapunjee, expect to pay Rs1,800 or perhaps more depending on the vehicle.

There are also no official exchange services in Dawkhi but if you ask around you will easily find someone who is willing to trade the cash at a reasonable rate. There are also a couple of basic hotels if you arrive late.

Akhuara/Agartala (*⊕ 08.00–18.00*) Among the crossings, this one is the closest, and often used by foreigners with an odd visa that specifies they should leave the country every 60 or 90 days. Despite the fact there is a Bangladesh visa office here, it is not recommended that visitors do visa runs from here as the visas issued tend to be very short unless you can convince the officials otherwise. While there is a direct daily bus service offered by BRTC operated by Shyamoli Paribahan (contact information as for Siliguri/Kolkata above), it is probably more scenic to take the train, not to mention much less stressful in terms of hectic road traffic.

The Upukul Express leaves Airport Station at 07.30 and arrives at Akhaura at 09.50. From there you can catch a quick rickshaw to the Sonali Bank to pay your Tk300 departure tax, and from the town you'll need to catch a *tempo* (Bangladeshi version of a *tuk tuk* – a noisy yellow-roofed three-wheeler) to the border 15 minutes away (Tk80 to hire the whole vehicle). After the formalities are complete, it's a quick rickshaw ride into Agartala. For getting to Dhaka by train, do the same in reverse, except you should aim to catch the Upukul Express at 17.40 as it returns to the capital.

Finally, if this is your first time in Bangladesh and you haven't yet got your hands on any taka, the Indian customs officials seem to be more than happy to oblige, although their rates put the hucksters to shame.

BY TRAIN When the new Maitree Express service began on 14 April 2008 (Bengali New Year), there was a great deal of fanfare – travellers could now travel from London to Dhaka entirely by train if they so chose. However, complaints of extreme delays at the border crossing means that the service isn't selling well, but will likely remain in service.

The train departs from Dhaka on Saturdays and Sundays at 08.30 from the Dhaka Cantonment Railway Station, on Airport Road just north of Baridhara DOHS. Expected check-in time is 07.00, but coming slightly after that time should be acceptable. It arrives in India anywhere after 20.30 (Indian time) and immigration formalities are completed at the border at Darsana (incidentally the location of Bangladesh's distilleries – yes, Bangladesh does make its own alcohol!). You need to purchase your tickets from the Kamlapur Railway Station (⏲ *09.00–17.00*). Advance tickets for air-conditioned first class are Tk1,912, air-conditioned chair Tk1,266 and shuvon chair Tk860. You must personally go to the station to collect the ticket. Bring your passport and an Indian visa.

From Kolkata, the train departs at 07.30 on Saturdays and Sundays from the new Chitpur Station (also known as 'Kolkata Station'). Tickets should be purchased at the Foreign Tourist Reservation Office of Eastern Railways (*West Fairlie Pl, 17 Netaji Subhas Rd, Kolkata;* ⏲ *10.00–17.00 Mon–Fri, 10.00–14.00 Sun & holidays*). Tickets for air-conditioned first class are US$20 or Rs980 at October 2008 exchange rate, air-conditioned chair US$20 or Rs580, non air-conditioned chair US$8 or Rs390.

BY CAR Travellers using their own vehicles on long-term overland journeys have reported having an excellent time driving the rural and village roads of Bangladesh, although the style of driving ranges from intimidating to downright dangerous. Serious overland travellers will have already prepared their *carnet du passage en douane* – essentially a document for your vehicle that guarantees you will not sell it abroad without paying import duties. The document allows you to cross borders freely. Some adventurers who have come overland from Europe will be disappointed to learn that there is no land border crossing to Myanmar, but some have compensated for this by shipping their vehicle from Chittagong to Singapore in order to drive through the rest of southeast Asia.

BY MOTORCYCLE The occasional foreigner can be seen driving around Dhaka streets on Chinese-made or Indian-made motorcycles, all of which provide independence and the best mobility to those willing to brave the roads. Other motorcycle enthusiasts have taken their bikes across India and into Bangladesh *en route* to northeast India. Again, a *carnet* is required in order to cross the border without hassle.

Finally, only the rarest breed of adventurer has purchased an Indian-made Royal Enfield motorbike and tried to drive it to Bangladesh without a *carnet*.

BY SEA Currently there are no passenger services allowing travellers to arrive in Bangladesh by sea. There may be opportunities to join a shipping vessel; those interested should contact the Bangladesh Shipping Corporation (*BSC Bhaban Saltgola Road, Chittagong;* ☎ *031 252 1162–8;* e *bsc_ctg@bttb.net.bd; www.bsc.gov.bd*) for further information.

HEALTH *with Dr Felicity Nicholson*

People new to exotic travel often worry about tropical diseases, but it is accidents that are most likely to carry you off. Road accidents are very common in Bangladesh so be aware and do what you can to reduce risks: try to travel during daylight hours, always wear a seatbelt and refuse to be driven by anyone who has been drinking. Listen to local advice about areas where violent crime is rife, and you'd be best not wandering around certain areas of the city late at night. Noise pollution is another major problem in Dhaka and Chittagong, so if you have sensitive ears bring a pair of earplugs. Sound-blocking earphones and a music device are even smarter for when you're stuck in traffic.

PREPARATIONS Preparations to ensure a healthy trip to Bangladesh require checks on your immunisation status: it is wise to be up to date on tetanus, polio and diphtheria (now given as an all-in-one vaccine, Revaxis, that lasts for ten years), and hepatitis A. Immunisations against rabies and hepatitis B may also be recommended.

Hepatitis A vaccine (Havrix Monodose or Avaxim) comprises two injections given about a year apart. In the UK, The course costs about £100, but may be available on the NHS; protects for 25 years and can be administered even close to the time of departure. Hepatitis B vaccination should be considered for longer trips (two months or more) or for those working with children or in situations where contact with blood is likely. Three injections are needed for the best protection and can be given over a three-week period if time is short. Longer schedules give more sustained protection and are therefore preferred if time allows. Hepatitis A vaccine can also be given as a combination with hepatitis B as 'Twinrix', though two doses are needed at least seven days apart to be effective for the hepatitis A component, and three doses are needed for the hepatitis B.

The newer injectable typhoid vaccines (eg: Typhim Vi) last for three years and are about 85% effective. Oral capsules (Vivotif) are currently available in the US (and soon in the UK); if four capsules are taken over seven days it will last for five years. They should be encouraged unless the traveller is leaving within a few days for a trip of a week or less, when the vaccine would not be effective in time. Vaccinations for rabies are ideally advised for everyone, but are especially important for travellers visiting more remote areas, especially if you are more than 24 hours from medical help and definitely if you will be working with animals (see *Rabies* page 56).

Experts differ over whether a BCG vaccination against tuberculosis (TB) is useful in adults: discuss this with your travel clinic.

In addition to the various vaccinations recommended above, it is important that travellers to Bangladesh should be prepared against malaria. For detailed advice, see page 48.

Ideally you should visit your own doctor or a specialist travel clinic (see pages 50–1) to discuss your requirements if possible at least eight weeks before you plan to travel.

Travel insurance Take out comprehensive medical and travel insurance. This should cover medical treatment and evacuation, accidents, cancelled flights and stolen cash, credit cards, passport and luggage. You should check any exclusions, and that your policy covers you for the activities you want to undertake.

Protection from the sun Give some thought to packing suncream. The incidence of skin cancer is rocketing as Caucasians are travelling more and spending more time exposing themselves to the sun. Keep out of the sun during the middle of the day and, if you must expose yourself to the sun, build up gradually from 20 minutes per day. Be especially careful of exposure in the middle of the day and of sun reflected off water, and wear a T-shirt and lots of waterproof suncream (at least SPF15) when swimming. Sun exposure ages the skin, makes people prematurely wrinkly; and increases the risk of skin cancer. Cover up with long, loose clothes and wear a hat when you can. The glare and the dust can be hard on the eyes, too, so bring UV-protecting sunglasses and, perhaps, a soothing eyebath.

Personal first-aid kit A minimal kit contains:

- Oral rehydration salts (widely available in Bangladesh pharmacies)
- A good drying antiseptic, eg: iodine or potassium permanganate (don't take antiseptic cream)
- A few small dressings (Band-Aids or plasters)

- Suncream
- Insect repellent; antimalarial tablets; impregnated bed-net or permethrin spray
- Aspirin or paracetamol
- Antifungal cream (eg: Canesten)
- Ciprofloxacin or norfloxacin, for severe diarrhoea
- Gut stopper like Imodium or Loperamide
- Calamine lotion for stings, rashes or bites
- Water purification tablets, like iodine
- Tiger Balm for muscle aches or pains and relief from mosquito bites
- Tinidazole for giardia or amoebic dysentery (see box on page 52)
- Antibiotic eye drops, for sore, 'gritty', stuck-together eyes (conjunctivitis)
- A pair of fine-pointed tweezers (to remove hairy caterpillar hairs, thorns, splinters, coral, etc)
- Alcohol-based hand rub or bar of soap in plastic box
- Condoms or femidoms

Malaria Along with road accidents, malaria poses another threat to the health of travellers in South Asia. It is unwise to travel in malarial parts of Bangladesh whilst pregnant or with children: the risk of malaria in many parts is considerable and these travellers are likely to succumb rapidly to the disease.

Malaria in Bangladesh The *Anopheles* mosquito that transmits the parasite is most commonly found in the Chittagong Hill Tracts region of Bangladesh. All other regions of the country are considered low-risk malaria areas, and there is no malaria in Dhaka. When visiting the CHT outside the main towns (Khagrachari, Bandarban or Rangamati), antimalarial drugs are definitely advised. If at all uncertain, however, visitors should err on the side of caution and take prophylaxis medication well before their visit to the CHT. Doxycycline is widely available and inexpensive as well.

Malaria prevention There is not yet a vaccine against malaria that gives enough protection to be useful for travellers, but there are other ways to avoid it; if planning to visit the remote areas of the Chittagong Hill Tracts, travellers must plan their malaria protection properly. Seek current advice on the best antimalarials to take: usually mefloquine, Malarone or doxycycline. If mefloquine (Lariam) is suggested, start this two-and-a-half weeks (three doses) before departure to check that it suits you; stop it immediately if it seems to cause depression or anxiety, visual or hearing disturbances, severe headaches, fits or changes in heart rhythm. Side effects such as nightmares or dizziness are not medical reasons for stopping unless they are sufficiently debilitating or annoying. Anyone who has been treated for depression or psychiatric problems, has diabetes controlled by oral therapy or who is epileptic (or who has suffered fits in the past) or has a close blood relative who is epileptic, should probably avoid mefloquine.

In the past doctors were nervous about prescribing mefloquine to pregnant women, but experience has shown that it is relatively safe and certainly safer than the risk of malaria. That said, there are other issues, so if you are travelling to Bangladesh whilst pregnant, seek expert advice before departure.

Malarone (proguanil and atovaquone) is as effective as mefloquine. It has the advantage of having few side effects and need only be continued for one week after returning. However, it is expensive and because of this tends to be reserved for shorter trips. Malarone may not be suitable for everybody, so advice should be taken from a doctor. The licence in the UK has been extended for up to three months' use and a paediatric form of tablet is also available, prescribed on a weight basis.

Another alternative is the antibiotic doxycycline (100mg daily). Like Malarone it can be started one day before arrival. Unlike mefloquine, it may also be used in travellers with epilepsy, although certain anti-epileptic medication may make it less effective. In perhaps 1–3% of people there is the possibility of allergic skin reactions developing in sunlight; the drug should be stopped if this happens. Women using the oral contraceptive should use an additional method of protection for the first four weeks when using doxycycline. It is also unsuitable in pregnancy or for children under 12 years.

Chloroquine and proguanil are no longer considered to be effective enough for Bangladesh but may be considered as a last resort if nothing else is deemed suitable.

All tablets should be taken with or after the evening meal, washed down with plenty of fluid and, with the exception of Malarone (see above), continued for four weeks after leaving.

Despite all these precautions, it is important to be aware that no anti-malarial drug is 100% protective, although those on prophylactics who are unlucky enough to catch malaria are less likely to get rapidly into serious trouble. In addition to taking anti-malarials, it is therefore important to avoid mosquito bites between dusk and dawn (see box, *Avoiding insect bites*, page 54).

There is unfortunately the occasional traveller who prefers to 'acquire resistance' to malaria rather than take preventive tablets, or who takes homeopathic prophylactics thinking these are effective against killer disease. Homeopathy theory dictates treating like with like so there is no place for prophylaxis or immunisation in a well person; bone fide homoeopathists do not advocate it. Travellers to Africa cannot acquire any effective resistance to malaria, and those who don't make use of prophylactic drugs risk their life in a manner that is both foolish and unnecessary.

Malaria diagnosis and treatment Even those who take their malaria tablets meticulously and do everything possible to avoid mosquito bites may contract a strain of malaria that is resistant to prophylactic drugs. Untreated malaria is likely to be fatal, but even strains resistant to prophylaxis respond well to prompt treatment. Because of this, your immediate priority upon displaying possible malaria symptoms – including a rapid rise in temperature (over 38°C), and any combination of a headache, flu-like aches and pains, a general sense of disorientation, and possibly even nausea and diarrhoea – is to establish whether you have malaria, ideally by visiting a clinic. Many of the clinics in the Chittagong Hill Tracts can test accurately for malaria, and some long-term residents of the hills recommend carrying a rapid test kit.

Diagnosing malaria is not easy, which is why consulting a doctor is sensible: there are other dangerous causes of fever in South Africa, which require different treatments. Even if you test negative, it would be wise to stay within reach of a laboratory until the symptoms clear up, and to test again after a day or two if they don't. It's worth noting that if you have a fever and the malaria test is negative, you may have typhoid, paratyphoid or dengue fever, which should also receive immediate treatment.

Travellers to remote parts of Bangladesh – for instance the Chittagong Hill Tracts – would be wise to carry a course of treatment to cure malaria, and a rapid test kit. With malaria, it is normal enough to go from feeling healthy to having a high fever in the space of a few hours (and it is possible to die from falciparum malaria within 24 hours of the first symptoms). In such circumstances, assume that you have malaria and act accordingly – whatever risks are attached to taking an unnecessary cure are outweighed by the dangers of untreated malaria. Experts differ on the costs and benefits of self-treatment, but agree that it leads to over-treatment and to many people taking drugs they do not need; yet treatment may save your life. There is also some division about the best treatment for malaria, but either Malarone or Coarthemeter are the current treatments of choice. Discuss your trip with a specialist either at home or in Bangladesh, especially if your posting will make you a long-term resident of hill tracts.

WATER STERILISATION You can fall ill from drinking contaminated water so try to drink from safe sources eg: bottled water where available. If you are away from shops in a remote part of the country and your bottled water runs out, make tea, pour the remaining boiled water into a clean container and use it for drinking. Alternatively, water should be passed through a good bacteriological filter or purified with iodine or the less-effective chlorine tablets (eg: Puritabs). If boiling your own water before drinking, it is recommended you boil it for at least 20 minutes. Deep-well tube water is available in some places and should be OK to drink if no other sources are available, but not in large quantities as many wells have been contaminated by arsenic in Bangladesh.

TRAVEL CLINICS AND HEALTH INFORMATION A full list of current travel clinic websites worldwide is available on www.istm.org/. For other journey preparation information, consult www.nathnac.org/ds/map_world.aspx. Information about various medications may be found on www.netdoctor.co.uk/travel.

UK

Berkeley Travel Clinic 32 Berkeley St, London W1J 8EL (near Green Park tube station); ☎ 020 7629 6233; ⏲ 10.00–18.00 Mon–Fri, 10.00–15.00 Sat

Cambridge Travel Clinic 41 Hills Rd, Cambridge, CB2 1NT; ☎ 01223 367362; f 01223 368021; e enquiries@travelcliniccambridge.co.uk; www.travelcliniccambridge.co.uk; ⏲ 10.00–16.00 Mon, Tue & Sat, 12.00–19.00 Wed/Thu, 11.00–18.00 Fri

Edinburgh Travel Health Clinic 14 East Preston St, Newington, Edinburgh EH8 9QA; ☎ 0131 667 1030; www.edinburghtravelhealthclinic.co.uk; ⏲ 09.00–19.00 Mon–Wed, 09.00–18.00 Thu/Fri. Travel vaccinations & advice on all aspects of malaria prevention. All current UK prescribed anti-malaria tablets in stock.

Fleet Street Travel Clinic 29 Fleet St, London EC4Y 1AA; ☎ 020 7353 5678; www.fleetstreetclinic.com; ⏲ 08.45–17.30 Mon–Fri. Injections, travel products & latest advice.

Hospital for Tropical Diseases Travel Clinic Mortimer Market Centre, 2nd Fl, Capper St (off Tottenham Ct Rd), London WC1E 6AU; ☎ 020 7388 9600; www.thehtd.org; ⏲ 09.00–16.00 weekdays; 24hr emergency available. Offers consultations & advice, & is able to provide all necessary drugs & vaccines for travellers. Runs a healthline (☎ *020 7950 7799*) for country-specific information & health hazards. Also stocks nets, water purification equipment & personal protection measures. Travellers who have returned from the tropics & are unwell, with fever or bloody diarrhoea, can attend the walk-in emergency clinic at the hospital without an appointment.

MASTA (Medical Advisory Service for Travellers Abroad), London School of Hygiene & Tropical Medicine, Keppel St, London WC1 7HT; ☎ 09068 224100; e enquiries@masta.org; www.masta-travel-health.com. This is a premium-line number, charged at 60p per min. For a fee, they will provide an individually tailored health brief, with up-to-date information on how to stay healthy, inoculations & what to take.

MASTA pre-travel clinics ☎ 01276 685040. Call or check www.masta-travel-health.com/travel-clinic.aspx for the nearest; there are currently 30 in Britain. They also sell malaria prophylaxis, memory cards, treatment kits, bed-nets, net treatment kits, etc.

NHS travel website www.fitfortravel.nhs.uk. Provides country-by-country advice on immunisation & malaria prevention, plus details of recent development, & a list of relevant health organisations.

Nomad Travel Stores Flagshipstore: 3–4 Wellington Terrace, Turnpike Lane, London N8 0PX; ☎ 020 8889 7014; f 020 8889 9528; e turnpike@nomadtravel.co.uk; www.nomadtravel.co.uk; walk in or appointments ⏲ 09.15–17.00 daily, with late night Thu. 6 stores in total countrywide: 3 in London, also in Bristol, Southampton & Manchester. As well as dispensing health advice, Nomad stocks mosquito nets & other anti-bug devices, & an excellent range of adventure travel gear.

InterHealth Travel Clinic 111 Westminster Bridge Rd, London, SE1 7HR; ☎ 020 7902 9000; e info@interhealth.org.uk; www.interhealth.org.uk; ⌚ 08.30–17.30 Mon–Fri. Competitively priced, one-stop travel health service by appointment only.

Trailfinders Immunisation Centre 194 Kensington High St, London W8 7RG; ☎ 020 7938 3999; www.trailfinders.com/travelessentials/travelclinic.htm; ⌚ 09.00–17.00 Mon–Wed & Fri, 09.00–18.00 Thu, 10.00–17.15 Sat. No appointment necessary.

Travelpharm The Travelpharm website (*www.travelpharm.com*) offers up-to-date guidance on travel-related health & has a range of medications available through their online mini-pharmacy.

Irish Republic

Tropical Medical Bureau Grafton St Medical Centre, Grafton Bldgs, 34 Grafton St, Dublin 2; ☎ 1 671 9200. Has a useful website specific to tropical destinations (*www.tmb.ie*).

USA

Centers for Disease Control 1600 Clifton Rd, Atlanta, GA 30333; ☎ 800 232 4636, 800 232 6348; e cdcinfo@cdc.gov; www.cdc.gov/travel. The central source of travel information in the USA. Each summer they publish the invaluable *Health Information for International Travel*.

IAMAT (International Association for Medical Assistance to Travelers) 1623 Military Rd, #279 Niagara Falls, NY 14304-1745; ☎ 716 754 4883; e info@iamat.org; www.iamat.org. A non-profit organisation with free membership that provides lists of English-speaking doctors abroad.

Canada

IAMAT (International Association for Medical Assistance to Travelers) Suite 1, 1287 St Clair Av W, Toronto, ON, M6E 1B8; ☎ 416 652 0137; www.iamat.org

TMVC Suite 314, 1030 W Georgia St, Vancouver, BC, V6E 2Y3; ☎ 905 648 1112; e info@tmvc.com; www.tmvc.com. One-stop medical clinic for all your international travel medicine & vaccination needs.

Australia, New Zealand, Thailand

TMVC (Travel Doctors Group) ☎ 1300 65 88 44; www.tmvc.com.au. 22 clinics in Australia, New Zealand & Thailand, including: *Auckland* Canterbury Arcade, 170 Queen St, Auckland; ☎ 09 373 3531; *Brisbane* 75a Astor Terrace, Spring Hill, Brisbane, QLD 4000; ☎ 07 3815 6900; e brisbane@traveldoctor.com.au; *Melbourne* Dr Sonny Lau, 393 Little Bourke St, 2nd Fl, Melbourne, VIC 3000; ☎ 03 9935 8100; e melbourne@traveldoctor.com.au; *Sydney* Dr Mandy Hu, Dymocks Bldg, 7th Fl, 428 George St, Sydney, NSW 2000; ☎ 02 9221 7133; f 02 9221 8401

IAMAT PO Box 5049, Christchurch 5, New Zealand; www.iamat.org

South Africa

SAA-Netcare Travel Clinics e travelinfo@netcare.co.za; www.travelclinic.co.za. 12 clinics throughout South Africa.

TMVC NHC Health Centre, cnr Beyers Naude & Waugh Northcliff; ☎ 011 214 9030; e traveldoctor@wtmconline.com; www.traveldoctor.co.za. Consult the website for details of clinics.

Switzerland

IAMAT 57 Chemin des Voirets, 1212 Grand-Lancy, Geneva; e info@iamat.org; www.iamat.org

COMMON MEDICAL PROBLEMS

Travellers' diarrhoea Travelling in Bangladesh carries a fairly high risk of getting a dose of travellers' diarrhoea, or the 'chitta shittas' as its sometimes referred to; perhaps half of all visitors will suffer and the newer you are to exotic travel, the more likely you will be to suffer. By taking precautions against travellers' diarrhoea you will also avoid typhoid, paratyphoid, cholera, hepatitis, dysentery, worms, etc. Travellers' diarrhoea and the other faecal-oral diseases come from getting other people's faeces in your mouth. This most often happens from cooks not washing their hands after a trip to the toilet, but even if the restaurant cook does not

TREATING TRAVELLERS' DIARRHOEA

Dr Jane Wilson-Howarth

It is dehydration that makes you feel awful during a bout of diarrhoea and the most important part of treatment is drinking lots of clear fluids. Sachets of oral rehydration salts give the perfect biochemical mix to replace all that is pouring out of your bottom but other recipes taste nicer. Any dilute mixture of sugar and salt in water will do you good: try Coke or orange squash with a three-finger pinch of salt added to each glass (if you are salt-depleted you won't taste the salt). Otherwise make a solution of a four-finger scoop of sugar with a three-finger pinch of salt in a 500ml glass. Or add eight level teaspoons of sugar (18g) and one level teaspoon of salt (3g) to one litre (five cups) of safe water. A squeeze of lemon or orange juice improves the taste and adds potassium, which is also lost in diarrhoea. Drink two large glasses after every bowel action, and more if you are thirsty. These solutions are still absorbed well if you are vomiting, but you will need to take sips at a time. If you are not eating you need to drink three litres a day plus whatever is pouring into the toilet. If you feel like eating, take a bland, high carbohydrate diet. Heavy greasy foods will probably give you cramps.

If the diarrhoea is bad, or you are passing blood or slime, or you have a fever, you will probably need antibiotics in addition to fluid replacement. A dose of norfloxacin or ciprofloxacin repeated twice a day until better may be appropriate (if you are planning to take an antibiotic with you, note that both norfloxacin and ciprofloxacin are available only on prescription in the UK). Ciprofloxacin is considered to be less effective in Bangladesh. If the diarrhoea is greasy and bulky and is accompanied by sulphurous (eggy) burps, one likely cause is giardia. This is best treated with tinidazole (four x 500mg in one dose, repeated seven days later if symptoms persist).

understand basic hygiene you will be safe if your food has been properly cooked and arrives piping hot. The most important prevention strategy is to wash your hands before eating anything. You can pick up salmonella and shigella from toilet door handles and possibly banknotes. The maxim to remind you what you can safely eat is:

PEEL IT, BOIL IT, COOK IT OR FORGET IT.

This means that fruit you have washed and peeled yourself, and hot foods, should be safe but raw foods, cold cooked foods, salads, fruit salads which have been prepared by others, ice cream and ice are all risky, and foods kept lukewarm in hotel buffets are often dangerous. That said, plenty of travellers and expatriates enjoy fruit and vegetables, so do keep a sense of perspective: food served in a fairly decent hotel in a large town or a place regularly frequented by expatriates is likely to be safe. If you are struck, see box for treatment.

Eye problems Bacterial conjunctivitis (pink eye) is a common infection in south Asia; people who wear contact lenses are most open to this irritating problem. The eyes feel sore and gritty and they will often be stuck together in the mornings. They will need treatment with antibiotic drops or ointment. Lesser eye irritation should settle with bathing in salt water and keeping the eyes shaded. If an insect flies into your eye, extract it with great care, ensuring you do not crush or damage it otherwise you may get a nastily inflamed eye from toxins secreted by the creature. Small, elongated red-and-black blister beetles carry warning colouration to tell you not to crush them anywhere against your skin.

Prickly heat This ailment is definitely a common problem in Bangladesh, especially during the hottest months of April–June. A fine pimply rash on the trunk is likely to be heat rash; cool showers, dabbing dry, and talc will help. Treat the problem by slowing down to a relaxed schedule, wearing only loose, baggy, 100% cotton clothes and sleeping naked under a fan; if it's bad you may need to check into an air-conditioned hotel room for a while.

Skin infections Any mosquito bite or small nick in the skin gives an opportunity for bacteria to foil the body's usually excellent defences; it will surprise many travellers how quickly skin infections start in warm humid climates and it is essential to clean and cover even the slightest wound. Creams are not as effective as a good drying antiseptic such as dilute iodine, potassium permanganate (a few crystals in half a cup of water) or crystal (or gentian) violet. One of these should be available in most towns. If the wound starts to throb, or becomes red and the redness starts to spread, or the wound oozes, and especially if you develop a fever, antibiotics will probably be needed: flucloxacillin (250mg four times a day) or cloxacillin (500mg four times a day). For those allergic to penicillin, erythromycin (500mg twice a day) for five days should help. See a doctor if the symptoms do not start to improve within 48 hours.

LONG-HAUL FLIGHTS, CLOTS AND DVT

Dr Felicity Nicholson

Any prolonged immobility including travel by land or air can result in deep-vein thrombosis (DVT) with the risk of embolus to the lungs. Certain factors can increase the risk and these include:

- Previous clot or close relative with a history
- People over 40 with increased risk in over 80s
- Recent major operation or varicose-veins surgery
- Cancer
- Stroke
- Heart disease
- Obesity
- Pregnancy
- Hormone therapy
- Heavy smokers
- Severe varicose veins
- People who are very tall (over 6ft/1.8m) or short (under 5ft/1.5m)

A deep-vein thrombosis (DVT) causes painful swelling and redness of the calf or sometimes the thigh. It is only dangerous if a clot travels to the lungs (pulmonary embolus). Symptoms of a pulmonary embolus (PE) – which commonly start three to ten days after a long flight – include chest pain, shortness of breath, and sometimes coughing up small amounts of blood. Anyone who thinks that they might have a DVT needs to see a doctor immediately.

PREVENTION OF DVT

- Keep mobile before and during the flight; move around every couple of hours
- Drink plenty of fluids during the flight
- Avoid taking sleeping pills and excessive tea, coffee and alcohol
- Consider wearing flight socks or support stockings (see *www.legshealth.com*)

If you think you are at increased risk of a clot, ask your doctor if it is safe to travel.

AVOIDING INSECT BITES

As the sun is going down, don long clothes and apply repellent on any exposed flesh. Pack a DEET-based insect repellent (roll-ons or stick are the least messy preparations for travelling). You also need either a permethrin-impregnated bed-net or a permethrin spray so that you can 'treat' bed-nets in hotels. Permethrin treatment makes even very tatty nets protective and prevents mosquitoes from biting through the impregnated net when you roll against it; it also deters other biters. Otherwise retire to an air-conditioned room or burn mosquito coils (which are widely available and cheap in Bangladesh) or sleep under a fan. Coils and fans reduce rather than eliminate bites. Travel clinics usually sell a good range of nets, treatment kits and repellents.

Mosquitoes and many other insects are attracted to light. If you are camping, never put a lamp near the opening of your tent, or you will have a swarm of biters waiting to join you when you retire. In hotel rooms, be aware that the longer your light is on, the greater the number of insects will be sharing your accommodation.

Aside from avoiding mosquito bites between dusk and dawn, which will protect you from elephantiasis and a range of nasty insect-borne viruses, as well as malaria (see page 48), it is important to take precautions against other insect bites. During the day it is wise to wear long, loose (preferably 100% cotton) clothes; this will keep off ticks and day-biting *Aedes* mosquitoes which may spread viral fevers, including yellow fever.

Fungal infections also get a hold easily in hot, moist climates so wear 100% cotton socks and underwear and shower frequently. An itchy rash in the groin or flaking between the toes is likely to be a fungal infection. This needs treatment with an antifungal cream such as Canesten (clotrimazole); if this is not available try Whitfield's ointment (compound benzoic acid ointment) or crystal violet (although this will turn you purple!).

Other insect-borne diseases Malaria is by no means the only insect-borne disease to which the traveller may succumb. Others include sleeping sickness and river blindness (see box *Avoiding insect bites*, above). Dengue fever is common in Bangladesh and there are many other similar arboviruses. These mosquito-borne diseases may mimic malaria but there is no prophylactic medication against them. The *Aedes* mosquitoes that carry dengue fever viruses bite during the daytime, so it is worth applying repellent if you see any of these mosquitoes around. After killing it, you can identify such a mosquito by the presence of white bands on its legs. These mosquitoes generally acquire the dengue virus after feeding on the blood of an infected person, and after an incubation period of eight to ten days the mosquito is capable of transmitting the disease for the rest of its life. Infected people are the main carriers and multipliers of this virus, generally circulating in the blood of the infected person at the same time that they have their fever.

Symptoms of dengue include strong headaches, rashes and excruciating joint and muscle pains and high fever. Viral fevers usually last about a week or so and are not usually fatal. Complete rest and paracetamol are the usual treatment; plenty of fluids also help. Some patients are given an intravenous drip to keep them from dehydrating. It is especially important to protect yourself if you have had dengue fever before, since a second infection with a different strain can result in the potentially fatal dengue haemorrhagic fever.

Bilharzia or schistosomiasis *with thanks to Dr Vaughan Southgate of the Natural History Museum, London, and Dr Dick Stockley, The Surgery, Kampala*
Bilharzia or schistosomiasis is a disease that commonly afflicts the rural poor of the tropics. It is an unpleasant problem that is worth avoiding, though can be treated if you do get it. This parasite is common in almost all water sources in Bangladesh. The most risky places are where infected people use water, wash clothes or bathe, etc.

It is easier to understand how to diagnose it, treat it and prevent it if you know a little about the life cycle. Contaminated faeces are washed into the lake, the eggs hatch and the larva infects certain species of snail. The snails then produce about 10,000 cercariae a day for the rest of their lives. The parasites can digest their way through your skin when you wade, or bathe in infested fresh water.

Winds disperse the snails and cercariae. The snails in particular can drift a long way, especially on windblown weed, so nowhere is really safe. However, deep water and running water are safer, while shallow water presents the greatest risk. The cercariae penetrate intact skin, and find their way to the liver. There male and female meet and spend the rest of their lives in permanent copulation. No wonder you feel tired! Most finish up in the wall of the lower bowel, but others can get lost and can cause damage to many different organs.

Although the adults do not cause any harm in themselves, after about four to six weeks they start to lay eggs, which cause an intense but usually ineffective immune reaction, including fever, cough, abdominal pain, and a fleeting, itching rash called 'safari itch'. The absence of early symptoms does not necessarily mean there is no infection. Later symptoms can be more localised and more severe, but the general symptoms settle down fairly quickly and eventually you are just tired.

Although bilharzia is difficult to diagnose, it can be tested at specialist travel clinics. Ideally tests need to be done at least six weeks after likely exposure and will determine whether you need treatment. Fortunately it is easy to treat at present.

Avoiding bilharzia If you are bathing, swimming, paddling or wading in fresh water which you think may carry a bilharzia risk, try to get out of the water within ten minutes.

- Avoid bathing or paddling on shores within 200m of villages or places where people use the water a great deal, especially reedy shores or where there is lots of water weed.
- Dry off thoroughly with a towel; rub vigorously.
- If your bathing water comes from a risky source try to ensure that the water is taken from the lake in the early morning and stored snail-free, otherwise it should be filtered or Dettol or Cresol added.
- Bathing early in the morning is safer than bathing in the last half of the day
- Cover yourself with DEET insect repellent before swimming: it may offer some protection.

HIV/AIDS The risks of sexually transmitted infection are extremely high in Bangladesh, whether you sleep with fellow travellers or locals. About 80% of HIV infections in British heterosexuals are acquired abroad. If you must indulge, use condoms or femidoms, which help reduce the risk of transmission. If you notice any genital ulcers or discharge, get treatment promptly since these increase the risk of acquiring HIV. If you do have unprotected sex, visit a clinic as soon as possible; this should be within 24 hours, or no later than 72 hours, for post-exposure prophylaxis.

In Bangladesh, HIV/AIDS prevalence remains extremely low, probably a result of the conservative culture of the country, although the incidence of more minor sexually transmitted diseases is high. For HIV/AIDS, occurrence rates are quite high amongst intravenous drug users and there is little knowledge or prevention action taken in the country. Therefore, it could become a high-prevalence area a few years down the track.

Rabies Rabies is carried by all mammals (beware the village dogs and small monkeys that are used to being fed in the parks) and is passed on to man through a bite, scratch or a lick of an open wound. You must always assume any animal is rabid, and seek medical help as soon as possible. Meanwhile scrub the wound with soap under a running tap or while pouring water from a jug. Find a reasonably clear-looking source of water (but at this stage the quality of the water is not important), then pour on a strong iodine or alcohol solution of gin, whisky or rum. This helps stop the rabies virus entering the body and will guard against wound infections, including tetanus.

Pre-exposure vaccinations for rabies are ideally advised for everyone, but is particularly important if you intend to have contact with animals and/or are likely to be more than 24 hours away from medical help. Ideally three doses should be taken over a minimum of 21 days, though even taking one or two doses of vaccine is better than none at all. Contrary to popular belief these vaccinations are relatively painless.

If you are bitten, scratched or licked over an open wound by a sick animal, then post-exposure prophylaxis should be given as soon as possible, though it is never too late to seek help, as the incubation period for rabies can be very long. Those who have not been immunised will need a full course of injections. The vast majority of travel health advisers including the WHO recommend rabies immunoglobulin (RIG), but this product is expensive (around US$800) and may be hard to come by – another reason why pre-exposure vaccination should be encouraged.

Tell the doctor if you have had pre-exposure vaccine, as this should change the treatment you receive. And remember that, if you do contract rabies, mortality is 100% and death from rabies is probably one of the worst ways to go.

Tickbite fever South Asian ticks are not the rampant disease transmitters they are in the Americas, but they may spread tickbite fever and a few dangerous rarities in Bangladesh. Tickbite fever is a flu-like illness that can easily be treated with doxycycline, but as there can be some serious complications it is important to visit a doctor.

Ticks should ideally be removed as soon as possible as leaving them on the body increases the chance of infection. They should be removed with special tick tweezers that can be bought in good travel shops. Failing that you can use your fingernails: grasp the tick as close to your body as possible and pull steadily and firmly away at right angles to your skin. The tick will then come away complete, as long as you do not jerk or twist. If possible douse the wound with alcohol (any spirit will do) or iodine. Irritants (eg: Olbas oil) or lit cigarettes are to be discouraged since they can cause the ticks to regurgitate and therefore increase the risk of disease. It is best to get a travelling companion to check you for ticks; if you are travelling with small children, remember to check their heads, and particularly behind the ears.

Spreading redness around the bite and/or fever and/or aching joints after a tick bite imply that you have an infection that requires antibiotic treatment, so seek advice.

Snake bite Snakes rarely attack unless provoked, and bites in travellers are unusual. You are less likely to get bitten if you wear stout shoes and long trousers when in the forests of Bangladesh, plus these will help ward off leeches. The only other time where there is a risk of snake bite is during the flood seasons in Bangladesh, when the snakes, like people, attempt to move to higher ground. Most snakes are harmless and even venomous species will dispense venom in only about half of their bites. If bitten, then, you are unlikely to have received venom; keeping this fact in mind may help you to stay calm. Many so-called first-aid techniques do more harm than good: cutting into the wound is harmful; tourniquets are dangerous; suction and electrical inactivation devices do not work. The only treatment is antivenom. In case of a bite that you fear may have been from a venomous snake:

- Try to keep calm – it is likely that no venom has been dispensed
- Prevent movement of the bitten limb by applying a splint
- Keep the bitten limb BELOW heart height to slow the spread of any venom
- If you have a crêpe bandage, wrap it around the whole limb (eg: all the way from the toes to the thigh), as tight as you would for a sprained ankle or a muscle pull
- Evacuate to a hospital that has antivenom. Most centres have a polyvalent antivenom, that includes the most common biting snakes in Bangladesh, but if not try ICCDR Travellers Clinic (*68 Shaheed Tajuddin Ahmed Sharani, Mohakhali; ☎ 02 886 0523–32; e info@icddrb.org; www.icddrb.org; ⏰ 09.00–12.00 & 14.00–17.00 Sun–Thu*).

And remember:

- NEVER give aspirin; you may take paracetamol, which is safe
- NEVER cut or suck the wound
- DO NOT apply ice packs
- DO NOT apply potassium permanganate

If the offending snake can be captured without risk of someone else being bitten, take this to show the doctor – but beware since even a decapitated head is able to bite.

IN BANGLADESH

Medical facilities Dhaka is the only place where somewhat decent medical facilities exist, but major procedures such as childbirth or surgery should definitely be undertaken abroad. Many expatriates head to Thailand for their regular medical treatments and more intensive diagnostic procedures. For less serious travel-related illnesses, International Centre for Cholera and Diarrhoea Research, Bangladesh (ICCDR,B) has a travellers' clinic which charges US$50 per visit for insured patients and US$15 otherwise. The clinic can also provide vaccinations as well. Appointments are recommended.

Emergencies are probably best handled at one of the major hospitals.

Apollo Hospital Hse 81, Blk E, Bashundhara; ☎ 02 989 1661/2; m 01713 046684, 01713 046685; emergency ☎ 02 989 6623; emergency m 01911 555555; emergency ambulance ☎ 01714 090000; e info@apollodhaka.com; www.apollodhaka.com

British High Commission Clinic Elizabeth Hse, Hse 23, Park Rd (cnr of Rd 6), Baridhara; ☎ 02 882 4345. Generally for high commission staff & British aid workers, but will likely point you in the right direction in the case of emergencies.

Dr Wahab's Medical Centre Hse 3, Rd 12, Baridhara; ☎ 02 882 1454. Can consult for acute but not life-threatening illnesses; also handles medical checkups for many international visa applications.

ICCDR,B 68 Shaheed Tajuddin Ahmed Sharani, Mohakhali; ☎ 02 886 0523–32; e info@icddrb.org; www.icddrb.org; ⏰ 09.00–12.00 & 14.00–17.00 Sun–Thu

Square Hospital 18/F West Panthapath, near Dhanmondi; ☎ 02 815 9457, 814 2431, 814 1522, 814 4400, 814 2333, emergency m 01713 377773–5; www.squarehospital.com

United Hospital Hse 15, Rd 71, Gulshan 2; ☎ 02 883 6000, 883 6444; m 01914 001234

SAFETY AND SECURITY

Bangladesh's security situation can be viewed from two perspectives. If you're at all an adventurous person who likes the unexplored and unknown, then Bangladesh can be a perfectly safe place to travel when taking local advice, and even female travellers have braved the country solo. But if you're the person responsible for writing government travel advisories, which will likely affect the decisions of thousands of potential visitors, you will find no shortage of fodder to help you describe Bangladesh as a security nightmare.

When I first arrived in Dhaka as a volunteer, the early 2007 election was just months away and what followed came as a real shock. When a supposedly neutral caretaker administration took control of the government in a bid to manage a free and fair election, the opposition cried foul and soon began a series of mass political strikes, which are known as *hartals* in south Asia. When these strikes happen, shops remain closed, buses and trains don't run, and most foreign aid workers are told to stay at home during the potential upheaval between police and political activists. There was an especially bad riot in November 2007 in which nearly 100 people were killed. Needless to say, it seemed outrageous to be volunteering in a place where political upheaval seemed as normal as the soup of the day.

Hopefully, your first impressions of Bangladesh's safety and security could only be better than this, but when dealing with Bangladesh's brutal politics, it's best to say that there is no way to predict what will happen or how that might affect security. During 2007–08, the prevailing state of emergency meant it was actually quite safe to travel around Bangladesh without fear of *hartal* hassle. Conversely, the weeks leading up to the election were like living in a prison security lockdown.

For travellers, the bottom line is that Bangladesh is a safe country in which to travel, with a caveat: *take local advice if unsure*. If you're in the planning stages it could be wise to check Bangladesh's headlines (see *Media and communications*, page 85). If it is anywhere near an election it is best to stay away unless you're a journalist or election monitor. This is not because you will necessarily be in any personal danger, it's just that a *hartal* can completely destroy your travel plans or itinerary.

Dhaka is a safe place, when you know how to play by its rules. Nonetheless, there have been incidences of muggings and robberies, and bag snatching among the expatriate community, particularly in the Gulshan and Mohammadpur areas, and particularly towards single females, moving around at night (see *Women travellers* opposite). Also there have been problems with robberies after late-night parties at clubs or private homes, and it is preferable to take a taxi instead of a rickshaw or take a ride from a friend with a vehicle, especially after 23.00. Victims of crime should contact their high commission or embassy for assistance before filing a police report. Women should not go to police stations alone. It is also prudent to withdraw cash from ATMs during the daytime and close to home. If you must arrange cash at night, do your best to get private transport arranged first.

Theft from households or hotels can be a problem. It is best to never leave cash, valuables and expensive mobiles exposed as these are easily pocketed by opportunistic thieves. Temptation can get the better of household staff who are the employees of expatriates: jewellery or cash can and does go missing frequently. Your best protection measure is to buy a lockbox for your valuables.

In order to stay safe, it is strongly recommended to abide by local customs and to stay informed about the current political situation, especially around active political periods. Between the overblown government advisories and the lax attitudes of locals who live under unsafe conditions, the true reality is that this adventurous destination has much to offer the street-smart traveller who is not only tolerant of the unknown, but seeks it with some well-heeded advice.

ROAD ADVICE The first and foremost risk in Bangladesh is the horrendous road traffic. Inside the cities, vehicles rarely move quickly enough due to some impressive traffic jams – something to be expected from one of the most densely populated countries in the world. The roads and highways outside the cities are markedly less safe however, because of higher speeds and decidedly insane overtaking practices. If you've hired a private vehicle, the words '*aste aste*' (slow, slow) can be used to command an over-eager driver to slow down, as you will certainly find their habituated lead foot pressing the gas harder and harder as the journey wears on.

If caught in, or anywhere near, a bad traffic accident in south Asia, it is best to evacuate the scene immediately. Such accidents usually culminate in large gatherings of people, some of whom may be quick to dispense mob justice. Newspaper stories of enraged mobs beating errant drivers to death seem to be the stuff of urban legend, but the frequency of first-hand accounts seems to prove otherwise. For personal safety reasons it is best to be far away from the centre of a traffic conflict well before the situation gets out of hand.

WOMEN TRAVELLERS It is an unfortunate reality that women need to be far more conscious and vigilant over their safety and surroundings whilst travelling in Bangladesh, because of cultural norms that people hold in the country. Attitudes towards women tend to be quite protective but people here are certainly less conservative than their religious brethren in Pakistan; they share more in common with their cultural relatives in West Bengal and India (and this isn't saying much as gender balance in India also remains far from ideal). Over the years it is pleasing to note that there has been a steady increase in the number of women visible in public surroundings, but there are still some precautions women should take.

The most common problem is verbal harassment, often in the form of cat calls (literally, meowing sounds) or loosely worded slights from immature teenagers. These should be disregarded and ignored. There have also been incidents of groping in extremely crowded places and again these pose mere nuisances more than any serious threat. Dressing more conservatively (eg: a *salwar kameez* – a loose-fitting shirt matched with a pair of baggy pants) will definitely help you attract less attention in this respect; as well as walking around in groups as opposed to alone, or with a male companion.

Single female travellers also attract a lot of attention while travelling, whether this is on public buses, launches or on trains. Again, it is not ill intentioned in most instances; it is mostly curiosity. It is the persistence of the attention that tends to be more draining than the actual attention itself. If travelling in well-touristed places like Cox's Bazaar, you will often find a group of people willing to 'adopt' a single female traveller for a period, which may help in keeping unwanted attention at bay.

Unfortunately, theft directed at single females, moving around at night (usually but not always after 22.00), seems to be a serious problem, especially in the expatriate areas of Dhaka. Far too many incidences have a single expatriate female riding a rickshaw well after dark, only to fall victim to drive-by bag snatchings. Some of these women have been pulled off the rickshaw entirely and dragged for several metres. These incidents occur mostly at night, on quiet or busy roads, but there is one common thread between them all: a single female is often the target victim. Some suggestions:

- Solo females should NOT travel around at night by rickshaw after 21.00–22.00. If you must travel, it is best to go in groups.

- Be vigilant while travelling/walking and keep aware of your surroundings. An alert-looking person, whose head is up and is watching the environment around them, presents less of a target than someone who is lost in their own world.
- Bags should be kept off the shoulder, so that if a bag snatching does occur, there is no risk of being dragged, which has actually caused the more serious injury in these incidences.
- A common myth is that poverty spawns these crimes, but in reality bag-snatching crimes are often committed by people with vehicles, which people in poverty cannot afford. It is theorised that it is actually young men, some of whom may be addicted to drugs, who commit these crimes and have the means (ie: a vehicle) to do so.
- If travelling out of the city at night, it is best not to accept food or drinks from strangers at train stations or bus stands, unless you see the drink being made or the food being prepared. In a recent theft, we heard of a drugging that knocked a single female unconscious. It would be a mistake to proclaim that all hospitality offered by strangers is malicious, especially in Bangladesh. But, by being aware of where a drink or food comes from, you can protect yourself.

DISABLED TRAVELLERS People with limited mobility will definitely find an added level of challenge within Bangladesh in terms of moving around independently, but there are plenty of helping hands available (for hire as well). Certainly the pavements are terrible, stair climbing is frequent and there are very few places that have provisions to cater to those with disabilities (ie: special lifts or reserved parking). While day-to-day tasks might prove to be a challenge, the flip side is that there are plenty of helpful hands around to assist with manual tasks. The country's leading organisation on disability is the Centre for the Rehabilitation of the Paralysed (*northeastern outskirts of Savar Bazaar, look for the sign on the Dhaka–Aricha Highway;* ☎ *02771 0464–5;* e *info@crp-bangladesh.org; www.crp-bangladesh.org*), popularly known as the CRP in Bangladesh. This socially conscious organisation has worked to rehabilitate tens of thousands of Bangladeshis, some of whom have been born with disabilities or who are disabled as a result of workplace injury. The ultimate goal is to reintegrate such individuals back into their home communities, with the means to make a living and remain useful members of society. The organisation's founder, Valerie Taylor, was in fact a VSO volunteer in East Pakistan, whose stay was interrupted by the Liberation War. She later returned to found the CRP and over the years it has grown into one of the nation's most famous success stories. Taylor was granted Bangladeshi citizenship in 1989 by Sheikh Hasina. For more information see page 158.

TRAVELLING WITH CHILDREN Travelling families would certainly find no shortage of interaction with local people, as children of foreign travellers will draw an extraordinary amount of attention, especially infants or young children. While families might enjoy some of the adventures provided by a stay in Bangladesh, the lack of tourist infrastructure means that families are best off sticking to Bangladesh's well-travelled routes. Journeys to Sundarban or Srimongol should top the list, as there are enough services and things to do that either destination will provide for an interesting and safe stay. Expatriates with families will soon meet other families in a similar boat, and should refer to *Chapter 3, Dhaka*, in a search for things to do around town – once again, river journeys would probably be the best option for families.

In terms of schools, Dhaka has quite a few choices of varying quality and fees. Below are the recommended schools.

FURTHER NOTES FOR DISABLED TRAVELLERS

Lieke Scheewe

Planning an accessible trip to Bangladesh may be challenging, as the required information is not easy to come by. Nevertheless, this colourful country can very well be enjoyed by anyone, with or without disability.

PLANNING AND BOOKING There are, to my knowledge, no travel agencies that run specialised trips to Bangladesh for travellers with disabilities. Yet, many travel agencies will listen to your needs and try to create a suitable itinerary. However, the easiest way may be to find local operators through the internet (*eg: Safari Plus; ☎ +880 2885 8736; www.safariplus.net; contact Md Ahsanul Huq*) and plan your trip directly with them, as they will also be available for you after arrival.

GETTING THERE At Zia International Airport in Dhaka you can expect reasonably good assistance and a narrow aisle chair to help you embark and disembark. There are also lifts.

ACCOMMODATION Finding accessible accommodation is not easy. In general, only top of the range hotels will have wheelchair accessible rooms, such as:

Dhaka Sheraton Hotel 1 Minto Rd, PO Box 504, Dhaka 1000; ☎ +880 2833 0001
Pan Pacific Sonargaon Hotel Dhaka 107 Kazi Nazrul Islam Av, GPO Box 3595, Dhaka 1215; ☎ +880 2811 1005; **f** +880 2811 3324; **e** mawal@panpacific.com

TRAVEL INSURANCE Most insurance companies will cater for disabled travellers, but it is essential that they are made aware of your disability. Examples of specialised companies that cover pre-existing medical conditions are:

Free Spirit ☎ 0845 230 5000; www.free-spirit.com
Age Concern ☎ 0845 601 2234; www.ageconcern.org.uk. Have no upper age limit.

FURTHER INFORMATION For further information on planning an accessible holiday visit www.able-travel.com, which provides many tips and links to travel resources worldwide.

American International School United Nations Rd, Baridhara; ☎ 02 882 2452; www.ais-dhaka.net. Dhaka's top international school, with the fees to match. Children of ambassadors & diplomats are all educated here.
French International School Plt 13, Rd 3, Baridhara; ☎ 02 881 9956; www.pedagogie.ac-toulouse.fr/eco-francaise-dacca. Offers a French- & English-language curriculum, the only international school in Dhaka to do so.
Grace International School Hse 78(B), Rd 23, Gulshan 1; ☎ 02 881 4469; www.graceinternationalschool.org. UK-certified education in a Christian environment, with mainly expatriate children attending.
International School Dhaka Plt 80, Blk E, Bashundhara; ☎ 02 881 7101–7; www.isdbd.org; Dhaka's 2nd choice, albeit in a bit of an odd location outside the diplomatic enclave.

WHAT TO TAKE

The great majority of travellers to Bangladesh, including expatriates, will find almost everything they need on the ground. Naturally, this doesn't include luxury food items such as alcohol, chocolate or fine coffees, but for just about everything else there is a local equivalent that will allow you to experience some of the local culture at the same time. On second thoughts, there is local alcohol, but as you'd expect from a non-alcoholic nation, it's quality is questionable.

Clothes-wise, you can bring as little as possible and have a tremendous range of items tailored during your stay in Bangladesh. Lightweight cotton is best, as new visitors might find they are sopping in their own sweat at first; this will eventually get better when they adjust to the heat (stay hydrated during those first few days!). At Dhaka's Banga Bazaar, there are plenty of items available from factory overruns, and given the prominence of the country's garment industry there is actually a pretty sizeable collection of items here – useful for picking up things like underwear, socks or even brand-name clothing at an extremely cheap price. Urban shops and boutiques use lightweight materials in their designs, allowing you to try out local styles. Culturally conscious women will need to dress more conservatively anyway, and so it follows that your first purchases might be a *salwar kameez*, which is a modest, loose-fitting pyjama-like outfit unique to India and Bangladesh. Shorts are not that common among men, and are considered to be especially casual.

If you're planning to travel to Nepal or the nearby mountains of Darjeeling, Sikkim or Bhutan, a warm jacket will likely come in handy, although you can purchase equivalents in these places. A lightweight rainproof jacket will also be useful if you are caught out in the weather and need to move. Swimsuits are hard to find here, but you won't be using them much in public anyway, although there are plenty of private swimming pools around.

Nevertheless, travellers will find a few other items helpful. Frequent power outages mean that it is handy to have a headlamp for reading and working in the dark, although storm lights are easy to purchase here. There is a good selection of shoes available but not in larger sizes (nine for women; ten for men). Hand sanitiser is especially useful as local people eat using their right hand. If you like to cook, a solid knife with a thick blade is essential as all the cooking knives are dull and prone to breakage. Laptops are good for watching DVDs although some apartments will come furnished with a DVD player. Rechargeable batteries come in handy as their quality is often very low in Bangladesh, but specialised computer markets do have these available. A travel-size mosquito net will also be a useful thing to have but most places provide nets or you can ask for one in hotels.

Tools- and electronics-wise, mobile-phone communication is quite common in Bangladesh, and so an unlocked GSM phone will prove convenient and it is free to receive local or international phone calls (although Skype is the cheapest option by far). A Swiss army-style knife or a multi-tool will be another useful accessory, not least as cheap can openers do break from time to time. Plug adaptors are available almost everywhere very cheaply, but a universal travel adaptor might prove valuable. You will find UK-style thick three-pronged plugs in newer buildings and standard round two-pin plugs in almost all other places. Although computer gear is widely available, most of it is cheaply produced imports from China and so you might prefer your own computer gear from abroad if you're a techie. Apple Macintosh service providers have just started reaching Bangladesh.

Toiletries are also easy to come by, although you may prefer some speciality items like tea tree oil (helpful for acne, cold sores, heat rash, insect bites and even fungus). Sunscreen is essential in the hot sun of Bangladesh summers, bring some with you as it's hard to find in Bangladesh. Same goes for tampons; ladies: they are sometimes available in Dhaka, but impossible to find in other areas. Towels are available locally, but you may want to bring a specialised lightweight travel towel if you know you'll be visiting some of the neighbouring countries. Shampoo and toothpaste are available at small shops in Tk2 packages to get you going while on the road or for the first few days in country. A *very* thin sleep sheet is handy when crashing out in ratty rooms, of which there are a fair number in Bangladesh.

You might like to bring a small, invaluable musical instrument. Bangladeshis are quick to break into song and being able to perform yourself is a real cultural icebreaker. Do note that good-quality guitar strings are not easy to find and local instruments tend to warp quite quickly in Bangladesh's humid climate. Photos of family and friends from home are good to have on you especially if you are visiting for a long time. Sunglasses, especially prescription sets, are a must, although contact lens solution is easily found in Dhaka. Zip-lock or specialised plastic bags can prove handy, especially while in the middle of Bangladesh's monsoon, where everything can become sodden if not well taken care of – technology and electronics gear will be happier inside these bags. A money belt is a good idea.

Specialised sporting equipment, such as tennis racquets and running shoes, is available here, but the quality and selection is decidedly lower than you're probably used to, but not bad nevertheless. Rock-climbing shoes are essential for climbers; as there is a workout gym at the American International School in Dhaka. Bicycle parts are hard to find but not impossible, but decent bicycles themselves are quite rare. Good tools for all of the above are hard to find for enthusiastic sports people.

Finally, there are no shortages of requests for passport photocopies and passport pictures when it comes to visa applications, local or otherwise. It's always good to carry these things with you in case you lose your passport – copies will help speed up the application process and help you deal with the necessary officials.

$ MONEY

For most travellers, money withdrawn via bank debit card is the easiest and most convenient way to get cash, as there are now ATMs in almost every major city of Bangladesh (this includes all the divisional capitals and most of the third-tier cities listed in this guide but not all, so do check ahead as there are some notable exceptions among the tourist destinations, like Srimongol or the Chittagong Hill Tracts). US dollars in cash is the next easiest option, although carrying large amounts of cash around, say US$500 or more, is discouraged. There are only facilities to change travellers' cheques in Dhaka and Chittagong (HSBC is best) and in this case it is best to stick with US dollars. If you're really in a pinch, HSBC or Standard Chartered ATMs will be able to advance Tk20,000 against a credit card, perhaps more at a teller, but the machine will help you avoid long queues at the bank.

MONEY TRANSFERS Wiring money into Bangladesh is not such a difficult process, and all you need to do is get the necessary banking information from your recipient. However, wiring money to yourself and withdrawing that money for business purposes can be troublesome given the complexity of local regulations to navigate in order to operate in Bangladesh. Do check with an attorney first and double-check anything that a government office tells you. It is highly recommended that you speak with the person in charge or find someone who is knowledgeable in such regulations when dealing with large amounts of money for business purposes, otherwise you may be told the wrong information which will cost you time and money in the end.

EXCHANGE Money exchangers are common in Dhaka, especially in the markets surrounding Gulshan One and Two circles, with pounds sterling, euros and US dollars for sale or purchase. You can also find exchange facilities for various currencies in Rifles Square in Dhanmondi. In the smaller towns and villages, most branches of the Sonali Bank will exchange US dollars but you'll probably find it easier to ask some intrepid entrepreneurs to exchange your cash at your hotel, and thus small denominations might be useful for this. Do check the rate first before agreeing to an exchange.

TIPPING In Bangladesh there is no standard for giving gratuities, but here are some rough guidelines. In most cases you can view a tip as a way of saying thank you, especially if the food, service or experience has met or exceeded your expectations. Usually 5% is enough, although more will not go unnoticed or unappreciated, especially if you become a regular customer at certain venues. Handing money directly to the staff you wish to thank is the best way to confirm the money goes to the right hands.

As you will be perceived as a wealthy foreigner no matter what your status, expect to be asked for '*boksheesh*' far more often than you should provide. The term is an all-encompassing one, and includes alms for the poor, tips for waiters, or bonuses for household or apartment staff. When to give and how much is a judgement call and a personal decision on your part. For waiters, the change from the bill, keeping this under 5%, is usually enough in basic restaurants. More upmarket places will usually add a service charge onto the bill, in addition to the government value-added tax, the amount of which varies depending on the service (usually 5–10% in restaurants or 15% in hotels). For household staff, one month's salary is expected as a bonus during Eid-ul Fitr.

BARGAINING Despite any markings such as 'fixed price' or even clearly indicated price tags, there is always room to negotiate in Bangladesh, and you will no doubt find yourself becoming a better bargainer after a stay here. Unfortunately, there is a general sentiment that foreigners are all rich and have taka to burn and so it will be hard, but not impossible, to get local prices. A good rule of thumb is to start with a price well below the initial offer (two-thirds or even half) and work your way upwards slowly, allowing plenty of room to meet in the middle. Do remember that a good deal is when the buyer and seller have reached a price that is fair to both parties, and unless you are a rock-bottom budget traveller your money will probably go a lot further in local hands than you may have imagined. Also keep in mind that value shows up in other ways, such as time, service and convenience, and with those bargaining bases in mind you should normally find the process to be a friendly one. For everyday items such as groceries, there are supermarkets that will save you the hassle of negotiating for every item, but certainly the freshness of items is less than if purchased in the open market. You can still support the little guy by going to the same vendors and eventually you will be given *bondhu* – friend prices – without the hassle of arguing. Finally, the last thing to consider is that bargaining takes time, so when you're in a hurry or it's late at night and there don't seem to be many other taxis in sight, then you may want to toss in the extra Tk10 it takes to get things moving.

GIVING TO BEGGARS One of the most difficult aspects of a stay in Bangladesh is the fact that there is a tremendous amount of begging, especially during the religious holidays and in Dhaka's smarter neighbourhoods. Quite simply, begging is a fact of life in Bangladesh and yet it remains extremely uncomfortable to be approached by those in need. Everyone handles being approached differently. By avoiding eye contact and shaking one's head slightly allows most beggars to understand that you have acknowledged their presence but are not going to give. This allows them to locate others who might do so more quickly. To give is purely a personal decision. It's worth knowing that giving to the poor is mandated under the tenets of Islam, so whether or not you do, someone else already is or else this behaviour would not continue as long as it has.

You may prefer to donate your money to a local development organisation, especially one that works directly with women or children as they form the most vulnerable sections of society in Bangladesh. Children working Dhaka's streets are very friendly and do enjoy conversation, especially with foreigners.

BUDGETING

Overall, Bangladesh is an extremely cheap place in which to travel, with some reporting that they have survived on less than US$4 per day, which is certainly not suprising given that most of the country makes it on less than US$2 a day. While you *could* make it on this amount, it's not really advisable to do so for health or sanitary reasons as low-cost food, served in downright dirty conditions, could be a trip-derailing gamble, compounded by a long recovery time if you're not staying somewhere you can recuperate properly. Cheaper transport is also less safe, as the drivers who are forced to stop most often also tend to be the wildest behind the wheel. Budget travellers would be better served by a budget of US$10 per day, which would allow for cleaner accommodation choices and healthier food. A mid-range traveller will find US$15–25 per day to be more than suitable, allowing the comfort of an air-conditioned room most nights and a filling meal at an upmarket restaurant at least once per day. Naturally all these numbers could double when staying in the big cities or when shopping. Budget even more if you plan on hard drinks, which are cheaper if you visit local bars.

Luxury travellers will have trouble finding things to spend their money on outside Dhaka and Chittagong, although some tours, especially boat trips, can run to over US$100 per person per day (hiring Contic's luxury boat could cost several hundred dollars per day). Car-hire prices have risen with worldwide fuel prices, with any car service outside Dhaka costing at least US$40–50 per day, and that's just for a sedan or microbus. Everyday items will usually be quite cheap: mineral water costs Tk10 for a 500ml bottle, and a pack of cigarettes usually less than Tk50. Local bus rides will usually be well under US$5 and luxury air-conditioned buses between divisional capitals just over US$10. Prices start to get a lot more expensive when dealing with imported items like cheese, alcohol and pasta, and although there are local versions of the same things, they tend to be of an inferior quality. Books can be much cheaper in Bangladesh although that's only when they are printed in India and not imported from outside south Asia.

GETTING AROUND

BY AIR The airline market in Bangladesh has just seen a few new competitors setting up shop, which at first was very good for local travellers but prices have since increased to the point where some might think twice before flying, especially because bus travel is just so cheap in comparison. At the time of research, routes were changing frequently to reflect the growing airline business in Bangladesh. Currently there are services between Dhaka and the major divisional cities (Rajshahi, Jessore, Chittagong, Sylhet and Cox's Bazaar; and with less frequency Barisal and Saidpur). At the time of research there was also a direct flight between Jessore and Chittagong, which would be very handy for mid-range travellers who want to travel between Sundarban and the Chittagong Hill Tracts, two of Bangladesh's best destinations, without having to go via Dhaka which would be something like a 16-hour bus ride – it's not unheard of.

Airline-wise, Biman Bangladesh is the country's national operator and given its reputation for erratic schedules, late departures and poor service, most people, even Bangladeshis, prefer other airlines. GMG Airlines is the country's oldest private operator although it seems to have fallen on hard times as of late flight frequency has decreased, but the service is still better than Biman. In 2006, United Airways (not to be confused with United Airlines in the US) opened operations in Bangladesh's domestic market, covering the major divisional cities and offering the best service so far. Just behind them is Royal Bengal Airlines, who also have comprehensive domestic coverage at similar prices, but using a smaller fleet than United, and hence fewer departures. Finally, Best Air began flying the Dhaka–Chittagong route in 2006, but has mainly focused on building its operations internationally and currently flies to Bangkok and Kuala Lumpur, and hopefully other cities soon. Just before publication it appeared that Best Air wasn't the best after all – it was about to go out of business.

Flight prices change frequently to reflect world fuel prices. At the time of research, domestic one-way flights were between Tk4,000 and Tk6,000, but flight specials that drop the price to Tk2,500 (including taxes) are not unheard of.

BY RIVER Compared with all other forms of transport, river journeys are the most 'Bangladeshi' way to travel, a type of journey you really can't experience anywhere else. Given the fact that the country lies at the mouth of the Ganges–Brahmaputra river basin, the world's largest delta, any journey to Bangladesh should include time spent on the water, whether that be a multi-day excursion to Sundarban, a cross-country journey on the rocket paddlesteamer or a day outside Dhaka on the Sitalakhaya. These trips allow for some real insight into the country and its inner workings, with the rivers serving as the arteries of the nation, the lifelines by which the remotest corners of an unexplored country can be reached. The rivers are also highly scenic places, where you will see people going about their daily lives or making a living from the water as fishermen, boat makers or transporters. All seasons are convenient for river travel, although during unstable weather periods such as minor tropical storms, it is riskier to travel by boat, but no more risky than a speeding public bus. The term 'launch' is used to describe river boats with sleeping facilities, such as those used for travel to Bangladesh's coastal south.

Whether or not to include a river journey depends on your time and budget during a short visit to Bangladesh – long-term visitors and expatriates will find that weekender journeys on the water are a great way to get out of Dhaka (see *Chapter 3, Dhaka*, page 153). If coming to or from Kolkata overland, spend time in Sundarban, as you will have a chance to stay on the water in a boat and see the wildest part of the country where tigers roam. Better yet, after touring Sundarban, you can catch the rocket paddlewheel as it departs from Khulna for Dhaka by co-ordinating your journey with a tour operator. Ensure your Sundarban departure or arrival dates include a trip on the rocket, which has twice-weekly departures from both Khulna and nearby Morrelganj, but the schedule changes frequently so you should check before booking..

There are many other options if the idea of seeing Bangladesh on the water appeals to you. Budget travellers will want to consider going from Sundarban to Chittagong entirely by public launch via Barisal, Bhola Island, Hatiya Island and Sandwip Island, which would take about two days if going straight through without stopping and costs less than US$30, even in first-class cabins. From Dhaka, other southern destinations include daily services to Barisal, Patuakhali (the gateway to the beach at Kuakata), Bhola and Hatiya by launch boat. Leaving by launch is one of the best ways to leave the stench of the city behind, and when feeling the cool air of the river blowing across your face, you'll be glad you experienced river travel, Bangladeshi style. Launches depart every evening from Dhaka's Sadarghat boat terminal, starting from about 18.00.

The launches are usually equipped with some basic cooking facilities and do offer meals to guests, and you will find the service staff to be quite eager to serve you meals, some of which are quite tasty, but have a look at what's on offer first. You can easily purchase fruit and snacks at the launch terminal. Depending on the launch, single and double cabins are usually available and cost Tk600 per person for Barisal, slightly more for destinations further away from Dhaka. Also some launches offer a lower price for singles and some don't, whereas others even have special VIP cabins that cost Tk1,500 offering private balconies, bathrooms and a big bed. Booking a ticket in advance is not easy without some knowledge of Bangla, in which case you're best off heading down to the terminal in the afternoon to secure a cabin. Foreigners are rarely turned away on the basis of no cabins. During Bangladeshi holidays, especially Eid, cabins are often sold off to the highest bidders, so it's best not to travel on the very overcrowded launches during those days. Finally, something must be mentioned of the safety record of Bangladeshi launch boats – they're not very good but they're definitely not worse than the buses. There are at least one or two sinkings every year, but it is usually on smaller boats and not the launches on the main routes.

BY BUS By far the cheapest and definitely the slowest form of transport is the public bus, which varies greatly in terms of comfort and price. This form of transport is probably the most accessible and has experienced the greatest growth in terms of luxury services as there are almost a half-dozen companies offering coaches with reclining leather seats, air-conditioned interiors, and in some cases, massaging chairs, at a cost that barely qualifies as splurging.

Regardless of the comforts, the roads can be quite hairy and bus journeys a stressful experience, especially to those who are extremely sensitive to unsafe driving, plenty of which happens in Bangladesh. If you feel unsafe, disembark at a major town or city, most of which offer direct, reserved chair coach services to divisional capitals.

Safety-wise, it is generally best to take the most expensive bus you can afford as these tend to have the least unsafe drivers who are generally more aware they're driving a pricy company vehicle. However, such buses are rarely available between smaller towns and your next best bet is a bigger chair coach bus, which stops slightly less frequently and lack the extraordinary number of paint scratches often seen on smaller buses – a sign that doesn't bode well when boarding an ultra-local public bus that looks like it's endured a few rollovers in its time. Each of the district cities usually has a central bus stand which connects to all other cities in the area, with services usually starting at dawn (06.00) until well after dusk (21.00 or 22.00). Travel at night is discouraged but sometimes unavoidable.

BY TRAIN The aging train system of the former East Bengal feels like it stopped being upgraded when the British left Kolkata in the first decade of the 1900s and moved the capital to Delhi. Were it not for the presence of a few new rail cars c2007, this assumption would probably not be far off the mark. Despite their age, the accumulated dirt and the noisiness of a rail car, Bangladeshi train journeys can still be preferable to hair-raising bus rides, especially if you manage to get your hands on sleeper tickets including air conditioning, something of an accomplishment in itself. You'll be surprised at the level of luxury available on an overnight train in Bangladesh – fresh sheets and plush interiors are not very common in these parts. The rails are also immune to traffic jams, which is something to consider depending on your planned arrival time, and especially if you plan to arrive into Dhaka in the evening.

Schedules are available online at the Bangladesh Railways website (*www.railways.gov.bd*), which is also starting to seem a little bit in disrepair, but is easier to use than first impressions suggest. First you can browse the site by departure city, and if you note the name of the train you'll be able to look it up by arrival city and find out when the train is scheduled to arrive. If you're ever unsure about the timing, asking a professional tour operator to help you plan might be prudent. For a small service fee they are usually able to purchase tickets for you, or especially for a group. The classes are known as air-conditioned sleeper, first-class sleeper, air-conditioned chair, reserved chair and finally shuvon class (unreserved seating). The kind of seats/sleepers available depends on the train and where it's headed; if you're OK with toughing it out you can show up just before the train departs and you'll likely get a sleeper for an overnight train. Some air-conditioned sleepers are reserved for government officials until the day of travel, and are therefore not released until that day, perhaps even just a few hours before the train's departure time. Otherwise you'll need to collect the ticket ahead of time by visiting the train station. Sleepers are usually four rooms to a cabin, although in some cabins there are only two – if you prefer privacy you could try buying all the bunks in a cabin. The cost of an air-conditioned sleeper is slightly more expensive than an air-conditioned bus for the same destination. For example, it costs Tk610 to travel by air-conditioned sleeper to Sylhet and Tk450 for the same journey on a luxury air-conditioned coach.

Most visitors like to try the train when travelling to Srimongol, Bangladesh's most popular weekender destination. From Dhaka, the four-hour daytime journey is quite memorable and scenic, especially after crossing branches of the Meghna after Ashuganj. Here there are some fine vistas over flooded fields, making this an excellent monsoon journey. Also, the seven-hour daytime journey from Chittagong to Srimongol is quite nice, and should be built into an itinerary if possible. Another memorable journey could be the trip between Kolkata and Dhaka on the new Maitree Express, which after a 40-year hiatus restarted on 14 April 2008, Bengali New Year. With the opening of the railway track over the Jamuna Bridge, destinations in northwestern Bangladesh also became a lot more accessible, and now have only slightly longer travel times than by bus.

BY PRIVATE VEHICLE Typically referred to as a 'reserved vehicle', hiring a car is definitely the most convenient way to travel around Bangladesh, allowing you to stop where requested and providing for some interesting journeys in the countryside. Naturally, it is also the most expensive way to travel, with a daily fee for a sedan vehicle costing about US$40–60 per day, depending on the distance travelled and where you go. Larger vehicles such as microbuses and multi-seat coaches can go well over US$100. Compressed natural gas (CNG) vehicles can be used east of the Jamuna and Meghna rivers as these areas are supplied regularly with natural gas; but in Rajshahi, Khulna and Barisal divisions, costs are significantly more expensive because natural gas is not available and petrol must be used (most vehicles can change between using CNG and petrol at the flip of a switch). You'll also get less far on a tank of natural gas, as CNG-equipped vehicles need to be refilled far more frequently and what you save in fuel costs could easily be lost in terms of the time it takes to refill. In Dhaka especially, there can be extremely long queues at the CNG pumps.

There are plenty of car services available and most guesthouses will be able to offer their vehicles for hire with driver, but do be aware that not many drivers speak decent English, so the words '*aste aste*' or 'slow slow' might come in handy. (See *Chapter 3*, *Tour operators*, page 118, for some local car-hire services.) Shop around and you'll be able to get a decent price.

BY BABY TAXI In the larger cities, taxis of various sizes are widely available and these are described in the relevant guide sections in greater details. In Dhaka, Chittagong and Sylhet, baby taxis use compressed natural gas for their fuel, and are hence called 'CNGs'. But in the countryside, your motorised transport options are more limited, especially where CNGs are not available. In the deep countryside you'll be lucky to find another form of baby taxi called a *tempo*, which is a colourful, yellow-roofed baby taxi not unlike the *tuk tuks* found in Thailand. These are not especially comfortable, but can help you get to remote sites where a rickshaw might take far too long. Often, these *tempos* substitute for local public transport and can be absolutely stuffed with passengers, so if you want a bit more comfort, try and hire the vehicle privately.

BY MOTORCYCLE It is possible to purchase a motorcycle or moped on the ground once you've arrived in Bangladesh, and after spending some time here you may find that Dhaka's immense traffic might push you into getting one, just for the sake of convenience. Journeys outside the city are only recommended if you have riding experience, as the drivers tend to be some of the wildest in south Asia. Also be aware that few insurance policies cover motorcycle accidents so if you do head out on the road, make sure you've got proper safety gear, some mechanic experience and drive *very*, *very* slowly.

Unfortunately your options for motorcycles are quite limited here, as *Easy Rider* culture has yet to flourish in the *desh*, and so the only bikes available locally are all 150cc or smaller. In motorcycle speak, that is quite small, something like saying you're going to have a round of 18 at the minigolf course. This is because Bangladeshi law has put a cap on the size of bikes that are permissible to import, but certainly a few more motorcycles and far fewer cars would help ease Dhaka's traffic woes. While such bikes might be adequate for getting around the city, they might be more prone to breakdown outside it and especially on long journeys. But every town has a repair shop and if you do decide on a motorcycle for travelling around the country you'll be able to get it fixed easily.

Enfield enthusiasts travelling from India won't be pleased to hear that Bangladesh officially requires *carnets* for Indian-registered motorcycles to cross into Bangladesh. These are almost impossible to get without having a residence in India you can register the bike to. However, there are urban myths about foreigners who have successfully obtained one.

Alternatively, you could apply for a 'temporary import' license from the Chief Controller of Import and Export Office in Dhaka. However, this is a lengthy process requiring a labyrinth of signatures and approvals, but it is a legal way to ensure the bike can enter Bangladesh.

If that fails, there are stories out there of officials willing to accept a declaration that you will return with the bike to the same border, which has occurred at the busy Benapol/Petrapol border between Jessore and Kolkata – the only way to know if you'll be allowed is to show up at the border and see what happens. Remember that if/when you get turned back from one place, that doesn't mean you'll receive the same response at other crossings.

As a last resort, it *is* possible to get a *carnet* for a Nepali-registered Enfield, but the costs are substantially higher than the Indian version.

In this way, highly adventurous travellers might consider adding Bangladesh to their overland itineraries with roads that are far superior in some places, especially in the less densely populated northwest. Plenty more information about Enfields can be found at the Horizons Unlimited website (*www.horizonsunlimited.com*).

ACCIDENTS There are far too many stories in the newspapers about angry mobs beating up drivers who have killed somebody, especially children, on

Bangladeshi roads, which is probably why many of same stories also end with 'the driver escaped the scene before he could be questioned'. Many of the local expatriate community prefer to hire drivers instead of driving themselves. Should you ever be caught in an accident outside the city, regardless of who is at fault, be aware that a large crowd of people will gather quickly to see what happened, and that a visible show of authority is important in order to keep the situation under control. Every accident is different, however, and there aren't really protections like insurance policies. In the end, the best safety measure you can take is prevention, achievable by driving safely and hiring good drivers and/or vehicles for your journeys.

ACCOMMODATION

Despite some recent improvements in the quality of accommodation across Bangladesh, travellers should maintain subdued expectations when it comes to finding fine beds, especially outside the main commercial cities. Luxury accommodation is still something of a novelty here, although the big hotel chains and some excellent guesthouses have set up shop in Dhaka. A boom in domestic tourism means that over the lifespan of this guidebook there will hopefully be some better options coming available in other locations, as rumours of new resorts and accommodation flutter around like flies at a streetside snack stall. But for the time being, standards remain low. Such is the reality of a country whose citizens have yet to afford travel for pleasure and become demanding consumers of travel.

UPMARKET ($$$$$$–$$$$$$$) As for the options that do exist, there is a full range of choices in Dhaka. At the top of the hotel heap are the luxury venues: hotels priced US$100 upwards are comparable to other international five-star properties around the world. While the international hotel chains top out at this price range, the lower end supports a few home-grown four-star options, which – at slightly cheaper prices – can offer extremely good value and you may be able to negotiate higher-end rooms at the same price. The choice depends on what kind of traveller you are or if you've been to Bangladesh before – obviously a five-star hotel experience tends to be more uniform across the world. A four-star choice might come with a couple of hidden surprises, both good and bad, such as excellent and more personal service, but less privacy.

ACCOMMODATION PRICE CODES

Because of the enormous price differences between the major cities (Dhaka and Chittagong) and the smaller divisional cities and towns (Rajshahi, Sylhet, Khulna or smaller), a wide range of price codes has been introduced to cover the range. Most of the smaller towns do not have upmarket accommodation; in these towns the most expensive places will rarely exceed US$30–40 per night. The prices here are based on a double room

$$$$$$$	Tk6,900+
$$$$$$	Tk4,800–6,900
$$$$$	Tk2,500–4,800
$$$$	Tk1,500–2,500
$$$	Tk700–1,500 (usually has AC)
$$	Tk300–700 (sometimes has AC option)
$	<Tk300

Underneath the top-end options, the pyramid widens and you'll find a few more venues offering unique accommodation experiences, priced at US$70–100 per night. These include half a dozen upper-end resorts scattered around the country (Panigram in Jessore will be the best when it opens in 2010, so that makes Nazimgarh the best at the moment). The Tea Resort at Srimongol needs some renovations: the Jamuna Resort seems like a nice escape (although its hundreds of hotel rooms mean that it isn't a terribly intimate place), a couple of heritage properties that offer guests a real taste of upper-end Bangladeshi culture and Mughal-style furnishings (Royal Resort at Tangail and Ideas Manzil in Dhaka are the notable properties), and a few hotels that maintain excellent standards in Bangladesh's main tourist destinations like Cox's Bazaar or Bogra (the base for exploring the Buddhist ruins of Paharpur). Good restaurants, well-appointed rooms and sparkling bathrooms are a given at all of these places. Swimming pools and gyms are usually available as well (but not always). Unfortunately, these places barely add up to a dozen choices, so if you're a high-end traveller looking for the cutting edge of luxury, check back with Bangladesh in a few more years. The country hasn't got the hang of luxury just yet.

MID-RANGE *($$$–$$$$$)* There are a range of cookie-cutter hotels in Dhaka and Chittagong that fit in the upper-end of this price range, between US$40 and US$70. These venues seem willing to drop their published prices before you even ask for a discount, sometimes up to 40% or even 50%. Such hotels would be good places to stay when given a deal as they also seem willing to toss in a few extras such as free airport transfers and breakfasts in their rates, something to consider while making reservation enquiries. There are literally half a dozen of these places scattered around Dhaka's diplomatic and business enclave which is why they seem to be the most willing to offer discounts. Facilities here will usually include an air-conditioned room, perhaps with some very nice verandas or terraces attached, and a spartan range of furnishing that would be good for a short-term, one- or two-month stay.

Lower mid-range travellers enjoy the best choices in terms of accommodation value in a visit to Bangladesh. At the top of the lower mid-range are a number of options, priced between US$25 and US$40. Options in this category almost always have a tidy, well-furnished air-conditioned room with efficient room service. These venues sometimes offer an attached multi-cuisine restaurant, a business centre, and broadband internet included in the price, but rarely a workout facility. This level of hotel is available in most major cities (eg: the divisional capitals and major cities like Rajshahi, Bogra, Rangpur, Khulna, Jessore, Sylhet, Mymensingh and Comilla; and the tourist destinations like Srimongol, Rangamati, Bandarban and Cox's Bazaar), although the smaller cities tend to have fewer options. The government-run Parjatan Hotels fit into the cheaper end of this category, and in some of the smaller cities they might even be the best hotel in town, although the ones that are over ten years old really show their lack of upkeep on the outside and inside.

At the bottom of the lower mid-range category, prices run between US$10 and US$25. The best of these options are some extremely friendly NGO guesthouses, most of which charge an absolute pittance for what they offer because they are non-profit organisations. Furnishings and rooms can be very basic but they're usually the cleanest places to stay in the most remote corners of Bangladesh. Well-prepared, tasty and moderately priced Bangla food made with caring hands is often communally served in heaping portions. Best of all, the service and the friendliness of the staff are unquestionably genuine (but be aware that NGO staff are not necessarily hospitality industry specialists), and you can literally rest assured that your money is supporting worthy causes. The biggest guesthouses even have some handicrafts on sale at their venues, allowing you to support the NGO's work directly while picking up some great souvenirs.

The hotels in this price range are usually well run, although the older places can be rough around the edges. It seems a simple proposition to do a paint job in places like this but owners seem to care very little for the upkeep, and so the newest hotels are the nicest places to stay. So, if you're reading this a few years after the publication of this guidebook, some of the recommendations within could be looking decidedly more worn in by the time you get there. Nevertheless, it is this class of hotel that has seen the greatest growth in Bangladesh, with a couple of new hotels to choose from in every big city. Facilities usually include televisions, tiled rooms, well-used-looking mosquito nets and a Western toilet or 'high commode', as it is sometimes referred to.

BUDGET ($-$$) Finally, budget hotels tend to be the Wild West of accommodation in Bangladesh, with the cheapest costing Tk60–100, or about US$1–1.25. Booking is not necessary at most places, unless otherwise specified, although if you arrive after dark you may find that all the cheapest rooms are taken already. These options also tend to be the oldest, smelliest and most mouldy rooms in the country, where you get exactly what you pay for. Ask to see the room before buying it, as the rule here is 'what you see is what you get'. The beds may appear unmade when you are shown the room as they will often lack sheets. But once you've purchased the room, staff will usually supply fresh sheets immediately. Some of these budget places have a 'VIP room' that is far less frequented than the cheaper options, and for Tk300–700 (US$5–10) more you might find a very decent room in a budget place where it turns into a good deal. These rooms are also typically on the higher floors, and so they have much more natural light and/or bigger windows. Sometimes there is even an air-conditioned room in a budget hotel, which is rarely ever purchased and just as good as any mid-range choices.

CULTURAL CONSIDERATIONS Bangladeshi culture dictates that men and women stay in different rooms unless they are married, and so travelling couples should simply introduce themselves as husband and wife regardless of their status. Additionally, male and female budget travellers, if wanting to share rooms, should also introduce themselves as husband and wife, in order to avoid potential hassle over room arrangements. Solo female travellers will also encounter potential hassles trying to stay at budget accommodation as women are often rarely seen in these places unless accompanied by a male such as a husband or colleague.

Non-smoking rooms are often not an option as almost the entire male population smokes cigarettes. The word 'hotel' can often dictate a restaurant or a place with rooms for rent, so if you're looking for a place to sleep you'll want to find a 'residential hotel' or '*oboshik hotel*'.

At all hotels and across all price ranges, privacy is often an issue as overzealous service boys may often come right into your room regardless of what you are doing, so lock your door if you want to stop this particularly intrusive behaviour. Even if you've sealed yourself in, you may find them knocking every five minutes, checking if you need tea, food or cigarettes. If you prefer to not be bothered, tell the management of the hotel what your needs are and then ask to be left alone. Also, most rooms have a buzzer that you can use to request service without having to leave your room.

EATING AND DRINKING

An unfortunate aspect of travelling in a poor country is that the notions of hygiene and cleanliness are far more basic here than in neighbouring countries, and even the hardiest of stomachs will eventually encounter an upset at some point during a stay in Bangladesh. Extra rice or bread might be served by hand; in most restaurants food is prepared ahead of time and left to stand for long periods, therefore eating earlier is better than eating later. These bouts of the 'chitta shittas' are often the topic of many conversations among resident expatriates and travellers, and you might be surprised at how frequently the topic of bowel movements is discussed, even at dinner tables. This is not meant to scare potential visitors to Bangladesh as there is plenty of good food in the country – you just need to know where to get it. In Dhaka, it is especially easy to get an upmarket meal that costs the same as it does anywhere else around the world with an almost comparable level of quality (never quite the same as home, however). Nevertheless, lowered expectations are helpful in the sense that fewer choices are available and often less healthy, especially when dealing with local food choices outside the main cities.

Oddly, there is an abundance of Chinese restaurants in Bangladesh, which have a decidedly darker (in the sense that they lack light but do not lack security) and more private atmosphere than the common eateries and are more expensive (but never outrageous, unless you are on a very tight budget). These places have wildly varying menus, but the most popular items among locals are the fried rice and chop suey dishes. You will also find various combinations of chicken, beef, vegetables and chilli served in various wet sauces, sometimes spicy. This is rarely 'authentic' Chinese food, but they do offer clean, healthy and well-cooked food at reasonable prices. A meal here will usually cost between Tk100 and Tk250 per person, which even if you are on a really tight budget you should be able to afford once every few days. These restaurants also feature cutlery, which might seem like a strange thing to think until you realise that most other meals are taken by hand (see below).

For menu vocabulary, see *Appendix 1, Language*, page 340.

CULTURAL CONSIDERATIONS In Bangladesh, the best food is often found at home, which is a good thing given that travellers and guests receive so many dinner invitations, sometimes from total strangers. It is not expected that you take up every invitation, but you should try out a few and get a taste of the best cuisine the country has to offer. Often, homemade meals are cooked with a lot of love and preparation, which does require time, and thus having dinner at a friend's house can become a multi-hour affair for which you should leave a lot of time and accept the fact that you will never be able to finish all the food prepared for you. Don't feel bad about this – it is their honour to host you as a guest and rest assured that

RESTAURANT PRICE CODES

Based on a main meal

$$$$$	Tk1,000+
$$$$	Tk500–1,000
$$$	Tk300–500
$$	Tk100–300
$	<Tk100

food is almost never wasted (very little at all is wasted in Bangladesh). You can repay the favour by sending some photographs or bringing some food contribution along (sweets like *rosh golla* or *misti doi* are a good choice – see below).

Food is eaten using the right hand in Bangladesh, and never the left hand as it is associated with ablutions. You are permitted to drink water using the left hand or break bread with it. Hand-washing facilities are available in every restaurant although soap is sometimes scarce, and thus it makes sense to carry an antibacterial hand sanitiser with you at all times. As a guest you will usually eat before the host family. This might make you feel uncomfortable, but it is the cultural norm in Bangladesh.

BREAKFAST The morning meal is consistently the best and most fresh meal available in any city, town or village of the country. Freshly baked tandoori *naan* or pan-fried *parata* (can be cooked with less or no oil if requested) served with a protein-rich thick *dal* and a spicy *momelette* (omelette with onion and green chilli) is available just about everywhere and costs less than US$0.40 or about Tk25. Most upper mid-range hotels with restaurants will be able to offer you a similar version of this breakfast delivered to your room although you will find fresher versions in streetside restaurants where the turnover is higher but the surroundings decidedly more dirty. These same hotels sometimes offer a 'western' or 'continental' breakfast which consists of white toast, a fried egg, banana, butter and jam if you're lucky, and a tea, or perhaps instant coffee, on request. At NGO guesthouses, this breakfast is often simpler but freshly prepared: often you can request a *chapati*, which is the non-fried version of the Bangladeshi flatbread or they might serve you the fried version, which is known as a *parata*. Finally, if you're the big-breakfast business-buffet type, you'll see these meals are often included while staying at a four- or five-star venue.

MAIN MEALS The quality of lunch depends highly on where you decide to take it. When travelling outside the main cities, there are significantly fewer food choices and you may end up taking lunches or dinners at local restaurants of varying quality. These highly frequented places are built for utility and fast eating far more than for the pleasure of enjoying food. Therefore, the food is prepared ahead of time and left to stand, sometimes for up to several hours, before being served to patrons who seem to want to eat as quickly as possible and then leave. A common lunch is a heaping plate of rice served with mushy vegetables (*sobji* or *bhaji*) and an oily meat or fish curry. Some restaurants serve chicken or mutton *biriyani* for lunch that is marginally more freshly cooked but still heavy on the oil. A few restaurants with a better reputation will also serve *bharta*, which is a freshly mashed vegetable, usually eggplant, potato or fish.

Dinner is a more elaborate affair, as the streets and laneways of most cities become throbbing and colourful veins of activity after the sun goes down. At this time there is a lot of food choice available, whether it be streetside *chatpoti* or *halim* (see *Snacks* below), or perhaps a few restaurants that do beef or chicken kebabs (*beef shikh kebab* or *chicken reshmi kebab*). The best of these places will also serve freshly baked tandoori *naan* and a cucumber salad alongside their dishes.

At the street-side stalls, breakfast can be served as early as 06.00 and sometimes as late as 09.30. Lunch is usually ready from 12.30 and stops late in the afternoon at about 15.00 (most restaurants maintain similar opening hours). Finally, dinner can be served any time from 07.00 to 10.00, although if you're taking it at a friend's residence be ready for it to run even later. Upscale restaurants generally maintain these hours, except during holidays like Ramadan, when most restaurants do not serve food during the day due to a lack of diners.

DESSERTS Bengali desserts are known throughout south Asia, with sweet shops found as far away as Delhi. Given the sweet tooth of most Bangladeshis, it's hardly surprising that every region has a famous dessert, with some notable examples including sweet yoghurt from Bogra (*misti doi*) to dough balls served in milk from Comilla (*rosh malai*). While travelling, these desserts make good gifts to bring local friends or hosts when they invite you over for dinner. At that same dinner, you might even be served homemade desserts despite your belly being terribly full already. Popular are *shemai*, a milk-based vermicelli dessert, and *payesh*, a rice version of the same thing.

More common are a number of *misti* (sweet) shops found in every city, town and village of Bangladesh. Here, the most common item is *rosh golla*, dough balls that resemble the doughnut holes served in pastry shops of Western countries. In Bangladesh, these same balls are soaked in sugary syrup, which shoots into your mouth or perhaps onto your neighbour with the first bite. You can be forgiven for eating only one as this dessert has just too much sugar in it.

SNACKS Bengali snack foods are also one of the main items you will see just about everywhere. The best of these snacks are the humble *phuchka* and *chatpoti*, often served from street carts, mostly in the cities but sometimes in the countryside as well. *Phuchka* is a combination of mashed potatoes and chickpeas, served inside small crispy shells, and topped with a sour tamarind sauce. *Chatpoti* is a plate of boiled chickpeas served with a topping of onions, coriander, chopped green chillies, grated hard-boiled eggs and more of those same crispy shells found in *phuchka*. Unfortunately the hygiene standards at these places varies widely so if you don't want to take any chances, your best bet is to try the *phuchka* in a couple of widely popular restaurants (namely the Dhaba in Dhaka and Chittagong, where they have a spicy version and an absolutely delicious yoghurt version that is quite possibly the best food item in the whole of Bangladesh). Vegetarians are also guaranteed to fall in love with this dish, especially the yoghurt version seen at more and more Dhaka restaurants nowadays. *Chaats* and *puri* dishes, which probably have their origin in Kolkata, are also making an appearance in some of Dhaka's newer cafés and restaurants, as they cater to a younger generation whose food tastes have gone well beyond the mutton *biriyani* crowd. Indian-style *dosas*, or Kolkata-style rolls, are sometimes found at similar venues.

There are other, homegrown snacks seen on just about every street corner of Bangladesh: dozens of deep-fried varieties crowd such food stalls. Most popular is the *shingara*, which is usually some mashed potatoes and/or a carrot/onion mixture wrapped in a thick pastry and then fried, or the *samosa* (pronounced 'shamosha' in Bangla), a deep-fried triangle-shaped vegetable pocket. You'll also sometimes see *piaju* (mashed lentils mixed with onions and fried) and *beguni* (battered slices of eggplant) served alongside, perhaps with a big pile of chow mein noodles too. A pile of dark chickpeas with a series of colourful green and red chillies means you're looking at *chana*, which is usually mixed with puffed rice (*muri*) and then served in a bowl with a spoon, probably one of the only non-fried dishes that qualifies as a common snack food. *Mughlai parata*, a scrambled egg with vegetables and spices and then fried inside a wrapped flatbread, is one of the most popular snacks, and often shared between several people in the early evening.

Finally, the last kind of snack worth mentioning is *halim*, which is actually a kind of lentil soup that is slow-cooked with beef, mutton or chicken and a range of delicious spices. Served hot from enormous pots outside restaurants, this soup is a fairly healthy dish and is found in most restaurants or snack stalls around the country during the evening.

Depending on your tolerance for heavy oils, most of these snacks are meant to be fast food and are best eaten in the early morning well before lunch (some people eat it as a late substitute for breakfast), or in the late afternoon well before dinner. The late selection often has much more variety than the morning. Around these times such snacks are the most fresh. Most of the snack carts are gone by 20.00, when people are either getting ready for their evening meal or going to a restaurant for a late dinner (often taken late, say 20.00 or 21.00).

FRUIT One of the great rewards for visiting Bangladesh during the hot and humid season is to taste what must be the most amazing and fresh fruit available on earth. Blessed with an extremely fertile and verdant landscape, the country produces its best fruit during what are known as the 'honey months', from June to August. To travel in the heat can be punishing but to taste the fruit fresh from the orchards is well worth the effort. Fruit really does taste far better here as opposed to when it is imported from across the world.

Topping the list are Bangladeshi mangoes, which are so abundant in the country during the month of June that prices often drop to less than Tk40 per kilogram (US$0.65) although they are available at higher prices until early August. As many Bangladeshis will surely tell you, the national fruit of the country is the jackfruit, which also comes to market around this time. Lychees – which originally came from China – also show up in June, as well as jackfruit and water-bearing green coconuts. During August, sweet guavas are sold from the street, followed by ripe jambura and fresh pineapple. Green papaya is available year round but ripens during the winter months.

ADIVASI FOOD Indigenous people, known as Adivasi people in Bangla, make some very different foods from their neighbours. In particular, the Chittagong Hill Tracts seem to have a very real love of fish-based flavouring that resembles Thai or Burmese cooking much more than south Asian cuisine (see *Chittagong Hill Tracts, Food and drink*, page 218, for more information).

A NOTE ABOUT RAMADAN Eating out is much harder during the period of Ramadan, a Muslim religious festival in which no food or even water is supposed to be taken during daylight hours. The fasting, called *roja* in Bangla, begins at dawn, after which many families have already awoken well before sunrise to have a quick meal. During the day, most restaurants – but not all of them – run a special *Iftar* service during this period, in which they sell a range of *Iftar* snack items that are usually packed off and taken home for eating the moment after sunset. *Halim* and fried items dominate these menus. The restaurants then usually reopen for regular dinner service in the evening although business often stays quite slow during this time.

Ramadan is a deeply religious time in Bangladesh, in which the citizens fast in order to remember the plight of the less fortunate in their society. It is also a time of giving alms to the poor and practising religious austerity with friends, family and colleagues. If travelling during this time, you might like to try a day of fasting to see how it feels, and certainly this voluntary starvation does bring on a kind of understanding as to why people seem quite droopy in the late afternoons.

Furthermore, not everyone sticks to the fasting period so rigorously, especially those who work in labour jobs like rickshaw pulling. Some restaurants and tea stalls simply put a curtain over their establishment to indicate that they are still serving food and its customers still do eat discreetly. Additionally, not all Bangladeshis fast during this period as it remains a partly personal choice.

DRINKING While most people don't mind if you drink, local people prefer to do it in private settings, which only makes sense given the prevailing Islamic culture of the country. When they do get their hands on the stuff they tend to shoot it back in large gulps as opposed to sipping it slowly and relishing it. As a result, if you do decide to offer drinks to your Bangladeshi friends/colleagues in a large party setting, get ready for some potentially lecherous or aggressive behaviour that can result from people who have little experience with alcohol, but really no more so than the drunken louts found in any Western country. That said, this is understandable given the restraint and tranquillity that Bangladeshis normally possess in more sober surroundings.

In terms of the law, Bangladeshis are not allowed to carry alcohol in their private cars without an alcohol licence. Such licences are only attainable with a doctor's prescription and hence the possession of alcohol can be legalised for 'medical reasons'. Also, there are a few bars in the big cities, although the police do raid these places once in a while, resulting in some interesting headlines in the local papers (usually somebody gets shot). There are also a few members' clubs in the divisional capitals that serve local and imported alcohol as well as imported beer. Technically, those who don't have an alcohol licence are not permitted to be drinking in these establishments but the raids are infrequent enough so that most people do it anyway. As a foreigner you are not required to possess such licences and you may find your Bangladeshi friends asking you to try and get alcohol on their behalf.

Amongst ethnic minorities, the story is naturally different. Because such people are either Buddhist or Christian, there is not only an acceptance of alcohol but there is often a culture surrounding it. Most of the people in the Chittagong Hill Tracts distil their own high-alcohol brews from rice, which are quite potent and belly warming and best not taken in too large a quantity (which is sometimes not an option depending on the vigour of your hosts!). Despite being called 'rice wine', the alcohol percentage makes it more like a hard-hitting spirit like whisky. In the Garo areas of Mymensingh, there is another kind of milder rice wine that is quite excellent and goes well with meals. The best time of year to visit these places is during the holiday seasons, where people are more naturally in a festive mood. For the Chittagong Hill Tracts, the best time is during Bengali New Year (14 April), and for the Garo areas of northern Mymensingh, the best time is around Christmas.

PUBLIC HOLIDAYS AND FESTIVALS

Making sense of Bangladeshi holidays is complicated by the fact that four different calendars combine to make up Bangladeshi holidays: the Gregorian, Islamic, Hindu and Buddhist calendars all contribute a few holidays each. The Islamic calendar is ten days shorter than the Gregorian calendar, and hence, Muslim holidays begin ten days earlier every year. The Hindu calendar is a lunar calendar and so the holidays stay around the same period each year. There is only one Buddhist holiday in May so thankfully that one is less complicated. Finally, the Gregorian calendar holidays are at the same time every year. Unless otherwise indicated, the religious holidays below are public holidays in which you can expect most government offices and shops to be closed.

RELIGIOUS HOLIDAYS

Buddha's birthday (*April or May*) Also known as Vesak or Buddhia Purnima, this holiday coincides with other countries that claim Buddhism to be one of their central religions, especially Thailand, Myanmar or China. In Bangladesh, the best place to enjoy this holiday is in the Chittagong Hill Tracts, but if you can't make it up there during this time, head to Dhaka's Dharmarajikha Buddhist Monastery, which usually puts on the biggest celebration in the city in conjunction with the Thai embassy.

Ramadan and Eid-ul Fitr (*one month long, begins late August 2009, early August 2010*) Visiting Bangladesh during Ramadan is definitely inconvenient but also very eye-opening. The idea of the holiday is to spread the wisdom of Islam and promote peace and brotherhood among Muslim people. In Bangladesh, Ramadan is also a time to give alms to the poor.

The most visible aspect of the holiday is the practice of fasting. Many families wake well before dawn to take breakfast, and then after sunrise, the more religious Bangladeshis don't eat or even drink water for the rest of the day. Most restaurants (but not all) shut down their regular daytime menu and serve *Iftar* instead, a series of traditional Ramadan snacks that most people gobble down in a rush to end the day's fasting at sunset. In Dhaka, you'll see that every restaurant posts massive banners advertising their *Iftar* specials, and then most people take a late-night meal at home before bed. Old Dhaka's Chawk Bazaar is one of the best places to enjoy the evening atmosphere, and see the largest range of traditional snacks on display, including gigantic 2kg *zilapis*, a fried sugar pretzel that you may or may not want to taste but is something extraordinary to see. Arrive in the early afternoon and you will also see the tremendous range of snacks on display.

Food aside, the atmosphere of Ramadan is also very special. In the towns and villages of the country, many families gather in the evenings after *Iftar* to shop, catch up or make plans for the end of the holiday period. Like Christmas, gift-giving between friends and family is becoming increasingly common, as it is traditional to don only new clothing at Eid-ul Fitr, which marks the end of the holiday.

Inside the city, Ramadan makes the streets even more frantic than usual. Most people, including some day labourers or taxi drivers, lacking food, water and even cigarettes, start to get very droopy-looking in the afternoon, especially on particularly hot days. Daytime traffic is even worse than usual as most fasters leave work early to take *Iftar* with their families.

A warning: the number of beggars on city streets increases phenomenally during this time, as many people from the villages come to collect alms from the wealthy in what is a circus-like display of disabilities and disfigurations. Do keep your head in check; this practice is just part of a culture that lacks strong social welfare institutions for its least fortunate people.

Travelling during this time is inconvenient but not impossible. More pre-planning than usual is required, especially if moving towards the end of the holiday. This is because most Bangladeshis make their way back to their home villages and towns during Eid, and use just about any form of transport available. The roofs of trains, buses and launches are all thronging with people, so if you're a photographer this is a mighty good time to be here. Tickets are not impossible to get, but they are often sold to the highest bidder, so be prepared to overpay up to 100% when dealing with transport prices during this time. But the experience of seeing millions of people on the move at once is something that cannot be experienced anywhere else.

The month finally culminates in Eid-ul Fitr, a multi-day holiday that is declared when the crescent moon is sighted in the sky and Ramadan officially ends. For this reason the holiday can vary by a day from year to year and it often falls to the government to declare which days will be holidays. Most shops and restaurants tend to stick to these schedules but you'll never know if anything is open or shut unless you try calling ahead or showing up at the door and seeing what happens. The hotels usually maintain a skeleton staff but be prepared for added inconveniences as well as the excuse that 'the cook has returned to his village'.

Eid-ul Adha (*early December 2009, late November 2010*) Also known as 'Bloody Eid', this holiday is meant to commemorate the fact that the prophet Ibrahim was willing to sacrifice his own son Ishmael to God. Just as Ibrahim was about to drive the knife into his son's heart, God put a ram in its place and spared Ishmael his life. Today the holiday is celebrated across the Muslim world in a similar fashion, although an animal is used for traditional sacrifice. The wealthy families purchase goats, cows and even camels for slaughter, and the culture dictates that two-thirds of the resulting meat is to be given to neighbours and the poor (one-third each).

The holiday is known as 'Bloody Eid' for a reason, in that the animals are traditionally slaughtered just outside the home and in the open. Depending on your tolerance for seeing blood, you may or may not wish to be out on the streets at this time, although the sounds of mooing cows and chopping meat may reach you anyway. Vegetarians need not apply.

Janmasthami (*early September every year*) This Hindu holiday celebrates the birth of Lord Krishna, and is marked by a public holiday in Bangladesh. There is no place where it is really celebrated, although if you go to any Hindu temple you will definitely see people making a visit to pray.

Durga Puja (*late September/early October*) Although this festival is more widely celebrated among the Hindu Bengali population of Kolkata, this is also a very colourful time to be in Bangladesh. The day marks the victory of Mother Durga over Mahishasura, a demon who been had granted invincibility against any man or god, but not a woman. Hence, Durga is always depicted armed with a spear, and defeating a dark-skinned demon and being chased by a tiger. There are also idols to the elephant god Ganesh, who symbolises wealth among wealthy Hindus.

In Dhaka, Shakhari Bazaar (or 'Hindu Street' as it is known among foreigners), is the place to be during this loud and outrageous holiday (see box in *Chapter 3, Preserving Old Dhaka*, pages 142–3, for more information on Shakhari Bazaar). Dozens of brightly coloured Durga idols are made from mud and displayed in homes and makeshift platforms through the neighbourhood, and there are a series of snack stalls, balloons and music decorating the street. On the final day of celebration, each of the Durga idols is loaded into a truck and rather unceremoniously dumped into the Buriganga River, symbolising Durga's departure from Earth.

Outside Dhaka, Durga Puja is also celebrated around the country, although it would be best to head southwest, where the concentration of Hindus is higher. Just outside Dhaka, there are a number of Hindu people living in the village of Dhamrai, which is just next to Savar. Contact Sukanta Banik of the Dhamrai Metal Crafts store (*Hse A71, Rothkhola, Dhamrai;* **m** *01713 003136, 01817 087732;* **e** *dmcsukanta@hotmail.com*) for more information.

Moharram (*late December 2009, mid-December 2010*) Not a public holiday, but definitely a major Islamic cultural event, signifying the start of the New Year. Usually this holiday is celebrated at Old Dhaka's Hussaini Dalan by the minority Shi'ite Muslim community of Bangladesh.

Bishwa Istjema (*February*) A little-known secret is that Bangladesh stages the second largest gathering of Muslims around the world at nearby Tongi. Over three million attendees were said to have come in 2007, although 2008 was cut short owing to inclement weather. The gathering is typically held in February each year, but the dates change. Some incredible photography opportunities can be had at this time of year, including trains that are completely covered with Muslim pilgrims going to join the congregation.

NATIONAL FESTIVALS AND HOLIDAYS

Ekushey (*21 February*) In the early days of the newly formed Pakistan, its government was quick to declare that 'Urdu and only Urdu' would be the national language of the new Muslim nation. This mistake gave the eastern wing of the country the fuel it needed to fan the flames of independence, which helped lead to the birth of Bangladesh. Known as International Mother Language Day, Ekushey marks the death of the first martyrs of Bangladesh. On 21 February 1952, five students were gunned down during language protests at Dhaka University by the police. The event is widely recognised as the seed that eventually culminated in Bangladesh's independence. On this day a large procession moves through the city towards Shaheed Minar, the Dhaka University memorial to these early martyrs.

Independence Day (*26 March*) Shortly after Sheikh Mujib Rahman all but declared independence during a historic speech at Dhaka's Ramna race course, he was arrested and shipped off to West Pakistan for trial. It was left to Major Zia to declare the independence of Bangladesh, which he did after storming the Chittagong radio station on the night of 26 March 1971, thus beginning the nine-month war in which anywhere between one million and three million lives were lost. During this national holiday, top political leaders and hundreds of visitors go to the National Martyrs' Memorial in Savar, where thousands of flower wreaths are laid down to remember the lives of those lost during Bangladesh's bloody war of independence. Otherwise, visiting the Liberation War Museum in Dhaka should be interesting at this time (see page 148).

Bengali New Year (*14 April*) The origins of this holiday are actually financial as opposed to cultural, as the Mughal tax collectors of historic Bengal needed to create a calendar that coincided with the yearly harvest as the Islamic calendar did not serve this purpose. Today, it is also a colourful and cultural time to be in Bangladesh, as many people take the holiday with their families and visit fairs and carnivals around the country. Although Bangladeshis hardly need the excuse to make great food, this is also an eating holiday: a battery of interesting foods will become available at the homes of neighbours and friends.

In Old Dhaka, there are some vestiges of a kite-flying festival that used to be held around this time, and there are even traditional wrestling events (called *bali*) in Chittagong. Also, there will be a number of events staged from Ramna Park and the Institute of Fine Arts at Dhaka University, including music shows and poetry readings.

Boiju or Boisabi (*14 April, celebrated in the Chittagong Hill Tracts*) Falling on the same day as Bengali New Year, this is also a great time to visit the Chittagong Hill Tracts, although the festival goes by different names depending on ethnic minority. Among the Marma people there is a wet version in which people throw water onto one another, reminiscent of Thailand's water festival. In other places, the holiday is typically celebrated with a battery of food and alcohol, including a special rice beer called *zu*. Tradition dictates that you must visit the homes of at least seven of your friends, family or colleagues, which after the fourth or fifth house does begin to resemble an untidy pub crawl if you let it get out of hand.

May Day (*1 May*) The international holiday for labour workers around the world. Ironically most people in Bangladesh still work on this day.

Day of Mourning (*15 August*) On 15 August 1975, Sheikh Mujib Rahman was assassinated along with most of his family. Only two daughters (one of them Sheikh Hasina) managed to avoid the slaying because they were out of the country at the time. Successive military and political governments kept their remembrances of the man a low-key affair until the Awami League took power in a 1996 election, and declared the day a national holiday. The holiday was in effect until 2002 when it was cancelled by the ruling Bangladesh National Party. As of 2007, respects are now paid to the man who fathered the nation and flags are flown at half mast at all government offices, but the day is not a public holiday.

Victory Day (*16 December*) Victory Day marks the end of Bangladesh's bloody Liberation War, the day that the Pakistani army officially surrendered to freedom fighters and the Indian generals who had supported them. As many Bangladeshis will proudly tell you, they have always won their freedom in December battles, including the 2008 election that returned the country to democratic rule. The holiday is marked by massive patriotic sentiment, flag waving on the streets and events at Dhaka's Liberation War Museum. The day is a public holiday and all offices are closed.

Christmas Day (*25 December*) In Bangladesh, Christmas is not celebrated with much fanfare but it is a public holiday given in view of the 1% of the population who are Christian – which still could be more than a million people given Bangladesh's massive population. Again, the Garo areas of the north would likely be the best place to visit during this time. Otherwise the expat community is fairly lifeless at this time of year.

MINOR FESTIVALS The following festivals and holidays are not considered regular government holidays but do hold special cultural significance and are well worth checking out during a long-term stay in Bangladesh of if you happen to be in the neighbourhood. Most of the Bangladeshi cultural holidays are celebrated at or around Dhaka University.

Falgun (*13 February*) This holiday marks the beginning of spring in Bangladesh, and the biggest celebration often takes place around Dhaka University campus.

Chobi Mela (*last three months of every year*) This annual photographic festival celebrates Bangladesh's well-established photojournalistic traditions, with photography from all over the world on display at various venues around town. Organised chiefly by the staff of Drik Gallery, the festival dates can be checked out at www.chobimela.org.

Rathayatra (*July*) Another major celebration of Bangladesh's Hindu community, in which several Jagannath chariots (called *rathas*) are pulled by devotees from temple to temple around Dhaka. At Dhamrai, a similar procession also occurs, although the original three-storey chariot, built by *zamindars* at Baliati, was destroyed by the Pakistani army during the Liberation War. The current chariot does not capture the former glory of course, but is worth seeing on a visit to Dhamrai.

Shab-e-Barat (*late July 2009, mid-July 2010*) Also known as the 'night of commission', this holiday is one of two all-night prayer nights in Bangladesh. It is said that one's fate is determined for the entire year.

Shab-e-Qadr (*27th day of Ramadan; mid-September 2009 and early September 2010*) This Muslim holiday is also known as the 'night of power', and marks the occasion when the Prophet Muhammad asked his followers to pray all night long in an effort to absolve their past sins. In Bangladesh, a few mosques will stay open through the night for the prayer, with many taking the next day off from work.

Prabarana Purnima (*late October*) Also known as Ashvini Purnima, this Buddhist festival is meant to reinforce the principles of right and wrong deeds among believers. In some places, particularly the Bandarbans, candle-bearing hot-air balloons are released into the sky.

Lalon Utsab (*17 October and March, celebrated in Kushtia*) Lalon Shah is the patron saint of Bangladesh's singing bards, the Baul people. Every year they hold two rambunctious music festivals in Kushtia. One celebrates his 17 October death anniversary and the other, larger bash commemorates his birth (held in March but the festival date changes). In terms of Bangladeshi cultural festivals, Lalon Utsab is definitely one of the best for its music, partying and reverie. Logistics for attending the festival can be difficult as thousands of people crowd Kushtia at this time. It is highly suggested that you ask a tour operator to make bookings and provide a guide for you, as crowd control can be an issue at the festival grounds and some women have reported harassment there, a situation that can be avoided by using a guide and having arrangements taken care of for you. As most of the people and music come out at night, female travellers will definitely feel more comfortable with male accompaniment. See *Chapter* 7, *Kushtia*, *Lalon Utsab*, page 283, for more information.

Ras Mela (*November*) Ras Mela actually comprises two festivals held at different ends of the country.

The first and probably larger of the two is held at Dubla Char, one of the southernmost islands of Sundarban. Thousands of Hindu devotees arrive here each year for a three-day festival that concludes with a ritual bath in the ocean at sunrise on the third day. The bath, said to absolve devotees of their sins, is taken here because this is also where the sacred waters of the Ganges meet the sea. This festival also marks the beginning of the fishing season for most of the temporary inhabitants of Dubla Char.

Ras Mela is also celebrated by the Manipuri people of the Sylhet Divison, particularly at Kartik-Agrahayan of Kamalganj in Maulvi Bazaar. The occasion is marked by traditional dance, song and celebration.

Wangala (*late November or early December*) Also known as 'Wanna' or the 'Hundred Drums Festival', this Garo celebration occurs at the onset of winter and the conclusion of the post-monsoon harvest. The Garo people are an ethnic minority who inhabit the hills of Meghalaya in India and the northern border areas of Mymensingh. To join this festival you can either travel up north to Madhupur, Durgapur or Askipara or head to the Tejgaon Church. The events are not well advertised so you'll have to ask around to find out when the exact date is.

Martyred Intellectuals' Day (*14 December*) In 1971, as defeat began to look inevitable for the Pakistani forces in Bangladesh they delivered a final debilitating blow upon their enemies before departing. About 250 journalists, doctors and academics were rounded up, beaten and then murdered just days before the war finally ended. Today, a decaying memorial to their sacrifice lies on a mass grave located at the western outskirts of Rayer Bazaar, a Dhaka neighbourhood west of Dhanmondi and reachable by rickshaw. Each year on 14 December, top government ministers visit the site to pay their respects to those who died in cold blood.

SHOPPING

RESPONSIBLE SHOPPING Bangladesh has been on the destination list of most fair-trade organisations for several years. Undoubtedly, the potential for fair trade to promote positive change is enormous. Better yet, most of the income that does exist in this sector reaches women, who unfortunately bear the brunt of the poverty suffered here.

Dhaka is the best place to survey the availability of such goods, and if you only have time to visit one shop in the city, you should visit Aarong (see *Chapter 3, Shopping*, page 138), the long-time haunt of middle-class Bangladeshis. Bedspreads, textiles, jewellery and several other well-made handicrafts and housewares are all available here, and all branches of the shop are packed to the gills on weekends and especially before holidays. Aarong is the retail arm of the Bangladesh Rural Advancement Committee, which also happens to be the world's largest NGO. Those armed with a little more time and a desire to spend their money even more meaningfully should also visit Folk International in Gulshan or check the listings in the Dhaka chapter for more responsible shopping suggestions.

For those interested in taking their shopping interest a little deeper inside Bangladesh, visit the **ECOTA Fair Trade Forum** (*6/4A Sir Syed Ahmed Rd, Mohammadpur, Dhaka; ☎ 02 812 6593; e info@ecotaftf.org; www.ecotatf.org*) and the **National Crafts Council of Bangladesh** (NCCB) (*2/8 Sir Syed Ahmed Rd, Mohammadpur, Dhaka; ☎ 02 914 0812*). The members of these organisations maintain production facilities throughout the country; the NCCB has previously arranged handicraft tours custom-tailored to visitor requests. So if you're interested in a handicraft tour with a focus on pottery, hand-blown glass, *nakshi kantha* (traditional weaving) or *jamdani saris* (made from a very special lightweight cloth, also known as muslin), these organisations would likely be very happy to guide you at low cost.

It's also interesting to visit NGO production areas out in the field, as many of these organisations do encourage their beneficiaries to begin small businesses of their own.

Below is a very small list of organisations associated with fair-trade businesses that come recommended; there are literally hundreds more out there. Feel free to contact them for more information:

Aranya 60 Kamal Ataturk Av, Banani; ☎ 988 2542; e aranya@citechco.net; www.aranyacrafts.com. A great shop for the environmentally conscious. Fabrics used in clothing, saris & scarves are handwoven & coloured with natural dyes. Fabric by the yard is also available.

Folk International Hse 19, Rd 108, Gulshan 2, Dhaka; ☎ 02 988 0784; e folkbd.leo2@gmail.com. Gulshan's best responsible shopping outlet. Has handicrafts sourced from around the country on display, plus a wide selection of books & textiles.

Hathay Bunano Hse 4, Rd 23A, Blk B, Banani, Dhaka; ☎ 02 988 6083; m 01732 701507; www.hathaybunano.com. Wholesale exporter of knitwear with a shop in the UK.

Tarango 282/5, 1st Colony, Mazar Rd, Mirpur 1, Dhaka; ☎ 02 801 4341, 802 0639; e wedptar@bdmail.net; www.tarango-bd.org. Offers some very well-designed jute products for wholesale export, with a particular focus on enabling women producers to start & run their own co-operative businesses.

UBINIG 5/3 Barabo Mahanpur, Ring Rd, Shyamoli, Dhaka; ☎ 02 811 1465; m 01715 021898. Has networks of fair-trade producers around Bangladesh; also features organically grown food at guesthouses near Tangail & Kushtia, plus an organic farming project in Ishwardi.

Viator Bangladesh Hse 60, Rd 7/A, Blk H, Banani; ☎ 02 987 2827; m 01717 925272; e viator@onenetbd.com; www.viatorbangladesh.org; One of the first organisations to focus on building fair trade within the Chittagong Hill Tracts. Has a shopping outlet in Bandarban & a guesthouse in Dhaka, with funding provided from a Norwegian partner organisation.

REGULAR SHOPPING Plenty of opportunities await potential shoppers, and naturally some of the best opportunities are in Dhaka. As Bangladesh doesn't have much of a tourist industry to speak of, there aren't many good shopping opportunities outside the capital, not yet at least. (See *Chapter 3*, *Shopping*, page 136 for more information.)

In terms of deals, clothing is probably the best as Bangladesh has managed to become a major garment production centre, especially of Western clothing. Many overruns are available in Dhaka's Banga Bazaar at prices that are a real steal.

Souvenir-wise, the industry is also not that strong, but you will find some wonderfully crafted goods, not only at Aarong. There are several unique stores in Banani and Gulshan, with Jatra earning a special mention for its unique offerings.

Rickshaws and their art tend to be a favourite among travellers and expatriate residents. You can even have an artist do a custom creation for you from photographs or purchase a rickshaw plate that features any one of a number of Bangladeshi themes. You could have yourself painted into a Dhallywood action film or depict yourself being chased by a tiger in Sundarban.

There are some things that shoppers should definitely avoid – one of these is the trade in archaeological goods such as terracotta or basalt statues. Unfortunately, many of Bangladesh's historical sites have been plundered of their finest artwork and sculptures, and travellers should not encourage this market without asking questions about where the goods come from first.

ARTS AND ENTERTAINMENT

Culture vultures on long-term visits to the country will find a vibrant artistic and entertainment scene in Dhaka. The website www.somewhereindhaka.net provides excellent up-to-date listings on some events in the city, including stage, film and food events. However, the great majority of other events are so poorly advertised that it often takes a detective mindset to figure out when and where to go. The best way is to ask around and figure out who's knowledgeable first. Then, once you discover who actually knows what they're talking about, you can follow their suggestions for what to do. Many of Dhaka's artistic organisations and galleries maintain in-house email lists broadcasting their events, but you must first get your email address on their list in order to get advance notice.

Getting up to speed on events in the expatriate scene is a similarly manual process: you visit the clubs and read the bulletin boards yourself for the latest information. These bulletin boards also feature classified ads, job postings for local help and flat availability.

ART Keeping in touch with Bangladesh's art scene is made easier when you know who to contact. The most active player is the Society for the Promotion of Bangladeshi Art (*www.bangladeshart.info*). The website leaves a lot to be desired but at least provides contact information from which you can find out more. The organisation hasn't been around for a long time, but long enough to have published a book that offers fairly definitive coverage of modern Bangladeshi art. It's also held a number of exhibitions over the years, some internationally.

MUSIC In terms of a local music scene, there's a fascinating fixation on rock music that has taken hold among Bangladesh's younger urbanites. To that end they like to attend loud concerts and play songs that were popular among punk rockers c1990. Covers of Pearl Jam's 'Jeremy' are tossed in for good measure. Bangladesh also has a homegrown version of Jimi Hendrix, a rock guitarist who goes by the name of Bacchu. His fingers literally dance on electric guitars at rock concerts, enthralling thousands of young onlookers with its almost unintelligible sound. Watching the local newspaper and asking among the younger generation will get you information on such events. Once again, the www.somewhereindhaka.net website also has the best listings for this sort of information.

A more traditional music experience is to seek an invitation to a private Baul music performance. The lyrics and melodies of these wandering bards espouse a minimalist philosophy that agrees with the mindset of most Bangladeshis. Furthermore, many Baul songs describe a humanist and secular way of life, reflecting the reputation of the patron saint of the movement, Lalon Shah, who also seems to appeal to many different segments of society in the country, regardless of religion, social status or even age.

Once again, the best way to obtain experiences attending one of these cultural events is to ask around and find out who's knowledgeable (ie: get yourself invited to something), and then award such an individual the honour of hosting you (a fact that becomes evident when they introduce you to everyone they know or even call their friends so that they can hear your foreigner voice).

THEATRE Bangladeshi theatre, like many other aspects of cultural life, is best experienced in the countryside. Among the villages and towns of the country, folk theatre and music – known as *jatra* – are often combined to transmit cultural ideas and practices. This aspect of Bangladeshi culture is used in the work of Rupantar (*www.rupantar.org*), an NGO based in Khulna. The programmes use folk theatre to spread awareness about the rights to democracy and gender balance amongst Bangladesh's poorest people.

In Dhaka, the most active theatre group is the Centre for Asian Theatre (*www.catbd.org*), which regularly holds performances at the Guide House and the Nilima Ibrahim Auditorium in the Mahila Samity (Women's Centre), both on Bailey Road. Other major venues for theatre include the Mahanagar Natyamanch Theatre, located near Ramna Park, and the Shilpalaka Art Academy in Segunbagicha. Contact the CAT for more information.

MEDIA AND COMMUNICATIONS

MEDIA Bangladeshis absolutely love to talk, something referred to as *adda*, or gossip. So, despite some historical causes for concern (eg: successive military governments), the country normally enjoys a vibrant and vocal media, much in line with the debating nature of its people. Several new television and radio stations have opened in the last few years, although their editorial tilts do tend to reflect the political realities of the day. There are two national English newspapers although the readership, and hence editorial coverage, focuses mostly on Dhaka and sometimes Chittagong. Community radio stations were also recently approved in principle by government regulators, but only time will tell whether or not these are successful in promoting grassroots awareness where it is arguably most required. One online newspaper (*www.bdnews24.com*) gives up-to-the-minute news coverage so if you need to know what's going on (political strikes, fog delays, etc), then check there.

At a more personal level, you will quickly notice that even the most basic hotel rooms feature televisions as a selling point, and more often than not these sets are hooked up to hijacked satellite signals. The BBC, Al Jazeera and CNN are available as well as a couple of English movie channels alongside the many Bangladeshi ones, many of which seem to broadcast a never-ending stream of Bangladeshi soap operas.

TELECOMMUNICATIONS Mobile-phone technology has witnessed an explosion in popularity as there are now well over 30 million subscribers in Bangladesh, with six mobile-phone operators competing for business here. The existing infrastructure and policies for landlines are poor (ie: government-operated), and so it is much easier to use a mobile phone for personal communication than a landline, not to mention being much simpler to obtain. To apply for a sim card you must bring two passport-size photographs and a photocopy of your passport, with the cost for a simple sim card and included talk time under Tk500.

The mobile companies are divided according to their telephone prefixes. At the top of the heap is Grameenphone whose numbers have the 017 prefix. Banglalink has the second largest subscriber base and its numbers begin with 018.

Local phone calls are extremely cheap – one benefit of living in a small country with huge numbers of potential customers. Most calls are under Tk2 per minute, but these can be even cheaper if you set up certain numbers as 'friends and family' contacts. Each mobile plan usually includes three of these numbers, and the cost is less than Tk0.25 per minute. International calls are more reasonable under the government's Economy International Subscribers Dialling plan, used by dialling

PHOTOGRAPHIC TIPS

Ariadne Van Zandbergen

EQUIPMENT Although with some thought and an eye for composition you can take reasonable photos with a 'point and shoot' camera, you need an SLR camera with one or more lenses if you are at all serious about photography. The most important component in a digital SLR is the sensor. There are two types of sensor: DX and FX. The FX is a full-size sensor identical to the old film size (35mm). The DX sensor is half size and produces less quality. Your choice of lenses will be determined by whether you have a DX or FX sensor in your camera as the DX sensor introduces a 0.5x multiplication to the focal length. So a 300mm lens becomes in effect a 450mm lens. FX ('full frame') sensors are the future, so I will further refer to focal lengths appropriate to the FX sensor.

Always buy the best lens you can afford. Fixed fast lenses are ideal, but very costly. Zoom lenses are easier to change composition without changing lenses the whole time. If you carry only one lens, a 24–70mm or similar zoom should be ideal. For a second lens, a lightweight 80–200mm or 70–300mm or similar will be excellent for candid shots and varying your composition. Wildlife photography will be very frustrating if you don't have at least a 300mm lens. For a small loss of quality, teleconverters are a cheap and compact way to increase magnification: a 300 lens with a 1.4x converter becomes 420mm, and with a 2x it becomes 600mm. NB: 1.4x and 2x teleconverters reduce the speed of your lens by 1.4 and 2 stops respectively.

The resolution of digital cameras is improving the whole time. For ordinary prints a 6-megapixel camera is fine. For better results and the possibility to enlarge images and for professional reproduction, higher resolution is available up to 21 megapixels.

It is important to have enough memory space when photographing on your holiday. The number of pictures you can fit on a card depends on the quality you choose. You should calculate how many pictures you can fit on a card and either take enough cards or take a storage drive onto which you can download the cards' content. You can obviously take a laptop which gives the advantage that you can see your pictures properly at the end of each day and edit and delete rejects. If you don't want the extra bulk and weight you can buy a storage device which can read memory cards. These drives come in different capacities.

Keep in mind that digital camera batteries, computers and other storage devices need charging. Make sure you have all the chargers, cables and converters with you. Most hotels/lodges have charging points, but it will be best to enquire about this in advance. When camping you might have to rely on charging from the car battery.

012 from any mobile phone. For countries with established mobile and landline networks (which includes Canada, the UK, the US, China, Hong Kong, Australia and many western European and southeast Asian countries), the cost works out to less than Tk8 per minute, sometimes even Tk6. Unfortunately this service is not offered to many other countries, such as Bangladesh's neighbours in south Asia. With the proliferation of different local phone systems around Bangladesh, don't be surprised to find that some landline numbers have five digits and others have six, while mobile numbers are 11 digits long. When calling any phone number (mobile or landline), always try twice as it doesn't always connect on the first attempt.

INTERNET Internet services are generally easy to find, especially in Dhaka. If connectivity is a concern of yours, call ahead and enquire with the hotel if it will be available in your room or not, although most upper mid-range guesthouses are now featuring broadband access direct from guests' rooms. Most main towns now feature an internet café somewhere near the main shopping districts, but these may not keep regular hours or have very high speeds. It's best to anticipate being offline most of the time while in rural Bangladesh.

DUST AND HEAT Dust and heat are often a problem. Keep your equipment in a sealed bag, and avoid exposing equipment to the sun when possible. Digital cameras are prone to collecting dust particles on the sensor which results in spots on the image. The dirt mostly enters the camera when changing lenses, so you should be careful when doing this. To some extent photos can be 'cleaned up' afterwards in Photoshop, but this is time-consuming. You can have your camera sensor professionally cleaned, or you can do this yourself with special brushes and swabs made for this purpose, but note that touching the sensor might cause damage and should only be done with the greatest care.

LIGHT The most striking outdoor photographs are often taken during the hour or two of 'golden light', after dawn and before sunset. Shooting in low light may enforce the use of very low shutter speeds, in which case a tripod/beanbag will be required to avoid camera shake. The most advanced digital SLRs have very little loss of quality on higher ISO settings, which allows you to shoot at lower light conditions. It is still recommended not to increase the ISO unless necessary.

With careful handling, sidelighting and backlighting can produce stunning effects, especially in soft light and at sunrise or sunset. Generally, however, it is best to shoot with the sun behind you. When photographing animals or people in the harsh midday sun, images taken in light but even shade are likely to look nicer than those taken in direct sunlight or patchy shade, since the latter conditions create too much contrast.

PROTOCOL In some countries, it is unacceptable to photograph local people without permission, and many people will refuse to pose or will ask for a donation. In such circumstances, don't try to sneak photographs as you might get yourself into trouble. Even the most willing subject will often pose stiffly when a camera is pointed at them; relax them by making a joke, and take a few shots in quick succession to improve the odds of capturing a natural pose.

Ariadne Van Zandbergen is a professional travel and wildlife photographer specialising in Africa. She runs 'The Africa Image Library'. For photo requests, visit the website www.africaimagelibrary.co.za or contact her direct at ariadne@hixnet.co.za

Technology-savvy travellers, on the other hand, will also quickly discover that Bangladesh offers excellent internet connectivity over the mobile network. Grameenphone has a flat-rate broadband plan that can be used in conjunction with a data-enabled mobile phone. The quality of connection can be variable depending on the time of day and location, but it is often enough to support internet telephone applications such as Skype and do basic web browsing. With a higher-end handset, it is possible to use such a connection to enjoy free phone calls with Skype. For city use it makes more sense to get a home broadband plan instead of relying totally on a mobile internet connection, but working travellers will discover that their office can easily move with them anywhere in Bangladesh – great when you're an active travel writer or journalist based in the country.

POSTAL SERVICE In terms of posting items abroad, Bangladesh's postal service is hit and miss. Outgoing mail seems more likely to make it than incoming mail, or the incoming mail sometimes takes months to show up. New credit cards sent by regular post have disappeared entirely, with unsuccessful fraudulent charges showing up at jewellers around the city. If something is very important to you, it is recommended that you use a courier service like UPS, DHL or FedEx to ensure safe delivery. For listings, see page 141.

BUSINESS

Patience is your best tool in setting up a business in Bangladesh, as the young country has still to set up standardised procedures for many business transactions, or it operates according to laws that have scarcely changed since the time of partition. Furthermore, reliable business information and advice is hard to come by. Government institutions, especially those meant to defend against corruption, tend to be weak and ineffective, and the country's infrastructure is already stressed under the demands of a burgeoning population. Uncontrollable delays are a frequent occurrence, but if you remember to stay patient the reward of success in Bangladesh is made all the more sweet.

All the negatives and cautions aside, things have changed a lot since 1971. Bangladesh's successes, especially in the ready-made garment sector, demonstrate that doing business here is possible. The country's best resource is undoubtedly its people, of whom this sector has already taken full advantage on its path to becoming an US$11 billion per year industry. More importantly, employment in the garment factories has focused on women, evident when the streams of colourful *salwar kameez*-clad workers change shift at the factories in and around Dhaka. Money from foreign remittances, mostly from Middle Eastern countries, is also significant, although both sectors did see trouble during the late 2007/early 2008 financial crisis.

Since the 1980s, Bangladesh's government has enacted policies meant to increase foreign investment in the country. But for all the friendliness and enthusiasm you may find from them in the initial meetings, do be aware that once you're in the door, that behaviour might soon switch to their next favourite activity: asking for money. As corruption has long plagued the government it is recommended that you do not participate by doing so yourself.

ETIQUETTE Business etiquette in Bangladesh requires some cultural awareness, especially of how Bangladeshi people communicate. Before the meeting, be aware that men and women interact differently. A firm handshake opens the meeting between men, but unless a woman offers her hand for a handshake, you should not offer yours. Business cards are usually exchanged after some small talk, and do be

FORMING A COMPANY IN BANGLADESH

Kristin Boekhoff, owner of Panigram Resort (www.panigram.com)

Like the road system of Bangladesh, the path to company formation is fraught with pot-holes, U-turns and unpaved roads, but for the intrepid entrepreneur starting a business here can be very rewarding. Foreigners are allowed to 100% own land and companies and they can repatriate 100% of their profits – a rare financial find in the developing world.

The tips below will help you navigate through this unmapped territory.

GET A GOOD ATTORNEY There are many professional, English-speaking attorneys; your local embassy should be able to provide you with a list. Meet with several attorneys to see which ones you have chemistry with, make sure that the firm has expertise in company formation, and get several quotes before selecting a barrister (prices can vary significantly!). I recommend Jamiruddin and Associates in Dhanmondi (*www.jamiruddin.com*).

SPEAK WITH THE BOARD OF INVESTMENT (BOI) All foreign companies need to register with the Board of Investment, so it is a good idea to get to know them early in the process. Their website (*www.boi.gov.bd*) has some good information.

SET UP A BANK ACCOUNT This sounds like an easy step, but it is actually quite difficult. You can't get a bank account until your company is registered and you can't get registered until you bring money in which requires you to have a bank account. The trick to escaping this roundabout is an encashment certificate. There are two ways to get this certificate: 1) exchange foreign currency (at least US$250 worth per company) at the airport, or 2) take taka from a cash machine, change it into dollars at a local money changer and then go to a large, reputable bank (like HSBC) and change the dollars back into taka. In both scenarios you need to ask for an encashment certificate.

FORM YOUR COMPANY You need the encashment certificate to form your company; your attorneys will complete this part for you. After your company is registered with the Registrar of Joint Stock Companies you can go to the bank and have them open a non-operating bank account. You will be able to deposit money into this account, but will not be able to take it out again until you register your company with the BOI and obtain the appropriate permits and visas.

REGISTER YOUR COMPANY WITH THE BOI You need to have land before you can complete this step. A lease or a *baina* (purchase option agreement) will suffice if you do not own land.

APPLY FOR YOUR WORK PERMIT, INVESTOR VISA AND TAX ID The BOI and your attorney will be able to help you. After you have these you can complete the opening of your bank account and will be able to withdraw your money.

This process is complicated and there are many twists and turns along the road. In order to give entrepreneurs a road map, I have created a series of detailed blog entries on company formation in Bangladesh. You can access them here: http://kboekhoff.blogspot.com/2008/12/forming-company-in-bangladesh-like-road.html.

aware that educational qualifications, especially prestigious ones, are fairly important to Bangladeshis.

First and foremost you will learn that Bangladeshi people tend to be indirect communicators. Instead of directly saying that something isn't possible, they will tend to say something like 'that may require some time', or 'we will try', instead of a flat-out 'no'. So if you're ever uncertain it is best to ask for clarification. Meeting timing can also be an issue, as things may or may not commence on time and their likelihood of running long is very high. It is more important to Bangladeshis to finish a meeting as opposed to controlling how long it takes, so expect your meetings to run longer than you plan for, and allow double the time to deal with the traffic before and after your meeting, especially in Dhaka.

Deference to the most senior member of staff or the people in charge is also quite important in Bangladeshi culture. Meetings are usually the place to disseminate decisions instead of making them. Rather, the most important decisions tend to be made in private consultation with higher authorities, especially when dealing with money. So, it is best to meet with the most senior person you can as they will tend to have the most decision-making power, but it usually doesn't take much time to establish who you need to speak with.

RESOURCES Bangladesh's Board of Investment (*www.boi.gov.bd*) is the government agency responsible for attracting investment to Bangladesh. Otherwise, the Economist Country Briefing (*www.economist.com*) is an excellent overall summary of the political and economic issues in the country. The Federation of Bangladesh Chambers of Commerce and Industry (*www.fbcci-bd.org*) and the Bangladesh Garment Manufacture Exporters Association (*www.bgmea.com.bd*) will also be good starting points for information.

CULTURAL ETIQUETTE

Western visitors will quickly find that while in Bangladesh, they are in fact the tourist attraction – for the local people, that is. For a country that still has so few foreign visitors and so many people, the sight of a traveller can quickly attract crowds of onlookers. This wouldn't be such an issue were it not for the fact that the concept of privacy is very different in Bangladesh (ie: there is none), and so the presence of visitors also turns heads, including those that should be looking at the road! Don't be surprised if you cause an accident, and do realise that it's not your fault. If you stay still for too long you will no doubt have a crowd on your hands, as it only takes two curious onlookers to generate a dozen more. Many visitors, especially female travellers, do complain that all the staring and attention can be very intimidating and unrelenting. But do realise that it's a form of flattery and the fact that in some of Bangladesh's backwater villages you may be the most interesting thing that's happened in the last several weeks. Welcome your new status as a foreign celebrity.

As to how to handle the crowd, it won't be long before one of the better English speakers steps forward and begins blurting out a volley of questions, and so you can try engaging with just one person instead of dozens. You can ask this person to take you somewhere where the crowds won't follow or even to shoo them away if you're trying to do something else like take photographs. Crowd control can also be handled by fellow travelling companions, which has the added benefit of allowing one person to distract the throngs and take the attention while the other person can snap photos surreptitiously. When it's particularly hot or especially crowded these onlookers can be especially infuriating, but it's best to take it all in your stride.

If you're a normally private person, leave that side of you at home. The unbridled curiosity and friendliness of Bangladeshi people shows up when dealing with the endless barrage of the same set of questions. At first this intense interrogation is both interesting and vigorous, but towards the end of a day it can be awfully tiring. It's OK to ignore people you do not wish to engage with, as rude as that may seem at first. If you have a mobile phone, do be reserved about giving out your number, unless you feel like having dozens of telephone friends who will eventually send your phone ringing off the hook. With over 30 million mobile subscribers, there are also inevitable random phone calls and wrong numbers. If there is a particularly persistent caller that you want to stop calling, a good trick is to answer the phone but not put your ear to it, thus using up the caller's taka while they talk to nobody. This usually stops incessant callers fairly quickly.

Hierarchy is an important aspect in Bangladesh society, and during a stay here you may encounter some awkward situations in which someone of higher status or authority treats someone with lower status like dirt. Conversely, status and prestige are considered highly important in most social interactions in Bangladesh and this is usually indicated by the presence of expensive clothing, jewellery, a nice watch, an expensive motor vehicle or a beautiful wife. As a foreigner you will instantly be given higher status than most other people despite your appearance, but if you dress the part you will be accorded an even higher status, something particularly useful when dealing with government officials or potential business colleagues. In other words, if you want to impress, you've got to play the part, despite the fact your society of origin may not be so vertically inclined.

Local clothing is not only comfortable but also demonstrates some cultural awareness. For men, new *panjabis* are almost always worn on holidays or religious events. The thigh-length shirt is typically white, although stylish or wealthy men usually diversify their colour choices. A shorter version of the shirt, called a *fatua*, is more popular among the younger generation of Bangladesh. For descriptions of women's clothing, see below.

GENDER On the whole, female travellers often have a tougher time in Bangladesh because of the conservative values of Islam. Often, it is less easy (but not impossible of course) for women to travel independently in the country, with the main annoyance being an overwhelming amount of personal attention and some isolated incidents of sexual harassment in the form of eve teasing (ie: whistling, calling names or making catcalls in the street) or groping in crowded places. There have also been accusations of rape made by foreign women against locals.

The female traveller's best tool is cultural knowledge and observation of how other women carry themselves in the presence of men. Long-term experience in the country will also show how empowered local women handle patriarchal attitudes. Independent travel certainly requires a strong mindset, although female travellers with experience in India will find Bangladesh to be more genuinely friendly, perhaps even easier and certainly less overtly sexual. Solo female travellers might find themselves temporarily 'adopted' by a group of other Bangladeshi travellers, especially if visiting the country's more touristed destinations. This can provide the cultural and physical space necessary to get to know members of a group. Sad as it may be, the presence of a male travelling companion does make travel much easier for women and can provide some mental and physical headspace.

Dressing conservatively is the simplest way to decrease (but never completely avoid) the amount of attention received. Local women often wear a *salwar kameez*, a long, loose-fitting shirt matched with a pair of baggy pants, all of which is meant to disguise the curvy parts of a woman's body. *Sarees* are also commonly worn in Bangladesh, a three-piece outfit that is draped over a woman's shoulder and wrapped around her torso, worn at special occasions such as weddings or perhaps business meetings. In Dhaka, and especially in the diplomatic enclave, attitudes tend to be much more liberal and so it is more common to see young women wearing jeans or T-shirts. But in the deep countryside of Bangladesh you may come across women wearing the full black *hijab* with not an inch of skin visible, not even the feet.

DOS AND DON'TS When it comes to interactions between people, there are a few no-nos that you will be forgiven for but if you come prepared you will be treated with even greater respect.

Men and women are not totally forbidden from interacting in public, but public displays of affection are generally frowned upon, whereas these same frequent displays between men make Bangladesh seem like a homosexual's paradise (that is exaggeration for effect, in case you're wondering). Men should not shake a woman's hand unless offered. Also, as the left hand is traditionally associated with ablutions it thus follows that most activities regarding cleanliness use the right hand, such as shaking hands, or handing someone a business card or money. Left-handers be damned.

Gesturing for someone to come closer is usually done with the arm up and the palm down, instead of gesturing with the finger and the palm up (which could be taken wrongly). The 'thumbs up' gesture is also considered rude in Bangladesh, but the 'A OK' sign is still positive.

Begging is something every visitor comes across in Bangladesh to various degrees; being aware that this is a behaviour supported by Islamic cultural practice goes a long way in understanding why there are so many beggars on Dhaka's streets, especially during the holy time of Ramadan, where many Bangladeshis open their hearts and wallets to the less fortunate in society. While the choice of whether or not to give is a personal one, do be aware that your money could better support organised social welfare organisations (see *Travelling positively*, below). Usually, a curt shake of the head and avoiding eye contact sends the message that you will not be giving, and although you might feel very rude doing so, try to remember that sustainable change comes from working at the systematic level (although that should never alleviate the pain of seeing someone in despair).

As described earlier, patience is a virtue that you will develop during a stay in Bangladesh, but when (and not if) you eventually lose your patience, a well-timed (or not so well-timed) display of emotion will usually help achieve a desired result or at least a real answer as to whether or not something is possible. People are quick to borrow from one another in Bangladesh, whether that be time, money or understanding, and on some days you may not feel like lending anybody these personal assets. Certainly, you may sometimes feel your kindness and patience are wasted on those who do not treat it the same way you do; most times this is an opportunity to learn more about Bangladeshi culture and you're best treating it as such.

TRAVELLING POSITIVELY

While traditional tourist thinking keeps people away from supposed disaster zones such as Bangladesh, there's another way of looking at such disheartening situations. Visits to the country are in fact a real opportunity to do something positive for communities in need, like building houses for cyclone or flood victims, or helping a slum education project to operate more efficiently and save costs. By contacting certain organisations before your arrival, it is often possible to set up low-cost volunteer placements that can make a holiday to Bangladesh both memorable and very positive for the local community. In Bangladesh, this form of travel is already fairly common and there are plenty of opportunities available to assertive volunteers.

STUFF YOUR RUCKSACK – AND MAKE A DIFFERENCE

www.stuffyourrucksack.com is a website set up by television's Kate Humble which enables travellers to give direct help to small charities, schools or other organisations in the country they are visiting. Maybe a local school needs books, a map or pencils, or an orphanage needs children's clothes or toys – all things that can easily be 'stuffed in a rucksack' before departure. The charities get exactly what they need and travellers have the chance to meet local people and see how and where their gifts will be used.

The website describes organisations that need your help and lists the items they most need. Check what's needed in Bangladesh, contact the organisation to say you're coming and bring not only the much-needed goods but an extra dimension to your travels and the knowledge that in a small way you have made a difference.

There are also a number of internships available in the country where, for a nominal fee, you can be exposed to the work undertaken.

A few caveats first: the country attracts a fair number of well-intentioned do-gooders wanting to save the world, but be aware that the experience of volunteering in developing countries such as Bangladesh often brings up more thorny questions than it solves. Much of the change these volunteers want to create manifests more in themselves than in their outside surroundings. In other words, if you come on a volunteer experience you must remember that local people are also here to teach you about yourself as much as they want to learn from you. It also helps to leave patronising attitudes at home – Bangladeshis have long endured negative perceptions of their country. For your sake and theirs, do remember that you are dealing with people who know what development is. The simple reality is that many Bangladeshis suffer for a lack of opportunity, whether that be fiscal, educational or employment. That probably also explains why when given the opportunity, most Bangladeshi people fervently seize it with both hands.

Pre-departure, the best thing you can do is your homework. Learn as much as you can and set your expectations properly about what you hope to achieve, and talk with former long-term visitors to the country if you can. Learn the local language as much as possible before your arrival, and do realise that the climate, food and cultural conditions of Bangladesh will take your health to task during a stay here. While this may seem very daunting, the intensity of the Bangladeshi experience will undoubtedly prove to be memorable and rewarding.

VOLUNTEER ORGANISATIONS

Bangladesh

Bangladesh Rural Improvement Foundation www.brif.org. Has worked with international volunteer-sending organisations in the past, but now accepts applications to volunteer.

Centre for the Rehabilitation of the Paralysed www.crp-bangladesh.com. Needs volunteer physiotherapists or occupational health therapists, but also accepts skilled volunteers for other tasks.

Habitat for Humanity Bangladesh e info@habitatbangladesh.org; www.habitatbangladesh.org. Supports groups of volunteers to do relief work but also regular construction programmes.

JAAGO Foundation www.jaago.com.bd. Accepts short-term volunteers for an education project based near Dhanmondi.

LAMB Project e stwc@lambproject.org; www.lambproject.org. A Christian hospital facility located at Parbatipur, 24km east of Dinajpur. Accepts short-term volunteers for various health-related needs.

The Dhaka Project www.thedhakaproject.org. Accepts volunteers for their project in which slum children are given free education, healthcare & food.

International

Australian Youth Ambassadors for Development (AYAD) www.ayad.com.au. Paid placements for recently graduated Australian youth. Has a significant presence in Bangladesh; opportunities here are based on the local skills required.

Hands on Disaster Response e info@hodr.org; www.hodr.org. Supported a volunteer team in reconstruction after Cyclone Sidr, but works in other disaster regions of the world. Volunteers are provided with meals & accommodation & only need to pay for travel expenses to get to the project site.

Idealist.org www.idealist.org. A repository of volunteer opportunities. Do your homework on organisations before accepting a post.

Volunteers for International Development Australia (VIDA) www.vidavolunteers.com.au. A similar programme to the AYAD programme, but for a longer placement period & focusing specifically on poverty-reduction activities.

Volunteers for Peace www.volunteerforpeace.org. US-based outfit with a database of international volunteering opportunities, including Bangladesh.

Voluntary Service Overseas Canada www.vsocan.org. Volunteer-sending organisation for professional, skilled workers. Typical placement is 2 years but short-term placements are increasingly common.

Voluntary Service Overseas UK www.vso.org.uk. Head office location of VSO, which also sends UK nationals to Bangladesh for volunteering.

INTERNSHIPS

Bangaldesh Rural Advancement Committee (BRAC) e internship@brac.net; www.brac.net/get_involved.htm. Also hosts research & student internships for those interested in familiarising themselves with the activities of one of the largest NGO in the world.

THE INTERNSHIP EXPERIENCE WITH THE RDRS

From previous experience, the RDRS has found that interns who are motivated and committed, adaptable and able to work on their own prove the best interns and both parties gain most from the experience. Although the RDRS provides reasonable living conditions in its guesthouses (there are five main guesthouses, in Dhaka and the field), living in northern Bangladesh can prove very challenging and demanding – there is little freedom of movement, and foreigners (especially women) attract attention wherever they go, which can be difficult for those not used to it. There is little or no evening social life. Visitors are expected to fit into prevailing cultural practices and norms so as not to cause offence. Visitors may also find the same Bengali food monotonous and unappetising for weeks on end. The summer months are also very hot and humid (averaging 34–36°C and with 95% humidity) which can be energy-sapping. Communications are also problematic. It is possible to telephone Europe or North America (though charges are high); email/internet communication exists. Owing to political circumstances there may be frequent strikes often extending for several days when all transport stops and interns should remain indoors. In the summer months, including the monsoon, flooding does occur which is unlikely to affect the interns directly but may limit their movement. Finally, the RDRS is a busy working NGO – there may be no staff member with much time to assist or supervise an intern, so the intern may have to fit into the travel arrangements of others to visit the field. Occasionally other interns can become disillusioned and this can unsettle even those who are relatively satisfied.

For those who can adjust to these conditions, an internship can be a rewarding experience and the RDRS has been privileged to have had a long list of interns who have adapted, and benefited personally from the experience as well as contributing to the work of the organisation and articulating its work abroad. The RDRS also has experience of a few who were not satisfied, or found the circumstances oppressive.

Normally, interns are expected to have some maturity – so anyone below age 23 would need to be highly motivated. Some previous exposure to developing countries will also help overcome the initial 'shock'.

Canadian International Development Agency www.cida.gc.ca. Offers some limited internships to Bangladesh through Canadian education institutions, particularly Humber College in Toronto (*www.humber.ca*).

Fulbright Program www.fulbright.state.gov. US State Department programme that sends American scholars to Bangladesh for courses of study or research projects.

Grameen Bank e g_iprog@grameen.com; www.grameen-info.org. Offers exposure internships at reasonable costs to students & researchers (for further details see box, page 17).

Rangpur Dinajpur Rural Service (RDRS) e rdrs@bangla.net; www.rdrsbangla.net. Northwest Bangladesh's best & largest NGO. Supports an internship programme from the North Bengal Institute in Rangpur (for further details see box opposite).

Transparency International Bangladesh e info@ti-bangladesh.org; www.ti-bangladesh.org. The organisation responsible for publicising the incidents of corruption in graft-ridden political system of Bangladesh. Naturally, internships here would be very challenging.

LIVING IN BANGLADESH

Nabil Ahmed, Kristin Boekhoff, Tuni Chatterji, Erin Lentz and Steve Micetic

Setting up as an expatriate in Bangladesh can be a laborious process, taking a lot of time and money. Try to allow several days over the first month for this process. Below are a few hints and tips for those relocating to the country.

FIRST STEPS Probably the first order of business when you arrive is to get a good map, several passport photos (necessary for mobile-phone contracts, etc), and a mobile phone.

Maps Maps are available on the street, but the best and most useful map for relocating expatriates is the Diggin Dhaka Map produced by Laura Bonapace. This is available from Amazon.co.uk before your arrival, or you can purchase it at the shops listed in maps section of the Dhaka chapter (see page 118).

Phones There are a lot of phone networks. Grameen tends to have the best coverage across Bangladesh, which is helpful if you will be in rural areas; folks based primarily in a city, may find it cheaper to use other networks such as Warid or Banglalink. Phones can cost Tk1,500–15,000 depending on quality. An international phone may work, but needs to be 'unlocked' before leaving home.

Phones can be purchased from major phone bazaars. You can try Rifles Square (*Rd 2, Dhamondi*); Genetic Plaza (*Rd 16 (new), Dhanmondi*); the northwest quadrant of Gulshan 2 circle (*Landmark Plaza and Taher Tower have several stores*); first floor of the SW quadrant to Gulshan 1 circle; Bashundara City. Alternatively phones are available from major phone centres (such as Grameen), but are more expensive.

To set up your phone you will need to bring three passport photos, your passport and a phone to a phone centre. There are Grameen Phone Centres on Gulshan Avenue on the east side of the street midway between Gulshan 1 and Gulshan 2 and on Road 16 (new) in Dhanmondi (you can check their office locations at www.grameenphone.com).

Phone rates (pre-paid) are currently Tk2 per minute and Tk1.5 per SMS. All phone operators provide the '012' service which provides discounted rates to most countries. Check with the mobile operator at the signup to find out what the rates are. A typical rate to a landline in Canada, the UK, the USA or Australia is Tk6 per minute; mobile phone calls are about twice that.

Landlines are difficult and time consuming to get – stick with a mobile phone.

Warning Be selective about who you give your number to. It is common for expats to have locals constantly calling them. Women are particularly vulnerable to this form of harassment. Try not to write your real phone number on any non-critical lists (ie: at drycleaners, tailors, internet cafés, etc). If you don't want a person who has requested your number to call you, it's OK to say 'no'. If you are a woman facing repeated calls, one option is to ask a man who speaks Bangla get on the phone pretending to be your husband. If you don't know the number and aren't expecting a call, don't pick up.

It's also worth signing up for voicemail. It is free with Grameen Phone; you just have to call their customer service number (121 from any Grameen phone) and ask for the necessary codes to set it up. Then, you can screen numbers you don't know.

Generally Bangladeshis don't use voicemail, so sometimes your Bangladeshi friends may still call five times and leave five messages. Also, there are charges every time you access your voicemail. Alternatively, use the SMS system to send messages – it is much cheaper and a common form of communication among expats and Bangladeshis.

SETTING UP HOME

Housing There are two options for finding a new apartment. The best is to wander the streets in the area you are interested in; available apartments will be advertised with a 'To Let' sign. Alternatively there are some real-estate agents in Gulshan/Banani area, although it is probably faster to find the apartment by yourself.

A few key questions that building managers can generally answer before viewing an apartment include:

- How many bedrooms?
- What is the price?
- What is the maintenance fee?
- Is there a security guard always on duty?
- Is there a generator and if so what does the generator run? Very few apartments will offer full generator support. Lights and fans are essential.

If you are happy with the specs you can ask to view the apartment. Alternatively, you can ring the landlord to negotiate the next phase. Some useful tips when viewing an apartment:

- Check the water pressure.
- Check cupboards for bugs and make sure that if there are locking closets, that the locks work or that a caretaker will come and fix them.
- Check the main door locks and see if there is a peephole.
- Location and noise level – if it is on a main road or near a school, it could be very noisy but if it is too remote, it could be hard to find transport from there and/or not be safe late at night (quiet streets off of main roads are ideal).
- Check whether there are any building sites near by. Building construction can take a long time and the constant tapping of hammers can be very disturbing.
- Be sure to negotiate the price; you can get a 5–20% reduction just by asking.
- Ask for a lease.
- See if there is a 24-hour security guard. If there isn't, you may have a curfew.
- Check to make sure that you can get out of your apartment in an emergency (ie: the front gate is not padlocked at night).
- Ask if the apartment has hot water (many places in Gulshan and Dhanmondi will have at least one bedroom with hot water).

Apartment leases tend to start at the beginning of the month, so if you are searching for housing mid-month, there will be fewer choices, but also fewer seekers. Try to bargain to reduce rental costs. When searching for housing, it is critical to consider where you will be spending the bulk of your workday. The traffic can be terrible. An hour commute in Dhaka is a lot more draining (pollution/noise/bad driving) than in other environments.

Housing in Bangladesh tends to be bare-bones. You will most likely need to purchase and install stove, light bulbs, refrigerators, ceiling fans, water heaters (if you want hot showers or hot water for dishes), air conditioners. If you have a caretaker in your building, for a fee he may be willing to buy and install light bulbs/fans/water heater, etc.

Some apartments are more expensive, but come with air conditioners and other appliances. It may make more sense to amortise the cost of these appliances over the course of nine months at a more expensive apartment rather than buying them.

There are cheaper options for apartments in Gulshan 2 and the diplomatic enclave. Walk through some of the residential areas and look for 'To Let' signs. Consider renting an apartment with roommates. This can greatly reduce the monthly cost of housing. Shared apartments can be located through adverts at local expat clubs or by word of mouth.

Sample prices

- Dhanmondi: three bedroom, 1,600 square feet costs Tk20,000 and Tk3,000 maintenance fee, water included.
- Niketan, Gulshan 1: two bedroom, Tk12,000 and Tk3,000 maintenance fee.
- Indira Road, Farmgate: three bedroom, 1,400 square feet costs Tk15,000 (plus water, gas, electricity).
- Gulshan 2: three bedroom, 1,850 square feet; four air conditioners, three water heaters, six ceiling fans and all light fixtures included costs Tk45,000 per month (asking rent was Tk50,000 per month) plus Tk3,000, Tk800 for water, gas included.

Utilities

Internet A wide variety of options are available, mostly localised by neighborhood.

- Shared 100kbps line in Dhanmondi costs Tk3,000
- Shared 70kbps line in Farmgate costs Tk1,500
- Shared 32kbps line in Gulshan 2 costs Tk1,300

Grameen phone offers internet service via EDGE modem (in mobile jargon this is known as 2.5G or 3G connectivity). It is about as fast as dial-up and draws down your pre-paid phone at Tk0.10/ KB, or you can purchase an unlimited broadband plan at Tk900 per month. The benefit is it provides internet in rural areas, where other connections are not available. If you have a PC, almost any phone with EDGE or GPRS connectivity should work. If you have a Mac, fewer phones are compatible.

Grameen CyberNet (*www.citechco.net*) is another that operates in Gulshan. Prices ranges from 32kpbs at Tk1,300 per month to 512kbps for Tk96,000 per month.

Gas Gas is billed by the burner in some neighbourhoods. In Dhanmondi, gas is Tk200 per burner (oven is not extra).

Electricity Here are some sample prices:

- Three-bedroom apartment with no air conditioner, about Tk500–800 per month
- With one bedroom's air conditioner running (just at night), expect to pay about another Tk1,000–1,500 per month

- Three bedroom with two–three air conditioners running part time in the summer is about Tk3,000–4,000 per month

Appliances Due to import duties, these tend to be extremely expensive. Also, in Bangladesh, it is very rare that any set price is actually set. Always be ready to bargain. You can find used items in large markets, such as the Gulshan 1 market. However, unless you know the person you are buying from these can be more of a hassle than a bargain.

If you do choose to purchase used appliances, it will be best to do so with a street-smart Bangladeshi friend and to demand a warranty. Get a one–two-year warranty with the terms of the warranty clearly written out because you will likely need to remind the shopkeeper that he did in fact promise to repair the item.

You can also check bulletin boards at the Nordic Club and Bagha Club for used appliances. If you can get them directly from an expat they may be more reliable.

Furniture There is a wide variety of furniture options. Panthapath Road, just west of the Sonargaon Hotel, has mostly new wrought-iron and cane furniture. There are some used furniture stores tucked away. Elephant Road shops also sell furniture as well as mattresses.

Karwan Bazar and New Market sell cheap 'deshi' furniture. If you ask for 'normal' or 'simple' furniture, you can get some serviceable, if not fashionable, furniture. The more you buy at a time, the better your bargaining power.

Bring measurements if possible, and remember that not staining the furniture (ie: leaving it in natural wood form) slightly increases the chance of termites, but dramatically decreases the price. Leave a deposit (less than half), but don't pay the full amount until it is delivered.

Deliveries tend to happen late at night (past 22.00), when *van-garis* can drive on main roads. In Gulshan they will also deliver during the day. You should be able to get different venders to co-ordinate to share one *van gari* for delivery. These should only cost about Tk200.

Near the Mohakali flyover are a number of cane furniture stores. Cane furniture tends to be cheaper than ready-made wood furniture. Bargain hard at Continental Cane for furniture sets.

Most of the expat clubs also have bulletin boards with postings of used things for sale. The Nordic Club, International Club and German Club have the best bulletin boards, but the American Club also has one as soon as you walk in the front door.

Custom-designed furniture is a great option if you're planning to stay permanently in Bangladesh. Furniture can be made to your specifications, including carvings for very low prices. Dola Furniture in the DCC Market in Gulshan 1 is recommended. The DCC Market is in the building on the southwest corner of Gulshan 1 Circle. You have to go inside the building, past the outer rim of stores. Once inside, ask for Dola Furniture. A photograph or drawing of what you want is useful and, as always, don't forget to bargain.

Water Water is delivered in 20-litre water-cooler containers. Each water delivery wallah works a particular area. Once you find housing, keep your eye pealed for delivery trucks or ask your neighbors (or local shops) who delivers their water. Finding a reputable water company is vital – ask around. Alpine Fresh, Purity, Prashanti Foods all deliver water and charge between Tk50–60 per bottle. Generally, you will have to purchase or rent a cooler from the water delivery store.

It is also possible to boil and filter your own water. Water filters can be purchased from many appliance stores and start around Tk1,500. Be sure that you (or your service staff) boil the water for 20 minutes. Then when it is cool put it into the water filter.

SERVICE STAFF

Hiring In Bangladesh, servants or *buas*, can be hired on a full-time or part-time (*chuta bua*) basis. A luxury of living in Bangladesh is being able to afford to have someone cook and/or clean for you. To find a *bua* you can ask people in your building or let security guard/caretaker/*daruwan* know you are looking (often under-employed *buas* periodically stop by apartment buildings to ask if anyone is looking for help). You can also find recommended *buas* and cooks at the expat clubs. Many folks who are leaving will often post the CVs of their former employees on the bulletin board. Most expat clubs (particularly the Nordic and the BAGHA club) have a 'help wanted' board that always has adverts for help (see *Membership clubs* on page 133 for listings).

Prices for *buas* can vary greatly depending on the neighbourhood and how often you want them to work, plus their associated skills (cooking, cleaning or minding children). In Gulshan 2, a *bua* who works six days a week from 08.00 to 12.00 costs Tk3,600 month. In Dhanmondi, prices could be up to a third cheaper. Many expatriates pay their service staff more depending on the other responsibilities given, anywhere between Tk5,000 and Tk10,000 depending on their tasks and abilities.

Most locally based expatriates also hire drivers, an understandable requirement given the hectic nature of Bangladeshi roads. Most drivers are hired and paid on a monthly basis and can also be recruited via the clubs. Some monthly car-rental services also include the driver as well, with the price ranging between Tk30,000 and Tk45,000 per month depending on the vehicle.

Management For many expatriates, living with service staff is a totally new experience; one in which the spectre of colonialism can be uncomfortably present. To steer clear of any problems, Westerners should be careful to treat staff with respect and to explain all assigned tasks in depth to avoid cultural misunderstandings. Ultimately, though, employing service staff can be a positive experience by allowing Bangladesh-based expatriates more time for creative pursuits while providing gainful employment for local people.

Employers should be aware that there will be requests for added money on top of the salary, as the employee will expect that their social well-being will also be provided for as well. Such requests should be considered on a case-by-case basis and it is OK to decline if the request seems unreasonable in some way. Many expatriates have also created a savings fund against the monthly salary of their employees, which could then be used to fulfil these added medical and/or educational requests.

Finally, a bonus is also expected at the conclusion of Ramadan each year. An extra one month's salary is typically applied; gifts of clothing or other goods are also appreciated.

Theft Petty theft among service staff is a common problem. Don't leave cash around; get a desk where you can lock the drawers or a safe where you keep your money or other valuables. In cases where you're unsure which member of staff might be guilty of the theft, the best solution we've heard is to gather all the staff and explain that the next time this happens all the staff will be fired regardless of who committed the crime.

INSECT CONTROL

Mosquitoes The simplest way to prevent yourself from being bitten by mosquitoes is protection. Mosquito nets are recommended for sleeping at night. You can buy ready-made square nets in most bazaars or you can have one made at a tailor's that specialises in bedspreads and mosquito nets (in Gulshan 2 Circle, on the northeast corner behind the inner row of stores there is a market – go east past the vegetables and you will find it). Having a custom-made circular net in 'American style' (Bangladeshi term) or 'princess style' (American term) will cost about Tk1,500 per net.

Second, Good Night or Mortein plug-ins are highly recommended. These are like Glade plug-ins and are filled with mosquito-repelling oil. They are odourless and non-toxic and can be purchased at any grocery store. Refills are available.

Mosquito repellent is available locally, under the brand name Odomos. It is a cream and costs Tk30 per tube. It is available at grocery stores like Nandan or Agora.

Cockroaches Insect powder and chalk available at the main grocery stores and small hardware stores can be used on the floors to kill cockroaches. Make sure all food items are off your benches – you don't want to be consuming this stuff. You can also hire (or have your landlord hire) a professional exterminator. Keep food covered and counters clean and periodically wipe out cabinets where food is stored. Buy a covered bin. Mothballs (available at grocery stores) placed in drains/sinks can keep cockroaches from coming out of the drains. Mothballs are poisonous so aren't recommended for kitchen sinks.

Visiting
Sundarbans, the world's largest
mangrove forest, with us, is more
than just a tourist tour – it is a
lifetime experience in one of
the last wildernesses on earth.
Conserving our natural resources
is a part of our mission. We
actively support ongoing
research activities in this
fragile ecosystem.
The Guide
Tours Ltd.
House 142, Road 12, Block E, Banani, Dhaka - 1213
Tel: 880-2-9862205, 9886983-4
theguide@bangla.net, www.guidetours.com
With us, you are never a stranger

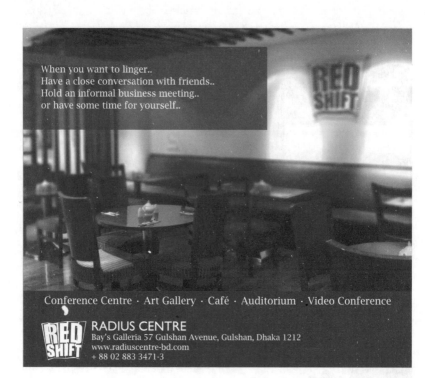

Part Two

THE GUIDE

3

Dhaka

Telephone code 02

Love it or hate it, the capital city is an essential ingredient of the Bangladesh travel experience. As the nation's heart and soul, the city has the best (great restaurants and extensive shopping) and the worst (prolific poverty and horrendous pollution) of everything. As much as some travellers – and even *bideshi* (Bangladeshi locals) – would like to pass it by, Dhaka is Bangladesh at its most raw and emotive.

Days begin with the morning *ahsan*, which, depending on how close you are to a mosque, may wake you well before dawn. Despite the early prayer call, most of the city's 12 million people stay in bed and even like to sleep in late. So, if you're touring Old Dhaka, moving before 08.00 is wisest (and coolest, temperature-wise, if it's a humid summer day in the capital). The morning is a great time to walk in a park, find a favourite tea stall and enjoy what is the most peaceful hour in Dhaka. Post-08.30, the city streets become an intense mosh pit of activity and they are not for the timid. Thundering buses, colourful rickshaws, smoking *tempos* and even horse-drawn carts vie for every inch of available asphalt, which makes getting around the city a nerve-rattling and toxic experience (never schedule too much in a day as the traffic tends to ooze, especially in the afternoon, plus take plenty of tea stops and you'll find it flows much more smoothly).

Early evening is the worst time to try and travel around the city, with commuters, shoppers and socialites all coming out of their homes at what seems exactly the same time. A flurry of cultural activity and interaction happens every evening at the city's art galleries, restaurants and bars (local or expatriate). Finally, around 22.00 things start to wind down, and by midnight, the shuttered shops, still streets and lack of nightlife make the city feel like a ghost town.

If you take it slow, you'll understand the real Dhaka behind its sullied façade. You'll see the colourful streams of *salwar kameez*-clad women walking to their jobs at one of the city's many garment factories. You'll soon tune into the colour and the vibrancy of the 'footpath markets' where vegetables of every hue catch your eye. You'll discover your favourite tea stall, and find yourself gravitating to it again so you can see the same smiling faces. And when you eventually leave the city for the countryside, the green hues of the rice paddies will have never looked so fresh. In short, Dhaka needs a little bit of time to warm up to, and so does Bangladesh.

To survive Dhaka, visitors require armaments: information is your best weapon as you can't necessarily rely on rickshaw or taxi drivers to know where you want to go, or even to understand your battered Bangla. Whenever you are lost, asking and confirming everything is essential. A sense of patience and a knack for adventure are your next best tools. Cross-city journeys are best augmented with an iPod and a pair of earphones, which also helps keep screaming car horns at bay. When kitted properly, Dhaka's delicacies – and there are many – do exist beneath its surface of dirt and pollution. Finally, don't forget to plan a journey out of the city (even just a few hours). For too many visitors and long-term residents, Dhaka is their only experience of the entire country, which is a shame given that the rest of the country is so gorgeous.

HISTORY

Dhaka's history essentially begins in 1608 when the Mughal rulers proclaimed it as the new capital of Bengal, and thus 2008 saw a few celebrations of Dhaka's 400th birthday. Before then, Dhaka was a functional trading port consisting of a small township served by many bazaars. It would not be until the Mughals relocated the capital from Sonargaon that the city began its expansion. The next century would see the city hosting a number of international interests with scores of Portuguese, French, English and Dutch merchants visiting Dhaka's trading ports, where a fine-woven cotton known as muslin was produced for export and famed internationally for its quality, showing up on the tailoring tables of Europe. These early economic successes prepared the city to one day become the future capital of East Pakistan and eventually Bangladesh.

In many ways, the history of Puran Dhaka (Old Dhaka) is the history of the city itself. Under the watchful reign of Mughal general Shaista Khan, the city saw its first period of rapid expansion from 1662 to 1689, because of the new administration requirements. A number of Dhaka's most famous buildings stem from this (eg: Lalbagh Fort, Choto Katra). Many city areas still retain their original names, reflecting the heritage of this period. For example, Old Dhaka's Tanti Bazaar and Shakhari Bazaar still house the Hindu professional groups of the day (*tanti* means weaver and *shakhari* means craftsmen); names like Harizabagh and Bakshi Bazaar are definitely of Mughal origin; places that end with *ganj* (eg: Nawabganj) denote business interests.

Dhaka's status as capital remained until 1717, when Murshid Quli Khan relocated the capital to Murshidabad, located in today's West Bengal, in an attempt to refresh the administration from some previous corruption. From that time onwards, the city housed only the deputy *subhadars* who were mostly subservient to their rulers in the west. When the British took control over Bengal in the mid 18th century, Dhaka's decline as a centre of trade and culture continued, so much so that the city was nearly reclaimed by the jungle; its population fell to 30,000 in 1840, when it used to be occupied by nearly a million people 200 years earlier during Mughal reign.

Nevertheless, the same year marked a change in Dhaka's importance as a regional administrative centre for East Bengal region, secondary to the British's administrative headquarters at Calcutta. Despite the decline, the British began to make political inroads with the Muslims of eastern Bengal, with whom they found a favourable counterbalance to the growing power of Hindu intellectuals from western Bengal. When Governor General of India Lord Curzon finalised the 1905 partition of Bengal, Dhaka was made the capital of the newly created province of East Bengal; it was also responsible for managing the affairs of nearby Assam. While the partition did not last long (in the face of relentless opposition it was annulled in 1912), it seeded the growth of Muslim separatist politics, a crisis that would beset Indian politics for the next several decades.

In 1947, British power finally came to an end and Dhaka became the capital of the newly created East Pakistan. For the next 24 years the city became the centre of agitation against western Pakistani dominance. The revolt began with the reaction to cultural imperialism in the form of the Language Movement. Eventually it led to the genocide of the Liberation War. On 16 December 1971, the Pakistani army formally surrendered at the Ramna race course, and Bangladesh was born after nine months of war.

GETTING THERE AND AWAY

For information on international destinations/arrivals, see *Chapter 2, Getting there and away*, pages 42–3.

BY AIR Zia International Airport [114–15] lies about 8km from the main embassy and commercial districts of Gulshan, Banani and Baridhara, and about twice that distance to Old Dhaka. At the time of research, the facility was getting a serious facelift, all of it funded by Bangladesh's major mobile-phone operators. Nevertheless, the moment you step out of the air-conditioned terminal building for the first time, you'll still be greeted with the shocking site of hundreds of people looking at you through a guarded security cage – welcome to your first sight of 'the real Bangladesh'.

The airport has a smaller domestic wing and a larger international one, with departures going upstairs, and new arrivals being greeted with a rather striking security cage downstairs. For a Tk200 entry fee, family and friends can wait inside the immediate arrivals area (ticket booths are on either entrance of the security cage). The international departure terminal features free internet terminals with spotty broadband service and an internet café where you can hook up your laptop, the Omni bookstore, plus an increasing number of duty-free and specialist shops. Most of the restaurants are either terrible or overpriced, but at least you can snack on something to kill time.

There is a currency-exchange service plus a Dutch-Bangla Banking Ltd (DBBL) ATM available in the international arrivals area, but do be warned that local taxi drivers often claim they have no *bantey* (small change) for Tk500 notes. Ask for small change at the exchangers.

Airport transfers If you are being met by hosts, you should wait on the inside of the security cage as outside vehicles can be driven in to load your luggage and trolleys can't leave the caged area. If arriving independently, leave the caged area and taxi drivers will find you well before you locate them. Fares vary considerably depending on the vehicle and your haggling skills/patience. It is best to see the vehicle first and then settle on a price. Judge by the number of other taxis waiting around and if they are numerous, then it should be easy to get a decent price. A pre-arranged transfer is recommended if arriving late at night, and most mid-range guesthouses do arrange this, with many even including it in their room rates.

Otherwise you could try the airport pickup service of Hertz Rent-A-Car (☎ *988 3411;* **e** *info@ipsslgroup.com; www.ispplgroup.com*), which will set you back Tk1,000 for the Gulshan/Banani/Baridhara areas. There is also a 'meet and greet' service being offered by UK-based tour operator Tiger Trails (*Hse 7, Rd 19/A, Sec 4, Uttara;* ☎ *893 1108, 892 3795;* **m** *01713 067848;* **e** *info@thetigertrail.com; www.thetigertrail.com*) that can arrange to assist newly arrived guests, for a Tk200 service fee. Most other tour operators will offer an airport transfer for Tk1,000 and up (for further details, see *Chapter 2, Tour operators*, page 118).

Taxi fares to Gulshan/Banani should cost no more than Tk150, and if you really feel like saving money, find a green baby taxi (known locally as CNGs) whose driver is willing to use the meter. This should cost around Tk80–100 for Gulshan/Banani. If you want the best prices possible, walk out from the terminal towards Airport Road, where there are regular public buses and baby taxis departing from the neighbouring train station for slightly lower fares.

Conversely, fares to the airport depend on the taxi's quality. Yellow Navana (☎ *955 8065*) taxis are the most expensive, and everything else can and should be judged by its cover (ie: the more battered-looking the vehicle is, the lower the price). When departing past midnight, it is best to hire a private vehicle whenever possible as finding a taxi on Dhaka's deserted streets can be difficult and perhaps dangerous.

Regular domestic flights travel to Chittagong (Tk5,495, including taxes), Sylhet (Tk5,395), Jessore (Tk4,895), Barisal (Tk4,495), Cox's Bazaar (Tk7,495) and sometimes Saidpur (Tk5,495). Tickets can be purchased on arrival at the airport but if it's anywhere near Bangladesh's holiday seasons you're better off booking first. Schedules for domestic flights change according to the winter/summer seasons so do check.

Airlines

✈ **Biman Bangladesh** Biman Bhaban, 100 Motijheel C/A; ☎ 955 3206, 716 8829; ☎ 955 4783; www.bimanair.com. Sometimes offers high-season flights to Chittagong & Cox's Bazaar.

✈ **Royal Bengal Airlines** Hse 56C, Rd 132, Gulshan 1; ☎ 988 2211; www.royalbengalairline.com. Flying to Chittagong & Cox's Bazaar at the time of research, although they were expected to expand domestic operations.

✈ **GMG Airlines** Banani: ABC Hse (Ground Fl), 8 Kamal Ataturk Av, Banani; ☎ 886 0935; Motijheel: Suite 1303, Senakalayan Bhaban, 195 Motijheel C/A; ☎ 711 4155–7; Sonargaon Ho☎ 107 Kazi Nazrul Av; ☎ 812 7372; Airport: ☎ 896 0404, 891 5699, 891 7221, 812 7742; www.gmgairlines.com. The oldest private operator.

✈ **United Airways** Corporate Office: 5th Fl, Uttara Tower, 1 Jasimuddin Av, Uttara; ☎ 893 2338, 893 1712; f 893 2339; Airport Domestic Terminal; ☎ 895 7640, 896 3191; m 01713 486660; Gulshan: Shop 219–221, Taher Tower, Gulshan 2 Circle; ☎ 885 4769, 885 4697, 886 1935; m 01713 486659; Kawran Bazaar: Shop 3, Level 2, Unique Trade Centre, 8 Pantha Path; ☎ 913 8238, 815 8046; m 01713 486658; Paltan: Oriental Trade Centre, 2nd Fl, 69/1 Purana Paltan Line; ☎ 935 2647, 935 2648; m 01713 486657; e info@uabdl.com; www.uabdl.com. Offers the most comprehensive domestic service for now. Let's see if they can keep it going.

By charter flight You have two options if you want to charter a flight: helicopter or seaplane. **Aero Technologies** (*Hse 347, Ln 5, DOHS Baridhara; ☎ 882 9525, 986 3035; m 01711 520359*) offers a charter helicopter service, costing Tk140,000 or US$2,000 per hour.

In a country that is over 50% flooded during the monsoon season, it makes sense to take a seaplane if you want to reach destinations as quickly as possible. **Mission Aviation Fellowship Bangladesh** (*Hse 299, Ln 4, DOHS Baridhara; ☎ 881 0164; f 881 0165; emergency m: 01711 533333; e bd-bookings@maf.org; www.mafbangladesh.org*) provides just that service. Chartered departures are said to cost at least Tk90,000 or US$1,200 per hour, but these prices could vary depending on destination.

BY TRAIN Bangladesh's aging railway system remains quite comprehensive, with journeys proving scenic and relaxing compared with the bat-out-of-hell buses careening over the country's highways. The Bangladesh Railway website (*www.railway.gov.bd*) used to be easy to browse, although it's now suffering from a lack of upkeep. You can look up departure and arrival times by city.

Trains depart from two locations in Dhaka because there is a different gauge system in place. All trains to destinations east of the Jamuna River depart from Kamlapur Station via the Airport Railway Station. All trains to destinations west of the Jamuna depart from the Dhaka Cantonment Railway Station.

The easiest way to catch eastbound trains is to look up your destination first and then catch the train from the Airport Railway Station [114–15] (see above for airport transfer information). Head to the airport but instead of turning left at the airport crossing, you'll see the train station less than 100m further ahead on the right, marked by a pedestrian overpass. Departure times listed below are from Kamlapur Station, but all trains pass by the Airport Railway Station anywhere between 20 and 45 minutes after the times listed below.

For westbound trains, head to the slightly closer Dhaka Cantonment Railway Station [114–15], which is just north of Baridhara DOHS residential area, about a 20-minute ride from Gulshan 2 when the traffic is good. The entrance to the station is on Airport Road.

TRAIN TIMETABLES

EXPRESS TRAINS FOR THE EASTERN CITIES (FROM KAMLAPUR RAILWAY STATION; ADD 20 MINUTES IF DEPARTING FROM THE AIRPORT RAILWAY STATION)

No	Destination	Train name	Off day	Dep time	Arr time
702	Chittagong	Subarna Express	Friday	16.20	22.40
704	Chittagong	Mahanagar Provati	None	07.40	14.45
722	Chittagong	Mahanagar Godhuli	Sunday	15.00	22.20
742	Chittagong	Turna Express	None	23.00	06.50
709	Sylhet	Parabat Express	Tuesday	06.40	13.15
717	Sylhet	Joyantika Express	None	14.00	21.00
739	Sylhet	Upaban Express	Wednesday	22.00	05.15
705	Dinajpur	Ekota Express	Tuesday	09.30	18.50
757	Dinajpur	Drutazan Express	Wednesday	19.50	05.10
751	Lalmonirhat	Lalmoni Express	Friday	21.30	07.20
712	Noakhali	Upakul Express	Wednesday	07.00	13.20
745	Mymensingh*	Jamuna Express	None	16.50	20.10
735	Mymensingh*	Aghnibina Express	None	09.50	12.40

*indicates that this is not the final destination of the train, just the major junction.

MAIL TRAINS FROM DHAKA (KAMLAPUR RAILWAY STATION)

No	Destination	Train name	Off day	Dep time	Arr time
2	Chittagong	Chittagong Mail	None	22.30	07.35
4	Chittagong	Karnaphuli Express	None	08.00	19.30
9	Sylhet	Surma Mail	None	21.00	08.10
12	Noakhali	Noakhali Express	None	20.10	05.00
49	Mymensingh	Balaka Express	None	10.30	14.30

DEPARTING FROM DHAKA (CANTONMENT RAILWAY STATION)

No	Destination	Train name	Off day	Dep time	Arr time
726	Khulna	Sundarban Provati	Thursday	06.30	17.00
764	Khulna	Sundarban Nishitha	Monday	19.20	05.55
753	Rajshahi	Silk City Express	Sunday	15.00	20.50
759	Rajshahi	Padma Express	Tuesday	23.45	05.35

Seat tickets for short-haul journeys can be purchased on arrival, but berth tickets should be booked in advance. It can be quite difficult to get first-class air-conditioned tickets as these are often reserved for travelling government officials until the very last day. For a service fee, tour operators can purchase tickets for you and take the hassle out of your journey. Otherwise you can go to one of the train stations first to pick up your ticket – Kamlapur, Banani Train Station and the Airport Railway Station all sell tickets for journeys from Dhaka. Kolkata tickets must be purchased from a special window at the Kamlapur Railway Station, even though the train departs from the Dhaka Cantonment Station.

Robberies have occurred at train stations. Two French travellers were mugged when they were taken to a private station waiting room and drugged when they were given drinks. They later woke up with all their valuables stolen. It is best to politely decline food or drink from strangers at the station unless you see it being prepared yourself.

The box above gives the train schedules, which may be subject to change. Do note that some of these trains have off days, where they do not run. Mail trains are

GETTING TO INDIA

SILIGURI SHYAMOLI PARIBAHAN (*departs Kamlapur Railway Station at 21.00 and transits through Gabtali Bus Station about 22.00;* ☎ *836 0241*) Operates a nightly service to Siliguri in conjunction with the BRTC, which is the eastern gateway to Nepal, Darjeeling or Sikkim. The bus arrives at the Burimari border at about 06.00. Customs clearance takes a few more hours, and about 15 hours later you arrive in Siliguri. Tickets can be purchased from any Shyamoli Paribahan office but it's probably easiest to meet the bus as it leaves the city from Gabtali Bus Station. There's also a Shyamoli Paribahan office just north of Asad Gate in Mohammadpur.

KOLKATA SHYAMOLI (*departs Kamlapur Railway Station;* ☎ *933 3803*) Also operates a service similar to its Siliguri trip, bound for Kolkata. Advance ticket purchase is recommended but not required. You can also use Green Line, Shohagh or Soudia S Alam services. The latter companies require you to switch buses after crossing the border at Benapol. The journey takes 11–12 hours, 3 of which are spent tussling with customs at both sides of the border, but it's a cheap way to go. Purchase your ticket at the Kalabagan bus counters at Russell Square in Dhanmondi.

AGARTALA This border is the closest destination for long-term expats who reside in the odd situation of having year-long visas, but maximum stays of three or six months. If you need to exit and re-enter the country this is the easiest place to go and the round trip only requires a day. You can catch any eastbound train (the Upakul Express headed for Noakhali is recommended; it departs from Kamlapur at 07.00, and arrives in Akhaura at 09.30). You'll also need to stop off and pay a Tk300 departure tax at Akhaura before the border formalities. After a few hours of exploring Agartala, you can catch the Upakul Express as it returns to Dhaka at 17.40 from Akhaura.

slightly slower, but that doesn't make much difference if it's an overnight train, and usually have sleeper cars attached.

For the Maitree Express service connecting Dhaka and Kolkata by train, see *Chapter 2, Getting there and away, By train*, pages 44–6.

BY BUS Dhaka has several bus stands and companies spread around the city. Which bus station and which company you choose depends on where you want to go.

For travellers heading to the major cities (Khulna, Jessore, Rajshahi, Bogra, Rangpur, Sylhet, Chittagong and Cox's Bazaar), the most convenient option is to head to Kalabagan on Pantha Path and take your pick of the several coach companies that have offices here (unless you happen to be staying closer to Old Dhaka, in which case you'll want to go to Arambag near the Kamlapur Railway Station). The company will then shuttle you to their main bus station or the bus will pass by Kalabagan on its way out of town.

Travellers heading to smaller cities need to choose from the three main bus stations: Gabtali and Kallyanpur bus stations for destinations northwest and southwest (NB the names Gabtali and Kallyanpur are used interchangeably), Mohakhali for cities in Dhaka Division or Sayedabad for anything heading south (eg: Barisal), southeast (Chittagong) or northeast (Srimongol). One exception is if you're heading to Sonargaon or Comilla – this bus departs from the Gulistan bus stand. The choice of vehicle for these cities is often a little less enticing, and if your destination is on a major route to somewhere else, it is advisable to try to take an air-conditioned coach if you can, simply because the drivers are safer.

Luxury air-conditioned bus services usually cost between Tk500 and Tk1,000, depending on where you're headed. Otherwise, non air-conditioned bus services to the more remote cities and towns usually stay under Tk500. You can call the counters listed below and shop around, although because competition is stiff there won't be much difference between companies.

For places more off the beaten track, read the relevant *Getting there and away* information to figure out which bus is best for where you're headed.

Kalabagan bus counters (aka Russell Square)

Green Line Lake Circus Rd; 911 2287. Recommended for transport to main divisional cities (Khulna, Rajshahi, Sylhet) & also offers a service to Bogra, Rangpur & Natore. Also offers upper-class 'Scania' service to Cox's Bazaar & Chittagong.

Neptune Russell Sq; 912 3092. Good at a pinch for Chittagong & Cox's Bazaar services, but vehicles not as top-notch as others.

Shohagh 64/3 Lake Circus Rd; 812 6293. A major company but lacking English speakers.

Silk Line 64/7 Lake Circus Rd; 914 3372; m 01713 093433; 99 Sukrabad; 812 0382; m 01714 087564. The recommended bus company for Chittagong & Cox's Bazaar, has a 'Saloon' luxury bus service with leather seats. Tickets Tk600 for Chittagong & Tk900 for Cox's Bazaar. Saloon service extra.

Soudia S Alam 13/1 West Panthapath; m 01197 015632–4. Newest competitor on the scene, featuring Mercedes Benz-built buses.

Arambag, Rajarbagh and Sayedabad counters

Green Line 9/2 Outer Circular Rd, Momenbagh, Rajarbagh; 833 1302–4, 835 3004–5, 934 2580; m 01817 043704. All Green Line buses depart from here & so check your departure time depending on where you're catching the bus.

Silk Line 167/8 Circular Rd; 710 2461, 719 1253; m 01714 087563, 01819 202028; 61/1-B Sayedabad; m 01714 087566.

Soudia S Alam 2 Baitul Aman Jame Mosque Market, Motijheel Circular Rd; m 01197 015636–8

Baridhara

Green Line Nadda Counter, Pragati Sharani Rd; m 01912 407157. A convenient place to buy tickets for luxury bus transport out of Dhaka, but you'll still need to get to a different location to catch the bus, based on where you're headed. At least this ticket counter is close to Gulshan. The counter is located on the east side of Pragati Sharani, on the northeast corner of the Baridhara residential area. See the map on page 120–1 [F1] for the exact location as Pragati Sharani is a very long road.

Uttara

Green Line Uttara; m 01716 976775

Neptune Uttara; 896 0993; m 01712 924641

Silk Line Hse 4, Rd 12; m 01716 308505, 01915 045586

BY LAUNCH BOAT One of Dhaka's great pleasures is to cruise away from the city on a launch in the fading hues of a Sadarghat sunset. In a country of rivers, launch travel is the way in this unique feature of the Bangladeshi landscape. Every evening, up to a dozen launch vessels, some easily four decks high, depart from the boat terminal for the south's major cities. The journeys can be long, but that's really quite the point of the adventure. There's very little to do other than read a book in the evening and wake up at your destination the next morning. Power is available so laptops can also be used, but do bring a plug adaptor.

For the ordinary traveller, your key destinations are Patuakhali (for its proximity to the beach at Kuakata), Khulna or Mongla via the rocket (as a logical launching point for ventures into the Sundarbans – see below) and Barisal (as a base from which to experience one of the hundreds of islands and *chars* of Bangladesh's south, most of which will be disappearing in the sea-level-rising scenario). Bhola might also prove to be an interesting destination, although the island is absolutely massive to cross from one end to the other. Unless it's

DISCOVERING BANGLADESH'S RIVERS

Journalist Christian Walsh once wrote that 'Leaving Dhaka is an involuntary experience. It spits you out.' As we idled amidst the seething toxic clouds of a Dhaka traffic jam – in an open-air baby taxi, no less – it was akin to being lodged in the phlegm of the city's toxic throat, preparing to be hawked out with projectile force.

It was Gulistan, and we were standing still. Translated as 'fragrant garden', the 'stan is a necessary rite of passage to reach Sadarghat (shod-or-ghat), the city's heaving boat terminal. Once you've run the gauntlet and surfeited yourself with exhaust, the reward of leaving Dhaka by launch is nothing short of bliss. It is the best way to get out in true Bangladeshi style: on the water, that is. The frothy spittle of the city simply sails away behind you, replaced with the cool air of a gentle evening cruise. Bringing a discreet celebratory beverage would not go amiss at this moment, given that glasses are always provided with your cabin.

Our destination was the southern township of Patuakhali, where we would then catch public transport to Kuakata. The south's landscape is unique in Bangladesh: it is where the mountains literally crumble to the sea. Massive quantities of monsoonal rainwater eventually empty into the Bay of Bengal each year, bringing with them the life-giving silt and minerals of the Himalayas. This phenomenon has helped sustain Bangladesh's massive population growth over the last few decades. Tidal flow also pushes back against this torrent, resulting in the floods that are the source of much grief for Bangladesh's millions. Yet, despite these miseries, southern Bangladesh holds an even darker promise, one that is now becoming an issue of intense contestation.

In early 2007, climate change finally attained mass awareness and even the leaders of the world's most polluting nations began rhetoric on the one issue that affects us all. Bangladesh was widely acknowledged to be one of the nations least responsible for climate change, yet its people would bear the worst of its impacts. And it would be here, in southern Bangladesh, where the most people would be affected. As sea levels rise, millions of people would be pushed inward by the combined forces of river erosion, land loss and fresh water scarcity. The same fateful year also saw Bangladesh mired by two bouts of flooding and pounded by a severe tropical cyclone, both of which killed thousands and left several million more even worse off.

Because of these reasons, the region needs more attention and more focus as the 'ground zero' point of where climate change forces will hit the most people and in the hardest way. Perhaps that is why many more visitors will come to these regions eventually, in a bid to stave off what will likely become the greatest challenge Bangladesh has ever faced.

holiday season in Bangladesh, arriving by 17.00 should allow enough time to locate the necessary launch and a cabin for the evening. For extra certainty, it may be best to book the ticket ahead of time – call the following booking numbers on the day of departure to reserve a cabin and confirm its price. Asking a Bengali speaker to help you book is wise.

Barisal Booking is not required as there are often 4 departures per night to/from Barisal. The launches begin leaving around 18.00, with the last departing around 20.30. Showing up by 17.00 will guarantee you a cabin on one of the launches. Single cabins are sometimes available at Tk350, although these are harder to get and you may end up in a double cabin charging Tk600 per bed. The prices are usually fixed in this case, unless it's the holiday season and demand is very high.

Patuakhali Has at least 2 launches per day. *Sundarban Five*; m 01714 017272; *Sundarban Six*; m 01712 151747. The preceding two boats depart on alternative days at 18.15 so one or the other will be available. VIP cabin Tk1,500; regular cabins Tk600. *Shaikat One*, Mr Samsu; m 01710 620742; *Shaikat*

Two, Mr Anwar; m 01920 206813. Also departs on alternative days at 17.45, so you'll catch one or the other launch. 11hrs either way. Regular dbl cabin Tk600, sgl Tk350.

Hatiya Island *Panama*; m 01711 349257; *Tipu 5*; m 01711 348813. 19hrs. Berth Tk600. Both launches stop over in Bhola in the morning the next day, & either launch runs on alternative days.

BY ROCKET When the rocket steamer service first commenced in 1956, the vessels may have actually 'rocketed' around the delta and were the fastest vessels of their time. Originally constructed in 1928, the rocket is still 'hammering around the Delta', as travel writer Jack Barker put it, and fortunately only one of the six original vessels is on the bottom of the Buriganga and four remain in operation to this very day. It is Bangladesh's most well-known journey, with its sloth-like speed actually quite a pleasure to enjoy.

There are two classes of cabin available: first class boasts air conditioning in double-bedded cabins (Tk1,190 for Khulna and Tk1,025 for Mongla) and is located at the front of the boat, where as the second-class cabins (Tk720 for Khulna) are located in the back and only offer fans. Even if you've purchased only a second-class ticket, the staff are normally pleased to let you sit in the front deck to enjoy the scenery going by. Food on the boat receives mixed reviews, but if your dietary requirements aren't too strict then you will be pleased. Standard Bengali fare is on offer, with toast and omelette available for breakfast and rice and curries available for dinner.

The (in)famous river journey can be booked ahead of time by liaising with the **BIWTC office** [144–5 E1] (*BIWTC Bhaban, 5 Dilkusha Commercial Area, Motijheel;* *955 9779, 891 4771*). Purchasing a ticket a few days in advance is recommended. Otherwise if you're based in Gulshan, **Guide Tours** [120–1 C4] (*Hse 142, Rd 12, Blk E; 988 6983, 986 2205; m 01711 696337*) can purchase the tickets for you, and for a small service charge you don't have to worry about getting down to the BIWTC office yourself. Assuming none of the other steamers breaks down or sinks before publication of this guidebook, departures run six times per week, but not all departures go all the way to Khulna or even Mongla, only Morrelganj. Full Khulna round trips run at 18.30 on Sundays, Mondays, Wednesdays and Thursdays from Dhaka, and depart from Khulna at 02.45 on Mondays, Tuesdays, Thursdays and Fridays. On the other days, the boats travel to Morrelganj, 90km before Khulna and 45km before Mongla. Schedules change frequently as sometimes the rockets are parked at dock for service or they are delayed owing to winter fog (worst in December and January). Call first and confirm departures before finalising your plans. Fares for Dhaka–Khulna are Tk1,190 per berth in air-conditioned first class and Tk720 for non air-conditioned second class (if you want a private berth you'll need to pay for a full cabin at double the cost).

If travelling to Sundarban, purchase a ticket for Mongla (Tk1,025; 1st class) as you need not travel all the way to Khulna only to turn around and come back again. Ask your boat operator to have the vessel meet you in Mongla, and you'll have less travelling time before you enter the forest.

GETTING AROUND

Overall, Dhaka is not a big city. But often what started as a 20-minute outward journey can turn into a two-hour return route. The terrible congestion suffered along the city's key arteries means that it is effectively quite hard to plan ahead. It is best to leave at least an extra hour for any cross-city journeys.

BY CNG If using a CNG (the green baby taxis), get prepared for a fairly serious haggle over the fare, although some drivers are willing to use the meter – always ask. Some drivers will use the meter if you offer Tk10 more (*beshi dosh taka*), or if

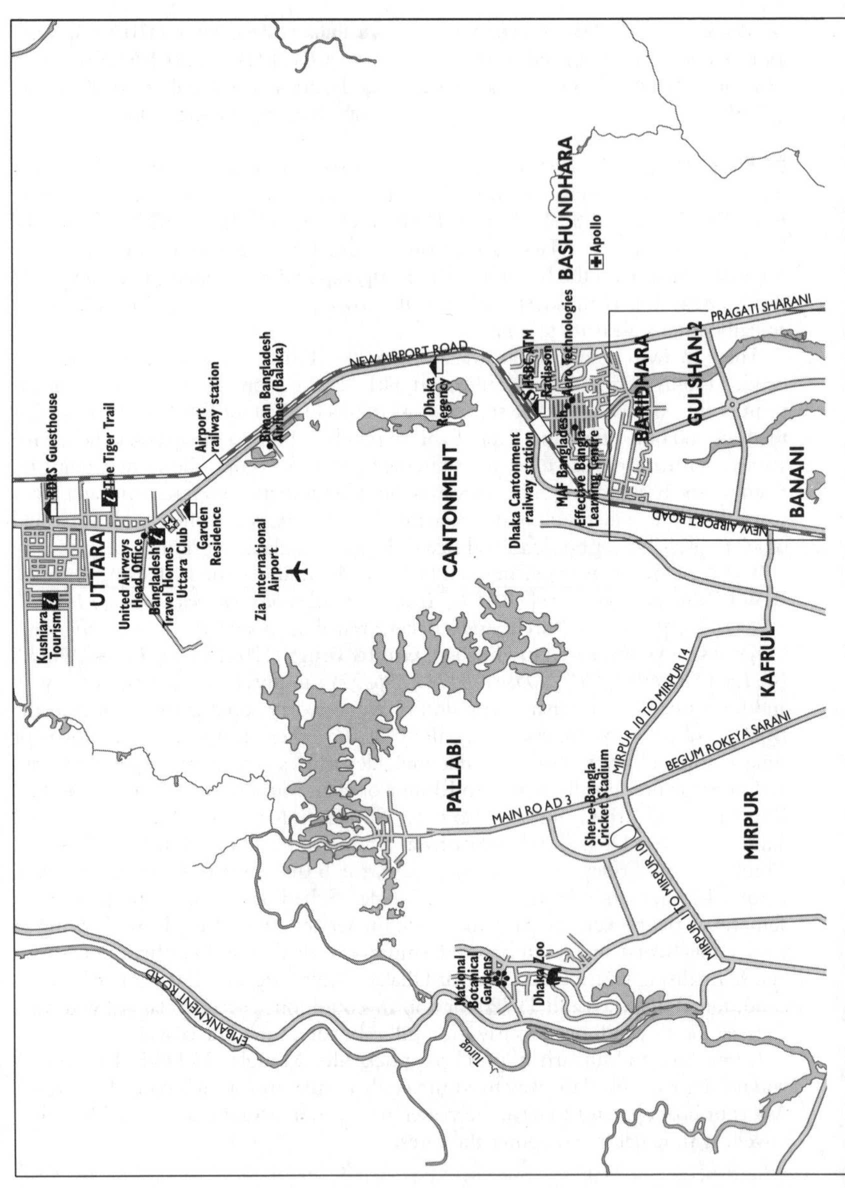

you're in a real hurry, offer them Tk20. Directions are rarely given using specific addresses. Instead, most drivers know an area by name or perhaps the Bangla name of a well-known building inside the area. Learning how to specify where you want to go and how much you're willing to pay is a real art form to getting around Dhaka, so don't expect to get the right price on your first go. In most areas of Dhaka there is a gathering place of CNGs, so if you're having trouble finding one, grab a rickshaw and ask for a CNG stand or walk to a bigger intersection.

Here are some rough ideas of fares. From Gulshan/Banani to Dhanmondi, expect to pay Tk70–90 for a CNG ride. For travel to Old Dhaka from

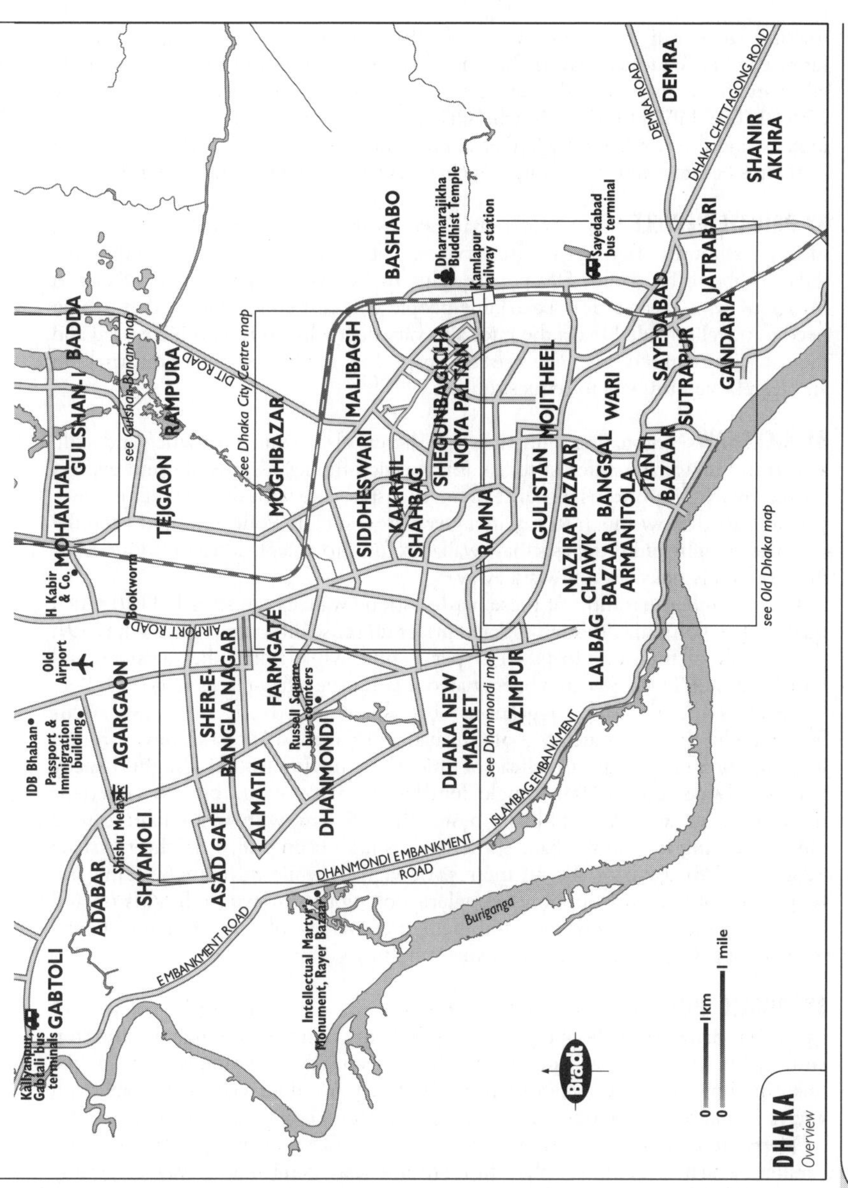

Gulshan/Banani, the fare will rise to Tk120–140 and if it's the middle of the day, with jams happening all along the way, the fare could inflate to over Tk150 or more. Drivers also tend to charge 10–20% more at night, when there are far fewer taxis on the road.

BY TAXI Fares for taxi rides also need to be negotiated beforehand, although once again, some drivers are willing to go on the meter right away. Yellow Navana taxis are the best available and most have working air conditioning, but you will pay a pretty penny for the luxury (at least three times the cost of a CNG). Other more battered-looking taxis can be used too, with the yellow ones offering the more knowledgeable/educated drivers. Blue and black taxis sound and feel like they could fall apart any moment, and they are not recommended for night-time travel but are perfectly fine during the day. Muggings have occurred during late cross-city journeys in taxis, and it is not known whether the drivers were co-conspirators or not. After 23.00 it is best to arrange a private vehicle whenever possible or travel in groups.

BY PRIVATE VEHICLE Several car-rental services are available around the city, with most guesthouses offering car-hire services. The going rate for an air-conditioned sedan is about Tk1,000–1,500 per day plus fuel costs, for use around Dhaka. A microbus with capacity for six to nine people will cost about double that. If you need to travel outside Dhaka the rates also vary depending on the vehicle used and the capacity required. See *Tour operators*, page 118, for more contact information and telephone numbers to request quotes.

BY RICKSHAW Negotiating with rickshaw drivers also requires patience and skill, as it is in the wallah's interest to ask for as much money as possible, and express serious dismay, humorous disbelief or angry displeasure with the given fare. Once you've learned how much to pay in a given area, stick to your guns and keep the negotiation light and if the rickshaw wallah refuses to accept, add a bit more, leave the fare on his rickshaw and walk away

Do remember that most of these hard-working wallahs can stretch Tk10 much further than you can, although inflated prices do cause difficulties for the locals. A general rule of thumb is to pay Tk1 per minute while riding the rickshaw, and hourly rates of Tk40–50 can be negotiated if you have a few places to go.

Again, some security suggestions: bag snatchings from rickshaws occur frequently in the expatriate areas of Gulshan and Banani. It's best to move around in groups or arrange transport ahead of time when moving around at night (usually but not always after 22.00). Single females seem to be the biggest target for rickshaw snatchings. A car pulls up beside the rickshaw, with an assailant leaning out, attempting to grab the bag. Some victims have been pulled off the rickshaw entirely and dragged for several metres. Be vigilant while travelling/walking and keep aware of your surroundings. An alert-looking person, whose head is up and is watching the environment around them, presents less of a target than someone who is not paying attention to their surroundings.

BY PUBLIC BUS Dhaka's bewildering public bus system largely consists of passengers dangerously hopping on and off moving vehicles, although they do stop entirely for women. Most ride under extremely crowded conditions, but a public bus can come in handy when there is absolutely no other vehicle available and you're in an area where rickshaws aren't permitted to cross major roadways.

There are two kinds of bus. The first is a kind of 'get on and get off anywhere' version, which is definitely the cheapest and least comfortable way of getting around Dhaka. The second is a 'sitting bus'. Bus stands for these buses can be identified by finding ticket sellers sitting under umbrellas at small tables by the side of the road. Simply walk up and state where you want to go and they will sell you the correct ticket and fare, plus point out which bus to catch.

BY BICYCLE Unfortunately, casual bicycle rental is not readily available in Dhaka but if you stay long enough you may befriend a fellow cyclist or find a decent used bicycle or mountain bike up for sale at the expat clubs. If you bring your own bicycle you'll find plenty of parts and technicians in Old Dhaka's Bangsal Road [144–5 D3] (aka Bicycle Street). Many Chinese- and Indian-made bicycles are sold

BUYING YOUR OWN RICKSHAW (AND RICKSHAW WALLAH)

Several expatriates have ended up buying rickshaws (along with befriending their associated driver) for personal use. Often, these are the most colourfully decorated rickshaws in Bangladesh, with personal photographs, paintings and plastic flowers covering every inch of available space on the rickshaw body.

The cost to purchase and outfit a rickshaw varies considerably, but a used rickshaw will cost about Tk10,000 and a 'fully loaded' decoration job another Tk5,000. Similarly, a new, fully decorated rickshaw should only cost a few thousand more. Laminated photographs can be nailed onto the rickshaw, plus the owner's name painted on the back. Normally, a rickshaw wallah pays about Tk75 per day to a rental garage for the rickshaw, and with most wallahs averaging Tk200 to Tk300 per day in the Gulshan area (one of the highest-paying places to be a rickshaw driver), the rental fee represents a significant cost to the wallah himself.

Nonetheless, some expat rickshaw owners have encountered problems when their wallahs ran into financial problems and sold their rickshaw to repay loans. Other issues include finding parking space for the newly decorated, beautiful rickshaw which is suddenly more valuable than an ordinary rickshaw. New components can sometimes be a target for theft at the rickshaw garage, so some expatriates have even offered their apartment parking spaces for the rickshaw. Despite these issues, owning a rickshaw does represent an interesting social experiment, allowing some insight into the life of these colourful vehicles and their drivers, each of whom symbolise the personality of Bangladesh.

from here, although the former are cheaply made and the latter extremely heavy. There is an informal group of cycling enthusiasts amongst the Dhaka expatriate community – ask around and you'll quickly find them.

BY MOTORCYCLE Motorcycle-owning foreigners, while rare, are not totally unheard of in Dhaka. Surely, the adventurous will find this the best and most efficient way to get around the city. The law stipulates that only 150cc motorcycles are permitted, therefore these are the largest sizes you'll find. New Chinese- or Indian-made motorcycles cost from Tk75,000 to well over Tk100,000. An international driving permit is required. Some expatriates have purchased scooters (about Tk60,000) to get them around the Gulshan/Banani area. You'll find plenty of motorcycle dealers in Dhaka's New Eskaton Road [124–5].

TOURIST INFORMATION

Bangladesh's national tourism organisation is called the Bangladesh Parjatan Corporation, or *Parjatan*, meaning tourism, for short. The organisation was largely ineffective and its materials well out of date, and so travellers might find the services of a tour operator (see listings below) more efficient and helpful in the search for information and guidance while considering a journey to Bangladesh.

TOUR OPERATORS Many of the local major tour operators are happy to provide information on what to do and how to go there, plus they can be used to purchase advance tickets for a small service fee if you cannot find the time. Below is a listing of the more established operators who actually own their own facilities and have provided services for foreign guests in the past (as opposed to domestic travellers, whose needs are very different).

Bangladesh Travel Homes Hse 13, Rd 6, Sec 1, Uttara; ☎ 895 0650; m 0152 483800; e info@bdtravelhomes.com; www.bdtravelhomes.com. Operates a hostel in Uttara.

Classic Tours and Travels Taher Tower 2nd Flr, Suite 313, Gulshan Circle 2; ☎ 988 2377; m 01556 360566; e info@classictours-bd.com; www.classictours-bd.com. Srimongol specialist, as well as other tours around Bangladesh.

Delta Outdoors Flat D, 6/F, Home Town Apartments, 87 New Eskaton Rd, Bangla Motor; ☎ 934 2689; m 01720 532059; e outdoors.delta@gmail.com; www.delta-outdoors.com. A highly adventurous bunch of young guys who operate inbound & outbound tours on request & are very responsive to the backpacking crowd.

Discover Tourism Unicorn Plaza, 40/2 North Gulshan Av; ☎ 882 8615; m 01715 207105; e discover@dhaka.net; www.discover-bd.com. Also operates tours on a request basis.

Galaxy Holidays Taj Casselina, 2nd Fl, 25 Gulshan Av; ☎ 988 8055, 988 3310; m 01713 005306; e info.holidays@galaxybd.com; www.galaxybd.com. High-end tour operator, mostly for outbound tours.

Green Channel Hse 11, Rd 1/A, Blk J, Banani; ☎ 989 4479, 881 8557; m 01730 012454; e info@greenchannelbd.com; www.greenchannelbd.org. Large group specialist (ie: hundreds of guests, conventions, etc). Specialises in transport & logistics.

Jatrik Travels Hse 15B, Rd 50, Gulshan 2; ☎ 2989 5362; e jatriktravels@gmail.com; www.jatrik.com. Operates specialised tours for university school groups, including tours of Grameen Bank & BRAC. Also features tours to Kushtia, for those interested in Baul music culture. No office address yet, call for information & they will be happy to come & meet you.

Journey Plus Suite 40/A, 1/F, Aziz Supermarket, Shahbagh; ☎ 862 8577, 966 0234; m 01819 227901, 01720 242942; e journey@bdcom.com, journeyplus@yahoo.com; www.journeyplus.com. Handles inbound travellers mostly from UK companies such as Explore. Also running some hotel facilities at Cox's Bazaar & St Martin's Island.

Kushiara Tourism Ltd Hse 40, Rd 3, Sec 13, Uttara; ☎ 893 2008–9; m 01711 392319, 01199 076408; e ktl@agni.com, info@touristhomebd.com; www.touristhomebd.com. Operates a guesthouse in Uttara, housed in an apt building. Fairly reasonable rates & optional 6hr or 12hr stays.

Petro Aviation Bldg 69/2, 4th Flr, Rd 7/A, Dhanmondi; ☎ 912 2621; e info@petroaviation.com; www.petroaviation.com. Offers full-service transport & guided tours throughout Bangladesh. Also offers Sundarbans trips. Despite being new entry to the tourism market, the company has an earnest desire & capacity to run professional tours.

Silver Wave Tours Ltd 3/F, Hse 5, Rd 17, Blk E, Banani; ☎ 883 7697; m 01713 452139; e info@silverwavetours.com; www.silverwavetours.com. Good for information & questions.

The Bengal Tours Ltd Hse 45, Rd 27, Blk A, Banani; ☎ 883 4716, 885 7424; e bengal@agni.com; www.bengaltours.com. Has boat facilities for Sundarbans tours, one of the best operators in town.

The Guide Tours Hse 142, Rd 17, Blk E, Banani; ☎ 988 6983, 986 2205; m 01711 696337; e theguide@bangla.net; www.guidetours.com. Bangladesh's most established tour operator. Has a range of services & 4 boats for touring Bangladesh & the Sundarbans. Also has a resort facility in the CHT. Recommended for professional service. Has experience supporting media & film-making crews.

The Tiger Trail Hse 7, Rd 19/A, Sec 4, Uttara; ☎ 893 1108, 892 3795; m 01713 067848; e info@thetigertrail.com; www.thetigertrail.com. Airport 'meet & greet' service worth checking out.

Time Travel and Tour 121 Motijheel C/A; ☎ 956 2315, 956 5427; m 01711 525489; e info@timedhaka.com; www.timedhaka.com. Inbound/outbound tour operator & immigration agent, seems like a professional outfit.

MAPS Several maps of the Dhaka city area are available, but the best and most useful of the bunch is the *Diggin' Dhaka* map created by Laura Bonapace. While it lacks written editorial reviews, it covers Gulshan, Banani and Dhanmondi's numerous entertainment and shopping venues, as well as airline offices, embassies, hotels, boutiques and so much more. For general purposes, Mappa [128–9 F5] (*112 Green Rd, Farmgate; ☎ 811 6710, 811 7260*) produces a detailed city map of Dhaka in addition to country maps. The company has also produced a few tourist guide maps to Cox's Bazaar, Sylhet and Chittagong.

Both maps should be available at Gulshan bookstores such as Words 'n' Pages [120–1 F9] (*Hse 7, Rd 7, Gulshan 1; ☎ 989 0832, 882 0417*) or Folk International (*Hse 19, Rd 108; ☎ 988 0784*). Otherwise try the mini book selections at Aranya or

Jatra [120–1 C4] (*60 Kamal Ataturk Av, Banani;* ☎ *882 6370*). You can also find plenty of maps at New Market's bookshops or ETC in Dhanmondi [128–9 C4] (*Hse 275, Rd 16 (Old 27), Dhanmondi;* ☎ *914 0089*). Otherwise you'll see them frequently being sold in the street.

Custom maps can be produced at the Centre for Environmental and Geographic Information Services [120–1 D6] (*Hse 6, Rd 23/C, Gulshan 1;* ☎ *882 1570, 881 7648–52; www.cegisbd.com*). CEGIS is easily Bangladesh's most professional mapping service and can consult on almost any GIS need.

WHERE TO STAY

Accommodation in the capital ranges from real budget accommodation to five-star services. The decision of where to stay depends on what you're doing in Dhaka. If it's business, and your contacts are in the Gulshan/Banani area, there are a lot of choices and some good deals to be had if you shop around. However, if you're doing anything finance-related you might be heading to Motijheel frequently, which can make for a hectic city crossing both in the morning and on the way back.

Budget travellers will find more options in the Motijheel area as well. Backpackers and adventurers should check out www.couchsurfing.com – a unique online project whereby members offer other members their couches/spare rooms or floors to crash on. Membership in the system is on a trust basis, and given the nature of Bangladeshi hospitality, this is a great way to find a free place to stay and have a local show you around at the same time.

GULSHAN/BANANI

Upmarket The most expensive rooms in Dhaka offer everything you could expect out of a 5-star experience, including the rates to match ie: US$100 plus). The lower end of the range offers better price/quality, ie: more for your dollars, and usually offers rates between US$70 and US$100. Breakfast is always included, as well as internet, business centre, television and backup generators – sometimes even AC-powering full-load generators.

Lake Shore Hotels & Apartments [120–1 C5] (60 rooms) Hse 46, Rd 41, Gulshan 2; ☎ 885 9991, 886 1787; f 886 0534; e info@lakeshorehotel.com.bd; www.lakeshorehotel.com.bd. A true hidden gem in Gulshan. If you or your organisation can afford it, the service & facilities are almost comparable to the big 5-star venues, but lacks the impersonality of chain hotels. Full-load backup power, AC in all rooms, 24hr room service, broadband in all rooms, business centre & security make this certainly one of the best hotels in Gulshan. Bar recently opened. Also has a few rooms with kitchenettes. $$$$$$$

Westin Dhaka [120–1 D4] (235 rooms) Hse 1, Rd 45, Gulshan Av; ☎ 989 1988; f 989 6661; e reservations.dhaka@westin.com; www.westin.com/dhaka. Among 5-star hotels in Dhaka, this is the newest option. Early reviews indicate that the hotel is still getting its kinks out. Local aid organisations or embassies will probably be able to get the best rates. Has spa & swimming pool & broadband in all rooms. This is the best hotel in Gulshan, so if your business is up here, this is where you'll want to be. $$$$$$$

Asia Pacific Hotel [120–1 E2] (50 rooms) Hse 2, Rd 2, Blk K, Baridhara; ☎ 881 5461, 881 5632, 881 5697; e asiaphtl@citechco.net; www.asiapacifichotelbd.org. Business & fitness centre plus small conference facilities make this hotel pretty much the same as all the others. The only difference is the secluded location in Baridhara. Furnishings are starting to look a little retro, however. B/fast inc. $$$$$$

Bengal Inn [120–1 D7] (25 rooms) Hse 7, Rd 16, Gulshan 1; ☎ 988 0236, 988 0610; f 988 0274; m 01815 655558; e info@bengalinn.com; www.bengalinn.com. Self-labelled as a boutique hotel, the Bengal Inn's sparkling new facilities look pretty good on first glance. Rates seem expensive, however, so enquire about discounts. Internet, airport transfers & b/fast inc. $$$$$$

Hotel Lake Castle [120–1 C2] (60 rooms) Hse 1A, Rd 68/A, Gulshan 2; ☎ 881 2812, 881 4137;

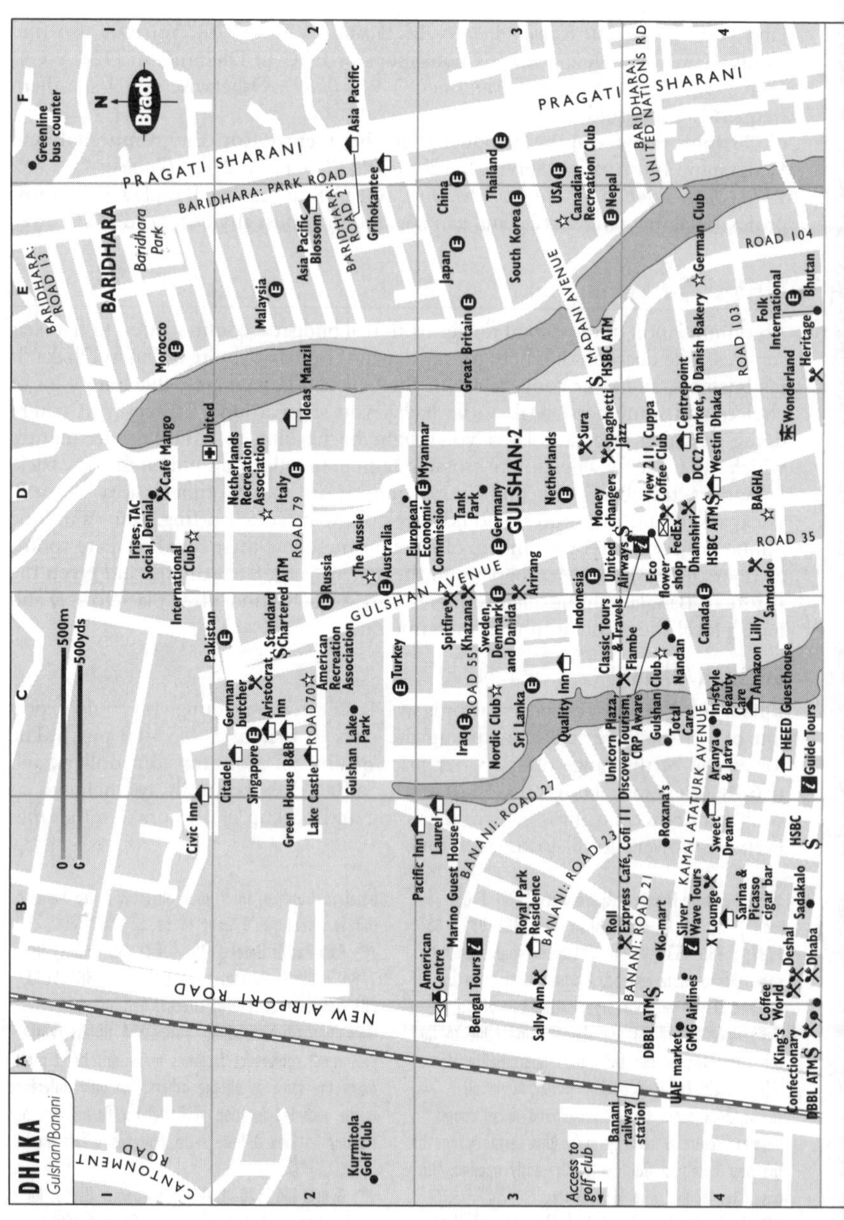

e htllake@agni.com; www.hotellakecastle.com. Impeccable service & facilities make this a standout in Gulshan. Not great for long-term stays, however. UN vehicles often seen parked out front. $$$$$$

Hotel Sarina [120–1 B4] (201 rooms) Hse 27, Rd 17, Banani; **t** 885 9604–10; **f** 988 9989; **e** sales@sarinahotel.com; www.sarinahotel.com. Banani's best upmarket hotel option, although sandwiched into the area's financial & university area. The rooftop restaurant does have good views. Also a pool on the top floor. Steep discounts offered to prestigious organisations. Unremarkable b/fast inc. $$$$$$

Hotel Sweet Dream [120–1 B4] (100 rooms) 60 Kamal Ataturk Av, Banani; **t** 987 3160; **e** reservation@hotelsweetdream.com; www.hotelsweetdream.com. Centrally located Banani

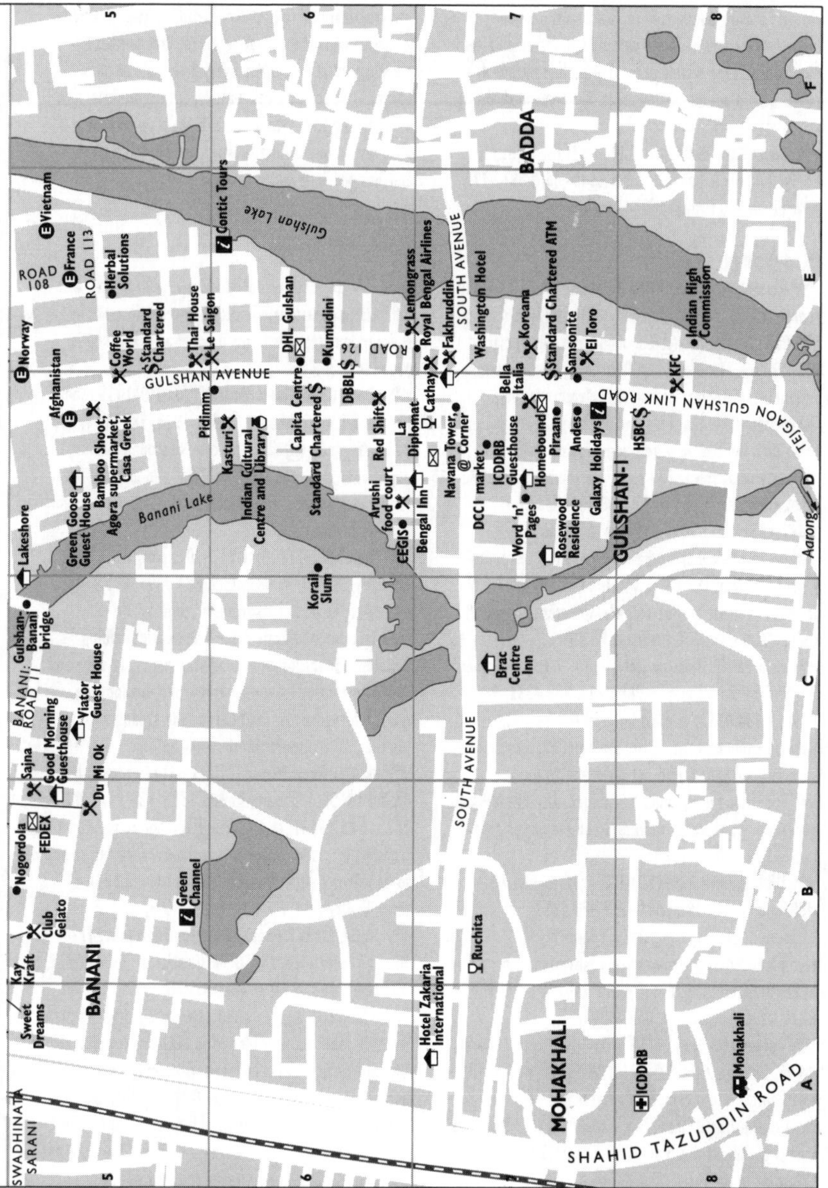

option, albeit seems expensive for the facilities – the typical combination of a small gym, wireless internet, AC rooms. $$$$$$

ICCDRB Guesthouse [120–1 D7] (7 rooms) Hse 12, Rd 12, Gulshan 1; ☎ 988 1073, 881 2029; e guesthouse@icddrb.org; www.icddrb.org. The guesthouse of Bangladesh's most famous diarrhoea research institution. Rooms offer wireless internet, satellite TV, en-suite bathrooms, full-load generator & a small fitness centre. Not bad value & certainly more comfortable than a hotel. 1 4-bed student room is available with approval from ICCDRB. B/fast inc. Recommended. $$$$$$

Ideas Manzil Guesthouse [120–1 D2] (4 rooms) Hse 19, Rd 79, Gulshan 2; ☎ 989 6791; e barrydison@yahoo.com; www.bisonhospitality.com. Dhaka's first heritage guesthouse. Owner Barry Ison promotes the richness of Bangladeshi culture. Restaurant has good homestyle versions of Thai & Indian food, served on a set menu basis at reasonable prices. Furnishings include 4-poster beds & antique sitting areas. Recommended. B/fast inc. $$$$$$

Royal Park Residence [120–1 B3] (60 rooms) Hse 85, Rd 25A, Blk A, Banani; 881 5945–46; f 881 5299; e reservations@royalpark-bd.com; www.royalpark-bd.com. One of Banani's best-kept secrets for accommodation. What's best is the little touches are taken care of at Royal Park. Everything could be more spacious (the rooms aren't massive) but the facilities, such as swimming pool, gym & sauna do make up for it. Also a good restaurant downstairs, which actually has a quite appetising-looking buffet. $$$$$$

Mid-range

Amazon Lilly Lake View Residence [120–1 C4] (20 rooms) Hse 28, Rd 19A, Banani; 881 2377, 881 2416, 989 0782; e lakeview@bol-online.com. The upmarket cousin of the Best Westen La Vinci. Small & intimate with restaurant, AC rooms, internet & conference facility. Otherwise little to make it stand out from the competition, other than the lake view from some rooms. $$$$$

Aristocrat Inn [120–1 C2] (21 rooms) Hse 12, Rd 68/A, Gulshan; 989 2327, 988 1014, 882 6617; f 882 1721; m 01817 019200; e a_inn@hotmail.com; www.aristocratinn.com. Steep discounts also available at this hotel, which doesn't have a lot of facilities to boast of, but simple is sometimes good. All rooms AC & transfer is included. $$$$$

Asia Pacific Blossom Hotel [120–1 E2] (36 rooms) 27 Park Rd, Baridhara; 988 0406, 988 4233, 988 9895; f 988 8512; e blossom@citech-bd.com; www.blossomhotel.net. Baridhara hotel offering facilities such as pool, gym & internet service in all rooms. Neighbourhood quite quiet & secluded. Also has full-load generator, so AC keeps running when the power goes out. $$$$$

BRAC Centre Inn [120–1 C7] (10 rooms) 75 Mohakhali Av; 988 6681–2; f 988 6683; e bracinn@bdmail.net. Doesn't come highly recommended as the rooms seem pushed into the bowels of the BRAC building, but if you're a visitor or guest of BRAC it's decent enough. $$$$$

Centerpoint Hotel [120–1 D4] (30 rooms) Hse 2A, Rd 95, Gulshan 2; 881 4211, 882 3583, 881 4458; e cpinn@bdcom.com; As a hotel that is extremely close to Gulshan 2 Circle, that's about the only thing that stands out about this place. Airport transfer & basic b/fast inc in the rates. $$$$$

Citadel Hotel [120–1 C2] (15 rooms) Hse 17, Rd 68/A, Gulshan 2; 988 2830, 988 4929; f 988 2463; e citadel@bangla.net. Not much stands out about this place, although a few rooms have nice balconies. Amenities are also not as good as neighbouring hotels & service appears lacklustre. $$$$$

Civic Inn [120–1 B1] (37 rooms) Hse 4/B, Rd 67, Gulshan; 881 7461, 881 7631, 881 6064; f 988 9589; m 01552 463275; e info@civicinn.com; www.civicinn.com. Secluded location for this hotel, with full backup generator, elevator & wireless internet in every room. Steep discounts on offer as everything is negotiable. $$$$$

Green Goose Guest House [120–1 D5] (15 rooms) Hse 30, Rd 38, Gulshan 2; 882 1928, 988 0050, 988 1283; e ggoose@citech-bd.com. Reasonable-value guesthouse in a good location of Gulshan 2. Has a few rooms with kitchens that could be more comfortable for long-term stays. $$$$$

Laurel Hotel [120–1 B3] (30 rooms) Hse 54, Rd 18, Blk J, Banani; 883 4009, 882 7399, 885 3747; f 883 4010; e info@laurelhotlbd.com; www.laurelhotelbd.com. Sounds amenable to doing discounts for corporate or long-stay guests. Save for odd smells emanating from the nearby lake, the location is quiet & tucked away. Facilities include broadband internet, AC & airport transfer. $$$$$

Marino Guest House [120–1 B3] (21 rooms) Hse 46, Rd 18, Blk J, Banani; 988 1585, 988 7173, 881 2028; f 882 9647; e marinobd@yahoo.com. Airport transfers included, rather tasteless decoration but seems to be willing to offer steep discounts from published rates. $$$$$

Netherlands Recreation Centre Guesthouse [120–1 D2] (15 rooms) Hse 33, Rd 74, Gulshan 2; 988 0931, 882 1892, 882 3877; e guesthouse@dutchclubdhaka.org; www.dutchclubdhaka.org. Definitely the best-value accommodation in Gulshan, as access to the centre's facilities is included with the price. With a bar, restaurant, swimming pool & tennis court, plus a library, pool room & TV room, this place is hard to beat. The only negative is that there is no gym at the club, but with the cheapest beer in town, you may not be exercising much anyway. $$$$$

Pacific Inn [120–1 B3] (22 rooms) Hse 12, Rd 18, Blk A, Banani; 988 7391, 988 4439; f 988 2326; e pacific@bol-online.com. Internet in rooms & transportation from the airport. Also known to do steep discounts for Grameen interns, making it actually a steal of a deal. $$$$$

Quality Inn [120–1 C3] (35 rooms) Hse 6, Rd 50, Gulshan 2; 988 1886, 988 1888, 883 2249; f 881

3220; m 01714 355500; e reservation@qualityinn.com.bd; www.qualityinn.com.bd. A well-located hotel with the basics in place. Bathtub & internet in every room, plus free airport pickup. $$$$$

Rosewood Residence [120–1 D7] (40 rooms) Hse 6/A, Rd 13, Gulshan 1; ☎ 988 0458, 989 0636–9; f 882 3784; e info@rosewoodresidence.com; www.rosewoodresidence.com. Decent facilities in a quiet location near the Gulshan lake. Has a gym, broadband in the room, & airport pickup service. $$$$$

Washington Hotel [120–1 D7] (75 rooms) 56 Gulshan Av, Rd 132; ☎ 885 1467–72; m 01817 046651; www.washingtonbd.com. Not exactly the White House, but definitely a good location in Gulshan. All rooms have split AC & there are gym facilities on site. Tour groups often stay here. Buffet b/fast inc. $$$$$

Good Morning Guesthouse [120–1 B5] Apt. B5, Rd 10/A, Hse 5, Blk H, Verona Verde bldg; ☎ 886 0050. e reservation@guesthouse-dhaka.com; www.guesthouse-dhaka.com. This guesthouse is actually an apt whose rooms are rented out on a daily basis or longer. Also a special place because the staff here are underprivileged youngsters, aged 16 & up. The guesthouse gives on-the-job training to these youths, who first attend a training course held by the development organisation that manages the guesthouse. Highly recommended, great value & a great place to stay for the knowledge that your money is helping fund the social development of the staff. $$$$

Viator Bangladesh Guest House [120–1 C5] Rd 7/A, Hse 60, Blk H, Banani; ☎ 987 2827, 987 1434; m 01717 925272; e viator@onenetbd.com, info@viatorbangladesh.org; www.viatorbangladesh.org. This simple & clean guesthouse deserves special mention because of its fair-trade & development activities. Well located within Banani & does the simple things well. B/fast inc & offers discounts to students. $$$$

Budget

HEED Guesthouse [120–1 C4] Hse 104, Rd 12, Blk E; ☎ 881 2390, 989 6028; e hlc@agni.com; www.heed-bangladesh.com. The HEED Language Centre in Banani also has a basic guesthouse in the same building. Meals are extra, but inexpensive. No hot water or backup power. Booking recommended – they are often full. $$$

Hotel Zakaria International [120–1 A7] (50 rooms) 35 Gulshan Rd, Mohakhali Wireless Gate, Mohakhali; ☎ 882 5003; e hzi@bdonline.com. Probably Gulshan's cheapest option; perfect for the capable adventurous traveller. AC & non-AC rooms available, plus a dark & seedy bar. $$$

Serviced apartments

Grihokantee [120–1 F2] (15 rooms) 4 Park Rd, Baridhara; ☎ 988 6645, 988 9409, 988 9452; f 9860141; m 01711 529082; e domus@accesstel.net; www.grihokantee.com. Extremely well designed & tasteful serviced apts in Baridhara, just adjacent to the Thai embassy. Apts come in various sizes & costs, but each has kitchen, laundry & a host of other facilities. Also a small gym dowmstairs. $$$$$$

Green House Bed & Breakfast [120–1 C2] (10 rooms) Apt 3W, Hse 10, Rd 68/A, Gulshan 2; ☎ 882 8411; m 01715 364721; e greenhousebd@hotmail.com; www.greenhouse-bd.com. Dhaka's only B&B venue, rather like a family homestay in some respects. Privacy is sometimes an issue but the at is very clean & there's a large kitchen in the lower flat. If no other guests you get the whole flat to yourself while enjoying all the eccentricities of Bengali home life. Credit cards not accepted. $$$$$

CENTRAL DHAKA

Upmarket

Dhaka Sheraton Hotel [124–5 C4] (272 rooms) 1 Minto Rd; ☎ 833 0001; f 831 2975; e sales@sheraton-dhaka.com; www.sheraton.com/dhaka. Dhaka's oldest 5-star property with established facilities & the most central location. A decision to stay here largely depends on where your meetings might be. If you need to be in Gulshan there are better options available. If you're dealing with government offices, however, this is the best place to be. $$$$$$$

Pan Pacific Sonargaon [124–5 B2] (277 rooms) 107 Kazi Nazrul Islam Av; ☎ 811 1005; f 912 7029; www.panpacific.com. There's something of a classic feel around the Sonargaon, which to some travellers could be described as simply aging or old. But a recent renovation has been done to counteract this, & it's certainly better located if your business is taking you to downtown Dhaka, so that might be the deciding factor. The regular range of 5-star facilities is available, including internet in the rooms, swimming pool & health club. $$$$$$$

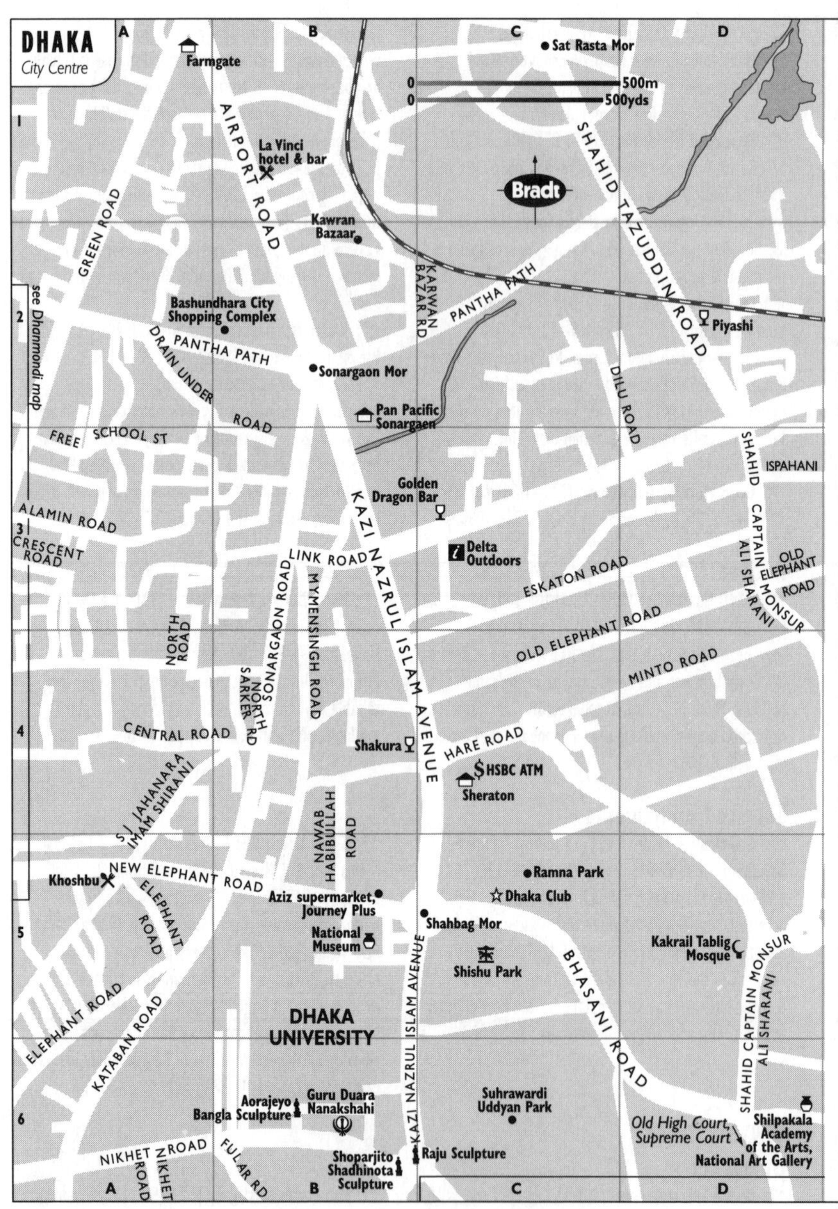

Hotel Orchard Plaza [124–5 F6] (70 rooms) 71 Nayapaltan (VIP Rd), Paltan, Motijheel; 933 0829, 933 1832, 933 3477, 934 7682; f 933 2369; e saleshop@aitlbd.net; www.hotelorchardplaza.com. Fairly professional choice if needing to be located in downtown Dhaka. Facilities make this a 3.5-star place, with internet in the room & a health club.Airport transfer & buffet b/fast inc. $$$$$$

Hotel Purbani [144–5 E1] (225 rooms) 1 Dilkusha C/A; 955 2229; f 956 2314; e purbani@bangla.net; www.hotelpurbani.com. Motijheel's aging starlet. It probably used to be the nicest hotel in town, say, 40 years ago, but nowadays things are just looking tired. $$$$$$

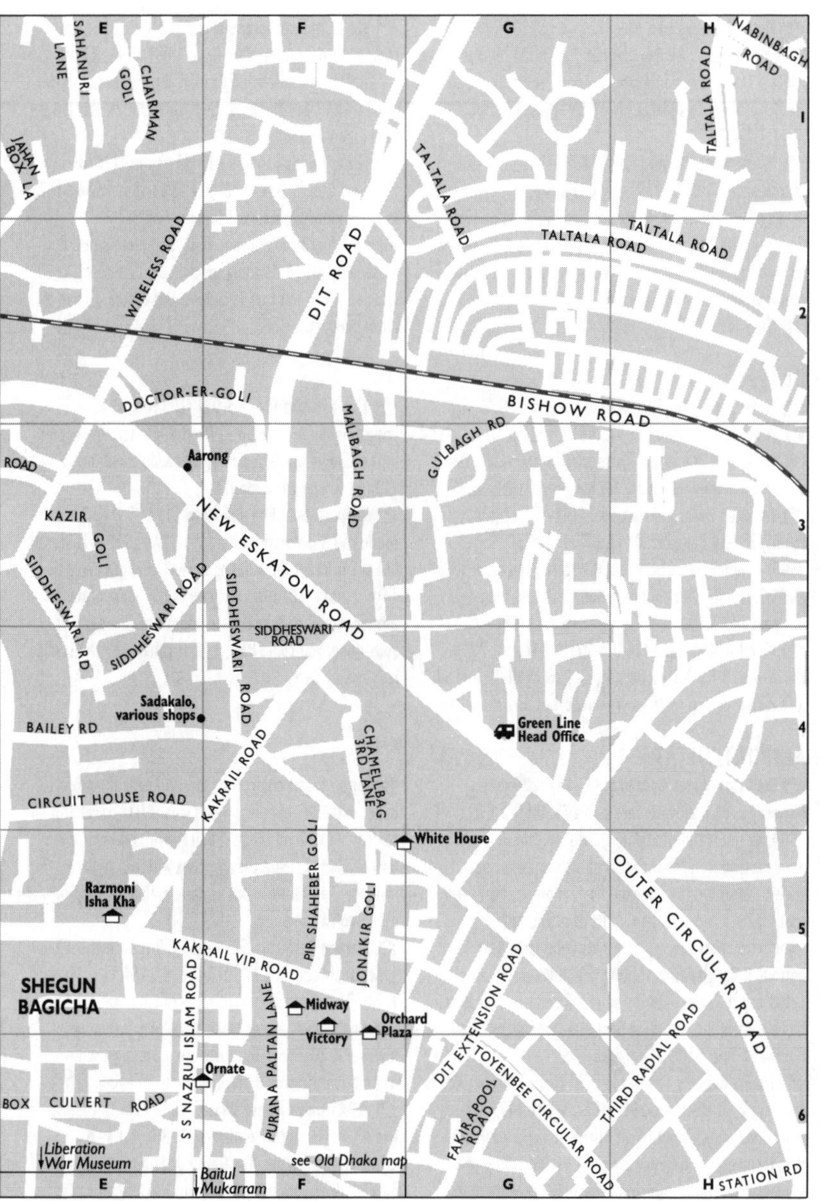

Mid-range

Hotel Victory [124–5 F5] (74 rooms) 30/A Nayapaltan (VIP Rd); 935 3055, 935 3088; f 935 3400; e info@hotelvictorybd.net; www.hotelvictorybd.net. Well-outfitted hotel, with similar facilities to the competition but slightly nicer & newer décor. Rates include transfer, internet, AC. Gym not so great, however. B/fast inc. $$$$$

Hotel Ornate [124–5 E6] (24 rooms) 30 Bijoynagar, Syed Nazrul Islam Sharani; 933 0219, 935 4434; f 933 4000; e ornate@dhaka.net. As one of the area's newest options, this property is true to its name. All rooms AC. Recommended & friendly service. Airport transfer & buffet b/fast inc. $$$$

Hotel Razmoni Isha Kha [124–5 E5] (70 rooms) 89/3 Nayapaltan (VIP Rd), Kakrail; ☎ 832 2426–9; f 831 5369; e razmoni@bdcom.com. Something of a seedy air about this place, which might just be your thing. $$$$

White House Hotel [124–5 F5] (45 rooms) 155 Shantinagar; ☎ 832 2973–6; f 831 7726; e seagull@agni.com. There's something good about the simplicity & reasonable prices of this hotel. All rooms AC with hot & cold water & internet service in the hotel room. Restaurant downstairs has extensive menu. $$$$

Hotel Midway International [124–5 F5] (66 rooms) 30 Nayapaltan (VIP Rd); ☎ 831 9315, 831 9345; f 831 5360; e hotelmid@aitlbd.net. Moderate budget option with clean rooms & the basic facilities. Has lower-priced non-AC rooms. $$$

Hotel Pacific [144–5 E1] (55 rooms) 120/B Motijheel C/A; ☎ 955 8148, 956 7583–85; f 956 5162; e resevation@hotelpacificdhaka.com; www.hotelpacificdhaka.com. Basic accommodation & reasonably priced. Nothing special but it's a good location if you want to be close to Old Dhaka & have a bit of comfort. $$$

Budget

Hotel Farmgate [124–5 A1] (82 rooms) 82 West Tejturi Bazaar, Farmgate; ☎ 912 0612, 911 8538; m 01712 848394; e hotelfarmgate@yahoo.com. One of Dhaka's best-value options for budget travellers. $$

Imperial Hotel International [144–5 D1] (50 rooms) 33–34 Bangabandhu Av; ☎ 955 4732, 955 9580; e hotelimp@bttb.net.bd. Pretty good value for an AC/hot-water budget hotel. Rough around the edges but passable. $$

Hotel Al Razzaque [144–5 D3] (40 rooms) 29/1 North–South Rd, Nazira Bazaar; ☎ 956 1990. Described as a rather devout male environment, but dirt cheap. $

Hotel Ramna [144–5 D2] (100 rooms) 45 Bangabandhu Av; ☎ 956 2279. Multiple styles of rooms in this budget place, including sgls & dbls with or without shared bathrooms. $

Kalpana Boarding and Hotel [144–5 D4] (56 rooms) 57 Shankhari Bazaar; m 01714 329481. Seems like the prices & the building haven't changed since the 16th century, when Old Dhaka was the heart of the former capital of Bengal. If rock-bottom cheap is just your thing, you could have a go at convincing the staff to let you stay here. $

AIRPORT/UTTARA

Radisson Water Garden [114–15] (204 rooms) Airport Rd, Dhaka Cantonment; ☎ 875 4555; f 875 4504; e reservations.dhaka@radisson.com; www.radisson.com/dhakabd. With its somewhat out-of-the-way location, the Radisson has a more exclusive feel that makes it a destination on its own. The hotel sometimes offers specials to expats (who have a work permit) & Bangladeshis seeking w/end luxury escapes. Call & ask the sales dept for more information. The hotel has all amenities, including pool, spa, broadband internet & fine dining. $$$$$$$

Dhaka Regency [114–15] (400 rooms) Airport Rd, Nukunja 2; ☎ 891 5463, 891 3912; f 891 1479; e www.dhakaregency.net. With British–Bangladeshi joint management, the Regency seems to be something of a homegrown venture, which may or may not work in its favour. Despite billing itself as '4 star', it has the look & feel of a 5-star facility, with prices being slightly cheaper than other 5-star choices. Its location near the airport might make it a big plus, which means less travel around the city. As with all things 'homegrown', however, there may be some unexpected surprises with a stay here – for instance the website is out of date, making it hard to even book a room online. $$$$$$

Garden Residence [114–15] (20 rooms) Hse 13, Rd 4, Sec 1, Uttara; ☎ 893 2076; f 893 2464; m 01713 162619; e admin@grdhaka.com. Guesthouse with decent looking facilities including internet & AC rooms, but rates are quite high, with negotiation this would become a better deal. $$$$$

RDRS Guest House Dhaka [114–15] (25 rooms) Hse 43, Rd 10, Sector 6, Uttara; ☎ 895 4384–6; e rdrs@bangla.net. The Dhaka guesthouse office of Rajshahi Division's most prominent NGO. Good value, training centre available, although not centrally located. $$$$

DHANMONDI

Ambala Inn [128–9 D7] (12 rooms) Hse 39, Rd 2, Dhanmondi; ☎ 861 9373, 861 0502; f 861 4490; e ambala@bangla.net; www.ambalainn.com. A moderate Dhanmondi accommodation option. Rooms are simple here & the hotel is in an excellent location in Dhanmondi. In-room refrigerator & AC. Airport & b/fast inc. $$$$

Ambrosia [128–9 E7] (12 rooms) Hse 17, Rd 3, Dhanmondi; ☎ 863 1409, 862 6237; f 966 8502; e ambrosia@bdmail.net. Spacious AC rooms within a garden area of an older Dhanmondi residence. Has a good feel. Internet available in the rooms. B/fast inc. $$$$

Roudrachhaya [128–9 C2] (10 rooms) 1/2 Asad Av, Blk A, Asad Gate, Mohammadpur; 812 3021; e hasab@bdmail.net; www.hasab.org. Spartan yet inexpensive guest rooms of the HIV/AIDS & STD Alliance Bangladesh (HASAB) offer the chance to learn about development work whilst supporting a local Bengali NGO. Close to major transport & the National Assembly. $$

Hotel Nidmahal [128–9 E4] (40 rooms) 105 Sukrabad, Mirpur Rd; 811 8452, 811 1750; e bankor@southnetbd.net. Cheap & close to the Dhanmondi area, although can be noisy at night. $

WHERE TO EAT

What follows is comprehensive coverage of Dhaka's upmarket eating options. Not all the options serve the dishes authentically and every menu has weaker and stronger choices. Just because a restaurant has higher prices doesn't always make the food more delicious, as there remains a sort of prestige associated with eating out in a fancy Dhaka restaurant. Nevertheless, there are some real standouts, and even a few places that manage to keep you coming back again and again, because of the great value and taste that they offer. These restaurants are recommended below.

If you're on an especially tight budget, you will find hundreds of restaurants serving mounds of rice alongside a thin *dal* and a rather oily curry. Eating this way will cost less than US$2 per day, even in Dhaka. Thankfully, this is not the case in Old Dhaka, where some of the city's most traditional food still lives on to this day.

GULSHAN/BANANI/UTTARA

South Asian

Khazana [120–1 D3] Hse 12, Rd 55, Gulshan Av; 882 1965; 12.00–15.30, 18.00–22.30. Authentic Indian food served in very comfortable surroundings. *Chana* salad recommended for vegetarians. $$$$$

Heritage [120–1 E4] Hse 10, Rd 109, Gulshan 2; 882 9359; 12.30–15.30, 18.00–22.30. Billing itself as Bangla-fusion cuisine, this restaurant is the product of British-Bangladeshi celebrity chef Tommy Miah, whose face beams out from a few billboards in the city. The Sylheti chef has attained a lot of fame in the UK, & opened this restaurant to bring the cuisine back to its roots. The restaurant receives mixed reviews from diners, however. $$$$

Sajna [120–1 C5] Hse 14, Rd 11, Banani; 881 1684; 12.30–15.30, 18.30–22.30. Dhaka's best variety of *dosas* (south-Indian style crispy pancakes). Otherwise decent northern & southern Indian food served in sparkling surroundings. $$$$

Kasturi [120–1 D6] Hse 25, Rd 24, Gulshan; 881 8548; 12.00–22.30. Also not a bad destination for just Bangla food, popular as a party/meeting centre & does a good job of catering for parties. $$$

View 2II [120–1 D4] 1/F Hse 11, Rd 46, Gulshan 2; m 01912 000339; 11.00–22.30. Kebab! Kebab! Kebab! Need more explanation than that? Prices could be better, but meat eaters will be in heaven. $$$

Arushi Food Court [120–1 D6] Hse 10, Rd 23, Gulshan 1; m 01720 106164, 01712 004400; 12.00–15.30, 18.00–22.00. With an open-air courtyard & your choice between several restaurants, this is one of Gulshan's most unique eating venues. You can choose *dosas* from Chaat Street itself, or choose basic Thai, Indonesian or Mexican meals from one of the other shops surrounding the courtyard. There is even an outlet of Paan Supari, where betel nut connoisseurs go to try some special varieties. Great value & highly recommended. Hard to find as there is no streetside sign. Look for the open doorway leading into a courtyard with some tables. $$

Dhaba [120–1 B4] Hse 100, Rd 11, Blk C, Banani; 11.30–22.00. The authors' personal favourite in Dhaka, squarely for its special *phuchkas*. The *dahi* variety, which is topped with yoghurt & freshly chopped tomatoes, onions & *chaat*, is healthy, vegetarian & delicious. $$

Dhanshiri [120–1 D4] Hse 32A, Rd 45, Gulshan 2; 988 2125; 07.00–24.00. Reasonably good Bangla food, even though the best Bangla food is always served at a friend's house. $$

Fakhruddin [120–1 E7] Gulshan 1 Circle; 12.00–22.00. This restaurant is famous for its *biriyanis* – a heaping rice dish cooked with onions, spices & chunks of meat. If you're trying to acquire a taste for the heavy dish, try this place out. Fakhruddin, the original proprietor, has now become a household name for the dish. $$

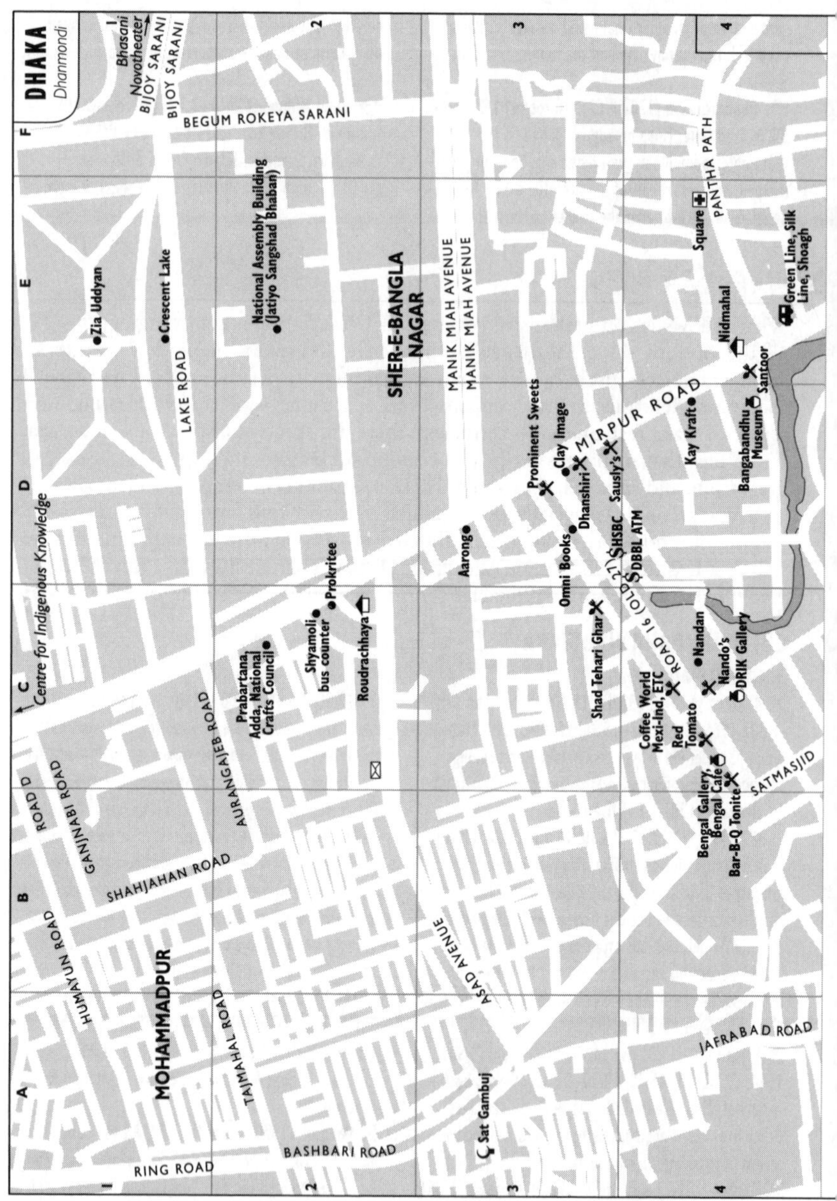

Asian

Arirang [120–1 D3] Hse 3, Rd 51, Gulshan 1; 989 6453, 989 6460; 12.00–15.00, 18.00–22.30. Upmarket Korean food that is of passable quality, & has sushi available too. Beer-drinking, tofu-eating vegetarians seem to like this place. $$$$$

Corner Thai [120–1 D7] 4th Fl, Navana Tower, Gulshan 1 Circle; 986 2588, 885 3851; 12.30–22.30. The best atmosphere for Thai food in town, although some debate whether Thai House is more authentic. Good nonetheless. $$$$$

Le Saigon [120–1 E5] 54 Gulshan Av; 882 0523; 12.00–15.00, 18.00–23.00. Authentic Vietnamese cuisine that comes highly rated from well-heeled locals. Definitely good for a treat. $$$$$

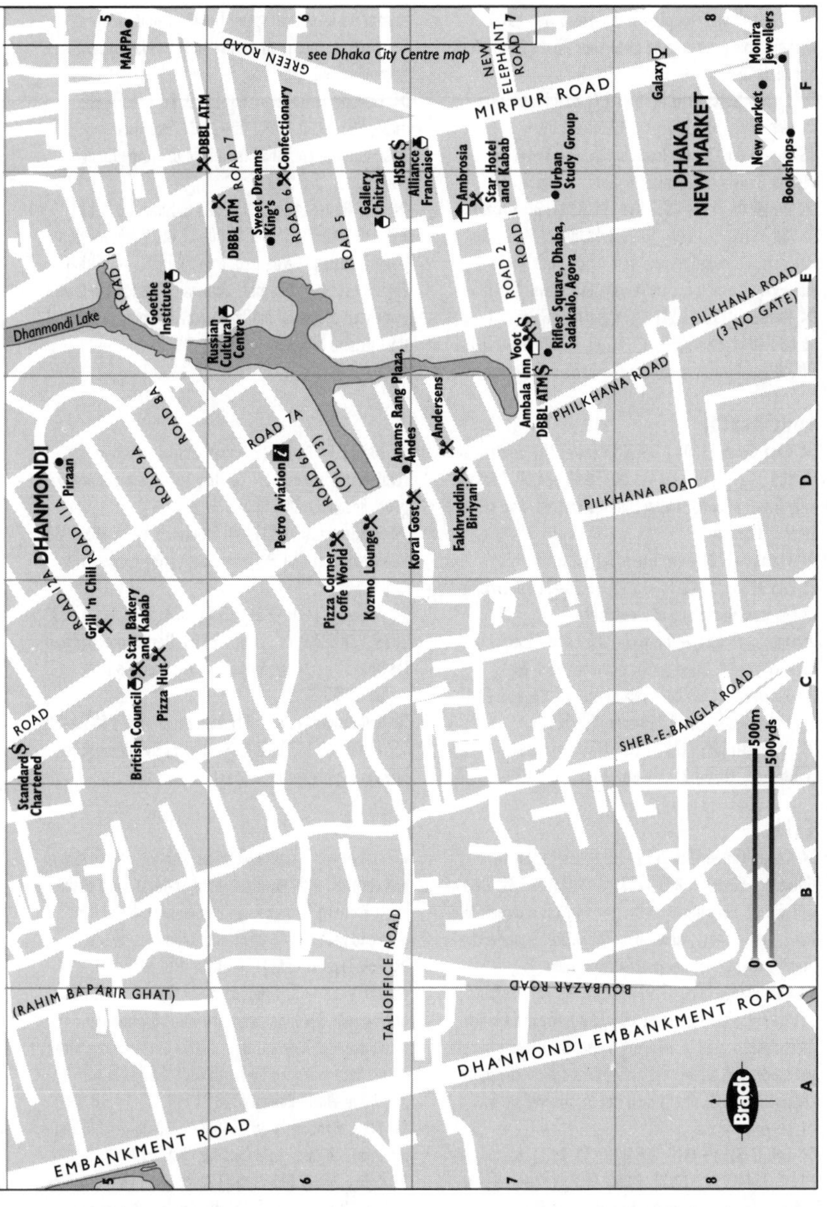

✕ **Samdado** [120–1 D4] Hse 27, Rd 35; ☎ 882 8499; ⏰ 12.00–15.00, 18.00–23.00. Dhaka's one & only Japanese restaurant, which for most of the local expats is a godsend. Evaluated by a regular standard of Japanese food, Samdado falls slightly short, but given the fact it's Bangladesh, the sushi here still tastes like manna from heaven. Sake sometimes available too. $$$$$

✕ **Sura** [120–1 D3] Hse 2, Rd 90, Gulshan 2; ☎ 882 1043; ⏰ 12.00–15.00, 18.00–22.00. Upmarket Korean fare served in nice surrounds. Also has *shabu-shabu*, a kind of Japanese fondue dish, on offer. $$$$$

✕ **Bamboo Shoot** [120–1 D5] 1/F RM Centre, 101 Gulshan Av; ☎ 988 8307, 882 1497; ⏰ 12.30–15.00, 18.00–22.30. Dhaka's best Chinese restaurant. With mainland Chinese management, those who have travelled to China will find this place a real treat. Also has 3 karaoke rooms for singing away your Dhaka blues. Book ahead. $$$$

✕ **Cathay Restaurant** [120–1 E7] Rd 133, Gulshan 1; ☎ 881 1793, 989 5087; ⏲ 12.00–15.00, 18.00–22.00. Chinese food that is a cut above the regular Bangla-fied Chinese options. $$$$

✕ **Du Mi Ok** [120–1 B5] Hse 154, Rd 11, Blk E, Banani; ☎ 988 5512. ⏲ 12.00–15.00 & 18.00–22.00. Korean fare that gets mixed reviews from locals, but if you're staying in Banani it is a convenient alternative. $$$$

✕ **Koreana** [120–1 E7] Hse 5, Rd 136, Gulshan 1; ☎ 882 4044, 989 9827; ⏲ 11.00–23.00. Beer, *soju*, BBQ & good prices make this Gulshan's best Korean restaurant (expect to spend Tk600–1,000 each). Definitely a place to make the meat eaters happy. Recommended. $$$$

✕ **Lemongrass** [120–1 E6] Hse 2, Rd 126; ☎ 988 3626, 881 6736; ⏲ 12.00–23.00. Expensive food in a so-so atmosphere. Good for a kind of escape though, nonetheless. $$$$

✕ **Thai House** [120–1 E5] 52B Gulshan Av; ☎ 882 2757; ⏲ 12.00–15.00, 18.00–22.00. While the décor leaves a little to be desired, true cuisinarts know that Thai House offers the most authentic Thai food in town, evidenced by the rotund Thai woman coming in & out of the kitchen. $$$$

Continental

✕ **Casa Greek** [120–1 D5] RM Centre, 101 Gulshan Av; ☎ 885 3447; ⏲ 12.00–15.00, 18.00–24.00. Dhaka's only Greek offering that gets mixed reviews. Also serves steaks. $$$$

✕ **Flambe** [120–1 C4] Hse 6, Rd 50, Gulshan 2; ☎ 885 3835; ⏲ 12.30–15.30, 18.30–22.30. Sizzling dishes have something of a notoriety around south Asia, & this particular restaurant specialises in it. Good for local-quality beef, & the lunch buffet has been recommended. Connoisseurs might be disappointed, however. $$$$

✕ **Spaghetti Jazz** [120–1 D3] 2/F Alam Arcade, 43 Gulshan Av (On Rd 91); ☎ 882 2062; ⏲ 12.30–15.00, 18.30–22.30. Authentic Italian cuisine served in comfortable atmosphere. Sizzling steaks & pizza pretty good. Recommended. $$$$

✕ **Spitfire** [120–1 C3] NWF8 Gulshan Av; ☎ 885 1930. Imported steaks for the true meat-eating crowd. $$$$$

✕ **X Lounge** [120–1 B4] 35 Kamal Ataturk Av; ☎ 882 2025, 988 8685; ⏲ 11.00–24.00. Destination hangout for Dhaka's party set. Sometimes has dance & food nights. $$$$

✕ **Bella Italia** [120–1 D7] 35 Gulshan Av; ☎ 885 1479. ⏲ 12.00–22.30. Good for your pizza fix, although the pizza is slightly better at Spaghetti Jazz. $$$

Cafés

✕ **Cuppa Coffee Club** [120–1 D4] Hse 11, Rd 46, Gulshan 2 Circle; ☎ 885 1727; ⏲ 10.00–22.30. Decent coffee, but more importantly, free wireless internet. Also has rotating photo exhibitions. The salads & sandwiches aren't bad, but not necessarily great value. $$$$

✕ **Café Mango** [120–1 D1] Hse 3A, Rd 72, Gulshan 2; m 01711 533531; ⏲ 11.00–22.00. Great for lunch meetings. Located in an aging house, the décor is simple yet modern, & serves reasonably priced & good-quality continental food, all of which can be followed up with a cappuccino. $$$

✕ **Cofi II Banani** [120–1 B4] Hse 34, Rd 21, Banani; m 01713 364499; ⏲ 10.30–24.00. Dhaka's newest & best coffee house, with an atmosphere that feels like an upmarket café anywhere else in the world. $$$

✕ **Red Shift** [120–1 D6] 5/F Bays Galleria, 57 Gulshan Av; ☎ 883 3473; e info@radiuscentre-bd.com; www.radiuscentre-bd.com; ⏲ 10.00–22.30. Gulshan coffee house with a fantastic terrace that affords splendid views of the city. The café is the centrepiece of the Radius Centre, a multi-purpose business & conference facility with the most modern amenities available in the entire city, without paying 5-star hotel prices. Also has an auditorium hall outfitted with movie projector, showing some of the latest Western & south Asian blockbusters. Email the centre to get on their movie notification list. $$$

✕ **Roll Express Café** [120–1 B4] Hse 34, Rd 21, Banani; m 01720 100016; ⏲ 11.00–22.30; Great *parata* rolls & a wide range of *chaats* & *phuchka*. Reminiscent of Kolkata street snacks but definitely nicer décor. Recommended for lunch &/or snacks. $$$

✕ **Coffee World Banani** [120–1 B4] 1/F Hse 90, Rd 11, Blk C, Banani; ☎ 883 6488; ⏲ 10.00–24.00. Chain places are so remarkably similar. $$

✕ **Coffee World Del Vista** [120–1 D5] 116 Gulshan Av; ☎ 883 7177; ⏲ 08.00–23.00. Prices reflect the calm environment more than they do the quality coffees. Pass on the food as well. $$

✕ **Sally Ann** [120–1 B3] Hs 96, Rd 23, Banani; ☎ 988 2836; ⏲ 09.00–19.00 Sat, 08.00–19.00 Sun–Thu, closed Fri. Has whipped cream, good tea & sometimes even sour cream too. Also serves waffles topped with cream that have been a hit among respite-seeking expats. Attached is an upmarket handicrafts shop. $$

Miscellaneous

✗ **El Toro** [120–1 E6] Hse 1, Rd 138, Gulshan 1; ☎ 885 2863; ⌚ 11.30–22.30. Excellent Mexican cuisine served in an imitation Mexican environment. On deeper reflection, the food here is like a Bengali remixed version of Mexican favourites. $$$$

✗ **German Butcher** [120–1 C2] Rd 69, Gulshan 2; ⌚ 09.00–12.00, 15.00–18.00. The 'German butcher' is what local expats use to refer to the Thai-German couple who sell imported cheese, sausages, meats & other treats from their private residence on Rd 69, just up the street from the American Club. Bring lots of taka as this is where you'll find the best meat in town. $$$$

✗ **H Kabir & Company** [114–15] 12 Abbas Garden, New Airport Rd, Mohakhali; ☎ 988 1936; ⌚ 10.00–17.00 Sat–Thu. If you're not one of the lucky ones with a diplomatic or club connection to booze, head to Kabir's for your home alcoholic requirements. Prices are sky high because it's duty paid, but at least you can take away. Hang around long enough & your Bengali friends will ask you to go to the store for them. $$$$

✗ **Club Gelato** [120–1 B5] Hse 50, Rd 11, Blk F, Banani; ☎ 881 5819; ⌚ 10.30–23.30. Real gelato comes as a real treat after a meal on Rd 11. $$$

✗ **KFC** [120–1 D8] Hse 10A, Rd 142, Gulshan 1; ☎ 989 4662; ⌚ 11.00–24.00. Needs no explanation, other than to say this is the real thing, unlike the dozens of other fried chicken shops in town. $$$

✗ **King's Confectionery** [120–1 A4] Hse 25, Rd 11, Blk F, Banani; ☎ 989 4312; ⌚ 07.30–22.30. Recommended for its brown & sugar-free breads. $$

✗ **O Danish Bakery** [120–1 D4] DCC Market 2, Gulshan 2; ☎ 988 0903; ⌚ 08.00–20.00. Freshly baked brown bread available here, but come before 11.00 as it sells out, or call ahead & reserve yourself a loaf. $$

DHANMONDI

South Asian

✗ **Santoor** [128–9 E4] Hse 2, Rd 11, Dhanmondi; ☎ 812 3336; ⌚ 12.00–15.00 & 18.00–22.00. Dhanmondi's best choice for Indian food, although not really worth going out of your way for it. $$$$

✗ **Bar-B-Q Tonite** [128–9 C4] Hse 58, Rd 16 (new), Dhanmondi; ☎ 811 2634; ⌚ 18.00–22.00. Despite branding itself the best kebab place in the subcontinent, some might beg to differ. Still has a decent outdoor eating area. $$$

✗ **Voot** [128–9 E7] Hse 35, Rd 2, Dhanmondi; ☎ 865 2194; ⌚ 12.00–22.30. A theme restaurant where the waiters try to scare you into eating makes this a really interesting experience. The food menu is also extensive, & even includes a low-calorie section. $$$

✗ **Adda** [128–9 C2] 2/8 Sir Syed Rd, Mohammadpur; ☎ 914 0812; ⌚ 08.00–20.00. A women-only eating venue on the top floor of Prabartana, where men are welcome but only as the guests/friends of women. A peaceful escape. Sign written only in Bangla. $$

✗ **Bengal Café Ltd** [128–9 C4] Hse 275/F, Rd 16 (new); ☎ 812 3115; ⌚ 10.00–15.00, 18.00–22.00. Great-value restaurant attached to the Bengal Gallery. Décor is relaxed & the food not bad. $$

✗ **Dhaba** [128–9 E7] 4/F Rifles Sq; ⌚ 12.00–22.00. Dhanmondi branch of this Bangladesh institution. The *dahi phuchka* & *gorom Phuchka* can't be recommended enough! $$

✗ **Dhanshiri** [128–9 D3] 2nd Fl, Orchid Plaza, Hse 2, Rd 28, Dhanmondi; ☎ 913 6722; ⌚ 11.30–22.00. Incredibly dark branch restaurant of the more well-known partner in Gulshan. Good specifically for Bangla food. $$

✗ **Khoshbu Restaurant** [124–5 A5] 1st Fl, 118/3 Elephant Rd; ☎ 967 5217; ⌚ 09.00–22.00. Delicious Bengali food that has earned it fame as one of Dhaka's best. Great if you're in the New Market area. $$

✗ **Korai Gost** [128–9 D7] 1st Fl, Hse 55/A, Rd 4/A, Sat Masjid Rd, Dhanmondi; m 01715 317116; ⌚ 07.00–24.00. With a range of well-cooked Bangla favourites, this place is showing the wear & tear of its popularity. Mostly university students crowding around. $$

✗ **Shad Tehari Ghar** [128–9 C3] 2/4 Blk C, Lalmatia; ☎ 911 8695; m 01195 057002; ⌚ 12.00–15.00, 18.30–22.00. Run almost entirely by women, this little restaurant still has Bangladesh's best chicken *reshmi kebab* & is a real hidden secret. Also serves tasty *chatpoti* & garlic *naans*. $$

✗ **Star Bakery and Kebab Ghar** [128–9 C5] 754 Sat Masjid Rd, Dhanmondi; ☎ 812 3549; ⌚ 12.00–23.00. Wildly popular *naan* & kebab place, if the crowds & lack of empty tables are any evidence. $$

✗ **Star Hotel and Kebab** [128–9 E7] Hse 16, Rd 2, Dhanmondi; ☎ 967 6847; ⌚ 07.00–23.30. Newer Dhanmondi branch of this Dhaka institution. You may be ushered upstairs to the more 'exclusive' section, but if you want kebab & *naans*, sit downstairs. $$

Continental

✕ **Nando's** [128–9 C4] Hse 43, Rd 16 (new), Dhanmondi; ☎ 812 2720, 812 1572; ⌚ 12.00–23.00. This international chicken chain has a venue all the way down in Dhanmondi & the locals love it. People going across town to eat here is not unheard of. The décor & atmosphere are a cut above the local shops, but did you come to Dhaka to eat at Nando's? The local roast chicken is pretty good too, to be honest. $$$$

✕ **Pizza Corner** [128–9 D6] Nilu Sq, Hse 75, Rd 5/A; ☎ 912 4079; ⌚ 10.00–24.00. Slightly cheaper prices than its more well-known competition. $$$$

✕ **Pizza Hut** [128–9 C5] 754 Sat Masjid Rd, Dhanmondi; ☎ 913 3576, 913 3599, 913 3750; ⌚ 11.00–23.00. When an area gets a Pizza Hut you know that it has 'made it' as an eating-out destination. Too bad it represents a decline in the quality of the options out there! $$$$

✕ **Kozmo Lounge** [128–9 D6] 3/F, Bikalpa Tower, Hse 74, Rd 5/A; ☎ 966 8773; ⌚ 11.00–22.00. When the items are actually available, it's not a bad place to eat. Also has band nights & poetry readings, making this a pretty interesting cultural destination when something is on. $$$

✕ **Red Tomato** [128–9 C4] Hse 50, Rd 27 (old), Dhanmondi; ☎ 811 7220; ⌚ 12.00–22.30. Pizzas, Thai, Indian & Bengali make this all-rounder a place that can please all. Also a pleasant upstairs eating area. $$$

Miscellaneous

✕ **Mexi-Ind** [128–9 C4] 2/F Hse 40, Rd 16 (new); ☎ 814 1738; ⌚ 12.00–16.00, 19.00–22.00. Who would have thought Mexican & Indian cuisine shared so many similarities? But in fact, they do quite well, according to people who have tried this place. $$$$

✕ **Andersen's** [128–9 D7] Hse 54, Rd 3A, Dhanmondi; ☎ 966 9689; ⌚ 10.00–24.00. Foreign joint-venture ice-cream shop. $$

✕ **Coffee World Dhanmondi** [128–9 C4] Concord Royal Court, Hse 275G, Rd 16 (new); ☎ 914 0089; ⌚ 10.00–20.00. Prices reflect the calm environment more than they do the quality coffees. Pass on the food as well. $$

✕ **Coffee World Nilu Square** [128–9 D6] Nilu Sq, Hse 75, Rd 5/A, Sat Masjid Rd, Dhanmondi; ☎ 912 4079; ⌚ 10.00–24.00. $$

✕ **Prominent Sweets** [128–9 D3] Dhanmondi Tower, Hse 4A, Rd 16 (new), Dhanmondi; ⌚ 11.00–23.00. Pricy but superior quality *mishti*, usually sold by the kilo. $$

✕ **Sausly's** [128–9 D3] Shop G6-7, Hse 1, Rd 15, Mirpur Rd, Dhanmondi; ☎ 912 6821; ⌚ 09.00–22.00. Snack shop that's OK for a cheap quick fix of something to eat. $$

PURAN DHAKA Dhaka's earliest eating traditions still manage to persist in the various remote corners of Old Dhaka – consider yourself forewarned: the following places are extremely hard to find. As you wander the streets you'll eventually notice a few unique items. A particularly delicious snack is the freshly baked *bakor khanni*, which is a flaky biscuit made in small tandoor ovens. If you're lucky you may even find a cheese variety as well. Other Old Dhaka meals include a range of *biriyanis* and *bhartas*, and at night the street is a furore of kebab-making activity.

✕ **Haji Biriyani** [144–5 C3] Bangsal Rd; ⌚ 12.00–22.00. This *biriyani* restaurant is a real Old Dhaka institution. At meal times there is a massive queue that stretches out the door. Although the Western palette might not detect the subtle differences between this & other *biriyanis*, the fact that it's served in a *shal pata* – something like a banana leaf – is quite innovative. $$

✕ **Star Kebab** [144–5 D4] Thatari Bazaar; ⌚ 11.00–23.00. Something of a late-night institution in Old Dhaka. Once all the store-owners have closed up shop, many of them congregate here to take their late evening meals before heading to sleep. *Biriyani*, & lots of it, is on offer. $$

✕ **Bailey Road Snack Stalls** [124–5 E4] Bailey Rd. This area also has a wide variety of street snacks, & may be worth checking out during Eid. Bailey Rd is closer to Kakrail & lies outside Old Dhaka. The Pithaghar restaurant does special varieties of rice-flour ingredient (*pitha*) during its seasonal time in winter. $

✕ **Chowk Bazaar Snack Stalls** [144–5 B3] Chawk Bazaar. Snack connoisseurs should make a visit to this place if they're in the Old Town, & especially in the early afternoons of Ramadan, where the greatest variety of *iftar* snacks are on offer. If you're not tolerant of fried food, then give this place a miss. $

✕ **Hotel Al Razzaque** [144–5 D3] 29/1 Nazira Bazaar, North South Rd; ☎ 956 6412; ⌚ 07.00–23.00.

Reliable cheap eats in Old Dhaka, a good place to head for after shopping in Bangsal Rd for rickshaw art. Especially famous for its mutton roasts. $

✕ **Nirob Hotel** [144–5 B3] 113/2 Nasimuddin Rd; ☎ 730 0149, 730 0265; m 01711 377217; ⊕ 12.00–22.30. Recommended for its excellent Bangla food. Not extremely clean but packed with crowds. Popular for multiple varieties of *bharta* (mashed vegetables), which should be especially pleasing for the vegetarians. $$

ENTERTAINMENT AND NIGHTLIFE

Entertainment options are rather poorly advertised in Dhaka despite the fact there is an absolute plethora of events to attend. Newspapers, the ideal source for such events, tend to provide coverage only after the event has happened. A starting point is to ask your colleagues or Bangladeshi friends what events are going on in the city as the most interesting events tend only to be spread by word of mouth. Otherwise you could try browsing www.somewhereindhaka.net to see if they have anything that takes your fancy.

The international jet-set might find Dhaka to be a bit of a letdown in terms of nightlife. But the reality is that there are many local drinking venues and events happening underneath the surface, but rarely are these places advertised or discussed openly. Depending on which way the political winds are blowing you could find a full-blown nightclub having a hip-hop party one evening or a near-complete shutdown of all drinking venues due to a temporary ban on imported alcohol.

LOCAL BARS Local bars generally open from the early evening, after work, but are always closed on Friday in lieu of religious concerns.

🍸 **Ruchita Bar** [120–1 B7] Parjatan Bldg, Mohakhali Av. Parjatan's in-house drinking facility. Does off-sales at expensive prices. $$$$

🍸 **Picasso Cigar Bar** [120–1 B4] Top Fl, Hotel Sarina, Hse 27, Rd 17, Banani. A men's cigar bar with great views of the city. Alcohol quantities vary depending on the prevailing political moods of the day. $$$

🍸 **Galaxy Hotel and Bar** [128–9 F8] New Market. Located down a dark alleyway with a barely noticeable sign, the Galaxy is a dark & smoky cave where your eyes will burn after 20mins, especially as you try & watch wrestling on the big-screen TV. For some, this might be considered atmospheric. $$

🍸 **Golden Dragon** [124–5 C3] 52/7 New Eskaton Rd. Also a reported drinker's den, so if you're going to check it out you may want to leave the female company behind. $$

🍸 **La Diplomat** [120–1 D7] Hse 7, Rd 20, Gulshan 1. Don't expect to be rubbing shoulders with any French ambassadors here. The 'Dip', like most other Bengali bars, is a smoke-filled darkened room where many of its patrons would rather not be recognised too easily. Definitely an experience, nonetheless. Beers cost upwards of Tk150, & 'tots', which are single-ounce servings of gin, vodka or whisky, are available from Tk70 to Tk150. Female patrons may feel slightly uncomfortable but with male company should be fine. $$

🍸 **La Vinci Hotel** [124–5 B1] 54 Kawran Bazaar; ☎ 912 4401. A bar on the top floor with apparently good views, but best to call & see if it's actually serving at the moment. The hotel itself gets terrible reviews from travellers. $$

🍸 **Piyashi Bar and Restaurant** [124–5 D2] Mogh Bazaar, Shaheed Tazuddin Rd. A haven for criminals & robbers. An interesting place to have a drink, although if you smell a police raid it would be best to steer clear! $$

🍸 **Shakura Bar** [124–5 B4] Opposite Sheraton Hotel. Long-running bar hidden away down a dark alley near the Sheraton. Use only in case of emergency. $$

MEMBERSHIP CLUBS Each of the foreign clubs requires club membership, which can be something of a nuisance to pick up depending on your nationality or your connections. Otherwise, knowing a few other friendly foreigners will help you out as most members can sign in guests. Once you're in, you purchase cash coupons to pay for your drinks. Most of the city's social life revolves around these clubs, which many people use to 'escape' the reality of Bangladesh. The never-ending circuit of parties and drinks does mean you'll often meet people who, despite having lived in Bangladesh for several months, have yet to leave Dhaka.

If you've done a good job networking with Bangladeshi people, however, you'll soon find yourself invited to one of the local memberships clubs (Dhaka, Gulshan and Uttara clubs) where the most elite rub shoulders.

☆ **BAGHA** [120–1 D4] Hse 17, Rd 44, Gulshan 2; ☎ 881 4644. Dhaka's most friendly expat club, with something of a pub feel about it. You need to be an EU national or work for a British aid organisation in Bangladesh to join. Most of the biggest drinkers hang out at this club but pay prices in pounds sterling for the privilege. Organises parties on a regular basis because it's not a diplomatic-sponsored club. $$$$

☆ **Dhaka Club** [124–5 C5] 1 Moulana Abdul Hamid Khan Bhashani Rd; ☎ 861 9180–4. The real old-school Dhaka wealth & political power call this recreation club home. An invitation here means you've made it into Bangladesh's most elite local circles. If you're invited as a guest, dress appropriately (covered shoes & a collared shirt). Foreigners can also become members for a price of Tk25,000 per year, so we've heard. $$$$

☆ **Gulshan Club** [120–1 C4] Hse 2, Rd 50, Gulshan 2; ☎ 882 7440. Club for the newest money Bangladesh has to offer. Facilities also include a guesthouse, pool & restaurants. Appropriate dress is required, membership restricted to Bangladeshi nationals $$$$

☆ **American Recreation Association** [120–1 C2] Hse 13, Rd 69, Gulshan 2; ☎ 882 1025. Dhaka's best b/fast &/or brunch. Does not accept members from other clubs without diplomatic associations, however. $$$

☆ **Canadian Recreation Club** [120–1 E3] UN Rd, Baridhara (next to American Embassy); ☎ 988 1208, 989 5223, 989 5139. A massive club with gorgeous facilities, but strangely, almost no people using it, let alone Canadians. If only Canadian taxpayers were to get wind of this. $$$

☆ **German Club** [120–1 E4] Hse 24, Rd 104, Gulshan 2; ☎ 882 7440. Haven't heard of many events happening here that engage the rest of the Dhaka expat community. $$$

☆ **International Club** [120–1 D1] Hse 5, Rd 74, Gulshan 2; ☎ 988 1712. Biggest melting pot of a club in Dhaka. Offers temporary memberships for short-term stays, regardless of nationality (US$75 joining fee, US$75 per month, 3-month validity). Wed barbecue nights popular. $$$

☆ **Nordic Club** [120–1 C3] Hse 18, Rd 55, Gulshan 2; ☎ 882 1331. Also another more ambitious & open expat club. Has food that is a cut above some of the other venues. $$$

☆ **The Aussie** [120–1 D2] Rd 83–84, Gulshan 2; ☎ 881 3105. Thu BBQ nights popular among the expat crowd – could it be Australia's reputation for meat? Something also of a drinker's den. $$$

☆ **Uttara Club** [114–15] Hse 6, Rd 9, Sec 1, Uttara; ☎ 891 2600. Uttara's drinking venue for the moneyed Bengali masses. Also has a guesthouse, tennis court & swimming pool. $$$

☆ **Netherlands Recreation Association** [120–1 D2] Hse 33, Rd 74, Gulshan 2; ☎ 882 3877. Also known as the Dutch Club, this is the quietest venue of the lot, but also offers the cheapest beer – Heineken, which is of course produced in Holland. $$

GALLERIES AND CULTURAL INSTITUTIONS The cultural life of Dhaka is much richer than people think, despite the fact that local cultural events are distinctly hard to find out about. Thankfully, there are some institutions that do use the benefit of technology to help spread ideas and information. Once again, the best way to find out what's going on is to ask work colleagues or to call. Some institutions have email lists where, if you can get yourself registered, you would receive notice about the events ahead of time.

Alliance Francaise [128–9 F7] Hse 26, Rd 3, Dhanmondi; ☎ 967 5249; e info@afdacca.com; ⌚ 15.00–21.00 Sat–Thu, 10.00–12.00 & 17.00–21.00 Fri. Regular rotation of cultural events & exchanges. Perhaps the most artistically focused foreign cultural institution of Dhaka.

American Centre [120–1 B3] Hse 110, Rd 27, Banani; ☎ 882 3440; e dhakapa@state.gov; dhaka.usembassy.gov/pas.html; ⌚ 09.00–16.30. Has a library of resources on America plus organises cultural exchanges.

Bengal Fine Art Gallery [128–9 C4] Hse 275F, Rd 16, Dhanmondi; ☎ 812 3115; www.bengalfoundation.org; ⌚ 12.00–20.00 Sun–Thu. Dhanmondi's fine-art venue, with a particular interest in painting & sculpture.

British Council [128–9 C5] 754B Sat Masjid Rd, Dhanmondi; ☎ 861 8905; www.britishcouncil.org/bangladesh.htm. English courses, art & science events, &

several outreach organisations around Bangladesh. Most established cultural institution of the bunch. Also maintains a library at Dhaka University (*5 Fuller Rd;* ⌚ *10.00–18.00 Sat–Thu, 15.00–19.00 Fri*).

DRIK [128–9 C4] Hse 58, Rd 15A, Dhanmondi; ☎ 912 0125; e office@drik.net; www.drik.net; ⌚ 15.00–20.00. Photography & art exhibitions with a social activist edge. Great website & the head of the organisation, Shahidul Islam, has some amazing photography at his blog: shahidul.wordpress.com.

Goethe Institute [128–9 E5] Hse 10, Rd 9, Dhanmondi; ☎ 912 6525; e info@dhaka.goethe.org; www.goethe.de; ⌚ 09.00–17.00 Sun–Thu. German cultural institution with events.

Gallery Chitrak [128–9 E6] Hse 21, Rd 4, Dhanmondi; ☎ 862 0345. Rotating exhibitions of photography & art. Call for the latest.

Indian Cultural Centre and Library [120–1 D6] Hse 35, Rd 24, Gulshan 1; ☎ 885 0141; e culture@hcidhaka.org; www.hcidhaka.org; ⌚ 10.00–18.00 Sat–Thu. Events, music & exhibitions from Bangladesh's big-brother neighbour. Sometimes even has yoga teachers in for 3-month-long sessions.

National Art Gallery [124–5 D6] Segun Bagicha. You could probably just show up here to see what's on, combined with a trip to Old Dhaka.

Russian Cultural Centre [128–9 E6] Hse 510, Rd 7, Dhanmondi; ☎ 911 8531; www.ruscultdhaka.org; ⌚ 09.00–17.00, Sun–Thu. Offers Russian language courses & has a gallery space.

Shilpakala Academy [124–5 D6] Segun Bagicha. Events are not well advertised here, although this is the institution responsible for promoting cultural affairs within Bangladesh.

FESTIVALS Every year there are a plethora of holidays and festivals to celebrate Bangladesh's recent history, as well as a smattering of religious and cultural holidays. Naturally, Dhaka lies at the centre of these celebrations, and it is good to hit the streets and join the masses of people moving around at this time, making for excellent photography opportunities. (For further details, see *Chapter 2, Public holidays and festivals*, pages 77–82.) Also check the *What to see* section later in this chapter for some information about the yearly events and where to participate.

SPORT Cricket matches in Dhaka are a frequent occurrence, with international teams often making visits. Despite Bangladesh's consistent losing streak there have been some serious upsets against the best teams by these 'cricket minnows', which most Bangladeshis will be happy to recount the story of, should you ask for it.

If you do hear about an upcoming match it's worthwhile making the time to take one in. With massive, cheering crowds and an unforgettable atmosphere, it's a fantastic cultural experience. Matches are held at the Mirpur Stadium [114–15] in Dhaka and tickets can usually be purchased beforehand at branches of the AB Bank around town. Naturally, only soft drinks are served from vendors at these matches but that shouldn't stop you from bringing your own. If you're staying long term, enquire at the American International School (*www.ais-dhaka.net*) about joining the community education classes.

✓ **Kurmitola Golf Club** [120–1 A2] Banani Cantonment; ☎ 875 2520, 875 2526, 875 2523; e kgcdhaka@hotmail.com; www.kgc-bd.com. A surprisingly good golf course & very good value for green fees (Tk600 per 9 holes; club rental Tk1,000) & also a surprising discovery given the scarcity of land in Dhaka. Also has a driving range for those interested in keeping their swing in shape. Expect to rub shoulders with a few army majors.

THEME PARKS

Fantasy Kingdom (*Dhaka–Ashulia Highway;* ☎ *883 3786, 989 6482; www.fantasy-kingdom.net.bd;* ⌚ *11.00–21.00 Mon–Thu, 10.00–21.00 Fri & public holidays ; entry & 2 free rides Tk220, or unlimited rides Tk450*) The most fancy of all the amusement park options in Dhaka, with rides, restaurants and big music events. The venue also has a high-class hotel on the premises, Motel Atlantis (*60 rooms, same contact info as above, rooms Tk2,400 and up*). Waterworld (*entry Tk250 for Waterworld only*) and Heritage Park (*entry Tk80*) also share the same location as Fantasty Kingdom. The former is a waterpark with slides and inner tubes and loads of people – you might have trouble finding a free space among the bathers and women visitors should dress modestly. The latter is a miniature exposition of Bangladesh's tourist wonders, as well as some village reproduction scenes populated with real villagers, where urbanites go to gawk at their rural roots.

Wonderland [120–1 E4] (*Gulshan Av; ⌚ 10.00–19.00; entry Tk50 & rides Tk20–40*) Visitors have described 'The Cave', one of the rides at Wonderland, as a rather surreal experience. With a 'dancing panda' and lighting straight out of *Leaving Las Vegas*, maybe this is a ride best taken under the influence, *Alice in Wonderland* style.

Shishu Park [124–5 C5] (*Shahbagh; ⌚ Oct–Mar 15.00–20.00; Apr–Sep 14.00–19.00 every Wed, street kids only; entry Tk8, per ride Tk6*) Situated adjacent to the National Museum, this children's park is moderate in size but could be fun for mixing it up with local families. There are 12 rides in total.

Shishu Mela [114–15] (*Shyamoli; ⌚ 10.00–19.00; entry Tk20 & each ride Tk25*) Fifty rides decorate this larger city amusement park located in the western end of the city.

SHOPPING

Bangladesh's burgeoning middle class means there is now more shopping choice than ever before, especially in Dhaka's main shopping areas. By far and away the most visible of these shops are the boutiques scattered around the city's main shopping districts. These break down into three areas. The shops of Gulshan/Banani carry the highest-quality items but also at the highest prices. Dhanmondi has another concentration of upmarket shops but with more accessible prices. Finally, the city's street markets carry plenty of overruns from the garment factories sold at rock-bottom prices.

GULSHAN/BANANI

Clothing/textiles

Andes [120–1 D7] ZN Tower, Hse 2, Rd 8, Gulshan 1; ☎ 881 4756, 989 4566; m 01712 649835; www.andes-ltd.com. Large array of *salwar kameez* for women (Bengali tunics & loose-fitting trousers) & *fatua* (light fitted shirts) for men. Other items include jewellery & housewares.

Aranya [120–1 E4] 60 Kamal Ataturk Av, Banani; ☎ 988 2542; e aranya@citechco.net; www.aranyacrafts.com. A great shop for the environmentally conscious. Fabrics used in clothing, saris & scaves are hand woven & coloured with natural dyes. Fabric by the yard is also available.

Denial [120–1 D4] Hse 3, Rd 72, Gulshan 2; m 01913 883728. Funky shop in the little enclave underneath Mango Café's Gulshan location.

Deshal [120–1 B4] Hse 9, Rd 11, Blk C, Banani; m 01817 549553, 01512 361139. Worth a visit, even if it's just to see the internal decoration. Inspired by paper recycling.

Kay Kraft [120–1 B4] Hse 26, Rd 11, Blk F, Banani; ☎ 914 1525. Clothes for men & women that scream Bengali.

Kumudini [120–1 E6] 74 Gulshan Av; ☎ 882 4284. An extensive collection of clothes, saris & handicrafts for the socially conscious shopper.

Nogordola [120–1 B5] Hse 3G, Rd 11, Banani; ☎ 987 2036. An extensive array of stylish Bengali clothing for both men & women, including silk *salwar kameez*.

Pidimm [120–1 D6] Hse 6, Rd 32, Gulshan 1; ☎ 885 6773. *Fatuas*, *salwar kameez* & upmarket handicrafts.

Roxana [120–1 B4] Hse 50A, Rd 23, Blk B, Banani; ☎ 988 2645; www.roxanadesigo.com. Each piece of Roxana's clothing is carefully created with subtle & stylish designs. Clothing appeals to both Islamic & Western markets.

Sadakalo [120–1 B4] Gulshan: Molly Capital Centre, 76 Gulshan Av; ☎ 883 1219; Banani: Hse 26, Rd 11, Blk D,

☎ 885 7414. In a country with so much colour try these unique black-&-white designs (*sadakalo*) for men & women.

Sweet Dreams [120–1 A4] Hse 24, Rd 11, Blk F, Banani; ☎ 986 0965. For women who care about what they wear under their clothes. Local & brand labels available. Men will have to wait outside at this shop.

Beauticians

Herbal Solutions [120–1 E5] Hse 11/A, Rd 113, Gulshan 2; m 01736 040462. A stylish beautician's offering beauty treatments in private cubicles. Bengali food is also available if you just can't leave without one more treatment.

In Style Beauty Care [120–1 C4] 10/F Taneem Sq, 158 Kamal Ataturk Av, Banani; m 01819 192208. A hairstylist from Bangkok occupies this top-floor salon. She's a popular gal so book ahead if you've got major work.

Total Care [120–1 C4] Hse 61, Rd 27, Banani; ☎ 986 1581. Large beauty parlour, offering all your beauty needs under one roof. Locally renowned hairstylist comes recommended, but book in advance. Services for both men & women.

Bangla classes

Effective Bangla Learning Centre [114–15] Hse 324, Ln 5W, Baridhara DOHS; m 01715 021687; e eblcbd@yahoo.com; www.eblcbd.com. Charges on an hourly basis at Tk500 per hr, but can work out a course fee on request. See website or email for a quote. Gets good reviews & teachers seem quite personal here.

HEED Language Centre [120–1 C4] Hse 104, Rd 12, Blk E, Banani; ☎ 881 2390, 989 6028; e hlc@agni.com; www.heedbangladesh.org. Dhaka's most established Bangla-learning centre. Can arrange group classes or private tutoring, but costs may run higher than if you manage to find a private tutor.

Books There's a selection of second-hand and new books at New Market. Magazines can be found at Etc in Dhanmondi or at the Gulshan/Banani newspaper stands on the main road.

Omni Books [128–9 D3] 2nd Flr, Hse 16, Rd 27, Dhanmondi; ☎ 02 8121472; ⏲ 09.30–20.00. Stocks international titles & often holds writers' events from the store.

The Bookworm [114–15] Twin Peaks Complex, Old Airport Rd, Tejgaon; ☎ 912 0387. A tiny little bookstore that seems to have such an odd location near the military airport. Other shops have better stock but you may find something here that you can't find somewhere else.

University Press Ltd [144–5 F1] 5th Flr, Red Crescent Hse, 61 Motijheel C/A, e 956 5441, 956 5444; www.uplbooks.com. For the most substantial collection of local books, including a few gems of photography & writing, visit the UPL's bookshop in Motijheel. Most of the collection is admittedly pulp, but among the collection are some compelling home-grown titles too.

Words 'n' Pages [120–1 D7] Hse 7, Rd 7, Gulshan 1; ☎ 989 0832, 882 0417. Carries a selection of newspapers, magazines, DVDs & of course, books. Has a café for reading & is a great space to relax in.

Custom clothing Tailoring can be hit or miss. This is not surprising when you think that most of their customers choose Islamic-style clothing that is very loose fitting. The best results are achieved when you provide a sample for tailors to copy, but allow extra time as most items will probably require a few tweaks.

A Rouf Tailors and Cloth Store [120–1 D7] 1/F Stall 68, DCC Market 1, Gulshan 1; ☎ 989 5257; m 01729 582087. Where expats go to get their glitterball costumes made & many other custom tailoring jobs. Always leave enough time to get garments fitted properly as each one will take 2 or 3 trips. Fitting area available in the shop.

Raj Leather Centre [120–1 D4] F-34 DCC Market 2, Gulshan 2; ☎ 989 5849. Custom leather goods including belts, shoes & clothing is available at this store; negotiate the price.

Arts and crafts

Aarong [120–1 D8] Tejgaon Link Rd; ☎ 882 1052, 882 5986. The country's most successful handicrafts & housewares chain store, with close links to its largest NGO BRAC. Shopping here is not for the tame or the timid, as swarms of shoppers descend on this institution particularly during the Eid's gift-giving frenzy.

CRP-Aware [120–1 C4] 2/F Unicorn Plaza, 40/2 Gulshan Av. Sales outlet for the products of the Centre for the Rehabilitation of the Paralysed. Handicrafts, gift cards, textiles & calendars are produced by people with disabilities at the Savar rehabilitation facility. Some of the artistry is even done by mouth-painting.

Folk International [120–1 E4] Hse 19, Rd 108, Gulshan; ☎ 988 0784, 989 6039. Traditional Bangladeshi handicraft selection with stock sourced from all over Bangladesh. A non-profit organisation & so the benefits are returned directly to the producers. Great selection & very friendly staff.

Haque Art Gallery [120–1 D4] F43, DCC Market 2, Gulshan 2. Where all the expats head to get their framing done, if the collection of business cards is any evidence.

Hossain Handicrafts [120–1 D4] G18, DCC Market 2, Gulshan 2; ☎ 986 2617. Antiques & brass dealer. You can probably find some unique items, but be careful what you buy: the antique trade in Bangladesh is responsible for much of the damage done to the country's most precious architectural sites.

Islam Handicrafts [120–1 D4] F26, DCC Market 2, Gulshan 2; ☎ 988 9147; m 01817 024515. Supposedly one of the best deals for pearls. Some have resold abroad for good profits.

Jatra [120–1 C4] 60 Kamal Ataturk Av, Banani; ☎ 882 6370. The city's smartest-looking boutique handicrafts store. A great place for souvenirs, clothing, gift cards, housewares. Truly one of the city's best shopping destinations.

Piraan [120–1 D7] Hse 22, Rd 10, Gulshan 1; m 01819 293643. Tiny shop with original designs of handicrafts & housewares.

National Crafts Council [128–9 C2] 2/8 Sir Syed Rd, Mohammadpur; ☎ 914 0812; m 01711 520 605. Organisation responsible for promoting & procuring unique handicrafts & supporting rural artisans. Definitely worth a visit!

Saju Arts and Crafts [120–1 D4] F28, DCC Market 2, Gulshan 2; ☎ 989 5940. Decent gallery space selling paintings by Bangladeshi artists.

Miscellaneous

Banani Decorators Hse 78/3, Mohakhali Commerical Area; ☎ 881 1489, 989 5564; m 01711 541910. Thinking of a rooftop party with a tent & tables? These guys can arrange the decorations.

Centre for Indigenous Knowledge Practice and Handicrafts [128–9 C1] 26/2 Dhaka Housing, North Abador, Shyamoli, Mohammadpur; m 01712 261550. Not much information on this small centre is publicly available, but it might be worth looking up if you want to source handicrafts from Bangladesh's indigenous people. Ask for Prabir Kumar Das Pujan, the centre's director.

Eco Flower Shop [120–1 D4] 10 Barun Bldg, Gulshan 2; ☎ 988 0548; m 01819 231692. Very friendly flower shop located right on the Gulshan 2 Circle. Flowers usually delivered in the afternoon.

George D'Cruze and Rekha Lucy D'Cruze 101/1-A Monipuripara; ☎ 911 4356, 811 6507; e gdcruze@bangla.net. Need some entertainment at a party? You may wish to call this magician couple for a show.

Interflora Hse 28, Rd 99, Gulshan 2; m 01711 537478, 01711 663472. Another decorator service, seems capable for floral arrangements & fancy table settings. Comes recommended. Call for consultation.

Samsonite [120–1 D7] Hse 1, Rd 138, Gulshan 1; ☎ 886 1386. Bangladesh retail outlet of this upmarket, high-quality luggage brand.

Tropikana [120–1 D4] G13, DCC Market 2, Gulshan 2; ☎ 883 3603–6; e tropigulshan@dhaka.net. Who would have thought to combine groceries & sporting equipment? But it works. This is Gulshan's best sports goods store; also can re-string tennis racquets.

Supermarkets

Agora [120–1 D5] RM Centre, 101 Gulshan Av; ☎ 989 2974. Dhaka's best Western-style supermarket.

Ko-mart [120–1 B4] Kamal Ataturk Av; ⏲ 11.00–20.00. An excellent supermarket that stocks Asian goods albeit at a steep price.

Nandan [120–1 C4] 4 North Av, Gulshan 2; ☎ 986 2637. Another large supermarket store with branches in Dhanmondi & Gulshan.

DHANMONDI

Andes [128–9 D6] Anam Rangs Plaza, Hse 61, Rd 6/A, Sat Masjid Rd, Dhanmondi; ☎ 911 2522; m 01711 470500; e aneela@andes-ltd.com. Dhanmondi location of this boutique clothing store. East-meets-West designs by Aneela Haque. Offers some extremely beautiful designs.

Kay Kraft [128–9 D4] Hse 1A, Rd 13, Dhanmondi; ☎ 987 2427. Male & female clothing that is quite accessible & of increasing quality. Also has a Gulshan outlet.

Piraan [128–9 D5] Hse 67, Rd 11/A, Dhanmondi; ☎ 912 8392; m 01819 293 643. Trendy local wear with a collection of jewellery & handicrafts, often imported from India. Opposite the Women's Sports Federation. Bigger than Gulshan version.

Prabartana [128–9 C2] 2/8 Sir Syed Rd, Mohammadpur; ☎ 911 8428, 914 0812; e udshamim@yahoo.com; www.prabartana.org. In a world dominated by men, this shop offers a little refuge. The atmospheric upstairs café is open to women & men accompanied by women. This fair-trade destination for discerning Dhakaites contains a bookshop with a collection of development & women-focused books. The downstairs fabric shop contains an extensive collection of handspun fabrics & clothing. Custom tailoring is available at the store (there's also a branch in Gulshan that just offers fabric)

Sadakalo [128–9 E7] 3/F, 351 Rifles Sq, Rd 2; ☎ 862 6282. Offers a unique series of *fatuas* & *salwar kameezes* that use only *sadakalo* (black & white) on its designs.

Sweet Dreams [128–9 E6] Hse 29, Rd 7, Dhanmondi; ☎ 815 2027. Racy outfits available here just for women.

Handicrafts

Aarong [128–9 D3] 1/1, Blk A, Lalmatia, Mirpur Rd; ☎ 811 1607. The best-stocked outlet of the highly successful handicraft, houseware & textile operation.

Clay Image [128–9 D3] 2/F, 22 Sunrise Plaza, 3/1 Lalmatia Blk A; m 01819 268470. Some funky pottery designs available here, a bit of a gem amongst other drab shops.

Prokritee [128–9 C2] 1/1 Blk A, Asad Gate Rd, Mohammadpur; ☎ 911 6461; m 01712 228019; www.prokritee.com. Gorgeous handicrafts, jewellery & gift cards.

Miscellaneous

ETC [128–9 C4] Concord Royal Court, Hse 275G, Rd 16 (new); ☎ 914 0089. 2-level variety store, with electronics, periodicals & a coffee shop.

Monira Jewellers [128–9 F8] 355/Ka, New Market; ☎ 862 8521. Silver is paid by the gram, making charge is additional; prices are negotiable.

Supermarkets

Agora [128–9 E7] Rifles Sq, Rd 2, Dhanmondi; ☎ 967 1046. Dhaka's best Western-style supermarket.

Nandan [128–9 C4] Hse 37, Rd 16, Dhanmondi; ☎ 812 7085. Another large supermarket store with branches in Dhanmondi & Gulshan.

REST OF DHAKA

Clothing

Aarong [124–5 E3] Mogh Bazaar: Aarong Plaza, 211 Outer Circular Rd; ☎ 933 4766, 936 0260; Wari: 1/F, 36/1 Rankin St; ☎ 711 4244; www.brac-aarong.com; ⌚ 09.00–18.30

Deshal [124–5 B5] 2/F, 124/A Aziz Market, Shahbag. Excellent selection of men's & women's clothing, made with some uniquely Bangladesh-flavoured designs.

Sadakalo [124–5 E4] 2 Property Arcade, Bailey Rd; ☎ 836 1653; Hse 9, Sec 7, Sonargaon Janopath, Uttara; ☎ 896 1138. Offers a unique series of *fatuas* & *salwar kameezes* that use only *sadakalo* (black & white) on its designs.

Miscellaneous

Ahmed Art Foundation [144–5 B2] 17 Hossaini Dalan Rd, Old Dhaka; ☎ 730 1401; m 01711 980173, 01817 070564. Artist Ahmed has been doing custom rickshaw art for foreigners for quite a few years. Provide him with a photo & some specifications of what you want & he will do a bang-up job. When you prepare the photo, make sure you pose with a machine gun (or however you choose).

Bashundhara City Shopping Complex [124–5 B2] Pantha Path; ⌚ 11.00–20.00 Mon–Thu, 14.00–20.00 Fri. The city's largest shopping complex also has a movie theatre & food court on the top floor. It suffered a major fire in early 2009, so some of the facilities may still be closed.

Dhamrai Metalworks Craft Hse A71, Rothkhola, Dhamrai, Savar District, 25km NW from Dhaka; m 01713 003136, 01817 087732; e dmcsukanta@hotmail.com. A brass handicrafts workshop run by the friendly Sukanta Banik. Housed in an aging Dhamrai *rajbari*, he & his family members are trying to maintain an ancient tradition of brasswork creation. The technique involves carving intricate statues from wax, from which a clay mould is made. Intricate brass statues of several cultural & religious creations are then made from the mould.

New Luxmi Bhander [144–5 D5] 118 Shakhari Bazaar, Old Dhaka; One of the many stores selling conch-shell jewellery on Hindu St.

Markets

Aziz Supermarket [124–5 B5] Shahbagh, north side from National Museum. Several young university designers have their shops here. Great place for cheap funky T-shirts of Bangladesh.

Banga Bazaar [144–5 C2] College Rd, Dhaka University south side. This large market is where many of the (seconds) overruns end up from the garment factories. Many good deals to be had, but it often involves sifting through bags of clothing to find what you are after. Changing rooms are not available, but if you get creative no-one will stop you trying on the clothes. If you have a specific want (ie: The North Face or other similar brand names) just ask around & somebody will guide you to the right shop.

IDB Bhaban [114–15] Agargaon, near United Nations Bangladesh headquarters. Dhaka's central computer market. Not terribly well stocked with the latest goods, but if you're looking for something random it's a good place to try first.

New Market [128–9 F8] South of Dhanmondi. If it isn't at New Market, Dhaka doesn't have it. As the city's biggest open-air market you should be able to find just about anything you need, & eat while you're at it. Jewellery, housewares, snacks, shoes; the list goes on.

Rifles Square [128–9 E7] Rd 2, Dhanmondi. Pirated DVDs seem to be a speciality of this market. Do drop by the 5th-floor Dhaba for a snack while you're here.

Stadium Market [144–5 E1] Motijheel. If you're outfitting a new mosque & need large sound equipment this is the place to come. Otherwise you'll find smaller sound gear & home electronics here.

UAE Market [120–1 A4] Kamal Ataturk Av, Banani. Saris, paintings & electronics can be had here at this collection of boutique shops.

OTHER PRACTICALITIES

BANKS HSBC, Standard Chartered Bank and DBBL have ATMs scattered around the city, but especially in the city's business areas (Motijheel and Gulshan). See the relevant maps for the locations. You'll also find a plethora of money-changing services in Gulshan, especially around the Gulshan 1 or Gulshan 2 circles.

$ **HSBC Gulshan** [120–1 B4] Hse SWG-2, Gulshan Ave; ☎ 9553053-6; ⌚ 10.00–15.00. Can exchange travellers' cheques, bring your passport. ATMs are at other locations (Westin Dhaka: Hse 1, Rd 45, Gulshan 2; Intersection of Gulshan North Avenue and Rd 92) if just needing cash withdrawal.

$ **HSBC Motijheel** [144–5 E1] City Centre, 103 Motijheel C/A; ☎ 9553053-6; ⌚ 10.00–15.00. Can exchange travellers' cheques. Has ATM.

$ **Standard Chartered Gulshan** [120–1 D6] 67 Gulshan Ave; ☎ 8833003–4; ⌚ 10.00–15.00. Can exchange travellers' cheques; bring your passport. Very busy location.

$ **Standard Chartered Motijeel** [144–5 E1] 5/A Motijheel C/A; ☎ 717 4127, 716 9438; ⌚ 10.00–15.00. Can exchange travellers' cheques, with passport. Also has ATM.

INTERNET Most guesthouses and hotels provide an internet service at varying rates and speeds, so if you do need to be connected during your visit choose a place that provides the service for the minimum amount of hassle, but do be wary that the smaller places may not have the technical support you need to get online, causing delays. Call first.

Otherwise, Gulshan and Dhanmondi's coffee shops are now offering free wireless internet if you have your own computer. **Cuppa Coffee Club** [120–1 D4] (*Hse 11, Rd 46, Gulshan 2 Circle; ☎ 885 1727*) has computer terminals for their customers.

Long-term visitors can subscribe to one of many internet services available to homes in the capital. The price of the broadband service depends on the data plan you subscribe to, but costs anywhere between Tk900 and Tk2,000 per month for unlimited data use. With Wi-Max connectivity, **Information Services Limited** gets excellent reviews for its consistent service and speed (*Ste 1103, Concord Tower; 113 Kazi Nazrul Islam Av; ☎ 832 1051; e sales@xpressbd.net; www.xpressbd.net*).

Those who travel outside Dhaka frequently may wish to consider subscribing to a mobile data service, which provides broadband internet services anywhere in the country where there is a mobile signal. **Grameenphone** (*www.grameenphone.com*) offers this service on an unlimited data plan basis for a measly Tk1,000 per month, which must make this service one of the best in the world. You also activate a daily service or pay by the kilobyte. Be warned, however, this service is only really useful if you spend a lot of time travelling the country and require internet access wherever you are. In Dhaka, you'll find there are frequent service drops and unreliable speeds. A home-based internet service may provide slightly better speeds for a cheaper price.

MEDICAL Doctors will advise you to have major medical procedures taken care outside the country (eg: giving birth, surgeries, major illnesses). Many expatriates travel to Bangkok for their regular check-ups and major procedures. For less serious travel-related illnesses, ICCDR,B has a travellers' clinic which charges US$50 per visit for insured patients and US$15 otherwise. Appointments are recommended.

Emergencies are probably best handled at one of the major hospitals (for further details, see *Chapter 2, Health, Medical facilities*, page 57).

✚ **Dhaka Medical College Hospital** Shahbagh, near Dhaka University; ☎ 862 6812; e www.dmchbd.com. 🕘 24hr emergency. Not really a preferred hospital if you're in serious need, but if you need one quickly, many local emergency cases are rushed here.

POST AND TELECOMMUNICATIONS Postal services in Bangladesh are often unreliable and there are mixed stories. One traveller had a replacement credit card mailed, but it never arrived, only discovering the card's fate when fraudulent transactions were attempted at jewellery shops around the city.

Mailing out items is similarly difficult. Trying to figure out the cost to send a large package abroad is difficult and you may be sent around to various desks, especially at the General Post Office [144–5 D1]. Generally the experience doesn't inspire trust so it would be best not to send items of substantial or sentimental value. Private services have fared better for having packages arrive on time, and for a similar quoted cost from the post office.

✉ **Bangladesh Post Offices** Gulshan: Hse 14, Rd 16, Gulshan 1; Mohammadpur: east side Mohammadpur Market, Asad Gate Rd; 🕘 10.00–16.00. Not highly recommended for anything other than lettermail &/or postcards, & even these are not guaranteed to arrive safely.

✉ **DHL Express** Head Office, 4/F Molly Capita Centre, 76 Gulshan Av; ☎ 988 1703; www.dhl.com.bd. Country office of DHL, where you can get information on shipping important documents or goods. Has several branch & express offices around town. See the website for locations, phone numbers & opening hours.

✉ **FEDEX Bangladesh** Corporate Head Office: Ibrahim Chamber, 95 Motijheel C/A; ☎ 956 5114; Banani: Hse 16, Rd 10A, Blk H, ☎ 988 1725, 882 0415; Gulshan: Bilquis Tower, Gulshan 2 Circle, ☎ 988 3287, 882 7771; www.fedex.com/bd. Bangladesh version of the international shipping brand, has a local company, Bangladesh Express, which manages local operations on FEDEX's behalf.

✉ **HomeBound** SW(A) 26 Gulshan Av; ☎ 989 5242, 989 5174, 989 5241, 989 4745–50; e commercial.dept@homebound.com.bd; www.homeboundbd.com. Service most used by expatriates for cross-country house moves. Has packing services & can consult on customs issues.

PRESERVING OLD DHAKA: SHAKHARI BAZAAR AND TANTI BAZAAR

Courtesy the Urban Study Group (e usg.dhaka@gmail.com)

The Shakhari and Tanti bazaars (*south entrance located on Johnson Rd, north entrance located at southern end of North–South Rd*) are a unique remnant of the glory days that Dhaka once had. They are the oldest surviving *mohalla* (traditional neighbourhood) of this historic city, a living testament to life as it has existed here for hundreds of years. Along with its adjacent areas, Shakhari Bazaar constituted the central area of pre-Mughal Dhaka which as early as the 16th century was a prosperous commercial centre. During much of the late 18th and 19th centuries, the surrounding areas of the *mohalla* formed Dhaka's urban core. During that time, Shakhari Bazaar was considered to be one of the two most prestigious neighbourhoods in the fledgling capital city.

Today it is home to a community, the Shakhari, which, through its history, habitat, craft and unique socio-religious practices, has become an icon of living heritage. By residing at the same place that their forefathers built over the centuries, this community continues to practise the original craft – Shankkha Shilpa – from generation to generation with the same devotion, artistry and precision that their forefathers once had. The Shakhari borrowed their name from the term *shakha*, a richly decorated bangle crafted from slices of *shakha*, or conch shells. Shakha has a tremendous religious importance to the Hindu community as a symbol of *shadhaba*, or a virtuous wife.

The *mohalla* is also shared by a few other artisan communities involved in the making of paper crafts, including colourful kites and paper garlands, as well as *sholapith* (popular ceremonial accessories for Hindu weddings) and *shilpata* (traditional musical instruments and clay sculptures for religious use).

The neighbourhood is actually spread out over a 300m stretch, lined by houses and shop fronts on the ground floor of buildings that are so narrow you feel like you could touch both sides at once. Most are two or three storeys high, and no more than 3–4m wide. The inner parts of the houses and upper floors are now used as residences. Most of these are broken up on the inside, with a series of courtyards and narrow winding

WHAT TO SEE

PURAN DHAKA (OLD DHAKA) The highlight of any visit to Dhaka is to take in a serving of the pulsing vibrancy and extraordinary atmosphere of Puran Dhaka (Old Dhaka). With its winding alleyways and frenetic buzzing energy, there is something to see around every corner and a walk here proves to be quite the photographer's delight. In order to get the most out of the experience, the services of the architects-turned-tour guides of the Urban Study Group are highly recommended (*2/F, Hse 29, Rd 1, Dhanmondi;* ↘ *861 7854;* m *01819 248408. Walks cost Tk500 per person*). Below are some of the key sights.

Sadarghat [144–5 D5] (*ghat entry Tk4*) Dhaka's heaving boat terminal is great fun to visit any time of year, but if you have the choice you should go just before Eid-ul Fitr, when millions of Bangladeshis make the journey home to their *baris* via launch. The terminal itself and all of its launches are absolutely stacked with people, making for some excellent photographic opportunities at what is a very special and memorable time of year. Throwing yourself into the crowd is akin to jumping into a heaving mosh pit, but the sheer number of people you can fit into one photograph is unparalleled.

At other times of year, the place still teems with people. Taking a small boat out on the river in the early morning is the best way to witness this. Several boatmen will approach you if you venture anywhere near the water, so hash out a price

staircases that open into richly decorated sky temple courtyards on the top floor. If you ask politely, you may be permitted to enter some houses to have a look.

The most historic of these houses are embellished with ornate decorations, using architectural styles that span 200, or sometimes 300 years. Others still show exotic surface decorations with symbolic religious motifs. Finally, the traces of Britain's colonial past are also etched on these buildings, some of which show a distinctly European influence.

Tanti Bazaar also shares a similar history. Spanning two major thoroughfares of Old Dhaka – English Road and Islampur Road – the bazaar is now home to dozens of goldsmiths and silversmiths. But from pre-Mughal times, this neighbourhood belonged to the *tanti* (weavers) community of Bengal and used to be where Dhaka's famous muslin cloth was produced. But when the British destroyed the cotton industry, the craftsmen switched to the jewellery trade, one that resulted in an economic boom that produced incredible urban development during the 18th and 19th centuries, making Tanti Bazaar one of the most elite neighbourhoods of Dhaka.

Over the last 30 years, however, sporadic incremental development along with lack of proper regulatory controls has meant that both neighbourhoods have been stripped of their grandeur by defacement or by redevelopment. In Tanti Bazaar, at least seven old buildings have been demolished, as the Department of Archaeology refuses to grant heritage status to these aging buildings.

In 2004, disaster struck when a multi-storeyed building collapsed in Shakhari Bazaar. As a result, a fair degree of criticism has rained down from different segments of society. Some have said that all the buildings are unsafe and should be demolished immediately. They say that the neighbourhood has become stereotyped as the ultimate example of urban congestion, blight and dilapidated residences. Conservationists in the community reacted, claiming the bazaar has preserved the area's unique and exotic cultural heritage and argue that it should be conserved on this basis.

before boarding and be prepared with the right amount of change when you're done. Excellent fares for the boatmen run to about Tk30–50 for half an hour, or Tk60–80 for an hour, but they'll try for every taka that they can.

The best way to see Sadarghat is for its intended purpose: plan a trip to Bangladesh's south via launch or rocket paddlewheel, and include some time to stop and look around the terminal before departure. To float away from Dhaka's intensity in a launch is by far the best way to leave the city behind.

Ahsan Manzil [144–5 C5] (*Near Sadarghat; www.nawabbari.com; ⌚ Oct–Mar 09.30–16.30, Apr–Sep 10.30–17.30 & 15.30–17.30 Fri–Wed; entry Tk2*) Also known as the 'Pink Palace', Ahsan Manzil holds a small collection of one of Dhaka's oldest aristocrat families. Historians may wish to visit the family's website for a much greater treasure trove of information, although you will find this is one of the few places where you can experience what the furnishings of the period were like. The palace first served as a government and trading centre. Lord Curzon, the former British viceroy of India, used to stay here when he visited Dhaka. After being sold to the Dhaka nawab family in the mid 19th century, they converted it into a private residence in the form it now has, but when the nawab died, the Pink Palace was left in a state of disrepair. Restored in 1985, it has served as a museum ever since.

Armenian church [144–5 C4] (*Armanitola*) Judging by the headstones of the tombs at the church, Armenians started coming to Dhaka in the late 17th century as

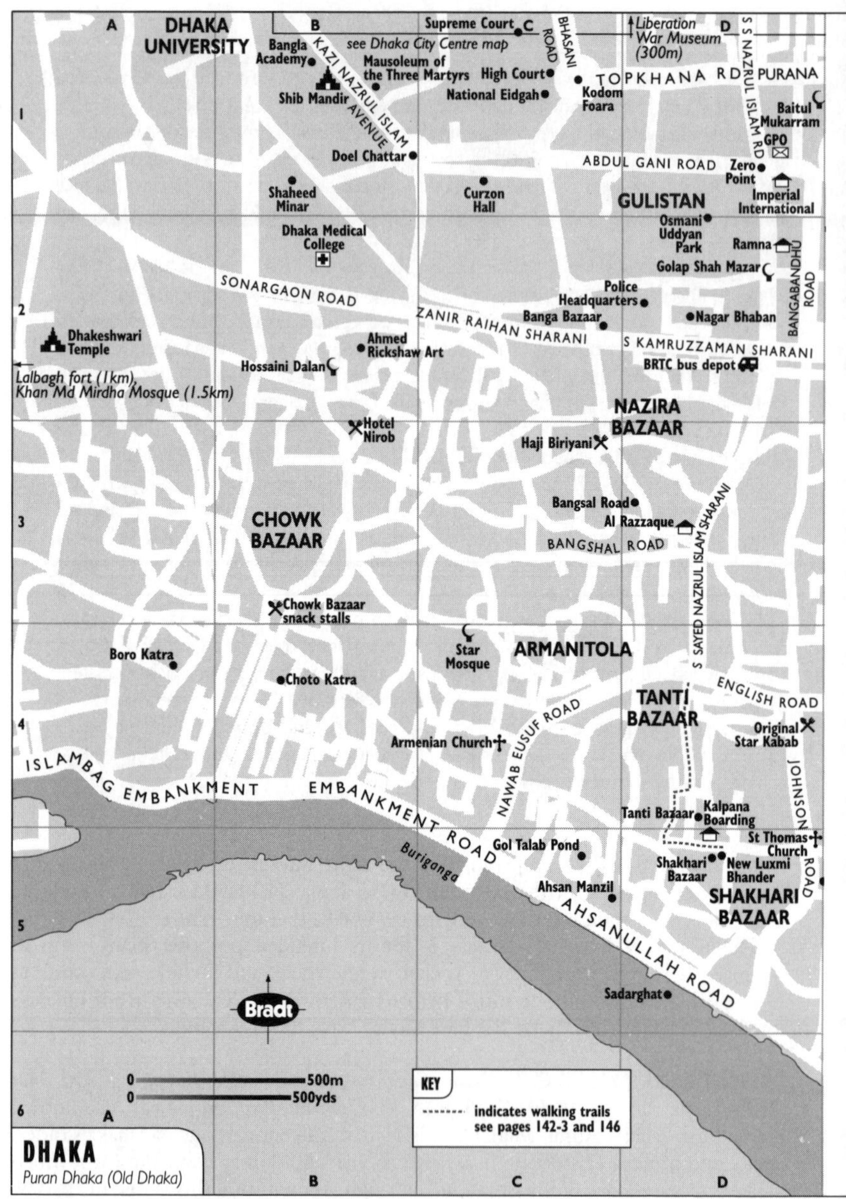

merchants and traders, although their history in the subcontinent is said to date back to the 12th century. Predominantly engaged in the city's muslin trade, they were known as the biggest buyers of Dhaka's famous cloth. Towards the mid 19th century, a few dozen families lived in Old Dhaka and because of their close ties to the British, they became rich landlords. The church, built in 1771, and the surrounding neighbourhood, Armanitola, stand as a testament to their presence.

Today the church is a rare oasis of peace and tranquillity inside Old Dhaka, and masses are held during Easter and Christmas. There is a chapel with a broad

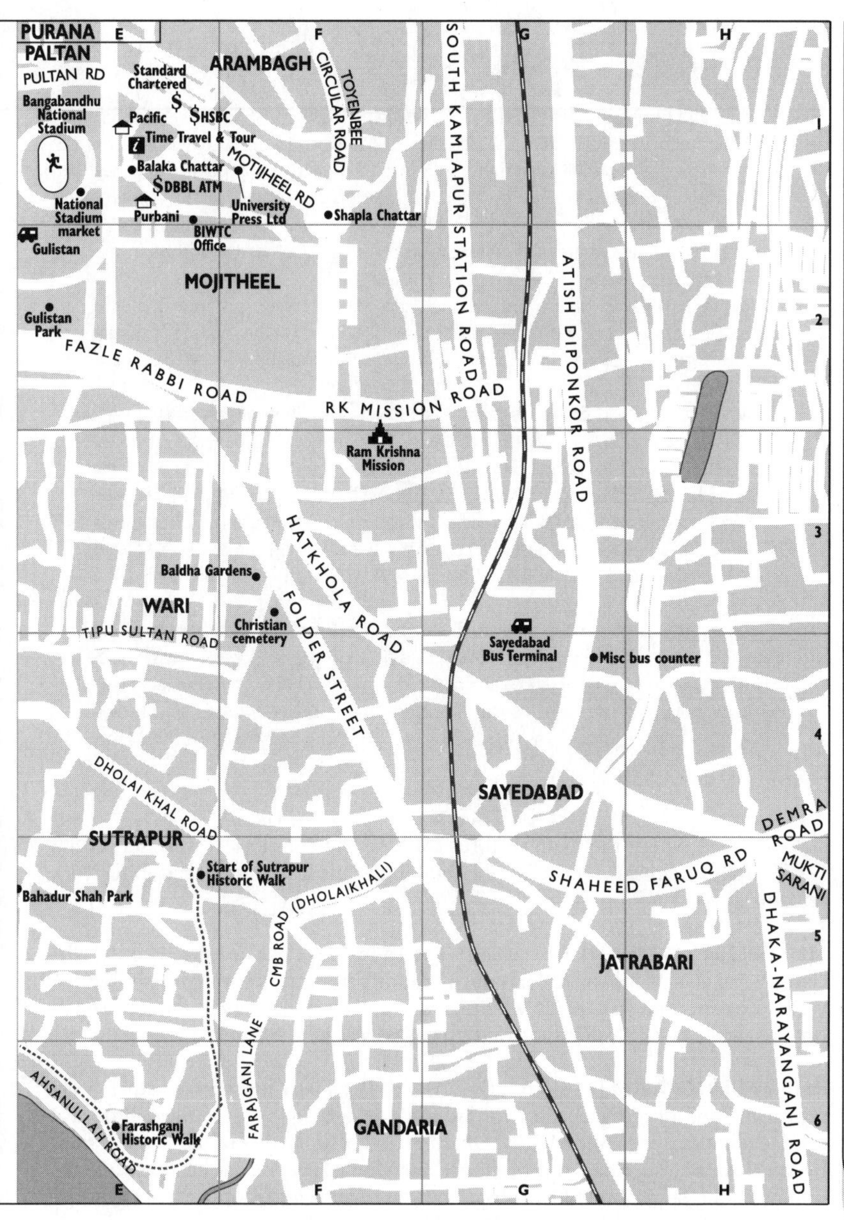

balcony upstairs, and a cemetery housing the graves of several Armenians who died here. When Mother Teresa visited Dhaka just after the Liberation War, she stayed here while she opened an orphanage for the rape victims of the war.

St Thomas Church [144–5 D5] (*54 Johnson Rd; 711 6546; e cbdacdio@bangla.net*) Sometimes referred to as the 'Church of Bangladesh', this small sanctuary is now the home of the Anglican mission in Bangladesh. Built in 1819 by convicts from the Dhaka Jail, the church uses the same style as others built around the

PRESERVING OLD DHAKA: SUTRAPUR AND FARASHGANJ

Courtesy the Urban Study Group (e *usg.dhaka@gmail.com*)

Sutrapur and Farashganj (*walk begins at intersection of Dohlai Khal Rd & Narindra Rd*) form another area of Old Dhaka. Located east of Shakhari Bazaar and bounded by the old stream of Dohlai Khal and the Buriganga River, they are generally identified as pre-Mughal Dhaka although the area's current form is a result of 19th-century development. Today, the conservation of this area is also hotly disputed and it remains to be seen whether its historical buildings will also be demolished in the name of progress.

At the north end of the area is the Binat Bibi Mosque, just north of the intersection of Narindra and Dohlai Khal roads. Built in 1457, the mosque is widely acknowledged to be one of Dhaka's first mosques, constructed well before Dhaka became the eastern capital of Bengal in the Mughal Empire.

Moving south, you enter Hrishikesh Das Road, a wealthy merchant of a later time who paid for the electrification of the area and hence the road was renamed after him. Houses No 42 and 111 show traces of the historic architecture of this period. Moving further south, you enter Reboti Mohon Das Road. His former residence was a grand palace, with dozens of rooms, courtyards and rooftop areas. Nowadays the house is a victim of a series of sublets but you can still walk around freely to explore and imagine the extravagance in which Reboti and his family used to live.

Turning the corner, you come to Boro Bari at 45 BK Das Road, an ornately decorated palatial home showing the influence of colonial style. Further west, Ruplal House shows the same influences and occupies a space right next to the river. It was originally built by an Armenian landlord named Aratun. Finally, the Lalkuthi Building was built on the occasion of the 1872–76 stay of the Governor of India, Lord North Brooke.

subcontinent, where the main features are a prominent clock tower and several Gothic-style archways. Most of the building's intricate stone and brickwork remains in good condition.

Star Mosque [144–5 C4] (*Armanitola*) The most endearing feature of this 19th-century *mosjid* is its mosaic decoration. The entire mosque is covered with flowers, vases, crescents and stars made with pieces of coloured glass and pottery plastered onto its walls. Look closely and you find a glass visage of Mount Fuji!

Boro and Choto Katra [144–5 A4, B4] (*Mitford Rd*) These illustrative names – *boro* means big and *choto* means small – indicate the relative sizes of these historical residences built during the Mughal Dhaka period. The smaller of the two was built by Subahdar Shaista Khan, one of the earliest Mughal generals of Dhaka, while the origins of the larger building are not known. Khan reigned over the city during some of its historically most productive periods. Today these two buildings are some of the oldest in Dhaka, which probably accounts for why they're falling to pieces now.

Chowk Bazaar [144–5 B3] The bazaar is Dhaka's central gathering place for *iftar* snacks during Ramadan. As the final prayer call booms from the Shahid Mosque (the bazaar's central mosque), hungry fasters begin chowing down mouthfuls of puffed rice and chickpeas. At other times of year, you will still find elaborate collections of fried culinary morsels.

Lalbagh [144–5 A2] (⌚ *Oct–Mar 09.00–17.00; Apr–Sep 10.00–18.00, closed Sun & Mon morning;* ☎ *967 3018; entry Tk50*) Decorating most of Dhaka's tourist materials is the 'Red Fort' (*lal* meaning red), and although it shouldn't be compared, Lalbagh lacks the same scope and scale of its Delhi namesake. Nevertheless, the fort remains historically interesting as a sign of the Mughals' increasing power in Bengal during the late 17th century. Construction began in 1678 under the direction of Prince Muhammad Azam although he couldn't complete it after he was sent to another posting. Ten years after its inception, Shaista Khan also didn't finish its construction and what is visible from today's excavations likely reflects where Khan's work left off. According to early illustrations of the fort, the Buriganga River flowed right in front of the southern gate.

Today, there are three main buildings on the site and the fort has been restored. The first is a small mosque located on the western side (or right side as you enter). To the left is the governor's former residence, which also contains an audience hall. Inside this building is a small museum containing some Mughal-era artefacts. Finally, the main building in the centre is the tomb of Pari Bibi, one of the few buildings that uses black basalt and Bangladesh-origin marble to decorate its interior.

Khan Md Mirdha Mosque [144–5 A2] (*500m west of Lalbagh*) An early Dhaka mosque built in the beginning of the 18th century, located near Lalbagh Fort and sharing some unique architectural features. The mosque may not be open when you want to visit, but if you ask around the caretaker might show up to let you in.

Dhakeshwari Temple [144–5 A2] (*Bakshi Bazaar on Dhakeshwari Rd)* Also near the Lalbagh Fort is the city's most prominent Hindu temple. The best time to visit is during Durga Puja, usually mid-October. At this time the temple throngs with trinket stalls, pilgrims and a prominent Durga idol. It is also where a procession begins during the Hindu holiday of Janmasthami, usually held in early September (varies according to the lunar cycle).

During the 1971 Liberation War, Dhakeshwari became a target of attack for occupying Pakistani forces. More than half of its buildings were destroyed and some of its custodians murdered, which is probably why the site's current buildings – one main temple and four small *mandirs* – remains quite simple in design.

Hossaini Dalan [144–5 B2] (*Hussaini Dalan Rd*) Dhaka's main Shi'ite mosque becomes the centre of attention during the first ten days of the Muslim month of Muharram, which usually falls in mid-December to mid-January. On the tenth day, mourners congregate to commemorate the death anniversary of al-Husain during the historic Battle of Karbala in Iraq. The soldier was a grandson of the Prophet Muhammad and so his loss has come to symbolise martyrdom among Shi'ite Muslims. Today, Hussaini Dalan is a picturesque mosque located on the northern fringes of Old Dhaka, where it has some extremely beautiful Arabic calligraphy decorating its front pillars. While in the area, do drop in at artist Ahmed's home to check out some amazing rickshaw art (see *Shopping, Rickshaw art*, page 140).

Baldha Gardens [144–5 F3] (*Wari;* ⌚ *09.00–16.30; Dec–Feb 17.00*) This tranquil garden was originally constructed by prominent landowner and plant lover Narendra Narayan Roy in 1904. After his death in 1943, the garden was left derelict before Roy's grandsons eventually donated the property to the Bangladesh Forest Department for restoration in 1962. Today the garden houses over 18,000 different plant species, many of whom Roy personally imported from countries around

Asia. Its overall layout is divided into two sections, named 'Cybele' and 'Psyche', the latter holding a massive sundial, a pond, climbing ivy and even an Egyptian papyrus plant. However, this part of the garden is often locked and you'll need to try and convince a caretaker to open it for you if you want to see it.

Across the street from the gardens is an aging Christian cemetery dating from the mid 18th century.

Bangsal Road (Bicycle Street) [144–5 D3] (*East entrance 1 block south of Al Razzaque Hotel and Restaurant on North–South Rd*) With several varieties of bicycles imported from India and China, cycling enthusiasts will get a kick out of Old Dhaka's pedal-powered neighbourhood. This is also the place to go should you want a local bicycle to get you around the city (if you're brave enough to take on the traffic). Rickshaw art, in the form of plates or seat covers, is also available from the shops in Nariza Bazaar. Look for the rickshaw hoods displayed prominently outside the shop, and inside you will find several choices of handmade or screen-printed designs.

CENTRAL DHAKA

Liberation War Museum [144–5 D1] (*Mukti Juddho Jaddughar, Shegun Bagicha; ☎ 995 9091–2; www.liberationwarmuseum.net; ⌚ Mar–Sep 09.00–18.00; Oct–Feb 10.00–17.00, closed Sun; entry Tk5*) Dhaka's best and most memorable museum. Situated in an old house, the exhibits lead visitors through a chronicle of the Liberation War and all its atrocities, including photographs, weapons and newspaper clippings from the period. There are also graphic displays of the war, including photographic records of rape and genocide, as well as information on the conditions of the refugees, mostly Hindus, who escaped to India. On a more pleasant note, the museum is a good place to visit during national holidays like Victory Day (16 December) and Independence Day (26 March), where colourful events are held to commemorate the main anniversaries of independence. Call for details.

National Museum [124–5 B5] (*Shahbagh, near Aziz Supermarket; ☎ 861 9639–9; ⌚ Oct–Mar 09.30–16.30; Apr–Sep 10.30–17.30, closed Fri morning & Thu; entry Tk5*) Bangladesh's state museum offers an extensive overview of the country's culture and heritage. There are a few gems among the dusty collections, including Zainul Abedin's stark series of charcoal drawings depicting the 1943 famine of Bengal and a massive 40ft boat that was constructed inside the museum for display purposes. Other exhibits cover the history, craftsmanship, ethnicities and art of Bangladesh.

Baitul Mukarram Mosque [124–5 B5] (*Motijheel, Topkhana Rd*) Bangladesh's state mosque was built in 1960, during Dhaka's rapid expansion as the capital of East Pakistan. The mosque's design is a real departure from tradition, as it lacks a tower and dome and is cube-shaped. The designer, Abdul Hussain Thariani, modelled the mosque after the Kaaba at Mecca, and included several other modernist touches like minimal ornamentation and decoration. During major Islamic holidays, the street in front of the mosque is closed down for mass congregational prayers. Permission to enter may be an issue because of security.

Dharmarajikha Buddhist Monastery [114–15] (*Sayedabad Rd, east of Kamlapur Railway Station*) This rarely visited monastery is an oasis of tranquillity near Dhaka's southern bus station at Sayedabad. Founded in 1962, the facilities consist of a prayer hall, a clinic, a shrine and the Dharmarajik Lalitakala Academy. The monastery also serves as a welfare and education centre for some of the community's poorest people, and has a collection of Buddha statues from around the world.

High Court [144–5 C1] This building is one of Dhaka's finest examples of European Renaissance architecture and a symbol of British influence in Bengal. It was originally constructed as the governor's residence after the 1905 partition of Bengal. But after partition was annulled less than a decade later, the building never actually housed a governor of the province. In 1947, there was a need for a high court building to meet the judicial requirements of the newly created East Pakistan. Nearby is the **Mausoleum for the Three Martyrs** and the **Supreme Court** building.

The court is another site for Eid-ul Fitr celebrations marking the end of Ramadan. You can come here to see throngs of Muslim men joining in the congregational prayers.

Suhrawardy Park [124–5 C6] Several historically important events took place here at this park, previously known as the Ramna race course. Sheikh Mujib Rahman almost demanded Bangladesh's independence at a massive rally attended by thousands shortly before his arrest and imprisonment in Pakistan. Nine months later this was the scene of the surrender of Pakistan at the conclusion of the Liberation War. Finally, on 17 March 1972, Mujib returned here with Indian prime minister Indira Gandhi to deliver a speech at another massive rally.

During Mughal rule, the area used to house the residences of several important generals and officials, although as Dhaka declined in the late 18th century so did Ramna. The area would not see rejuvenation until 1825, when a demolition and reconstruction programme eventually saw the race course constructed here.

Today the park is a pleasant place to walk around, as well as its surrounding areas (see below). This is especially the case for young canoodling Bangladeshi couples, who find quiet places in the park to have private conversations. At the park's north end, the **Shishu Park** *(closed Wed except for street kids)* is a children's amusement park with rides, and to the northeast is the massive **Ramna Park**.

Dhaka University [124–5 B5] When the British began courting Muslim rule in Bengal, they created several institutions to facilitate the development of its less educated eastern half, namely Dhaka University. The institution was widely recognised as Dhaka's best educational facility and one of the most prominent in Asia. It also used to be a significant source of dissenting voices in the country, a place where the tenets of the wider society could be challenged and debated. But during the latter half of the 20th century, the university faced several difficulties that hampered its progress as an institution of higher learning. During the Liberation War, the university was one of the Pakistani army's first targets – scores of the nation's best professors and students were murdered on the first fateful day of the attacks.

Furthermore, the violence didn't end there. The last few years have seen the campus become the target of intense political violence, where the two big parties, via professors, rallied the nation's malleable young minds to create chaos and havoc upon demand. Sadly, this has often resulted in a total closure of the university for long periods at a time and the grandeur of the university seems tainted because of this.

Despite these discouraging signs, there are still some worthy architectural and cultural sites scattered around the campus, including the picturesque Curzon Hall, which is a unique blend of European–Mughal architecture, and whose peaceful grounds prove for an interesting visit. The **Central Shaheed Minar** commemorates the Language Movement of 1952, which represents the country's earliest longings for independence. Each year during Ekushey (21 February, International Mother Language Day), the monument becomes the focal point for a procession of patriotic citizens who come to mourn the loss of the country's earliest martyrs.

Other sites around the university include several sculptures commemorating the youthful and bloody history of Bangladesh. These include several lining the university's north side along Nilkhet Road: the Aparajeyo Bangla sculpture, the Shoparjito Shadhinota and the TSC Chattar Raju sculpture.

Aparjeyo Bangla means 'Invincible Bangladesh' and was created by artist Syed Abdullah Khalid in commemoration of victory during the Liberation War.

Created by female artist Shamim Shikdar, **Shoparjito Shadhinota** means 'Self Achieved Freedom'. Before its inauguration several hardline Islamists threaten to destroy it, but in the end it didn't happen. The **Chattar Raju** sculpture, known in Bangla as *Shontrash Birodhi Raju Sharokh Bhaskarjya*, or the 'Raju Memorial Sculpture Against Terrorism' is dedicated to a student who was killed during political violence, a notorious problem at university campuses across the country.

National Assembly Building [128–9 E2] (*Jatiyo Sangsad Bhaban, Manik Mia Av*) Bangladesh's signature parliament building is the most unique structure that the country has, and stands as a testament to the youthful spirit of the country and its people. Known as the largest legislative complex in the entire world, the building was originally designed by American architect Louis Khan. The architect's monolithic style is unmistakable in the design: its towering walls are recessed by

COMMUNITY SPIRIT *Andrew Morris*

You could easily spend years in this city and not even know of its existence. Hidden away in the triangle formed by upmarket Banani and Gulshan, and bustling Mohakhali, a stone's throw but also a universe away from the villas and the trendy boutiques, the slum area of Korail is an island of poverty in a sea of affluence. But you won't find despair or self-pity here. This makeshift community of over 100,000 residents (that number alone bigger than the population of dozens of fully fledged towns back home) is characterised above all by resilience and determination.

Korail is just one of many slum areas in Dhaka, each different in its own way. Similarly, the Spanish NGO most active here since 1999 is not the only body involved in this kind of work. But this is where I've pitched up, and Intervida are my hosts for the day, and it seems that many of the insights and lessons here are indeed replicated in other disadvantaged areas of the city, so it's worth pursuing and looking more closely at this one example.

As you enter, the roads narrow and the buildings huddle in. The shops and houses, mostly made of corrugated iron, stand defiant but also precarious, under a sky as flat and white as paper. This community, I am told, is lucky – they have access to some basic sanitation and amenities that other slums can only aspire to, but you are always aware in a place like this that its very existence is under constant threat, subject to the capricious whims of administrations keen on quick fixes. Nevertheless, today life goes on as usual: the area has the feel and sound of a busy marketplace. There are stores selling brightly coloured mattresses, DVDs and groceries. A tailor is putting the finishing touches to a pair of trousers, while next door freshly pressed shirts hang from a thin rack. Tinny rock music blares from speakers wired up to the walls. Old women peer warily as they walk past, and in the gutters the pie-dogs lap at the fetid greenish water. Piles of rubbish line the roadside.

There are several babies and toddlers playing naked in the lanes. Somewhere amongst all these shacks are the homes of all these people milling around. The dominant

geometric shapes such as triangles and squares, all of which allow large amounts of natural light into the building complex. The building is surrounded by several lakes framed in geometrical shapes, said to symbolise the rivers of Bangladesh.

Interestingly, the construction of the building was commissioned in 1962, well before Bangladesh came into being, and was completed more than 20 years later in 1982. During the Liberation War the work stopped entirely, but then the newly formed government decided to begin it again in 1974 without any changes in the design. The original cost estimate put the building at US$15 million, but when it was completed, construction firms had spent US$32 million. In the words of the jury for the Aga Khan Awards for Architecture:

> Faced with an imposing architectural work of extraordinary power, clarity of form and beauty, the jury could not help but question the compatibility of Sher-e-Bangla Nagar with the needs and aspirations of a poor country. Yet, a review of the building's design and construction plans on site studies reveal that over time it has come to enjoy overwhelming approval, it stands as a symbol of democracy in Bangladesh and has influenced the country in a variety of beneficial ways. Reaching beyond the architecture of the immediate area, the building has assimilated important archetypes of the region among other ways through the extension of its parks and water pools. The architect has re-interpreted and transformed these ideas through a process that applied concepts of construction technology to conditions specific to the Dhaka locale. The result is a building that while universal in its source of forms, aesthetics and technologies, could be in no other place.

colours here are metal-grey and mud-brown, never more so than in times of flooding, when these tiny walkways are quickly waterlogged. But there are also occasional flashes of bright blue and yellow: these are the colours of the uniforms worn by the children to whom Intervida is offering a helping hand.

In Korail, the community pooled their resources to purchase the land for the *pathshala*. To step into the little schoolyard is to enter a vibrant world abuzz with energy and colour. Small classes of uniformed children at work on their various activities, in bamboo classrooms decorated from floor to ceiling with the pictures and poems created by the children themselves. The teachers, whose salaries match those of their government school counterparts, are still to some extent locked into a methodology which emphasises rote memorisation at the expense of active learning, but at the very least they have fashioned a positive and encouraging environment, unlike some of the dreary cobweb-laced classrooms I have seen in regular primary schools.

After a day like this among those who eke out a life in Korail, you are struck both by the contrast with the people in the smart neighbourhoods all around, and by how much we actually share. That evening, an image returned to my mind and refused to subside. Sitting in the daycare centre, I'd looked through a gap in the wall, only to realise with a start that I was looking into someone's home. An almirah, with carefully folded shirts in a pile, a television perched high above a few schoolbooks. And there, no more than a few feet away from me, a handsome teenager, looking intently into a heart-shaped mirror, brushing his hair, peering at his teeth, and, finally satisfied, making his way out into the morning. Despite the obvious difference in living standards between him and just about anyone reading this, what he and his neighbours also want from their lives is more of the things they find pleasant, and fewer of the hardships. He's looking for contentment, and just a small piece of dignity. In this, of course, he's no different from you and me.

Tours of the National Assembly building can be arranged by local tour operators (see page 118) or by the Urban Study Group (*2/F, Hse 29, Rd 1, Dhanmondi;* ☎ *861 7854;* m *01819 248408; cost on donation basis*). However, this needs to be arranged well in advance, as permission is required for security reasons. Photography is not permitted inside the building.

Sat Gumbad Mosque [128–9 A3] (*Ring Rd, Mohammadpur*) Dating from 1680, the seven-domed mosque is said to be the finest example of Mughal-style architecture in Dhaka.

Intellectual Martyrs' Monument [114–15] (*Rayer Bazaar, West Dhanmondi*) When the Pakistani army began its genocide during the Liberation War, they immediately targeted the nation's best minds. Their goal was not complicated – by destroying the intelligentsia they believed they could more effectively control dissent against their rule. On 12 December 1971, two days before the war ended, they rounded up about 250 journalists, doctors, professors, engineers and writers and took them to torture cells around the city. Two days later, most had been murdered and dumped into mass graves. The monument commemorates this last atrocity of the war. To learn more about those fateful days, visit www.bangladeshgenocide.com. Be warned – the website is not for the faint of heart.

Unfortunately, the monument itself is not in great shape and perhaps more interesting is the embankment area surrounding it. Rayer Bazaar lies at the intersection of the Dhaka countryside and its urban core, but manages to feel a world apart. It's a scenic place to take photographs and see how most of Dhaka's millions truly live.

Bangabandhu Sheikh Mujib Museum [128–9 D4] (*Hse 10, Rd 11;* ☎ *811 0046;* ⏲ *10.00–17.00 Thu–Tue; entry Tk10*) On 15 August 1975, army gunmen stormed the sheikh's home and gunned down more than 20 people there, including the sheikh himself and all of his family members, save for Sheikh Hasina and Sheikh Rehana, who were out of the country at the time. Today his home has become this museum, which contains a decidedly political slant on the man accorded the title 'Father of Bangladesh'. As to why the sheikh was murdered, see *Chapter 1, History, Early days of Bangladesh*, page 11.

Kawran Bazaar [124–5 B2] Located in the heart of the new city and housing most of the major media outlets, Kawran Bazaar isn't so much a 'sight' as a place to get a feel for Dhaka's thronging heartbeat. Between the office buildings and the railway artery, the bazaar hums with activity at all times of the day. At night, trucks are permitted onto the city's streets and so this is when activity swells beyond belief. Most of the city's fresh goods are brought here first, where scores of workers then load massive baskets of fruits and vegetables onto their heads to get them to smaller markets around town. If you do decide to visit, it would be best to go in a group and arrange transport.

Bhasani Novotheater [128–9 F1] (*Bijoy Sharani, east of Zia Uddyan Park*) The country's only planetarium features a dome-shaped theatre and celestial exhibits that give Bangladeshis a taste of the galaxy. It's a good place to take the kids for an afternoon.

Dhaka Zoo [114–15] (*Mirpur, northwestern city outskirts;* ☎ *803 5035, 900 2020;* ⏲ *07.00–18.00 Mon–Sat; entry Tk10*) Given the fact your likelihood of seeing a tiger in the wild is quite low (even in Sundarban), you'd best head here if you want to see the predatory feline up close and personal. Otherwise, the zoo has well over 100 species of animals, including lions, leopards, monkeys, chimps and many more. When Mahatma Gandhi said 'The measure of a society can be seen by how well its people treat its animals', he was right on the money. During the winter, especially January, is a great time to visit, as the zoo becomes a layover location for several varieties of migrating birds.

National Botanical Gardens [114–15] (*Mirpur, next to the zoo and accessed through the same gate;* ☎ *803 3292;* ⏲ *09.00–16.30; entry Tk5*) The city's botanical gardens are an extremely tranquil place in the morning and also serve as a great birdwatching destination in winter, like the zoo.

The garden's 40ha contains over 1,000 different species of local and imported plants – definitely a botanist's dream.

Korail Slum [120–1 D6] (*Banani Lake; Tk2 ferry ride*) While it might seem a little odd to be listing a slum as a tourist destination, the Korail slum is unique because it is 'an island of poverty among a sea of affluence', according to writer Andrew Morris (see box on pages 150–1). From the lofty apartments of Gulshan, the wealthiest neighbourhood in town, Korail is completely visible and its inhabitants live a very public life. Many of its shacks perch precariously on bamboo stilts above Banani Lake. Getting here is another adventure in itself: first you clamber onto the wooden ferry boats with the locals and then you can walk through the slum to the other end. If you prefer something more informative and instructive, contact **Intervida Bangladesh** for more information (*Hse 504, Rd 34, new DOHS Mohakhali; www.intervida.org*). The Spanish development agency has set up a number of *pathshalas* in the Dhaka slums, which provide free education to the children of these neighbourhoods.

DAY TRIPS FROM DHAKA

Armed with a sense of adventure and a sincere desire to see the heart and soul of Bangladesh lying just beyond the city borders, there are plenty of day-trip options in and around Dhaka. Listed below are a few suggestions that only require a one-day trip, although a few accommodation options are listed below for those seeking an overnight escape. Otherwise, you can check out *Chapter 4, Dhaka Division*, for more information.

Before your departure, here are some logistical suggestions. Those with some extra cash will find it best to organise a group of friends/fellow travellers and hire a shared vehicle for the day, although this isn't necessarily the cheapest route. Public buses are available to all of the below destinations for a fraction of the price, but you do get what you pay for: several hours of hair-raising start–stop driving that can be unbelievably dangerous in one moment and absolutely standstill in the next – quite possibly the cheapest rollercoaster you've ever ridden.

On the return journey do be aware that city dwellers all have the odd habit of returning at the same time after dusk, so it's best to depart as early as possible in the morning (06.00–06.30 is best) so as to make the return journey earlier and easier on your crew. While such an early start might sound a bit ridiculous for a weekend trip, you'll believe it when you're back before nightfall and not in the grip of a terrible traffic jam in the dark.

BOAT TRIPS Perhaps the best way to explore the areas surrounding Dhaka is by boat. There are a few options of how to do this, each offering a varying level of service and exposure to local travel.

Organised tours

Contic Tours and Cruises [120–1 E6] (*4/F, Hse 23, Rd 121, Gulshan 1;* ☎ *881 4824;* m *01711 402513;* e *mail@contic.com; www.contic.com*) Offers high-end, well-serviced boat tours, either around Dhaka or on the Jamuna River. They have three boats – the *B613*, the *Fleche D'Or* and the *Little Prince* – each suited for varying numbers of passengers, service and length of trip. Overnight stays on the luxurious *B613* will cost US$180 or more per person, with six passengers needed for departure. The company is the creation of French–Bangladeshi couple Yves and Runa Marre, who have worked hard to preserve Bangladesh's boatbuilding traditions through their work. Their associated NGO, Friendship, also has a floating hospital project working in some of the poorest river island areas of the Jamuna.

The Guide Tours [120–1 C4] (*Darpan Complex, Gulshan 2;* ☎ *988 6983, 986 2205;* m *01711 696337;* e *theguide@bangla.net; www.guidetours.com*) Operates a cruising yacht called the *SB Ruposhi* just for exploring the Sitalakhya River around Dhaka. Organising a trip does require some pre-planning as you'll want to round up some friends/fellow travellers in order to minimise the cost of the boat hire. A typical day includes an afternoon departure, followed by an evening barbecue while watching the sunset. A day tour or sunset cruise costs Tk2,500 or more per person, with a minimum departure of ten people.

The Boat Consortium Long-term residents in Bangladesh may eventually bump into someone who has membership in 'The Boat Consortium', a group of expatriates who have purchased and refurbished three vessels explicitly for taking leisurely cruises around the city. Generally these kinds of events will be by invitation only and involve significant quantities of alcohol.

Tongi This is the option for travellers willing to strike out on their own, in search of a random Bangladeshi adventure. First, you head to Tongi by baby taxi and disembark at the Tongi Bridge. From there, ask around until you can find a *tolar*, or motorised passenger boat, to take you to Ulukhola, located approximately 12km (8km as the crow flies) along the Tongi River. Should a *tolar* prove difficult to find, some travellers have hired a rowboat and the journey took about two hours.

Once past the city limits, the views are sublime and allow excellent glimpses into local life along the river. During the monsoon season, the river is flooded on all sides, but during the dry season there will be plenty of opportunities to see life up close and enjoy the peace and quiet. At Ulukhola, you can visit the Church of St Augustine of Hippo, dating from 1925. The humble church is located in Mathbari village, and still functions as a welfare organisation.

To return to Dhaka, you'll need to catch a rickshaw to the N105 Highway, also known as the Dhaka Bypass Road on some maps. Ask a rickshaw wallah to take you to a bus or CNG stand and bargain your way home.

CYCLE TRIPS Those based in Dhaka and working full time will find that the weekends can sometimes be too short for escapes too far out of the city. But armed with a good map, a keen sense of direction (or a mobile enabled with Google Maps) and a sturdy bicycle, it is easy to go exploring the rural areas northeast of Bashundhara for a few hours. The best tool for checking out cycling routes is Google Earth. There are hundreds of little pathways snaking through gorgeous rural countryside, all of which lie tantalisingly close to the city. After a few canal and river crossings, there are paths of various qualities, including bricked paths, dirt roads and tarred roadways suitable for motorcycles and even cars.

Because of the differing qualities of path, a bicycle equipped with a front shock absorber is best, although it's not absolutely required. There is a small group of expatriates who make exploratory trips every weekend. If you ask around you'll locate the group and can join them for a ride, although they tend to be very well equipped and pretty fit riders. A temporarily loaned bicycle is also not too hard to find, but does require some networking first.

SONARGAON Sonargaon ('Golden City' in Hindi) served as an eastern capital of Bengal at various points throughout Bengal's pre-Mughal history, although at times it was only a subsidiary capital to Gaur at Rajshahi. Prior to the 13th century it was a centre of Hindu power, although when the Muslim generals and governors starting showing up in the late 13th century, most of them used Sonargaon as their base because of its strategic location at the convergence of the then Brahmaputra (now Jamuna) and Meghna rivers. When the Mughals took power in the early 17th century, they saw Dhaka as more strategically protected from Arakanese invaders and hence decided to relocate the capital to Dhaka. From that time, the area experienced a serious decline and not many of its historic buildings still remain.

At its zenith, however, Sonargaon was known as the 'Golden City', and a number of specialised industries sprung up to support it. It was the trading centre of Bengal's famous muslin cloth, and north of Sonargaon at Murapara there are still remnants of this industry – a few villages with specialised *jamdani* weavers still inhabit the area. However, most of the textile skill was destroyed under British colonial rule. Today, Sonargaon feels like a bit like a ghost town in which the atmosphere of the Hindu *zamindars* (landlords) lingers among the old mosques, *rajbaris* and architecture that survived the decline.

Getting there and away Reaching Sonargaon is quite easy by public bus. Take any Mograpara-bound bus from Dhaka's Gulistan Bus Station and enjoy the local ride (45mins; Tk50). From there, plenty of rickshaw wallahs can ferry you around the site.

What to see

Mograpara Mograpara is now a bustling village situated on the southern end of the Dhaka–Chittagong Highway. Unfortunately, most of its mosques haven't survived and are now lying in ruins, with most visitors passing them by in favour of the more picturesque Painam Nagar. Nevertheless, it is worth making the journey to visit the Tomb of Sultan Ghiyasuddin Azam Shah, as well as the other mosques and tombs of the village.

Painam Nagar Positively *the* highlight of a visit to Sonargaon, Painam Nagar houses a few dozen aging *rajbaris* that rich Hindu *zamindars* built at the beginning of the 20th century. They are not, in fact, the buildings of Old Sonargaon – those are in Mograpara. Today you can wander around the settlement and imagine what life must have been like here at the turn of the century, although the inhabitants who live there now are mostly squatters who lack other places to live. Most of the *zamindars* fled their mansions during the partition of India in 1947, or later on during the Indo–Pakistan riots of 1964.

Near the end of the strip of old buildings you will also find one labelled the 'Sonargaon Art Gallery', at which artist Aminul Islam does a series of drawings and paintings depicting scenes from Bengal.

Awal Manzil Just 500m up the road from the end of Painam Nagar, there is one regal house that nobody seems to know about. Awal Manzil (sometimes referred to as Poddar Bari) has been well maintained by a caretaker who seems reluctant to have too many visitors. But with a few reassuring words of Bengali and a small *boksheesh* (judgement call required), you can go in and have a look at one of Sonargaon's finest buildings. Inside the house, there is a fabulously decorated courtyard, private pond and *naach ghar*, or dance hall, where some regal parties must have been held at the turn of the century, before Hindu–Muslim violence drove the original owners away.

Sadarbari (*⌚ 10.00–17.00; compound admission Tk4; museum Tk3*) This aging *rajbari* now houses a folk art museum and is one of the oldest buildings still standing in Sonargaon. Embellished with a picturesque façade and a nearby pond, it is worth having a gander. Just nearby there is a modern museum building with some rather dusty exhibits.

Goaldi Mosque This historic mosque lies on a pathway that few visitors bother to check out. Built in 1519, this small, single-domed mosque is characteristic of pre-Mughal architecture. You can easily walk there in about 15 minutes from the folk art museum. Instead of entering the ticket area that contains the folk art museum, continue along the road towards Painam Nagar, but take the first left after a few hundred metres. Then, weave your way through the serene local villages heading northwest (a few turns are involved), asking your way there.

Sitalakhya River at Demra, Rupgonj and Murapara These areas used to be the centre of the muslin-weaving industry in pre-Mughal Bengal, before most of it moved to Dhaka's Tanti Bazaar. Nowadays, the historic fabric faces an uncertain future as its weavers cannot sustain themselves financially, with its most skilled craftspeople switching over to the better-paid jobs inside modern garment factories. A finely made *jamdani* is said to take two to three months to create, but today, most of its practitioners take shorter periods to produce cheaper, perhaps more inferior, designs.

To get here, head out of town on the Dhaka–Chittagong Highway. About 10km from Dhaka's Jatrabari crossing circle (one of the last major urban traffic crossings with impenetrable traffic jams, after which there is an unmistakably smelly fish market) drive for about 10km and then turn left after crossing Demra Bridge over the Sitalakhya River. After another 4km, turn left into a village road that leads back towards the river and follow that for another 5km. This will get you to the village of Gandharbapur, the home of the Murapara Zamindarbari, a stately looking residence in the countryside overlooking a pleasant pond. From here you can ask around for the weaving villages, which should be located further north along the road.

LOHAGANJ AND MUNSHIGANJ This sublimely scenic area lies near the massive convergence of the Meghna and Padma rivers, the place where all of the subcontinent's water makes its last journey towards the Bay of Bengal. There isn't much here in the way of classical tourist 'sites', but a journey here, just one hour from the city borders, does offer some great vistas over the river landscape.

Getting there and away Buses for the Mawa Ferry ghat depart from the Gulistan bus stand (1hr; Tk60). Visitors can make for the rather precariously located Padma Resort, popular among the massive crowds of picnicking Bangladeshis (*Lohaganj, Munshiganj, 6km east from the Mawa ferry ghat;* ☎ *815 2324;* **m** *01713 033049; www.padmaresort.net; 16 duplex cottages with fan rooms; Tk3,000 b/fast inc or Tk2,000 for day use, Tk300 pp for lunch*). Although the resort seems crowded during the day it becomes quiet in the evening as not so many guests choose to stay overnight. The area is especially scenic during the rainy season, when the river's flooded waters flow underneath the resort's cottages – it is precarious in the sense that stilts keep the cottages above water during the monsoon. To experience this 'waterworld' phenomenon, visit between July and October. For the rest of the year, the area turns into an enormous river beach, scenic in another way. It is best to contact owner Mohammed Ali before visiting so that arrangements can be made before your arrival. Bangladeshi food is served but other things may be able to be cooked on request.

SAVAR This area, about 15km from Gabtali Bus Station, is better known as Dhaka's export-processing zone. Here, many of the city's garment factories send their resulting materials for packaging and processing. Along with the Gazipur and Ashulia areas, a great majority of what are Bangladesh's biggest industries run from this area.

Most of these factories line the highway towards the National Martyrs' Memorial, along with dozens of brick-making kilns, marked by their smokestacks poking up from the rice patties, giving the landscape an eerie industrial look. Silt from flooded areas is the source of the mud necessary to produce these bricks, most of which is mined directly from the riverbeds by hand and dumped into overladen boats that seem only inches from sinking. Workers then pile the mud into trucks to take it to the kilns, where it is then formed into brick shapes, fired and then trucked to the city for construction. If it ever seems that Dhaka is a giant construction zone, the answer is yes, it is, and at the outskirts of the city is where it all begins.

Getting there and away To get there by bus, go to the Gabtali bus stand and find an almost full bus heading for Sha-var Bazaar (Savar Bazaar) or Manikganj or by specifiying the memorial's name in Bangla (*jat-ee-yo shm-ree-tee shod-oh*) (1hr; Tk20). Otherwise a CNG ride will cost you about Tk100, but you'll probably find a driver willing to make the round trip for Tk250–350, more if you plan to stop in Dhamrai.

What to see

National Martyrs' Memorial (*Jatiyo Smriti Souddho in Bangla; entry free*) The monument gracing every Tk500 note in Bangladesh is situated here, about 22km from the city border, 8km past the main Savar Bazaar. The structure, a result of a design competition held in 1978, consists of seven isosceles triangles and was the conception of architect Syed Moinul Hossain. Around the monument itself are a series of mass graves, plus some well-tended gardens. To reach it requires a climb up and down a series of stairs, which are meant to symbolise Bangladesh's struggle for independence. If you wander inside the monument, you get an even better appreciation for its beauty and design. Finally, it does look rather regal at night when it is lit up, and processions are held here every 26 March to commemorate independence.

Dhamrai (*5km past the National Martyrs' Memorial, village just a few hundred metres past the Dhamrai bus stand, turn right after the Alta Pharma Factory*) Situated just beyond the National Martyrs' Memorial is the village of Dhamrai, a predominantly Hindu village with a few interesting sights. The oldest part of the village has a few aging *rajbaris* and the Jagannath Chariot, used in processions held during the Rath Jatra Hindu festival in late June or early July. Otherwise, Dhamrai is the second-best place to experience Durga Puja, the largest Hindu festival across Bengal.

Thousands of people come from nearby villages to watch the ceremonial dumping of the goddess into the river. If you come on a Friday or a Monday you will also experience market day in the village.

The **Dhamrai Metal Crafts Workshop** (m *01713 003136;* e *dmcsukanta@hotmail.com*) is housed inside one of the old *rajbaris* of the village. The proprietor, Sukanta Banik, has been trying to preserve his family's tradition of brass making, using the 'lost wax technique'. Craftsmen first create intricate Hindu and Buddhist designs on pieces of wax, from which clay moulds are formed. During the firing process the wax melts away. The resulting mould is then filled with molten brass or bronze, producing a unique piece that has no exact equivalent. The designs are quite beautiful but they are also expensive, ranging from a few thousand taka to well over Tk100,000 for the largest and most intricate designs.

Centre for the Rehabilitaton of the Paralysed (*northeastern outskirts of Savar Bazaar, look for sign on Dhaka–Aricha Highway;* *771 0464–5;* e *info@crp-bangladesh.org; www.crp-bangladesh.org*) In Bangladesh, there is definitely no lack of disabilities amongst its people. Some of these are from birth defects, others come from workplace injuries. Concepts like 'worker's compensation' and disability insurance simply don't exist here. Since 1979, the CRP has worked with disabled people, (mainly those with spinal injuries), with the hope of reintegrating them into society. To this end, there are a number of trainings conducted here at the centre, including an electronics lab, textile production and a woodworking shop.

Visitors are welcome at the centre and can have a brief guided tour of the facilities by former patients. Gift cards and handicrafts are available here for purchase. If you can't make it to the CRP itself, do visit CRP-Aware (*2/F Unicorn Plaza, 40/2 North Av, Gulshan*) to purchase some of the handicrafts or clothing made by patients of the centre.

DEMORPARA, PUBAIL The area immediately northeast of Dhaka is rural and lush, and makes for an escape barely one hour's drive from the city. At the Demorpara village of the Pubail, 15km northwest of the city limits, the **Pubail Retreat** (*Pilotbari, Demopara, Pubail, Gazipur;* m *01521 108520, 01819 262030;* $$$$) offers serviced day trips and overnight stays in open-air accommodation. The 25-acre property is spread amongst the homes of a local fishing village. There are two fan rooms available with shared bathrooms, but what would be more memorable is a sleep in the open air under one of the various bamboo canopies spread around the retreat grounds – staying here would be more like a serviced camping trip or even a homestay. Tasty local meals are also available for visiting guests and the retreat also organises exposure visits to the surrounding village areas. An overnight stay for two starts at Tk16,000, which includes transfers, meals and accommodation, but the price drops to Tk3,000 per person for a group of 10. If you're interested in visiting, your best bet is to contact owner Kamal Mahmood to make your arrangements.

MANIKGANJ Two lesser-known *rajbaris* make for some interesting journeys for those with the vehicular ability to explore the Manikganj area, 30km beyond the National Martyrs' Memorial. The Baliati Zamindarbari (Palace) used to be the home of Sukhendu Roy Chowdhury's father, who was a Hindu landlord of the area. Today, Mr Sukhendu and his family live in New Delhi, having escaped from Bangladesh during the tumultuous time surrounding partition. After posting pictures on the internet, Chowdhury contacted us with this fascinating story:

I was told that when I was one year old, my mother left Baliati with her sons including myself. My father, with his adamant attitude, continued there for three more years and finally arrived at our refugee camp near Bishnupur, West Bengal with five rupee to spare. It was a double tragedy in respect of money matters. Soon, my elder brother became a teacher in the refugee camp and we were seven mouths to be fed. It was already a miserable life that we were leading at that time before father came and joined. He did nothing as he could not leave his Zamindar's nature.

No one is living there as far as I know. I am 54 years old now and live in Delhi with my small family and do outsourcing work for an American company. My mother suffered a lot in the hands of my tyrant father. We brothers and sisters were also scared of our father. My parents are now no more and my other brothers and sisters are in West Bengal.

Somehow the name Baliati has a magic spell on me having heard about it from my mother a number of times. You can see my email address is also baliati@gmail.com. I would like to pay a visit to Bangladesh as and when the opportunity comes.

If you avail yourself of the opportunity to visit Baliati, do send a message to Mr Sukhendu with your photographs as he would obviously appreciate it.

Further onwards towards the Jamuna River is the Teota Palace, another British-era mansion with some extraordinarily beautiful buildings. Best among these is the family's Hindu temple, a three-storey affair topped with majestic hive-like towers, located beside a pond. The *rajbari* itself still has some intricate building decorations intact as well.

Getting there and away To reach Baliati, you need to turn right off the Dhaka–Aricha Highway approximately 8km before reaching Manikganj. The turn-off lies just before a pair of signs welcoming you to the Manikganj district. There is a small Department of Archaeology sign marking the turn-off that's better seen when approaching from the west. Teota is several kilometres south of the Aricha ghat. Head there first and then ask your way there.

Where to stay **Proshika**, one of Bangladesh's largest NGOs, has a training centre with clean and comfortable rooms. The grounds are peaceful and the meals served pretty good, making it an excellent venue for a family-orientated one-day escape from Dhaka (*Saturia Thana, Koitta village, Manikganj;* ☎ *801 5812, 801 6015, 801 6759, 801 5945;* **m** *01714 085921 (Mr Bashir); www.proshika.org/hrdct_n.htm;* $$$$).

SHISHU POLLI PLUS (*Tengra, Sreepur village, Gazipur;* ☎ *02 895 3308;* **m** *01199 850145;* **e** *info@sppdbd.org; www.thesreepurvillage.org*) Shishu Polli Plus is the local name for 'the Sreepur Village', a charity project started by British Airways stewardess Pat Kerr way back in 1981. As the story goes, Kerr was determined to make a difference amongst children of a local orphanage she began visiting during flight layovers. Eight years later in 1989, her efforts culminated in the Sreepur village, a safe haven for underprivileged women and children at a location about 70km north of Dhaka. Currently, the village provides healthcare, education and shelter to 100 women and over 400 children who would otherwise have no place to go. The village also provides vocational and business training to its residents, the end goal being to have them reintegrate into the wider community. The village welcomes visitors; do bear in mind that the organisation needs donations in order to continue its community rehabilitation work. Regular updates are available on the organisation website.

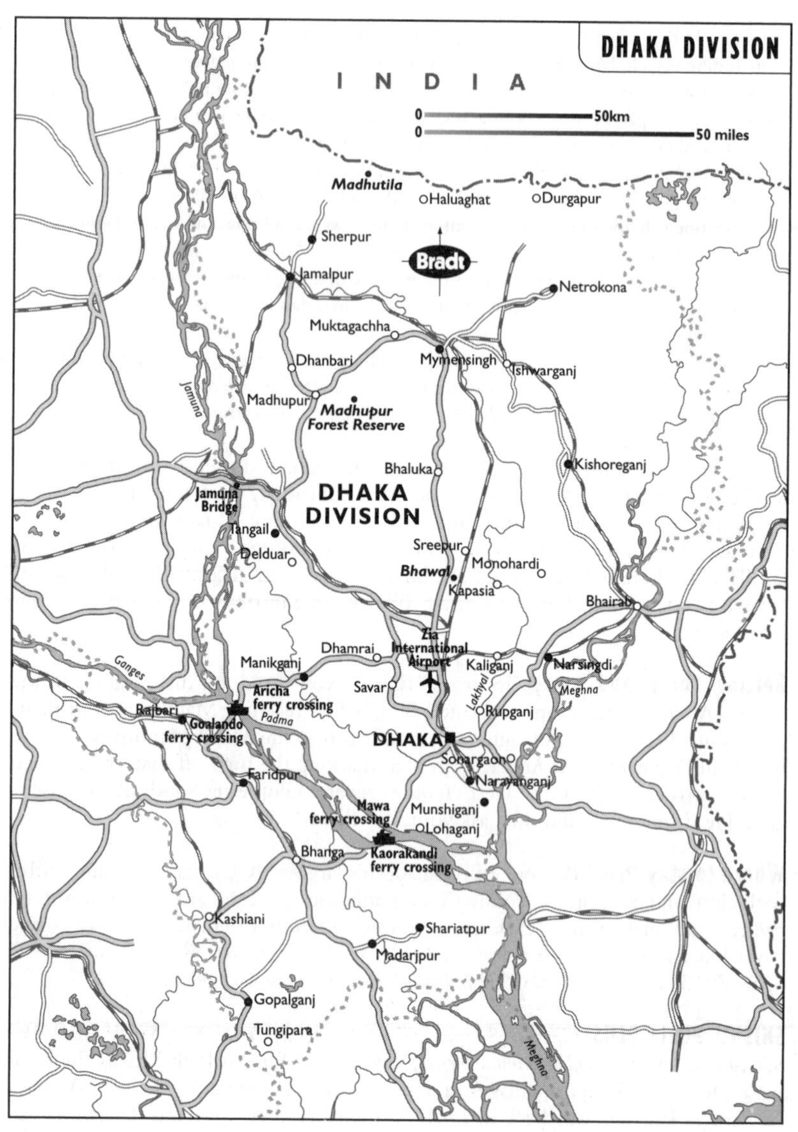
DHAKA DIVISION
INDIA
0 50km
0 50 miles
Madhutila
Haluaghat
Durgapur
Sherpur
Bradt
Jamalpur
Netrokona
Muktagachha
Mymensingh
Ishwarganj
Dhanbari
Madhupur
Madhupur Forest Reserve
Jamuna
Kishoreganj
Bhaluka
Jamuna Bridge
DHAKA DIVISION
Tangail
Sreepur
Delduar
Monohardi
Bhawal
Kapasia
Bhairab
Zia International Airport
Dhamrai
Manikganj
Kaliganj
Narsingdi
Ganges
Savar
Aricha ferry crossing
Lakhyal
Meghna
Rupganj
Rajbari
Goalando ferry crossing
Padma
DHAKA
Sonargaon
Faridpur
Narayanganj
Mawa ferry crossing
Munshiganj
Lohaganj
Bhanga
Kaorakandi ferry crossing
Kashiani
Shariatpur
Madarjpur
Gopalganj
Tungipara
Meghna

4

Dhaka Division

Bound by the Garo Hills of Meghalaya and stretching just south of the Padma River, the Dhaka Division includes the capital city and the area immediately surrounding it. Its most scenic areas lie directly adjacent to the hills bordering India. During the monsoon, a torrent of crystal-clear water streams from the hills, and spills into Bangladesh's northern region, an attraction that isn't even known to most Bangladeshi people.

Fortunately, the division's proximity to Dhaka means it's easy to get there, and a number of tourism businesses have opened up to attract city dwellers seeking weekend escapes. There are a number of resorts with full facilities, especially around Tangail, which offer a high standard of amenities (high for Bangladesh, of course). But the most adventurous will want to head straight for the northern border, where indigenous Garo culture and some very scenic rivers and hills await.

MYMENSINGH *Telephone code 091*

This medium-sized town is built along the south bank of the Old Brahmaputra River, where the bulk of this mighty river used to flow until it changed course during the 18th century. Historically, the region shared the same history and fate as the rest of Bangladesh, but did spring some insurgency of its own in the form of the Sannyassi Revolt of 1772–90. After the British pacified the rebellion, the region became a major production centre of jute and remained so until the natural fibre was eventually taken over by synthetic products in the late 20th century.

Mymensingh was also the hometown of one of Bengal's most famous artists, Zainul Abedin. The painter is most well known for his depictions of the 1943 famine of Bengal, where he depicted the gaunt, starving figures using stark coal sketches. Today there is a museum for the artist in Mymensingh. Finally, the town is also a centre of education in the north, and the Bangladesh Agricultural University is situated in the eastern part of town.

While the town itself possesses some relics of the British Raj, it serves better as a base for exploring and enjoying the nearby ethnic diversity of the north. All along the Indian border, Garo villages lie just under the hills. With matriarchic societies, Christian beliefs and a propensity for homemade alcohol consumption, it is this group of people that makes Mymensingh a fascinating – not to mention easy – place to visit.

GETTING THERE

By bus Buses depart regularly from the Mohakhali Interdistrict Bus Terminal in Dhaka, located just south of the Mohakhali flyover. Several direct chair coaches are available to Mymensingh (3hrs; Tk100), Jamalpur, Haluaghat and Durgapur; with no bridge crossings, connections here are good. These depart through the day but don't go too late or you'll be stuck with a slower bus (some travellers have advised that you avoid Rashik Transport buses). And before you board, ask for a 'direct,

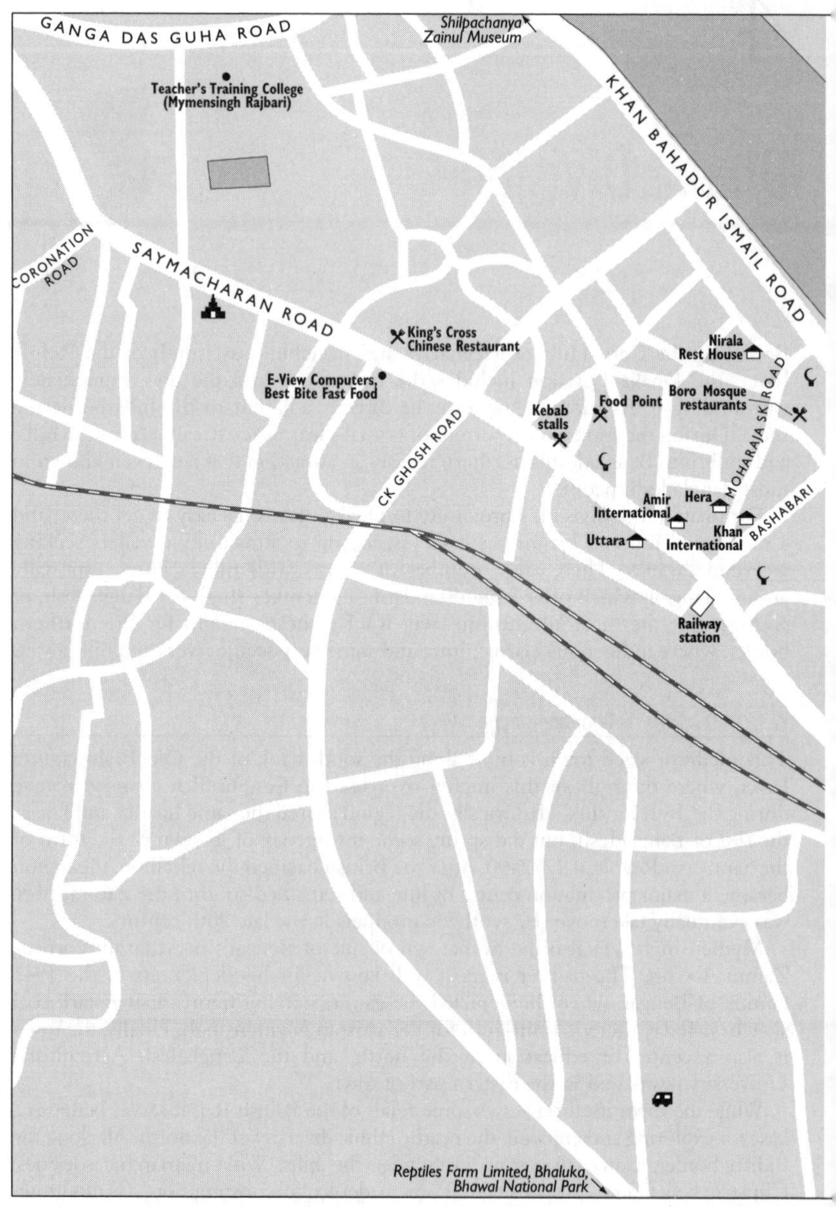

express bus, stopping ney!' and make sure you see it before buying your ticket as some buses will be far nicer than others. If you don't like what you're seeing, shop around.

Buses to Dhaka depart from the Mahstandar bus stand, a few kilometres south of town. For Haluaghat, Birisiri and Durgapur, head to the bus stand near the Bangladesh–China Friendship Bridge.

By train Albeit slightly slower, the train does offer more comfort than the bus and it's an OK alternative. For Dhaka departures, see the schedule on page 109.

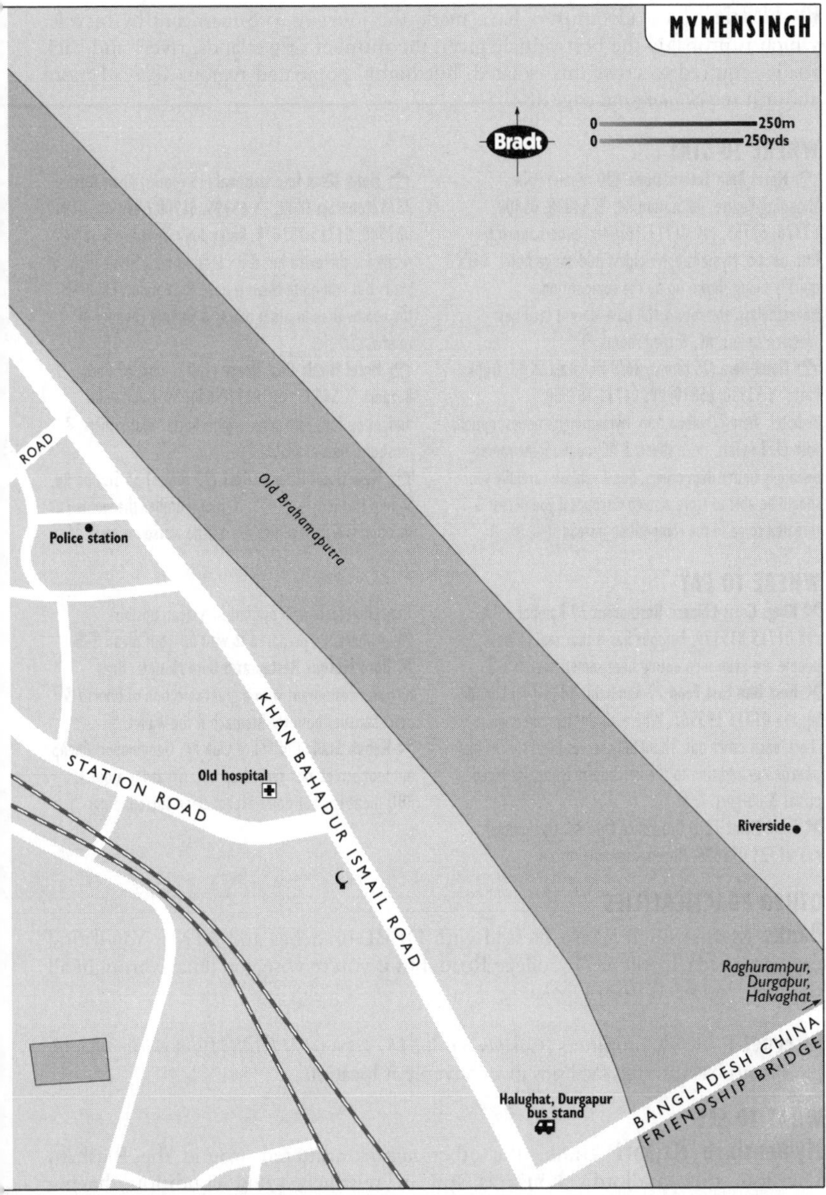

MYMENSINGH

TRAIN TIMETABLE

No	Destination	Train name	Off day	Dep time	Arr time
746	Dhaka	Jamuna Express	No	05.03	08.20
50	Dhaka	Balaka Express	No	15.00	18.55
736	Dhaka	Aghni Bina Express	No	19.20	22.35
38	Chittagong	Mymensing Express	No	05.20	21.50

By bicycle Some adventurers have made the journey to Sunamganj by bicycle, which is probably the best vehicle given the number of wetlands, rivers and back roads required to cross this isolated, but highly populated region. To read more about it see *Sunamganj*, page 183.

WHERE TO STAY

Hotel Amir International (30 rooms) Palika Shopping Centre, 46 Station Rd; ☎ 54030, 65400, 63376, 62755; m 01711 167948; e heroamir@bttb.net.bd. Mymensingh's oldest mid-range hotel, & it's quickly being shown up by the competition. Nevertheless, the rooms still have decent facilities: Western toilets, AC, & tiled rooms. $$$

Hotel Hera (25 rooms) 36/B Moharaja SK Rd, Trunk Potti; ☎ 53930, 65810; m 01711 167880; e hotel_hera@yahoo.com. Mymensingh's newest option, with tiled rooms, clean sheets & AC rooms. Some rooms definitely better than others, but if you ask carefully you should be able to score a steep discount if you persist & threaten to go to the competition instead. $$$

Hotel Khan International (15 rooms) Khan Plaza, 33/A Moharaja SK Rd; ☎ 65995, 61900 (res); m 01817 087588, 01715 281678. Rates don't include tax so be ready for the extra hit, & it's located up a whole flight of stairs but still quite clean & new. More natural light in the rooms than in other places & slightly cheaper AC rooms. $$

Hotel Nirala Rest House (100 rooms) 67 Chota Bazaar; ☎ 54285; m 01719 644629. Good-value budget option, with some rooms better than others, & mosquito nets available. $

New Hotel Uttara (Res) (20 rooms) 55 Station Rd, Shahid Market; ☎ 54455. Men outnumber the women at this hotel, & its facilities are a little worse for wear. $

WHERE TO EAT

Kings Cross Chinese Restaurant 29 Rambabu Rd; m 01715 815399. Rumour has it that real Chinese people are even seen eating here sometimes. $$$

Best Bite Fast Food 27 Rambabu Rd (1st Fl) Canada Sq; m 01716 195567. Where all the teenagers go to check each other out. Thankfully serves local snacks like *phuchka* in addition to the ketchup/mayonnaise-laced pizzas & burgers. $$

Food Point 12/D Old Police Club Rd, Ganginapar; m 01723 098696. More reasonably priced Thai/Chinese/Bangla options in a clean upstairs atmosphere. Be prepared to wait for your meal. $$

Boro Mosque Restaurants Boro Mosque. High turnover restaurant with a great selection of *bhorta* & *dals*. Satisfies both the stomach & the wallet. $

Kebab Stalls Old Police Club Rd, Ganginapar. Cheap outdoor street eats served up hot. Great for a quick BBQ meat fix, but don't expect clean surroundings. $

OTHER PRACTICALITIES

Banks Mymensingh is also blessed with DBBL branches and ATMs. You'll find one at Canada Tower at 71 College Road, but if you're wise you'll have brought all the cash you need from Dhaka.

Internet E-view Computers (*Canada Sq;* ☎ *61574;* m *01711 148319;* e *eview_mym@yahoo.com*) has internet facilities in a convenient location.

WHAT TO SEE

Mymensingh Rajbari Unlike the other *rajbaris* scattered around the Rajshahi Division, this landlord's house is still in relatively good condition, having undergone a restoration job a few years back. Today the building is being used as a teachers' training college, but much of the old structure remains. Originally built in 1905, the building still shows much of the British colonial influence. One of its most unique features is a Classical statue of a semi-nude nymph that greets you just as you walk in the gate, surrounded by a dry fountain.

Shilpacharya Zainul Abedin Museum (*Adjacent to Shaheb Quarter Park;* ⌚ *10.30–17.30 Sat–Wed, 15.30–19.30 Fri, closed Thu; entry Tk2*) This humble gallery (*shongorshalla* in Bangla) is a small tribute to Zainul Abedin (1914–76), who is often referred to as

'Shilpacharya' among Bangladeshis, meaning 'great teacher'. Abedin was born in an undivided India but lived through partition and the Liberation War. His most famous charcoal drawings of the 1943 Bengal famine are not on display here at the museum, but instead at the National Museum at Shabagh in Dhaka. Instead, 53 of his oil paintings are displayed at this Mymensingh museum, most of which depict scenes of rural Bengal. So if you're in the neighbourhood, it's worth paying homage to the man who painted some of Bengal's most haunting images of poverty and famine. To reach the gallery, head to the northwestern tip of the Shaheb Quarter Park, which runs alongside the river. The gate of the gallery is at the end of the park.

Old Brahamaputra River Mymensingh is built all along the riverfront. As a result the town stretches far from east to west. Many of the local people like to head out on boats to enjoy the river, and you can do the same for a price. How much you pay directly depends on the amount of Bangla you have and your negotiation skills. A reasonable fare would be Tk30 for a 30-minute trip or Tk50 for an hour.

AROUND MYMENSINGH

Finally, the best of what Mymensingh has to offer. Most of the following locations are accessible by public bus.

DURGAPUR UPAZILLA This isolated *upazilla* (Bangladeshi name for the area constituting a municipality) of northern Bangladesh has long been a centre of Garo and Hajong activity. With its beautiful panoramas of the Himalayan foothills and the emerald-coloured Someshwari River, it has started attracting the attention of many Bangladeshi adventurers and photographers. Christian holidays are an especially festive time to visit the area, as people are in a celebratory mood (with the help of some hard drinks, of course). This place won't remain a secret for much longer!

Getting there Direct buses to Birisiri, a village of the Duragpur area, are available from Dhaka's Mohalkhali bus terminal. The ride would take just over five hours, and some of it on bumpy backcountry roads (Tk350).

Where to stay Durgapur has only basic hotel facilities, most of which can accommodate backpackers and those visiting for a shorter period. Enquire around the Durgarpur Bazaar, but don't expect luxury accommodation, just beds in a room with a squatter toilet attached. At Birisiri you can stay at the **Tribal Cultural Academy** (*℡ 095 25 56266;* m *01731 039769, contact Shalil Chambugong;* $) or the **YWCA** (m *01712 042916, contact Omita Shangma;* $). Booking ahead is not really required but it helps to let them know you're coming. The YWCA is said to have the newest and most comfortable facilities, although no air-conditioned rooms are available. The cost per bed will be Tk150 or less. All of the above places should be able to provide meals on request, although give them plenty of advance warning.

What to see From Birisiri, the best thing you can do is hire a boat for a few hours to get you right up to the hills. Head for Ranikhong, where a Christian mission and church is situated on the top of a hill. From there you can journey to Bijoypur by rickshaw, the home of more Garo villages and the monument of Rashmoni Hajong, one of the female leaders of the Tonko Andolon movement. Rashmoni is famed as one of the earliest female martyrs against so-called British imperialism.

Birisiri also has a **Tribal Cultural Academy** that you can drop into anytime during the day for some information and/or recommendations for places to see.

HALUAGHAT AND ASKIPARA Haluaghat is simply a ramshackle town of tin shacks and village chaos, but upon coming here you soon notice there is a distinct diversity among its faces, as the Garo people are more numerous the further north you go. Just a few more kilometres away lies the Indian border. You can either stop at Haluaghat and ask after accommodation at the Oxford Christian Mission (ask your way there), or press onwards to the village of Askipara, a beautiful Garo village that lies just under the Garo Hills of Meghalaya. Visitors will find a Garo indigenous craft and weaving centre led by women, as well as a 100-year-old Anglican church in Panihata (another 20 minutes by motorcycle or one hour walk). From the top of the church, the view of Meghalaya State and Bugai River is beautiful. If you ask around, you'll probably be able to stay with one of the friendly villagers of the region. Better yet, you may be directed to the house of a local headman, who is rather accustomed to seeing the occasional smiling foreigner(s) showing up on his doorstep. If you prefer a more official introduction, send an email to the **Bangladesh Indigenous People's Forum** (e *sanjeebdrong@gmail.com, drong03@yahoo.com*) and the folks there will be happy to tell you more.

Haluaghat lies north from Mymensingh, about one hour by public bus (head to the bus stand near the bridge in the east part of town). To reach Askipara, the best way is to hire some local motorcycles from the bazaar at Haluaghat for the 30–minute ride.

REPTILES FARM LIMITED (*Dhaka: Ste 2B, Hse 1/8, Blk D, Lalmatia;* m *01713 038796; Farm Office: Hatiber Mouza, Uthura Union, Bhaluka Thana;* m *01714 090497;* ⏲ *Dec/Jan 10.00–12.00, 14.00–16.00 Fri/Sat; entry Tk250 adults, Tk200 children*) Bangladesh's sole institution devoted to the conservation of saltwater crocodiles. While the farm is in the market of crocodile skins, the owners seem to be very passionate in promoting knowledge about this highly misunderstood predator. The manager is a friendly and knowledgeable man who will happily walk you around and give you straight facts. For example, when asked how many fingers have been lost, he said 'eighteen fingers, four legs. We count every one.'

Officially, no visitors are allowed outside specific visiting hours as it's obvious that the owners don't want their operation to be overrun by hordes of Bangladeshi tourists, but being a *bideshi* helps a lot. Kindly asking the guard at the front gate to speak with the manager will help, or if you call first and explain the purpose of your visit they should extend their normal hospitality towards foreign guests.

Getting there This oddity is located a short distance off the Dhaka–Mymensingh Highway. First, head for Bhaluka. About 4km past the Bhaluka bus stand, turn left at the Bhora Duba Bazaar, and then continue for 12km towards Uthura. From here, you should start asking after the '*Kumir* project' (Bangla for crocodiles) and locals will show you the rest of the way.

SHOLAKIA A locality near Kishoreganj Town, famous for holding the largest prayer gathering in Bangladesh during Eid–ul Fitr, the day of celebration after the end of Ramadan, About 300,000 men are said to take part in this congregational prayer each year. Kishoreganj is roughly 120km northeast of Dhaka, and 100km southwest of Mymensingh.

BHAWAL NATIONAL PARK A picnicking destination for busloads of Bangladeshi holidaymakers that does have some tracts of forest wilderness lining the Dhaka–Mymensingh Highway. If stuck in the region at night you could stay at the

GARO PEOPLE OF NORTHERN MYMENSINGH

Isaac Sairs

Although the exact number is unknown, Bangladeshi anthropologists estimate that about 100,000 Garo people are found as far northwest as Rowmari and as far east as Sunamganj, with the highest concentration found in villages around Mymensingh. Many more live on the Indian side of the border as well. Their unique ethnicity and racial makeup derives from their Mongoloid origins, and some historians believe they actually originate from Qinghai province in China, having resided first in Tibet and Bhutan on their journey to the current homelands in the Meghalaya Hills.

Fruits and rice are the principal foods of the Garo diet, and their cuisine is very distinct from Bangladeshi offerings. Like the Chinese, Garo people have little reservations with respect to food and do take pork regularly in their diet. They also brew their own rice beers and wines, which are quite heartily consumed on the occasion of visiting guests or during holidays such as Christmas. The largest non-Christian Garo festival is called Wangala, and is often celebrated in early December.

Speaking of religion, the bulk of the Garo people are Christian, although some of the neighbouring Hajong people still call Hinduism their religion. Under British rule, those willing to convert were given land and titles, whereas in the previous ownership system, the area was owned collectively by a tribe and cultivated under a village collective. Despite the conversions, they retained many other non-religious practices, especially those related to marriage and matriarchy – women are the heads of the households here.

The matriarchy beliefs spring from a Garo myth that a woman named Nantanupanta created the earth from a handful of soil taken from the bottom of the ocean. Today, the lineage of families follows the female line, and when a woman dies, her assets are passed to her eldest daughter. Young girls also receive priority in terms of education and resources, and upon marriage, it is the males that move into the woman's house and not the other way around.

When partition came around, it created a Hindu Bengal, and a Muslim Bengal, but left the indigenous people in between. Many of the Garos and most of the Hajong left for India at partition. In the early 1960s there were anti-Hindu/Christian riots stemming from the Indo–Pakistan war and more left for the hills. During the Liberation War, many were forced to move to refugee camps immediately across the border, and many died. Shortly after the establishment of Bangladesh, Muslim settlers began to move in, and even more Garo left.

After decades of interaction with the people of the plains, the Garo people now find themselves more integrated in wider Bangladeshi society. Whether this is by design is not known, but certainly the traditional ways of life these people once held are now harder to find among their villages than before.

Happy Day Inn (*20 rooms;* **m** *01911 004801–4;* **e** *resort@bnk.com.bd*) that lies 100m south of the Bhawal park gate. It's gaudy tiled rooms do offer air conditioning and televisions, but lack charm.

TANGAIL *Telephone code 0621*

There's not much reason to stay in Tangail itself, but there is a good reason to stop here if you're sightseeing and passing through the region, plus there are a few totally unknown resorts nearby. The main attraction here is the Atia Mosque, a wonderfully decorated mosque set in tranquil countryside, embodying both the sultanate and Mughal architectural forms.

GETTING THERE Express public buses are available from the Mohakhali bus stand in Dhaka. From Tangail, there are departures all day to Dhaka (2.5hrs; Tk60), Mymensingh (2.5hrs; Tk60) and Madhubpur (1hr; Tk30). The bus stand is located on the Dhaka–Mymensingh Road that leads towards the Jamuna Bridge.

WHERE TO STAY

SSS Resthouse (12 rooms) Zila Sadar Rd, Akurthakur para; m 01712 799428. A very clean & quiet option that is well out of the thronging bazaar area, but you do pay more for the privilege. All the rooms have AC. B/fast inc. $$$

Hotel Silicon (19 rooms) Khan Supermarket, Mohen Rd; 53994; m 01911 105020. Friendly folks here at this smaller hotel, located upstairs from a clinic. The rooms here are of the basic tiled/attached bathroom variety with fans & mosquito nets. Slightly preferable over the Polash Bari (see below), as it's not as old. $$

Polash Bari (46 rooms) Mosjid Rd; 53154; m 01711 237738. Cheap sgls here in an aging building pressed into the heart of Tangail's market area. Atmospheric perhaps, but noisy also. AC rooms available for the extra bucks but if you're going to splash out, the SSS is better. $

WHAT TO SEE

Atia Mosque Built in 1609 by Sayyid Khan Panni, the Atia Mosque combines both Mughal and pre-Mughal architecture to create one of the country's most interesting mosques. Over the central entrance there is a stone inscription written in Persian, which bears the name and date of the building. The mosque's graceful curves embody the Mughal style, whereas its terracotta plaques represent the sultanate style.

To get here, you need to go southwards 5km from Tangail Town, along the tarred road to Nagapur. Pass through Victoria Road and the crowded Six Annas Market Road, and you'll shortly reach the Delduar and Nagapur roads. Veer right and cotinue for another 4km. The turn-off to your left is marked by a sign in Bangla, and the mosque is several hundred metres down the road, by a pond.

AROUND TANGAIL

DHANBARI ROYAL RESORT (*20 rooms; Dhanbari; 02 913 0900; m 01911 956 357; e resort@lighthousebd.com; www.lighthousebd.com/resort*; $$$$) Three resorts lie due north from Tangail and perhaps the most interesting of the three is the Dhanbari Royal Resort, a sprawling complex that houses the buildings of Bengal's earliest nawab families. The nawabs were the local officers of the Mughal court, but were also highly placed in the British colonial government as well. One of its most prominent members, Nawab Bahadur Syed Nawab Ali Choudhury, was the first Muslim minister from undivided Bengal during British rule. His forefathers were mystic Islamic saints hailing from Baghdad, and were the first managers of the Dhanbari *zamindar* estate. A 700-year-old mosque stands as testament to their presence. Today the property is Bangladesh's only heritage resort, and offers guests a taste of nawab lifestyle in the peaceful countryside.

The resort is situated on the Madhubpur–Jamalpur Highway at the town of Dhanbari, and it takes about four hours to reach the resort, including the time needed to get out of Dhaka. At Elenga, turn right to go towards Madhubpur, and then at the Madhubpur roundabout turn left and travel another 16km. Direct buses leave Mohakhali bus stand at Dhaka for Dhanbari frequently. The closest railway station from this resort is 40km away at Jamalpur.

MADHUBPUR FOREST A long-time home to several generations of Mandi people (also referred to as Garo people), the Madhubpur Forest counts some amazing tracts of sal trees. Unfortunately, this treasure of a forest is slowly disappearing.

After several decades of economically driven Bangladesh Forest Department policies, there have been far too many stories of eviction, land grabbing, murder and banditry arising from Madhubpur. Today, a drive along the Tangail–Mymensingh road reveals a tree-lined road that seems to promise a forest paradise. Monkeys can be seen preying on passing banana carts. But as soon as you proceed further into the forest, the changes become more obvious. Many of the native sal trees have been replaced by rubber and banana plantations, and there's even a shooting range of the Bangladesh army in the forest's northern reaches. Groups of picnickers crowd the forest on weekends, wielding massive speakers and leaving loads of litter.

Certainly, there are still some pockets of the forest that remain untouched and worthy of exploration, but these areas are slowly shrinking under the pressures of a burgeoning population. Visiting the nearby Garo villages would certainly be a pleasant experience; the Garo villages of Pirgacha are rumoured to be excellent places to visit and stay for a day or two.

JAMUNA RESORT (*Hundreds of rooms; Jamuna Bridge, Bhuapur; Dhaka booking office:* ☎ *02 814 2971–3;* m *01711 816807; Resort:* ☎ *031 441 4041–44;* m *01713 049347;* e *jrl@bol-online.com; www.jamunaresort.com;* $$$$) This sprawling complex features modern buildings and accommodation, and also modern prices. There are tennis courts, a swimming pool, billiards hall, restaurant, conference facilities and cottages. All of it is situated on the east bank of the Jamuna Bridge; the resort can arrange boat trips. This is not a bad place to escape for a while but is probably better used as a conference or training facility for anywhere from a dozen to a few hundred guests. The resort's massive facilities are well maintained and there's a museum (⌚ *10.00–16.00 Sat–Thu; entry Tk10*) on site that covers the construction of the bridge.

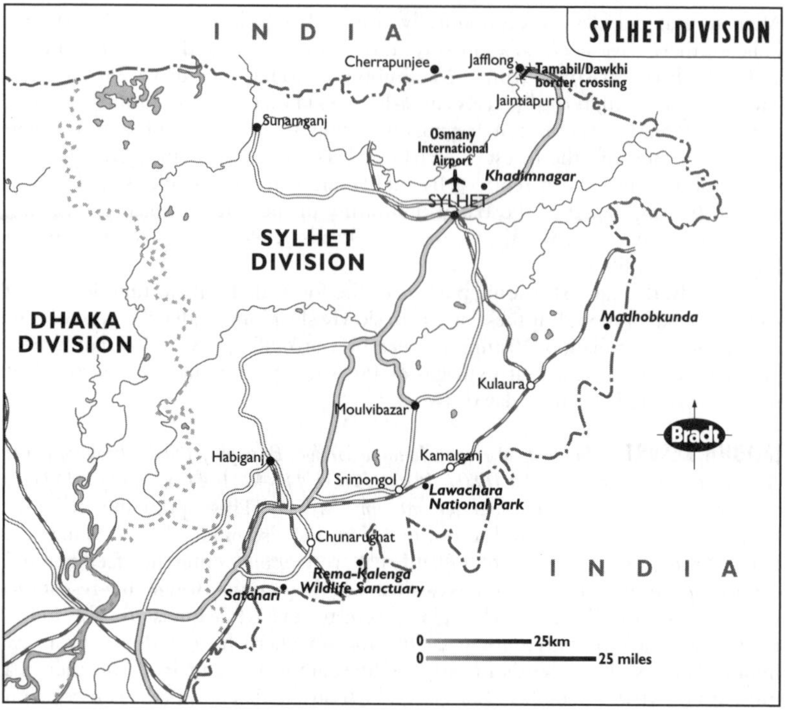

SYLHET DIVISION

INDIA
Cherrapunjee
Jafflong
Tamabil/Dawkhi border crossing
Jaintiapur
Sunamganj
Osmany International Airport
Khadimnagar
SYLHET
SYLHET DIVISION
DHAKA DIVISION
Madhobkunda
Kulaura
Moulvibazar
Habiganj
Kamalganj
Srimongol
Lawachara National Park
Chunarughat
Rema-Kalenga Wildlife Sanctuary
Satchari
INDIA
Bradt
0 25km
0 25 miles

5

Sylhet Division

Excluding the Chittagong Hill Tracts, the Sylhet Division holds the greatest variety of landscapes to explore in Bangladesh. With low rolling hills carpeted by tea plantations, scattered patches of tropical forests, and massive wetland marshes, the variety of countryside scenery inside Sylhet remains ripe for exploration. And if that weren't reason enough to visit the division, then perhaps you might want to experience the homeland of so many British Bangladeshis – the people who would eventually found the curry shops populating London's Brick Lane. Curry here definitely isn't made the same way it is over there, however.

Ethnically speaking, the division has populations of Manipuri, Khasia and Tripura people, all of whom live in villages scattered throughout the hills and practising Buddhism, Hinduism and even Christianity. While the Manipuri people have largely integrated into Bangladeshi society as artisans, businesspeople and jewellers, the Khasia and Tripura people have largely stayed separate from mainstream society.

Tea plantation workers, largely from Bihar and Orissa, form another ethnic minority, as they were brought by the British during the colonial days, and retain distinct facial features. Speaking of tea, it is also the region's biggest export item, with tea estates scattered throughout the countryside, but especially concentrated around Srimongol. Because of the naturally cooler and wetter climate of Sylhet, this product is grown in abundance and sold mostly for export to countries like Pakistan and even Russia.

Natural wonders dot the landscape of the division. The Lawachara National Park is one of the precious few natural places where you can see wild Hoolock gibbons in pristine virgin rainforests. During the monsoon, the hills surrounding Sylhet all dump their waters into the Surma's massive depressions, called *haors* in Bangladesh. The largest and most pristine of these is the Tanguar Haor. During the dry season, these winter wetlands house dozens of northern migratory birds, a sight which is nothing short of paradise for the birdwatcher.

Finally, the British connection of Sylhet makes it worth visiting all by itself, if only to see what billions of dollars of foreign remittances can do to a place in a very short time. It depends how you work the numbers, but some say that 2008 could bring a 44% growth in foreign remittances, based on numbers calculated from the record-breaking third quarter but then the financial crisis swept the world. At the time of publication, several countries had decreased or stopped entirely their intake of foreign workers from Bangladesh as a result of the crisis, thus cutting the potential for growth in foreign remittances. Nevertheless, aside from Dhaka, this is Bangladesh's wealthiest region, and it shows.

While the region doesn't compete with nearby Darjeeling for the size of its hills or the quality of its tea, Bangladesh adventurers will find it delightful to explore. For travellers with only a short time available, the region is easily worth three to five days in a two-week itinerary, or several successive weekend visits for the

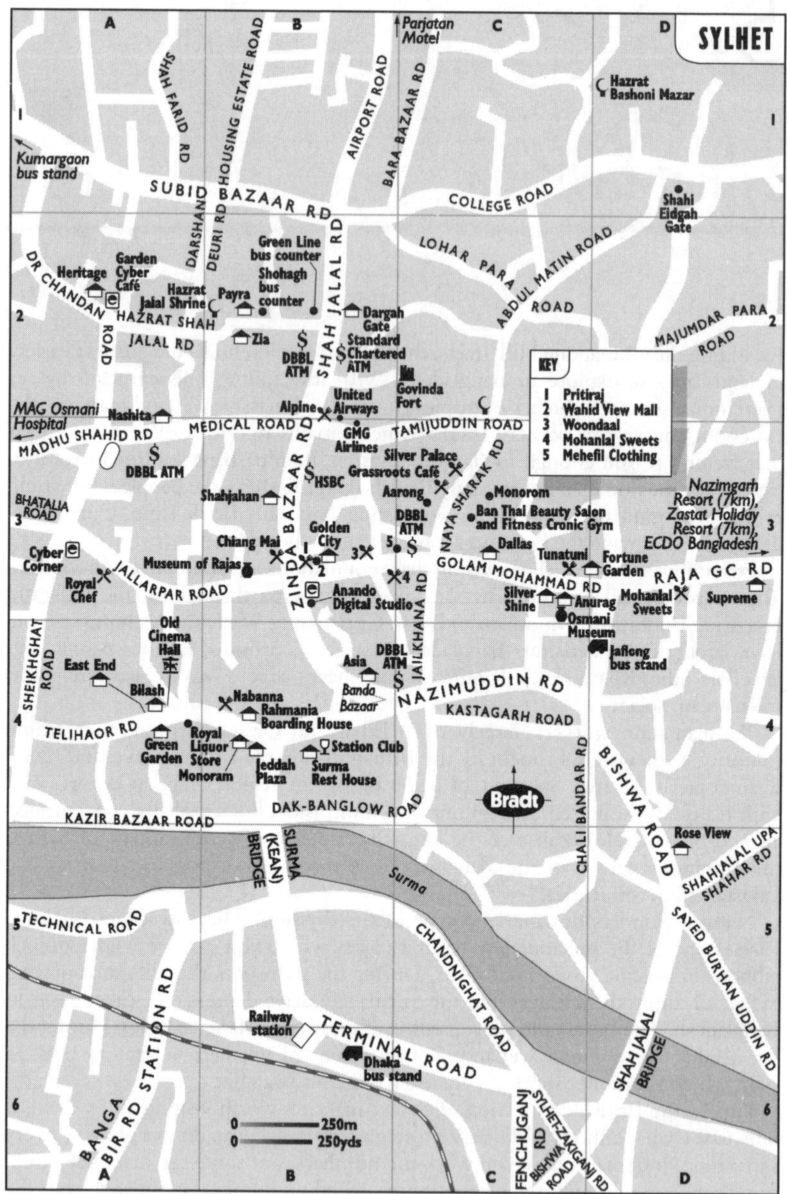

resident expatriate. With so many hilly hidden trails and dirt tracks, cyclists and motorcycle riders have raved about the potential for two-wheeled explorations, but you do need to bring your own bike for now. It's only a matter of time before some enterprising Bangladeshi companies organise cycle tours of the region.

Finally, a special mention must be made of Cherrapunjee, the self-proclaimed 'wettest place on earth', which lies just on the other side of the northeastern border with India. India visa holders should not miss the opportunity to take a holiday on the other side of the border (for further details, see *Cherrapunjee*, page 181).

HISTORY

Like the rest of Bengal, not much is known about Sylhet's ancient history. Like the rest of Bengal, the territory was previously ruled by Indo-Aryan Brahmins, although the presence of Khasi-style megaliths in Jaintiapur seems to indicate strong cultural influences from nearby Assam and Meghalaya. It is likely that the Kamarupa kingdom, which ruled Assam between the 4th and 12th centuries, either controlled Sylhet for a short period or maintained significant trade and/or political connections.

By the 14th century, Islam began making its presence known when Shah Jalal arrived in Sylhet in 1303, all the way from Mecca via Delhi and Dhaka. The messianic Muslim saint is said to be one of earliest pioneers of Islamic culture in Bangladesh, responsible for mass conversions of Bengalis from Buddhism and Hinduism. Today he is still revered. Making the journey to his shrine is a major religious pilgrimage for tens of thousands of Bangladeshis, not to mention the country's top political leaders who seek the blessing of the creator over their earthly affairs.

When the Burmese became more successful in their expansionist exploits from the east, they eventually came knocking on Sylhet's door when they invaded Assam in 1817. Sylhet then became more strategically important to the British, who began incorporating governance of the region into their greater Bengal affairs several years earlier. It was during this period that Sylhet's linkages to Britain strengthened.

Some historians theorise that the enterprising Sylhetis believed tea garden labour was below their station, and so many of its men instead chose to go to sea as sailors on British trading vessels. By the turn of the 20th century, thousands of these Sylheti sailors worked for the company, and these 'native seamen' became known as Lascars. When World War I broke out, the demand for these sailors increased and they became the mainstream workforce of Britain's merchant vessels.

As devout Muslims, they still maintained their culinary practices, and hence the smell of curries was said to waft across the London docklands. When one of the ex-seamen set up a curry shop in London's Commercial Road in the 1920s, it would later become the roots of London's Brick Lane. Today, the Bangladeshi restaurant industry is estimated at £4 billion per year, and many of the younger generations of Bangladeshis have grown up as British as they come.

LANGUAGE

With influences from the surrounding areas of Assam, Meghalaya and Tripura, it is hardly surprising there is a unique linguistic identity amongst the people of Sylhet. The language shares linguistic ties with Assamese and Bangla, although it is not mutually intelligible to either language, and thus maintains its own identity. About 10% of Bangladeshis speak or understand Sylhoti, with well over ten million speakers worldwide. The main difference between Sylhoti and Bangla is a replacement of the 's' consonant with an 'h'. Regardless of that fact, most people in Sylhet do understand Bangla.

SYLHET *Telephone code 0821*

Filled with shopping malls, new money and congestion, the Old Town of Sylhet is mostly utilitarian. Its roads are choked with rickshaw and vehicular traffic, and you often find yourself competing with industrious mall-hoppers for space. On the other hand, the greater urbanisation has brought a greater choice of hotels, restaurants and shopping outlets, of course. And, once you leave the comforts of the city, you can easily take the time to discover what Sylhet is really about.

On first glance, Sylhet is all about shopping. Some of the best discount clothing outlets you'll find anywhere in the country are here, a result of so many Bangladeshis visiting from the UK, looking to shop. Sylhet is also growing the country's earliest 'luxury accommodation' and has a few resorts to offer.

While they still have a long way to go in terms of service, some 'five-star' properties have been selling at extremely discounted rates. You would do well to check out these properties before they start charging the rate that they advertise in their brochures. Remember, in the language of business in Bangladesh, everything is negotiable.

For a few languid explorations close to the city, there are many things to check out beyond Sylhet's shopping malls. A couple of tea gardens offer a spot of green amongst what turns out to be a well-planned city outside its congested heart. With vehicular access (there are plenty of gas-run CNGs in Sylhet), you can easily take a jaunt to gaze at the hills and discover the crystal turquoise water deposited fresh from the hills of Meghalaya – definitely the most pristine water in Bangladesh.

GETTING THERE

By air Sylheti Bangladeshis seem to be leading the airline industry with recent capital investments in the form of two new domestic airlines that opened for business in 2007 with some support from non-resident Bangladeshis (NRBS). In addition to GMG Airlines, Royal Bengal Airlines and United Airways (not to be confused with United Airlines in America), began domestic coverage and are in stiff competition with one another for dominance in the skies. It's always worth enquiring for specials on this route, so shop around.

✈ **GMG Airlines** 1st Fl, Firoz Centre, Chowhatta; ☎ 721225–30; Airport; ☎ 720072. Offers twice-daily flights to Dhaka at 13.30 & 16.25.

✈ **Royal Bengal Airlines** Hse 10, Lichu Bagan, Majumdari; ☎ 283 1001, 283 1002; Airport; ☎ 283 1111. No Sylhet flights at the time of research but may start up again soon.

✈ **United Airways** 5 Niloy Chowhatta; m 01713 486654; Airport; m 01713 486653. Daily flights. Fare specials sometimes available as low as Tk3,000, but most times the fare is up around Tk5,495.

By train Using the train to Sylhet is more comfortable but not necessarily faster given the fact the road is pretty good between here and Dhaka. The only drawback is that the bus travels to the Sayedabad bus terminal, which is much less convenient for getting to the diplomatic areas around Gulshan/Banani, as that usually adds at least an hour to the journey in a smog-ridden taxi. If your ultimate destination in Dhaka is the northern part of the city, the train is recommended. (For departures to Sylhet from Dhaka, see *Chapter 3*, *Dhaka*, page 109.) For Chittagong the train is recommended as there is no direct bus connection. Sightseers will also want to consider the daytime journey as it is quite scenic. Tickets for air-conditioned/non air-conditioned berths are Tk610/Tk425 (there's a '+1' class on the night train which means a cabin with only two bunks in it; couples should enquire). Otherwise, air-conditioned/non air-conditioned seats are Tk400/270 and other unreserved classes as cheap as Tk95.

By bus Shohagh, Green Line and Silk Line all service Dhaka from Sylhet's main bus terminal [172 B6], referred to as the 'Dhaka terminal'. Depending on the level of comfort you desire, the fare will be between Tk200 and Tk400, perhaps more if you take a high-end luxury bus with three seats to a row. Buses depart all day, almost every hour, from 06.00 until 23.30.

TRAIN TIMETABLE

No	Destination	Train name	Off day	Dep time	Arr time
710	Dhaka	Parabat Express	Friday	15.10	21.10
718	Dhaka	Jayantika Express	None	07.30	14.35
740	Dhaka	Upaban Express	None	21.30	05.30
720	Chittagong	Paharika express	Saturday	10.10	19.45
724	Chittagong	Udayan Express	Sunday	21.10	06.20

From Dhaka, take a bus from the city's Sayedabad bus terminal, in the southeast.

For Jaflong, buses used to leave from Sobhanighat, about 500m west of the Supreme Hotel. However, this bus stand has relocated to the northwest corner of Upashahar where it meets Mira Bazaar [172 D4]. Ask your way to the bus stand or check the map. Be aware that it might move again.

Sunamganj travellers should make for the Kumargaon bus stand [172 A1]. Go north on Airport Road and take the next left after passing the road that leads to Hazrat Shah Jalal's shrine and travel northwest until you find the bus stand.

For Mymensingh, there is no direct highway available but that doesn't mean there's not a way. The problem is that the area between the two cities is mostly flooded wetland during the monsoon season and mostly marshy bogs during the dry season. Some travellers have reported a boat service being available from Sunamganj to Dharmapasha, a five- or six-hour journey, from which there is a local bus available from nearby Mohanganj. This service could change from year to year, however.

To India See box, *Crossing at Tamabil/Dawkhi*, page 180, for details on arranging onward transport to India.

GETTING AROUND

To/from Osmani Airport Plenty of taxis and CNGs await to take you on the 7km ride into town. Expect to pay Tk100–150 for a CNG or Tk200–250 for a taxi.

By rickshaw This is the most common way of getting around Sylhet's central area. The normal Tk1 per minute charge applies here. If you've just arrived from the train, taking a rickshaw over Sylhet's Kean Bridge [172 B5] is a real experience. Owing to the bridge's incline, brigades of borrowed hands help get the rickshaws up and over the bridge, and the wallah pays them Tk1 each.

By CNG Northeast Bangladesh also features the country's most available gas deposits. Hence CNG baby taxis, which don't pollute as much, are widely available here.

VOLUNTEERING

ECDO Bangladesh [172 D3] 2nd Fl, 17 Urmi, near to Forhadkha Pool, West Shibgonj; e info@ecdo-bd.org; www.ecdo-bd.org. The Ethnic Community Development Organisation is one of the few development groups representing the ethnic minorities of the Sylhet division. See box on pages 182–3 for more information.

WHERE TO STAY

Upmarket

Nazimgarh (48 rooms) Khadim Nagar, 7km NE of Sylhet; 287 0338, 287 0339; e reservation@nazimgarh.com. Upmarket resort offering tours of the local area & tea gardens. The most notable trip is a speedboat ride to Lalakhal. Will be good value when the spa, health club & gym are built, but for now, the rates are expensive. $$$$$$

Mid-range

Rose View Hotel [172 D5] (150 rooms) Plt 2, Blk D, Shahjalal Upashahar; ☎ 721835, 283 1508–14, 283 1516–21; e sales@roseviewhotel.com; www.roseviewhotel.com. One of Sylhet's newest 5-star options. Negotiation is necessary as their published rates are exorbitant. $$$$$

Surma Valley Rest House [172 B4] (6 rooms) Shahjalal Rd, Sylhet; ☎ 712671. Definitely worth the extra money for its peace & quiet, plus proximity to Sylhet's only watering hole, the Station Club. Recommended. $$$$

Zastat Holiday Resort (30 rooms) Khadim Nagar, 7km NE of Sylhet; ☎ 287 0040; e zastatholidayresort@zakariyacity.com. Sells packages that revolve around its resort. Good for large groups of people. Décor of the rooms is best described as 'colourfully tacky', as is the rest of the property. Swimming pool looks undeniably good, however. $$$$

Heritage Hotel and Restaurant [172 A2] (18 rooms) Ornab 16, behind Mira Maidan Point; ☎ 810237; m 01713 310179. Nice place well off the main strip, & in a quieter residential neighbourhood of Sylhet also recommended but must book ahead. $$$

Hotel Anurag [172 C3] (105 rooms) Dhupadighi North; ☎ 715717, 714489; m 01712 093039. Marbled goodness, & again, very popular with locals. Book ahead. $$$

Hotel Dallas [172 C3] (36 rooms) North Jail Rd; ☎ 720945, 720929; e hoteldallassylhet.com, hoteldallassylhet@yahoo.com. Pretty spotless, comfortable & new. Recommended. $$$

Hotel Fortune Garden [172 D3] (33 rooms) 29/A Bongobir Rd, Naiorpul; ☎ 715590, 722499; m 01552 427842; e www.hotelfortunegarden.com. One of Sylhet's more expensive options, but not necessarily worth the extra money. $$$

Hotel Golden City [172 B3] (40 rooms) East Zinda Bazaar; ☎ 812846; m 01714 674738. Nice place although really confusing room pricing. $$$

Hotel Supreme [172 D3] (38 rooms) Jaflong Rd, Mira Bazaar; ☎ 813168, 813169, 720721; m 01711 197012; e hotelsupreme@btsnet.net; www.hotelsupreme.net. Good-value hotel with a great restaurant downstairs, although because of this you need to book well ahead of time. $$$

Parjatan Motel [172 C1] (35 rooms) Boroshola, Airport Rd; ☎ 712426. Aging concrete block, although in a pristine location on a hill near the northern tea gardens. $$$

Budget Budget accommodation is spread over two areas of Sylhet:Telihaor and Shah Jalal Dargah. Telihaor is the older of the two and many of the rooms on offer are well used, whilst the Shah Jalal Dargah is surrounded by dozens of hotels catering for pilgrims to the Shah Jalal Mazar (mausoleum) [172 B2], and families. and therefore ideally placed if you've come to experience the region's religious importance. There are also a few options in the city centre.

Hazrat Shah Jalal Shrine area (also known as Dargah Gate)

Hotel Zia [172 B2] (24 rooms) Dargah Gate; ☎ 711888; m 01717 726896. Cheap & easy going. $$

Hotel Dargah Gate [172 B2] (75 rooms) Just north of Dargah Gate; ☎ 718848. Cheap but somewhat smelly in some of the rooms. Some rooms better than others. $

Hotel Payra [172 B2] (40 rooms) Dargah Gate; ☎ 723457; m 01711 322010. Another one of the *mazar*'s many hotels. $

Central area

Asia Hotel [172 B4] (24 rooms) Banda Bazaar; ☎ 711278; m 01558 323032. Another central option with an OK restaurant downstairs. $

Hotel Shahjahan [172 B3] (28 rooms) Shahid Mansion, Zinda Bazaar; ☎ 719516; m 01712 120389. Undergoing some renovations at the time of research, so looks rough on the outside. Worth a look now to see if the newness is still good! $

Telihaor

Hotel Bilash [172 A4] (78 rooms) Telihaor Rd; ☎ 714659. Slightly nicer than its neighbours. $$

Hotel Green Garden [172 A4] (68 rooms) Telihaor Rd; m 01726 499128. Overpriced for its room quality. $$

Hotel East End [172 A4] (64 rooms) Telihaor Rd; ☎ 719212. Middle-aged but seems to be aging well. Friendly service but rooms could be cleaner. $

Hotel Monoram [172 B4] (30 rooms) Telihaor Rd; 717307. Tucked-away budget option & some rooms reasonably clean. Can't complain for the rock-bottom price offered by this hotel! $

Jeddah Plaza Hotel [172 B4] (23 rooms) Telihaor Rd Surma Market; 811844; m 01726 357129. Make sure you try out the price flexibility & meet the lovely Shahjahan, the young but enthusiastic manager who would love to serve as your guide to Sylhet. $

Rahmania Boarding House [172 B4] (47 rooms) Telihaor Rd; 714919. With peeling pain on the walls & a continuously damp feeling, this place is rough around the edges but dirt cheap. $

WHERE TO EAT

Hazrat Shah Jalal Shrine area (also known as Dargah Gate)

Alpine Restaurant [172 B2] Chowhatta; m 01715 195550. Set over a couple of floors the Alpine is reasonably clean, & has kebabs on offer in the evenings. $$

Central Area

Royal Chef Thai and Chinese Restaurant [172 A3] 758 Lama Bazaar; m 01712 246424. Clean enough with the prerequisite darkness, but with its Thai–Chinese–Indian multi-cuisine selections, this restaurant offers nothing out of the ordinary, cuisine-wise. $$$

Silver Palace [172 C3] Nahar Tower, Nayasharak; m 01711 975019. One of those places equipped to have a massive Bangla party. $$$

Tunatuni [172 C3] Ajit Complex, Dhopadighirpar (North); m 01720 630730. An eclectically painted exterior lends to the even more curious culinary experience found on the inside. For pure novelty factor this place is interesting, if not for the food. $$$

Zinda Bazaar

Chiang Mai [172 B3] Zinda Bazaar. Why are all Bengali restaurants so darn dark? When I visited it was so dark I couldn't see the overpriced prawn dish I ordered. $$$

Pritiraj [172 B3] Zinda Bazaar, Hajari Supermarket; m 01711 940575. Popular with the locals for kebabs, typically served after 16.00. Recommended for a local feed. $$

Woondaal [172 B3] East Zinda Bazaar; m 01717 020505. Superbly clean & well decorated, with a substantial Indian menu. Recommended. $$

Dhanshiri Restaurant [172 B3] Zinda Bazaar. Located upstairs, this busy & inexpensive restaurant offers good views of the street below along with its standard rice, *dal* & curry offerings. $

Grassroots [172 C3] Inside Aarong, Nayasharak; m 01199 304370. Don't expect the same level & quality you find at the Grassroots cafes in Dhaka, but good for a fast-food hit. $

Mohanlal [172 B3, D3] Zinda Bazaar & several other locations around town. A popular *mishti* store run by Hindus. The *shondesh* is extremely good, & while Nescafé doesn't substitute for the real thing, this is about as close to a comfortable coffee shop you can have while in Sylhet. $

Telihaor

Nabanna [172 B4] Taltola; m 01721 228049. Cheap as chips with excellent *halim* (slow-cooked mutton in a curry soup) & hop-to-it service. Recommended. $$

Pipasa Restaurant [172 A4] & **Jamunia Restaurant** Telihaor. Both offering budget Bangladeshi b/fasts of freshly baked *naan* bread & *dal*, although probably not as strong with the lunch & dinner offerings. $

ENTERTAINMENT AND NIGHTLIFE

Station Club [172 B4] Shahjalal Rd, behind Surma Valley Guest House; 18.00–22.00. Drinks are cheap, once you've coughed up the Tk100 entrance fee. Invitations normally required but if you play the foreigner card you'll have no problem. $$$

SHOPPING

Aarong [172 C3] Nayasharak; 815988, 713150; 10.00–20.00. The Sylhet branch of this Bangladeshi chain outlet offers goods that make excellent gifts for friends or additions to a comfortable home.

Bandar Bazaar [172 B4] The city's central shopping bazaar, stocked with all sorts of goods, even those smuggled from India. Located in the heart of the city, south of Zinda Bazaar.

Ban Thai Salon & Fitness Chronic [172 C3] Nayasharak Rd; ☎ 0605 4010944 (NB include zero); ⌚ 10.00–20.00. The place to get a work out in, while staying in Sylhet & get prettied up before your next jaunt.

Monorom [172 C3] Nayasharak Rd; ⌚ 11.00–20.00. Direct competitor with the nearby Aarong for locally produced handicrafts & textiles. Worth checking out for the different selection from Aarong, but the goods not quite as high quality.

Royal Liquor Store [172 A4] Telihaor; ⌚ 10.00–17.00. With a little convincing the staff here are willing to sell liquor to foreigners.

OTHER PRACTICALITIES

Banks There is an HSBC branch with ATM [172 B3] (*Hse 1, just south of Chowhatta crossing;* ☎ *2830053–7*) in Zinda Bazaar. There is also a Standard Chartered branch [172 B2] (*Nirvana Inn, Ramer Dighir Par, Mirzajangal;* ☎ *721206–8*) just at the end of the road leading from Dargah Gate. Finally, you'll find a DBBL ATM [172 A3, C4] near Bandar Bazaar beside the Asia Hotel.

Internet Plenty of cybercafés can be found if you ask around. Mid-range hotels normally have their own computer facilities, including Hotel Supreme [172 D3] and Surma Valley Rest House [172 B4]. One of the better cybercafés in town is the Garden Cybercafé [172 A2] located near the Heritage Hotel.

Medical The MAG Osmani Hospital [172 A3] (*Badhon, Nawab Rd*) and the Northeast Sylhet Medical College (*South Surma*) are the best in town. But you wouldn't want to head to these places unless you were desperate or badly injured.

WHAT TO SEE

Shrine of Hazrat Shah Jalal (Dargah Gate) [172 B2] This large complex is an active mosque, a *mazar* (tomb) and a family destination all at once. If you come during prayer times, especially on Friday, you'll find yourself awash in a sea of pilgrims, many of whom have made the trip up on the weekend to visit the shrine (and book up most of the hotel rooms in Sylhet as well). Interestingly, there is a separate prayer room just for women here too. A set of stairs leads up to the *mazar*, but before climbing it you'll be asked to remove your footwear. For a few taka, these can be deposited with a caretaker for safekeeping or taken with you to see the shrine. Respect for the religious sanctity is requested and women may not be able to see the *mazar* as it requires passing through the mosque. The tomb itself is covered with a decorative brocade and at night there are sometimes candles, creating a unique atmosphere. The old legends say that the sacred catfish in the shrine's pond are the former black magicians of Govinda of Gaur.

Govinda Fort [172 C2] (*also known as Rama Raja's Tilla;* ⌚ *9.00–16.30*) When Hazrat Shah Jalal defeated the Hindu king Govinda, legend has it that Allah caused an earthquake that destroyed Govinda's fort. Today none of the ruins are left but this hillock is a good place to walk to for some heady views of the city.

Museum of Rajas [172 B3] (⌚ *09.00–17.00 Mon–Sat*) This small museum is the former house of Hasan Raja (1854–1922), a Sylheti poet who wrote many songs on the topic of truth beyond the material world. He was also a prominent and successful landlord who owned many acres around Sylhet. The museum holds some of his family heirlooms and gives a spot of history of Sylhet; definitely worth a visit if you're in the area.

General Osmani Museum [172 C3] (🕘 *Apr–Sep 10.30–17.30 Sat–Wed, 15.00–18.00 Fri; Oct–Mar 09.30–16.30 Sat–Wed, 15.00–18.00 Fri*) During the Liberation War, General Osmani (1922–84) and his brimming moustache led the freedom fighters to victory with the assistance of the Indian military. As is evident from the possessions of his old house, he lived a soldier's life and was not prone to extravagance and is now buried at the Shah Jalal Mazar like a fellow warrior saint. A few war slogans also decorate the humble museum.

AROUND SYLHET

TEA ESTATES

Malnicherra and Laakatoorah tea estates (*Airport Rd*) Located just on the road to the airport, many people (especially couples) come here for afternoon gossip to escape the hustle and bustle of the city. Both estates are not really open for 'tours' but if you play dumb and ask for a manager, they may be gracious enough to give you a quick tour. Both tea estates line the road to the airport, and so if you just park your car and wander around on the hilly pathways it may be simpler than trying to see the tea factory itself.

Just north of these tea estates and closer to the airport is an amusement park accessible from the Parjatan Hotel hilltop. It's a decent place to come for views of the city or have a wander around the hills. Vigorous walkers would definitely enjoy it here.

Khadim Nagar National Park (*Khadim Bazaar, 7km from Hotel Supreme on Tamabil Rd*) This national park is one of Bangladesh's newest, and has a small and secluded tea garden on its grounds. There is a 12km dirt road leading a circuit around the park that would be fun to explore by bicycle or on foot. You can catch a Jaflong-bound public bus and disembark at Khadim Bazaar, then you'll need to ask your way to the Khadim cha bagan (Khadim Tea Garden). On the way you could check out the shrine of Hazrat Shah Paran (*a couple of km before Khadim Bazaar; marked by a white gate with 2 green domes*), also a destination of many Muslim pilgrims paying homage to this relative of Shah Jalal.

JAINTIAPUR (pronounced *'JOINT-ah-poor'*) About 40km up the highway to Tamabil lies the town of Jaintiapur. Historically, the place may have been some sort of base of the Jaintia kingdom, before the British annexed the region in 1935. Today very little remains of that history, save for a dilapidated *rajbari* and a Kali temple on its grounds. There are also a series of about 20 striking stone monoliths spread around the *rajbari*, something like Bangladesh's 'mini Stonehenge', except these stone obelisks have been around for a few hundred years. The monoliths also exist in Assamese Khasi towns as well. To get here you can take a Jaflong-bound public bus from Sylhet and by notifying the bus conductor where you want to go they'll tell you when to hop off. The journey takes about one hour and is on good roads. This is a great place to go, just for the adventure of finding it.

LALAKHAL The best river beach in Bangladesh. Surrounded by hills on one side, a gigantic river beach on the other, and an emerald blue ribbon running through it all, this is one of Bangladesh's pristine locations that the Bangladeshis themselves have yet to discover, although it might soon be more accessible by road, unless the ecotourists get to it first. For now you can only take a speedboat hired from the Nazimgarh Resort (see page 175).

Just before Jaintiapur, the road crosses over the river as it weaves its way towards Tamabil. From here, country boats make the journey upriver carrying cargoes but travellers will want to hire transportation. So far, only the resort offers the private

CROSSING AT TAMABIL/DAWKHI

TAMABIL Tamabil is the name of the minuscule town on the Bangladeshi side of the Indian border, where there is an official land crossing. The officials here don't see so much traffic and so it is one of the least busy road border crossings out of Bangladesh and surrounded by some impressive scenery on both sides of the border. Crossing this way into or out from Bangladesh is not necessarily the most logistically simple, but it is certainly one of the most beautiful. The hills of Meghalaya stand like sentinels along Bangladesh's northwestern border, and are said to contain some of the wettest places on earth.

TO INDIA For Tamabil/Dawkhi, hiring private transport for this 53km trip is inexpensive and worthwhile (hire a CNG for Tk250–300, taxi Tk400–500). You need to stop first at Jaintiapur's Sonali Bank (about 13km before Tamabil, soon after crossing the river bridge (⌚ *09.30–16.30 daily*) to pay your Tk300 departure tax – don't spend your last taka until you've paid these fees. Then, have your transport take you to the immigration/customs post at Tamabil. Using public buses will accomplish the same thing for under Tk100, but will take twice the time.

After clearing these formalities you can find a public bus to Shillong if you cross before 11.00, but there are not many hotels in Dawkhi, save for a small hotel on the hill above the Sikh temple. You may be better off travelling direct to Shillong (4hrs; Rs1,500) or Cherrapunjee (2.5 hrs; Rs1,800–2,000).

Official exchange facilities are not available in Dawkhi but if you ask around you'll find a trader in the market who deals in currency exchange as well as fish.

TO BANGLADESH From Shillong, catch a public bus or a share taxi from the queue at Bara Bazaar (Rs70 for share taxi to Dawkhi, departs when full). India customs and immigration are straightforward, and there is no long walk involved in no-man's-land as at other land crossings.

Once across, you'll probably find a friendly customs official who volunteers his services in setting up your transport to Sylhet (2.5hrs; Tk500). Otherwise you could crash the night in nearby Jaflong, where there are some budget hotels. It is best to stay if it's already rather late and you prefer not to be travelling at night. Have some US dollars ready for exchange if you can't find a person willing to change rupees.

transport necessary to get up here quickly with a group of people. But those who enjoy trekking would love this journey upriver, as you could easily flag down passing boats and hitch a ride. The one drawback is that this could easily be a very muddy experience during the rainy season.

JAFLONG

Just beyond the border crossing at Tamabil, this is one place that Bangladeshi people have discovered *en masse*. Jaflong is famous for one thing that Bangladesh lacks: solid rock. In a mud-filled country devoid of rock, Jaflong is one of the few places you can buy rock by the truckload.

Hundreds of Sylhetis come here for the weekend. They watch gigantic loaders pile rocks onto cargo ships, which are then toted to shore and broken down, almost by hand. The sight of dozens of workers pounding down rocks with sledgehammers is actually quite interesting. Photographers have found this place absolutely amazing for its scenes of gritty labour and well-built men, and so do dozens of Bangladeshi holidaymakers, apparently.

GETTING THERE AND AWAY To get here, take the public bus (2hrs; Tk40) from the Jaflong bus stand near the MAG Osmani Museum. (Ask a rickshaw wallah to take you to this bus stand as it has moved several times; see map, page 172.) This bus usually stops at Mamar Bazaar, where the road forks in two directions. Going straight will take you to the tourist facilities at Jaflong, and the site of where all that rock is pounded down by hand. Turn left and you will head towards Jaflong Bazaar, the direction of the Jaflong Tea Estate.

WHERE TO STAY

Hotel Paris (56 rooms) Mamar Bazaar; m 01711 345092. Certainly not the cleanest digs, but at the price charged for a dbl room & an attached bath, you can't really complain. There are a couple of deluxe rooms that might prove more appetising if you can afford it. $$

Hotel Parjatan (36 rooms) Mamar Bazaar; m 01712 516420, 01724 926898. Facilities here are basic but clean, & don't yet show the abuse of overuse. Rooms available with or without bathroom. $$

WHAT TO SEE

Jaflong Tea Gardens After passing through Mamar Bazaar, the road continues for a few more kilometres up to a shallow riverbed that can be crossed using a passenger ferry (Tk2). A large tea garden awaits on the other side, explorable on foot, rickshaw or by bicycle, if you've brought one. There is a processing factory here and a network of pathways leading around the gardens, plus some friendly villages to stop in for tea.

West Jaflong Khasi villages and hills dot the areas just on the other side of the Jaflong River. You can cross the riverbed on foot during the dry season or catch a ferry across during the wet season and explore these villages by foot. The village of Shangram lies on the west side, and is visible from the east bank, marked by a series of tall betel nut trees, unmistakable because of their thin trunks. The hilly terrain and the varied cultures would make this an excellent exploratory trek for those who like exploring with their own two feet.

Boat rides Many of the visiting Bangladeshis have made a trip out of going right up to the hills in a boat for cruising around with their families. The clear, coloured waters of the river coming out of the Khasi Hills are quite beautiful to behold.

CHERRAPUNJEE *Telephone code +91 3637*

This little-known escape from northeast Bangladesh is one of the highlights of a visit to this region, and yet this ecotourism-friendly destination remains woefully under the radar of many Bangladesh travellers and *bideshi* residents. In 2007, 12,646.8mm of rain fell on Cherrapunjee, re-earning it the title of the 'wettest place in the world' (it competes with nearby Mawsynram for the title each year), a fact that has made many wannabe meteorologists visit the place.

While you might get images of total downpours, visiting 'the wettest place in the world' at the wettest time of year is actually quite interesting, and contrary to expectation, it doesn't rain all day all the time during the monsoon. With a wide selection of treks through the nearby hills, plus a number of lookout points offering stunning views into Bangladesh, this is a very scenic and memorable place to visit.

If this wasn't enough to convince you already, there is one last highlight worth mentioning: the region's famous 'living root bridges'. By placing thin betel nut tree trunks across the path of growing roots, the Khasi villagers here have managed to

THE ETHNIC COMMUNITIES OF SYLHET

Courtesy Ethnic Community Development Organisation (ECDO), Sylhet(www.ecdo-bd.org); Partner organisation of VSO Bangladesh

The main ethnic groups in Sylhet are the Khasi, Manipuri, Garo, Patro, Bishnupriya, Tripura and Santal, although ECDO's non-formal survey identified 35 indigenous groups in total. Among these groups the Manipuri and the Khasi are greatest in population in Sylhet Division. Each group has distinct linguistic and cultural practices.

It is estimated that more than 100,000 indigenous people (1.5% of Sylhet Division's population) live in Sylhet Division with various unique difficulties. The problems of discrimination and human rights abuses on the basis of ethnic origin against the indigenous and tribal peoples have been exacerbated by a lack of specific legal mechanisms against such discrimination.

The location of the indigenous people of Sylhet Division has produced some unique problems that are different from the indigenous communities in the Chittagong Hill Tracts (CHT) region:

- The Sylheti indigenous peoples are dispersed in small pockets of settlements that are surrounded by the areas inhabited by mainstream people
- The Sylheti indigenous community's self-government system is not formally recognised by the law
- Sylheti indigenous people have no direct representation at national level
- Instances of land dispossession suffered by Sylheti indigenous people are perhaps even more widespread than in the CHT region

More specifically, some of the main issues that face the indigenous people of Sylhet Division include:

create, over dozens of years, bridges made entirely from the roots of living *Ficus elastica* trees. They're an amazing sight to behold, albeit very difficult to get to. Be warned that even the fittest trekkers will find these hikes pretty strenuous and so if you're here to see the bridges bring a good pair of shoes and a good rain jacket if it's the rainy season. There may even be a few leeches too.

GETTING THERE From the Bangladeshi border, the easiest way is to arrange a private jeep or taxi with a small group of people to get you to Laitkynsew village (2hrs; Rs1,800–2,000). If your budget allows for only public buses, you may need to get to Dawkhi very early in order to not miss the 11.00 bus to Shillong, from which you'll need to take another public bus to Sohra (another name for Cherrapunjee), and then a jeep the rest of the way there. Again, if you're simply on holiday from Bangladesh, it may be worth spending the extra money here to speed up your transport and bringing friends to split the bill.

WHERE TO STAY There are some accommodation options in Sohra, but if you've come all the way from Bangladesh you'll want to book and stay at the **Cherrapunjee Holiday Resort** (*6 rooms; Laitkynsew village, Cherrapunjee, Meghalaya;* ☎ *+91 3637 264218–20;* **m** *+91 94361 15925;* **e** *cherrapunjee@hotmail.com; www.cherrapunjee.com;* $$$). The wonderful hosts at this tiny guesthouse serve up delicious meals and offer comfortable accommodation with hot water and fans. There's also the option of camping outside during the dry season. Room prices vary, depending on the views, with tents costing Rs500.

- Little education among ethnic groups. This is particularly evident in the Khasi community where education of children rarely progresses past primary level. The cause of these problems can be attributed partly to the remoteness of ethnic community villages; there are no secondary schools located nearby. Language also creates a problem as many lessons are conducted in Bangla and not the mother language. High illiteracy rates of guardians also lead to an indifference towards the value of education.
- Remote locations of villages means that medical facilities are far away and very difficult to access. There are generally no people with formal medical training in the villages. Consequently, typical diseases with symptoms such as diarrhoea, fever and reproductive health problems are highly prevalent, and in the Khasi hilly areas, malaria is also present. Water and sanitation problems aid and create water-borne diseases. There is a general reluctance to attend mainstream health facilities owing to a fear of discrimination and an inhibition of cultural practices and rituals.
- Employment problems are prevalent throughout indigenous communities. These problems are a product of the isolation of their communities and an unwillingness to integrate into mainstream society. In Manipuri communities for example, employment initiatives are lacking and only a small minority attend higher education. There is no organised training, market place or co-operative for local craft making. As a result, market prices for cultivated products are often not known and indigenous people are often given an unfair price for their traded products.
- Land issues pose a huge threat to the livelihood and future of all indigenous communities in greater Sylhet region. The communities lack official documents which certify ownership of their land and therefore have no legal support for their land. There is a great need for legal assistance to ensure their land is protected, as land grabbing by a few corrupt members of the mainstream community and some corrupt government officials is debilitating for indigenous communities.

SUNAMGANJ *Telephone code 0871*

If you're supremely adventurous or a keen birdwatcher (perhaps both), Sunamganj is where you'll want to head. The remote township offers some very unique opportunities to explore Bangladesh's endangered wetlands, some very special places where thousands of migratory birds make their winter stopovers. You can hire a launch from the Sachna ghat in Sunamganj for roughly Tk2,000 per day, depending on the number of people you have and how far you want to go.

It takes four days to make a return journey to Tanguar Haor, the most pristine of these wetland wildernesses, with most of that time spent chugging along in the boat. But overnight adventurers could wake up in wetland paradise, watching the sunrise over an enormous marsh landscape teeming with birdlife.

GETTING THERE Public buses depart from Sunamganj's bus station in Sylhet, on Amberkhana Road for the 70km journey (2.5hrs; Tk50). Motorcyclists have reported that the road is quite good up to Sunamganj.

To/from Mymensingh Another option for overland travellers is to try and make the journey to Mymensingh via Sunamganj. From the small town, you catch a launch to Dharmapasha, near Mohanganj, where there are basic hotel facilities available, or a friendly villager who will probably put you up for a night if you ask around. The five–six-hour boat journey travels through flooded wetlands and village landscapes, a backwater route – literally.

Some travellers have reported successful crossings in reverse, doing the journey by bicycle. One motorcyclist even attempted to cross via the Hobiaganj to Kishoreganj route, but got waylaid by an unstable bamboo bridge. Mohanganj can be reached by public bus from Mymensingh (about a 50km journey for the cyclist). Basic accommodation is available there, and the launch leaves from nearby Dhamapasha. It should be stressed that this route may change from year to year depending on where the water from the monsoon goes.

TOURS Enquire at the Bangladesh Boat Owners' Association (☎ *0871 55996*) at least a day before you plan to arrive, and be aware that this will be an adventure trip. Ask for Farouk Miah. There are two boats; both sleep four comfortably. Food costs extra and will have to be pre-organised. Give a cash advance for petrol and other necessities. Remember water, bedding, a torch, mosquito net and binoculars.

SRIMONGOL *Telephone code 08626*

Srimongol is the epicentre of tea-growing culture and should be included in every traveller's itinerary during a visit to Bangladesh. With its picturesque scenery, increasing tourism infrastructure and dominant tea culture, it really is one of Bangladesh's stand-alone destinations. Better yet, it's easy to get to by private car or by train from Dhaka, although the latter is the better choice to have a bit of interaction with the locals.

If there was any institution that best symbolised the former British influence on the country, it would be the tea-drinking tradition that lives on to this day. In every village, city and slum of Bangladesh, there is always a humble tea stall where, for just a few taka, you can sit down and have a genuine conversation and a snack with passing locals (who often offer to buy the tea for you in their overwhelming kindness). During more politically heated periods, these tiny tea stalls become fierce battlegrounds of verbal debate. Over mud-coloured, sugar-laden cups of *cha*, the ubiquitous tea stalls are the best places to sit down and get a feel for 'the real Bangladesh', offering an opportunity to pause where you are, whether you're riding the maelstrom of human activity in Dhaka, or breathing in the clean air of a peaceful rural vista.

In Srimongol, tea begins its life as a leaf on one of the hundreds of thousands of tea bushes carpeting the low, rolling hills. From early April until late November, dozens of female tea pickers roam the gardens delicately plucking the leaves from the waist-high bushes. The pickings then end up in massive bundles perched on their heads as they return to the factory – a picturesque sight to behold. After drying and fermentation, the tea is then rolled into tiny balls and sold as black tea around the world. Most of the export teas end up in Russia or Europe.

Some tea connoisseurs are surprised at the quality of Bangladeshi tea, noting the flavour is far from subtle. In Bangladesh, the tea is usually served with milk and heaping mounds of sugar (if you prefer your tea less sweet, ask the seller to make it *chini chara*, which means sugar-free, although the use of sweetened condensed milk means that sugar is never totally avoidable). Otherwise, some tea sellers can make *lal cha* (red tea). This is tea served without milk, and sometimes with a piece of ginger or cardamom for flavour. Because the tea is often steeped for long periods before serving, a bit of milk is often required to cut back the bitter taste.

Venturing through the region on two wheels (motorised or mechanical), is easily the best way to explore the region.

HISTORY The practice of tea growing actually began in the hills of nearby Assam (present-day Meghalaya) in the early 19th century and provided the seedl for Bangladesh's future industry. Bangladesh's very first tea garden was actually

above **Prayers in front of Buddha at the beachside town of Kuakata** (BM) page 288

right **Durga Puja: a Hindu festival celebrating the triumph of Mother Durga over Mahishasura the demon, Dhaka** (BM) page 79

below **An awesome sight: Islamic Eid prayers** (BM) page 22

above **Frenetic energy of New Market, Dhaka's biggest market** (CZ) page 140

below **It's common for groups of friends to share a bowl of food during *Iftar* – right hand only though!** (BM) page 78

right **Tea break, Khulna** (BM) page 253

below ***Iftar* snacks for sale** (ML) page 132

bottom **Limes, tomatoes, chillis and beans on sale at a street market, Old Dhaka** (BM) page 140

above **Ferry madness at Sadarghat** (BM) page 142

below **Board a local ferry for an overnight journey to Bangladesh's riverine south** (MC) page 66

right **Traditional sailing boat**
(BM) page 33

below **Spot endangered Ganges river dolphins on your journeys downstream**
(E&R Mansur/BCDP)
pages 268–9

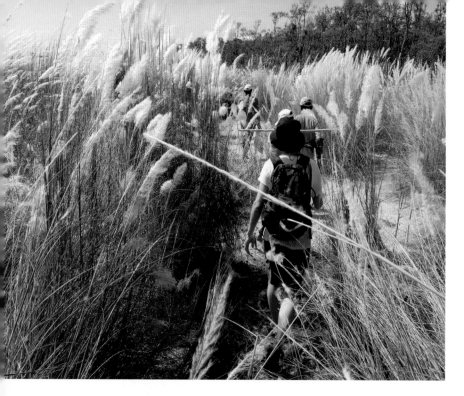

above **Walking through *ghoshful*, Sundarbans** (BM) page 264

below **Sunset at Cox's Bazaar – the world's longest natural beach** (BM) page 231

right **Karnaphuli River, Chittagong Hill Tracts** (BM)

page 214

below **Bangladesh's most isolated people live on shifting river islands known as *chars***

(ML) page 311

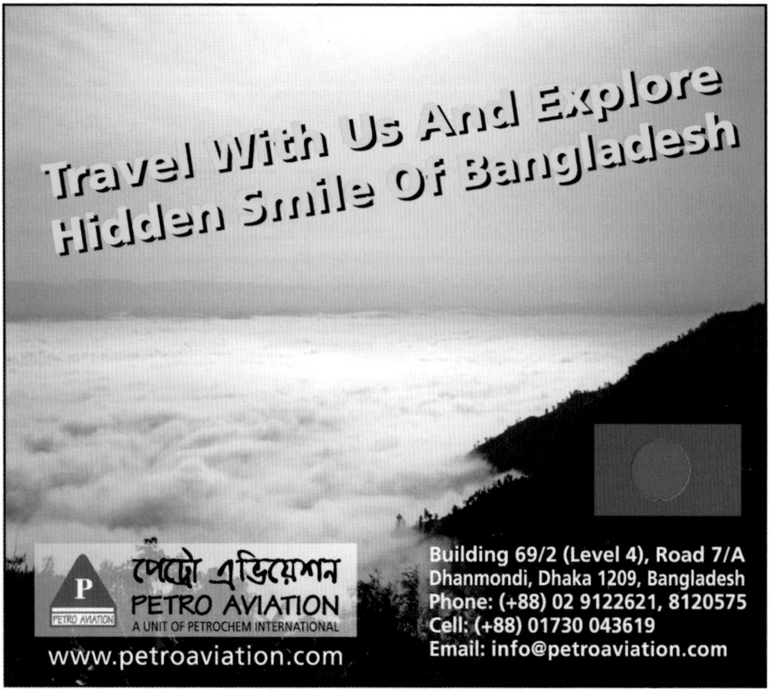
Travel With Us And Explore
Hidden Smile Of Bangladesh
পেট্রো এভিয়েশন
PETRO AVIATION
A UNIT OF PETROCHEM INTERNATIONAL
PETRO AVIATION
P
www.petroaviation.com
Building 69/2 (Level 4), Road 7/A
Dhanmondi, Dhaka 1209, Bangladesh
Phone: (+88) 02 9122621, 8120575
Cell: (+88) 01730 043619
Email: info@petroaviation.com

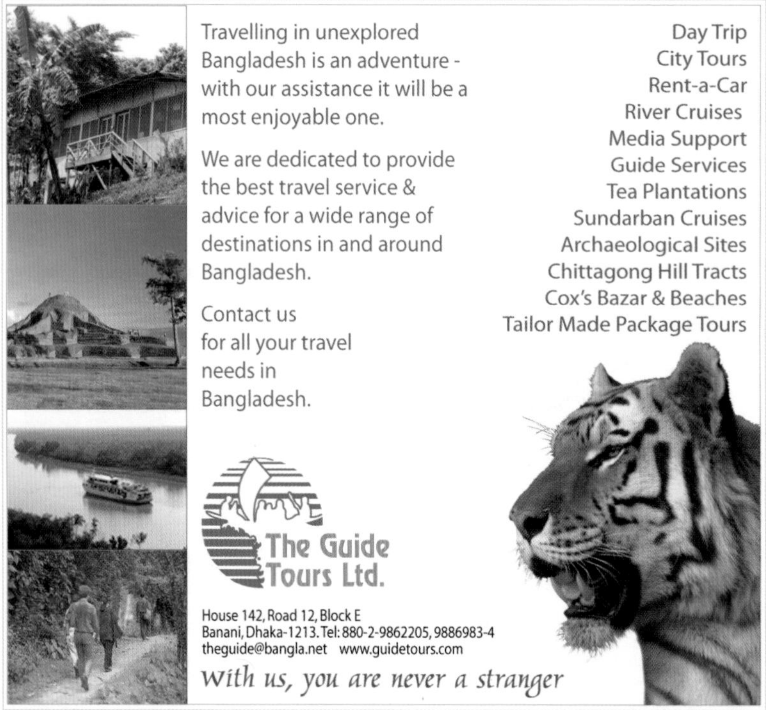
Travelling in unexplored Bangladesh is an adventure - with our assistance it will be a most enjoyable one.
We are dedicated to provide the best travel service & advice for a wide range of destinations in and around Bangladesh.
Contact us for all your travel needs in Bangladesh.
Day Trip
City Tours
Rent-a-Car
River Cruises
Media Support
Guide Services
Tea Plantations
Sundarban Cruises
Archaeological Sites
Chittagong Hill Tracts
Cox's Bazar & Beaches
Tailor Made Package Tours
The Guide Tours Ltd.
House 142, Road 12, Block E
Banani, Dhaka-1213. Tel: 880-2-9862205, 9886983-4
theguide@bangla.net www.guidetours.com
With us, you are never a stranger

established in Chittagong in 1840, at a location where the Chittagong Club now stands, but the first commercial tea garden, Malnicherra in Sylhet, would not come along for another 17 years. The tea grew so well here that by the turn of the century there were over 150 tea estates, with the highest density of them concentrated around Maulvi Bazaar (which includes the township of Srimongol). Today the majority of the estates are owned by Bangladeshi companies, although a good chunk still have their ties to Britain.

Managers of the earliest estates soon discovered that the locals were not suited to plantation work, and so they were forced to bring in labourers from Bihar and Orissa, which at the time were the poorer parts of British India. After their importation, these workers maintained separate identities from the surrounding Islamic culture. Because of this, they have different facial features and actively practise Hinduism amidst the villages attached to the tea gardens where they live. After partition in 1947, the industry was quite strong and tea production increased as large quantities were easily shipped to West Pakistan. When the Liberation War broke out, many of the workers were targets of genocide or harassment by Pakistani forces. Factories were left derelict. As a result the tea industry was devastated during these years and never recovered its former lustre.

Today the tea estates in Bangladesh produce about 55 million kilogram annually, making Bangladesh the ninth-largest producer of tea in the world.

GETTING THERE AND AWAY

By train Travelling by train is easily the best and simplest way to get to Srimongol from Dhaka and/or Chittagong as the timings are quite convenient, even for a weekend visit. (The night train timings are terrible, however, as they are geared to get people to Sylhet early in the morning.)

From Dhaka, it is easiest to catch the morning or afternoon train from the Airport Station. The departure times listed below are from the main train station, but all trains pass by the Airport Station on their way out of town, anywhere between 20

TRAIN TIMETABLE

TO SRIMONGOL (FINAL DESTINATION SYLHET)

No	Origin	Train name	Off day	Dep time	Arr time
709	Dhaka	Parabat Express	Tuesday	06.40	14.27
717	Dhaka	Joyantika Express	None	14.00	18.47
740	Dhaka	Upaban Express	None	22.00	02.45
723	Chittagong	Udayan Express	Saturday	21.00	05.55
719	Chittagong	Paharika Express	Monday	10.10	14.27

FROM SRIMONGOL

No	Destination	Train name	Off day	Dep time	Arr time
718	Dhaka	Jayantika Express	Thursday	09.45	14.50
710	Dhaka	Parabat Express	Tuesday	16.49	21.25
740	Dhaka	Upaban Express	None	00.08	05.05
720	Chittagong	Paharika Express	Saturday	12.30	19.45
724	Chittagong	Udayan Express	Sunday	23.13	06.20
709	Sylhet	Parabat Express	Tuesday	10.53	13.15
719	Sylhet	Paharika Express	Monday	14.27	17.20
717	Sylhet	Jayantika Express	None	18.47	21.00
739	Sylhet	Upaban Express	Wednesday	02.45	05.15
723	Sylhet	Udayan Express	Saturday	03.28	05.55

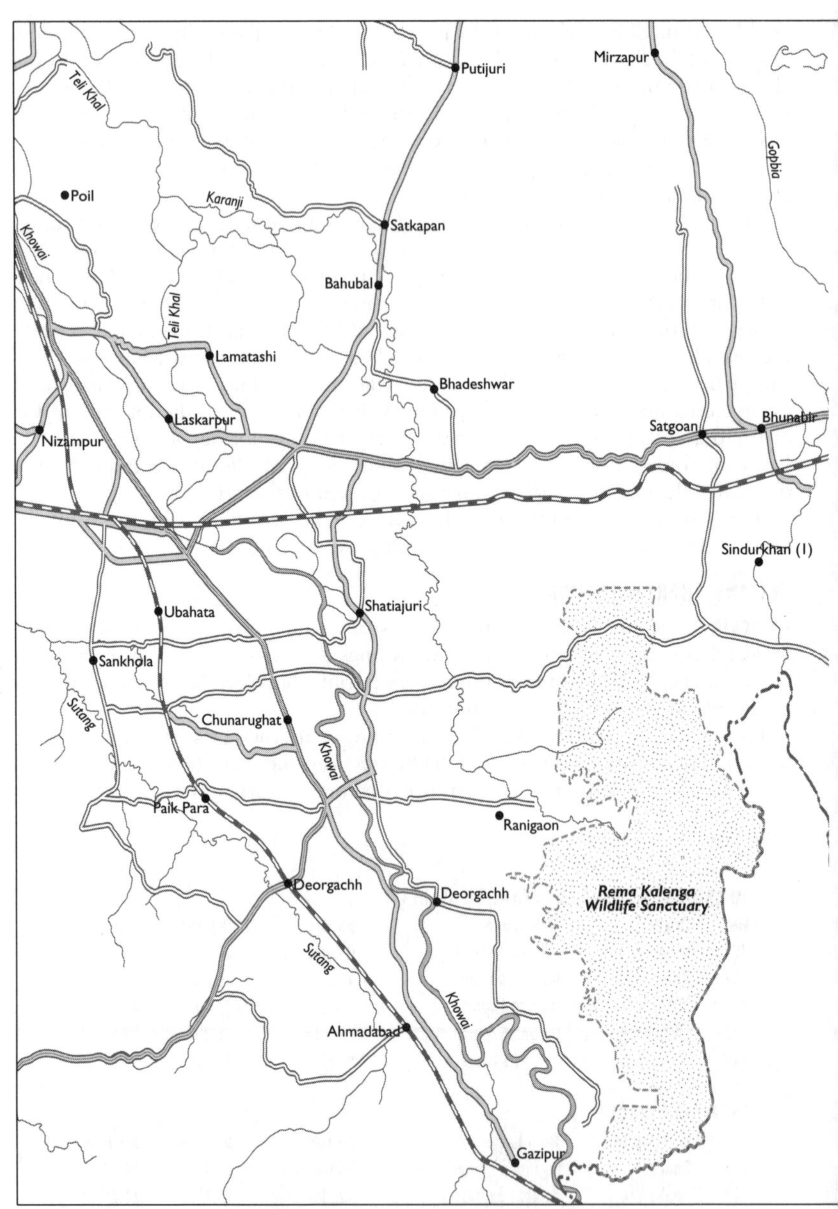

minutes and 45 minutes after the times listed below. You can purchase a ticket when you get there by just explaining which train and where you want to go; you'll have a choice of two classes – unreserved or chair. Cheap is more interesting and fun for the five-hour journey, as you'll interact with more people. But if you want a chair to chill out in and snooze, pay more. Ask when to disembark the train so you don't miss your stop – these trains continue on to Sylhet. As a rule you will probably arrive a few minutes late as opposed to a few minutes early, but anything is possible. Tickets cost Tk300/200 for air-conditioned/non air-conditioned seats.

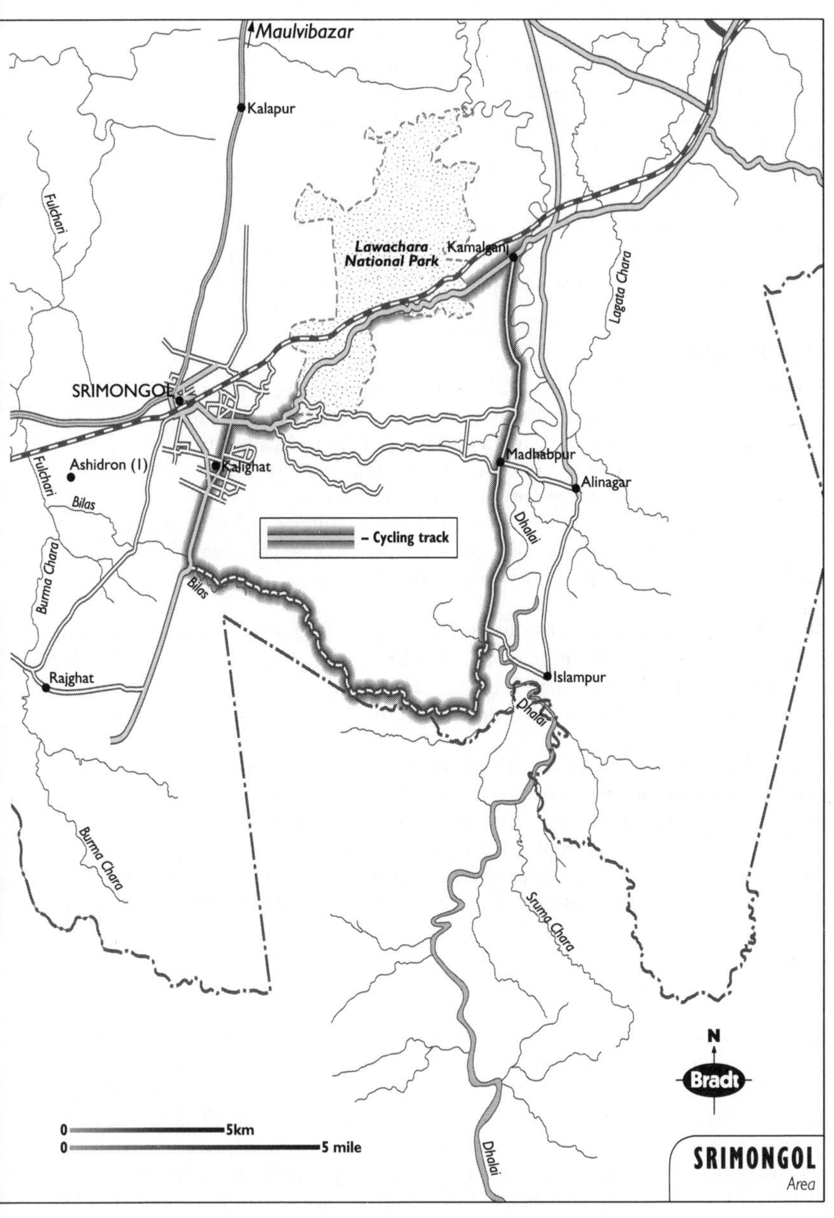

From Chittagong, the daytime journey is also pleasant and comfortable, with varied scenery along the way and plenty of fruit, *chanachur* (Bengali snack mix of peanuts, *chaat* and spices) and tea sellers coming by to keep you fed and caffeinated (Tk490/320 for a non air-conditioned berth/chair).

By bus While the train is the preferred option for getting to Srimongol, sometimes you'll be stuck taking the bus, but avoid it if you can. There are not many connections to Srimongol because it does not lie directly on the Dhaka–Sylhet Highway.

From Dhaka, head to Sayedabad Bus Station and look for the Hanif Enterprise, Shyamoli Paribahan or Maulvi Bazaar city buses. The last offers an air-conditioned service but only twice per day. If you show up at any time you'll usually be able to board a Srimongol-bound bus within an hour or two. From Srimongol, the above bus companies have counters on the Habiganj Road just west of the Noor Foods Restaurant. The journey runs from 06.20 to 00.45 with several departures every hour (4hrs; Tk250).

To get to Sylhet, there is a direct bus line called 'Habiganj Express' that departs from a stand further down the Habiganj Road from the Dhaka bus counters. The bus starts in Habiganj and stops in only major towns (such as Srimongol) *en route* to Sylhet (2hrs; Tk40).

GETTING AROUND

Arrival The town itself is small and you can walk across it in less than 15 minutes, but the region's main highlights out of town would make for longer walks (the rainforest is about 8km east of town and the Nilkantha Tea Cabin 4km). Outside Srimongol the car traffic is very thin and the atmosphere peaceful and so walking is recommended but perhaps not for everybody.

Getting to accommodation outside the town requires a rickshaw or a CNG. If you book ahead someone will come to meet you and take you there free of charge. You need to let them know your arrival time, however.

By bicycle The region is perfectly suited for bicycle exploration and you can easily bring your own bike on the train or rent bicycles in Srimongol (Tk150–200 per day). Contact Shablu of Classic Tours and Travels for more information (m *01718 155492*) or enquire at your hotel and they can probably make arrangements for you.

Locally available bicycles tend to be the heavy Chinese-made one-speed contraptions and sometimes have some problems with their brakes (the bicycles at the Tea Resort are especially rickety and poorly maintained). So if you're not able to arrange a bicycle ahead of time, do be aware that the bike you get will be half of the adventure in Srimongol, but it should be fine as the hills are not very high and as long as the brakes work you should be fine. Rickshaw-repair wallahs are easy to find if you have any major problems such as a flat tyre.

Motorcycles are not available for private hire in Srimongol. Not yet at least. We think they should be.

By CNG As there is a giant natural gas field not far from Srimongol, CNG baby taxi transport is widely available for buzzing between the tourist sites if you have little time. These can easily be flagged down around town near the bus and train stations. Normally, hiring a CNG for a few hours costs between Tk250 and Tk400. With a higher number of tourists here than in other places, beware of overcharging. Negotiate everything firmly and ask questions, but don't get carried away as Tk20–30 makes a far bigger difference to a local than it does the foreign visitor.

TOUR OPERATORS

Classic Tours & Travels Dhaka: Ste 313, 2nd Fl, Taher Tower, Gulshan 2; m 01556 360566, speak with Razu; Srimongol: Railway Station Office; m 01718 155492, speak with Sablu; e info@classictours-bd.com; www.classictours-bd.com. While many other tour operators offer trips to Srimongol, Classic Tours is the only operator that maintains an office in Srimongol with a full-time local guide/staffer from the region. While the office itself is stuffed into the back of a tiny store, the people here do know Srimongol better than many of the other operators. Single female travellers or groups would probably benefit most from their services. They can hire bicycles, organise transport & make accommodation bookings & you will benefit from the relationship they have with the local contacts.

Nishorgo Eco-Guides www.nishorgo.org. Nishorgo was a USAID-funded programme that helped to develop the nature-guiding skills of several locals in the Srimongol area, some of whom come from the indigenous communities around the forest. If you check the Nishorgo website you will find a list of their guides at the various Nishorgo protected sites around the country, as well as information on the protected areas & Nishorgo's work. Each guide speaks suitable English, so if you want the most amount of interaction, then these young locals would be the way to go. You can try Mr Dhiraj Shing (m *01190 270716; Manipuri*) or Mr Benedict Daring (m *01723 760499; Garo*), both of whom are members of Srimongol's indigenous community. They would also be good sources of information if you wanted to know about indigenous festivals of the area or wanted to see a cultural performance of the Manipuri people.

Rashed Husan RK Mission Rd; m 01711 078362; e enjoylife_45@yahoo.com. Rashed & his brother are enterprising local tour guides who speak excellent English & can help take the hassle out of a trip for you. You can call them & let them know your needs & see what kind of prices they offer.

WHERE TO STAY

Srimongol Town

Hotel Plaza (15 rooms) College Rd; m 01711 390039. Without a Bangla sign this place is a little bit hard to find, & once you clamber up the darkened stairs you'll find the rooms here more spacious than the competition, but not really anything special. AC rooms available. $$

Tea Town Rest House (28 rooms) 3rd Fl, Razzaque Tower, Hobiganj Rd; ☎ 71065; m 01718 316202. Boasting friendly staff, this is the best resthouse in Srimongol Town, although some rooms lack light & the feel isn't so homely. AC rooms available. $$

Hotel Biroti (15 rooms) Chowmohona; m 01715 526044. With its central location & all the associated traffic this hotel is hard to recommend except for the cheaper prices. Rooms have standard amenities: attached bathroom, mosquito net & sometimes clean sheets. $

Hotel Grameen (12 rooms) Puran Bazaar; m 01715 526044. This is the newest budget hotel in Srimongol, & opened in 2008. This means it is the cleanest for the time being. Mosquito nets & attached bath included. $

Hotel Nilima (37 rooms) Hobiganj Rd; ☎ 71304. A hotel as old as Srimongol itself, it seems. Earns the distinguished entry as the cheapest in town. $

Outside Srimongol

Tea Resort (14 2–3-bed bungalows for a total of 30 rooms, plus 6 hotel-style rooms) Kamalganj Rd, 10min rickshaw ride; m 01712 916001, 01712 071502; e tearesort@yahoo.com. With steadily rising prices & very little spent to maintain the place, the Tea Resort has a bit of a tea-stained reputation among some travellers, but for the time being it is one of the only choices that upmarket travellers have in Srimongol, & so with your expectations set properly you may in fact be surprised to see the resort's swimming pool & tennis court. Private bungalows are spread around the property & offer a modicum of privacy but lack luxurious comfort. They are furnished with the bare minimum of facilities to earn the name 'resort', such as beds, AC & hot water. Some bungalows have kitchens but no utensils to cook with, & refrigerators but no potable water – bad if you've decided to have a few drinks in the evening & really need to rehydrate in the morning. If the bungalows are out of your price range, there is a block of hotel rooms but these are also similarly uninspiring but ultimately satisfactory given the lack of choice . All in all it will be good when someone finally clues in that they could make a lot more money if they improved the service & facilities of the resort. If staying here, you'll be better prepared if you regard it as a camping expedition & bring a few of the extra little luxuries that make a holiday pleasurable as such luxuries have yet to reach this place. Check-out time is 11.00 & prices listed already include the VAT (15%). Meals average Tk900–1,000 per day & are usually served on a fixed basis. A small tip: straight out from the gate of the tea resort & across the field there is a small stream where you can take a few drinks & set up a small fire for the evening, or take the kids to play on the small sandy beach by the riverbed. $$$$

Nishorgo Nirob Eco-cottage (3 rooms) Radhanagar, 20min rickshaw ride from the train station; m 01715 041207. Nishorgo's flagship project of creating 'eco-cottages' began here at this small village just a few kilometres outside Srimongol & a 45min walk from the Lawachara rainforest. The concept was to employ locals to house visiting guests & provide some of the capital necessary to build facilities for them. At the Nirob Eco-cottage, 1 room is housed in a standard concrete building but the other 2 are bamboo huts nestled in a lemon

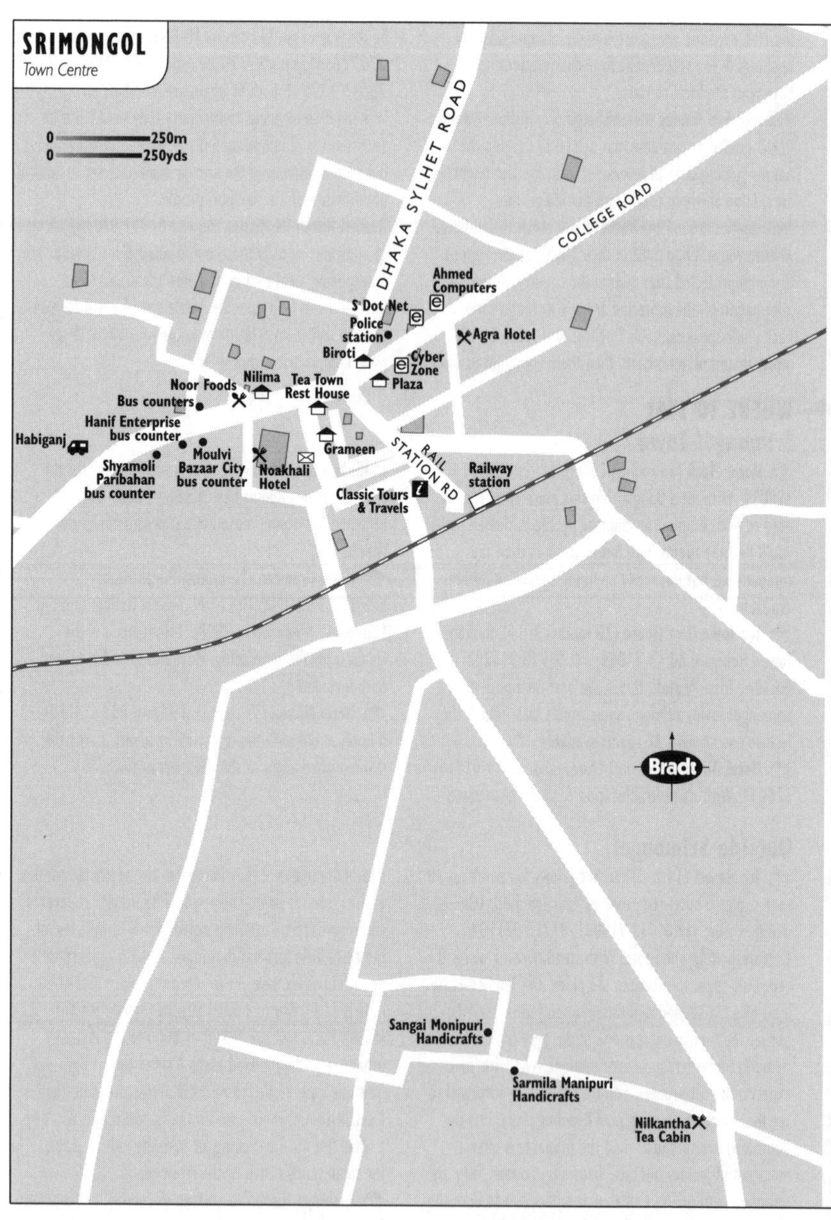

grove tucked away at the back of the property, with a small flowing stream behind it, perfect for dipping on hot days. Needless to say, this is a secret spot that won't remain hidden for long. Calling ahead for booking is essential. Facilities include hot water on request, meals, & a power supply system that can run computers, chargers & lights even when the power goes out. Mr Shamsul is the one you want to speak with. B/fast inc. $$$

Nishorgo Nandan Eco-cottage (2 rooms) Uttar Baligaon, Karamat Nagar; m 01711 731551. The second of Nishorgo's eco-cottages, offering similar facilities but not the beautiful bamboo hut. If Nirob is already booked this would be a great choice as well. Facilities are the same: 2 dbl-bedded rooms with attached bath & basic food served. Mr Anando is the proprietor here. $$$

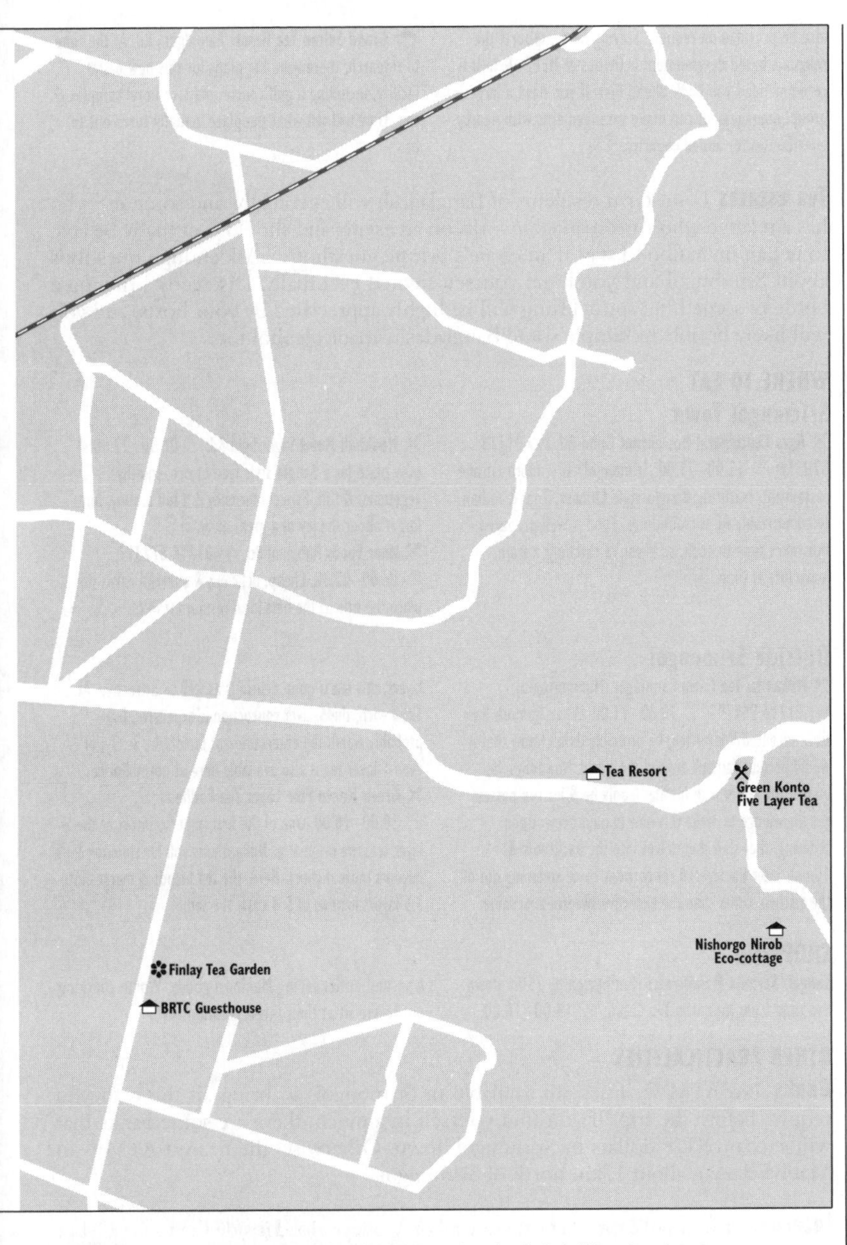

BTRI Guesthouse (6 rooms) Just off Kamalganj Rd before reaching the Tea Resort; m 01711 867485. Rooms at the guesthouse of the Bangladesh Tea Research Institute are available but it is best to call this place & book ahead if you can as it tends to fill up with BTRI officials. The guesthouse facilities (rooms with attached bath, no hot water/AC) are as old as Bangladesh itself, but if you head here expecting 'retro' style & facilities, then the price seems to match the expectations (meals Tk250 per day). $$

HEED Guesthouse (5 rooms) Kamalganj, 16km outside Srimongol town, past the Lawachara rainforest; m 01719 773689. A decent option outside Srimongol, bathrooms are shared in some of the rooms but the basic facilities are kept very clean. Kamalganj is accessible via bus stand near the train station. Food can also be provided on request. Staying here supports the religious-based development activities at HEED, & so it is recommended you book ahead first. If you have a large group, management can make arrangements with nearby guesthouses for added capacity. $$

Grand Sultan Tea Resort Kamalganj Rd. At the time of research, there were big plans for this new 6-star facility, including a golf course, massive hotel complex & spa. Time will tell what the place actually turns out to be.

Tea estates Long-term residents of Bangladesh will eventually find someone who has a relative who runs/manages/works on an estate, and should eventually be able to net an invitation to stay at an estate's private guesthouse. Ask enough questions about Srimongol and you'll get yourself invited eventually. Discreetly bringing a bottle of something spirit-lifting will be highly appreciated by your hosts, and you will likely be able to sample some Bangladeshi-made alcohol too.

WHERE TO EAT

Srimongol Town

Agra Continental Restaurant Guho Rd; m 01716 570916; 12.00–23.00. Srimongol's first multi-cuisine restaurant, featuring Bangla-style Chinese, Thai & Indian in comfortable AC surroundings. Food is well prepared but takes time to cook, so if you're catching a train, leave lots of time. $$

Noakhali Hotel Sagordighi Rd; 06.30–22.00. A busy place for a Bangla-style feed of rice, squishy vegetables & fish. Expect efficiency & a full tummy, but forget about the joy of a great meal. $$

Noor Foods Habiganj Rd; m 01718 672317; 06.00–22.30. Cheap, delicious & cheerful earns this place the title as the best local restaurant in town. $

Outside Srimongol

Nilkantha Tea Cabin Ramnagar (Munipuripara); m 01716 969797; 10.00–17.00. When Ramosh Ram Gour invented 5-layer tea, he probably didn't know that it would become famous around the world. Nowadays, he guards the secret with his life – only he & his son possess the knowledge to make this now famous brew. Upon ordering, they shut themselves into the backroom & 10mins later the layered concoctions come steaming out of the kitchen. Other than the excessive sweetness of some layers, this tea is quite delicious as well as attractive. At Tk50 each, the 5-layer concoction is expensive, but probably worth the entertainment factor. 4-, 3-, 2-, or even 1-layer tea is also available here at normal prices.

Green Konto Five Layer Tea Radhanagar; 10.00–18.00. One of the first impersonators of the 5-layer tea, the original at Nilkantha is still far superior & its flavours more distinct. Here, the tea blends & merges into 3.5 layers instead of 5 & costs the same.

SHOPPING

Sangai/Sarmila Handicrafts Manipuripara, 250m down the road from Nikantha Tea Cabin; 10.00–16.00. A second outlet selling Manipuri goods. Worth checking out to see what their latest creations are.

OTHER PRACTICALITIES

Banks No ATM facilities are available in Srimongol, so bring all the cash you require before the trip. If you find yourself in a pinch, there are some banks that will exchange US dollars in Srimongol Town. Otherwise, the nearest ATM is in Maulvi Bazaar, about 17km north of Srimongol.

Internet Srimongol's internet cafés are all on College Road inside the town. Cyber Zone is near the Hotel Plaza; look up for the sign. S Dot Net and Ahmed Computers are 150m further down the road.

Medical The nearest medical emergency facilities are in Sylhet, but Dhaka will have more professional diagnoses available.

Post office The Srimongol post office is in the old bazaar, on the same road as the Hotel Grameen.

THE HOOLOCK GIBBONS OF LAWACHARA

Petra Osterberg, from the Nishorgo booklet The Vanishing Ape

In Bangladesh, there are only about 200 Hoolock gibbons (*Hoolock hoolock*) left scattered in 22 small populations. Lawachara National Park is home to the largest remaining population, consisting of around 60 individuals.

Gibbons are small apes and belong to the taxonomic family Hominidae, which also includes great apes and humans. Apes are different from monkeys because they lack tails and have larger brains and longer childhoods.

After a gestation period of seven months the female will give birth to a single baby that she will carry and nurse for two years. The baby is born light-coloured and will gradually turn black during the first two years. Juveniles and males are black with white eyebrows, whereas females will change back to a light colour upon reaching maturity. Sexual maturity is reached between six and eight years of age, but a female living to 30 years can only produce five or six babies in her lifetime.

Gibbons live their whole adult lives in monogamous relationships with a single partner and their dependant offspring. As young adults, the gibbons will leave their parents and start looking for partners and new territories. Neither sex will reproduce before they have stable partners and territories of their own.

Gibbons depend on a variety of fruit trees to provide them with ripe fruit throughout the year and they supplement their diet with young leaves, buds, flowers and insects. Figs are the most important food, since these fruit are available year round in natural forests. In Bangladesh many forests are planted with commercially valuable tree species and the diversity of fruit trees is limited. Hence, many gibbons suffer periodical starvation during non-fruiting seasons and this can reduce the number of young reaching adulthood.

Each gibbon family has a territory of around 30ha, which it will defend from other gibbons. To announce the territory, the couple perform loud song duets in the mornings. A gibbon's whole life depends on the forest and it will never leave the safety of the treetops to cross open land between forest patches. Because deforestation has seriously fragmented Bangladesh's forests, many gibbon populations – even individuals – have become completely isolated from others of their kind.

The Hoolock gibbon is listed as Endangered by the International Union for Conservation of Nature (IUCN) and the national classification in Bangladesh is Critically Endangered.

Lawachara National Park, together with the surrounding West Bhanugach Reserve Forest, is the only place in Bangladesh with a sustainable gibbon population, but even here the apes will only survive if the forest is efficiently protected against illegal logging. Tourists should not forget to pay the visitor fee to the national park and to hire a local guide so that the people can benefit from forest conservation.

WHAT TO SEE

Lawachara National Park The Lawachara National Park is one of the few places in Bangladesh where you can see Hoolock gibbons in their national habitat. The park began its life as a timber plantation but eventually evolved into a natural semi-evergreen forest. It now supports several different kinds of wildlife, and serves as a watershed for the region. The canopy is multi-storeyed and the trees mostly deciduous, although the under-canopy trees are predominantly evergreen.

Walking through a piece of pristine wilderness in Bangladesh, however small, is quite a pleasure. By heading out here nice and early (ie: 06.00–07.00) you will have the chance to see the wildlife at its most active, especially the endangered Hoolock gibbons of the forest. You can also stop by two forest villages inhabited by Khasi people: Lawachara Punji and Magurchara Punji, although do remember to request permission before taking photographs as some of the villages are frequented by busloads of Bangladeshi tourists as well.

The park is bordered by the Bhanugach Reserve Forest to the north, tea estates to the west and east and Tripura villages to the southwest. Over 27,500 people are directly dependent on the park and its natural resources for their survival, and the neighbouring tea reserves do put enormous pressure on the forest for fuel wood and timber.

Without the potential increase of ecotourism to this ecologically sensitive area, most of these villages would have no alternative source of income. So if you decide to tour the forest, employ a guide (see *Tourist information*, *Nishorgo Eco-Guides*, page 189), and let them tell you the story of the forest from their eyes.

Lawachara walking trails Three designated forest trails are available in the park: a half-hour trail, a one-hour trail or a three-hour trail. This is a similar set-up enjoyed by all the national parks and wildlife sanctuaries that developed under the Nishorgo Programme. Each of the trails has signboards at their respective starting points with maps. If you feel confident navigating yourself, then the trails should be quite easy to navigate. Otherwise it is best to hire a Nishorgo ecotour guide so you don't get lost.

Tea estates With an increasing amount of visitors wandering around the tea estates, they aren't as easy to tour as they used to be. Some guards will turn you back before you've even poked your head into the factory, but if you look around you may eventually find an estate that will let you see the production process. Again, it is best to hire a guide to facilitate an introduction through a connection they may have, as opposed to walking up to gates unannounced. The real tea tasters will probably want to start by contacting the Bangladesh Tea Research Institute.

But if you just have a passing interest, the Zareen Ishpahani Tea Estate is easily accessible on foot from the Tea Resort. Take the road to Kamalganj and then turn right a few hundred metres past the Tea Resort gates at the village road, where a yellow and red sign points the way. The Zareen Estate is another 1.8km down the road, and their factory is hard to miss. Alternatively you could visit Finlay Tea Garden. Special access is required to enter the estate and must be arranged by invitation. Contact James Finlay Limited (*www.jfbd.com*).

Madhubpur Lake This small but peaceful lake is accessible from the town of Kamalganj and makes for an excellent bicycle journey. First, travel 12km along the main road from Srimongol to Kamalganj (that passes by the Tea Resort). After the road comes out of the hills and straightens out, travel a further 1.8km where you will hit the main Kamalganj junction, and turn right. After a further 7.3km southward travel you will find the Madhubpur Tea Gardens, where you should again turn right and start asking your way to the lake.

To return, you can either travel back by the same route or cross the hills again using the paths on the north side of the lake. The criss-crossing route leads through villages, hills and great scenery – ask locals for the directions to Srimongol and they'll point you the way. Once you come out of the hill range on the west side, turn right again to start making your way back to the Kamalganj–Srimongol road.

Indigenous villages Dozens of indigenous villages dot the hills and forests of Srimongol and Kamalganj. If you'd like to visit one, it is strongly suggested you contact a Nishorgo eco-guide as they will be able to properly describe the cultural differences you see when you visit the village. The villages near or within the forest are Lawachara Punji, Marhil Punji and Magucherra Punji.

AROUND SRIMONGOL

CYCLE TRIPS Cyclists and motorcyclists have raved about the two-wheeled explorations offered in and around the hills and tea plantations of Srimongol. With plenty of pathways and back roads to explore, and not many people around, this is a great place to escape while getting some real exercise and fresh air at the same time. Refer to the Srimongol Area map (pages 186–7) for potential cycle routes.

SATCHARI NATIONAL PARK The newest of Bangladesh's protected areas was created to preserve the precious remaining hill forest patch of the Raghunandan Hill Reserve Forest. In Bangla, *sat chari* means 'seven streams', which bears testament to the streams flowing through this forest that sustain the local area with water. The main ecological function of preserving it is to prevent soil erosion of the hills, retain water and provide a carbon sink. The forest also provides habitat for threatened natural species, including some very rare Hoolock gibbons.

This park is also surrounded by a number of tea estates, villages, towns and paddy fields. Only one village, Tiprapara, is located inside the park and has 24 Tripura families. People from the 14 other surrounding villages all depend on the forest resources to various degrees. Fuelwood, house-building materials, timber, bamboo cane plans and vegetables are all used by the local people. In some cases it is their only means of survival, but in others it is a profit-making venture.

Getting there The park lies along the old Dhaka–Sylhet Highway and it's therefore easy to access. From Dhaka it takes about 2.5 to three hours. At Madhabpur's Saiham Circle, turn right off the N2 Highway and go a short distance towards Chunarughat. Eventually you will find the Satchari Range Office where the trails begin.

What to see Like Lawachara, three forest trails of different lengths are offered here. There is a short half-hour trail, an extension one-hour trail or a three-hour trail. Guides are recommended unless you are an experienced trekker.

REMA-KALENGA WILDLIFE SANCTUARY Officially established in 1982, this sanctuary is a part of the Tarap Hill Reserved Forest, which is the largest remnant of upland natural forest in the country and lies adjacent to the border with India. With several hills and low-lying valleys, it is perhaps the prettiest and quietest of the area's three protected areas, but that's because it's also hardest to reach. Like the Lawachara forest, the upper canopy is mainly composed of deciduous trees while the lower canopy is evergreen.

A total of 22 villages have a stake in the forest. The majority are ethnically Bengali but there are also Tripura, Santal, Telugu and Urang indigenous people as well. Without any other form of income, most of the people here are highly dependent on the forest for their livelihoods, as the majority of them (80% or adults over 30) are illiterate. Furniture shops crowd nearby Chunarughat and most of the resulting product goes to Dhaka.

Getting there Only the adventurous should consider this journey: the sanctuary lies 130km northeast of Dhaka and about 30km southwest of Srimongol and is currently very difficult to reach. First, you need to reach Chunarughat, which lies along the old Dhaka–Sylhet highway. Turn right at the Saiham Circle off the N2 Highway (the new Dhaka–Sylhet highway), and travel towards Chunarughat. From there you need to take a motorcycle for another 45 minutes, fording one stream and crossing a rickety wooden bridge. A motorcycle is probably the only vehicle that could do this, and then only during the dry season. From Srimongol, a 4x4 vehicle might be able to make it, but the road (or lack thereof) is not good. Make for the Hooglicherra Finlay's Tea Estate, and access is from there. If you plan to visit here it is recommended that you call a Nishorgo guide first to help get you to the sanctuary. They can receive you at Chunarughat or Srimongol first.

Where to stay Accommodation is offered at the **Nishorgo Taraf Hill Eco-Cottage** (*2 rooms; Kalenga village; contact Abdur Rahman Lashu;* m *01711 442247; 01711 967089;* $$$). There are also three designated walking trails for the area and so you may wish to take a Nishorgo guide for your walk, but always ask for the price of guidance first to avoid any nasty surprises later – there is clearly a dual pricing system for foreigners in effect at this place. Contact Mr Abdur Rahim (m *01913 933449*) or Razu Chakraborty (m *01913 367799; 01721 968171*) for this purpose, but be aware that they don't speak much English.

MADHABKUNDA WATERFALLS (*entry Tk50 for foreigners*) Madhabkunda has long graced the tourist brochures of Sylhet since the inception of Bangladesh, and so the falls here are quite well known amongst Bangladeshi people. While it is hardly Niagara, the falls can be quite impressive during the rainy season when flowing at full force, but they slow to a trickle during the dry season, making some wonder why they made the journey all the way here. There's a picnic area around the site run by Parjatan plus a restaurant, so you can easily take a simple lunch and enjoy the countryside journey to and from the site. To get here you probably want to hire private transport from Srimongol (by CNG: 4hr round trip; Tk500).

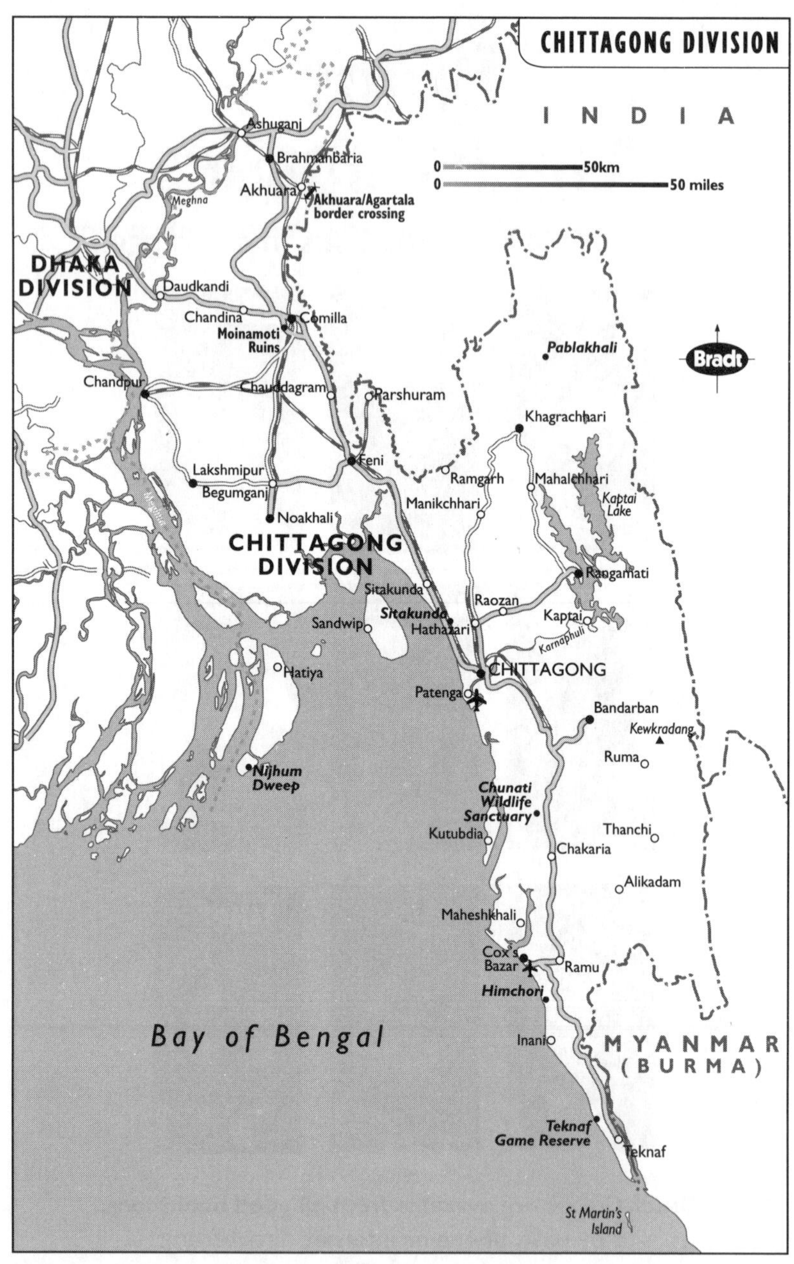
CHITTAGONG DIVISION
INDIA
0 50km
0 50 miles
Bradt
Ashuganj
Brahmanbaria
Akhuara
Akhuara/Agartala border crossing
Meghna
DHAKA DIVISION
Daudkandi
Chandina
Comilla
Moinamoti Ruins
Pablakhali
Chandpur
Chauddagram
Parshuram
Khagrachhari
Feni
Lakshmipur
Begumganj
Ramgarh
Mahalchhari
Manikchhari
Kaptai Lake
Noakhali
CHITTAGONG DIVISION
Rangamati
Sitakunda
Raozan
Sitakunda
Kaptai
Sandwip
Hathazari
Karnaphuli
Hatiya
CHITTAGONG
Patenga
Bandarban
Kewkradang
Ruma
Nijhum Dweep
Chunati Wildlife Sanctuary
Kutubdia
Thanchi
Chakaria
Alikadam
Maheshkhali
Cox's Bazar
Ramu
Himchori
Bay of Bengal
Inani
MYANMAR (BURMA)
Teknaf Game Reserve
Teknaf
St Martin's Island

6

Chittagong Division

In many ways, Bangladesh's southeastern division offers the most variety to travellers. Here you'll find the world's longest natural beach, as well as the country's highest region, the Chittagong Hill Tracts. The variety in between is stunning: at Teknaf Game Reserve, wild Asian elephants roam the tropical evergreen forests; in Bandarban, exploring the hilly topography, tasting Adivasi food and drinking fiery rice wine makes you change your definition of Bangladesh; at Nijhum Dwip, a mangrove forest filled with spotted deer awaits visitors who dare to make the long but scenic river journey to Bangladesh's coastal south.

Unfortunately, all this potential has meant that the region has been targeted for the greatest domestic tourism expansion in Bangladesh. Not all of the signs are encouraging. For instance, Bangladesh's sole coral island, St Martin's, did at one point have a sustainable development plan that was created in conjunction with private industry. But then the island was 'sold out' to private developers who then went about building dozens of concrete monoliths, putting the tiny island well on the path of ecological destruction. Who would have thought that an under-travelled country like Bangladesh could suffer from too many tourists? At Cox's Bazaar, the forest of hotels is almost impenetrable, and during Bangladesh's holiday season, even this capacity is stretched to its very limit – coming during low season is much more pleasant (not to mention cheaper).

Despite these disturbing developments, you can rest assured that Bangladesh's normal array of travel frontiers awaits you at every turn. There are even some promising ecotourism initiatives afoot in the region. By supporting them travellers contribute money towards the development of local communities. Listings of these outfits can be found in *Chapter 2, Conservation, Nishorgo eco-guides,* page 28.

CHITTAGONG *Telephone code 031*

Bangladesh's second city is at first a slap in the face: a teeming mess of highly decorated trucks choke the already polluted air (in Dhaka, these polluting vehicles are not permitted inside the city during the day, but in Chittagong the port necessitates truck traffic). As a city it has little to offer bar its people, who are renowned, at least locally, for their generous hospitality. If you stay long enough you will probably have the opportunity to dress in sari or Punjabi (formal dress for women or men) and attend one of the numerous weddings in town, the 'happening events', where you – not the bride – will become the centre of attention.

With four million people, Chittagong is developing rapidly. In GEC Circle – one of the city's main intersections – new buildings pop out of the ground like poppies in spring. The city plays an important role in the country's economy, housing a large majority of its industries. The Old City originally centred on the port, which played a significant role in Bangladesh's history and remains important to its economic development.

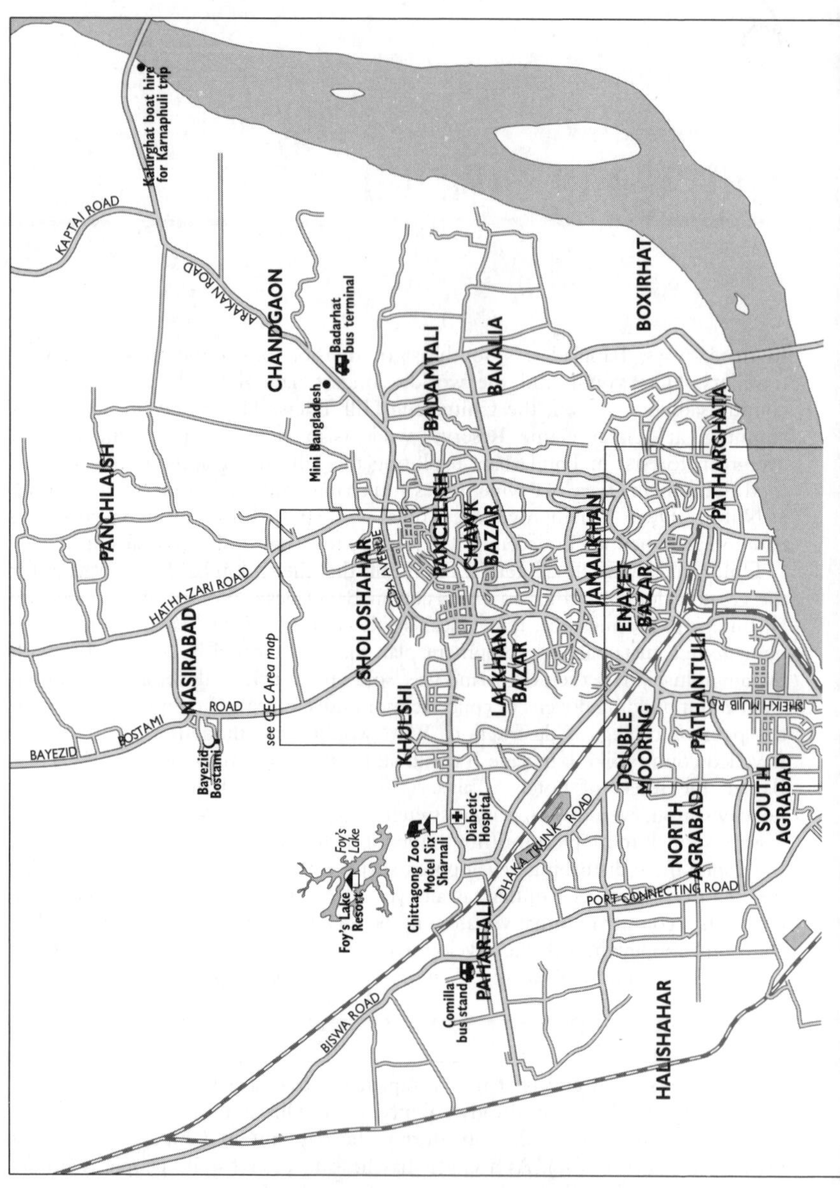

Amongst the clamour of hammers on bricks, the *azan* call to prayer also bellows across this city, welcoming you to the area where early Arab traders first entered Bangladesh. Nowadays, full cover is increasingly common and female travellers will receive a warmer welcome if they dress conservatively. Traditional *salwar kameez* is most appropriate (thigh-length top and loose-fitting trousers)

Unlike Dhaka, there are only a few luxurious respites, but this is changing rapidly. More than anything else, Chittagong offers an odd entanglement of religion, capitalism and life that spills onto its hilly streets.

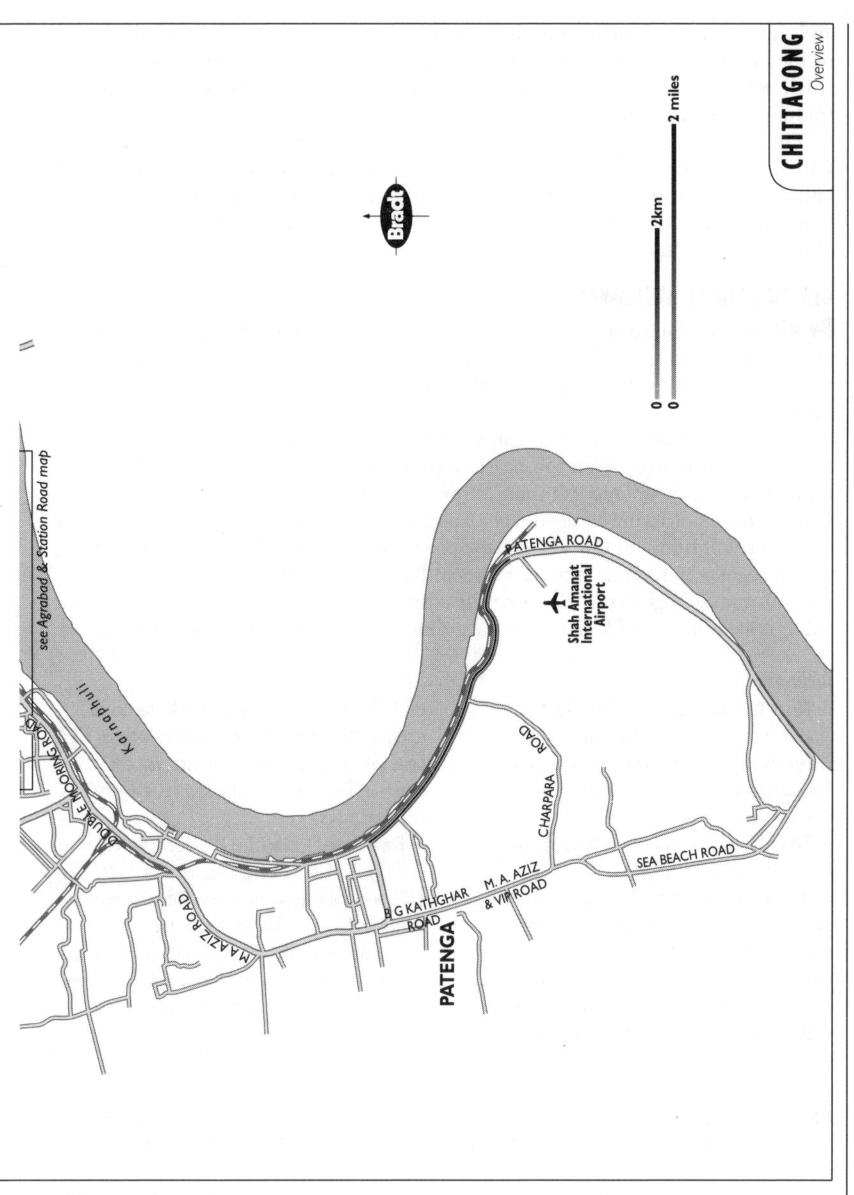

HISTORY Chittagong's history is in fact the history of the entire division, which centres on the development of the seaport. The land was originally under the control of the Arakanese, but their reign was eclipsed by Arab traders who arrived in AD900 and introduced Islam. The Arakans eventually succeeded in reclaiming their lands, but not before Portuguese settlers and Mogh pirates had their turns at influencing the trade and culture of Chittagong as well. Christianity's first steps in Bangladesh are largely attributed to the work of the Portuguese settlers, who arranged the construction of the first churches in Bengal, near modern-day Kolkata and in Chittagong. The Mughals eventually took control in the mid-16th century and the region has remained under Muslim control ever since. But small pockets of the groups mentioned above still have a presence in the city today, including a small minority of Burmese people who came down from the eastern hills for trading activity as well.

These settlers and traders brought new religious (the Portuguese set up the first Christian churches) and economic changes that influenced the character and culture of Chittagonians. Given these influences, it is hardly surprising that Chittagong has a unique language, spoken by some 14 million people, that is almost unintelligible to Bangla speakers.

GETTING THERE AND AWAY

By air From Chittagong, you can fly to/from Dhaka, although occasionally there are also flights to/from Cox's Bazaar or Jessore as well (there is probably still not enough demand to make these regular routes, so call and enquire for the latest information).

The Shah Amanat International Airport is located in Patenga, roughly 30–40 minutes (15km) away from the heart of the Chittagong. If staying at a mid-range hotel, you may be able to ask them to pick you up at the time of booking, saving you the hassle of trying to negotiate a taxi yourself. As you exit the airport a sea of taxi touts will find you quickly. A baby taxi CNG ride should cost around Tk120, with a regular taxi expect it to cost one-and-a-half times more than that.

A 30-minute flight to Dhaka normally costs Tk5,000, but you can sometimes find a discounted flight forTk3,500. See the airlines listings below for more information.

Airlines

✈ **Biman Bangladesh** Biman Bhaban, CDA Av; ☎ 650671–5, 650866; www.bimanair.com; Undependable at best, dangerous at worst. Even Bangladeshis don't use Biman's domestic services unless they have to.

✈ **GMG Airlines** GEC Circle, Husna Mansion, 1702 CDA Av; ☎ 655659–61; Hotel Agrabad; ☎ 718147, 723151; Airport; ☎ 740285–6; m 01711 796640; www.gmgairlines.com. Oldest private operator for domestic flights in Bangladesh. Flies Dhaka twice daily most days. Fare is equivalent to the other operators, when there's a special it can be as low as Tk3,500.

✈ **United Airways** Golden Plaza (4th Flr), 1692 CDA Av, ☎ 255 2435; m 01713 486 663; Airport; m 01713 486664; www.uabdl.com; At the time of research offers domestic flights to Dhaka between 3 & 5 times per day. If purchased in advance, you can sometimes find fares under Tk4,000, but a regular price fare is Tk5,495.

✈ **Royal Bengal Airlines** 2nd Flr, Ayub Trade Centre (2nd Flr), 1269/B Sheik Mujib Rd, Agrabad; ☎ 251 4202; www.royalbengalairline.com; The other major carrier to Chittagong, but less frequent than United Airways. Also offers Tk3,500 ticket specials for advance bookings on the Chittagong–Dhaka route, but full fare is usually Tk5,495 & up. Fares & specials change frequently.

By bus Chittagong is served by several major bus companies. Overnight coach services are available as well, but the hair-rising driving and unending Hindi music don't allow for much sleep.

The main bus counters are all located near GEC Circle along Zakir Hossain Road, just past Pizza Hut, although a few have offices near the train station as well. Tickets should be purchased at least one day in advance in order to secure a departure time and a favourable seat position. However, NGO staff and/or frequent business travellers may be able to reserve by phone and pay when you show up. Most companies use air-conditioned coaches and offer regular departures to Dhaka and Cox's Bazaar, so if one company is sold out just try one of the others.

For Rangamati (2.5 hours) or Bandarban (3 hours), you need to go to Chittagong's Badarhat bus terminal, located in the northern part of the city. Only local public buses serve this route, with departures leaving at least every two hours, more in the morning. Definitely no pre-booking service available here, but thankfully the roads to the hills are good and the journey not too long.

Coach companies

Baghdad Express Zakir Hossain Rd. New bus company operating luxury Mercedes-built coaches to Cox's Bazaar & Dhaka. Fares range between Tk600 & Tk1,000.

Green Line Zakir Hossain Rd, 630551, 842994; Station Rd, 631288; m 01817 210286. Offers a luxury 'Scania' service to Cox's Bazaar & Dhaka, with seats that even have massagers built into the chairs. Sometimes these don't work & (ironically) end up being a pain in the backside for the entire ride. Fares range from Tk600 to Tk1,000.

Neptune Zakir Hossain Rd, 613511; Hotel Golden Inn, Station Rd; 611004–8. Less frequent AC departures than the above 3 companies, but a more competitive price if you're looking for cheaper transport to Dhaka or Cox's Bazaar. Fares range from Tk500 to Tk800.

Shohagh Paribahan Zakir Hossain Rd; 618930, 616520; m 01711 798344. Frequent departures to both Cox's Bazaar & Dhaka. Fares range from Tk600 to Tk1,000.

Silk Line Zakir Hossain Rd; 612527; m 01819 310825. Offers a 'saloon' bus service with extra-large leather seats & 3 to a row in addition to regular Volvo buses, which have 4 seats in a row. One of the best luxury services, although departures are not as frequent as other companies. Fares range from Tk600 to Tk1,000.

Soudia S Alam Zakir Hossain Rd; m 01197 015610–2; 01197 015636–8, 01197 015632–4. New Mercedes-Benz coach service between Dhaka (Tk600) & Cox's Bazaar (Tk400).

By train Travellers should check the useful Bangladesh Railways website (*www.railway.gov.bd*) to figure out which train they need before heading to the station. The station is located on Station Road in the heart of Chittagong and easily accessible by baby taxi from GEC Circle or Agrabad. The ticket windows are open whenever the trains are running. Advance bookings are required, especially around holiday seasons like Eid.

To Dhaka Having seen drivers on the Dhaka–Chittagong Highway in action, getting the train to Dhaka certainly seems the less stressful option. There are two nightly departures (see table below) which cost Tk660/435 (air-conditioned/non air-conditioned sleeper; 10hrs) respectively. Air-conditioned sleepers are hard to buy as they are often reserved for government officials until the last minute, especially from Chittagong. Otherwise three daytime departures will set you back Tk430/290/150/125 for an air-conditioned seat/first-class seat/shuvon/unreserved (8hrs).

To Srimongol/Sylhet The daytime journey from Chittagong to Srimongol has been highly recommended by travellers thanks to the great views of the surrounding countryside. It departs at 08.00 and arrives at 14.27, and tickets cost Tk320/210/190 for a first-class seat/chair/unreserved seat, a journey of about 7hrs. Another overnight train arrives at a punishing 03.28. Consider the day train if including Srimongol in your itinerary. Travellers heading to northeast India can also take this route to get to Sylhet.

TRAIN TIMETABLE

No	Destination	Train name	Off day	Dep time	Arr time
701	Dhaka	Subarna Express	Friday	07.00	13.00
703	Dhaka	Mohanagar Probhati	None	07.15	14.00
721	Dhaka	Mohanagar Godhuli	Sunday	15.00	21.30
741	Dhaka	Turna Express	None	23.00	06.00
719	Sylhet	Paharika Express	Monday	08.00	17.20
724	Sylhet	Udayan Express	Satruday	21.00	05.55

By launch Travelling by river boat is invariably the slowest option, but it's perhaps the most interesting. There is no direct service to Dhaka, but you can get there via Barisal if you've got a couple days and want to see the rivers. The service to Sandwip (berth in double cabin Tk540; 3hrs) and Hatiya (berth in double cabin Tk1,000; 6hrs) runs every Sunday, Tuesday and Thursday departing at 09.00. The Thursday departure goes all the way to Barisal (berth in double cabin Tk1,200; 22hrs), returning on Friday. Enquire at the BIWTC office (☎ *613358*) in Sadarghat for bookings.

GETTING AROUND Chittagong is cheaper than in Dhaka to get around. A CNG (green baby taxi) ride from the port area to GEC Circle should cost Tk50–70, and between Agrabad and GEC about the same. Many locals use rickshaws to get between places in the city, although the presence of hills means that your rickshaw wallah might be working a little harder than expected. The usual 'one taka per minute' rule applies for rickshaw rides.

ORIENTATION Chittagong is divided into two new areas that are on almost opposite ends of the Old City. GEC Circle is the city's newest district and most of the best restaurants, hotels and cultural activities are located here. This area is the best spot to be for travellers. The junction between CDA Avenue and Mehedibagh Road forms the heart of GEC and serves as a great reference point, known to all local taxis. Most services for travellers can be found in the shopping complexes surrounding GEC Circle. There is a fair collection of computer goods, photo-printing stores, stationery and internet cafés located here.

The other main district is situated in Agrabad, which serves as the commercial centre of the city. Traders and corporate offices reside here and this is where all the money changes hands. You'll want to be based in Agrabad or Station Road here if your business is taking you to the port area.

The Old City, like Dhaka, centres on the port. Most of the imported goods end up in markets around the train station and Jubilee Road areas, which also house the city's cheapest hotels and restaurants. Budget travellers will want to look up hotels in this area.

TOUR OPERATORS

Bangladesh Ecotours 263 Jubilee Rd; ☎ 623451; m 01711 264827; e didar@bangladeshecotours.com; www.bangladeshecotours.com. Chittagong's one & only local tour operator, this unique outfit specialises in Chittagong Hill Tracts tours & treks. Comes highly recommended for their knowledge & experience of this secluded & hard-to-reach region. Their tiny office is difficult to find so head to the Tower Inn on Jubilee Rd first & call from there. Can arrange Chittagong Hill Tracts permits on your behalf – a service that saves you the trouble of dealing with the security officials.

WHERE TO STAY Hotel prices are higher compared with other cities and many establishments quote in US dollars, but are usually willing to offer discounts faster than you can even ask for them. Refer to the price code system on the inside front cover for the listings below.

GEC

Upmarket

The Peninsula Chittagong (122 rooms) Bulbul Centre, 486/B OR Nizam Rd, CDA Av; ☎ 285 0860–69, 616722; f 624385, 632506; e reservation@peninsulactg.com; www.peninsulactg.com. 4-star facilities at 5-star prices & definitely not the same brand as other Peninsula hotels. Nonetheless, this is probably the best hotel in town, with a well-stocked bar to match. Bring your credit card. $$$$$$

Mid-range

Grand Park Hotel (20 rooms) Av Centre, 787 CDA Av; ☎ 620044, 286 2044; f 617586; m 01818 111541; e facl@myway.com. This well-appointed guesthouse is CDA Av's best business-traveller choice with a business centre. Laundry service & b/fast inc. $$$$$

Harbour View Hotel (21 rooms) 721 CDA Av; ☎ 615020, 615034, 617821; f 617868; e hview@spctnet.com; www.harbourviewbd.com. Expensive for what you get, considering the rooms are rather dark & smoky & better hotels are available in the area for similar prices. The Royal Park Inn would be a better, more intimate choice. $$$$$

Hilltop Inn (10 rooms) Hse 6, Rd 2, Khulshi; ☎ 655762, 255 0957; m 01814 142909. e htopinn@yahoo.com. Situated right next to the World Food Program's offices in the residential area of Khulshi, this quiet & well-serviced guesthouse has to be one of Chittagong's best choices for the well heeled. The restaurant isn't superb, but the peace & quiet is. $$$$$

Hotel Lord's Inn (68 rooms) Hosna Kalam Complex (opposite Ocean City), CDA Av; ☎ 255 2671–4; f 255 2673; e info@hotellordsinnbd.com; www.hotellordsinnbd.com. This hotel complex offers every single service under one roof, & an army of people to service you. Best for the Bengali businessman. $$$$$

Meridian Hotel (64 rooms) 1367 CDA Av; ☎ 654000–01, 654299; f 650154; e meridian@techno-bd.net. Service at the Meridian seems organised, even if the hotel is aging. Do ask for a room that faces away from the road. $$$$$

City Inn Hotel (16 rooms) 576/577 OR Nizam Rd; ☎ 650981, 655968; f 655968; e cityinn@spnetctg.com; www.cityinnbd.com. A little bit rough around the edges, but the rooms do have refrigerators. Better value is had in the hotels at the located closer to the GEC Circle, such as the Royal Park Inn. $$$$

Hotel Silmoon (42 rooms) 134/A CDA Av, Dampara; ☎ 628302, 286 0755; f 2860756; e hsilmoon@bbts.net; www.hotelsilmoon.comemail. Terribly noisy location for this terribly tacky hotel. $$$$

Royal Park Inn (18 rooms) 1702 CDA Av; ☎ 658689, 652881; m 01817 712355, 01811 506873; e hotelroyalpark@link3.net. After a hike of stairs, you arrive at this secluded hotel, which has nicer bathrooms & clean rooms done right & is cheaper than its neighbours. Not a bad option. $$$$

Budget

Hotel Abakash (12 rooms) 654 OR Nizam Rd; ☎ 633960; m 01558 673021; e hotelabakash@yahoo.com. GEC's cheapest choice, if you think you can sleep through the thunder of one of Chittagong's busiest intersections. $$

Agrabad

Hotel Agrabad (110 rooms) Agrabad C/A; ☎ 713311–8; f 710572; e info@agrabadhotels.com; www.agrabadhotels.com. Dhaka booking office: Agrabad Group, 7th Flr, 61 Motijheel C/A; ☎ 02 955 0861/01713 193343; e hotel@agrabadgroup.com. Primarily for business & leisure travelers, facilities include internet, TV channels & 24-hour room service. Although some of the rooms have a retro feel, others are newly renovated & ensure that guests enjoy a comfortable stay. 2 restaurants available: Manini offers Chinese, while Mallika entices guests with continental fare. Car rental, travel agencies & airline offices are situated nearby. Guest airport pick-up & drop-off service is available on request. $$$$$$

Hotel Saint Martin (74 rooms) 25 Sheikh Mujib Rd; ☎ 725961, 712107–9, 710624; f 710659; m 01817 260325; www.hotelsaintmartin.com.bd. Despite its age, this hotel has been in business for a long time, so they must be doing something right. The building is a monstrosity from the outside. Has a bar. $$$$$

Landmark Hotel and Restaurant (28 rooms) 3072 Sheikh Mujib Rd; ☎ 252 3598, 727299; f 252 3597; m 01820 141995, 01731 886997; e landmark@ctgtel.net. One of the newer Agrabad hotels, it's smaller & has a Bengali boutique-hotel feel – if such a thing exists. $$$$$

Hotel Hoque Tower (62 rooms) 500/A Sheikh Mujib Rd; ☎ 713828; m 01819 323876. Cheap for the area, with fan rooms & attached bathrooms. $$

Hotel Parabat (94 rooms) 472 Sheikh Mujib Rd; ☎ 726168, 721187. One of Agrabad's cheapest options, with fan rooms & private bathrooms, but not much in the way of luxuries. $$

Jubilee and Station Road

Mid-range

Foy's Lake Resort (11 rooms) Foy's Lake; ☎ 256 6080, 256 6070; m 01913 531480, 01913 531481. A nice location, isolated from the rest of the tourist fodder at Foy's Lake, but geared primarily to the well-heeled domestic honeymooners seeking a lakeside escape for a day. Not much to do except float around the lake in a

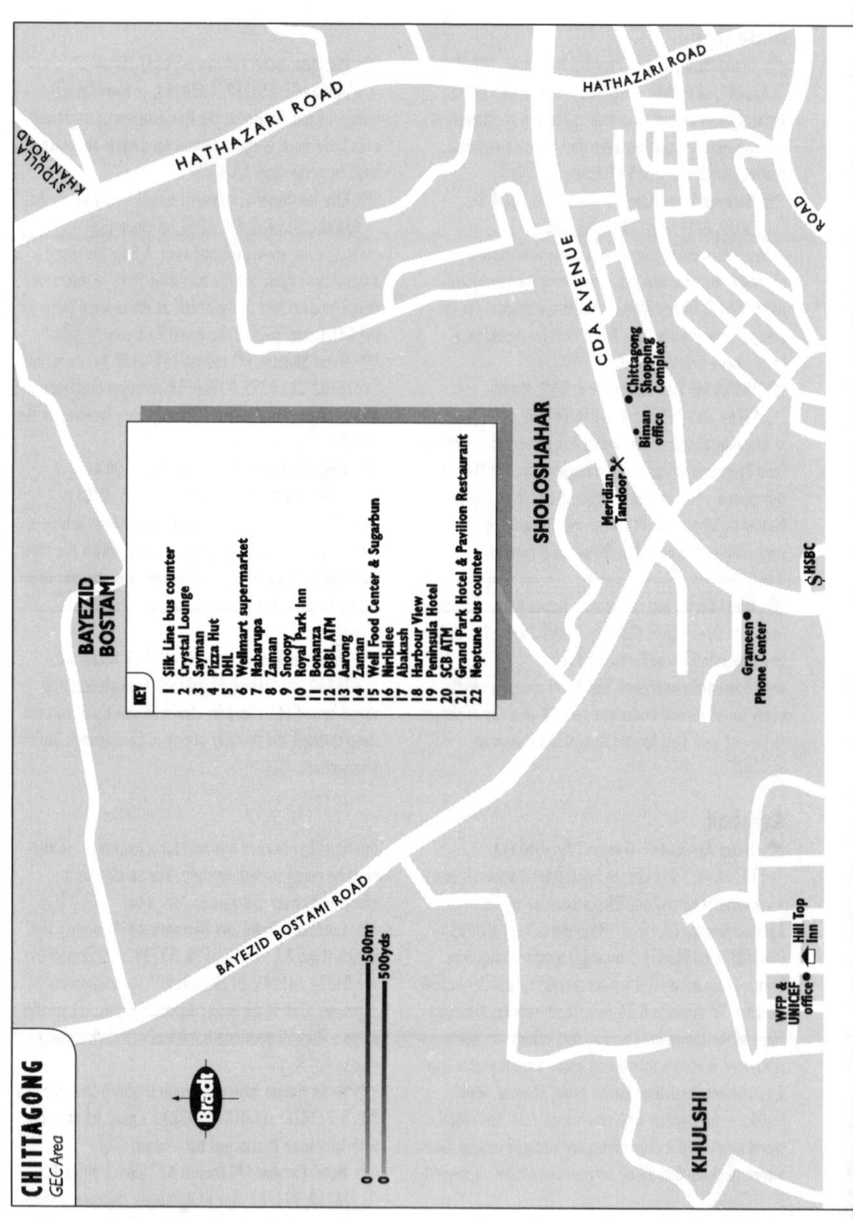

boat & pretend you're a famous actor/actress in a Bangladeshi soap opera. $$$$$

Tower Inn Chittagong (88 rooms) 183 Jubilee Rd; 842 6912, 842 6946; f 615662; e info@hoteltowerinn.com; www.hoteltowerinn.com. Billed as the city's only boutique hotel, it has a wide range of modern services & facilities such as a business centre, AC rooms, in-room internet, credit card facility, car rental, restaurant & 24hr room service. Certainly the best hotel in the area if you can afford it. $$$$

Asian SR Hotel (55 rooms) 291 Station Rd; 285 0346–8, 636383, 637872; f 634881; e info@asiansrhotel.com; www.asiansrhotel.com. Easily Station Rd's best choice, with a great rooftop view over the city. Recommended. $$$

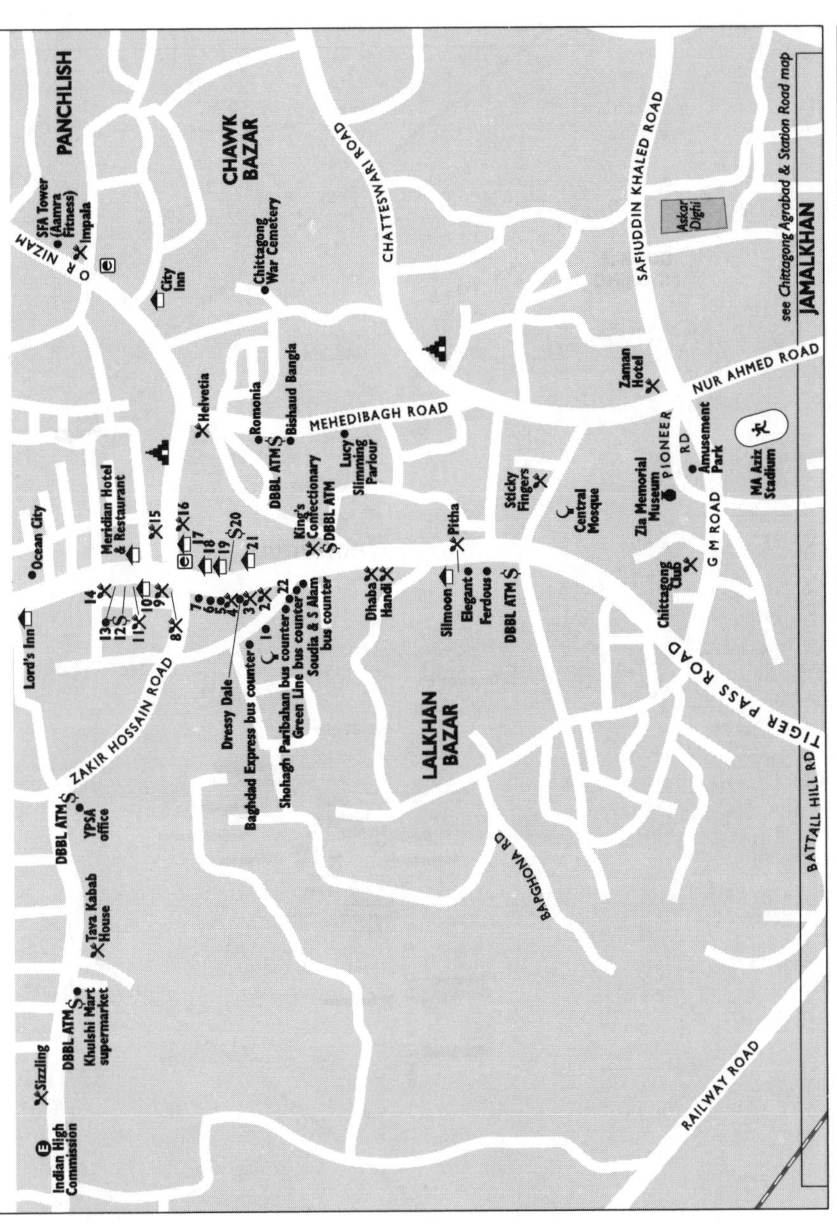

Golden Inn (40 rooms) 336 Station Rd; ☎ 611004–8; f 610683; m 01711 819025. Old stalwart of Station Rd & a good option if you're looking to save a couple of hundred taka. $$$

Hotel Al Faisal International (40 rooms) 1050 Nur Ahmed Rd, Stadium; ☎ 619000, 613936, 636844; f 610326; This well-established hotel is one of Chittagong's oldest, but its service is friendly & straightforward, making it excellent value & a good place to stay. $$$

Hotel Bandargaon (25 rooms) 875 Jubilee Rd, Enayat Bazaar; ☎ 637686. A decent mid-range choice for this area with fan & AC rooms, but privacy at this hotel can be an issue. $$$

Hotel Regent Park (65 rooms) 4/A Jubilee Rd, New Market; ☎ 285 2072, 285 2073; f 615435; m 01914

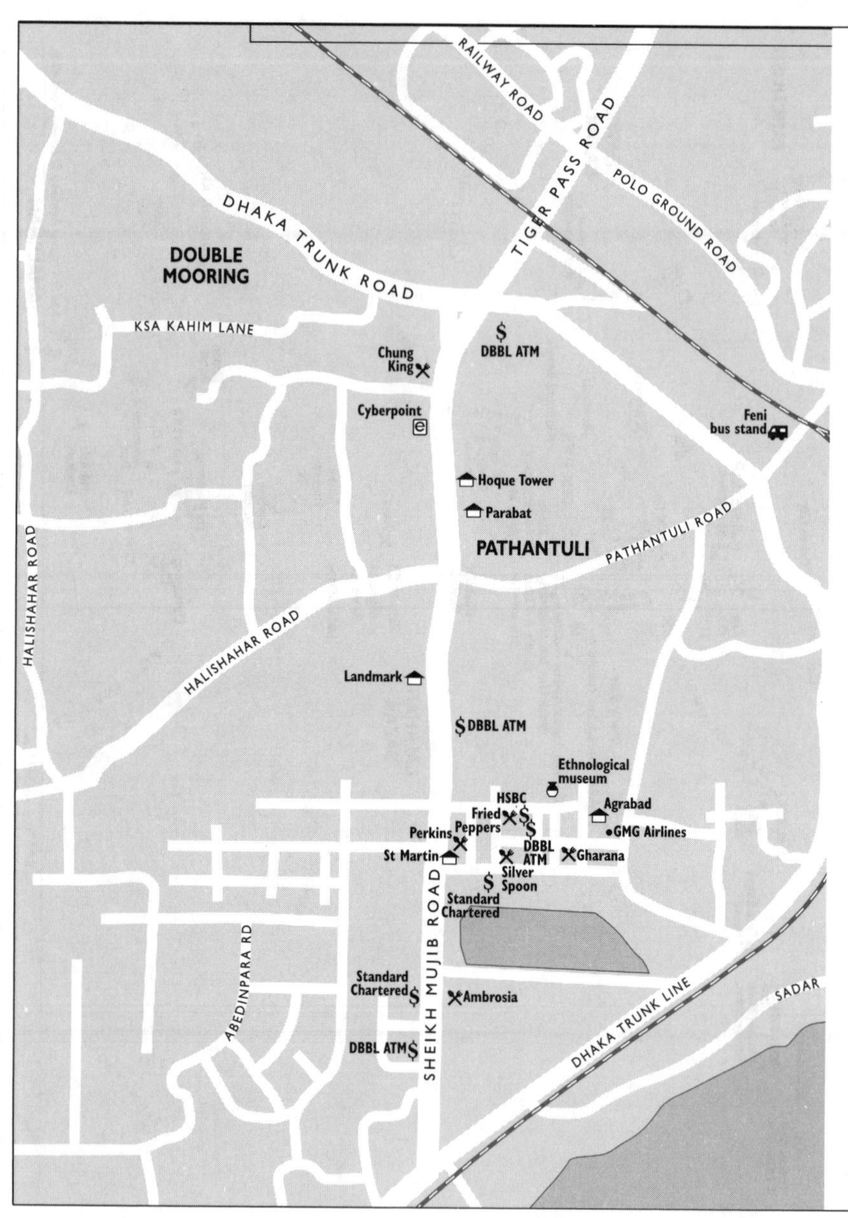

123602, 01818 503633; e hotelregentpark@yahoo.com. A more affordable option than the Tower Inn, but certainly closer to the noise, hustle & bustle of New Market area. $$$

Motel Six Sharnali (36 rooms) Foy's Lake Gate; 0443 3340751. Gaily painted hotel, primarily for large groups of domestic tourists visiting Foy's Lake from out of town. $$$

Budget

Hotel Sylhet Super (18 rooms) 16 Station Rd; 841451, 841452; f 632265. If your primary purpose in Chittagong is a night at the bar, make a discreet enquiry here. Otherwise the hotel is forgettable. $$

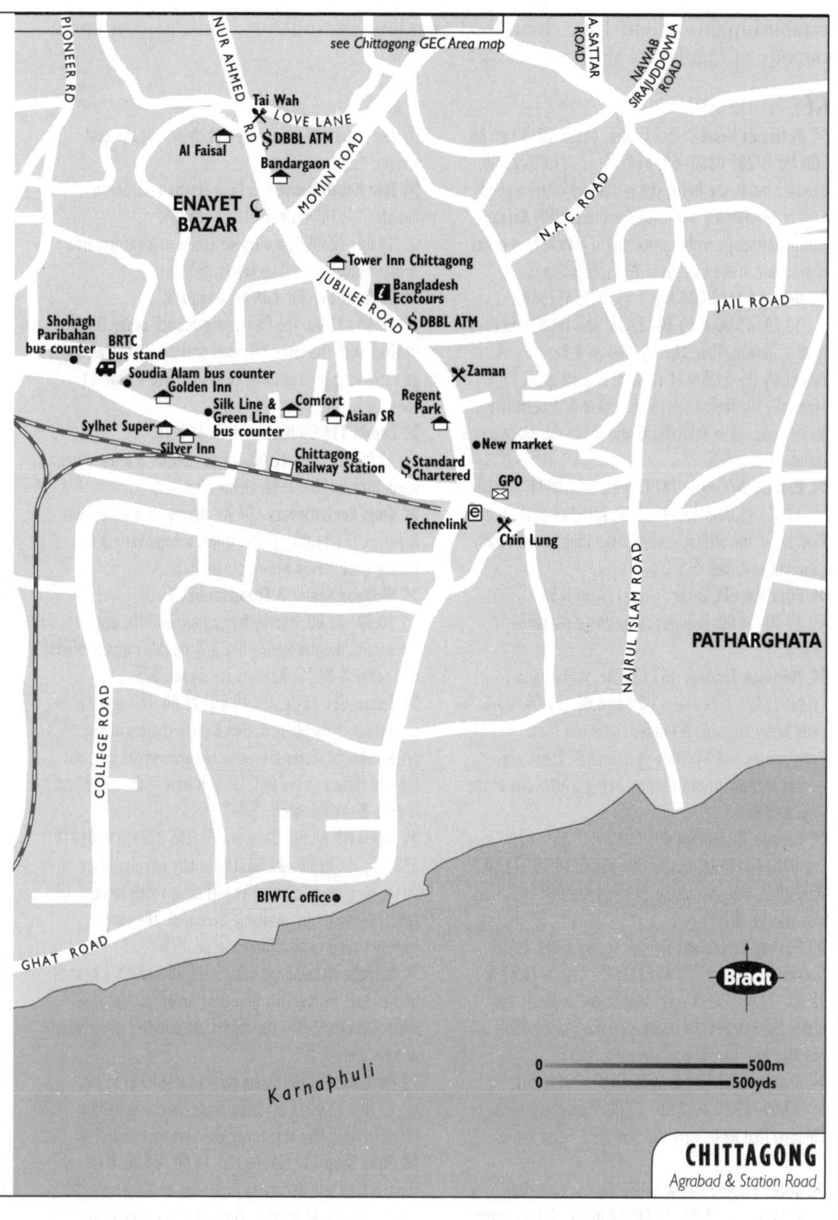

Hotel Comfort (25 rooms) 734 Station Rd; ☎ 624346, 624348. Dark, dank & dirt cheap sums this hotel up. $

Hotel Silver Inn (30 rooms) 335 Station Rd; ☎ 632757; m 01814 462510, 01725 977320. Don't expect silver spoons at this cheap dive. $

WHERE TO EAT Unless otherwise noted, most restaurants in Chittagong are open for lunch and dinner, bearing in mind that Bangladeshis do prefer to eat late (lunch is typically from 13.00–14.00 and dinner after 20.00). The upscale restaurants will definitely serve made-to-order meals out of these times, but the smaller, cheaper establishments might have their food standing around for awhile if you come outside of regular mealtimes.

GEC

✕ **Peninsula Hotel** Bulbul Centre, 486/B OR Nizam Rd, CDA Av; ☎ 285 0860–69, 616722; ⊕ 11.00–23.00. Situated inside the hotel, the restaurant offers a good variety of relatively authentic food, especially Korean cuisine, although with a price tag to match. Real coffee is available in the café, as is Wi-Fi. $$$$$

✕ **Bonanza** 1692 CDA Av; ☎ 652079, 652564; ⊕ 12.00–15.00 & 18.30–22.30. This restaurant does it all – Korean, Thai, Chinese, Indian & Bangla – & thankfully the quality of all them is quite good, especially the Indian selections. Polite & unobtrusive service plus white tablecloths also make this place a real standout. $$$$

✕ **Pavilion** Av Centre, 787 CDA Av; ☎ 620044, 286 2044; ⊕ 12.00–15.00 & 18.30–22.30. Attached to the Grand Park Hotel, this well-appointed restaurant serves reliably good Indian dishes. $$$$

✕ **Pizza Hut** GEC Circle; ☎ 632733, 614656; ⊕ 11.00–23.00. Requires no further explanation. $$$$

✕ **Meridian Tandoor** 157 CDA Av, Sholashahar; ☎ 650154; ⊕ 12.00–15.00 &18.00–22.00. Dark with heavy curtains & hidden away like most Bangladeshi multi-cuisine restaurants. There are decent Indian options despite being a little out of the way. $$$

✕ **Sayman Restaurant** 805 CDA Av; ☎ 635669; m 01819 318593; ⊕ 12.00–15.00, 18.00–22.00. Only offers Bengali cuisine, but you can find favourites like *bhorta*. $$$

✕ **Sizzling Restaurant** Sanmar Spring Valley, Zakir Hossain Rd, Khulshi; ☎ 657221; ⊕ 12.00–15.00 & 18.00–22.00. Didn't seem frequented by locals too often, but you get the impression this place is more popular with Bangla party groups. $$$

✕ **Snoopy** 1702 CDA Av, GEC Circle; ☎ 651201; ⊕ 12.00–15.00 & 18.00–22.00. Passable versions of Chinese/Thai food – try the *pad thai*. Good value. $$$

✕ **Sticky Fingers** 300/A Raboti Mohan Lane, Dampara; ☎ 627631; ⊕ 12.00–15.00, 18.00–22.00. Sometimes recommended by Chittagonians, with all your multi-cuisine favourites, like American chow mein & chilly chicken –that's the spicy kind of chilly, not the cold variety. $$$

✕ **Tava Kebab House** 6/5 Zakir Hossina Rd, South Khulshi; ☎ 614246; m 01912 685389; ⊕ 18.00–22.00. Has outdoor tables in a garden area. Recommended for kebab lovers. $$$

✕ **Dhaba** MM Ali Rd, CDA Av, Dampara; ⊕ 18.30–22.00. The Chittagong branch of the Dhaka Dhabas, with the same delicious *phuchka*. Popular, so go early as they sometimes run out of stock. Doesn't open for lunch. $$

✕ **Impala** 136 OR Nizam Rd; ☎ 654410; ⊕ 12.00–15.00 & 18.00–22.00. *Dosas* & a few other south Indian choices. Recommended. $$

✕ **Kings Confectionary** CDA Av, across from Dhaka bus counters; ⊕ 11.00–22.00. Offers a large variety of bakery goods, even brown bread. $$

✕ **Wellfood Center & Sugarbun** GEC Circle; ⊕ 10.30–22.00. Hooray for cappuccino! The upstairs restaurant, despite feeling like a McDonald's inside, offers real coffee & Baskin Robbins ice cream. $$

✕ **Zaman** GEC Circle; ⊕ 10.00–22.00. This popular restaurant chain offers decent Bangla choices at low prices. Several stores are scattered around the city, but the one closest to the GEC Circle is best – the *mugh dal* is thick & the fish fresh. $$

✕ **Handi** MM Ali Rd, Dampara; ☎ 285 3711; m 01819 638013; ⊕ 12.00–22.00. This wildly popular place serves up a range of cuisines including south Indian (*dosas* & *chaats* are available here too). The curries, however, tend to be lathered in oil. $$

✕ **Helvetia** Mehedibagh Rd; ⊕ 11.00–22.00. A branch of the chain restaurants that does American fast food more accurately than the others. Definitely a clean place to have a meal. $

✕ **Niribilee** 654 OR Nizam Rd; m 01815 675528; ⊕ 07.00–22.00. A fantastic place for cheap Bangla b/fast in GEC. Also serves excellent cream custard. $

✕ **Pitha Shop** 134 CDA Av; ⊕ 11.00–21.00. If for some reason you're craving *pitha* out of the winter season, you could try this glorified snack shop to see what they have on offer. $

Agrabad

✕ **Ambrosia** Jibon Bima Bhaban, 1053 Sheikh Mujib Rd; ☎ 251 3576, 251 3460; ⊕ 12.00–16.00 & 19.00–23.00. Agrabad's newest & fanciest joint offers a gut-bursting buffet. $$$$

✕ **Chung King** 304 Sheikh Mujib Rd; ☎ 712358; ⊕ 12.00–15.00 & 18.30–22.30. Old Chinese standby but not worth visiting, unless you are seeking shelter from the summer sun. $$$

✕ **Silver Spoon** 99 Agrabad C/A, Sattar Chamber; ☎ 727423, 728102; ⏲ 12.00–15.00 & 18.30–22.30. Watch out for the monosodium glutamate in the Chinese food here. $$$

✕ **Fried Peppers** Daar-E-Shahidi, 69 Agrabad C/A; ☎ 723407; ⏲ 12.00–15.00 & 18.30–22.30. Standard Bangladeshi fare, cooked in a standard way. Certainly no lack of choice. $$

✕ **Gharana** 93 Agrabad C/A; ☎ 251 2415; ⏲ 12.00–15.00. Where most of the local office workers head for cheap lunch. *Biriyani* power! $$

✕ **Perkins** 26 Agrabad C/A; ☎ 724510; ⏲ 12.00–15.00 & 18.30–21.00. Has the same Perkins name as the North American chain restaurant but instead serves decent Bangla food. $$

Jubilee and Station Road

✕ **Chittagong Club** Circuit House Rd; ☎ 635747; e info@chittagongclubbd.com; www.chittagongclubbd.com; ⏲ 08.00–24.00. Members only but those with connections might get access. Has a guesthouse, bar & restaurant serving upscale Bangladeshi food such as *naan* & curries. $$$$

✕ **Tai Wah Restaurant** 1052 Jubilee Rd (Near Lover's Lane); ☎ 616505; ⏲ 12.00–15.00 & 18.30–22.30. Chittagong's most authentic Chinese restaurant, with an actual Chinese chef. Also serves Korean. Did somebody say beer? Foreigners can get it here (Bangladeshis are forbidden by law to drink alcohol), but be prepared to pay. $$$

✕ **Chin Lung** 48 Shahid Sarwardi Rd; ☎ 633976; m 01819 645067; ⏲ 12.00–15.00 & 19.00–22.30. This little Chinese establishment is probably Chittagong's very first restaurant; it certainly looks that way from the inside. The faded décor easily lives up to the claim. $$

ENTERTAINMENT AND NIGHTLIFE There isn't much to do in Chittagong in the evenings, although beer can be purchased at Patenga Beach and the port area in the evenings if you enquire discreetly with locals. Otherwise the Peninsula Hotel's bar is well stocked and their upstairs terrace offers decent views of the city but you'll be paying through the nose for the privilege of drinking in public. Thursdays are barbeque night, where for Tk1,599 per couple you get fed, can buy booze and dance with wealthy Chittagonians.

SHOPPING Chittagong offers very few things of note that you can't purchase elsewhere, although **Bishaud Bangla** (*792/A Mehedibagh Rd;* ☎ *285 4595;* m *01713 109940;* e *bishaudbangla@yahoo.com; www.bishaudbangla.com*) is an island of Bangladeshi culture in Chittagong. It has a well-stocked bookshop, and sells handicrafts and funky T-shirts. Come prepared with a wad of money and a few spare hours, because this is not a place you'll want to leave quickly or empty-handed. It also serves a great array of snack food if you start to feel light-headed.

Lucy Slimming Parlour (*14/15 Mehedibagh Rd;* ☎ *285 2451*) is one for the girls: one of the first and largest beauty parlours in Bangladesh. Visit on a winter Friday, when brides are busy being transformed into porcelain dolls. It is also a good place to get a sari tied or traditional *mehendi* (henna tattooing) done.

The Chittagong branch of **Nabarupa** (*809 CDA Av;* ☎ *840777; www.nabarupa.com*) is the place to buy saris, in case you end up being invited to one of the local weddings. Excellent custom tailoring (or copying) for suits can be had at **Elegant** (*Moon Plaza, Lal Khan Bazaar, 89 CDA Av;* ☎ *638445*) and **Ferdous** (*downstairs from Elegant;* ☎ *615369*), although the former is preferred and the latter hit and miss. **Dressy Dale** (*SA Complex, 805 CDA Av;* ☎ *637081*) offers upmarket ready-made garments, with homegrown Bangladeshi designs.

Romonia (*868 Mehedibagh Rd;* ☎ *637167*) is a tiny rural crafts store with a few gems and **Aarong** (*GEC Circle;* ☎ *654030*) offers a range of household items and textiles like the other Dhaka branches.

If you're staying for a long period, visit **New Market** (*south end of Jubilee Rd*) for your houseware items.

Aamra Fitness (*SFA Tower, Panchlaish]*) is a women-only gym where long-term residents of Chittagong might like to escape the crowds for an air-conditioned workout.

Chittagong's newest shopping centre is the **Ocean City** shopping mall (*CDA Av*), just a short skip from GEC Circle. The mall is mostly filled with upmarket clothing outlets that serve Chittagong's middle classes.

Chittagong Shopping Complex (*CDA Ave, near Biman Bhaban; ⌚ 11.00–20.00*) is a handy shopping complex if setting up a home in Chittagong. *Salwar kameez* available. You'll need to bargain hard as the prices here are not as competitive as at New Market, but it's definitely less frenetic.

Khulshi Supermarket (*6/5 Zakir Hossain Rd; ⌚ 10.00–20.00*) is an essential for those with fussy dietary habits and like to cook their own food. Has a decent supply of Asian cooking needs and breakfast cereals including muesli. Fruit and vegetables are also available with no need to bargain, but this comes at a cost in quality. The freshest fruit and vegetables are always available at the markets. You could also try **Wellmart** (*805 CDA Ave; ⌚ 10.00–20.00*). Located closer to GEC, this supermarket is a handy respite when you simply can't handle the smells and sights of shopping in the local market. Imported food is also available including frozen cheese and butter.

OTHER PRACTICALITIES

Banks Standard Chartered in Agrabad or GEC, or HSBC in GEC can assist you in changing travellers' cheques or cash. DBBL ATMs are scattered around town. ATMs at any other banks tend to not accept international debit cards.

$ **HSBC GEC Office** Hosna Kalam Complex, Plot No. 3439, CDA Av; ☎ 255 1501–4
$ **HSBC Agrabad Office** Osman Court, 70 Agrabad C/A; ☎ 724406, 723750, 711154, 710008
$ **Standard Chartered Main Branch** Ispahani Bldg, Sheikh Mujib Rd, Agrabad; ☎ 711833–8, 714890–1
$ **Standard Chartered Agrabad Branch** 31 Agrabad C/A; ☎ 714907–8, 710081, 713341
$ **Standard Chartered GEC ATM** Peninsula Hotel, Bulbul Centre, 486/B OR Nizam Rd, CDA Av

Internet These are plentiful in GEC Circle (see maps, pages 206–7). Otherwise most of the mid-range hotels have computers equipped with internet for use by their guests.

e **Dot Com** 945 OR Nizam Rd, GEC Circle; www.dotcombd.com
e **Grameen Phone** 1012/A, CDA Ave, East Nasirabad; www.grameenphone.com. Offers broadband internet over mobile network (see page 87 in *Media and communications* for more information).

Assistant Indian High Commission (*Plt 2111 Zakir Hossain Rd, Khulshi; ☎ 654148, 654201; e admin@bbts.net; www.ahcictg.net*). A bureaucratic nightmare, but easier than going to Dhaka if you are in the region. Bangladeshis queue at the front counter, but foreigners are required to go around the back of the building behind the main entrance – you will be directed where to go by the guards. Always allow extra days when applying for Indian visas. Getting a visa in Dhaka is recommended as the staff there are slightly less rude and bureaucratic.

Medical Hospitals are not up to speed in Chittagong and for major medical procedures, patients should travel to Dhaka if possible (or better yet, Bangkok). For immediate emergencies, the Medical College Hospital in Mehedibagh (intersection of Mehedibagh Road and OR Nizam Road near GEC Circle) might be able to help you out, but don't expect much in the way of services.

Post Chittagong's central post office (*Station Rd*) is near the train station, towards New Market. DHL (*JB Complex, 805 CDA Ave; ☎ 635545-6; ⏲ 10.00–19.00*) offers an expensive but reliable international courier service.

WHAT TO SEE

Chilla of Hazrat Sultan Bayazid Bostami (*Nabi Nagar, north of GEC; ⏲ 09.00–17.00; entry free*) Dozens of pilgrims come to see the giant tortoises here. The animals are believed to be evil spirits who were forced to assume their current form when they incurred the wrath of the Muslim saint Bostami, who originally hailed from Iran and visited Chittagong during the 8th century. Worshippers feed the spirits scraps of food (if you feel like participating in this ceremony, you can buy bananas and bread on the road leading up to the shrine). Once fed, the mud on the tortoises' backs is used for ritual cleansing.

Sadarghat Chittagong's oldest area, close to the port is a good way to spend a day exploring the city's busy river life, especially when combined with a couple of hours in a boat on the Karnaphuli. Walkers might also want to check out nearby **Paterghatta**. With its Christian churches, the previous Portuguese influence on Chittagong is evident.

Anderkilla The city's most historically important mosque, the **Shahi Jama-e-Masjid**, built in 1670, is sited here, and has an impressive minaret whose design is Turkish in origin. Nearby the **Chilla of Badar Shah** commemorates a Sufi. Also close by is Chittagong's version of Dhaka's more well-known 'Hindu Street' with music shops crowding its laneways.

Zia Memorial Museum (*Stadium; ⏲ 10.30–16.30 Sat–Wed, 15.00–20.00 Fri; entry Tk2*) For a taste of recent Bangladesh history, visitors should drop by this museum which houses the radio transmitter that Zia used to declare the independence of Bangladesh. There are also photographs and background information on the man who was eventually assassinated by his own military men just a few years after he took power (refer to *Chapter 1, History, East Pakistan*, page 10 for more information).

World War II Memorial Cemetery (*Mehedibagh*) The cemetery lies in a peaceful location well off the main drag and is popular with canoodling couples. Take a moment to reflect amongst the memorials dedicated to the Allied and Japanese soldiers who died fighting on the Burma front during World War II. The entire site is very peaceful and well maintained.

Hilltop walks Chittagong is surrounded by hills and taking a quick stroll across them is an excellent, quick way to get off the beaten track and meet people who rarely see foreigners. **Khulshi Hills** (*just behind the Dhaka bus stand*), **Battali Hill** (*near Tiger Pass Road*), **Fairy Hill** (*High Court*) and **DC Hill** all make for interesting wanders around the city, and give good views once you've made it to the top. Sadly these areas are also prone to mudslides during the monsoon – so do take care. You'll notice that several people who come to the city in search of work have been forced to live in these dangerous areas and sadly some are killed when a hill collapses every couple of years.

Ethnological Museum (*Agrabad C/A, near Agrabad Hotel; ⏲ Oct–Mar 09.00–17.00 Tue–Sat, 13.30–17.00 Mon; Apr–Sep 10.00–18.00 Tue–Sat, 14.30–18.00 Mon*) This run-down museum contains interesting displays on the culture of local hill tracts tribes, but tends to portray these societies as backward and unevolved and is therefore somewhat depressing. The garden in front of the museum provides peaceful respite from the buzz of Agrabad.

Foy's Lake (Pahartali Lake) (*entry Tk120/60*) This amusement park offers the standard version of Bangladesh entertainment – loud music and lots of people – and now surrounds this city lake. However, the inner sections of the park adjoining the lake are a pleasant place to be, especially in a boat.

Mini Bangladesh (*Chandgaon; ⌚ 10.30–21.00; entry Tk90 adults, Tk50 children*) This is exactly what the name says: a collection of Bangladesh's tourist sites miniaturised and squished into one lovely complex. There's also a revolving restaurant (*entry Tk75, Tk75 inc food*) offering not-so-great food but good views over Chittagong.

AROUND CHITTAGONG

KARNAPHULI RIVER (*Boats leave from Kalurghat*) One of the most relaxing ways to spend a day is to cruise upriver towards the Chittagong Hill Tracts (CHT). Special CHT permits are required to cross the army checkpoint upriver, but moving away from the hum of the city to the more peaceful hilly environment makes the journey worthwhile. You can disembark just before these checkpoint posts and visit tea estates kept on either side of the banks – albeit only with an entourage of police. Arranging such a trip is easier with a local guide, who can deal with the police and security requirements as well as hiring a boat for the trip. There is no entry fee for the tea estates; you can just ask the boatman to stop for awhile and wander around.

The hum of the boat motor is far from soothing, but doesn't diminish the fun of lying back on the deck and seeing the transition of cityscape to rural environment. If you're lucky you'll see sand dredgers toiling away in the water, fishermen working five lines at a time, and bamboo being transported downriver. Try to head back well before dark, so you have time to see the sunset from Chittagong docks.

Boats can be hired from the old bridge at Kalurghat, for around Tk3,000 per day. If you can manage to bring a cook or a supply of food, there are small beaches along the route where you can have a lazy lunch and cool off with a swim in the clear green water.

PATENGA BEACH (*3km past the airport*) A visit to Chittagong isn't complete without watching the sunset at the festival-like Patenga, where weekend visits are extremely popular among locals. Only a few bathers dare the rocks and pollution, but it's still a great place to take *cha* and people watch. Absurdly priced beer is sometimes available here, but it depends on the mood of the government officials of the day.

PARKI BEACH (*17km south from Chittagong*) This is a fairly unknown beach across the Karnaphuli River at Anwara and quite muddy during low tide, 40 minutes' drive from Chittagong. Peaceful views of both the Karnaphuli River and the sea are found here, as well as views of the big ships anchored at the outer dock. Not great for swimming, however.

CHITTAGONG SHIP-BREAKING YARDS Owners and workers are now reluctant to let foreigners into the ship-breaking yards closest to Chittagong, but visitors trying to enter the shipyards closer to Sitakund (see opposite) have had better luck. Try and wear decent shoes because it's a filthy process and the beach is often muddy and covered in chemicals from the ships. Those with a passing curiosity should consider searching among the markets beside the Dhaka–Chittagong Highway, where a great deal of the goods salvaged from the ships is sold.

SITAKUND *Telephone code 03028*

Time seems to have stood still in Sitakund, a village 37km north from Chittagong on the Dhaka–Chittagong Highway. The place is synonymous with the controversial ship-breaking yards (see box on page 216), but ironically the village itself lacks anything related to the industry and Sitakund slips by mostly unnoticed, except during the ten-day Shiva Chaturdashi Mela Festival that takes place every year in late February. Thousands of Hindu pilgrims camp along the roadside and the village itself comes alive with food and trinket stalls thronging with people. The main pilgrimage occurs during the first three days of the festival.

GETTING THERE AND AROUND Sitakund is most easily accessed by CNG baby taxi from Chittagong – from GEC circle you can find drivers willing to do the ride for about Tk200. Otherwise you can pick up a Comilla-bound public bus from Alangkar (Tk40) .

On arrival, rickshaws ferry people to the base of the Chandranath Temple hill but the walk up is pleasant if the weather is good.

WHERE TO STAY AND EAT When visiting Sitakund it's better to stay in Chittagong, but if you want to be based at the village you could try emailing YPSA, the local Chittagong-based NGO listed below. There are several basic restaurants, ie: shacks, serving pretty much the same food.

Ayesha Villa (4 rooms) College Rd; ☎ 56242; e disc@ypsa.org; www.ypsa.org. A local Chittagong-based NGO with basic rooms at a training centre just off the Dhaka trunk highway, a Tk8 rickshaw ride from College Road. Call in advance to organise accommodation & basic meals.

WHAT TO SEE

Chandranath Temple *(45mins' walk from Sitakund Town, east from the bazaar; ⌚ all day; entry free)* Nestled on the edge of the eco-park and located at the end of College Road, Chandranath Temple is the most famous of Sitakund's 220 Hindu temples. Pilgrims with walking sticks hike to the top of the hill to pay homage; non-believers can enjoy spectacular views across the Bay of Bengal on a clear day.

Sitakunda Botanical Garden and Eco-Park *(Dhaka–Chittagong Highway, 0.5km south of Sitakunda bazaar; ⌚ 10.00–17.00; entry US$8 for foreigners, Tk8 for locals)* Sitakund's eco-park, located just off the Dhaka trunk highway, charges absurd ticket prices and is hardly worthwhile. However, entering the eco-park enables you to drive to the top of the hill, which makes the trip to Chandranath Temple significantly easier. The eco-park has a waterfall to see and a few birds amongst the forest but otherwise provides no other facilities to visiting guests.

Ship-breaking yards Visitors have had an easier time getting access to the ship-breaking areas via Sitakund, mostly because there aren't so many other camera-wielding travellers knocking on doors trying to take a peek. To visit the yards from Sitakunda, you'll need to hire a taxi to head south along the Dhaka–Chittagong Highway until you start seeing piles of recycled goods from

CHITTAGONG SHIP-BREAKING YARDS

Midori Courtice

The industry of dismantling ships on the beaches of Bangladesh is becoming widely known around the world, mostly for its notoriety as one of the world's most dangerous professions, both from an occupational and environmental standpoint. It is also worth noting that almost all the steel being used in construction throughout Bangladesh today comes directly from the melted down, re-rolled hulls of these massive vessels. It is a vital industry for a nation that is developing at an exponential rate, and it creates much-needed work for thousands of Bangladeshis.

A lesser-known fact is that the majority of these workers are not from the bustling, southern port city of Chittagong where the ships end up. Rather, they migrate from the rural, impoverished northwestern regions of the country. With no secure employment and frequent flooding in these areas, ship-breaking means a regular stable income, no matter how dangerous. Recruitment generally occurs in between rice harvests and plantings when work is scarce and men will jump at the opportunity. The average working lifespan of a ship-breaker is 15 years, at which point they are often too injured to continue. They will return to their villages in the north, crippled, blind or with diseases yet to appear, such as those of the lung, caused by years of inhaling asbestos. With no compensation or social programmes in place, communities rely on the constant flow of younger, robust workers to leave for the yards and send home remittances.

the ships available for sale – this indicates the presence of a shipyard on the beach. Turn westward on any small village road and you'll eventually find a shipyard to explore; whether or not they permit you to enter and take photographs is another matter! Be prepared as it can be very difficult traipsing through the mud to get closer to the ships.

CHITTAGONG HILL TRACTS

This section has been kindly checked by Sophie Grig at Survival International. Bradt entirely support responsible travel and urge travellers to prevent intruding on the lives of CHT's tribal people; ensure you ask permission before entering their villages.

With its folding hills, clouded valleys and varied peoples, the undulating scenery of the Chittagong Hill Tracts (CHT) offers a thrilling escape from what can be a rather homogenic existence in the delta below. Over 11 different tribes inhabit villages dotting the hills, most of which remain totally unexplored and unexploited by even the strongest forces of globalisation – mobile-phone operators were not permitted to set up in the hill tracts until very recently. Much of this is owed to the region's remote, rugged terrain and the unresolved issues surrounding the armed insurgency. Sometimes, it seems that the powers that be, such as the army or security forces, would rather keep the affairs of the hills hidden from view. So let's call a spade a spade: the CHT is Bangladesh's dirtiest little secret.

HISTORY Locals are keen to point out that during British colonial times, the people of the CHT enjoyed a special status. Under the Hill Tracts Act of 1900, the indigenous people here were given a great deal of autonomy in return for economic provisions (eg: taxes to the Crown raised from the sale of cotton). Deputy commissioners were assigned to the regions, but circle chiefs were left to deal with the social and administration issues. The British rarely interfered with their internal affairs.

Later, during the partition of India in 1947, the British rather hastily decided that the CHT should become part of East Pakistan, on the shaky basis that the peoples' economic livelihoods were dependent on East Bengal (present-day Bangladesh). Others argue it was instead a bit of poorly conceived trading of territories: since some prime bits were given to India, other bits had to be given to Pakistan to appease both sides. Despite the fact local people were already hoisting the flags of India, the Pakistan regiments quickly pacified them and set about administering their new country.

In the early days, the Pakistani administration was too busy to pay much heed to indigenous leaders. After a military regime took over in 1963, even more rights and freedoms were disregarded. Kaptai Dam was constructed in 1962 by the Pakistani authorities, and the resulting lake flooded immense tracts of arable lands, causing huge numbers of people to be displaced from the most agriculturally productive low-lying lands. Today, these people still lack a place to reside, and the issue of recurring displacement continues to inflame tensions between the central government and local people.

When 'liberation' came in 1971, the nation's earliest administration also refused to award any sort of autonomy to the CHT people. This was on the basis of the newly established 'Bangladeshi means Bengali' identity, which the hill tract people never completely subscribed to (but were never directly opposed to either). Many indigenous people even participated in the liberation struggle while still others sided with Pakistan.

Thus were sown the seeds of a long period of discontent that eventually culminated in an armed insurgency. During the late 1970s and early 1980s, the final straw came: the government began forcibly moving settlers from the poorest regions of Bangladesh into the CHT. The local people mobilised under the name of Shanti Bahini and began fighting back.

The conflict reached one of several peaks in 1981, with atrocities occurring on both sides. Thousands of hill refugees fled to India for fear of persecution. When General Ershad took over in 1983, government policy towards the CHT shifted towards engagement instead of containment. Large massacres continued to take place throughout the 1990s, in particular at Logang in 1992 (1,200 killed) and Naniachar in 1993 (100 killed, 500 injured). Finally, 15 years (and three successive governments) later, a peace treaty was signed after multiple rounds of negotiations on 2 December 1997.

A decade later, most of the terms of the peace treaty remain substantially unimplemented, the underlying issues have not yet been addressed, and a simmering discontent still brews beneath the surface in the CHT. The fact remains that there is a distinct ethnographic and social identity amongst indigenous people, and most would be happily Bangladeshi if that didn't always mean Bengali. Nowadays, there are still tensions in the CHT because of land grabbing and violence by settlers who are still handed rations by the government-controlled army. Human rights violations, intimidation, arbitrary arrests and torture of the tribal people, by the army (and the Bengali settlers), remain rife.

However, there are some promising signs of change on the horizon. Awami League (the political party which signed the peace accord) came back into power in January 2009 and has pledged to fully implement the peace accord. And in April 2008, the government announced it would finally allow mobile network operators to enter the region, which has long stood as a symbol of the repression of the area.

An excellent documentary, *Teardrops of Karnaphuli*, directed by Tanvir Mokammel, is worth seeing before any visit to the CHT. Apparently, it has been banned in Bangladesh, so you'll have to try and find it at home.

CHT TRIBES At the time of partition, Jummas made up 98% of the population of the CHT. Now – as a result of the government's settlement programme – it is barely 50%. In the main town areas of Rangamati, Khagrachari and Bandarban there is a Bengali majority. There are 11 major ethnic groups in the CHT (and two sub-groups) compromising about 1.5 million indigenous people (the last census was in 1991). The great majority are Chakmas, mostly concentrated in the Rangamati area and making up roughly half of the indigenous population. Chakmas are the most integrated and well organised among the ethnic groups, which might account for the fact they are relatively well off in terms of education and wealth. They are also Theravada Buddhist, keeping in line with their neighbours to the east. Their lands also sit astride the main trade route to and from the CHT and, as a result, they find themselves in a position of relative power. They also speak a language that is a variant of the Chittagonian.

Marma people are the next most numerous group and are mostly concentrated in Bandarban, the southernmost of the three CHT districts. Their language and script are direct derivatives of Burmese. Tripuras are the third commonest group, although substantial populations reside in India. Finally, the Bawm people are perhaps the fourth largest group, and, thanks to the missionary visits of the early 1900s, are Christian in religion.

Most of the tribes practise a sophisticated form of shifting cultivation, to get the best out of the steep slopes, using only a small proportion of their land at any time. This practice is known locally as Jhum cultivation, giving rise to the name 'Jumma' to describe the tribes in the area. Given the increasing land pressure from settlers, their way of life is facing serious threat.

HEALTH Falciparum malaria poses a serious threat in CHT. It has killed soldiers and foreigners and also nearly killed some CHT guides who didn't take precautions. Mosquito nets, malaria prophylaxis and insect repellent are absolute musts if travelling to remote villages. Otherwise, visits to the area surrounding Bandarban Town and Milonchari (around the Hillside Resort) should be OK without taking anti-malarials – however, it is better to be safe than sorry. If you're concerned, carry malaria prophylaxis with you and take it according to the prescribed schedule – sometimes up to a week before your visit.

FOOD AND DRINK Food is much more delicious in the Chittagong Hill Tracts, especially during the holiday time. One particular local speciality, *parjan*, is a jungle-curry more reminiscent of the hill tribes of Thailand. These curries might taste a little fishy – a result of the dried fish used as the major source of sodium.

Adventurous eaters will also find their Scoville units (Scoville is a scale of spicyness) going off the chart: Adivasi *khabar* is far spicier than Bengali cuisine, so consider yourself warned. Reportedly, the spiciest chillies in the world originate from nearby Nagaland in India, and after you've tried the food in the CHT, you won't disagree.

By combining pork and local rice wine, one will find one's tolerance, both religious and alcoholic, tested by a true hill tracts visit. The people here are largely Buddhist and so have no reservations against pork or alcohol. Often the containers the latter is stored in are heavily contaminated, so it is essential you obtain your alcohol from a reputable source (if you see others drinking in a residence, or at the drinking venues in the hills, it is probably OK).

The best time to enjoy the hospitality of the hill tracts people is during the 'Boiju' festival (known as Sangrai among the Marma people of Bandarban). During the festival, local tradition dictates that you must visit at least seven houses of your families and colleagues. A special rice beer, called *zhokang*, is prepared for this holiday. When served chilled, its yeasty taste is extremely enjoyable and lacks the alcoholic drop-kick of traditional rice wine. The only caveat is that the Boiju festival runs at the same time as Bengali New Year, *pohela boishak,* every 14 April. Both festivals are colourful and jubilant, making it a difficult decision to choose where to spend the holiday. But if you're looking for an 'escape' from Bangladesh, visiting the hills during this time might just be the thing.

ORIENTATION Three districts form the CHT: Bandarban is the most scenic and interesting to visit because of its location inside a valley of the Sangu River; Rangamati is the most accessible of the three hill districts and features the Kaptai Lake and the largest selection of restaurants and hotels; Khagrachari is the least developed of the three districts and some would say the most isolated, although that might be considered a positive, depending on what kind of adventure you seek.

GETTING THERE AND AWAY Getting to Rangamati and Bandarban is more easily accomplished from Chittagong by virtue of proximity, but all three destinations can be reached from Dhaka via day/overnight bus; **Soudia Alam** (*67 Kamlapur Railway Station Rd; ☎ 02 8315087*) is the most commonly used bus company to reach all three destinations, and coaches depart from the Kamlapur Railway Station (timetables are given in the individual relevant sections below). Your best bet is to show up at least an hour early to confirm a ticket or call ahead with the help of a Bangla speaker. Otherwise, you can consider flying to Chittagong or taking the train down; the latter is far more environmentally friendly and air-conditioned first-class tickets are an absolute pleasure (see *Dhaka by train*, page 108). A private vehicle to/from the hills usually costs between Tk2,500–3,000.

RISKS ASSOCIATED WITH VISITING Despite the 1997 peace treaty, there are still outbursts of violence and the occasional kidnapping in CHT: in 2003 armed gunmen stormed Guide Tours' Hillside Resort and a ransom had to be paid for the safe return of the manager. Tensions between the settlers and Jumma people can spill over into violence, and occasionally there are armed battles between different insurgency groups. These, although not aimed at tourists, could be dangerous for visitors who are in the wrong place at the wrong time. As a result of these incidences the army carefully manages the security of the region and provides high levels of protection (as a result, they will need to be informed of your visit beforehand). Travellers should always enquire about the current level of threat before deciding to travel in the region; it's possible things will get worse again.

PERMITS It remains essential to obtain a permit before entering the CHT. Even if you have a permit, police officers sometimes insist you are accompanied everywhere by police escorts – especially outside the three main towns of Rangmati, Bandarban and Khagrachari. Whether you need police is a matter of negotiation and the presence of an experienced tour guide might make the difference. If the police insist you keep security with you, you can debate the number of officers you have to take with you, and a good thing too because you are expected to pay for transport for the entire entourage. As a result, it is often easier to explore the regions closer to town.

Due to a kidnapping in July 2007, Bandarban is the tightest in terms of security restrictions, which could severely impact the enjoyment of a visit – if you're a *bideshi*, or foreigner. Security may need to accompany you if you venture outside the main bazaar areas and into the hills, whereas Rangamati receives the most tourist traffic and therefore the least amount of hassle coming from security agencies. Often you don't need to take guards just to make a journey onto the lake, but sometimes the police will insist that you do.

Life is made a lot easier if you have connections inside the hill tracts or a justifiable reason for visiting, such as working with indigenous development organisations. If you are a *genuine* volunteer these organisations can act as your 'reference', in that they can help you get a permit or show you around some of their working areas. They can also introduce you to how the local culture here differs from the flatlands below. Do your homework first.

Group travellers may find that the assistance of a local tour operator, such as Chittagong's Bangladesh Ecotours (see page 204) or Dhaka's Guide Tours (see page 118), might ease their journey to the hill tracts and smooth the way with permissions and police escorts, especially useful given the fact these companies have a vested interest in treating their guests to a positive hill tracts experience. But it is expected that you also hire these companies for their services, which will cost more than if you make a visit on your own.

Individual travellers who simply want to tour the hill tracts will find that the easiest and cheapest way to get a permit is to spend a few hours in Chittagong visiting the Chittagong Divisional Commissioner on Chatteshwari Rd (🕘 *09.30–16.30 Sun–Thu*). Upon arrival in the hills, it is suggested that you report to the local police station, especially if you will be making a journey to more remote sections of the hills.

RANGAMATI (*Telephone code 0351*) Rangamati serves as the hub for most of the NGO and business activity in the CHT, and as such is the most established tourist destination among the three districts. It also lacks the tight security restrictions that can bog down visits to Bandarban or Khagrachari, so if you're looking for the least amount of hassle during your CHT visit – official or tourist – Rangamati is the place to be.

The region's prime scenic attraction, Kaptai Lake, holds a beautiful but ghastly story. In the early 1960s, Kaptai Dam was built to meet growing electricity demands. The resulting lake displaced over 100,000 indigenous people, and government promises of compensation (emotional or financial) fell by the wayside. Many of the displaced, mostly Chakmas, eventually became refugees in India.

While the lake itself is quite beautiful and tranquil, today it remains a bone of contention: local people don't even benefit from the electricity of the dam and discontent still simmers below the surface.

Getting there and away Like all the hill districts, prior approval from the District Commissioner is required before your visit, so the appropriate paperwork can be forwarded to the army checkpoints (see *Permits*, page 219).

The Dhaka–Rangamati route is best serviced by S Alam bus company, which departs from their counter near the Kamlapur Railway Station at 08.00 and 20.30 (7hrs; Tk330). From Rangamati, the same service returns to Dhaka at 09.00 and 19.30 and arrives seven hours later. There is also a direct air-conditioned service by Shyamoli that runs at night from Dhaka and during the day from Rangamati.

For Chittagong, S Alam or Shyamoli Paribahan offices at the Badarhat Bus Terminal have regular services departing every other hour through the day for the three-hour journey. It is also possible to travel directly to Bandarban via private transport without rerouting through Chittagong via direct road, but make sure you have your permits prepared for such a journey.

Getting around Rangamati is just a little too big to walk everywhere and one of those rare places in Bangladesh where you'll find no rickshaws because of the hills. Instead, share baby taxis buzz up and down the main road, which stop for passengers anywhere and charge based on the distance travelled – usually just a few taka for Rangamati's short distances. When you want to get off just tap the shoulder of the driver, which is what the locals do. The only time you'll face a difficult negotiation is if you visit the Parjatan tourist complex, where regular shared-taxi services don't exist and the drivers charge a premium for hiring the whole baby taxi to get there or away.

Where to stay

Hotel Sufia (42 rooms) Kathaltali; 62145, 61174; f 61648. Best-value hotel in Rangamati based on central location, service & quality. The room interiors are only so-so, but most of them have balconies, some of which look right onto the lake. Take a pass on the b/fast & see if they'll give you a discount instead – the food is far too oily & not very fresh. Instead, head to the bamboo shack next door for a local b/fast of hot *naan*, *dal* & omelettes. $$$

Motel George (5 rooms) College Gate; 63348. This hotel may be far from the heart of town, but the rooms are clean, simple & big enough to play football in. Tiled Western bathrooms are available in the best rooms. $$$

Parjatan Motel (22 rooms) Deer Park; 63126, 61046. Great location if you want peace & quiet, although aging like the rest of the Parjatan facilities across Bangladesh. The furnishings feel like they're at least 20 years old. Has a decent restaurant, which offers ridiculously overpriced beer, & a bar. $$$

Hotel Anika (18 rooms) Reserve Bazaar; 62132. Cheap, basic (but clean) rooms in the heart of the bazaar. $$

Hotel Green Castle (39 rooms) Reserve Bazaar; 61200. Rooms are large & clean, but the staff generally unwelcoming. Has large balconies overlooking the lake. $$

Hotel Dignity (16 rooms) Main Rd near the bazaar; 62364. Basic budget option lacking the dignity of its namesake, but with a good location very close to the heart of the bazaar. $

Hotel Paharika (18 rooms) Reserve Bazaar; 62176. Smoky, but the cheapest hotel in town for budget seekers. $

Where to eat

Jum Food Garden Tobolchari; 63400. Above-average Bengali food served in Rangamati's most bizarrely painted room. $$$

Peda Ting Ting Kaptai Lake. Located on an island on the lake, this scenic restaurant has a steady stream of visitors who make the lunch stop on the way back from the Shuvalong Waterfall. Peda Ting Ting actually means 'full stomach', understandably so because this restaurant features tasty indigenous food that's worth stopping for. However, don't expect everything on the menu to be available at the time you arrive. The best dish is a curried chicken served in a bamboo dish. $$$

Thai Mart Restaurant T&T Rd; 62493. Not exactly Thai nor Mart, this restaurant serves up a range of Bengali & Adivasi food. It is one of the best restaurants in town food-wise & its décor is very homely. $$$

The Roof Restaurant Dolbee Shopping Complex, Banarupa; 62969. This open-air restaurant has a welcoming atmosphere & serves some tasty indigenous dishes, as well as Chinese & Bangladeshi cuisine. It's extremely popular with locals. $$$

Hotel Green Reserve Bazaar; 61199. A reasonably clean-looking & inexpensive choice serving standard Bengali fare. $$

Kebang Opposite the post office; 63546. Offers big helpings of pork – need we say more? Again the food here is pre-prepared, but if you show up around feeding times, say just after noon or at 19.30, it'll be delicious & relatively fresh. $$

Mejang Rajbari; 62944. Lovingly referred to as the UNDP staff's cafeteria, Mejang serves up excellent fish-based Adivasi food. Note that prices are based on portions & are prepared ahead of time so may not be ultra fresh. Serves lunch primarily, although they will fetch you dinner &/or rice wine if you show up looking hungry. $$

Grishanova Kathaltali, Tobolchori Embankment Rd. Floating restaurant on the lake, which serves so-so food. But at least it floats! $

Upaban Restaurant Banarupa. Clean restaurant near the fruit & veg market serving standard Bengali fare like *ruti*, *parata* & *bhaji*. $

Shopping Rangamati has the best selection of indigenous textiles and handicrafts for sale among the hill districts. If you're after indigenous cloth for tailoring purposes, check out the **Bangladesh Small Cottage Industries Corporation (BSCIC)** (*62981*) store near the stadium. If you'd prefer to buy pre-made indigenous-style clothing or handmade household items, visit the cluster of stores

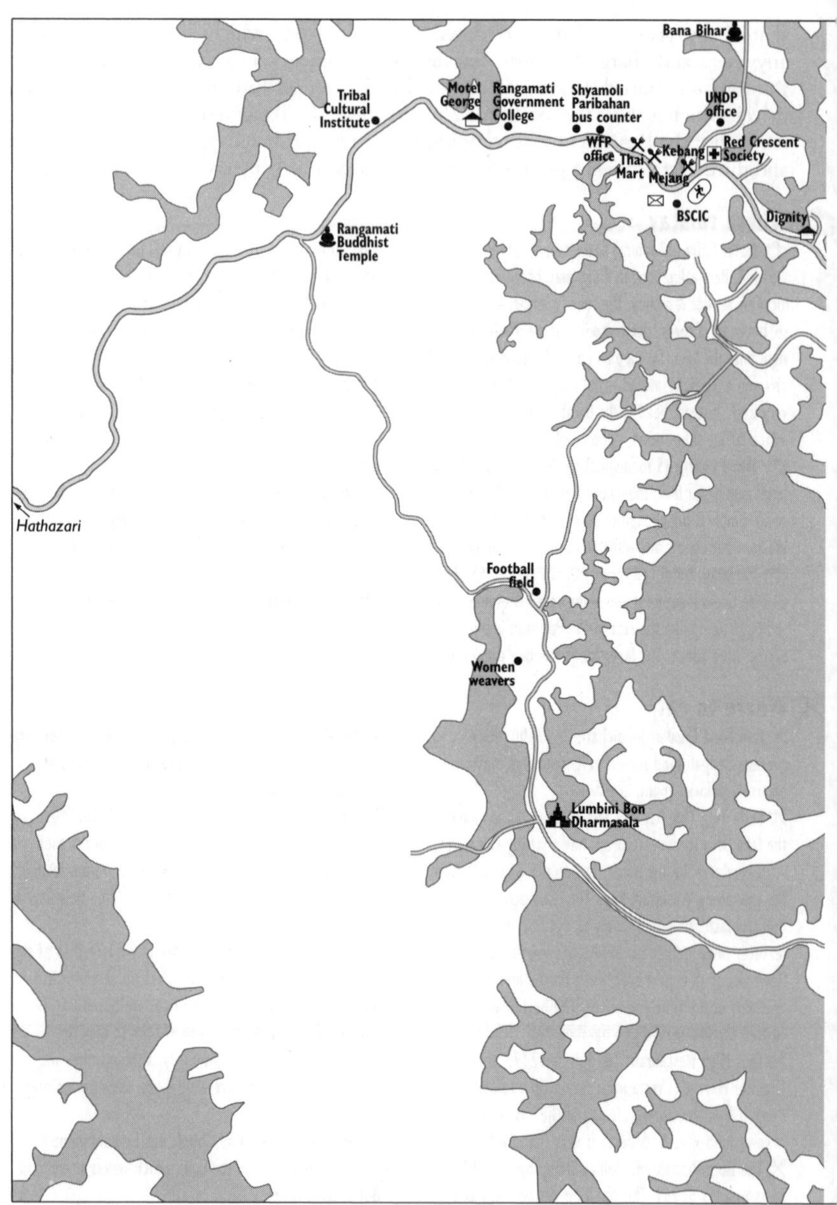

at the **Burmese Market,** situated between the Parjatan Hotel and Tobolchari. Finally, the **Nakshi Craft and Fashion** (*62494 or 63338*) at Kathalthali has more indigenous clothing and crafts. There's also a fashionable store next to **Mejang**, across from the stadium. There's even a **liquor store** near the main market selling varieties of Bangladeshi-made alcohol from Darsana.

On **market** days (Wednesday and Saturday), many of the local farmers bring a huge variety of fruits and vegetables not seen in Bengali markets or other days. Interesting to visit at any time of year as different items come into season.

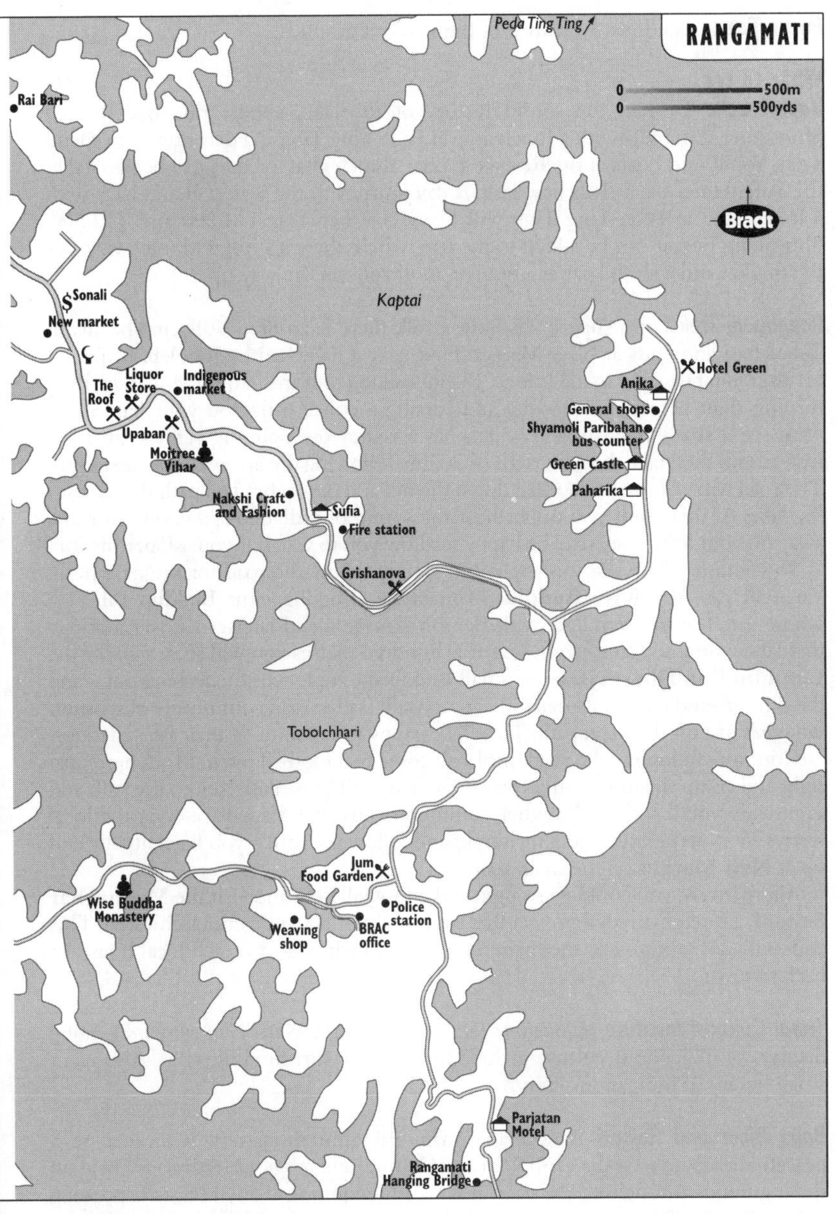

Other practicalities

Banks A branch office of the Sonali Bank (⌚ *09.30–16.00 Sun–Thu*) is located opposite the New Market building, but they can only change US dollars cash to Bangladeshi taka. Best to come prepared with cash from Chittagong.

Medical Serious medical emergencies are best handled at Chittagong or, better yet, Dhaka. For minor treatments, there's a Red Cresent clinic located near the stadium.

Post office Located just a bit west of the stadium grounds.

What to see

Kaptai Lake Despite the sordid history of the lake, a boat ride over to the Shuvalong Waterfalls with a lunch stop at Peda Ting Ting is a decent way to spend a day. You'll find boats at the Reserve Bazaar launch ghat, or they can be booked at the Sufia Hotel's travel agency desk. A day journey to the waterfall and back with a lunch stop at Peda Ting Ting will likely cost between Tk1,200 and Tk1,500. Shuvalong Bazaar can be added to the trip, where there's a hill with nice views of the market and a sloth bear at a bizarre 'mini zoo' on the way up.

Rangapani Trek For a superb 2.5-hour stroll, there is an 8km walk that begins in Tobolchari and ends at New Market. First, take a baby taxi to Tobolchari and get off after you cross the metal bridge. Begin walking onwards from the market, then turning right before the mosque and passing a police office on your left. You'll soon see a small Bengali sign which has a red arrow pointing right – turn left instead and then take the next right (this time following the arrow of the next sign). The road will eventually proceed down the hill and onto a bricked path that crosses the lake. At this point you might hear the sound of indigenous weavers working away on your left. They may be happy to allow you to watch if you ask permission.

To continue the walk, turn right and simply follow the road for the next hour. You will pass the **Wise Buddha Monastery** (Buddhangkur Buddho Bihar) – whose gate features two deer with Bengali signage – and later cross over a bridge that takes you into Rangapani. After few hundred metres you will see a sign for the **Lumbini Bon Dharmasala** – a small Buddhist temple worth checking out – and then the ground rises to a small hill where you'll find a small community of **women weavers** just off the main path. They'll be happy to sell some of their latest designs.

Continue following the road until you come to a football pitch. From here turn right and go up the hill; it offers excellent views of Rangamati. Rejoin the path and eventually you'll follow the other commuters crossing a small lake via the local ferry. Once on the other side, turn right and follow the path – you'll eventually end up at **New Market** on the main road.

Alternatively, you could go straight at the football field and visit the **Moanaghar School**, a foreign-funded project that supports over 600 indigenous children. This path will also take you to the main road from which you can catch local transport back to town.

Tribal Cultural Institute (*Chittagong Rd; ⏲ 10.00–16.00 Sun–Thu; entry free*) Aging displays of indigenous culture include maps of the surrounding areas. Also has a small library of indigenous culture.

Bana Bihar and Rajbari Rangamati's main Buddhist monastery is located on a peaceful headland near the UNDP office. Cultural and religious festivals are held on these grounds throughout the year; it is worth enquiring if anything is happening before you visit. The Chakma king's residence is on a nearby island and accessible by a quick ferry ride. Although the residence is not open to visitors there is a friendly monastic community on the island and a large bronze statue of Shakyamuni worth having a gander at. The monks here will also be glad to sit and have a chat with you.

Kaptai National Park At the time of research, this national park was just being listed in a new Nishorgo guide to Bangladesh's national parks. There was also word of some kind of guesthouse inside the park. Check out www.nishorgo.org for the latest information.

Buddhist temple (*Chittagong–Rangamati Rd*) Rangamati's main Buddhist temple is an interesting place to chat with the monks and soak up a the different religious reality of the hills.

BANDARBAN (*Telephone code 0361*) Bandarban, or the 'dam of monkeys', is the hill tracts' southernmost district, and were it not for some incredibly prolific security restrictions placed on foreign visitors, it would be the jewel in the hill tracts' crown. Its attractions are irresistible: Bangladesh's highest peaks line the landscape while villages of various ethnicities dot the hills. Travelling on the region's meandering mountain roads offers unforgettable vistas onto the land below. Finally, the Sangu River cuts a life-sustaining ribbon through it all, supplying local people with their livelihoods. One of the most common products, seen lining the riverbanks during the low water of winter season, is tobacco.

Bandarban's ethnic population is dominated mostly by Marmas, of which Bandarban is the historic home of the Bohmong Circle Chief, better known as the Marma king. If you want to go back further in time, Mru people are said to be the original inhabitants of the region, which only changed with the decline of the Mughal Empire in the mid 19th century. Today the Mru remain the most traditional of the hill tracts people: they shun outside influence and maintain their traditions vehemently to this day.

While the town itself is quite scenic, visits into the surrounding hilly countryside should be the aim of every visitor. A road extends deep into the district and at the time of research ended at Thanchi. Halfway along this road, there's a turn-off for Ruma Bazaar at Chimbuk Hill. Unfortunately, these areas are also deemed the least secure area by the Bangladeshi government. Insurgent rebel groups are said to be operating in the remote parts of the jungle, and security hiccups such as the 2007 kidnapping of two Bangladeshi nationals of a Danish NGO mean that it isn't as easy as it should be to explore all the wonderful scenery and culture Bandarban has to offer. Foreign tourists might be saddled with security precautions in the form of rifle-toting police. They will probably escort groups or individuals, although if you have employed the services of an experienced tour guide, they may be able to take responsibility for your safety while in the hills by requesting that police do not accompany visiting guests.

Getting there and away Like all the hill districts, prior approval from the District Commissioner is required before your visit, so the appropriate paperwork can be forwarded to the army checkpoints. A tour operator such as **Bangladesh Ecotours** (*263 Jubilee Rd, Chittagong;* ☎ *031 623451;* m *01711 264827;* e *didar@bangladeshecotours.com; www.bangladeshecotours.com*) can handle it for you. The Dhaka–Bandarban route is again best serviced by Soudia S Alam, whose buses depart from their counter near the Kamlapur Railway Station at 08.30 and 23.15 (7hrs; Tk350). From Bandarban, the same service returns to Dhaka at 09.15 and 20.00 and their office is closer to the main jeep stand.

For Chittagong or Cox's Bazaar, head to the main bus stand where you'll find Saudia, Purabi or Purbani hourly services, although you should expect a lot of stops along the way – to be expected for the cheap fares (Chittagong 2.5hrs, Tk60; Cox's Bazaar, 2.5 hrs, Tk85).

Getting around Most of Bandarban is flat and walkable, although you will find some areas with inclines but nothing a rickshaw puller can't handle. Jeeps can be hired at the stand across from the Hotel Hillbird (rates negotiable, depending on where you want to go) or you can hire a noisy baby taxi near the Green Hill Hotel if it's night-time and you don't have to travel too far. Expect to pay at least

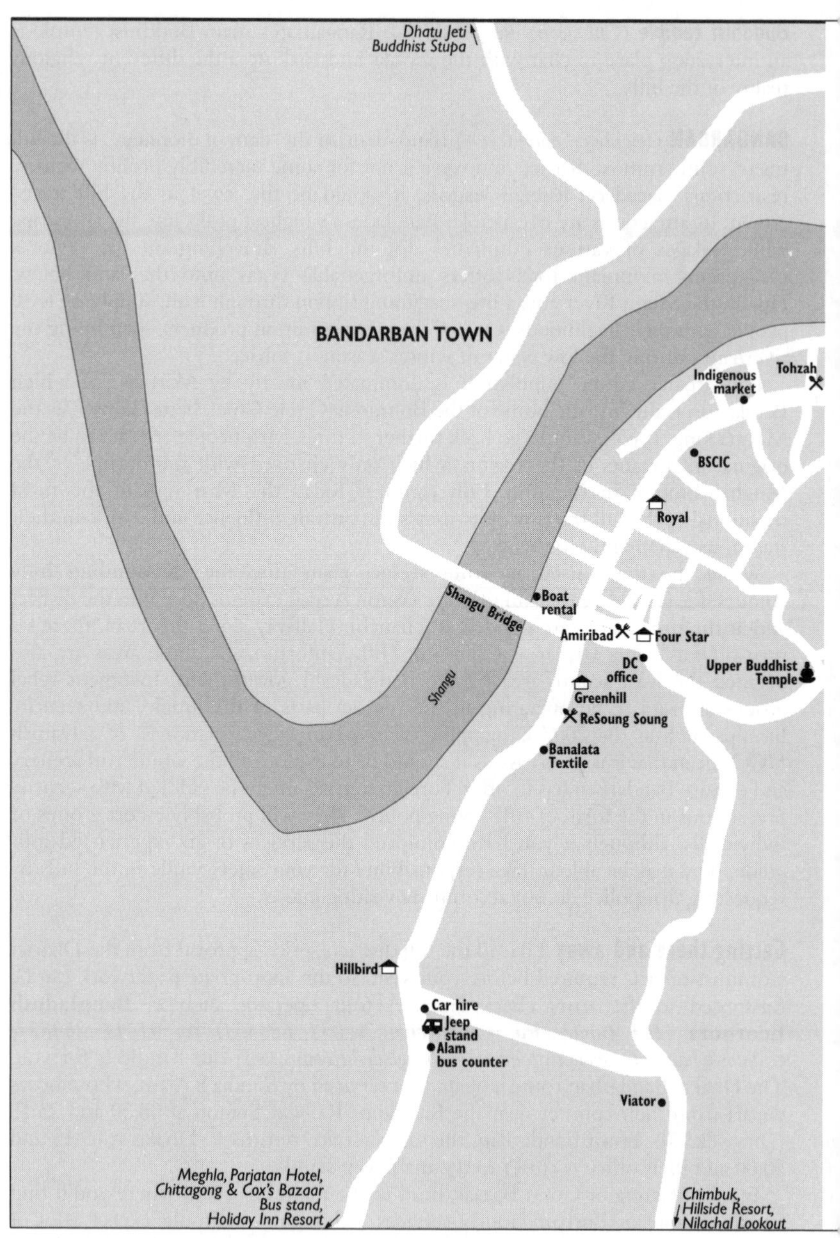

Tk100 for a noisy baby taxi ride up to Hillside Resort, with a jeep costing at least twice that.

Where to stay

Upmarket

Hillside Resort (14 rooms) Milonchari, Chimbuk Rd; 02 988 6983, 02 986 2205 (Dhaka office); f 02 988 6984; m 01199 275691 (direct line). Perched on a hilltop 15mins' drive from town, this Guide Tours-owned

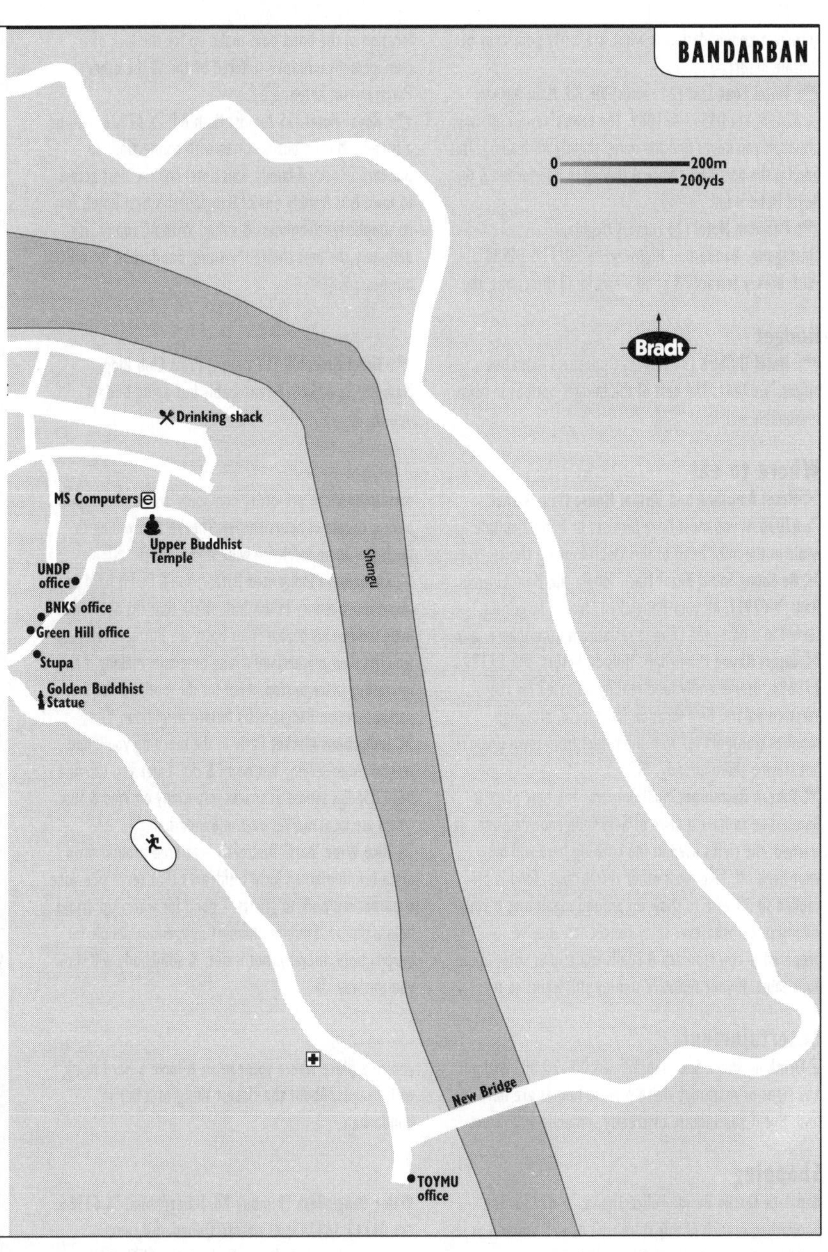

property offers a well-serviced retreat with a fantastic view of the hills. Guests have a choice of dorm rooms, duplex rooms or even individual cottages. Security is still sometimes a concern around the resort, but at the time of research you are free to hike to the nearby villages or the Shailopropat Waterfall without police escort. $$$$

Mid-range

Holiday Inn Resort (3 rooms) Meghla, Chittagong–Bandarban Highway; 62896. Popular as a lunch stop among the day-tripping busloads of domestic tourists visiting Meghla, but does offer some basic cottage accommodation in what is a fairly poor copy of Hillside Resort. $$$

Hotel Four Star (24 rooms) VIP Rd, Main Bazaar; 62466; m 01553 421089. The town's newest offering, although you might find the name slightly misleading. This hotel is the next best choice if staying in Bandarban & the Royal Hotel is full. $$$

Parjatan Hotel (26 rooms) Meghla, Chittagong–Bandarban Highway; m 01720 149801. With breezy terraces & good views in all directions, the location of the hotel does make up for the lack of management initiative suffered by this & the other Parjatan-run hotels. $$$

Royal Hotel (25 rooms) Main Rd; 62926. Run by a friendly Marma businessman with connections to Bandarban's royal family, this hotel has the best access to town & is frankly one of Bangladesh's best hotels for its simplicity, cleanliness & value. With AC rooms, it's definitely the best choice if visiting Bandarban for official business. $$$

Budget

Hotel Hillbird (34 rooms) Opposite S Alam bus office; 62441. The best of the budget options in town, reasonably well kept. $$

Hotel Greenhill (17 rooms) Press Club Bldg, Main Rd; 62574. A reasonable but aging budget option. $

Where to eat

Hotel Amiribad and Biriani House Main Bazaar; 62036. If you must have *biriyani* or Bangla cuisine while in the hills, head to this clean-looking choice. $$

Re Soung Soung Razar Mach Songlagan, Main Cinema Hall; 62917. All your Banglafied Chinese favourites, served in a darkened Chinese restaurant atmosphere. $$

Riggri Khyog Milonchari, Hillside Resort; m 01199 275691. User-friendly food readily adjusted for the Western palate. Best location for a meal, although requires transport to/from the resort from town if you're not staying there already. $$

Tohzah Restaurant Modhumpara. The best place in Bandarban to have a taste of fiery indigenous cuisine. Be warned: the chillis used in the cooking here will blow your head off. Like most other restaurants, food is pre-cooked so it's wise to show up around mealtimes if you're willing to eat whatever spicy concoction they've prepared – cow stomach & snails sometimes show up on your table. If your sensitive tummy still wants to try something local, pre-order non-spicy dishes like *napi* & pork a couple of hours earlier. They're also willing to fetch you some local rice wine if you desire. $$

Chanachaya Indigenous Bazaar. You'll find it hard to spend much money in this little shack that sits above the main indigenous bazaar. Your hosts are Burmese refugees who left their motherland a long time ago, making it an interesting place to stop, if not for the food, but for the perspectives on Bangladesh's forlorn neighbour. $

Indigenous market Early in the morning you'll find several shops serving hot *naan* & *dal*. Later you can find fresh noodles served as snacks, especially on Wed & Sun, which are local market days in Bandarban. $

Rice Wine 'bars' Discreetly scattered around town are a few unmarked local residences that serve rice wine & barbecued pork to guests – good for warm-up drinks before dinner. Enquire amongst indigenous people for *gorom pani*, literally, hot water, & somebody will show you the way. $

Entertainment

Drinking shack See map; 16.00–20.00. Without any signs or markings these private homes are hard to find. But if you inquire discreetly someone will direct you to a place where you can sit & have a hard drink with friends. About the closest thing to a bar in Bandarban.

Shopping

Banalata Textile Beside Police Thana; 62735. The Bandarban branch of this store isn't as well stocked as its companions in Rangamati & Cox's Bazaar.

Bangladesh Small Cottage Industries Corporation (BSCIC) Indigenous Bazaar; 62465. A great place to buy raw materials that can be tailored elsewhere.

Viator Bangladesh Chimbuk Rd, Hafezghona; 63386; m 01717 364445; e viator@onenetbd.com; www.viatorbangladesh.org. Perhaps the CHT's first indigenous fair-trade store, recently opened. Part of Viator Bangladesh's fair-trade initiatives.

Other practicalities

Internet MS computers (*Upper Buddhist Temple; 11.00–18.00*) has dial-up internet connection available here (Tk20 per hour).

Medical The Bandarban Sadar Hospital is located on the road to the new bridge, going south out of the main town area. Best used only in serious emergencies. Can do malaria tests if required.

What to see

Supreme Bliss Buddhist Pagoda and Monastery (*entry Tk50 donation*) Situated on a hilltop just outside the main town lies *dhatu jetee,* an elegant Buddhist pagoda and active monastery. Several young monks are more than happy to show you around and practise their English. Donations go towards the monks' education and the construction of more monastery buildings. It's a 20-minute rickshaw ride from the main baby taxi stand or a one-hour walk on the road beside open fields and villages. From the taxi stand go across the bridge and follow the road past the army base and police line offices.

Other Buddhist locations In town are the two **Upper Buddhist Temple complexes**, where more modest monastery building plans are under way and there are a few gorgeous pagodas on the hilltops. There is also a **Golden Buddha** statue and stupa located on the hills just in front of the complex on Hospital Road.

Shangu river trip Just underneath the bridge from the taxi stand, local boats can be hired for river sightseeing. Expect to pay roughly Tk600 per hour for an engine boat, and a quarter of that to be paddled around the river. During the dry season the river may be running too low to do a journey; moving downstream or upstream will provide scenic views either way.

Nilachal Lookout Accessible by jeep or by foot, this scenic viewpoint offers vistas of the ocean and the surrounding hills on clear days and is well worth the trip. From the jeep stand it would be a steep two-hour return journey by foot; energetic hill walkers would take three to four hours to get there and back or longer if returning via Milonchari.

Hatibanda Trek Starting from Hillside Resort, it is possible to take the steep but short uphill walk to Nilachal and then return to town or the resort via the Tripura village of Hatibanda. Roughly two hours is required, but the security personnel at Hillside Resort make this trip a little harder to arrange. A guide from the resort is recommended for this trip.

Shailopropat Waterfalls Although the falls are dry for most of the winter, there are a few indigenous entrepreneurs who sell textiles to visitors here and it could make for an interesting visit during the wet season. It's about 4km up the road from Hillside Resort.

Meghla (*entry Tk10*) The designated picnic park for domestic tourists who usually come by the busload, armed with massive cooking pots, paper plates and enormous speakers – all of which can be very distracting for visitors seeking tranquillity and nature amongst the hills. Nevertheless, if visited in the late afternoon or early morning, the circular path of the park is well worth the entry fee. Indigenous women from the neighbouring villages sell *dabba pani*, or coconut water, to refresh you along the way.

AROUND BANDARBAN Before 11 January 2007, foreign visitors didn't need police escorts to move around the hills, but since then, when the State of Emergency was declared, the security situation in the CHT has deteriorated and the corresponding freedoms of its people have been reduced enormously, with all visits, official or tourist, requiring a police escort. It is disappointing to know that the army and government are restricting exposure to areas that they themselves say could be used to promote tourism in Bangladesh. In 2009, the situation improved somewhat, and only those venturing into the deeper part of the hills required a police escort. Until all the security restrictions are lifted, however, the destinations described below are some of the hardest to reach and for all the wrong reasons.

Chimbuk Hill and Ruma Bazaar These are often combined into a single day trip, requiring jeep transport to/from Bandarban. The road winds along the hill and offers some great views on its way to Chimbuk Hill. Then, it forks downwards and then promptly ends at a bend in the Sangu River at Ruma Bazaar, upstream from Bandarban. After crossing the Sangu in a local boat, you can explore the bazaar and village. Figure on approximately Tk3,000 to hire a jeep for the day, including fuel costs. Bangladesh Ecotours has previously arranged homestays in Ruma, and there are two basic guesthouses here: the Moung Hotel and the Hilton Inn Residential. These can be booked ahead of time with the help of a tour operator. The guides from Bangladesh Ecotours can arrange cultural programmes and homemade meals with their contacts in Ruma Bazaar.

Kewkradang One of Bangladesh's tallest peaks, although there is some debate as to whether Tajingdong is higher. At 882m, getting to Kewkradang involves a rewarding multi-day trip that may prove too difficult and/or frustrating for individuals to arrange given all the security hullabaloo surrounding visits to Bandarban for foreigners. But those spectacular views of empty hillside scenery, plus the pleasure of reaching this unknown corner of Bangladesh makes the journey highly worthwhile.

Persistent visitors can arrange trekking permission themselves, but it is highly suggested that travellers employ the services of a tour operator who has some contacts within the region. This can help ease your journey and maybe – just maybe – you will become free of the police escorts for your trip.

Reaching the summit of Kewkradang requires a three-day trek from Ruma Bazaar, the first rest day taken at Boga Lake. The first six-hour day follows a stream riverbed route into the hills and requires more than 50 stream crossings, although during the dry season you often do not need to take your shoes off in the later half of this day. The last hour is a slog up a steep hill that finally opens up to a view of Boga Lake. On the second day, you will make for Kewkradang, a return journey of about five hours. Finally, for variety's sake, you can return via the scenic jeep track that leads from Boga Lake and offers some fantastic ridge and valley views, another four-or-five hour walk, including rest stops.

A solid pair of shoes is essential, although you may wish to bring a pair of flip-flops or sturdier sandals for the many stream crossings required on the first day of the trek. Tents are not essential as there are some villages along the way, including a guesthouse at Boga Lake managed by the Bawm community. Water purification tablets are also recommended, and there are some available in Bandarban pharmacies although the resulting chlorinated taste isn't much to look forward to. Antimalarials should top everyone's packing list – malaria has killed some would-be adventurers who didn't take precautions. Finally, visitors will benefit from the experience of a local guide, first to deal with all the police inquiries that still surround visits to the hills, but also to for the benefit of being introduced to the local indigenous communities in a positive way.

Thanchi At the end of the road is the scenic village of Thanchi, where tobacco fields line the riverbanks and at the time of research there was a new bridge being built to cross the Sangu River. There is no doubt that this will bring more development and Bengali settlers into this remote but definitely not unpopulated area. Primarily Tripuran, there is also a Christian mission out here, as well as some development projects that have met with mixed success. For instance, a government hospital building lies unused for lack of doctors who are willing to staff the area. Finally, Thanchi is also where the last kidnapping of an NGO worker by 'Burmese rogue forces' occurred. He was later 'rescued' by Bangladeshi army forces.

COX'S BAZAAR *Telephone code 0341*

One of Bangladesh's claims to fame lies here at what they call the longest beach in the world, but despite it being 120km long, that claim is not entirely true: Cox's Bazaar is in fact the world's second longest beach, the longest being Cassino Beach in Brazil, which stretches for well over 240km. However, it has been pointed out that part of Cassino Beach is manmade, whereas Cox's Bazaar is entirely natural and unbroken.

Nonetheless, these semantic disputes have not diminished the enthusiasm that domestic Bangladeshi tourists have for Cox's Bazaar, and a good stretch of that 120km beach is mostly empty and undeveloped. If the number of hotels in the main town is any indication, this place might well be Bangladesh's most visited tourist destination. During the height of the season and especially during the winter holidays, the number of people concentrated at the beach is enough to drive any peace-seeking traveller completely nuts, but thankfully most of the tourists tend to congregate in one place. Tranquillity seekers need only keep walking southward, and soon enough the crowds fade away and you're left with only the sound of the ocean lapping the shore. Better yet, escapes to the nearby islands or forests show that this region is indeed one of Bangladesh's most diverse, geographically speaking. With its varied hilly scenery and some rare patches of forest, all of it attached to a long stretch of empty beach, it's a great place to explore for a few days once you get out of Cox's Bazaar itself.

Cox's Bazaar takes its name from Captain Hiram Cox, an officer appointed by the British government in the late 18th century to settle a long-standing dispute between Arakan refugees fleeing Burma and the local Rakhine populations. Although Cox died before he could complete his work, the town was still named after him.

The beach itself is nice enough, although the water will always be brown because it is still filled with the silt of the Himalayas by the time it reaches Cox's Bazaar. Surfers are not totally unknown at Cox's Bazaar but the waves are rarely big enough to attract serious attention.

Foreign guests should remain culturally aware: Bay of Bengal-watch this is not. Bangladeshi women never swim in bikinis or even fitted bathing suits. Unless you wish to invite unnecessary attention and harassment, you'd best do as the locals do and swim in a *salwar kameez*, even though the extra clothing makes it hard to deal with the ocean currents. Males have it a bit easier and will create no additional attention by swimming in just a pair of shorts.

GETTING THERE AND AWAY Cox's Bazaar is well served by all major airlines and bus companies, although there are many more departures during the busy season. Fares vary in accordance with rises and falls in worldwide fuel prices, but travelling by bus is economical, albeit time consuming, but you have plenty of companies to choose from. At the time of writing United Airways and Royal Bengal Airlines were the most reliable carriers with three and two flights a week respectively. GMG

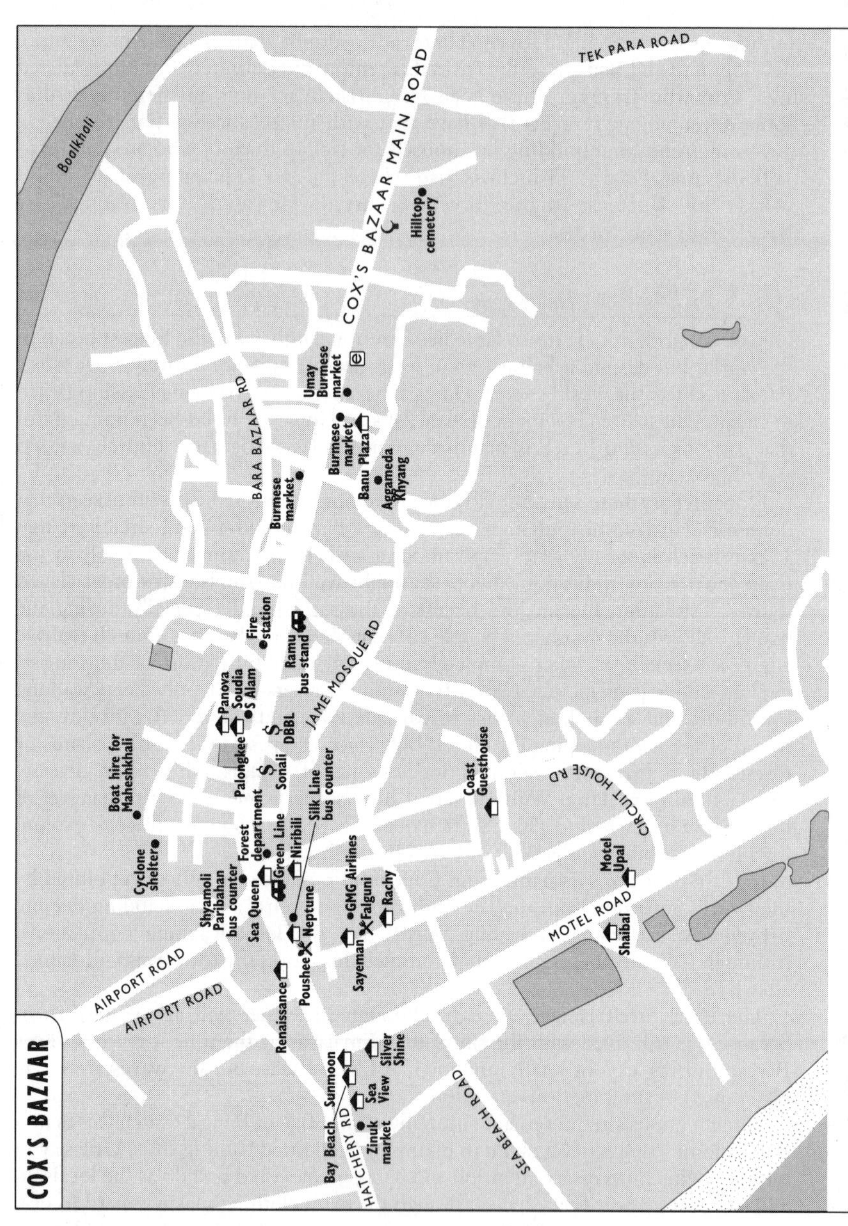

had ceased flying to Cox's Bazar and flights on Biman Bangladesh are few and far between: they take bookings but cancel the flight at short notice if they do not have enough passengers to break even.

By air

✈ **Biman Bangladesh** Motel Upal, BPC Holiday Complex; ☎ 63461, 63721. Tk4375 Dhaka.

✈ **GMG Airlines** Hotel Sayeman; ☎ 63900–4; m 01711 890076; www.gmgairlines.com. Oldest private operator.

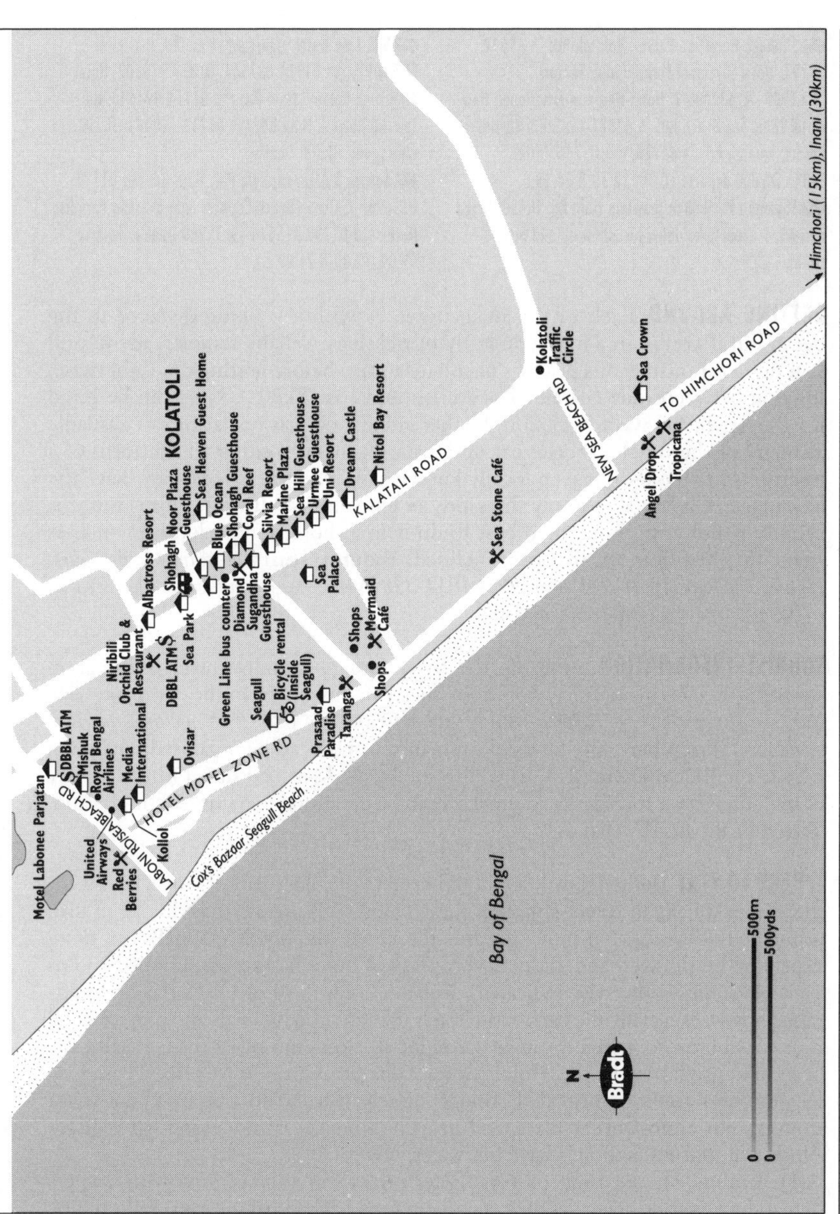

Royal Bengal Airlines Hotel Mishuk, Sea Beach Rd, Hotel Motel Zone; 64748; m 01727 093065, 04433 339348; www.royalbengalair.com. Tk7,495 Dhaka. Departures on Thu & Sat.

United Airways Hotel Kollol, Sea Beach Rd, Hotel Motel Zone; m 01713 486652. Tk 7495 Dhaka, Tk 3495 Chittagong. Departures on Sun, Tue & Thu.

By bus

Green Line Main Rd, Jhawtala; 62533; m 01817 210286; Kolatoli Main Rd; 63747. Tk800 (Volvo)/1,000 ('Scania') Dhaka, twice daily. Tk250 Chittagong, daily departure 16.00.

Shohagh Hotel Sea Palace; Kolatoli Rd; ☎ 63692, 63792; Hotel Sayeman; Muktijuddho Sarani; ☎ 63900–4, 63703–7; Hotel Media International, Hotel Motel Zone, Sea Beach Rd; ☎ 62881–5; Saint Martins Resort, Kolatoli Rd; ☎ 64726, m 01711 400222. Tk845 Dhaka, departs 10.30, 12.30 & 21.15.

Shyamoli Paribahan Jhawtala Main Rd. Tk450 Dhaka non-AC, 5 departures daily. Just show up and buy a ticket.

Silk Line Hotel Sagargaon, Main Rd, Jhawtala; ☎ 51097; m 01714 087561, 01819 379502; Hotel Albatross, Kolatoli Main Rd; m 01714 094646; Hotel Sea Hill Kolatoli Main Rd; m 01713 160003. Tk250 Chittagong, Tk800 Dhaka.

Soudia S Alam Laldighi Par, Main Rd; m 01197 015626–7; Ocean Beach Counter near Prasaad Paradise Hotel; m 01197 015624–5. Tk900 Dhaka, departs 09.00, 12.00 & 21.00.

GETTING AROUND Each of the main hotels is within walking distance to the beach but if you're in a hurry, an army of rickshaw wallahs stands ready to pull you there for outrageous prices – negotiate a price before getting on. Otherwise, moving between Jhawtala and Kolatoli should cost Tk20. CNGs can be hired for the day if you wish to explore further afield, and private car hire is available at many of the hotels. Private car options are generally either in the form of a microbus or an old-style jeep locally known as *chandergari*. *Chandergaris* have the advantage of being able to ply the sandy beach (magical during sunset) but this activity is not entirely legal so best to do it in a more remote location such as Inani Beach if you are that way inclined. **Bangla Tours** (*Dream Castle Guest House, Kolatoli;* m *01911 886199, 01911 328154;* e *banglatours@gmail.com*) can make travel arrangements for you.

TOURIST INFORMATION Probably the most foreign-friendly travel information source is the Mermaid Travel Solution office run directly from the Mermaid Café (*between Sugandha & Kolatoli Beach;* m *01730 093 620-2;* e *mermaidtravels@gmail.com*). From here, any kinds of tours or transport can be organised, including trips to the Pachar Dwip Art Village, also run by the Mermaid staff. Otherwise, any of the hotels have tour desks where trips can be organised to Saint Martin's Island, Teknaf or the nearby islands.

WHERE TO STAY Budget travellers should head to the older part of Cox's Bazaar for the cheapest beds in town, although these come with the associated level of dirt, grime and noise. As you move towards the beach, the hotels gradually get more expensive and newer, and almost every class of hotel has air-conditioned rooms available (unless otherwise indicated). Kolatoli holds most of Cox's Bazaar's mid-range hotels, especially the back-road hotels that offer better deals and quieter hotel rooms as buses do arrive through the night all along the main road. Finally, the beachside properties in the Hotel Motel Zone are Cox's most pricey, based on location and facilities provided. Budget hotels usually do not have hot-water showers but almost every place will provide a bucket of hot water on request. Almost all mid-range hotels have hot water, however.

Depending on the time of year, hotel prices can vary greatly, with owners demanding every single taka they can during the heart of the season, followed by steep discounts of 40% during the low monsoon season. It's best to avoid coming to Cox's Bazaar during Bangladeshi holidays, unless you're prepared to hunt for rooms or have something booked well in advance.

Old City

Mid-range

Hotel Bay Beach (54 rooms) Motel Rd, Old Zinuk Market; ☎ 63830, 62723; m 01734 334234. Recently taken over by new management. Well located but looking a bit worn around the edges & overpriced. $$$

Hotel Sayeman (75 rooms) Muktijuddho Sarani; t 63235; f 64231; m 01711 022088; e sayeman@bttb.net.bd. An aging & massive stalwart of Cox's Bazaar that was probably pretty good in its time. The swimming pool looks pretty secluded here at least. $$$

Renaissance (32 rooms) Jhawtala, Main Rd; t 64712; m 01711 282804; e cox@abnetbd.com. Expensive but well-maintained hotel close to the old side of town. Rooms are tiny, but they're clean & the facilities are new here. Recommended if the budget permits. $$$

Budget

Hotel Banu Plaza (50 rooms) Burmese Market, Main Rd; t 64368, 64097; m 01712 084276. A friendly & reasonably priced place, but could be cleaner. $$

Hotel Niribili (40 rooms) Shahid Sharani Rd; t 64324, 63202; m 01811 337723. So-so place with decent grounds for the hotel, reasonably close to the beach. A fair budget option. $$

Hotel Rachy (28 rooms) Muktijuddho Sarani; t 64452, 63455; m 01818 041081, 01819 519979. Better location for the quietness, & friendly staff. Rooms could be better taken care of, however. $$

Hotel Sea Queen (108 rooms) Jhawtala, Main Rd; t 63789, 63878; f 63688; m 01819 321888; e seaqueen@gshakti.com. Another massive hotel complex, but good value for budget seekers. $$

Hotel Sea View (30 rooms) Hatchery Rd, Jhawtala; t 64491, 63518; f 63519. Rooms have balconies & Western toilets. Mirrors by the beds might tickle your fancy. $$

Hotel Silver Shine (104 rooms) 26 Motel Rd; t 64610, 64897; f 64693; m 01199 276184; e hotelsilvershine@yahoo.com. Big rooftop & good location for this hotel. Some rooms offer more light & better views than others. Decent value. $$

Hotel Sunmoon (31 rooms) Motel Rd; t 63231; m 01711 315627. Decent but aging. Location is also good. $$

Hotel Palongkee (50 rooms) Laldighi Par; t 63873, 63677, 63597; m 01711 172035. Features a restaurant but the rooms & interiors are awfully dark & foreboding. $

Hotel Panova (86 rooms) FA Chowdhury Rd, Laldighi Par; t 63282; f 64382; m 01711 946417. Big place situated on decent grounds & budget friendly, although pricier rooms also available. $

Hotel Motel Zone Road and nearby

Upmarket

Praasad Paradise (40 Rooms, 10 cottages) Hotel Motel Zone Rd; t 64403, 64113, 01726 070148; www.praasadcox.com; e info@praasadcox.com. A hotel with prices like the Seagull but not quite the quality of its neighbour. Its restaurant offers a decent outdoor BBQ every night during the season. $$$$$

Seagull Hotel (75 rooms) Hotel Motel Zone Rd; t 62480–91; f 64436; e seagull_cox@yahoo.com; www.seagullhotelbd.com. Cox's Bazaar's one & only 5-star option. Bike rental available plus a bar, 5 restaurants, full services such as restaurant, swimming pool & room service. $$$$$

Mid-range

Hotel Media International (100 rooms) Hotel Motel Zone Rd; t 62881–5; f 62047; m 01711 341164, 01819 519719. Not a bad-value hotel with good service, but geared to large groups & conferences. Recommended. $$$

Hotel Mishuk (70 Rooms) Hotel Motel Zone Rd; t 64320, 62808; m 01715 946471. Another large complex close to the beach. $$$

Hotel Ovisar (38 rooms) Hotel Motel Zone; t 63061; m 01819 821774, 01710 807996, 01914 591353. Nothing special about this place, but it's next to the beach. $$$

Hotel Shaibal (24 rooms, 4 cottages) Hotel Motel Zone Rd; t 63274; f 64202; e info@bangladeshtourism.gov.bd; www.bangladeshtourism.gov.bd. Beachside option, although it is still a Parjatan Hotel which means that the building is old & the upkeep spotty at best.Only worth it if nothing else seems available. Cottages on offer as well. $$$

Parjatan Motel Labonee (60 rooms) Hotel Motel Zone Rd; t 64703; f 62223; m 01716 382032. One of the better Parjatan Motels in Cox's Bazaar, or at least one of the newer ones. $$$

Budget

COAST Guesthouse (6 rooms) Luciana Bldg, New Circuit House Rd, Baharchara; t 63186; f 63189; m 01711 881646; e info@coastbd.org, rmccxb@coastbd.org; www.coastbd.org. COAST is an

NGO serving Bangladesh's coastal poor people; they have a small training centre & office tucked away near the Circuit Hse. Accommodation here is basic but clean & comfortable, plus it lacks the impersonality of the big hotels. Food is served a fixed-menu basis, & it's very cheap. A good option if you are comfortable with spartan accommodation. Prior booking definitely necessary as they may have training sessions on. No AC rooms are available. $$

Hotel Kollol (80 rooms) Sea Beach Rd, Hotel Motel Zone; 64748; m 01727 613258, 01819 548434. This massive complex should have something for everyone, & occupies a prominent location very close to the beach. Slightly cheaper than the Hotel Ovisar or the Parjatan Motel Labonee. $$

Kolatoli

Upmarket

Hotel Sea Palace Ltd (253 rooms) Kolatoli Main Rd; 63692, 63792, 63794, 63826, 63853; e seapalace@gmail.com, cxb@hotelseapalaceltd.com; www.hotelseapalaceltd.com. Cox's Bazaar's newest hotel complex, with a 5-star wing & a 3-star wing to match budgets. Quality corresponds decently to price, & visiting international aid workers often stay here. $$$$$$

Mid-range

Uni Resort (53 rooms) Kolatoli, Main Rd; 63181, 63191; f 62824; e uniresort@gmail.com; www.uniresort.com. A one-stop shop for hotel & entertainment. Also one of Cox's Bazaar's newest properties with the fairly high prices to match the newness. Might be a good deal in the off-season however. $$$$

Silvia Resort (27 rooms) Kolatoli, Back Rd; 62495, 62496; m 01819 391541; e silviars@gshakti.com; www.silviaresort.com. More expensive rooms than other hotels but provides more exclusivity, better furnishings & privacy, if that's what you're after. $$$$

Dream Castle Guest House (24 rooms) Kolatoli Main Rd; 64628; m 01711 134435. On the main strip but has the advantage of feeling slightly more like a home than a big hotel. $$$

Hotel Coral Reef (54 rooms) Plot 47, Blk B, Kolatoli; 64469; m 01818 080651; e hotelcoralreef@yahoo.com; www.coralreefcoxsbazar.com. Discounts offered during the off season. One of the better hotels in the Kolatoli area. $$$

Hotel Marine Plaza (35 rooms) Kolatoli, Main Rd; /f 64146; m 01716 742464; e hotelmarineplaza@yahoo.com. A cut above the other rooms on Kolatoli Rd, but probably noisy like the others. $$$

Hotel Sea Crown (50 rooms) Marine Dr, Kolatoli New Beach; 64795, 64474, 02 882 2043, 02 882 0402 (Dhaka booking office); f 02 882 5197; www.hotelseacrown.com. The Sea Crown's location makes it a standout, being directly across the street from the beach. Prices are a bit high, but if they give a discount it'd be a good place to stay. $$$

Hotel Sea Park (50 rooms) Kolatoli, Main Rd; 51078; m 01913 617599. Another of the cookie-cutter hotels in Kolatoli. $$$

Nitol Bay Hotel (37 rooms) Kolatoli Beach Rd 64278, 63677, 01715 946355, 01199 741090; e nitolbay@bttb.net.bd, bayresort@nitolniloy.com; www.nitolbay.com. One of the oldest hotels in Kolatoli. Quality food, swimming pool & rooftop facilities. Recommended. $$$

Budget

Albatross Resort (53 rooms) Kolatoli Rd; 64684, 62889, 01818 540177, 01816 033445. $$

Blue Ocean (18 rooms) Kolatoli, Back Rd; 63207, 62135; m 01711 785381, 01583 310726. With clean rooms & a good location off the main Kolatali Rd, this hotel offers good value for the area. $$

Hotel Daffodil International (45 rooms) Sea Beach Residential Area, Lighthouse, Kolatoli Rd; 62544, 01815 123855, 01818 470338; e info@hoteldaffodil.com; www.hoteldaffodil.com. Slightly better quality than the other Kolatoli establishments. $$

Noor Plaza Guest House (21 rooms) Kolatoli, Back Rd; 62051; m 01726 043415, 01735 430616. Off the strip, quieter & cheaper, but dark. $$

Sea Heaven Guest Home (40 rooms) Kolatoli Main Rd; m 01726 519323, 01818 711185, 01710 112405. Another Kolatoli Rd hotel, this looks a little more appealing from the outside & offers slightly lower prices than the nearby Blue Ocean or Shohagh guesthouses $$

Sea Hill Guest House (80 rooms) Sea Beach R/A, Kolatoli Rd; 63088, 62777; m 01815 075698. Another one of the standard hotels on this strip, this hotel doesn't have much that sets it apart from the Marine Plaza Hotel or the Urmee, its immediate neighbours. $$

Shohagh Guest House (32 rooms) Kolatoli, Back Rd; 62561; m 01712 802954. Green monster of a building, but with decent enough rooms on the inside. $$

WHERE TO EAT All bar the cheapest hotels can do a simple *paratha–bhaji* breakfast while some of the newer hotels, especially in Kolatoli, have multi-cuisine restaurants.

Beachside, Kolatoli

Upmarket

Mermaid Café Between Sugandha & Kolatoli Beach; m 01730 093620–3. Easily Cox's Bazaar's best food, environment & service. The young entrepreneurs running this café are all about bringing real beach culture to Cox's Bazaar. Prices are not cheap, but the quality is very good & the chefs do know what they're doing. You might not want to take your meals anywhere else after eating here. Real filter coffee also available here, although do expect to wait a long time for your freshly prepared meal. $$$$

Seastone Café Nestled in beside the Mermaid Café, this newly renovated café offers both European & Bangladeshi cuisine. Its 2nd-floor cushion deck offers one of the best views in Cox's Bazar. It's also the first café in Cox's Bazar with an espresso machine, offering real coffee. The pizzas are a favourite with resident foreigners in Cox's Bazar. $$$$

Mid-range

Niribili Orchid Club & Restaurant Kolatoli; 63194, 64334. Where most of the wedding parties & events are held, otherwise not serving food like a regular restaurant. Handy if you've got a big group to cater for. $$$

Taranga Sea Beach Rd, Hotel Motel Zone; 64793. BBQs from 17.00 make this beachside option a pretty good place to try for kebabs & *naans*. $$$

Angel Drop Marine Dr, Kolatoli. Uninspired service makes this place a bit of a letdown but it might be a nice place to have a soft drink & watch the sunset over the Bay of Bengal. $$

Diamond Restaurant Kolatoli. Recommended by locals for slightly higher-quality Bangla cuisine. $$

Poushee Restaurant Muktijuddho Sarani; 62343. Utilitarian Bangla cuisine that's good for a quick feed. $$

Falguni Restaurant Muktijuddho Sarani; 63455. Bangla cuisine served in a sterile atmosphere. $$

Red Berries Beach Rd, Labonee Point; m 01715 653020. Western-style fried fast food but a nice terrace upstairs. $$

Tropicana Marine Dr, Kolatoli. Location, location, location. Situated in a wooden building right over the beach, this up-&-comer seems to be surpassing the rapidly fading Angel Drop Café & will hopefully stay in business. Offers standard Bangla & 'mini Chinese' fare. $$

SHOPPING

Burmese Market Cox's Bazaar has long been home to ethnic groups hailing from Burma, some of whom have managed to integrate into Bangladeshi society & even set up stores selling their goods to tourists. Just beneath the Aggameda Khyang, dozens of stores are labelled in both Bangla & English but they do offer goods that you don't find in other places, such as textiles & even Burmese jewellery, if you search hard enough. Otherwise, gaggles of friendly street children will approach you on the beach carrying seashells tied onto strings.

VOLUNTEERING

COAST Bangladesh www.coastbd.org. One of the country's loudest NGOs when it comes to voicing concerns over climate change. They are already working with groups of people who have migrated to Cox's from nearby islands, especially Kutubdia, an island that will eventually disappear underwater in the next 40 years. According to COAST this is due to river erosion & climate change. Their staff are helpful & accommodating plus they do have a simple guesthouse & training centre in Cox's Bazaar which serves meals. See *Where to stay*, page 235, for more information.

OTHER PRACTICALITIES

Banks Two DBBL ATMs are available. The first is in the Old City next to the Green Line office on Jhawtala Road. The second is at the Niribili Orchard Club in Kolatoli.

Sonali Bank (*Jhawtala Rd; ⌚ 11.00–15.00*) can exchange dollars at a pinch but you might have better luck enquiring at your hotel if you're really in need of exchange.

Bicycle rental (*Seagull Hotel*) Rents bicycles to its guests but may be able to hook non-guests up if you really want to cycle around Cox's and you ask politely.

Internet Available at shops on the far end of Cox's Bazaar's main road near the Burmese market.

Medical Cox's Bazaar lacks decent medical facilities, but for immediate emergencies there are a cluster of clinics across from the fire station on the Old City's main road.

Post Available on Motel Road just at the edge of the Hotel Shaibal grounds. It's poorly marked; look for the red letter box.

WHAT TO SEE

Aggameda Khyang An active Buddhist monastery in the town, and with a few decorative buildings. It can be worth a visit when combined with a shopping jaunt to the Burmese Market. Just behind it are a collection of Buddhist buildings spread amongst the trees and hills, and is an interesting area to explore by foot as the hills gradually rise and fall throughout the area.

AROUND COX'S BAZAAR

HIMCHORI AND INANI BEACHES Himchori and Inani are two quieter beaches that are now more readily accessible following the construction of the new Marine Drive Road. There is now no doubt that the area will be considered for the future development of Cox's Bazaar, but thankfully both beaches still remain peaceful and secluded.

Himchori is 15km south from Cox's Bazaar, and Inani about 30km. Getting here involves a private car hire only, as no public buses ply the road yet.

RAMU AND LAMA BAZAAR The remains of several Buddhist communities are spread around the villages and hilltops surrounding Cox's Bazaar. The most prominent are housed at Ramu, a village located 15km out of town and accessible by public bus. Here you'll find the ancient and picturesque U Chitsan Rakhine Temple which still serves as an active monastery. In nearby Lama Bazaar, the Boro Khyang holds Bangladesh's biggest bronze Buddha, cast in traditional Arakanese style. The people here are a mix of Rakhine and Barua communities. Barua is the name for ethnically Bengali Buddhist people, who may be the descendants of Bangladesh's ancient communities of the 8th to the 13th centuries.

To get there, take the public bus from the Ramu bus stand, a few hundred metres' walk past the Burmese market. It's unmarked – ask for directions.

MOHESHKHALI AND SONADIA ISLANDS These islands are close by Cox's Bazaar and can make for interesting day trips and strolls. Moheshkhali in particular is quite hilly and fringed with mangroves. There are a few temples here too: the **Adinath Temple** is dedicated to Shiva, whereas the modest **Buddhist Pagoda** attracts a few visitors. Sonadia has become more well known for its community of fishermen. To get here the best way is to go by speedboat from Cox's Kastura ghat (Tk75). These usually depart when full but should you need to charter your own, expect to pay about Tk1,500–2,000 to get to either of the islands, with Sonadia costing more than Moheshkhali as it's farther away. There are some very basic hotels near the ghat on Moheshkhali.

CHUNOTI WILDLIFE SANCTUARY (*80km from Chittagong, 90km to Cox's Bazaar on the Chittagong–Cox's Bazaar Highway*) There are two trails here offering good views of the forest and its wildlife. There is also another Nishorgo eco-cottage recently established here, allowing visitors to stay near the sanctuary and enjoy the walks. The **Nishorgo Potrhikrit Eco-cottage** (*Banapukur village, Chunoti district, Lohagora Upazilla;* m *01814 157310*) is run by the friendly Nasir Uddin, although do be warned: his English is limited. The two-room facility costs Tk500 per night and has attached bathrooms. Trained eco-guides are also available: try Mohammad Ali (m *01722 422992*) or Nezam Uddin (m *01818 416236*).

TEKNAF *Telephone code 03426*

Situated on the very southeastern tip of the peninsula, Teknaf is a scenic region to travel through at all times of the year, although if you want to visit some secluded beaches you'd best do it in winter while the village roads are dry and passable. Once you depart from Cox's Bazaar, the winding highway road follows a series of curves that offer vistas over expansive rice fields, salt farms and through rippling hilly landscape.

A second inside road goes to Teknaf from Cox's Bazaar along Marine Drive. Close to Cox's Bazaar, the road is good. But after passing Inani Beach it deteriorates quite quickly and is only traversable by motorcycle. Even 4x4 jeeps would likely get bogged in the deep sand. The other option is to drive directly along the beach, but the presence of river crossings might make that a fairly wet proposition.

The area's unexplored gem is the Teknaf Game Reserve, where wild elephants still roam and a gorgeous virgin evergreen forest lines the hills. Studies have indicated that in the 1980s the Teknaf range had almost 100% forest cover and today only 8% of that remains. If new ecotourism projects in the region are successful, however, there is a chance that the remaining forest could survive, but the livelihood requirements of the local people need to change.

The town itself, a haven for smuggled goods, proves for an interesting wander: hundreds of shops line the streets carrying goods from nearby Myanmar, a massive bazaar that has become a serious tourist attraction for domestic travellers and holds a few gems you can't find anywhere else.

GETTING THERE AND AWAY Buses depart for Teknaf every hour from the main bus terminal at Cox's Bazaar. These are generally the slow, pick-up-and-drop-off-anyone variety. The local bus terminal is located well away from the beach along the main road, and is best accessed by a short CNG baby taxi ride (Tk50). The journey takes 2.5 hours and costs about Tk90. A privately hired vehicle will make the journey for Tk2,000–2,500 and is probably a better option for a group of travellers who would like to see the more empty stretches of beach at Teknaf.

WHERE TO STAY AND EAT

Mid-range

Fardin Nishorgo Eco-cottage (2 rooms) Dumdumia, 5km north on the Teknaf–Cox's Bazaar Highway; m 01715 921892; www.nishorgo.org. Basic roadside accommodation nestled against the eastern side of the Teknaf Game Reserve near the newly built visitors' centre. Excellent views all around. Bangla meals available while staying, but be prepared to wait as everything appears to be slow-cooked. Highly recommended. $$$

🏠 **Hotel Ne-Taung** (22 rooms) St Martin's Island ferry ghat; ☎ 75104; m 01814 882706. Parjatan's aging contribution to Teknaf tourism that is the best-equipped place to stay in the area, with AC rooms & hot water. $$$

Budget

🏠 **Hotel Dwip Plaza** (15 rooms) Bus station, Main Rd; m 01818 050052. If odorous & noisy hotels are just your kind of thing, you can't go wrong here. $$

🏠 **Hotel Hilltop** (15 rooms) Main Rd; m 01817 311117, 01710 478 375. Not the best option but close to the Cox's Bazaar bus stand. $$

🏠 **Hotel Pleasure Inn** (15 rooms) Upper Bazaar; ☎ 75083; m 01815 334385. Teknaf's newest accommodation & more centrally located in the bazaar. AC rooms available. $$

WHAT TO SEE

Teknaf Game Reserve This is the area's prime scenic attraction with plenty of forest trails available for **day trekking**. With virgin evergreen and semi-evergreen forest, it is one of the last remaining refuges for some highly endangered animals, especially wild elephants. Sightings sometimes occur on the eastern side close to the highway in the mornings. In the afternoons, you'll have a decent chance of seeing them if you head into the forest. There is also a beautifully designed **visitors' centre** at the game reserve gate, across from the Fardin Nishorgo Eco-cottage at Dumdumia village. Here you'll find a fairly good introduction to the wildlife and nature inhabiting the forest, plus an introduction to the fragile ecosystem still in evidence at the reserve.

A small network of **forest trails** is available. The most easily accessed trails are from the visitors' centre, and can be tailored according to the length of walk you wish to take (one hour, three hours or five hours; a packed lunch would be handy); beware of leeches during the rainy season and bring protection or wear long socks). It is best to pick up maps and information at Nishorgo's Banani office (*Hse 68, Rd 1, Blk I, Banani;* ☎ *02 987 3229, 02 987 1553; www.nishorgo.org*) before heading out, but there are signboards and information at the visitors' centre as well. From the visitors' centre, there is a three-hour trek up **Toingya Hill** for views of the Bay of Bengal and Myanmar.

Perhaps the wisest course for trekking is to hire a **Nishorgo-trained eco-guide** to point out the natural features of the forest and help you get around the network of trails without getting lost. Mr Salauddin is one such guide, who also helps to run the Fardin Nighorgo Eco-cottage (see *Where to stay and eat* for details). Otherwise the contact information for other guides is available on Nishorgo's website.

Shaplapur is a region of the reserve that is currently under development and is located on the western, beach side of the reserve. At the time of research, the Whykheong–Shaplapur Road was under construction and hard to cross during the monsoon season. But for those with the means to hire a suitable vehicle, the **Kudum Cave Trail** is a one-hour walk that begins from Harikhola village halfway down the Shaplapur Road. According to local Chakma villagers, bats have occupied this cave for hundreds of years.

ST MARTIN'S ISLAND

St Martin's Island is Bangladesh's one and only coral beach island. Among locals, its name is Narikel Jinjira, or Coconut Island. But before you start dreaming of drinking from a coconut in a hammock by the beach, you should know the behind-the-scenes story. St Martin's is what tourism in Bangladesh becomes when left in the hands of purely profit-seeking enterprises and when government

ROHINGYA REFUGEES

The Rohingya are a Muslim minority group who mainly originate from the northern Rakhine state of Myanmar. During 1991, they began to cross over into Bangladesh under threat of Burmese military oppression and genocide. The majority of the refugees ended up in the Nayapara refugee camps, which were then mainly supported by the United Nations High Commissioner for Refugees programme. Travellers will see the signs for the UN camps along the highway while they travel towards Teknaf.

Up until mid 2008, visitors *en route* to St Martin's Island used to be greeted with the feral site of the Tal refugee camp as they boarded the ferry to the island. As Tal camp refugees were not recognised as such by the UNHCR programme, they received no assistance from any agencies, international or Bangladeshi, until Doctors Without Borders (also known as Médecins Sans Frontières) intervened in 2006. When MSF started attracting international attention towards the abject conditions of the camp, officials took notice and moved the camp to a new facility at Leda Bazaar, well away from the well-travelled Cox's Bazaar–Teknaf Highway and the view of tourists travelling it.

Today, however, these refugees remain stateless as they have been for almost a decade. Unsurprisingly, they refuse to return to Myanmar – forced repatriation programmes of the early 1990s only brought on waves of new refugee arrivals in the years following. Recent signs have shown that despite the move, the withdrawal of MSF's health provisions has resulted in decreased health among the refugees, which only increases the need for a solution to be found soon.

officials fail to manage tourism development properly. Thousands of migratory birds used to seek refuge here, sea turtles laid eggs and the coral reef grew as it had for millions of years. Nowadays, the island bustles with migratory tourists and growing piles of plastic.

Most of this tourist gold rush was funded from the outside, and it looks just like that. As you approach the island, garish concrete monoliths litter the beachside, dwarfing the small unobtrusive local bamboo village huts, with most of these hotel rooms resembling prison cells – nothing a good paint job couldn't fix. Nonetheless most hotel owners refuse to focus on upkeep when hotel rooms are fully booked during the peak season.

Despite these discouraging signs, a visit to the island can still be rewarding. One simply needs to get to its less frequented places and stay well away from the crowds. The island is actually a long strip that stretches 9km from tip to tip, and takes a good half day to walk completely around it. Cherradhip, in the southernmost part of St Martin's, becomes completely inaccessible during high tide as it is only connected via a small strip of land. Here, there is some basic and quiet accommodation well away from the masses.

GETTING THERE AND AWAY Getting to the island can be done in two ways. Easier, but not necessarily cheaper, is to arrange a package visit through a tourist operator in Cox's Bazaar (Mermaid Café or Bangla Tours comes recommended; see *Cox's Bazaar, Tourist information*, page 234), who can offer a two-day trip which includes a tourist bus to Teknaf with boxed breakfast, ferry transport to the island and accommodation when you arrive. In theory this sounds easier, but you'll likely be booked in with groups of domestic travellers and locked into a hotel you might not necessarily enjoy.

It may therefore be better to negotiate with an operator to join on the bus/ferry combination but then choose your own accommodation when you arrive on the island. Local buses depart from the Cox's Bazaar bus terminal and cost Tk90. If you choose the local bus be aware that you might miss the ferry. The frequency of the ferry departures depends on the number of tourists currently shuttling between Teknaf and the island – this can be up to 3,000 people per day during the height of the season. Two classes of ticket are available based on whether you want to be above (Tk540) or below (Tk450) deck. Tea and snacks are available on board, the ships are big and the journey – mostly along the Myanmar coastline – is quite scenic.

For those with a sense of adventure, you could try chartering a country boat or catching one that carries locals and island supplies, although the journey is longer and if the seas are rough, you'll feel every bump and wave along the way. Prices depend on the number of passengers but you can expect it to be cheaper but much less comfortable than the big ferries.

ORIENTATION AND GETTING AROUND On arrival, you will see the main hotel area and the island's northern portion, called Narikeldia. If you head straight into the village and walk about 1km and over a small bridge, you'll come to Uttarpara, from where if you turn left you will find the best guesthouses and beach bungalows. It takes about two hours to walk to Dakhsinpara, which is the southern, less populated part of the island. Plenty of boats await to ferry people around the island and especially between the main ferry ghat and Cherradhip, which is in the southernmost part of St Martin's that is occasionally cut off from the rest of the island when the tide is high. Expect to pay Tk150 for a return journey to/from Cherradhip. Rickshaws are available in Uttarpara in the north of the island.

WHERE TO STAY Accommodation is primarily concentrated in the area immediately adjacent to the ferry *ghat*, where hundreds of tourists step off the boat and head directly to hotels. For a quieter experience, head to the peaceful and more intimate surroundings of Uttarpara.

Blue Marine Resorts (34 rooms) Delpara; ☎ 0341 62100, 62500 (Cox's Bazaar booking). Tempting-looking balconies but definitely one of the big hotels. $$$

CTB Resort (16 rooms) Main Ferry Area; ☎ 02 717 0158 (Dhaka booking); m 01731 121425. Upstairs rooms preferred & slightly cleaner. Dorm rooms also available. $$$

Hotel Rayad (11 rooms) Main Ferry Area. One of the first options when you step off the ferry. Has a decent courtyard in the front. $$$

Prince Heaven (20 rooms) Main Ferry Area; m 01720 948527. Still under construction, garish feel, intrusive service. Use in emergencies only. $$$

Sailor Moon Resort (4 rooms) Uttarpara; ☎ 02 935 9909, 935 7687 (Dhaka booking); m 01814 298077 (St Martin's). Big rooms, secluded feel, teems with the atmosphere that other hotels lack. Has hammocks out front. Recommended. $$$

St Martin's Resort (16 rooms) Main Ferry Area; ☎ 02 835 8485, 934 2351 (Dhaka booking); m 01552 372269. Not much to recommend here, as upkeep isn't up to speed. $$$

Ocean View Guest House (10 rooms) Main Ferry Area; ☎ 02 935 7687 (Dhaka booking); m 01817 050631, 01815 681611. Falling to pieces & hardly recommended, but there if you're desparate. $$

Shemana Pereye Resort (10 rooms) Uttarpara; m 01819 466059, 01819 018027, 01911 225911. The island's best accommodation. Wood & bamboo bungalows located right on the beach, with great restaurants & friendly helpful staff. Dorm rooms & tents available. Recommended. $$

WHERE TO EAT The best option is to buy a fresh fish from the market near the ferry ghat and take it to your hotel where they can cook it to your preference. However, another option is to try one of the restaurants crowding the main ferry area, most of which are set up inside atmospheric gardens offering the normal range of Bangla cuisine – especially fresh fish. None particularly stands out, so take your pick.

OTHER PRACTICALITIES

Electricity The only electricity available is through generator power in the evenings at some guesthouses.

Telecommunications St Martin's is connected to the mainland by mobile phone, with all the major companies offering coverage.

ACTIVITIES The island has an established diving outfit but whether it operates to any international standard is unknown – divers and snorkellers might be better off bringing their own gear if they can. **Dive Bangladesh** (m *01917 823523, 01711 671130;* e *rescue_diving2005@yahoo.com; www.oceanicbd.com*) is an initiative of some former navy divers. Underwater expeditions should be organised well in advance as all the necessary equipment didn't seem to reside on St. Martin's. Call first to sound them out. Prices are approximately Tk2,500 per hour, or Tk1,000 for a guided snorkelling trip (Tk500 to rent the equipment and set off on your own).

The whole island takes about four hours to **walk** around, roughly a 9km journey. Otherwise a **fishing trip** can be taken, where you'll be taken out on a boat with the locals (2hr trip; Tk300–400p). Finally, most of the freshest catch is sold during the **morning fish market** near the ferry ghat, which is the best time to pick up your dinner for the evening and bring it to your hotel for preparation.

NOAKHALI *Telephone code 0321*

In an already under-travelled country, Noakhali must be one of the country's least-travelled regions and also one of its least understood. Nevertheless, a serious helping of travel by launch makes it a fascinating region to explore for its river character and its unique place in the history of partition. Another unknown fact is that Noakhali has a substantial export market: labour from the region often heads to the Middle East from here so don't be surprised if you see men wearing Arab-style dress here.

HISTORY In the year leading up to India's partition in 1947, Noakhali bore witness to some of the greatest Hindu–Muslim violence seen on the subcontinent. The extent of the riots and murders was so bad that the great Mahatma Gandhi himself came to the region in early 1947 and spent some of his last months in Noakhali walking barefoot from village to village, pleading for peace among Hindu and Muslim residents of the region. In total he spent four months in the region before returning to Kolkata, just before partition became inevitable. After East Bengal became East Pakistan, most of Noakhali's Hindu residents left the region in a mass exodus to West Bengal, which would again happen during the Liberation War.

GETTING THERE AND AWAY You have a few options for reaching the Noakhali region, which depends on how long you want to stay and what you're there to see. Don't expect luxury transport, however. If you're looking to leave the area, head to Comilla and from there you can catch connections to all the major cities.

By bus Direct buses leave from Dhaka's Sayedabad Bus Station for Maijdi (the local name for Noakhali) and Sonapur (a town closer to the coast and home of the Char Development and Settlement Programme (CDSP) although if you're the adventurous type who is out to see the rivers, it is much better to travel by launch.

Head to the Sayedabad Bus Terminal, tell them you're headed for Noakhali and you'll be shown the correct bus to take.

By train A six-hour train journey on the Upakal Express gets you from Dhaka to Noakhali, departing at 07.00 and arriving at 13.00; it makes the return journey at 14.15, arriving at 20.45.

By launch This is perhaps the most interesting way to go. Plenty of private launches ply the route between Dhaka and Chandpur, which is the first stop for many of the southbound launches heading to Barisal, Hatiya or Bhola islands. Timetables mean that departures to these places are at odd times, however. From Chandpur you can catch local public transport to Maijdi via Lakshimipur and destinations beyond.

WHERE TO STAY, EAT AND WHAT TO SEE

CDSP offices BWDB Compound, Sonapur, Noakhali; 61428; e cdsp@bttb.net.bd; www.cdsp.org.bd. Those with legitimate interests in the *char* phenomenon may be able to stay at the CDSP offices. Their head office is located at Sonapur, near the coast. It also has satellite offices at project sites with guestrooms. The rooms are plainly but comfortably furnished with beds, mosquito nets & tables, although the bathroom is seldom attached. $$ for room & board.

Gandhi Ashram Trust Jayag village, 30km north of Maijdi village; 0322 18083; m 01711 408226; e info@gandhiashrambd.org; www.gandhiashrambd.org. Today there is a modest memorial museum paying tribute to Gandhi & his peace mission in Noakhali, as well as an NGO created in his name, the Gandhi Ashram Trust, which does development work in the local area with both Muslim & Hindu people. By calling ahead you may be able to stay here. $$

HATIYA ISLAND

Bangladesh's second biggest island is situated well off the mainland, but feels even further away. It is this region where Bangladesh's rivers and landscape become indistinct from one another. In some places, the mighty Meghna River generates new land through silt deposition; in others it is eating away the land directly beneath villagers' homes through erosion. Above all, it's a fascinating place to travel as rivers replace roads in areas like this.

At Hatiya Island, the lead attraction is Nijhum Dwip (pronounced 'deep', meaning island), a smaller island off the southern tip of Hatiya that has a massive population of chital, or spotted deer. Normally these would be tiger prey but because there are no tigers, the population has exploded. Visitors now come to see the impressive sight of hundreds of these deer grazing in the island's fields. Nijhum Dwip also has a modest, muddy beach, but thankfully it lacks anything resembling a Cox's Bazaar-style hotel development.

GETTING THERE AND AWAY Hatiya itself is very accessible as launches leave six days a week from Dhaka's Sadarghat and arrive at Hatiya's Tomaruddin ghat, which is really just an eroding pile of mud from which you disembark the launch. (*Panama Launch booking* m *01711 349257; Tipu 5 booking* m *01711 348813, 17.30 departure; 19hrs; Tk600 pp for a berth in a sgl or a dbl cabin.*) Note that these same launches also stop at various places on Bhola Island along the way. Otherwise, you can catch the launch to Barisal every Thursday (15.00 departure, but this can vary greatly!) or return to Chittagong via Sandwip every Friday night late (01.00 but check with locals for the latest).

For Noakhali, there is a morning ferry service from Hatiya's northern ferry ghat to the mainland that drops you off at Steamerghat, about 20km from the nearest major town of Sonapur, but *tempos* are waiting to ferry people back and forth on

SOLUTIONS FOR CLIMATE CHANGE?

Most people assume that Bangladesh is slowly going underwater due to climate change. But the truth is that there is actually a net accretion of land when silt is deposited from the major rivers and new land is formed, called a *char* in Bangla. The Char Development and Settlement Programme (CDSP) is a joint collaboration between several Bangladeshi government agencies and funded by the Netherlands – a fellow low-lying country with more means to deal with the sea-level rise that might occur under a global warming scenario. An illustrative quote from their website explains the phenomenon:

> The central part of the coastal zone of Bangladesh where major rivers flow into the Bay of Bengal is, in physical terms, the most dynamic part. The flow of water through the Meghna/Padma river system causes loss of land through erosion, but at the same time the gradual deposit of silt carried down by that same system results in the formation of new land. The silt flows into the Bay and is then pushed back by tidal movements to the area in front of the coastline. It takes an average of 20 to 30 years from the first deposits to the emergence of new land.
>
> In the beginning it will be just mudflats, used for fisheries. Gradually the land will be more accreted and grass will grow. When the land is higher the first crop can be planted, usually aman rice. If it is high enough, the land can be embanked to create a polder. A general rule is that this can only be done if the land falls dry at mean high water level in monsoon time. These newly accreted lands, in the different phases of development, are the chars.

According to the official policy, newly emerged land is transferred to the Forest Department for a period of 20 years, for plantation and management of forests, especially mangroves. This is to accelerate accretion, stabilise the land and to protect the main land against storms and cyclones. However, due to a tremendous pressure for land in Bangladesh, the new lands are encroached upon by settlers – in most cases from victims of erosion elsewhere – before the 20-year period has elapsed. They live on the *chars* in a harsh environment on land with limited economic value and without title. This has set the stage for *char* development activities.

The CDSP helps displaced people find security and titles to newly generated lands in an organised way, while building the necessary embankments and infrastructure to protect these newly built settlements from extreme weather events like cyclones. However, the scale of their work is not enough to compensate for the massive numbers of displaced people that occur every year in Bangladesh around its coastal regions. Nevertheless, the programme shows what is possible especially if the doomsday climate change scenario eventually materialises.

rough roads. Because these ghats move frequently owing to embankment construction it would be wisest to ask locals which ghat to head to and at what time, before attempting to move from Noakhali to Hatiya.

WHERE TO STAY **Ochkhali** has a few basic hotels, which you can stay at before making the journey onwards to Chittagong, Barisal or back to Dhaka. No luxury surrounds here, but certainly some gorgeous countryside to explore.

Dwip Unnayan Songstha (2 rooms) Sayadia Bazaar; m 01712 580080. Guesthouse of the Island Development NGO, which is happy to have guests. Friendly & located on pleasant grounds. Also best if you wish to hook into the development activities on the island. The phone number will connect you to an

English-speaking director of the NGO named Shamsut Tibriz. You are welcome to stay here but you should call first to see if the room is free & explain who you are & what your interest is on Hatiya Island. $$

Hotel Singapore (20 rooms) Shahjahan Supermarket; m 01711 589510. Friendly, located in the centre of the market & even a generator. No AC rooms available, however. $$

Salma Rest House (10 rooms) Beside HEED & BRAC offices; m 01720 698111. Relatively clean, commode toilets, closer to the NGO offices. If for some reason you can't get a room at the above 2 places, Salma comes in a reliable 3rd. One VIP room is available at Tk1,000 with AC, but electricity is fairly inconsistent at Hatiya anyway. $$

NIJHUM DWIP

Nijhum Dwip is a coastal island that borders Hatiya and is being promoted as a tourism destination despite the fact almost no infrastructure exists here and it's extremely hard to reach. But if that's the sort of challenge that turns you on, the reward includes a secluded mangrove forest that hides the herds of chital and a mostly muddy beach offering fantastic views into the Bay of Bengal. The journey itself is also quite scenic, but long.

GETTING THERE AND WHERE TO STAY From Tomaruddin ghat, where you arrive when coming from Dhaka, there are two ways to get to Nijhum Dwip. The first is by a service trawler, said to depart twice a week from Tomaruddin and heading directly to Nama Bazaar on Nijhum Dwip – the problem is that even locals seem confused as to when this service is supposed to run, so be prepared to go overland instead of by trawler. A chartered boat will be totally unaffordable for an individual traveller as the 2.5-hour journey could cost several thousand taka.

If travelling overland, you need to take a rickshaw to Ochkhali, the island's main town. Then you can catch a shared jeep or *tempo* (Tk250 for private hire) and drive for about two hours to the Mukteria ghat, which is on the southern tip of Hatiya. Here a ferry service can get you to the northern end of Nijhum Dwip (a 15min crossing), and from there it's another three hours' walk to Nama Bazaar, at the southern tip of the island, where the beach and the **Nijhum Resort** awaits you (*6 rooms; Dhaka booking office* ✆ *02 935 1100–1, 02 935 7095–6;* m *01552 420602, 01190 635565; has generator*; $$$). Come prepared with water and food and you shouldn't have major problems reaching the resort by late afternoon as the entire route is populated and you'll find many villagers willing to point you in the right direction.

If this all sounds a bit daunting, the journey itself makes it worthwhile, and as long as you come prepared, it will prove to be a unique adventure through beautiful countryside. Once you make it, there is a decent guesthouse awaiting you at Nijhum Resort. A group of people might be able to hire the boat necessary to go directly to Nijhum from Tomaruddin, making the journey much simpler, and the folks at the Dhaka booking office can help make such arrangements.

COMILLA *Telephone code 081*

Comilla holds Bangladesh's third most prominent Buddhist site at Moinamoti. The ancient monastic complex would be worthy of further exploration save for the fact that some of its most important buildings lie within a military cantonment, with travellers requiring a battery of permissions to view it. Unfortunately, this does seriously detract from a visit. But for those travelling through with their own vehicle, it would be worthwhile to break the journey at Comilla and to view the ruins at Salban Bihar for a taste of Bangladesh's Buddhist past.

Comilla has also attracted a fair bit of notoriety as the Bangladeshi home of *rosh malai* – the famous Bangladeshi desert is made of small *rosh golla* dough balls served in milk, making a slightly sweet dessert that is simple in its presentation. Even the highway restaurants serve it and if taken home can be served chilled or frozen.

GETTING THERE AND AWAY Depending on the highway traffic, Comilla is about 2.5 hours away from Dhaka and three hours from Chittagong.

By bus A direct, non-stop service is only available to/from Dhaka with departures every 20 minutes departing/arriving from Sayedabad Bus Station in Dhaka and arriving at Comilla's train station. **Tisha** (*Train Station Rd; ☎ 65856, 66519*) and **Asia Line** (*Train Station Rd; ☎ 72642*) are the two best companies, and a coach chair seat costs Tk100.

For Chittagong, buses depart from the Chowk Bazaar bus stand, 2km past the main market, and arrive at Alangkar, near Chittagong's city gate at the start of the Dhaka–Chittagong Highway. The journey takes four hours and costs Tk300.

By train A train service is also available to Dhaka, Chittagong and Sylhet. For Dhaka, expresses depart at 10.03, 16.22 and 01.48 (4.5hrs). Chittagong has departures at 11.24, 16.02 and 02.55 (3.5hrs). Sylhet has two departures at 10.50 and 23.52 (6hrs). Availability of berths or air conditioning varies from departure to departure.

GETTING AROUND Comilla itself is a mostly walkable city, but you'll find no shortage of rickshaws waiting to get you around the bustling city area. Shuttling between the city and Moinamoti Ruins, however, is a different story. The ruins are about 5km from the centre of town and on the other side of the Dhaka–Chittagong Highway. CNGs are easy to find in town, and a queue of baby taxis are sometimes waiting outside Salban Vihara to get you back.

TOURIST INFORMATION Guides for Moinamoti are best sourced from Dhaka with tour operators (see *Chapter 3*, page 118).

WHERE TO STAY

Mid-range

Vita World (10 rooms) Choira, Chowddogram; Dhaka–Chittagong Highway; m 01819 212293; e info@vitaworldtourism.com; www.vitaworldtourism.com. It might seem odd to have a highway hotel promoted as a bilateral joint-venture project, but with Japanese flags flying high over Vita World's shimmering & shiny building, that's exactly what it is. With 3 restaurants, a conference room & prices quoted in dollars, it is quite the facility. It's located 30km from Comilla Town. $$$$

Bangladesh Academy for Rural Development (BARD) (40 rooms) BARD Campus, Kotbari; ☎ 76424, 76428; e bardbd@hotmail.com; www.bard.gov.bd. For those with a legitimate reason to visit the BARD training centre (or legitimate sounding, at least), this will be Comilla's best place to stay. Housed on a beautiful campus & surrounded by the nearby ruins, those with connections may be able to request a tour of the ruins inside the cantonment area but that depends on which way the political winds are blowing. Permission requests to stay should be addressed to the Director General by email, explaining the purpose of the visit & your background. $$$

Hotel Ashik (22 rooms) 186 Nazrul Av (beside Modern School); ☎ 68781; m 01711 964064. Expensive aging rooms with mismatched décor, but still one of Comilla's best hotel options for those with the means. $$$

Budget

Hotel Sonali (43 rooms) Town Hall Supermarket, Kandirpar; ☎ 63188, 73188; m 01819 879688, 01723 000900. Comilla's most centrally located hotel, but above a busy market & quite noisy. TV & hot water available in more expensive sgls/dbls. $$

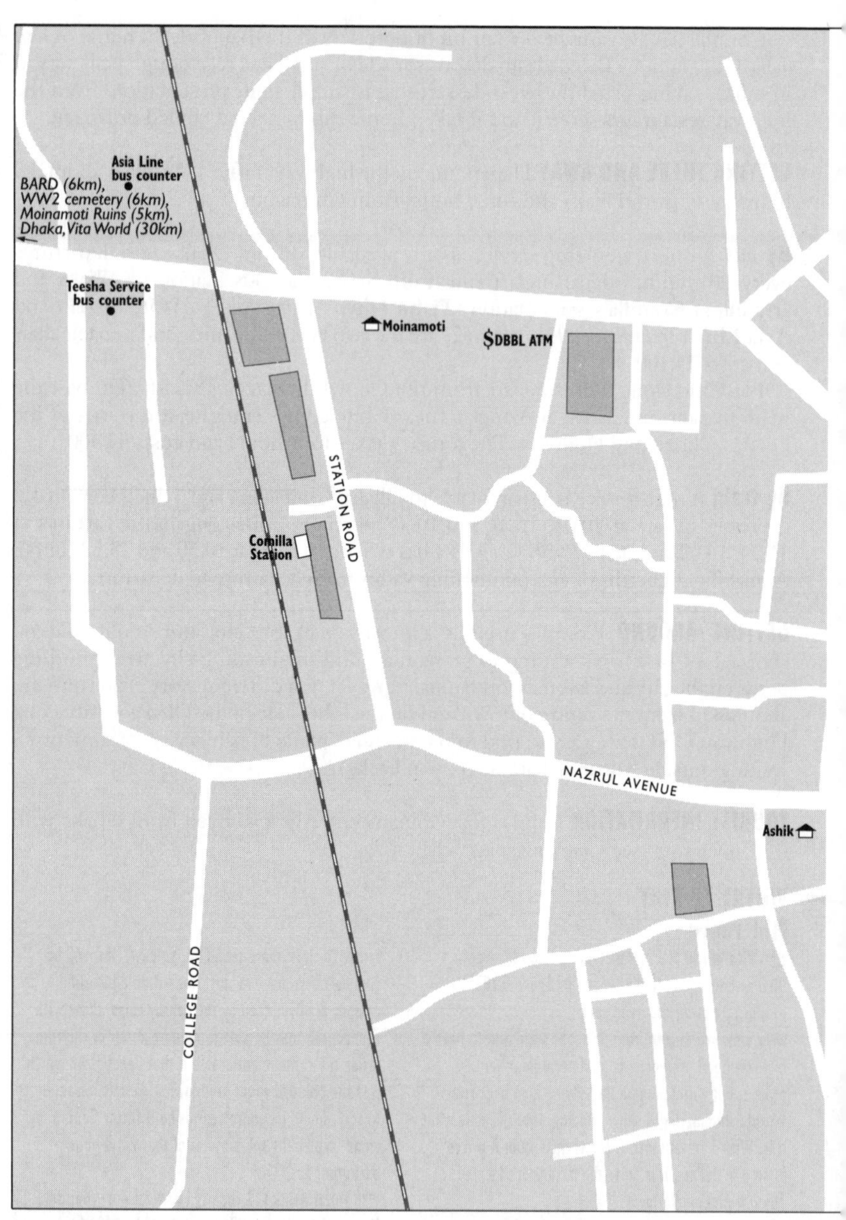

Hotel Fatema (12 rooms) Zila School Rd; m 01722 108821. Cheap, albeit dark. The quietest budget option, but not central. $

Hotel Moinamoti (39 rooms) Race Course (near train station); 68255. Not as old as nearby budget options, but definitely noisy. $

WHERE TO EAT

Silver Spoon Badurtala; 61684. Even the half portions are massive. A bit under-frequented albeit decent enough for a change-up from local cuisine. $$$

Vita World m 01817 123320/01711 876405. Dhaka–Chittagong Highway. Offers an OK buffet around the clock for highway travellers. $$$

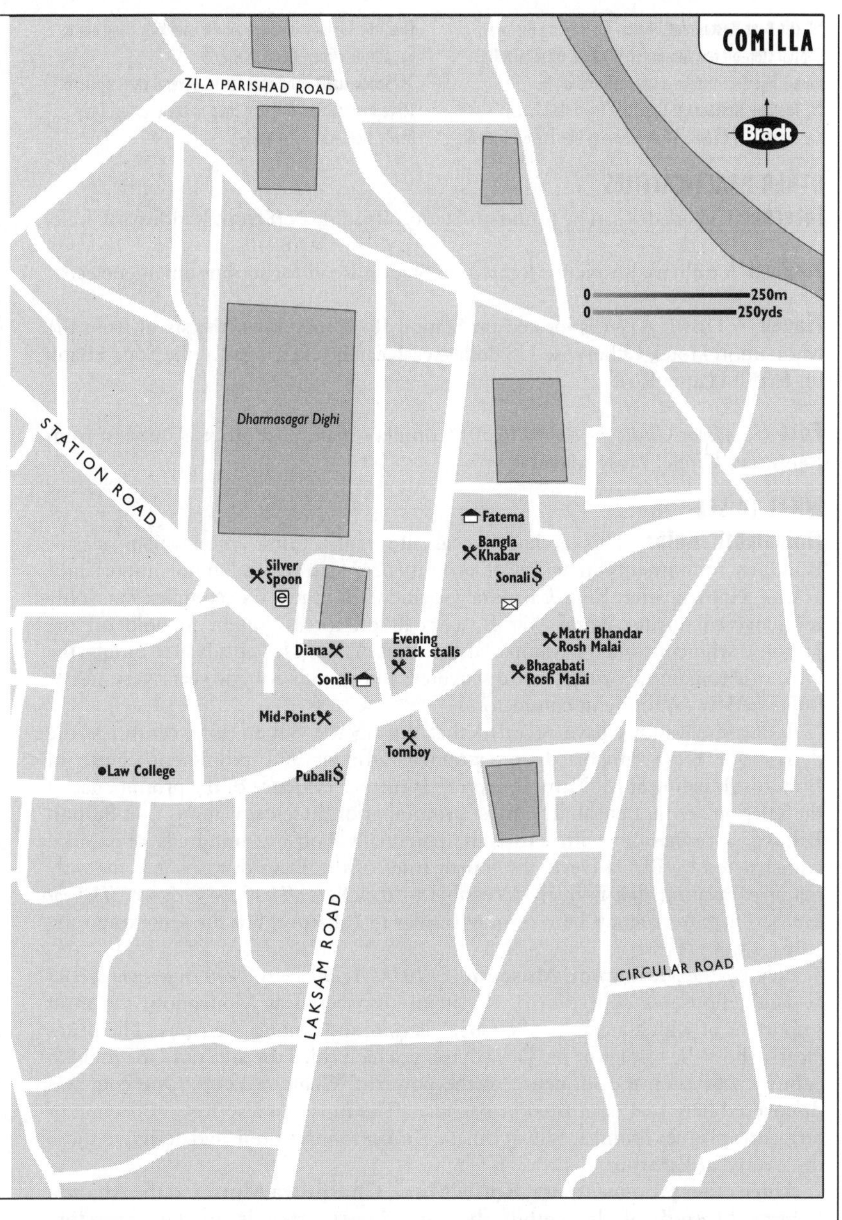

✕ **Bangla Khabar** Zila School Rd; ☎ 62340. Range of Thai, Chinese & Bangla options served in a clean & well-lit atmosphere, unlike the darkened caves these kinds of restaurants normally occupy. $$

✕ **Mid-Point Restaurant** Kandirpar Circle; ☎ 71202. Tasty *halim*, rotisserie chickens, fresh kebabs & hot *naans* at great prices. Easily one of the busiest & best restaurants on Kandirpar Circle. $$

✕ **Bhagabati Pera Bhander** Monoharpur. A friendly *rosh malai* alternative to the well-frequented Mati Bhandar. $

✕ **Hotel Diana** Kandirpar; ☎ 64773. Another high-turnover joint featuring the meaty favourites of Bangla cuisine. $

✕ **Mati Bhandar** Monoharpur; ☎ 76233. Supposedly Comilla's best *rosh malai*. Has the number of customers as evidence. $

✕ **Off Beat Restaurant** Dhaka–Chittagong Highway. Chosen stop-off restaurant for Silk Line travellers. Has simple but decent take-away *rosh malai*. $

✕ **Tomboy Restaurant** Opposite Town Hall Gate, Kandirpar; ☎ 62662. With offerings like French fries & Thai, the Tomboy is where all the cool kids hang out to get a little closer. Good music. $

✕ **Snack stalls** Kandirpar Circle. Several carts open to serve fried snacks & Halim soup in the evening. Only hardy stomachs need apply.

OTHER PRACTICALITIES

Internet Cybercafés can be found on Station Road just off from Kandirpar Circle.

Medical A military hospital is located on Station Road for serious emergencies.

Money A DBBL ATM is located on Station Road just down the street from the Moinamoti Hotel. Otherwise US dollars cash can be exchanged at the Sonali Bank on Fazlul Haque Road.

Post (*Kandipar Circle; ⏲ 10.00–16.30*) Comilla's main post office is out east from Kandirpar Circle; easily walkable.

WHAT TO SEE

Moinamoti Ruins This archaeological site ranks third among Bangladesh's Buddhist monuments in terms of prominence, stature, and more importantly, access. Named after King Chandra Govinda's mother, the complex was only rediscovered during World War II, as coalition forces sought to hold off the Japanese who controlled Myanmar at the time. As they set up advance camps, the bulk of Moinamoti's ruins was discovered and in subsequent years very nearly bulldozed by cantonment contractors.

Today, excavations have revealed that during the 8th to 13th centuries, the dynasty of Deva supported an extremely affluent and prominent centre of Buddhist learning at Moinamoti, serving as further evidence of the prominence of the religion across Bengal. The most prominent of these excavations is at **Salban Bihara**, a monastery with 115 cells, potentially housing hundreds of monks. Constructed by Bhava Deva, the fourth ruler of the Deva dynasty, it is the only major excavation that is freely accessible to travellers (*Tk50 for foreigners, Tk5 for locals*). The construction here is quite similar to Paharpur, but the same imposing stupa is not present.

Nearby, the **Moinamoti Museum** (*⏲ 10.00–17.00; entry Tk50 for foreigners, Tk5 for locals*) houses a collection of the items discovered at Moinamoti, the most important of which are a set of copper plates found among the ruins. The plates clearly show the lineage of the Deva dynasty, which ruled the area until the mid 8th century, and later, the influence of the powerful Chandra kings. One coin was discovered here that originated in Baghdad. The museum also has a collection of terracotta plaques found at Salban Bihara, similar in inscription and design to those discovered at Paharpur.

Three other prominent sites, **Kotila Mura**, **Charputra Mura** and the **Ananda Vihara Mound**, all lie within the cantonment grounds and are therefore inaccessible to casual travellers who can't be bothered dealing with the paperwork required to make a proper visit. Kotila holds three Buddhist stupas that represent the three jewels of Buddhism: Buddha, Dharma (Buddha's teachings) and Sangha (community). Charputra is another shrine atop a hill a few kilometres from Kotila. Finally, Ananda Vihara is another monastic complex that didn't survive the cantonment onslaught – most of its archaeological treasures were plundered in the mid 1940s.

World War II cemetery With all the talk of World War II, it would only make sense to pay a visit to Comilla's beautifully maintained war memorial, where Japanese, English, French and Indian (which may include some Bangladeshi) soldiers lay next to one another in death, even if they fought on opposing sides during the war.

AROUND COMILLA

AGARTALA Agartala stands tantalisingly close to Comilla and Dhaka, and those who have the odd situation of six-month visa validity but only three-month stays should consider making their visa renewal run through this border as it's the closest land crossing to Dhaka and Chittagong. The Samatat Express departs for Akhaura from Noakhali, passing through Comilla at 09.06 daily.

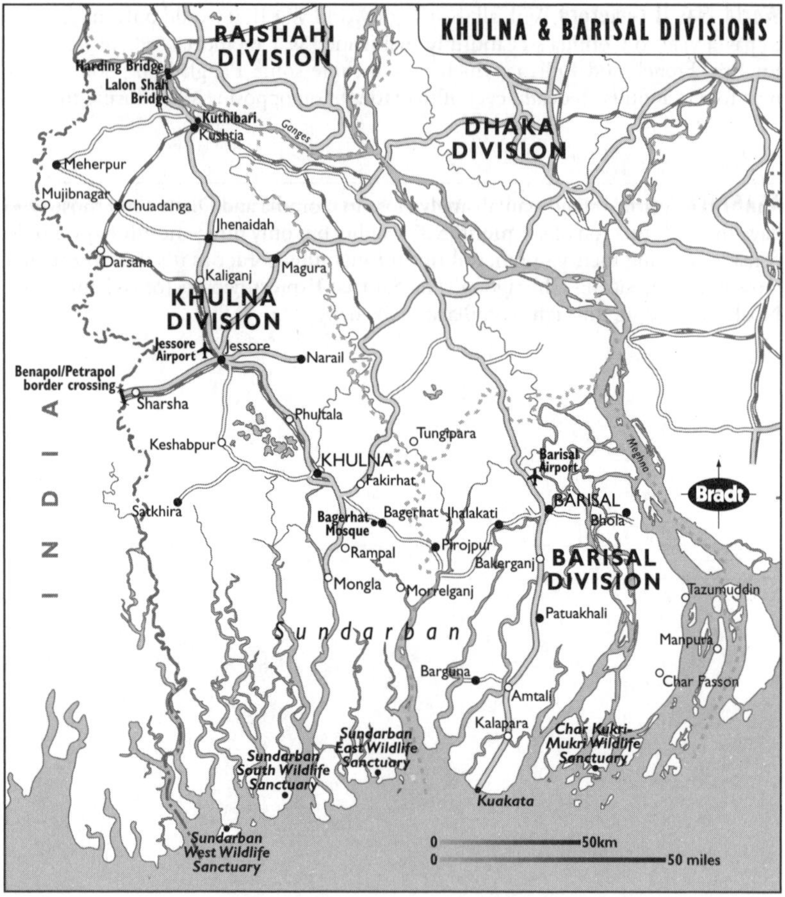

KHULNA & BARISAL DIVISIONS

RAJSHAHI DIVISION
DHAKA DIVISION
KHULNA DIVISION
BARISAL DIVISION
INDIA
Harding Bridge
Lalon Shah Bridge
Kuthibari
Kushtia
Ganges
Meherpur
Mujibnagar
Chuadanga
Jhenaidah
Darsana
Kaliganj
Magura
Jessore Airport
Jessore
Narail
Benapol/Petrapol border crossing
Sharsha
Phultala
Keshabpur
Tungipara
KHULNA
Fakirhat
Satkhira
Bagerhat Mosque
Bagerhat
Jhalakati
Pirojpur
Rampal
Mongla
Morrelganj
Bakerganj
Barisal Airport
BARISAL
Bhola
Meghna
Tazumuddin
Patuakhali
Sundarban
Manpura
Char Fasson
Barguna
Amtali
Kalapara
Kuakata
Char Kukri-Mukri Wildlife Sanctuary
Sundarban East Wildlife Sanctuary
Sundarban South Wildlife Sanctuary
Sundarban West Wildlife Sanctuary
0 50km
0 50 miles
Bradt

7

Khulna and Barisal Divisions

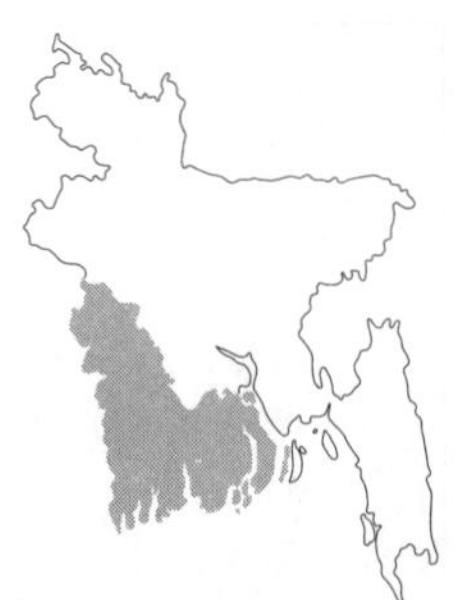

The south and southwestern regions of the country are where Bangladesh's rivers reign supreme over its pan-flat landscape. Several braided threads of the Padma and Meghna rivers break off from the main channel and meander southwards, a phenomenon that makes this region of Bangladesh particularly fertile and lush. Sundarban, Bangladesh's main wildlife refuge and the world's largest mangrove forest, lies in the southwest corner of the country adjacent to the border with India. Travelling by river to the region is an absolute must. Bangladesh's famous rocket paddlesteamer journey offers a fantastic opportunity to experience this landscape from the deck of its most historic vessel. For those journeying between Kolkata and Dhaka, there are plenty of reasons to break the journey here and explore riverine Bangladesh.

KHULNA *Telephone code 041*

Of the Bangladeshi divisional capitals, Khulna is the most orderly. With long curving roads and little vehicular traffic, the city is easy to navigate and lacking the same amount of congestion and pollution that riddles bigger cities like Sylhet and Chittagong. The Rupsa River is the city's dominating feature, bracketing the urban area to the east.

During pre-partition times, Khulna had a greater industrial importance than it currently occupies. Jute used to be a major export of the area, but nowadays the country's 'golden fibre' is no longer produced or processed in sizeable quantities. Today, shrimp is the major export, and visitors should be aware that some environmental concerns have been raised from the ecologically destructive farming practices which produce quick profits that rarely reach the people whose lands pay the price. (See box *Shrimp farming*, page 260, for more information.)

The majority of trips to the Sundarbans begin from Khulna, and so it is the best base from which to mount a trip to the forest. The major Sundarban tour operators have offices here (see *Tourist information* below for more information).

GETTING THERE AND AWAY From Dhaka, Khulna can be reached by bus, boat, train or air via Jessore. Visitors coming from Benapol should head to Jessore first and then catch a local bus to Khulna.

By air Travellers with limited time available can take flights via Jessore, approximately 1.5 hours away from Khulna.

Airlines

✈ **GMG Airlines** 1 KDA Av, Senakalyan Bhaban; ☎ 732273, 810881; m 01711 296110; e khl@gmgairlines.com; www.gmgairlines.com. Offers twice-daily flights at Tk4,895 plus Tk120 for transport.

✈ **United Airways** 2nd Fl, City Trade Centre, 75 KDA Av; m 01713 398784. Has a twice-daily service from Jessore (transfer departs 08.45 & 16.00 from their Khulna office). Fares are the same as GMG plus a Tk150

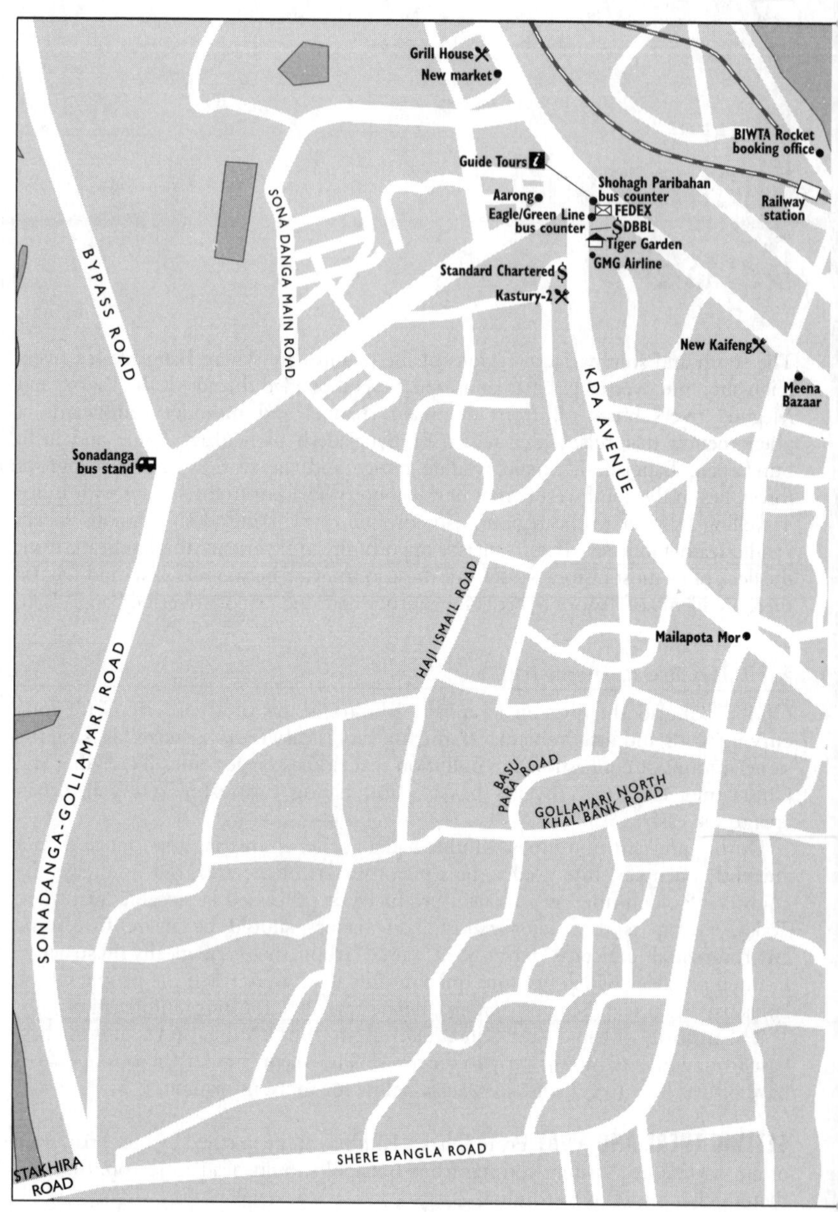

transfer charge from Khulna. There are periodic specials in which the fares drop to as low as Tk2,500 – call & see as it may make it worthwhile to save time. Jessore–Chittagong flights were in service for a short time, but this service was stopped because of a lack of demand. Nevertheless, for travellers wishing to get from the forest to the beach in a hurry, it may be worth checking if these flights have been reinstated. Otherwise you'll need to travel via Dhaka.

By bus **Green Line** (*KDA Av, near Royal Hotel; ☎ 813887–9; m 01730 060037*) (Dhaka 8hrs; Tk650), **Eagle** and **Shohagh Paribahan** each have daily and

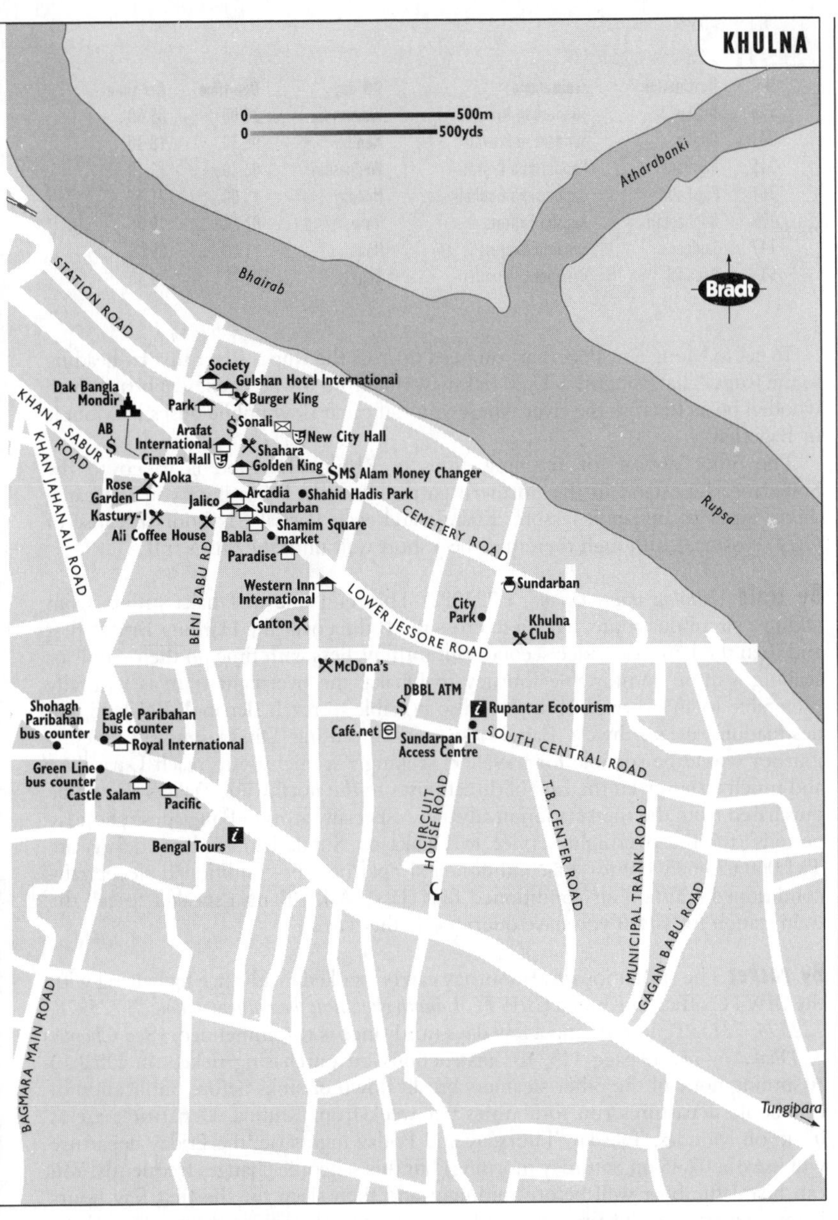

overnight services to/from Khulna from Dhaka. Green Line's air-conditioned buses offer the greatest degree of comfort and have three daily departures at 08.15, 14.45 and 22.00 from Khulna, and 08.00, 15.00 and 23.00 from Dhaka's Kallyanpur (NB The names Gabtali and Kallyanpur are used interchangeably) bus stand. The journey can take longer because of delays or queues at the Aricha–Goalando ferry crossing, although this is infrequent. If the Green Line bus is sold out you will likely be able to catch a ride on the Shohagh or Eagle services next door to the Green Line office.

TRAIN TIMETABLE

No	Destination	Train name	Off day	Dep time	Arr time
725	Dhaka	Sundarban Nishitha	Wednesday	20.00	05.50
763	Dhaka	Sundarban Provati	Monday	08.30	18.30
715	Rajshahi	Kapotaskha Provati	Wednesday	06.30	13.10
761	Rajshahi	Kapotaskha Godhuli	Monday	15.00	21.45
727	Nilphamari	Rupsha Express	None	07.50	19.05
747	Saidpur	Simanta Express	None	21.00	05.50
53	Benapol	Benapol Commuter	None	07.15	09.50

To get to Mongla or Bagerhat you need to cross the Rupsa River first by heading to the Rupsa ghat, roughly a Tk20 rickshaw ride from town. Then, you board small wooden boats to cross the river where you can catch slow public buses to Mongla or Bagerhat.

The other option for reaching cities in Khulna Division is to go to the Sonadanga bus stand in the northern part of the city. From here you can catch direct buses to Benapol, Jessore, Kushtia and even Barisal (six hours because of ferry crossings), although there may be a short wait until the bus is full.

By train (*Khulna train station;* ☏ *723222*) The train line to Dhaka suffers from taking a circuitous route, having to cross the Padma over the Harding Bridge first and then the Jamuna Bridge second. But for travellers with time on their hands or seeking a more comfortable journey to Dhaka, the overnight train is naturally preferable to an overnight bus. It is also possible to reach Benapol, Rajshahi and destinations in northwest Bangladesh, circumventing Dhaka entirely. Such a journey would be suitable for travellers seeking a scenic way to reach Darjeeling and much faster given the lack of direct buses to the northwest. Tickets should be purchased from the train station in advance, especially around Bangladeshi holiday periods (for the overnight service to Dhaka on Sundarban Nishita, tickets are Tk1,060/625/625/420 for air-conditioned sleeper/non air-conditioned sleeper/air-conditioned seat/non air-conditioned first class). Ask a Bangla speaker to call the train station for you if you have queries on other fares.

By *rocket* The (in)famous river journey can be booked in advance by liaising with the BIWTC office in Khulna (*BIWTC Launch ghat, near the railway station;* ☏ *725978, 722394, 721532*). Purchasing a few days in advance is recommended. (See *Chapter 3, Dhaka by rocket*, page 113, for instructions on purchasing tickets in Dhaka.) Assuming none of the other steamers breaks down or sinks before publication of this book, departures run four times per week from Khulna. Departures are at 02.45 on Monday, Tuesday, Thursday and Friday nights (ie: the Friday departure will leave at 02.45 on Saturday morning) but this schedule changes frequently. You can board the boat well before midnight and then sleep for the first few hours before departure. Call first and confirm departures before finalising your plans, and be prepared to adjust should the boat be fully booked or delayed owing to bad weather (first-class cabins are sometimes all taken).

If travelling to Sundarban from Dhaka, purchase a ticket for Mongla as you need not travel all the way to Khulna only to turn around and come back again. Ask your boat operator to have the vessel meet you in Mongla, and you can simply step from one boat to the other and have less travelling time before you enter the forest.

There are two classes of cabin available. First class boasts air conditioning in double-bedded cabins and is located at the front of the boat and costs Tk1,190 per berth, whereas second-class cabins are located in the back and only offer fans, costing Tk720 per berth. If you're travelling solo you might get a room mate for the journey unless you decide to buy the whole cabin. Even if you've only purchased a second-class ticket, staff are normally pleased to let you sit in the front deck to enjoy the scenery going by. Food on the boat receives mixed reviews, but if your dietary requirements aren't too strict then you will be pleased. Standard Bengali fare is on offer, with toast and omelette available for breakfast.

GETTING AROUND Khulna is small enough such that everywhere is accessible by rickshaw or by long walks. As usual, area names or major landmarks are helpful when describing where you want to go. Note that Khan-A-Sabur Road and Lower Jessore Road are used interchangeably to refer to one of Khulna's main streets on the map.

TOUR OPERATORS The operators listed here are those who only maintain Khulna offices. If based in Dhaka, you can shop around by checking *Chapter 3*, *Tour operators*, page 118.

Bengal Tours Dhaka Hse 45, Rd 27, Blk A, Banani; ☎ 02 883 4716, 885 7424; e bengal@agni.com; www.bengaltours.com; Khulna 236 Khan Jahan Ali Rd; ☎ 724355; m 01711 275231. A tour operator with specialised Sundarban boats.

Guide Tours Dhaka Hse 142, Rd 12, Blk E, Banani; ☎ 02 988 6983, 986 2205; e theguide@bangla.net; www.guidetours.com; Khulna KDA Bldg (ground flr); ☎ 731384; m 01711 298000. Bangladesh's best operator to the Sundarbans. Offers different styles of travel to Sundarban (eg: research &/or media support as well as standard tours). You can put together a group of people yourself or try & join an already scheduled departure, but this will be a more expensive trip.

Rupantar Ecotourism 8 Hazi Mohsin Rd (1st Fl); ☎ 811424; m 01711 829414, 01711 841276; e info@rupantareco-tourism.com; www.rupantareco-tourism.com. Khulna-based start up with the ability to organise cultural performances in local villages, & with a true focus on promoting ecotourism in Sundarban. Very friendly.

Hotel-organised day trips can also be organised from the Western Inn International or the Royal Hotel International.

WHERE TO STAY

Mid-range

Hotel Castle Salam (60 rooms) G-8, KDA Av; ☎ 720160; m 01711 397607. Truly overpriced & well past its sell-by date. Other travellers have reported being sick from the restaurant. $$$

Hotel Royal International (41 rooms) A-33, KDA Av; ☎ 813067–9; m 01718 679900. Despite looking very new & shiny, the hotel didn't give great impressions of its service & facilities, especially when given a room that had a giant hole in the wall where the AC unit should have been. Rumours of bad management float around this place. Extra 5% sgl supplement. $$$

New Hotel Tiger Garden (55 rooms) 1 KDA Av (Shiv Bari More); ☎ 721108; m 01712 257030; e zakirskb@yahoo.com. The appearance of the lobby is deceiving considering the poor state of the rooms. This place is best avoided if possible. $$$

Western Inn International (34 rooms) 51 Khan-A-Sabur Rd; ☎ 810899, 810928; m 01711 431000; e western@khulna.bangla.net, western@bttb.net.bd. Khulna's best service, restaurant & hotel all rolled in to one. Rooms with terraces are excellent. Pretty hard to say no to this place when visiting Khulna & that's why you must book ahead when staying here. $$$

Budget

Hotel Golden King (30 rooms) 25 Sir Iqbal Rd; ☎ 725917; m 01718 208072. Slightly odorous rooms that are quiet & tucked away off the street, but also up many, many flights of stairs. $$

Hotel Jalico (30 rooms) Jalil Tower, 77 Lower Jessore Rd, Khulna 9100; ☎ 811883, 810933, 725912, 725649; m 01715 743477. Decent tiled rooms with friendly service, up & away from the street. Not very private, but definitely good value. $$

Hotel Pacific (13 rooms) G9 KDA Av, Khan Jahan Ali Rd, Royal More; m 01712 136247. Sheets not all clean, but it's cheaper than the more upmarket Castle Salam & Royal International. $$

Hotel Park (44 rooms) 45 KD Ghosh Rd; ☎ 720990; m 01716 522810. Better managed than some of the other hotels in the area & reasonably clean. Worth the extra bucks. $$

Hotel Paradise (15 rooms) 60 Khan-A-Sabur Rd; m 01719 124200. Reasonable enough fan rooms for the price, although spending a little bit more at the Western Inn, just up the street, is tempting, especially when you consider the private balconies. $$

Hotel Rose Garden International (24 rooms) 81 Cemetery Rd (near Dak Bangla Mosque); ☎ 722530; m 01711 279437. No English sign at this place, so you'll have to ask around in order to find it, but it's worth the challenge. Located upstairs & away off the main strip, the space is bright during the day thanks to an open-air floor plan. Has a good feel & makes guests feel like they are part of Khulna's laid-back atmosphere. The rooms represent good value for this price range. $$

Gulshan Hotel International (37 rooms) 3 KD Ghosh Rd; ☎ 723368. At this hotel, you are greeted with a multi-coloured *paan spigot* before you even reach reception. Cleanliness is obviously an issue here, but you might call that character. $

Hotel Arafat International (28 rooms) 136 Sir Iqbal Rd; ☎ 725819, 722584; m 01711 582021. Showing some heavy wear & tear – the rooms reek of smoke & sweat. $

Hotel Babla (15 rooms) 65 Lower Jessore Rd; ☎ 813641; m 01711 335882. There are better budget places in town. $

Society Hotel (50 rooms) 27 Telatola Rd, Khulna 9100; ☎ 720995. Cheapest in town & certainly not the tidiest. Well kept enough for a quick & dirty Khulna stay. $

WHERE TO EAT

Canton Chinese Restaurant 4 Ahsan Ahmed Rd; ☎ 732403; m 01711 482088. Looks clean & decent, on par with the other Chinese restaurants on this street. $$$

Grill House and Restaurant KDA New Market; ☎ 730245. Locals rave about the place, although that might be for a lack of competition that serves kebabs. $$$

McDonas Chinese Restaurant 12 Ahsan Ahmed Rd; ☎ 731756. Bangladesh's only 'McDonas', with a funky yellow arches sign to boot. Sorry, no hamburgers available here, however, but heaping plates of chow mein! $$$

New Kaifeng Chinese Restaurant 132–3 Khan-A-Sabur Rd; ☎ 720259. Clear view of the busy street down below, although the location of this place is out of the way if you're just looking for a hit of Bangla–Chinese food. $$$

Western Inn International 51 Khan-A-Sabur Rd; ☎ 810899, 810928, 724754, 720637. Consistently good Indian & Bengali food is served here; definitely ranks as one of Khulna's best. Fish tikka highly recommended. $$$

Aloka Restaurant 1 Khan-A-Sabur Rd; ☎ 732342. Great Bangla food served in clean surrounds. Food is prepared in advance but as long as you come during mealtimes it will be tasty. Recommended. $$

Kastury-2 Kastury Plaza, 73 KDA Av; ☎ 813461. Carbon copy of the Kosturi-1. AC place to chill out for a meal. $$

Kastury-1 10 Cemetery Rd; ☎ 723757. Reasonably priced but dishes served are a bit heavy on the oil. $$

Shahara Hotel and Restaurant 107 Sir Iqbal Rd; m 01719 654561; ⏲ daily all day. High-turnover place, which might be its saving grace. $

ENTERTAINMENT, NIGHTLIFE AND SHOPPING The **Khulna Club** (*1065 Khan-A-Sabur Rd; ☎ 724193, 720229; m 0171 067123; e info@khulnaclub.com; www.khulnaclub.com*) is an old bastion of drinking stalwarts, but its atmosphere feels more like a dark room where Bengali men go to escape their wives for a while. Foreigners may be able to get themselves an invitation by asking local contacts, as you need to be signed in by a member. Make sure you wear covered shoes and a collared shirt. The club also has a tennis court and billiard table.

Overpriced beer is usually sold out of a few of the hotels, including the Western Inn International, but this comes in handy if you want to have a drink during your Sundarban trip.

New Market (*Khan-A-Sabur Rd, north of Shiv Bari Mor*) is where most of Khulna's shopping action takes place. Groceries and snacks for the boat trip can be picked up at **Meena Bazaar**, but you'll find that most tour operators provide far too much food given the fact you'll be spending most of your time sitting around on the boat.

OTHER PRACTICALITIES

Banks There are a number of DBBL ATMs in town, but the easiest to find is at the Hotel Tiger Garden, attached to the GMG Airlines office at 1 KDA Avenue. There is a Standard Chartered Bank just across the street from here that can change travellers' cheques and dispense cash as well.

Internet You can head to **Café.net** (*2/5 Babu Khan Rd; m 01711 047377*) for all your web needs.

Post office The main post office is near the shiny and new-looking KDA City Corporation office.

WHAT TO SEE

Dak Bangla Mondir (*Dak Bangla Circle; ⌚ 09.00–17.00; entry free*). This city temple is a community gathering place for most of Khulna's Hindu population, and so the nearby shops sell some colourful Hindu goods, including beaded wedding saris at excellent prices. The temple was recently renovated for its 200-year anniversary. A nearby **Dak Bangla Mall** sells electronics for those in need as well as English newspapers.

Sundarban Information and Education Centre (*K D Ghosh Rd; ☎ 720665; e dfo@khulna.bangla.net; ⌚ 9.00–13.00 & 13.30–16.00 Sat–Wed, 09.00–14.00 Thu; entry free*). This forestry office museum has a small selection of natural items on display, including a 10ft tiger skin whose origins are unknown. In addition to some basic information on the Sundarbans, you could also enquire about tours from here.

AROUND KHULNA

SHEIKH MUJIB MAUSOLEUM After his bloody assassination on 15 August 1975, the sheikh's final resting place would eventually be his birthplace at Tungipara. Despite being largely credited with the founding of Bangladesh, the sheikh never received proper honour, although that fact largely depended on which political party was in charge at the time. Today there is a small monument honouring him. In recent years, the country's political leaders have made the journey here to pay their respects. To get there, catch a public bus to Gopalganj from Khulna and then disembark at Tungipara.

Where to stay Parjatan has a hotel at Tungipara called the **Hotel Madhumati** (*22 rooms; ☎ 06655 56349; AC rooms available; $$$*).

FISHING OTTERS OF GOPALGANJ AND NARAIL In the local villages of these two areas near Jessore (they are equally close to Khulna), there are a few villages which still employ this ancient method of fishing. Trained, tame otters are used to herd fish into waiting nets. Finding these villages would prove difficult without the assistance of a guide. Inquire with the Guide Tours office for more information (see *Khulna*, *Tour operators* listings on page 257).

BAGERHAT *Telephone code 046*

Not much is known about the shadowy figure of Ulugh Khan Jahan (also known as Khan Jahan Ali), the founder of Bagerhat's 15th-century mosque city. Formerly known as Khalifatabad, the pioneering Muslim Sufi located his mosque city next

SHRIMP FARMING IN BANGLADESH: SMALL FRY OR THE BIG FISH?

As you travel the rivers and roads in the remote corners of the Khulna Division, particularly the areas around Mongla and Satkhira (although there are other shrimp farms in Chittagong Division too), you will inevitably come across some permanently waterlogged, tree-less landscapes that seem wholly out of place with the village landscapes seen everywhere else in the region. Where once rice or trees grew, there are now massive ponds, bound by mud banks on all sides. If you spot this scenery, you've spotted a Bangladeshi shrimp farm. The reason the landscape seems so out of place is that shrimp farming requires semi-saline water, the same kind of water that flows in and out of the Sundarbans.

Over the last few years, the tiny crustacean has become the focal point of an intense debate in Bangladesh. On one hand, shrimp has become the second largest export earning industry after the garment industry, and this brings valuable and much-needed foreign currency into the country. Most of the shrimp heads off for dinner tables in the US or western Europe, but Japan and southeast Asia also account for some of the export value as well. In 2007–08 fiscal year, the industry earned over US$515 million in Bangladesh – obviously no small fry.

On the other hand, some development agencies have been quick to point out that very little of this incredible profit reaches the landowners and workers whose now salinated lands become infertile and useless for agriculture. Reports of violence and coercion have trickled out from the villagers who have protested this destruction of their land. Some say they their livelihoods have been destroyed, but have no alternative other than to continue working for the meagre wages offered by shrimp industry.

Not all of Bangladesh's shrimp industries should be tarred with the same brush, as there are some businesses that are conscious of what they are doing and the resulting social and ecological impacts, although environmentalists might say that there is no such thing as an ecologically friendly shrimp farm. It should be noted that there are two kinds of shrimp: both salt (*bagda*) and fresh (*golda*) water shrimp farms. The freshwater shrimps can be farmed in rice paddies which gives more income to the farmers; Grameen and the Bangladesh Rural Advancement Committee (BRAC) have some projects promoting this form of cash crop. However, without responsible management, future shrimp production could come at an even greater cost to Bangladesh's precious mangrove forest at the Sundarbans and the people who rely on it for their livelihoods.

As for the choices of individual travellers, it is best to enquire where the shrimp on the table comes from: river shrimp and sea shrimp, plus the *golda* (farmed freshwater) variety are more ecologically friendly than the *bagda* (farmed saltwater) variety. *Golda* shrimp are the bigger, blue colour lobster-like variety, whereas farmed *bagda* are grey and smaller than *golda*.

to a now moribund branch of the Bhairab River, in an area that was likely a part of Sundarban during his time. Historians speculate that Khan Jahan was either forced by political instability or commissioned by the sultanate of Delhi to establish the outpost of Islam in this remote corner of India. The prolific builder likely braved tigers, wild jungles and humid swamps in his frantic construction of over 360 mosques, water tanks, bridges, roads, palaces and even his own mausoelum – a remarkable accomplishment that eventually earned the ancient city a spot on the list of World Heritage Sites.

Today, the great majority of Bagerhat's monuments lie in ruins, although the prime attractions have been restored and prepared for tourist visits. The historical nature of these buildings does demonstrate the vigorous commitment of Bengal's earliest Muslim rulers to spreading the word of Allah, but what is perhaps most memorable about a visit to Bagerhat is the wonderful countryside and friendly villagers between all the mosques and temples, and the rich natural surroundings they inhabit. If you do choose to visit Bagerhat, make it a long, languid day and you will find plenty of friendly adventures to keep you entertained.

GETTING THERE AND AROUND Unless you're a Mughal architecture buff who would like to spend more time exploring the different mosques, Bagerhat is best fit into a half- or full-day trip from Khulna or as a stop *en route* to Mongla. From Khulna, first head to Rupsa ferry ghat and cross the river on tiny pedestrian boats (Tk2 for entry to the boat terminal). Then, a series of Bagerhat- (1hr; Tk20) or Mongla-bound (1.5hrs; Tk25) public buses will be waiting for you on the other side. Bagerhat lies just off the Khulna–Mongla road, so if you're trying to get to Mongla from Bagerhat, you might be better off taking a public bus to the main road first.

In Bagerhat, rickshaws or rickshaw vans are available to ferry you between the two principal sites (Shait Gumbad Mosjid and Khan Jahan's Mausoleum). At Dosani Mor (a traffic crossing on the Khulna–Bagerhat Highway, about 2km from the mausoleum road), asking around could get you some motorcycles (with drivers) to ferry you between the sites (Tk150–200 per hour) or drive you back to Khulna (Tk600).

WHERE TO STAY AND EAT Bagerhat doesn't have the same facilities as Khulna. At a pinch, however, the **Hotel Al Amin** (*26 rooms; Kendriyo bus stand;* ☎ *863168;* m *01711 398811;* $$) is Bagerhat's best choice for an overnight stay if you wish to spend time exploring the countryside and the temples nearby, and isalso good as a rest stop between Mongla and Khulna. There is a range of rooms to suit budgets but it can be busy, so call ahead.

WHAT TO SEE Dozens of mosques and temples dot the countryside around the city of Bagerhat and archaeologists could easily spend a few days discovering them all – regular travellers will probably only need a day. The most comprehensive guide is *Discover the Monuments of Bangladesh* by Dr Nazimuddin Ahmed, available at the University Press bookshop in Dhaka's Motijheel district (see *Dhaka*, *Bookshops* on page 137). The book provides the most detailed coverage of Bagerhat and a comprehensive map for exploring the area. Below are some of the highlights.

Shait Gumbad Mosque As it's the principal monument amongst the ruins of Bagerhat, it is linguistically educational to learn that this stark and simplistic mosque actually has a highly misleading name. In Bangla, *shait gumbad mosjid* means '60-domed mosque', when in fact there are 77 small domes and another four on the corner turrets. Surrounded by well-kept grounds and exuding an air of peace, the mosque's blocky façade remains bare and unplastered, perhaps even 'noble' as one archaeologist calls it. Inside the mosque, a series of repeating columns and curving arches create a kind of mesmerising effect no matter which way you look.

The mosque is one of the first monuments on the Bagerhat–Khulna Road (when coming from Khulna) and if riding a public bus you should be able to hop off here. Entry tickets are Tk50 each for foreigners, perhaps a bit extortionate considering that Bangladeshis pay Tk1 for the same privilege, but do remember that they'll probably still make more money based on the volume of people coming to look at the mosque. The price does include an entrance ticket to the site museum that is worthwhile for the photographs in case you don't have time to visit all the mosques in person. Nearby, the stout-looking Singar Mosque lies across the road and features just a single but very wide dome. Likewise, the Bibi Begni Mosque and the Chunakhola Mosque are situated on the western side of the Ghora Dighi water tank, both even larger than the Singar Mosque.

Khan Jahan Mausoleum Situated on the northern bank of a water tank known locally as *thakur dighi* lies the single-domed Mausoleum of Khan Jahan, which is open for pilgrims to pay homage to the man whose relentless building efforts created the city we see today. As a heavily fortified, singled-domed mosque, the building shares similar traits to the other buildings the area. Attached is a second mausoleum of almost identical construction, which is the tomb of Pir Ali, a close associate of Khan Jahan. Attached to the complex is the Dargah Mosque, still an active place of prayer. You may be asked to remove your shoes while walking in the complex.

Finally, swimming in the water tank is not suggested. There are a couple of resident crocodiles that you may see while visiting the *mazar* (mausoleum). You might even catch a local feeding a chicken to the croc as an offering, believed to be some kind of living representation of the holy saint.

Nine-domed mosque Located in the western bank of *thakhur dighi* (pond), this mosque has been extensively restored both inside and outside. The western wall (that faces Mecca), has a number of insets (*mihrabs)* adorned with terracotta floral scrolls and flower motifs. The nearby Zinda Pir Mosque and *mazar* just to the north are also worth a gander although it is falling to pieces in the jungle due to lack of maintenance.

Ronvijoypur Mosque The mosque's 11m–wide dome is the largest in Bangladesh. It can be viewed on the way to see the Khan Jahan Mausoleum and lies on the opposite side of the Khulna–Bagerhat road from the mausoleum.

Kholda Math For a spot of adventure, consider the 10km journey to this 20m Hindu pagoda hidden in the village north of Bagerhat. The spire was built in the 17th century by a Brahmin court adviser, and sports some extremely intricate terracotta work, albeit in various states of decay. It's not easy to get to but does provide some excellent countryside views along the way.

The best way to get there is to head to Dosani Mor, 2km east from the Khan Jahan Mausoleum. From here you can hire a *tempo* or baby taxi (see page 261), or perhaps even a couple of motorcycles (with drivers) to take you to the site, or if you have lots of time (one hour each way) then a rickshaw will do. Be warned that the road is bumpy in some parts.

MONGLA *Telephone code 04662*

Unless you're a budget traveller seeking the cheapest way to visit Sundarban, there's really little reason to consider Mongla as anything other than a transit point to the majestic wilderness just south from here. The riverside town has an inactive seaport and a government-run Parjatan hotel (see below), and also features a whole lot of hustlers who'll want to take you to the forest for a day and won't take no for an answer. For this reason it is best to mount a trip to Sundarban from the more professional outfits in Khulna or Dhaka. That said, this still remains the cheapest way to see the northern tip of Sundarban.

GETTING THERE AND AROUND

By bus From Khulna, there are regular public buses leaving from the opposite side of the river at the Rupsa ferry ghat (1hr; Tk25). From Mongla, you can catch a Khulna-bound bus outside the Parjatan hotel, which is on the northern bank of the river.

By rocket Mongla isn't all bad – it's actually most handy as a transit point, especially for travellers coming from Dhaka on the rocket. With some pre-departure planning, it is a good place to disembark from the rocket and join a Sundarban journey. To do this properly you need to instruct a tour operator to have their boat meet you at Mongla between 16.00 and 18.00. You will then take your first night at the edge of the forest.

A few things to be aware of: ensure your rocket travel isn't one of the twice-weekly departures that travels only to Morrelganj, 45km before Mongla on a journey to Sundarban; otherwise the tour operator may need to arrange transport from Morrelganj to Mongla by road to pick you and your group up, adding to the cost of a trip.

This may change, but currently the rocket travels to Khulna via Mongla four times a week, every Sunday, Monday, Wednesday and Thursday. Call the BIWTC offices in Dhaka/Khulna to confirm (*Dhaka* ☎ *02 955 9779; Khulna* ☎ *041 725978, 722394, 721532*).

Going the other way is slightly more difficult as the rocket comes in from Khulna at about 04.30 and so it would be difficult to get a proper night's sleep. It is also suggested that you arrange your ticket in Khulna first instead of at Mongla, as it will be easier to confirm a cabin in person as opposed to over the phone at Mongla.

WHERE TO STAY AND EAT

Hotel Pashur (16 rooms) Northwest riverbank, Khulna Rd; ☎ 75100; m 01816 879874; e bpcho@bangla.net; www.bangladeshtourism.gov.org. The government-run Parjatan facility is Mongla's best accommodation option, albeit pricey if you're on a budget. There's a restaurant, hot water & AC/non-AC rooms available. The management here is also keen to help you organise trips to Sundarban, but do your homework first before signing up for a trip (see Sundarban, page 264). $$$

Hotel Bangkok (20 rooms) Southeast riverbank; m 01711 397531. Friendly staff here & reasonably clean rooms (some with bath) make this a better budget choice than the other places. $

Hotel Singapore (10 rooms) Southeast riverbank; m 01728 456022. Just opposite the Hotel Bangkok, but definitely lacking the cleanliness of the city it is named after. Some rooms have attached bathroom. $

WHAT TO SEE

Sundarbans Museum (*near Hotel Singapore; ⏲ 09.00–18.00 Sat–Thu; entry free*) A small room holds a number of exhibits from Sundarban, including a dolphin, eels and several kinds of fish. All in all, it's a rather garish display of the wildlife but does show some of the animals you might not otherwise see in the forest.

Boat day trip Many Bangladeshis make the trip down to Mongla to do tours into the forest, but given some economic limitations they might often hire a boat and simply cruise to the Karamjol Wildlife Centre less than an hour away. The centre is essentially a miniature zoo that houses some spotted deer, snakes and crocodiles in caged enclosures. For Bangladeshis this facility at least serves to expose some of the wildlife in Sundarban to which they might not otherwise be aware of. Furthermore, this kind of journey doesn't require permits or armed guards (for the tigers), which doesn't push up the price of a trip to Sundarban (Tk200 per entry to Karamjol plus a Tk1,000 boat charge).

For an excursion deeper into the Sundarbans, management at the Pashur Hotel can offer a single day trip including food and forest permissions at about Tk2,000–2,500 per person, with a minimum group size of five or six (cheaper per person if more people visiting). For longer, planned excursions you are best off using one of the tour operators listed below and arranging your trip from either Dhaka or Khulna.

SUNDARBAN

Sundarban is Bangladesh's must-see place. If you manage only one trip suggested in this book, make sure you spend a few days in Bangladesh's most pristine and abundant wilderness. Moonlit evenings spent stargazing from a boat deck amidst the simultaneous pulsating glow of fireflies are among the most memorable you can have in Bangladesh. Letting the calm serenity of the jungle replenish your Dhaka-battered nerves makes Sundarban actually feel like an escape. Finally, it's fascinating to ponder the notion that tigers stalk people amongst these dense jungles (you're perfectly safe on a boat, however), and that this is the last remaining stronghold for the Royal Bengal tiger in the entire world.

GEOGRAPHY At 10,000km^2, Sundarban is the world's largest continuous mangrove forest, of which almost two-thirds belong to Bangladesh and one-third to India. From the coast of the Bay of Bengal, the tidal forest stretches approximately 80km inland and acts as a natural barrier for the adjoining areas. The forest protects the low-lying delta from tidal surges and cyclones and traps nutrients and sediments carried by the waters of the Padma (Ganges) and Jamuna (Brahmaputra) rivers from the north into the sea. About one-third of this vast forested area is permanently underwater, although inundation levels vary with tides and freshwater inflow. The seasonal variation of freshwater inflow influenced mainly by the monsoon rainfall creates an ever-changing environment; inhospitable for humans and challenging for fauna and flora. Through manmade alterations to the natural waterflow, the natural seasonal fluctuation has been seriously disrupted, resulting in rising salinity and increasing sedimentation rates especially in the western Sundarban, directly and irreversibly affecting the biodiversity of the Sundarban Forest.

FLORA AND FAUNA Despite the inhospitable and ever-changing environmental factors, Sundarban teems with an extraordinary range of specialised species, adapted to this distinctive environment. Chief among these are mangroves, featuring special root systems ensuring sufficient oxygen intake despite daily inundation, extracting excess salt and adding to the structural support. Most mangroves generate viviparous seedlings dispersed by water. Of the world's approximately 50 recognised mangrove species, Sundarban features about 20. The name of the forest is most likely a derivative of one of its common mangrove species, the *sundari* tree. Wood from these magnificent, tall mangrove trees is of high value and traditionally used for building the boats that frequent the mangrove channels during the fishing tides.

Sundarban is home to Bangladesh's national animal, the Royal Bengal tiger, of which an estimated 400 prowl the forest. Unfortunately it is quite rare to catch a glimpse of this majestic big cat, and perhaps this is a good thing given the history of human–tiger conflict in this area (see box, page 266).

You have a much better chance of spotting the tiger's preferred prey, chital or spotted deer, as they often congregate in open spaces or along the shores. You might also be fortunate enough to see barking deer or muntjak, wild boar, otter,

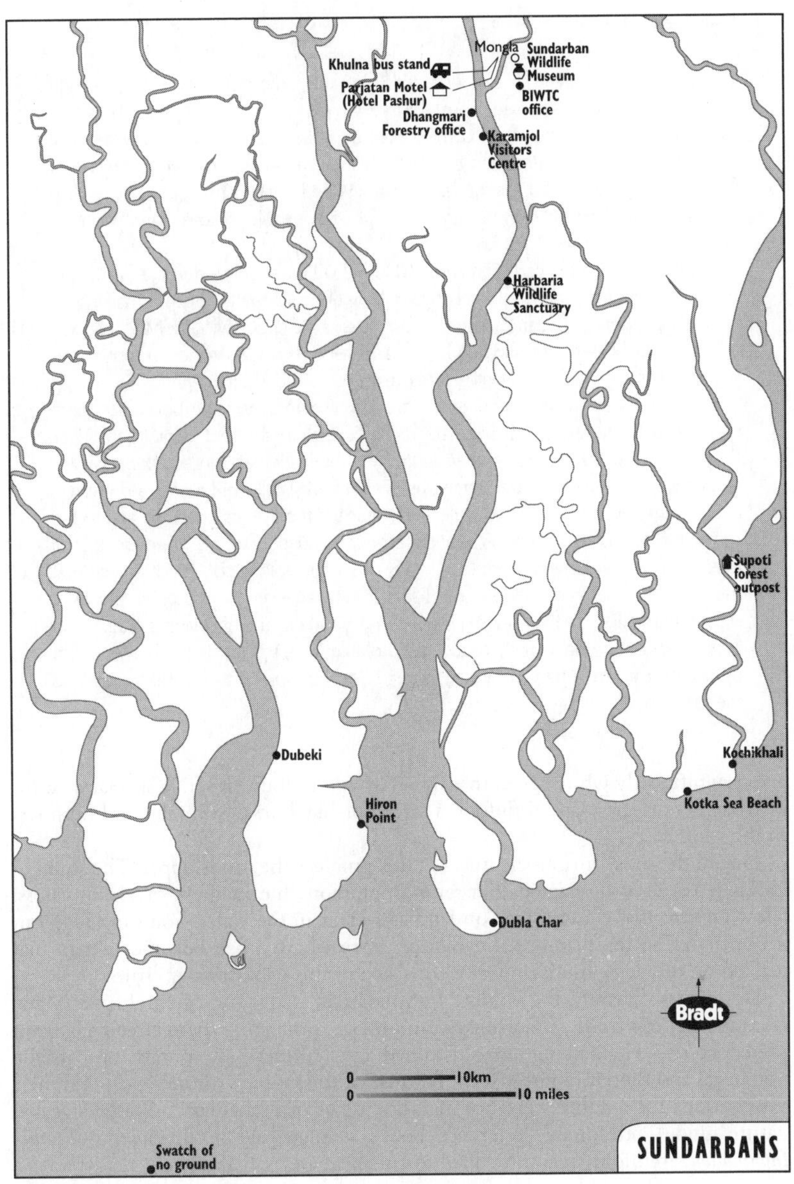

rhesus macaque, fishing or leopard cats. While amphibians are rare in these mangroves, reptiles including water monitors, snakes and the enormous estuarine crocodiles are spotted fairly regularly. The aquatic life is incredibly diverse: look out for the Ganges River and Irrawaddy dolphins frequently surfacing at confluences throughout the year.

Birds abound in the nutrient-rich ecosystem of the Sundarban Forest, especially during the winter months when migratory species join the residents. During the early morning creek explorations, the jungle reverberates with the song of birds including nine species of colourful kingfishers, amazing varieties of woodpeckers

HUMAN–TIGER CONFLICTS

Tigers originally evolved in east Asia, following the large populations of deer and cattle species that dispersed from northern regions into south Asia. They are carnivorous, most of their food coming from ungulates (cattle, deer and wild boar). Their canine teeth are designed to inflict a killing bite on its prey, while the rest of the teeth are adapted for tearing apart flesh. When hunting, the tiger's stripes help keep it hidden from its prey and its powerful body enables it to make a final rush once it is close enough for a kill.

Today there are only an estimated 5,000–7,000 wild tigers left in the world and research indicates there are probably between 400 and 500 remaining in Sundarban (India and Bangladesh). The existence and behaviour of the national animal of Bangladesh are surrounded by a battery of myths, stories, rumours and legends. Yet very little factual information exists on Sundarban tigers.

Why do these myths and legends persist? For many years the population here was one of the least studied. Since 2002, the Forest Department 'Sundarbans Tiger Project' has entered this research vacuum by collaborating with international wildlife and conservation experts, training teams of local field staff, forest guards and villagers in an attempt to understand and effectively manage the threats posed by and to the remaining Sundarban tigers. An estimated 100–200 people are killed or injured every year in Sundarban, more than in any other tiger-range country. It is clear that the protection of both people and tigers is ultimately in the hands of the local stakeholders. By creating alternative income sources, the growing pressure on Sundarban can be significantly reduced. A notable NGO, Rupantar, has recently set up an ecotourism wing that directly engages local people in tourism activities (see the following box).

and magnificently white egrets that fly off as you pull up closer. A special treat for birdwatchers is the masked finfoot, a rare coot-like bird nesting in good numbers in the southeast.

One of the most curious creatures in this jungle is the mudskipper. The strange-looking fish is well adapted to a semi-amphibious life in these brackish waters, allowing it to move and forage on land as well as in the water. You can't help but imagine that in the primordial evolution story where a fish becomes a man that walked on two legs, mudskippers were a step in this evolutionary chain.

Despite its diversity, the wildlife in Sundarban is shy and often elusive. Many creatures benefit from extraordinary camouflage, protecting them effectively from predators and challenging unaccustomed eyes. Others are purely or partially nocturnal and therefore rarely seen. Because of this, some visitors report that their expectations for wildlife were not met, but a pair of binoculars, a knowledgeable nature guide and suitable reference books as suggested in *Appendix 2, Further Information*, are highly recommended to enhance your satisfaction.

LIFE AROUND SUNDARBAN Sundarban (in Bengali, *sundar* (pronounced 'shundor') means beautiful and *ban* forest) was declared a Reserved Forest under the management of the Forest Department of the government of Bangladesh in 1875. Human encroachment had swallowed more than half of the forest's total area over the previous 200 years. Luckily the loss of forested area seems to have been stabilised for the time being. There are no permanent human settlements within the Reserved Forest, but villages surround Sundarban all along its inland borders. Well over five million people use the forest to support their livelihoods. The main forest products are fish, crustaceans, wood, shells, thatching materials and delicious wild honey – available at the Guide Tours offices and speciality stores in Bangladesh. The mostly manual, traditionally sustainable harvesting methods are regulated under the supervision of the Forest Department (see *Threats*, below, for more information).

April and May are the months for honey collection in Sundarban, an occupation that is probably one the most dangerous jobs in Bangladesh owing to the high risk of tiger attacks. If visiting Bangladesh during this time, it would be a unique opportunity to see the honey being collected by the *mawalis* (honey collectors). The collectors comb through the forest in small groups, making loud noises and setting off firecrackers to scare off any nearby tigers. After tying together a bunch of fallen forest debris to create a makeshift torch, they then smoke the bees inside the large hives hanging from tree branches. A second *mawali* then climbs onto the branch and cuts away a chunk of the hive – never all of it – and drops its valuable honey into the waiting hands of a fellow collector.

FESTIVALS There are two major festivals worth visiting in the Sundarban region: the Ras Purnima Mela (late November or early December, held in various locations along the coast of Bangladesh) and Bonbibi Mela (mid-January, the date changes according to the lunar calendar). During Ras Purnima, tens of thousands of Hindu pilgrims travel to Dubla Island for the two-day festival, joining the thousands of fishermen in the temporary fishing villages. Bonbibi Mela, on the other hand, celebrates the 'lady of the forest', to whom the villagers pray for protection and safe returns from the forest. In honour of the forest goddess clay statues in little shrines are erected along the forest edge and within the villages. During Bonbibi Mela the old figurines are replaced, colourfully painted and decorated with ornaments.

As the legend goes, there was once a malicious man who offered his young nephew to the demon of the forest, Dokkhin Rai, in return for seven boats of honey and wax. Just as the demon, who sometimes takes the form of a tiger, was about to attack the boy, he called out to Bonbibi who saved his life. The villagers believe that those who enter Sundarban with *pobitro mone* and *khali hate* (a pure heart and an empty hand), respecting the fact that both animals and people are dependent on the forest and take only what they need from it, will be protected by Bonbibi.

THREATS Unfortunately, the future of Sundarban is as uncertain as the future of Bangladesh itself. With growing evidence of a sea-level rise and the severely depleted freshwater flows owing to upstream dams and barrages, it is disheartening to imagine that Sundarban (and its inhabitants) will be one of the first places to disappear. Sundarban protects the low-lying country from tidal surges and cyclones. When Cyclone Sidr struck in November 2007, it hit eastern Sundarban and the adjoining coastal areas. An estimated 30% of the forest was damaged. The devastation to unprotected human settlements and agricultural lands was however far worse. The forest, left to its own devices, is recovering quickly from the disaster. The unprotected coastline is prone to further natural calamities occurring with increasing strength and frequency.

An additional large threat Sundarban faces comes from the massive un-selective catch of fish fingerlings and crustaceans. This unsustainable practice supports the county's second-largest foreign-currency earner and export product, shrimp, while destroying the fish stock of south Asia's richest fish nursery. Commercially valuable catches for local fishermen and the prey of aquatic animals including freshwater cetaceans (such as Irrawaddy river dolphins) are declining at an increasing rate.

THE BANGLADESH CETACEAN DIVERSITY PROJECT

Through studies conducted in 2002–05, the Wildlife Conservation Society (WCS) identified a 120km-wide belt of estuarine, coastal and pelagic waters in Bangladesh as a hotspot of cetacean abundance and diversity that is in urgent need of conservation. This prime cetacean habitat extends across the world's largest contiguous mangrove forest, the Sundarban Reserve Forest, and offshore to a 900m undersea canyon known as the Swatch-of-No-Ground. The area supports extraordinary whale, dolphin and porpoise diversity, and several species that occur here in significant numbers are regionally at risk.

The northern waterways of the mangrove forest encompass the farthest downstream range of the 'endangered' Ganges River dolphin or shushuk (*Platanista gangetica*). In a generally narrow geographic band, occurring within the same habitat, is the farthest upstream distribution of a seasonally mobile population of the Irrawaddy dolphin (*Orcaella brevirostris*). Farther offshore but still occurring in habitat influenced by freshwater inputs is the Indo-Pacific humpback dolphin (*Sousa chinensis*) and finless porpoise (*Neophocaena phocaenoides*). Then, a relatively short distance from the fluvial habitat of shushuks, is the Swatch-of-No-Ground. Here, a burst of biological productivity created by upwelling currents supports large groups of Indo-Pacific bottlenose dolphins (*Tursiops aduncus*), pantropical spotted dolphins (*Stenella attenuata*) and spinner dolphins (*S. longirostris*), as well as a probable resident population of Bryde's whales (*Balaenoptera edeni*).

The diversity of cetaceans occupying this relatively small area is remarkable, and rigorous abundance estimates of shushuks, Irrawaddy dolphins and finless porpoises indicate that large populations of these species remain. In fact, the Irrawaddy dolphin population in Bangladesh is probably the world's largest, possibly by an order of magnitude. However, optimism about the long-term survivability of cetaceans in these

Forest management under the Forest Department has been far from perfect. Like many institutions in Bangladesh, this department has suffered from endemic corruption resulting in deforestation and loss of habitats throughout the country. But there is yet hope for this globally unique and important ecosystem: new approaches to sustainable uses, scientific research aimed at conservation of fauna and flora and collaboration with local communities are being introduced. By supporting the Forest Department programmes and conservation initiatives as well as acting as a responsible tourist when visiting Sundarban, you can significantly contribute to its protection.

TOURS It is a hassle to arrange your own boat, supplies and the required entry permits to the Sundarban Forest.

You'll find several local operators offering tours to Sundarban but there are only a few companies that actually own the necessary facilities to run a Sundarban trip, or have guides specifically designated for these nature cruises.

Because the biodiversity is highest in the far southeast where you can also enjoy pristine beaches facing the Bay of Bengal, it is best to spend at least three or four days for a Sundarban tour. Ensure your tour includes stops at Kotka and/or Kochikhali in the Southeast Sanctuary – perhaps the nicest places in Sundarban for enjoying the beach and taking adventurous treks through the forest.

If you don't have the time or budget for an overnight tour, you can arrange your own day trip aboard a local 'jolly' boat hired from Mongla. A recommended stop is the Harbaria Forest Station on the Passur River, which has a nice boardwalk through a beautiful sundari grove – the sundari being the tree that the Sundarban takes its name after. The visitors' centre at Karamjol is crowded on Fridays and Saturdays, but offers

waters is tempered by increasing threats from incidental killing in gill-net fisheries, depletion of prey due to a loss of fish and crustacean spawning habitat and to massive non-selective catch of fish fingerlings and crustacean larvae. An additional threat is declining freshwater flows from upstream abstraction and the compounding effects of sea-level rise.

The Bangladesh Cetacean Diversity Project (BCDP) seeks to ensure the long-term protection of cetacean diversity while the current population sizes of several species at risk are known or appear to be sufficient for long-term persistence if threats can be reduced. With a successful effort, Bangladesh could serve as a critical safety net for freshwater and coastal cetaceans whose populations are disappearing elsewhere in Asia.

The strategy of the project is to work closely with government agencies, fishing communities, local NGOs and nature tourism operators to develop and implement a conservation plan that protects the range of cetacean diversity inhabiting the estuarine channels of the Bangladesh Sundarban and surrounding marine waters including the Swatch-of-No-Ground. Major emphases are on (1) conducting sound science for supporting development of a conservation plan that includes establishing a protected area network; (2) involving and providing training and technical support to local scientists, resource managers and nature tourism operators to execute effective conservation actions and conduct rigorous research and monitoring; (3) consulting with and enlisting the support of government officials and local people for implementing the Conservation and Protected Area Plan; and (4) communicating research results and conservation progress through publication of technical papers and production of popular media.

If you are interested in supporting BCDP or want to learn more about their work, please visit www.shushuk.org.

an arboretum as well as some enclosures with deer, donkeys and crocodiles. A few travellers have recommended Mr Ferdous at the Hotel Pashur for boat bookings. Otherwise, boatmen will easily find you if you hang out around the Mongla ferry ghat.

Guide Tours (*Dhaka: Hse 142, Rd 12, Blk E, Banani;* ✆ *02 988 6983, 02 986 2208;* **m** *01711 696337;* **f** *02 988 6984;* **e** *theguide@bangla.net; www.guidetours.com. Dhaka Sheraton: Sheraton Hotel Lobby, 1 Minto Rd;* ✆ *02 833 0001 ext 4451;* **m** *01711 696331. Khulna: KDA Bldg, Ground Fl, Shivbari Mor;* ✆ *041 731384;* **m** *01711 298000*) have offices in Khulna and Dhaka. They are the most experienced and largest Sundarban tour operator, with three specialised cruising vessels. Their freshly prepared meals are renowned, as are their knowledgeable guides and friendly crew. You can put together a group of people yourself for an exclusive tour or join one of their scheduled tours. Check for their special cruises starting or ending in Dhaka. The company also actively supports various conservation programmes and offers its expertise and logistics to researchers, wildlife photographers and film crews. Visitors are welcome to join the research expeditions to the Bay of Bengal, Swatch-of-No-Ground – a deep undersea canyon located 50km out in the Bay of Bengal, where dolphins and whales can often be seen during the winter season. **Bengal Tours** (*Dhaka: Hse 45, Rd 27, Blk A, Banani;* ✆ *02 883 4716, 02 885 7424;* **f** *02 988 6381;* **e** *bengal@agni.com; www.bengaltours.com. Khulna: 236 Khan Jahan Ali Rd;* ✆ *041 724355;* **m** *01711 275231*) is another tour operator with specialised Sundarban boats.

Rupantar Eco-tourism (*Khulna: 8 Hazi Mohsin Rd, 1st Fl;* ✆ *041 811424;* **m** *01711 829414, 01711 841276;* **f** *041 720629;* **e** *info@rupantareco-tourism.com; www.rupantareco-tourism.com*) is a Khulna-based outfit with the ability to organise cultural performances in local villages.

MUSIC AND SOCIAL CHANGE

Rupantar Eco-tourism (RET) is a tourism-promotion organisation that works to highlight the scenic beauty of Sundarbans, using a novel approach that involves local people. The organisation deeply believes that tourism can be a pathway to reduce the poverty of the people dependent on the Sundarbans' resources. In this context, RET has patronised and trained-up several folk groups to represent the local cultural heritage to Sundarbans visitors. By including Sundarban information in the folk songs, it also becomes a medium of dissemination of ideas and opinions that ultimately favour conservation of this precious wilderness. Although the concept is quite new, RET would like to enlarge the programme when the organisation's capacity increases. For the time being, the organisation invites all guests to enjoy its cultural programmes and become a part of Sundarban conservation, thereby sustaining the local heritage while reducing the poverty of rural people.

Journeys can also be organised from the Western Inn International or the Royal Hotel (see *Khulna*, *Where to stay*, page 257 for details).

JESSORE *Telephone code 0421*

For travellers coming overland from Benapol, Jessore is a fantastic introduction to the new country. Compared with Kolkata's urban sprawl, Jessore is small and walkable with its centre being the most interesting area: it's a warren of twisting laneways that make for interesting explorations especially at night. The bazaar comes alive with some intense shopping and gossiping activity; it's especially nice to wander this area and take tea stops along the way, gossiping with the local people. If arriving in the evening it would be smart to break the journey here before heading on to Sundarban or northwards to Kushtia.

HISTORY Of all the major towns and cities of Bangladesh, Jessore shows the greatest ties to a past linked to Kolkata's former glory as the capital of India. The city has a number of aging buildings that show the colonisers' influence over its architecture, the most notable of which is the massive old court house which serves as the city's central landmark. Before Bengal became East and West Bengal in 1905, there was no division between the two regions here as there is today. In the 1947 partition of East Pakistan from India, not only was Bengal again divided, so too was the division of Jessore. Later on, during the Liberation War, Jessore was a hotbed of resistance activity. At the war's outset, a contingent of Bengali soldiers posted at the Jessore cantonment mutinied against the Pakistani army on 29 March 1971. Later in the war, Jessore was also the scene of a pivotal battle between the Indian and Pakistani forces. With the latter completely demoralised and dissolute, resistance was weak and Jessore became the first liberated region of Bangladesh on 7 December 1971 and precipitated the Pakistani army's quick defeat.

GETTING THERE AND AROUND Jessore is easily accessible by bus and train, as it lies along the highway route to Khulna, less than 1.5 hours away. It also lies about the same distance to the border at Benapol. The town is easily enough to explore on foot or by rickshaw. Unlike all the other cities in Bangladesh, in Jessore there are rumours that you can hire motorcycles for getting around – the local name for these is 'helicopter'. Enquire around the local bus stand and see if you can get a two-wheeled lift.

By air

✈ **United Airways** Jessore Airport; m 01713 398783. Offers a twice-daily flight to Dhaka departing 10.10 & 18.10. Fares are sometimes on special for as low as Tk3,000 but are normally Tk4,995.

✈ **Royal Bengal Airways** Jessore Airport; ☎ 67434; m 01713 123276. Also offers twice-daily flight to Dhaka, departing 10.35 & 18.35. Latest advertised specials had the fare as low as Tk2,500 if purchased 72hrs ahead of time, but the regular price fare is Tk4,600.

By bus **Green Line** (☎ *68389;* m *01712 897578*), **Shohagh** and **Eagle** all service the Dhaka–Jessore route, and have bus counters on MK Road, just east of High Court Mor in Jessore. From Dhaka, you can catch Green Line or Shohagh buses at either Gabtali or Kalabagan bus counters. Green Line offers six departures per day on air-conditioned buses, coming from either Benapol or Khulna (from Jessore 09.00, 11.00, 12.00, 16.30, 17.00 and 23.30; Tk570). Shohagh also offers an air-conditioned service. Eagle buses are not as nice but they are cheaper (Tk520). The length of this trip depends on potential delays at the Goalundo–Aricha ferry crossing, but should take less than six hours and can sometimes be as short as five.

From Jessore's main bus stand, located east of the heart of the city, you can take direct buses to Kushtia (3hrs; Tk60), Khulna (1.5hrs; Tk35) or Benapol (1.5hrs; Tk37).

By train It is easier and faster to get to Jessore by public bus than it is by train, but it might be more comfortable, albeit much longer, to go by train to Dhaka (trains take a circuituous route across the Padma and Jamuna via special rail bridges). For overnight services to Dhaka on Sundarban Nishita, tickets are Tk1,060/625/625/420 for an air-conditioned sleeper/non air-conditioned sleeper/air-conditioned seat/non air-conditioned first class. If you prefer a scenic slow journey to Dhaka, there's also the Sundarban Provati. Ask a Bangla speaker to call the train station for you if you have queries on other fares. Many Khulna-bound trains depart through the day and night, at 03.05, 03.41, 09.55, 12.26, 15.15, 16.15 and 18.55.

WHERE TO STAY

Luxury

Panigram Resort and Spa (10 rooms, 10 bungalows still under construction at time of publication) 22km northwest of Jessore; e info@panigram.com; www.panigram.com. Though the Panigram Resort is still under development, it is positioning itself to be one of Bangladesh's premier resorts. Designed by an award-winning Bangladeshi architect to be a modern interpretation of Bangladeshi village architecture, the resort uses traditional, sustainable materials, such as mud & bamboo, but with all the modern amenities of a high-end resort found anywhere else in the world. Built at the intersection of two rivers, Panigram (literally 'water village') aims to give its guests a taste of Bangladeshi village life. Boat trips on the river, rickshaw & bicycle rides through the countryside, guided tours of local archaeological sites, & visits to a nearby pottery

TRAIN TIMETABLE

No	Destination	Train name	Off day	Dep time	Arr time
725	Dhaka	Sundarban Nishitha	Wednesday	21.25	05.50
763	Dhaka	Sundarban Provati	Monday	09.55	18.30
715	Rajshahi	Kapotaskha Provati	Wednesday	07.56	13.10
761	Rajshahi	Kapotaskha Godhuli	Monday	16.21	21.45
727	Nilphamari	Rupsha Express	None	09.06	19.05
747	Saidpur	Simanta Express	None	22.21	05.50
53	Benapol	Benapol Commuter	None	08.45	09.50

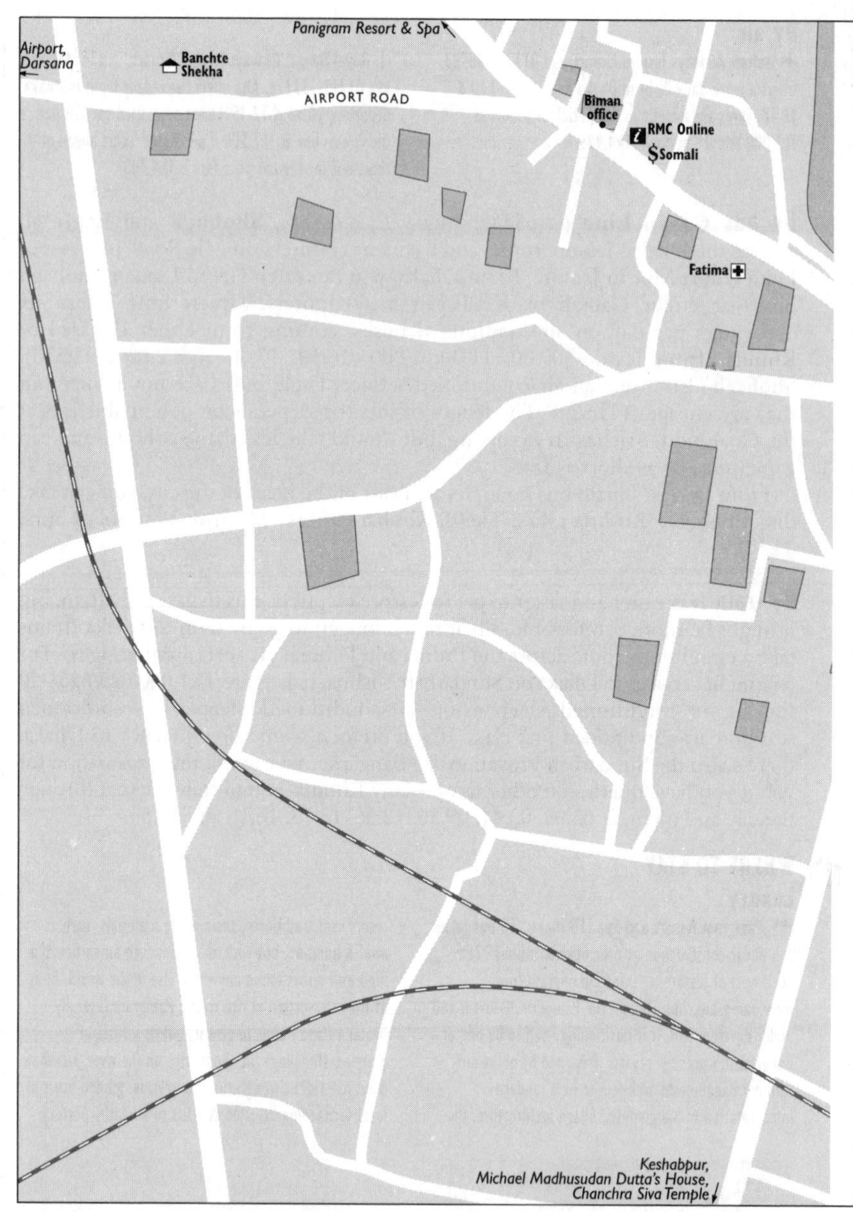

village are on offer. The resort is also committed to social responsibility, & will be partnering with local NGOs on various 'voluntourism' projects that will give guests the opportunity to reach out to the host community. The final resort will have 10 separate bungalows (Tk10,500–40,000), a guesthouse with 10 rooms (Tk4,500–10,000), restaurant, bar, spa, wellness centre, swimming pool, playground, tea house, hammock house, organic gardens & a small conference centre. With development & management by foreigners, expectations are high that Panigram will raise the bar for resorts in Bangladesh. The opening date has not currently been set, but conversations with the owner reveal that it may open on a limited basis as early as winter 2009. Check the website for further details. $$$$$$

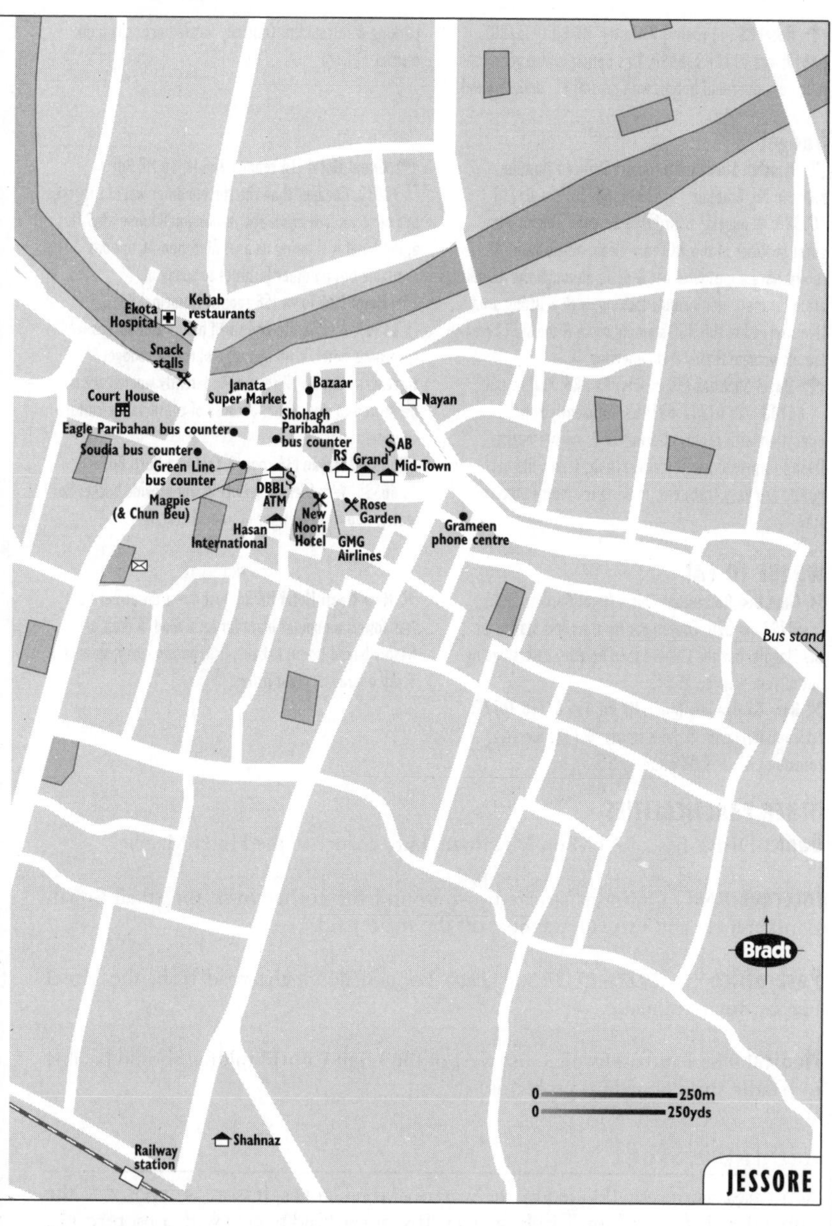

Mid-range

Hotel Hasan International (45 rooms) 15 Keshoblal Rd, Mikepotti; 67478, 65893; m 01712 110108; e hotel@bttb.net.bd. The newest of the upper-end hotels in town. Rooms are well furnished & comfortable, & there's a restaurant & business centre & also a conference facility. Service is sometimes an issue here. $$$

Hotel Magpie (34 rooms) Chitra More, Garikhana Rd; 68772–3; m 01711 365079; e hotelmagpie@yahoo.com. With AC rooms, satellite TV & restaurant, this hotel is a good choice & steep discounts are offered on request. Competition in the area is stiff. $$$

Hotel RS (44 rooms) RS Tower, MK Rd; 61881, 62617; m 01711 238556. This option is also good in terms of upper-end hotels, with central AC, underground parking & restaurant. Centrally located near the bank district. $$$

Budget

Banchte Shekha (16 rooms) Shaheed Mashiur Rahman Rd, Arabpur; 68885, 66436; m 01713 400388; e angela_bsjsr@yahoo.com. The on-site guest facilities of this NGO are clean, albeit basic. All rooms have a mosquito net & desk, although the AC dbls are a bit more comfortable looking, with a sitting area. Meals served in the NGO's dining room & the staff here are all women! Highly recommended. $$

Hotel Shahnaz (30 rooms) Rail Rd, Rail Bazaar; 66740; m 01712 631403. Efficiently run operation with rooms offering TV & private baths. Owing to proximity to train station, seems like its guests are very transient, making it a noisy place to stay. $$

Grand Hotel (14 rooms) 2nd Fl, 36 MK Rd; 73038. Cheaper than the surroundings would suggest, but once you see inside the rooms you'll know why. This aging hotel is showing its age. AC & non-AC options available but no other facilities to speak of. $

Hotel Mid-Town (58 rooms) Municipal Rd; 66501. A mosquito-coil smell hangs around this cavernous hotel. With its range of rooms, budget travellers will be well served. Apparently women are not permitted to stay alone, because of conservative culture considerations. $

Hotel Nayan (35 rooms) Kapuriya Purti Rd; 66535. Very friendly service & will provide bucket hot water. Rooms show signs of wear & tear. $

WHERE TO EAT

Chun Beu Restaurant Chitra More, Garikhana Rd; 68773 ext 220. Convenient for travellers staying at the Magpie, but the Chinese food here isn't worth going out of your way for. $$$

Rose Garden Jess Tower, MK Rd; m 01718 767298. Appropriately dark & quite empty. But the food is consistent & offers OK value. $$$

New Noori Hotel MK Rd. Just down the street from Jess Tower, a popular place for local food. A feast of freshly baked *naan*, kababs, fish, potato curry, spinach & *dal* offered at great prices. $$

OTHER PRACTICALITIES

Banks DBBL has an ATM on MK Road, kitty corner to the Hotel Magpie.

Internet RMC Online is situated just around the corner from the small Sonali Bank branch, and in a laneway just off the main road.

Post office (*10.00–15.00 Sun–Thu*) Located down the road from the Hotel Hassan International.

Medical The Fatima Hospital just west of the High Court building should be able to handle simple medical problems.

AROUND JESSORE

As an area constantly flooded by the waters of the Ganges, Jessore is exposed to the mineral-rich silts of India's holiest river. If you can find a local with a motorcycle, and hire them for a day, it would be the best way to explore this area.

NALDANGA HINDU TEMPLES Tucked away at the Kaliganj Upazilla in Jhenaidah district is a temple complex built in 1656 by Maharaj Indranarayan Debroy dedicated to the Hindu goddess of death and destruction, Kali. Locals say that the Kali idol here was brought all the way from Varanasi. After some restoration work in the 1980s some of the temples were later defaced by religious rioters, and today many of the temples at the complex are decaying. Kaliganj is located about 25km north of Jessore on the Kushtia–Jessore road. Catch a Jhenaidah-bound public bus and disembark at Kaliganj. From there ask a local rickshaw wallah to take you the rest of the 30-minute journey.

DARSANA (*Bangladesh–India train border, known as 'Gede' on the Indian side*) This remote village of the Chuadanga district hides a little-known secret. Bangladesh produces its own alcohol here, with labels that proudly state: 'Brewed in Bangladesh'. Very few have actually been to see the production facilities as the brews are extremely deadly if taken in large quantities. Rum, vodka, gin and whisky are your choices, but for a taste it might be a wonderful adventure to see Bangladesh's one and only liquor factory.

The Chuadanga district borders the Jhenaidah district, which lies to the northwest of Jessore. To get there, private transport is a must. Head north on the highway to Jhenaidah towards Kushtia, but turn left at Kaliganj after about 25km. From there, turn northward at Jibannagar. Now, start confirming with locals you are heading in the right direction by asking them the direction to Darsana. Expect to take a left turn at a few kilometres from Jibannagar. All in all, the journey should take two to three hours. A bicycle or motorcycle would be perfect for this sort of journey.

CHANCHRA SIVA TEMPLE One of the best examples of the 'composite style' of architecture that combines Hindu designs with the sloping-roof form of Bengali huts. Dating from 1696, the most beautiful aspect of this temple is the terracotta plaques decorating its outer walls. Finally, the main entrance of the east doorway has a rectangular frame with a curve, corresponding with the sloped roof.

The temple is not well known by locals. To get here you need to travel the Jessore–Khulna Highway for 2km until you see the connecting tarred road to Keshabpur. From there, start asking local villagers how to get there. You could also combine this trip with a visit to Michael Madhusudan Dutta's house.

MICHAEL MADHUSUDAN DUTTA'S HOUSE This famous poet (1824–73) was destined to live an eccentric life, despite his humble origins. Dutta was born in Sagardori, located on the outskirts of Jessore, and took the bulk of his education in Kolkata. During college he converted to Christianity and added 'Michael' to his name, and it was during this early period that the intellectual was recognised for his literary talent and poetry. Dutta also had a penchant for languages, learning English, Latin and Greek through his college education. In 1861, he wrote his most well-known literary work. In the words of Rabindranath Tagore, 'The Epic Meghnad-Badh is really a rare treasure in Bengali literature. Through his writings, the richness of Bengali literature has been proclaimed to the wide world.' In 1862, Dutta moved to Europe, spending time in both England and France, and eventually returned to Kolkata in 1867. A man of stormy passions, Dutta was not given to managing his health and financial affairs, and as a result he died quite prematurely in 1873. His grave is in Kolkata, but his headstone is embossed with the following poem, emblematic of his colourful life:

> Stop a while, traveller!
> Should Mother Bengal claim thee for her son.
> As a child takes repose on his mother's elysian lap,
> Even so here in the Long Home,
> On the bosom of the earth,
> Enjoys the sweet eternal sleep.

Poet Madhusudan of the Duttas

'SEPTEMBER ON JESSORE ROAD' BY ALLEN GINSBERG

Poet Allen Ginsberg was an American activist who penned many criticisms of his country's military decisions, especially the Vietnam War. During his travels in India he spent a period in Kolkata during the time of Bangladesh's Liberation War and later wrote a poem describing the intense misery of refugees that he personally witnessed on a visit to the camps. Several million fled for Kolkata during the Liberation War. While the poem's cadence strikes as little more than a nursery rhyme, its words still induce nausea and sadness. This is probably what Ginsberg intended, although what is less known is that he had planned to make the poem a song, which he later did.

Millions of babies watching the skies
Bellies swollen, with big round eyes
On Jessore Road–long bamboo huts
Noplace to shit but sand channel ruts

Millions of fathers in rain
Millions of mothers in pain
Millions of brothers in woe
Millions of sisters nowhere to go

One Million aunts are dying for bread
One Million uncles lamenting the dead
Grandfather millions homeless and sad
Grandmother millions silently mad

Millions of daughters walk in the mud
Millions of children wash in the flood
A Million girls vomit & groan
Millions of families hopeless alone

Millions of souls nineteenseventyone
homeless on Jessore road under grey sun
A million are dead, the million who can
Walk toward Calcutta from East Pakistan

Taxi September along Jessore Road
Oxcart skeletons drag charcoal load
past watery fields thru rain flood ruts
Dung cakes on treetrunks, plastic-roof huts

Wet processions Families walk
Stunted boys big heads don't talk
Look bony skulls & silent round eyes
Starving black angels in human disguise

Mother squats weeping & points to her sons
Standing thin legged like elderly nuns
small bodied hands to their mouths in prayer
Five months small food since they settled there

on one floor mat with small empty pot
Father lifts up his hands at their lot
Tears come to their mother's eye
Pain makes mother Maya cry

Two children together in palmroof shade
Stare at me no word is said
Rice ration, lentils one time a week
Milk powder for warweary infants meek

No vegetable money or work for the man
Rice lasts four days eat while they can
Then children starve three days in a row
and vomit their next food unless they eat slow.

On Jessore road Mother wept at my knees
Bengali tongue cried mister Please
Identity card torn up on the floor
Husband still waits at the camp office door

Baby at play I was washing the flood
Now they won't give us any more food
The pieces are here in my celluloid purse
Innocent baby play our death curse

Two policemen surrounded by thousands of boys
Crowded waiting their daily bread joys
Carry big whistles & long bamboo sticks
to whack them in line They play hungry tricks

Breaking the line and jumping in front
Into the circle sneaks one skinny runt
Two brothers dance forward on the mud stage
The guards blow their whistles & chase them in rage

Why are these infants massed in this place
Laughing in play & pushing for space
Why do they wait here so cheerful & dread
Why this is the House where they give children bread

The man in the bread door Cries & comes out
Thousands of boys and girls Take up his shout
Is it joy? is it prayer? "No more bread today"
Thousands of Children at once scream "Hooray!"

Run home to tents where elders await
Messenger children with bread from the state
No bread more today! & and no place to squat
Painful baby, sick shit he has got.

Malnutrition skulls thousands for months
Dysentery drains bowels all at once
Nurse shows disease card Enterostrep
Suspension is wanting or else chlorostrep

Refugee camps in hospital shacks
Newborn lay naked on mother's thin laps
Monkeysized week old Rheumatic babe eye
Gastoenteritis Blood Poison thousands must die

September Jessore Road rickshaw
50,000 souls in one camp I saw
Rows of bamboo huts in the flood
Open drains, & wet families waiting for food

Border trucks flooded, food cant get past,
American Angel machine please come fast!
Where is Ambassador Bunker today?
Are his Helios machinegunning children at play?

Where are the helicopters of U.S. AID?
Smuggling dope in Bangkok's green shade.
Where is America's Air Force of Light?
Bombing North Laos all day and all night?

Where are the President's Armies of Gold?
Billionaire Navies merciful Bold?
Bringing us medicine food and relief?
Napalming North Viet Nam and causing more grief?

Where are our tears? Who weeps for the pain?
Where can these families go in the rain?
Jessore Road's children close their big eyes
Where will we sleep when Our Father dies?

Whom shall we pray to for rice and for care?
Who can bring bread to this shit flood foul'd lair?
Millions of children alone in the rain!
Millions of children weeping in pain!

Ring O ye tongues of the world for their woe
Ring out ye voices for Love we don't know
Ring out ye bells of electrical pain
Ring in the conscious of America brain

How many children are we who are lost
Whose are these daughters we see turn to ghost?
What are our souls that we have lost care?
Ring out ye musics and weep if you dare–

Cries in the mud by the thatch'd house sand drain
Sleeps in huge pipes in the wet shit-field rain
waits by the pump well, Woe to the world!
whose children still starve in their mother's arms curled.

Is this what I did to myself in the past?
What shall I do Sunil Poet I asked?
Move on and leave them without any coins?
What should I care for the love of my loins?

What should we care for our cities and cars?
What shall we buy with our Food Stamps on Mars?
How many millions sit down in New York
& sup this night's table on bone & roast pork?

How many millions of beer cans are tossed
in Oceans of Mother? How much does She cost?
Cigar gasolines and asphalt car dreams
Stinking the world and dimming star beams–

Finish the war in your breast with a sigh
Come fast the tears in your own Human eye
Pity us millions of phantoms you see
Starved in Samsara on planet TV

How many millions of children die more
before our Good Mothers perceive the Great Lord?
How many good fathers pay tax to rebuild
Armed forces that boast the children they've killed?

How many souls walk through Maya in pain
How many babes in illusory pain?
How many families hollow eyed lost?
How many grandmothers turning to ghost?

How many loves who never get bread?
How many Aunts with holes in their head?
How many sisters skulls on the ground?
How many grandfathers make no more sound?

How many fathers in woe
How many sons nowhere to go?
How many daughters nothing to eat?
How many uncles with swollen sick feet?

Millions of babies in pain
Millions of mothers in rain
Millions of brothers in woe
Millions of children nowhere to go

Today, Dutta's house has been restored and is adorned with some of his possessions. Sagardori lies 8km southwest from Keshabpur, which is about 30km from Jessore through some beautiful countryside, about a one-hour drive.

BENAPOL/PETRAPOL

There isn't much to this border town except a couple of hotels, some warehouses and a fair amount of transport facilities. On the Bangladeshi side of the border, the name of the crossing is Benapol, and on the Indian side it is called Petrapol.

GETTING THERE AND AROUND

Border crossings Many travellers cross here into or out of Bangladesh. Previously a 'change of route permit' was required if entering Bangladesh by air and exiting by land, but this is no longer the case. The border is open every day 06.00–18.30, but the least busy time is in the middle of the day, from about 11.00.

From India Crossing into Bangladesh is fairly straightforward, although there can sometimes be crowds of people if you arrive when the major companies are processing their busloads of people. From Kolkata, **Green Line** (*9A Marquis St; ☎ 2252 0571*), **Shohagh** (*23 Marquis St; ☎ 2252 0757, 2252 0696; e shohagh12@sify.com*) (Rs250 to Petrapol and Tk675 from Benapol to Dhaka), **Shyamoli Paribahan** (*10 Marquis St; ☎ 2252 0693, 2252 0802*) (Rs250 to Petrapol and Tk600 to Dhaka) and **Soudia S Alam** (*23 Marquis St; ☎ 6536 4547, 3023 0679*) all have services to the border, but each one (except for Shyamoli Paribahan) requires a change of vehicle. Most of the buses depart in the morning but there are usually a few early afternoon departures. It is best if you book ahead. The bus offices are just east of the intersection of Marquis Street and Rafi Ahmed Kidwai Road, close to Kolkata's backpacker district on Sudder Street.

Immigration and customs on both sides are usually fast enough as they are typically more concerned with the busloads of Bangladeshis than they are with individual foreigners. Also note that you will find several people who want to 'help' you through customs in the hope that you will use them to change money or take their taxi, acting almost as if they are customs officials. Don't hand your passport over to anyone not behind a desk or wearing a uniform.

The nearest ATM is in Jessore but you will find plenty of people on both sides willing to change a small amount of money at indecent rates; ask around.

Some motorcycle riders have managed to cross here while others have been turned back on the whim of the customs officials on duty, regardless of any paperwork you have. Otherwise, a *carnet du passage en douane* is definitely required to take a motor vehicle across.

Once on the Bangladeshi side, the bus company offices are further up the road, as well as a United Airways office (twice-daily flights from Jessore to Dhaka are offered, which could be worthwhile if there is a special fare available, say Tk3,000 or less, otherwise Tk4,895). If you're carrying a lot of gear you'll find plenty of rickshaw vans waiting to take you to the nearest bus counters where you can catch onward transport. Otherwise public buses for Jessore (1.5hrs; Tk37) and Khulna (3hrs; Tk70) are available throughout the day.

From Bangladesh A Tk300 departure tax is levied on all travellers exiting Benapol; this must be paid first at a small shack inside the immigration office compound, which is on the left side of the road if coming from Jessore. All foreign passports are processed at a window in the arrivals side of the building.

Customs is on the right side of the road and must be cleared before departing Bangladesh.

WHERE TO STAY AND EAT

Parjatan Hotel (18 rooms) Main Rd, 2km from border crossing; ☎ 0421 75411. Definitely Benapol's nicest hotel. There is also a restaurant. Like all other Parjatan facilities, this place is overpriced & there are probably better-value choices in town, although this hotel, at 5 years old, is newer than most other Parjatan establishments. $$$

KUSHTIA

Nestled on the southern bank of a branch of the Padma River, this sizeable town might be called the cultural home of Bengalis for two reasons. The first is that Kushtia is the location of the final resting place of Lalon Shah, whose teachings, spirituality and philosophy carry great importance among Bengalis regardless of religion, class or country. The second reason is to pay a visit to Rabindranath Tagore's Kuthibari, where the Nobel laureate spent a number of years writing his finest poems and stories, some of which were heavily influenced by the humanist philosophies of Lalon Shah and his Baul followers.

Every year there are also two multi-day folk music festivals held on the grounds near Lalon Shah's *mazar* (gravesite). For a few days before and after 16 October, hundreds of Baul people gather to commemorate Shah's death anniversary every year, an event that attracts thousands of people. On the occasion of Dol Purnima, whose dates change every year, hundreds of followers do the same thing.

GETTING THERE

By bus From Dhaka, three bus lines service Kushtia directly. The best of the three is the **SB Super Deluxe bus line** which departs from Kallyanpur/Gabtali in Dhaka (m *01199 340748*), with departures at 08.00, 09.30, 12.00, 14.00, 15.30, 17.00, 20.00 and from Kushtia's Dhaka bus stand at 07.30 and 10.00, and then every two hours thereafter until 20.00 (Tk280). Despite the super name, the line doesn't offer an air-conditioned service but has comfortable enough buses to do the six-hour ride without much trouble. Booking isn't necessary unless you're trying to get to the Lalon festivals, in which case you should show up at least an hour earlier than the time you hope to go. **Hanif Enterprise** (m *01713 402660*) offer an hourly service from 05.45 to 23.00 (Tk280) and **Shyamoli Paribahan** (m *01711 942709*) also service the route hourly from 05.15 to 22.45(Tk250).

By train Kushtia does not lie on the major rail routes, save for one that connects Rajshahi and the Goalando ferry ghat. The Madhumati Express passes through on its way to Goalando at about 09.00 and returns to Rajshahi via Kushtia at about 18.00.

GETTING AROUND Kushtia is fairly spread out but you'll find no shortage of rickshaws and rickshaw vans to shuttle you around. A van is usually just a bit more expensive (depending on the number of passengers) but the normal Tk1 per minute usually applies.

TOURIST INFORMATION AND TOUR OPERATORS

UBINIG Kushtia (*entrance at the tourist market just outside the entrance to Lalon Shah's mazar*) This organisation is unique among Bangladeshi NGOs in that it promotes holistic development and puts that into practice with its activities. Mostly, this

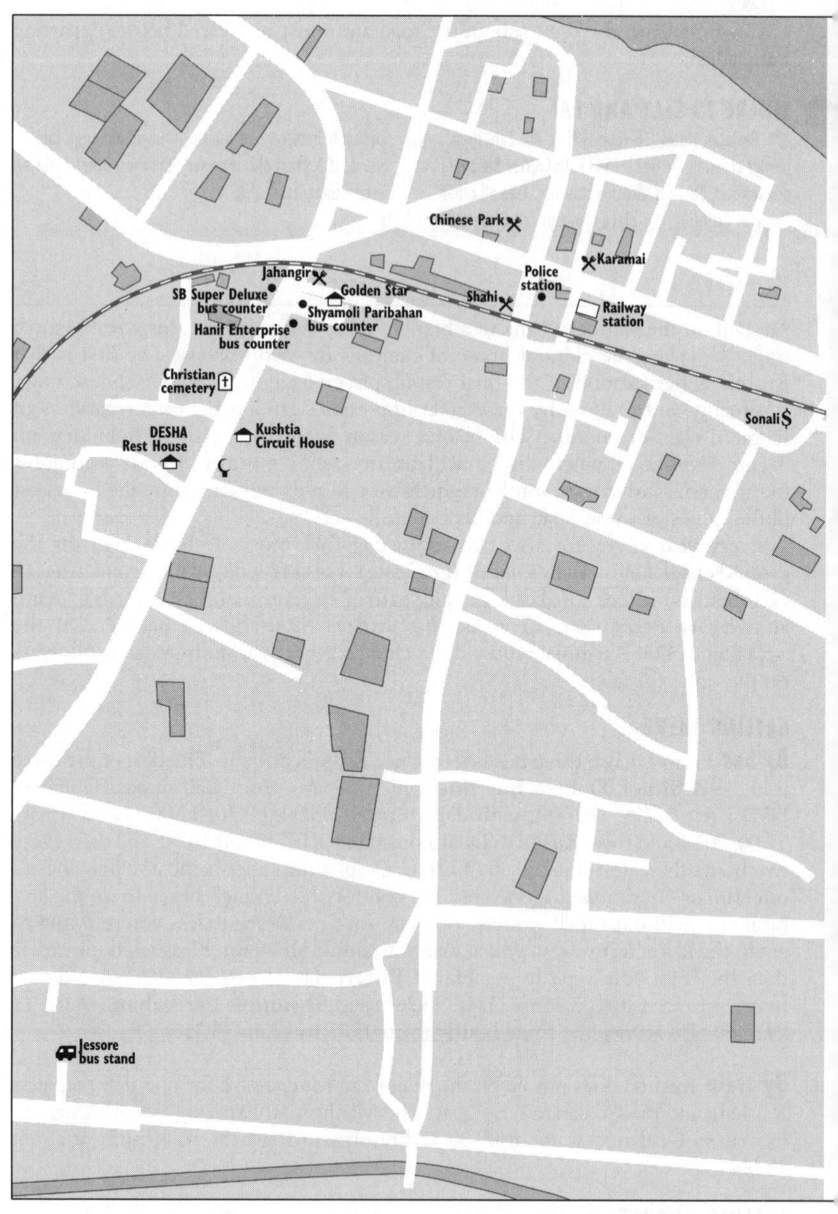

involves the empowerment of the neglected parts of Bangladeshi society including women and farmers. UBINIG is the abbreviation of the organisation's Bengali name, Unnayan Bikalper Nitinirdharoni Gobeshona. In English, this translates into Policy Research Centre for Development Alternatives.

At Kushtia, UBINIG works through its partners to promote organic farming and holistic lifestyle. Many of its publicised materials shun development as the West has defined it; instead it tries to promote and refine indigenous farming practices that have lasted for thousands of years. In a sense, the organisation's

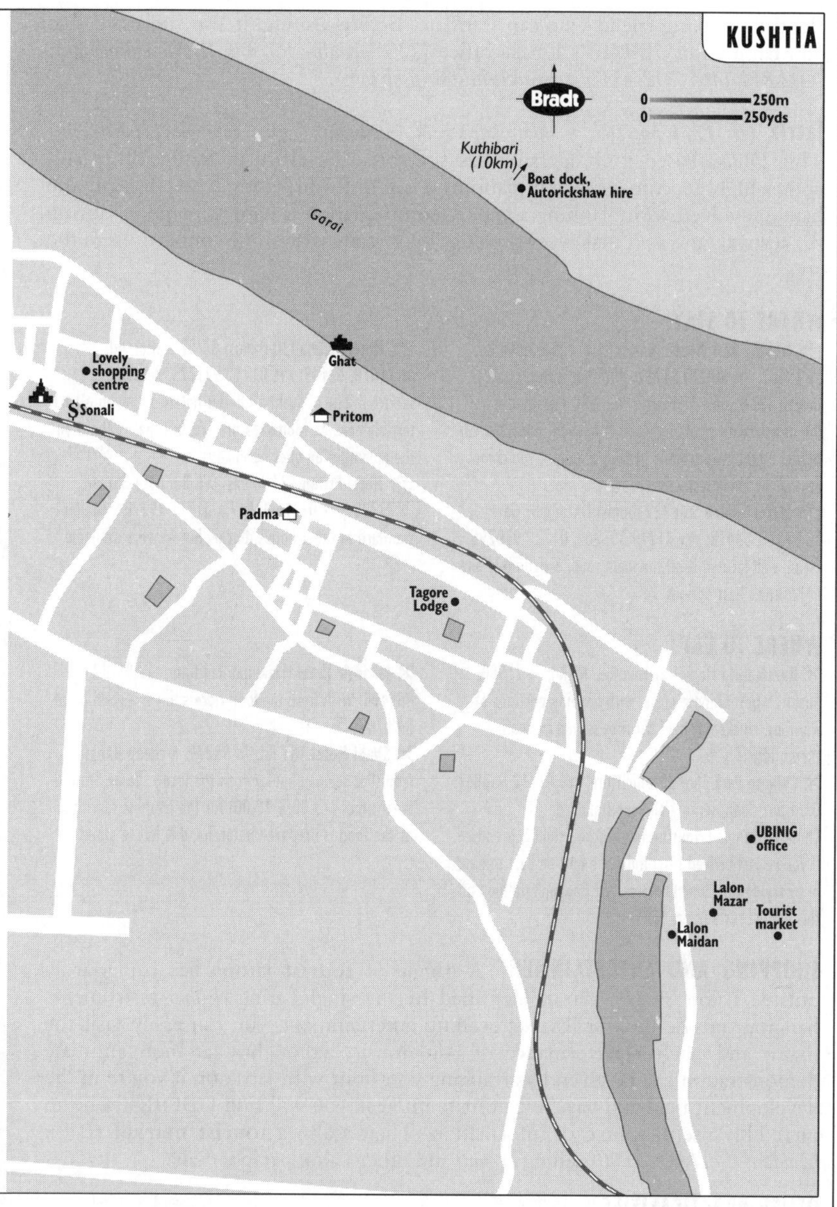

activities are really the embodiment of what Lalon Shah espoused in his songs and poetry. Today there is a small guesthouse at the UBINIG facility and you can visit their seed bank to learn more. The organisation also hosts evening music sessions so if you drop by during the day and express a genuine interest in Baul subculture, you may be invited to listen to the music later in the evening – definitely a unique experience.

Unfortunately, not much English is spoken locally here, so if you want to learn the inside story of this unique subculture of Bangladesh, you'd best bring a

Bengali-speaking friend who can translate. Before visiting, it also suggested that you liaise with UBINIG's Dhaka office (*22/13 Khiljee Rd, Blk B, Mohammadpur;* ☎ *02 811 1465, 812 4533;* e *nayakrishi@siriusbb.com*).

Jatrik (m *1711 546765;* e *info@jatrik.com, jatriktours@gmail.com; www.jatrik.com*) This Dhaka-based tour operator has some real expertise in Baul culture and comes highly recommended if planning a trip to Kushtia, simply to eliminate the hassle involved with planning a trip. Accommodation is hard to come by during the festivals and so it makes sense to use a company with some connections in the area.

WHERE TO STAY

DESHA Rest House (6 rooms) 317 Jhenaidah Rd; ☎ 73402; m 01720 51212. With hot water, clean sheets, TVs & some AC rooms, this NGO guesthouse has the nicest facilities of any place in Kushtia. But it's small so you might have trouble getting a room if you come during the Lalon festivals. $$$

Hotel Golden Star (29 rooms) Mazampur Gate; ☎ 61675, 54418; m 01719 305264, 01722 930295. Clean, well located & off the main road, & definitely one of Kushtia's best options. $$

Hotel Padma (30 rooms) 86/57 Station Rd; ☎ 71678, 62143; m 01712 921223. Reasonable service in one of Kushtia's better hotels, although it isn't terribly new. AC rooms feature TVs, but that is about all the amenities on offer here. $$

Hotel Pritom (31 rooms) SCB Rd, Boro Bazaar; ☎ 73798; m 01716 418175, 01711 352704. Similar standard as other hotels, bucket hot water is available. $$

WHERE TO EAT

Karamai Ma Mony Supermarket, NS Rd; ☎ 71580. Kushtia's best Chinese place, with heaping portions of wontons, chicken or beef stir fries served in clean surrounds. $$$

Chinese Park Thana Traffic More; m 01712 568861. Dark but clean, serving all your standard Chinese–Bangla favourites like chicken chilli & fried rice. If you've just arrived from India it might be best to ease in by trying out some Chinese-style Bangladeshi food at this hidden restaurant. $$

Jahangir Hotel Mazampu Rail Gate; m 01712 469494. With fresh tandoori *naans* this is a good place for b/fast. $

Shahi Hotel T&T Rd; ☎ 55279. A cheap Bangla feed that seems popular with the locals. Come around meal times (13.00 & 19.00) for the freshest servings, as the food is prepared beforehand & left to stand. $

SHOPPING AND ENTERTAINMENT A gaggle of **tourist shops** lies haphazardly outside Lalon Shah's Mazar, identified by the single-string *ek-tara* instruments hanging outside their stalls. For evening entertainment, you can easily visit the mazar and catch a performance of Baul music, although a far more intimate demonstration can be given by arranging your tour with Jatrik or, if you're in the development field and have a legitimate interest, you will find UBINIG to be an incredibly useful source of information. There's also a **tourist market** (*Lalon Maidan;* ⏱ *11.00–20.00*) selling *ek-tara* and other Lalon paraphernalia.

OTHER PRACTICALITIES

Banks There are no ATMs in Kushtia, with the nearest being at Jessore. Money can be exchanged at the Sonali Bank on Kushtia's main road.

Medical Unfortunately, there aren't many decent medical facilities in Kushtia. Serious emergencies should be transferred to Dhaka or nearby Jessore. Be aware that some of the Lalon Shah festival visitors may be smoking marijuana, and thus you should be aware of your own safety at all times. Some female visitors of the festival have also been victims of harassment after dark.

WHAT TO SEE

Lalon Utsab (*Held at the grounds outside Lalon Shah's mazar, mid-March and mid-October every year*) Lalon Shah is the patron saint of Bangladesh's Baul people, a group of singing, marijuana-smoking bards who espouse a love of the land while shunning the mainstream. Twice a year, they gather to celebrate their saint's birth and death. The larger of the two festivals is held in March (dates change from year to year), and commemorates the Baul poet's birthday in 1776; the second is held during Lalon's death anniversary, usually between 16 October and 19 October. Lalon holds a special place in Bengali culture, in that the secular and humanist philosophies in his songs largely reflect the tolerant mindset of most Bangladeshi people, regardless of religion.

Tagore Lodge (*Main Rd*) The unmistakable pink building just up the street from the Padma Hotel is also a former residence of Rabrindranath Tagore. The outer fence of this residence is decorated with his poems. Tagore probably spent more time at his Kuthibari country house.

Kuthibari (*🕘 09.00–16.00 but closes for prayer on Fri & for lunch every day; entry Tk100, additional Tk250 for transport*) When Rabindranath Tagore came to Bangladesh in 1880, he did not depart for over ten years. In the spirit of 1906's Bengali nationalism, he penned *Amar Sonar Bangla*, one year after the first partition of Bengal. The song later became Bangladesh's national anthem. Tagore's list of achievements is long, and at Kuthibari you can see some of the vistas that inspired him.

You can picture Tagore observing the local life from his houseboat and then writing his impressions. Simultaneously, his *zamindar* duties required him to make important tax decisions that would directly affect people's lives. And so his writings were inspired by some dramatic stories of love and loss.

Today, Kuthibari is his home, and quite a wonderful adventure to get to. First you cross the Gorai River by passenger ferry, sometimes with dozens of other people. Then you arrive at the opposite bank, and clamber onto a motorised *'nazaman'* (a noisy vehicle made from the parts of an irrigation pump) and then travel for 9km to reach Tagore's former home (Tk250 return journey if you take the whole vehicle but probably less if you negotiate). Rickshaws are also available but will add at least two hours to the journey – great if you're not in a hurry and certainly much cheaper. There used to be motorbikes but then they were taking all the business and so they were outlawed.

AROUND KUSHTIA

MUJIBNAGAR The home of Bangladesh's first government-in-absentia was located at this remote village of Kushtia district. When the Pakistanis began their murder spree at the advent of the Liberation War, what was left of Bangladesh's top political brass set up camp at Meherpur, which briefly became a base for radio broadcasts during the war until it was shelled out by the Pakistani army. This early incarnation of Bangladeshi radio would later become the Bangladesh Betar, or Radio Bangladesh.

Today there is a humble monument at Mujibnagar commemorating the founding of the government in exile. Like the ascending triangles of the National Martyrs' Monument, Bangladesh's gradual evolution to a standing position is represented by a series of slowly rising triangles. Fortunately the war only lasted nine months. Had Sheikh Mujib not returned from his imprisonment in Pakistan due to unforeseen circumstances, perhaps Mujibnagar would now have a different name.

No national highways lead to Meherpur, and so you may wish to arrange private transport if your political orientation is decidedly 'boat' (boat is the symbol of the Awami League) and you want to see this modern monument to Bangladesh's history. Because of its inaccessibility, you may want to include it as part of a larger tour of Kushtia by employing the services of a tour operator like Jatrik (see tourist information above); otherwise you may be able to hire a vehicle from one of the town's bigger hotels like the Padma or the Golden Star, usually between Tk2,000–3,000 per day.

BARISAL *Telephone code 0431*

The Barisal Division used to be a part of the Khulna, until it was given its own administrative control in the mid 1990s. Today, it is a bustling port town, through which many goods pass through *en route* to/from Dhaka on their way to destinations south and southwest from here. Despite the high river traffic there isn't much industry to speak of here, just a continuous movement of fruit, vegetables and fish onto and off from boat launches. The city is mostly built around the riverbank but spreads out as you move further away from the ghat.

Interestingly, there are far more rivers than roads in this area, and because of this travel can be arduous, but this provides the opportunity to enjoy the rural scenery surrounding Barisal, some of which is the most lush and pretty in Bangladesh.

GETTING THERE AND AWAY

By boat Launches are easily the best way to come to/from Barisal, as you have the option of travelling in any direction depending on where you're headed, plus the benefit of sleeping on board the boat while you travel. Schedules are prone to change because of bad weather or the fact that launches are sometimes parked for repairs. Contact the Bangladesh Inland Water Transport Corporation (BIWTC) (enquire at the Barisal launch ghat) to confirm.

To Dhaka There are four regular daily launch services from Dhaka's Sadarghat terminal. Advance tickets for cabins are not normally required if you show up at least one hour before the boat's departure. During the Eid holidays, tickets become scarce as boat operators try to make as much money as possible from local travellers trying to get home for the holidays. Launches typically leave in the evening between 17.30 and 20.00 and cost Tk250–400 for a single room (not always available) or Tk600–800 for a bed in a double room (you may get a room mate, but this is perfect if travelling in a pair). Cabins usually come with fresh bedding, fans, power outlets and even a television. A few of the private launches have a 'suite room' with private balcony and bathroom for Tk1,500 and up.

Otherwise you can also try catching the rocket's daily service to/from Barisal, which will have a similar cost to the private launches, leaving at 18.30 each day. But without prior booking you may not be able to get a cabin. Deck class usually costs under Tk100, which might be fun if you're a nocturnal person or don't mind crashing on a boat deck. Rockets are also available to Khulna and Mongla four times per week on Monday, Tuesday, Thursday and Friday at 06.00 (14hrs for Khulna; 12hrs for Mongla).

To Chittagong and Hatiya There is also a weekly service every Friday from Barisal to Chittagong, with stops at Hatiya and Sandwip islands along the way. A berth in a double cabin costs Tk1,200 per person. This long but picturesque journey (22hrs) would certainly be less arduous for travellers seeking the scenic way to reach Bangladesh's southeast directly from Sundarban.

By air **United Airways** (*47 Sadar Rd, opposite Ali International Hotel;* m *01713 365095, 01713 365097*) is the only operator serving Barisal, although every airline changes its flight schedules frequently. At the time of research, they flew three times per week on Sunday, Tuesday and Thursday, departing Dhaka at 14.20 and returning from Barisal at 15.30 (Tk4,495 one-way).

By bus No air-conditioned bus services are available for Barisal, and the journey to Dhaka is complicated by the Mawa–Kaorakandi ferry crossing, which takes two or three hours, perhaps longer during the dry season. The whole journey could take up to seven hours. With a comparably better safety record (but still far from perfect), launches are much more convenient and interesting. **Eagle Paribahan** (a local bus company) offers a regular service on chair coaches from 07.00 to 23.00 (6hrs, depending on ferry crossing time; Tk300).

GETTING AROUND Barisal is definitely a rickshaw-sized place, but if you're interested in exploring the local area you will find a baby taxi stand near the main bus terminal.

WHERE TO STAY

Hotel Athena International (40 rooms) Katpotty Rd; 65109, 65233; m 01712 261633. Barisal's newest option, offering rooms with AC, Western toilets & mosquito nets. A special VVIP room available for those who consider themselves *very very* important people.Parking space is tiny but available. $$$

Rose Valley VIP Guesthouse (3 rooms) 4th Flr, Rose Sky Bhaban, 42, C&B Rd; m 01711 359055. Clean rooms with attached bathrooms, all of which feature hot water & lots of light are the attracting feature of this tiny guesthouse, which is actually an apt converted into guestrooms. 3 varieties of rooms are available to suit different budgets, with the cheapest starting at Tk400. B/fast not inc. $$$

Hotel Ali International (38 rooms) Sadar Rd; 217 3103; m 01711 262201. An aging but old stalwart of Barisal. Bathrooms attached & AC rooms available. Rooms are smoky. $$

Hotel Huq International (28 rooms) Sadar Rd; 217 3750; m 01718 587698. Worse for wear, but probably the best of the budget places. $$

Hotel Imperial (29 rooms) KB Hemayet Uddin Rd; 64379, 64479; m 01711 585758. Now 12 years old but the rooms, most of which are attached bathroom with fans, are still in reasonable condition. $$

Hotel Paradise One International (35 rooms) Hospital Rd; 217 3069; m 01718 335104. Unforgettable green paint job, smoky rooms, balconies pleasant but could be noisy with traffic during the day. No parking here. $$

WHERE TO EAT

Best Food Garden Police Line Rd, near Zila School; 64721. Looks interesting, with Bangla–Chinese options. Dark plastic interiors make the décor of this place decidedly odd. Sgl & full portions available. $$$

Garden Inn Restora Alhaj Dr Sobahan Complex; m 01711 183488. Pretty good Bangladeshi food – that is, it's a little less heavy on the oil than in other places. $$$

Green Chilli Bogra Rd Mor; 65142. They say that they have *bhorta* (delicious mashed vegetables) available but ask before sitting down. $$$

The River Café Police Line Rd; 217 5714. Pizzas, salads, tandooris & kebabs served in Western fast-food surrounds. Not a bad spread – should be something for everybody. $$$

Yan Thai Chinese Restaurant Subho Plaza (1st Flr), East Bogra Rd, Barisal (just off Sadar Rd); m 01711 589185. Décor needs a serious upgrade but the people seem friendly & the food is standard Chinese–Bangla fare. $$$

Royal Coffee House Obiruchi Complex, Sadar Rd; 217 4675. 'Mini Chinese', which means noodles & fried rice, served in extremely dark surrounds. But maybe that's just what you want. $$

Royal Restaurant Obiruchi Complex, Sadar Rd; 217 4675. An older establishment that serves up a good *biriyani* in a reasonable portion (not too much), but a bit tucked away. $$

Shokal Sondar Sadar Rd. Tasty b/fast place on the main drag. Omelettes & *paratas* & thick *dal* served early in the morning, usually from 06.00. $

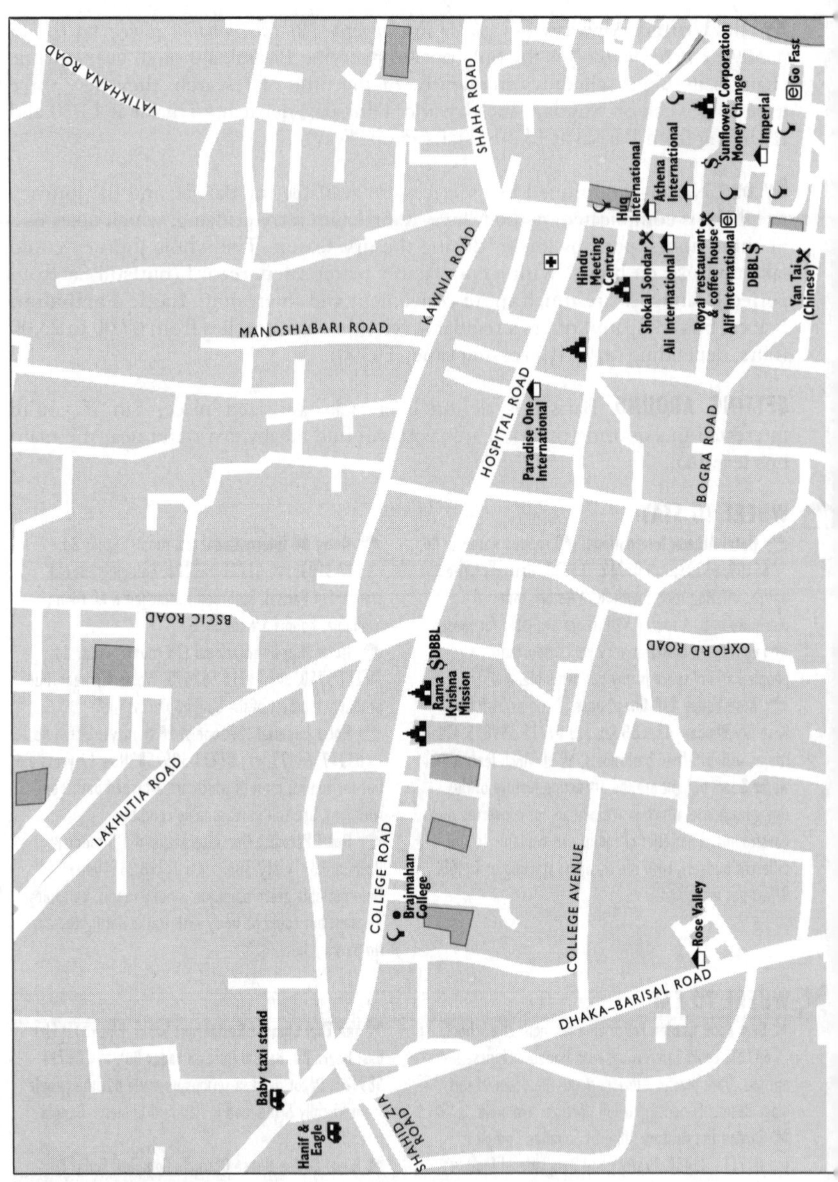

OTHER PRACTICALITIES

Banks DBBL ATMs are found in multiple locations on Sadar Road and Police Line Road. Cash can be exchanged at the Sonali Bank, also on Sadar Road. **Sunflower Corporation** (*Katpotty Rd*; ⌚ *11.00–20.00*) can change US dollars to taka if required.

Internet Plenty of cybercafés inhabit Sadar Road, Barisal's main street. You can try the services at the **Alif International** (*Sadar Rd*) or the aptly named **Go Fast Internet Café** (*Chowk Bazar Rd*). Both will run you Tk20 per hour of browsing.

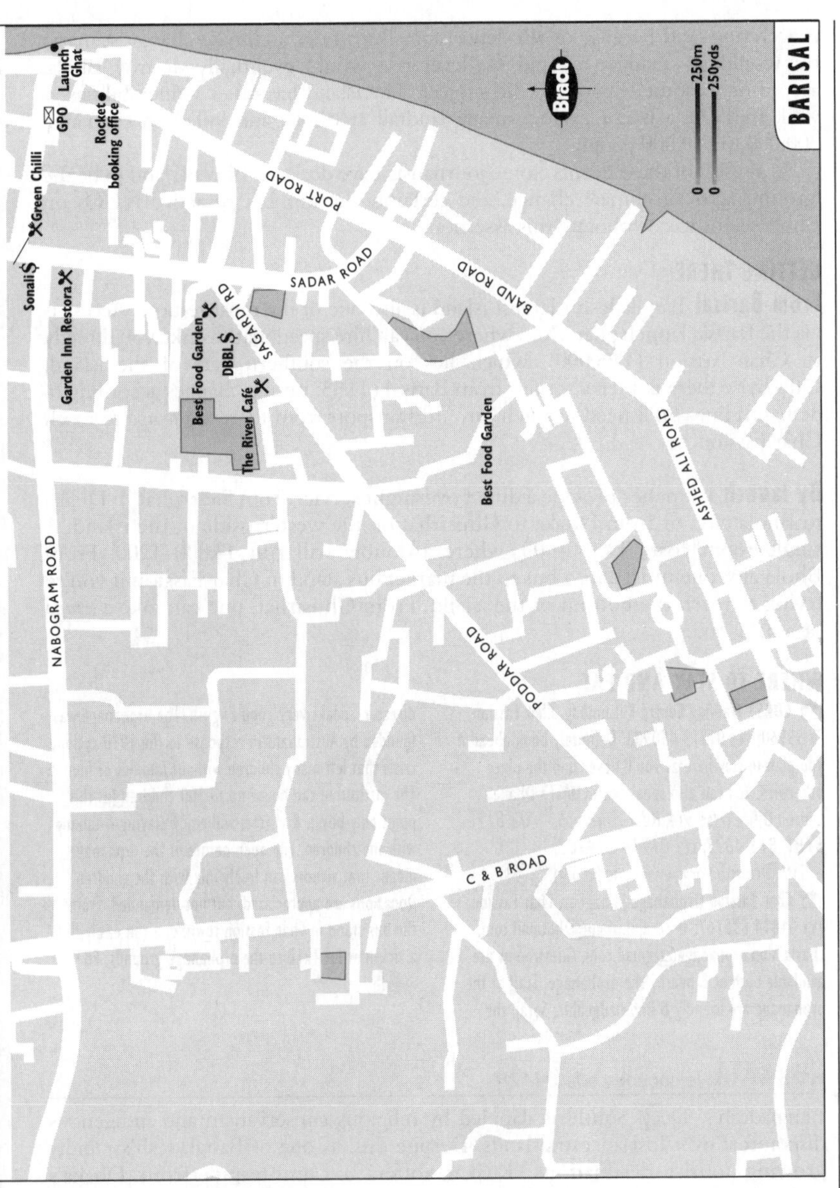

Medical At the north end of Sadar Road is a local hospital.

Post offices Barisal's post office is located in Fazlul Haque Road, near the launch ghat.

BHOLA ISLAND *Telephone code 0491*

Bangladesh's largest island lies squarely in the path of the Meghna River, which means that at one end it suffers from destructive river erosion while at the other it is accreting land because of silt deposition. But under a climate change scenario this could all change: a rapid sea-level rise would eventually destroy Bhola, according to some experts on the subject. The island has other vulnerabilities as well. In 1970, a major cyclone made landfall at Bhola, and killed an estimated 300,000 to 500,000 people.

As a result of these events, some journalists have declared Bhola Island to be the 'ground zero' of climate change, and certainly the number of active NGOs on Bhola seems to corroborate this assertion.

GETTING THERE

From Barisal Bangladesh's largest island is also one of the most remote. Access is via the Barisal launch ghat, from where you can hire speedboats to take you directly to Char Fassion (Tk5,000), which lies on the southern part of the island. Otherwise there is a ferry service from Barisal (Tk55; timing changes according to demand) but you'll need to catch onward transport from there via *tempo* to reach Char Fassion.

By launch Launches provide a direct overnight service from Sadarghat in Dhaka to Bhola city; or from Dhaka to Ghusirhat on the western side of the island. A single room costs Tk400-600, where a double will run Tk800–1200. From Bhola city, one must take a bus to the market bus stand in Char Fassion if you're trying to reach the bottom of the island. From Ghusirhat, one can take a *tempo* or a baby taxi.

WHERE TO STAY AND EAT

COAST Training Centre Kulsumbag, Char Fassion; 55960; m 01713 450983. Definitely book ahead if you plan to stay here as you'll never find the place otherwise. You can also speak with COAST's Dhaka Liaison Office (*Hse 9/4, Rd 2, Shyamoli;* *02 812 5181, 815 4673;* m *01714 014203,* e *info@coastbd.org; www.coastbd.org*). $$$

Char Fassion Orphanage Jinnaghar, Char Fassion; m 01814 636167; e serajul.islam@hotmail.com, charfassion.orphanage@gmail.com. Guestrooms are available both at & nearby the orphanage. Staff at the orphanage are friendly & knowledgeable; Seraj, the director, speaks very good English. The orphanage was founded by Australians in response to the 1970 cyclone crisis that left many children without families or homes. The institution can house up to 100 children (at this point only boys), & visitors will enjoy playing & talking with the children. The open nature of the orphanage means that visitors can freely mix with the children. Donations are appreciated, but not demanded. From the bus stand in Char Fassion town, one can easily find a rickshaw for Tk10 to the orphanage grounds. FB $$$

KUAKATA *Telephone code 04428*

Bangladesh's 'Deep South' is dappled by religious conservatism and indigenous discomfort over lost ancestral lands. Despite this, as one of Bangladesh's rapidly growing tourist destinations, Kuakata offers a calm respite from Dhaka's suffocating intensity, without the commercialisation of Cox's Bazaar.

Located 320km south of Dhaka and 70km south of Patuakhali, Kuakata is connected to the rest of the mainland by a series of river crossings. The dusty, laborious bus journey meanders through an increasingly rural landscape. As you journey southward, men from the modern workforce are slowly replaced by chickens, farmers and veiled women. It feels like an adventure in *The Wizard of Oz* where at the end of your journey you'll discover romance as you stroll hand-in-hand along an isolated beach. But like the movie, the romance must be inside because other local tourists are seizing the opportunity to watch the glistening light of a waking and setting sun play upon the ocean.

CYCLONE ORPHANS *Tiffany Hodge*

I have been travelling to Char Fassion, Bhola, since 2001, and I keep making my way back every few years. The Char Fassion Orphanage is my primary destination in this part of Bangladesh. The orphanage, built after the 1970 cyclone that killed hundreds of thousands in southern Bangladesh, was once run by Australians. Now the institution struggles financially, but the staff works hard to maintain it. Seraj, the director, grew up in the orphanage after his own father died and can advise the children on the basis of his personal experiences. I have had the chance to meet many of the children over the years, all with their own interesting personalities and stories. Despite the hardships they have endured, they are joyful, spirited, and friendly. Some of the children come to the orphanage when they are very young, perhaps six or seven, and stay until they are 16 or 17, when they have passed their metric exams.

The children are not adoptable, as might be the case in other countries. In Bangladesh, a child is considered an orphan if he or she has lost his or her father. Many of the boys in the Char Fassion orphanage lost their fathers in fishing accidents, as fishing is a major business in the Bay of Bengal. But despite the fact that one cannot adopt a child, the visit is always memorable. Those who are interested in the education of children in Bangladesh may enjoy the opportunity to learn more about the educational system and its challenges, and perhaps work with the children in their studies. Environmentally interested folks will have the opportunity to see the effects of climate change on a delta island community. Anyone interested in visiting the deltas of Bangladesh for any other reason will find a comfortable place to stay, and will be welcomed by a warm and friendly group of people who are intimately familiar with the region. The Char Fassion Orphanage offers one of the best opportunities to experience rural Bangladesh.

Locally known as Sagar Kannya (Daughter of the Sea), the long strip of dark, marbled sand stretches for about 30km. Although the main strip of beach is littered by deckchairs, motorbikes and touts promising adventure, we did manage a peaceful hand-in-hand walk along the warm foreshore waters.

Spat out as you are from Dhaka's disarray at Sadarghat, lazing on the launch for the overnight journey to Patuakhali is the way to begin your journey to Kuakata. Branded as the place 'where the sun meets the sea', Kuakata is veiled by an intriguing cultural diversity. Here the ocean breeze wisps away the heaving insanity of Bangladesh's bustling development and leaves you wishing you could stay longer.

GETTING THERE

By launch The best option to travel from Dhaka is the overnight launch departing daily in the evening from Sadarghat to Patuakhali. From the Patuakhali boat terminal, catch a ten-minute rickshaw ride to the bus stand and board a local rickety bus to Kuakata (about 3hrs). The Ruchita Hotel and Restaurant – about halfway between the boat and bus terminals – is a good place to stop for Bengali breakfast of chapatis and dhal before catching your bus.

Patuakhali launches

Sundarban Five Mr Mamun; m 01714 017272. Departs every other day at 18.15.

Sundarban Six Mr Raja; m 01712 151747. Departs every other day at 18.15. VIP cabin Tk1,500; regular cabin Tk600.

Shaikat Two Mr Anwar; m 01920 206813. Departs every other day at 17.45.

Shaikat One Mr Samsu; m 01710 620742. Departs every other day at 17.45. Regular dbl cabin Tk600; sgl Tk350.

The Sundarbans boats are slightly newer, but also more expensive. Alternatively you can catch an overnight bus from Dhaka, although it's debatable how much sleep you'll get.

WHERE TO STAY

Mid-range

Annando Bari Guest House (16 rooms) m 01711 006026. On the outskirts of town, serenely located adjacent to the mobile tower, you can't miss this hotel. Rooms are overpriced but large & the VIP room even has a carpet. $$$

Hotel Neelanjana (28 rooms) Opposite Rakhine Womens' Market; 56017–18; m 01712 927904. Clean & spacious but lacks character. A safe option if you want AC & a Western toilet. $$$

Hotel Sky Palace (31 rooms) 556026, 56027; m 01727 507479. A Bangladeshi attempt at luxury; at the time of writing the innards were still exposed, but completed rooms were bright & clean with a pleasant vista over a small lake. They also offer a small cottage on the beach. $$$

Kuakata Guest House (19 rooms) Main Rd; 56024; m 01719 589752. The outside is more inviting than the inside, but staff seem friendly & honest. $$$

Parjatan Holiday Homes (25 rooms) Main Rd; 56004. Resembling an aging prison hall, its exterior is far from welcoming, but rooms are clean with hot water & Western toilets. $$$

The Golden Palace (10 rooms) m 01711 441 622. From the beach junction; turn right, 1km down the road. For a moderately priced hotel near the beach this is a great option. Rooms are clean & staff very helpful; they'll even supply hot water on request. It's a quiet place to escape, bathe in the sun & enjoy life passing by from your balcony. $$$

The Village (2 rooms) West Kuakata beach; m 01711 623901, 01726 707154. Individual bungalows built in the style of the indigenous Rakhine community located in a secluded stretch of woodland 5mins from the beach. Western & local cuisine served. With Western management, this place won't remain a secret for long! $$$

Budget

Cottage Sweet Home (7 rooms) Embankment Rd; m 01722 061105. Garish & overpriced, but clean. $$

Hotel Al-Hera (12 rooms) m 01716 900403. Young touts will try & lure you into this hotel, just off the main road into town. The cold concrete floors & painfully pink walls are uninviting, as are the small bathrooms with squat toilets. If desperate, cheaper rooms are available downstairs & prices are negotiable if you arrive during the afternoon in low season. $$

Hotel Graver Inn International (15 rooms) Sea Beach, Kuakata; 56007; m 01718 230920. Clean & well-run hotel, although slightly overpriced. If you're willing to forgo a balcony & light, cheaper darker rooms are available on the ground floor. $$

Hotel Roney (6 rooms) Main Rd. Nasty but cheap, if that's what you like. $

Hotel Sagar (16 rooms) m 01716 762601. Good budget option with a friendly family feel. $

Hotel Sekander (4 rooms) m 01712 445487. Dark, hidden hotel on Kuakata's main strip. A dirt-cheap option. $

Hotel Sykat (12 rooms) Embankment Rd. A cheap option in the centre of town, if you don't mind mosquitoes. $

Hotel Symoon (4 rooms) Main Rd. At the time of writing the hotel was incomplete. $

Ryaj Hotel (4 rooms) Main Rd. A tin shack on the main road is Kuakata's rock-bottom hotel option: don't expect much. $

The White House (8 rooms) Main Rd. Far from the presidential palace, it's cheap but smelly. $

WHERE TO EAT

Khabar Ghar Pach (Food House 5) Located in a small lane just at the end of the highway road, near the beach. Despite its utilitarian name, it's the best restaurant choice of an unruly lot, on the basis of food quality & relative lack of oil. Come around meal times for the freshest offerings & if you're kind to the staff they might even be able to make fresh *chapatis* for you, or perhaps other dishes on request. $$

The main street in front of the Parjatan has a number of local restaurants, all of which seem to be serving the same oily stuff.

OTHER PRACTICALITIES

Banks No banks or ATMs are available in Kuakata, or nearby Patuakhali, so bring all the cash you need from Barisal or Dhaka. You can probably change money at the Parjatan if need be.

Medical There are no hospitals or clinics in Kuakata, so be careful if you decide to take a motorcycle for your explorations.

Media Bangladesh's alternative beach destination has an entire website devoted to it (*www.kuakata.info*). Check it out for the latest news and a few recommendations/ photos.

WHAT TO SEE

Gangamati On the eastern end of the beach is Gangamati, an evergreen mangrove forest and snippet of the original Kuakata. When the Rakhines settled in the area in 1784, Kuakata was part of the larger Sundarbans Forest. The Sundarbans is now a distant one hour by speedboat. As a mangrove forest, Gangamati, like the Sundarbans, offers some protection against tidal surges, but it too is being threatened by logging and deforestation.

The best way to reach the forest is by foot or by motorbike along the beach, where a fleet of flag-flying fishing boats can be seen trawling the coast. Choosing to visit Gangamati in the late afternoon is a perfect time to watch the sun cast shadows on the abstract exposed mangrove roots.

Rakhine villages The Rakhine community, like the forest, is becoming increasingly diminished, although its cultural influence remains. Kuakata takes its name from the Rakhine people: as *kua* means well and *kata* means to dig. It is said that the Rakhines dug a well when they first settled to supply drinking water. The small Buddhist community nestled within this conservative Islamic belt, which offers more than just religious variance. Traditional weaving and different grades of home-brewed rice wine produce a unique coastal spirit (you can ask for it by mentioning the words *gorom pani*, literally 'hot water'). Handicrafts are available at the Rakhine Mohila Market (Women's), where you can buy directly from indigenous women to ensure your contribution returns to the community.

Superficially, harmony appears to be brewing between the Bangladeshis and Rakhines. A government-funded temple is currently under construction, designed to replace the original Buddhist temple that was destroyed during the 1970 cyclone. The temple will house the locally renowned 80-year-old brass Buddha. The undercurrent however is that of developing tourism rather than cordial indigenous relations.

Less impressive aesthetically, the 21ft Buddha, housed in a rustic temple in Misripara, 6km northwest of Kuakata (as the crow flies), is a great excuse for an adventure. Hired motorbikes (with or without driver, Tk200 per hour) can take you along the dirt roads that pass paddy fields and villages, where fuel sticks, drying rice and the occasional cow compete for space. Friendly villagers will stop to chat and point you in the right direction, should you decide to drive yourself.

Fatra Char On a calm day, a visit to Fatra Char makes a wonderful excursion for the day. A jungle island lying on the extreme eastern rim of the Sundarbans, it takes about an hour by hired boat to reach. The Forestry Department has created an ideal picnic spot in a forest clearing where a freshwater pond offers a refreshing dip. As evening descends the visitor can hear howling jackals and the thrilling call of various jungle birds, although one must bear in mind the tides and the return journey.

Negotiating the hire price for a boat to Fatra Char can be a little tricky, especially for foreigners, so be prepared to bargain hard with the fishermen on the beach, having a figure of at least Tk500 in mind for the return journey.

Shopping Kuakata's Rakhine minority seems to be the most industrious when it comes to creating products for tourists. The clothing and textiles seem especially well made. At the **Rakhine Women's Market**, you'll find plenty of these goods and more. Inquire at the **Ma Than Shop** (*Shop 10, Rakhine Mohila Market;* **m** *01718 512573*) for some interesting background on the Rakhine roots of Kuakata.

Rajshahi Division

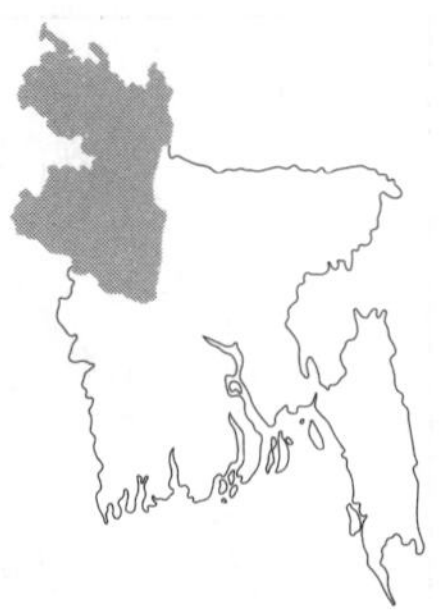

The Rajshahi Division is often referred to as Golden Bengal, and comprises Bangladesh's largest division. Overwhelmingly rural in character, the entire division is as flat as a pancake and possesses very little in the way of industrial development. On its eastern side runs the Jamuna River, the scene of much destruction and loss during bad flood years, and yet millions of people persist in living in the heart of its most flood-prone regions. To the north, the climate and the people are decidedly more chilled out, and these are some of the most tranquil places the country has to offer. The central and southern parts of the division hold a treasure trove of architectural wealth, although sadly many of these gems are slowly crumbling to pieces, their history poorly understood and undervalued by even Bangladeshi people. But the truth is that Rajshahi Division used to comprise the heart of Bengal, and several expansive kingdoms have ruled the surrounding regions from here. Despite the lack of maintenance, the architectural sites remain picturesque places to visit and explore especially if you know their history, and with more foreign visitor arrivals there will definitely be an increased need for preservation.

The entire division can be broken into three parts. The area comprising Rajshahi, Pabna, Natore and Shahjadpur can be loosely grouped together and if you want to taste the freshest mangoes on earth you'll want to spend some time in May or June here. Secondly, the monuments of Paharpur and Mahasthan are an easy day's travel from Bogra, which is also a great place to take a side trip on the Jamuna River. Finally, the far north region comprising Rangpur, Dinajpur and their surroundings are a destination all on their own. There are tea gardens tucked away in the northwest corner of the country, anthropological mysteries in the form of the India–Bangladesh enclaves, and even more opportunities to explore the *chars* of the Jamuna River.

While this division doesn't have the must-sees of the other regions, true Bangladesh adventurers know that Rajshahi holds the greatest number of surprises; experiences that, like hidden gems, only show themselves to those who endeavour to seek them out.

With regards to trip planning, be aware that Rajshahi is now far better connected to the rest of Bangladesh than it used to be, with the 1997 opening of the Jamuna Bridge. However, bus journeys can still be quite long, and so if you don't like the thought of sitting on a bus for several hours, consider taking an overnight train instead, which is especially useful for getting to the more remote parts of the region. While these journeys are also long, at least you can sleep and move around on the way to your destination – surely this is a way to enjoy the journey as opposed to suffering through it on a jittery public bus. (See *Chapter 3*, *Dhaka*, *Train timetable*, page 109, for more information.) Major destinations by train include Dinajpur, Rajshahi and Lalmonirhat. Finally, two-wheeled explorers will find the rural realms of Rajshahi to be a real paradise, especially up in the far northwest corner of the country where it is the least densely populated, and from where on clear days there are views of the Himalayas to be had.

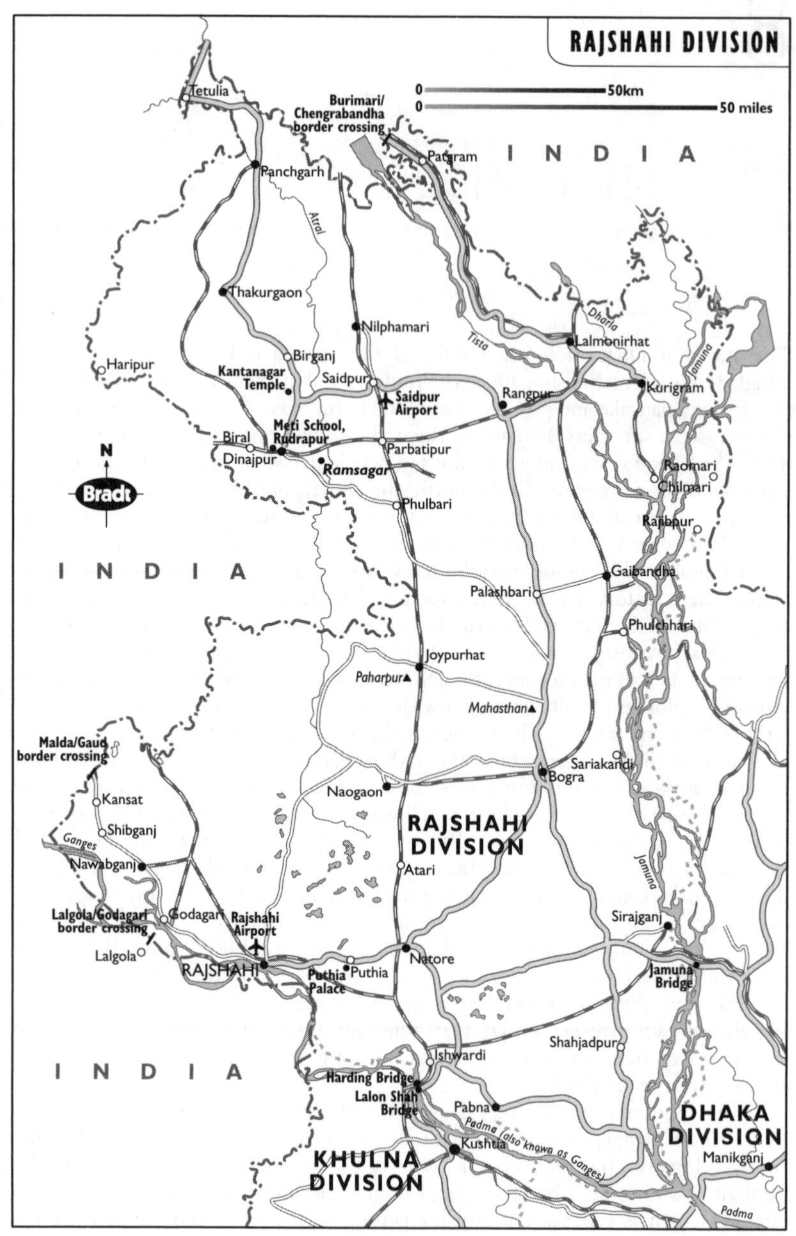

RAJSHAHI *Telephone code 0721*

With its tranquil avenues and predominance of rickshaws, Rajshahi is the kind of city you want to explore slowly. With only 700,000 people living here, the municipality captures the character of the rest of the division in the sense that it all feels so much less crowded here than everywhere else, a real respite from the frenetic nature of other Bangladeshi cities.

TRAIN TIMETABLE

No	Destination	Train name	Off day	Dep time	Arr time
754	Dhaka	Silkcity Express	Sunday	07.15	13.00
760	Dhaka	Padma Express	Tuesday	16.00	21.35
716	Khulna	Kapotaksha Godhuli	Wednesday	14.00	20.40
762	Khulna	Kapotaksha Provati	Monday	06.50	14.00
731	Nilphamari	Barendra Express	Friday	14.45	21.00
733	Chilahati	Titumir Express	None	06.30	13.40
756	Goalando	Madhumati Express	Wednesday	06.00	11.45

In terms of history, the city itself is a fairly modern invention. A few hundred years ago, the Ganges used to flow along the modern-day Hooghly River in West Bengal, towards Kolkata. But when it changed course, it began flowing along what is known as the Padma River in modern Bangladesh. This probably gave rise to the prosperity currently enjoyed by Rajshahi, but the written history of the city doesn't go back much further than the early 19th century.

Today, the number of educational institutions headquartered here is quite impressive, and Rajshahi has become a centre for higher education in the region. It is also a base for exploring the mango orchards and a few of the ancient temples of the Kingdom of Gaur.

GETTING THERE

By train From Dhaka, trains for Rajshahi depart from the Dhaka Cantonment Station north of Baridhara DOHS, including the Padma Express overnight service. (See *Chapter 3*, *Dhaka*, *Train timetable*, page 109, for more information.) You can also go to Jessore and Khulna via train, which is probably nicer than the stop-and-go public buses.

By bus **Green Line** (*across from the train station;* ☎ *812350;* m *01730 060050*) is the only major bus company that runs an air-conditioned service to Dhaka. There are three daily departures each way, at 07.00, 15.00 and 20.20 from Green Line's head office in Rajarbagh, arriving 20 minutes later at Kalabagan, and returning at 08.00, 15.00 and 23.00 from Rajshahi (Tk500). Otherwise if you head to Gabtali or Kallyanpur (Dhaka's northwest bus stations) you'll find buses departing regularly for Rajshahi (5–6hrs) with cheaper tickets.

For other destinations in Rajshahi, there are plenty of buses departing from the bus stand near the train station. Head there, announce your destination and the bus conductors will herd you onto the right bus. You might not be asked to pay or be given a ticket until the bus starts moving.

To India Two border crossings to India are available from Rajshahi, although no regular transport links are available to/from either; using them would thus be very time consuming and is therefore not recommended, but if you have your own vehicle and a *carnet* then you're probably the adventurous type who wants to know about such backwater border crossings anyway.

The first crossing is at Malda/Gaud, just a few hundred metres away from the Choto Sona Masjid. On the Bangladeshi side, the road runs right up to the border and a few trucks cross here occasionally. There is an immigration checkpost as well as customs, and foreigners can cross here as long as their visas have already been obtained. From Rajshahi, you would need to catch a public bus towards Chapai Nawabganj, and then potentially change buses to get to the border town at Bhola

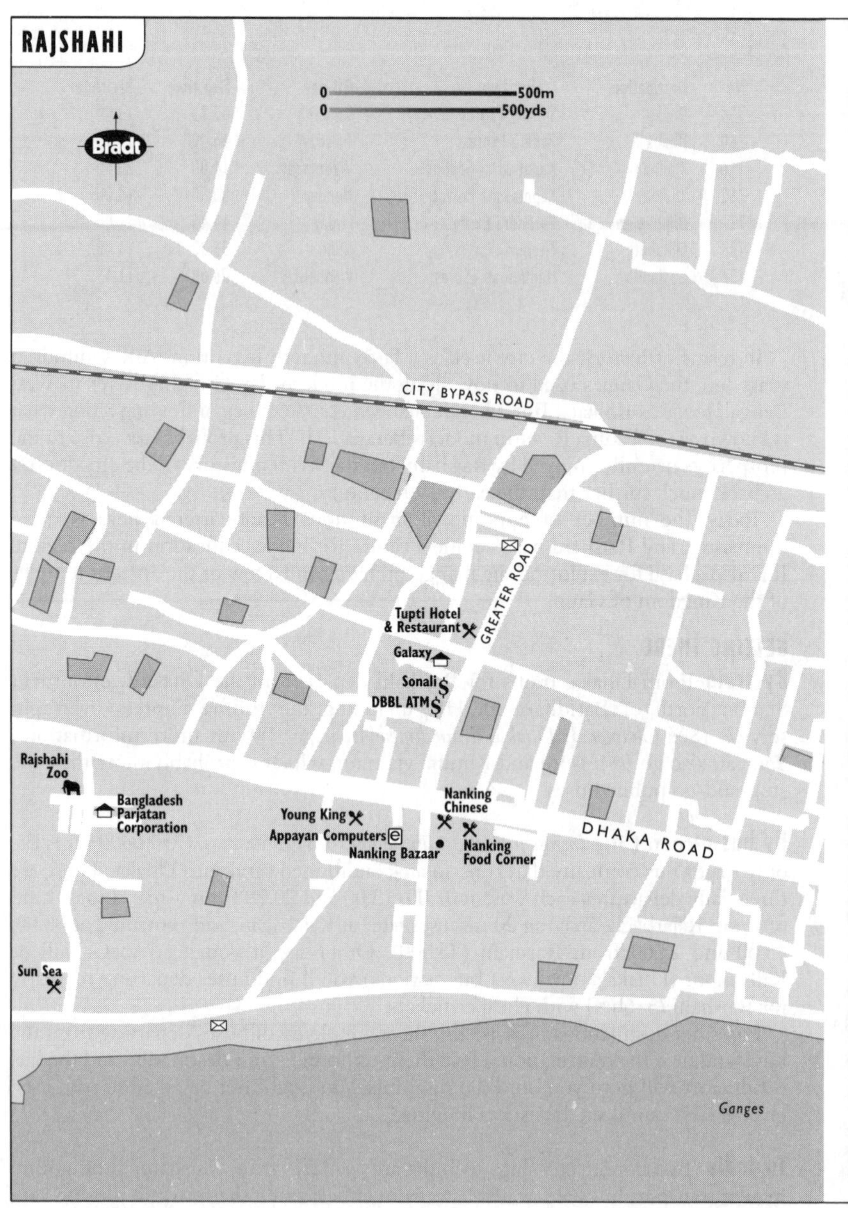

Hat. Once across, the town of Malda is about 14km away along a fairly broken road. There is no public transport or taxis available here so you may need to hitch a ride for your onward transport.

The other crossing is Lalgola/Godagari. First head to the town of Godagari where the border is quite well marked. Then you need to board a boat to cross the Padma if it's the wet season; during the dry season you may be able to walk across. On the Indian side, there is a train station, and the immigration and customs offices are nearby.

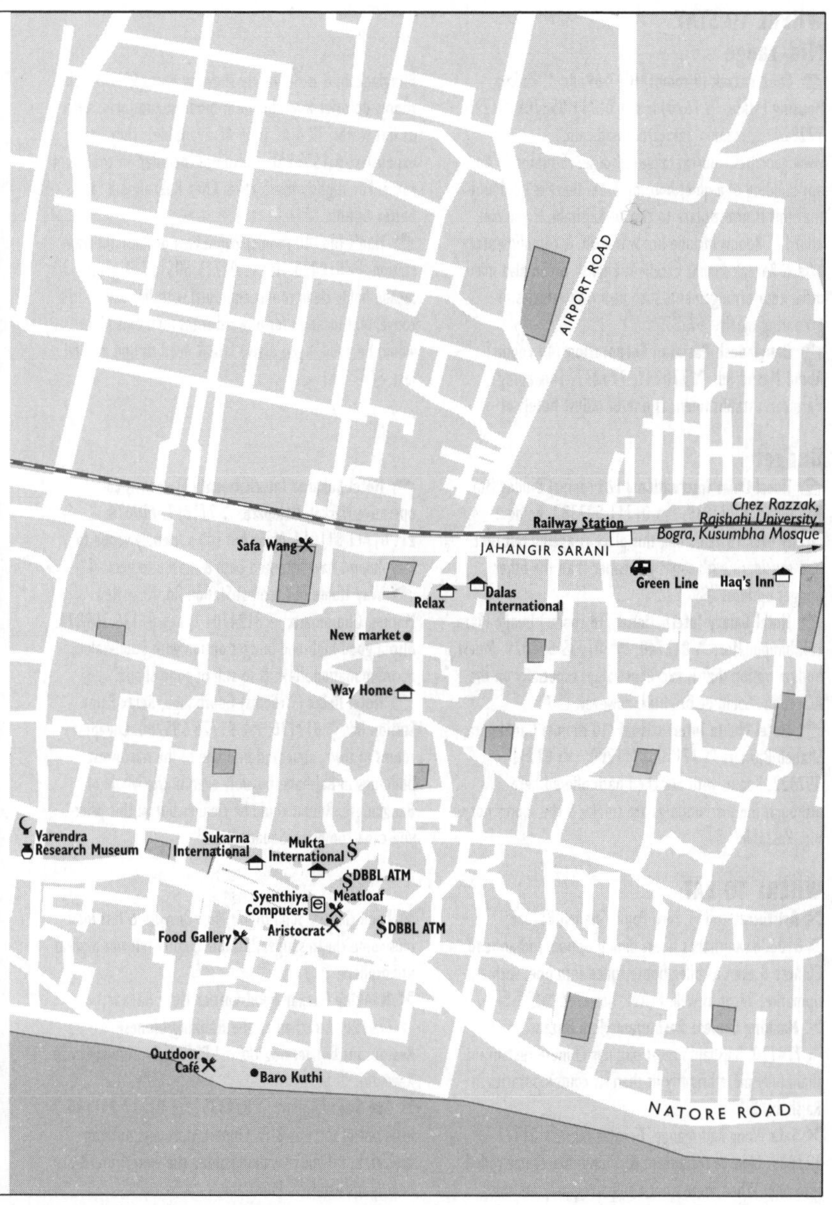

GETTING AROUND Rajshahi is mostly a rickshaw city. If you want to hire a vehicle for exploring nearby destinations you could enquire at Chez Razzak or Parjatan (see page 298 for contact details). The cost for this should be between Tk1,200 and Tk1,500 plus petrol.

TOUR OPERATORS Both the Parjatan and Razzak of Chez Razzak (see page 298) will be happy to answer your questions but you'll probably get better and more personal service at the latter.

WHERE TO STAY

Mid-range

Chez Razzak (9 rooms) Hse 169, Rd 4, Padma Housing Estate; ☎ 762011; m 01711 958708, 01715 772824; e razaak_rzk@hotmail.com; www.geocities.com/razzakguesthouse/. Situated in an apt building of a quiet housing area, there is no doubt that this is nicest place to stay in Rajshahi, if you can afford it. Rooms include hot water, AC & complimentary b/fast. Razzak speaks excellent English & can also make other tour arrangements such as hiring vehicles or preparing meals. $$$$

Bangladesh Parjatan Corporation (49 rooms) Abdul Masjid Rd; ☎ 770247, 775237. This aging Parjatan establishment is one of oldest hotels of Bangladesh, & is definitely showing its age. While the rooms do offer a modicum of modern comforts, such as hot water, TV & AC (non AC available), they are expensive. A 15% VAT is also not included in the room rates. For slightly more taka, Chez Razzak is a far better option. $$$

Haq's Inn (40 rooms) 200m east of Rajshahi train station; ☎ 810420–1; m 01715 605157. A giant glass façade holds clean rooms equipped with hot water, in a convenient location for onward transport. This place would be good if you arrive late & need to find a hotel fast. $$$

Budget

Hotel Dalas International (28 rooms) Bindur Mor, Rail Gate; ☎ 773839; m 01711 802387. Being a facility over 10 years old, this place is ageing but isn't bad considering it's slightly cheaper than the other budget options. $$

Hotel Galaxy International (36 rooms) Image Plaza, Lakshmipur Mor; ☎ 812740; m 01735 692029. A new budget option that is excellent value, especially on the AC rooms. Could be brighter, however. $$

Hotel Mukta International (40 rooms) Ganakpara, Shaheb Bazaar; ☎ 771100, 771200; m 01711 302322. Rooms with attached bath offered here although the surroundings are smoky & the rooms not so big. Passable. $$

Hotel Sukarna International (33 rooms) Co-operative Market, Malopara; ☎ 771817, 770670; m 01711 811014. Aging but still a friendly venue to stay. Rooms have attached bath & mosquito nets. $$

Way Home (44 rooms) Station Rd, Near New Market, Ghoramara; ☎ 812470–1; m 01135 209874. Also a good high-end budget option with good-value accommodation. New, & so still in good shape. $$

Hotel Relax (9 rooms) Gourhanga, Relax Point, Station Rd; ☎ 812170; m 01726 585280. Cheapest rooms in town, squeezed into one of the narrowest buildings in Rajshahi, possibly even in the whole of Bangladesh. Rooms could be cleaner but at this price you can't complain. Squat loos. $

WHERE TO EAT

Aristocrat 2nd Fl, Zero Point, Shaheb Bazaar; ☎ 810688. Rajshahi's finest dining option. Indian food, Chinese & even a coffee house rolled into one, with upmarket décor as well. Pricey, however. $$$$

Nanking Chinese Restaurant Moni Bazaar; ☎ 774120. Rajshahi's most popular Chinese restaurant, thankfully more brightly lit than its contemporaries in Rajshahi. $$$

Safa Wang Kadirgange, Greater Rd; m 01711 127009. Chinese restaurant & community centre rolled into one. When there's not a massive party on, this would be a good place for stomach-cooling fried rice. $$$

Young King Kazihata. Standard Chinese–Bangla cuisine, except this restaurant is even more dimly lit than usual. $$$

Food Gallery Sona Dighir Mor. *Biriyani* & fast food plus some cheap soups. Passable quality but not a great atmosphere. $$

Nanking Bazaar Food Corner Moni Bazaar; ☎ 774120. Attached to the Nanking Chinese Restaurant but serving *dosas*! Definitely a must-try in Rajshahi. $$

Sun Sea Islampur; ☎ 811335; m 01712 951740. A little out of the way & its Chinese cuisine is nothing special, but if you're walking along the waterfront & are nearby it's handy to know about. $$

Tupti Hotel and Restaurant Lakshmipur Mor; ☎ 811328. Quick & dirty but good for a fast b/fast & fried snacks. $

Outdoor café Riverside; ⌚ 12.00–20.00. An OK place to stop in for a quick drink or a snack while walking along the riverside.

ENTERTAINMENT AND NIGHTLIFE Alcohol can be purchased locally in Rajshahi, but you'll have to ask around as it's illegal for Bangladeshis to drink (but that doesn't always stop them). There are occasional rumours of alcohol smuggled across the border from India. Otherwise there isn't much in terms of nightly entertainment in this laid-back town.

SHOPPING

New Market (⌚ *11.00–20.00*) Bazaar atmosphere which might be handy if searching for random electronics, Rajshahi silk or housewares.

OTHER PRACTICALITIES

Banks DBBL ATMs are available in Rajshahi, and if you need to change cash you can do it at the Sonali Bank near Lakshmipur Mor.

Internet

Syenthiya Computers Near Zero Point, just behind Aristocrat Restaurant. Tiny little cybercafé with helpful staff.

Appayan Computers Around the corner from Nanking Chinese Restaurant. A little internet café with just a couple of computers, but friendly people.

Medical There's a hospital near the university campus, but the best nearby facility is the Khwaja Yunus Ali Medical College and Hospital at Sirajganj (*Enayetpur Sharif, Sirajganj; ☎ 0751 63761–3; m 01716 291681*). This hospital could probably handle serious emergencies a bit more competently.

Post office (*Greater Rd;* ⌚ *10.00–16.00*) Located on the west side of town.

WHAT TO SEE

Waterfront Rajshahi sits on a large swathe of riverbank near the Padma River. Many locals like to walk here during the early evening and take in the sunset. A barrage of food vendors and snack sellers come out at this time and the atmosphere is friendly and jovial. Walking along the embankment and taking in the views, or taking a local boat out onto the Padma, is a nice way to spend the afternoon.

Varendra Research Museum (⌚ *10.00–16.30 Sat–Wed, 14.30–17.00 Fri; entry free*) Definitely one of Bangladesh's best museums, with some excellent Hindu and Buddhist relics on display. Some of the moderately sized collection was excavated locally from the Paharpur and Mahastan archaeological sites, whereas other pieces come all the way from the ancient city of Mohenjo Daro in Pakistan. The museum's work is also tied to Rajshahi University, and is also an active research centre of Bengal's ancient history. Sadly, a lack of funding has prevented it from expanding its displays and increasing its research capacity. The museum's five galleries take just under one hour to explore.

Rajshahi University The Rajshahi University campus is airy and dispersed, and maintains an excellent and peaceful atmosphere, except when political activities are at their height, of course. At the **Martyrs' Memorial Museum** (*Shahid Smriti Sangraha Shala;* ⌚ *10.00–17.00 Sat–Thu, 15.00–17.00 Fri; entry free*) there is a small but decaying collection of mementoes from the war. Among them are some bloodstained uniforms and some of the weaponry used by the freedom fighters. There are also photographs of many martyrs who died during the war, but not much explanation either in English or in Bangla about who these slain heroes were. Nevertheless, the museum is worth a short visit to reflect on the country's past, especially if you won't be travelling through Dhaka to see the main Liberation War Museum.

Rajshahi Zoo (*Entrance opposite Parjatan Motel; ⌚ 11.00–17.00; entry Tk5*) A somewhat depressing experience given the condition of the animals and the size of the enclosures, but does offer some open space to walk in.

Baro Kuthi (*Near the waterfront*) You may not want to bother making the journey to see Baro Kuthi as it's just an aging building from the outside and bears little testament to its sordid past, but do take the time to learn a bit of interesting history: this sordid place used to be the scene of countless atrocities committed by angry *zamindars* against revolting villagers.

During the late 18th and early 19th centuries, the British made large investments in indigo, a plant which yields the rich purple colour seen in saris and other decorative clothing. The dye was known around the world, although the trade was hardly profitable for the farmers who grew it. They instead chose to focus their efforts on jute and rice, much to the dismay of some angry landlords who lost a fortune as a result. The landlords then turned to torture and murder to keep the indigo production going. Most of their gruesome work happened in the indigo production factories, and Baro Kuthi was one such place.

Towards the late 1850s, the increasing violence spread across all the indigo-growing districts, with resistance swelling from the peasants forced to grow that which would destroy their livelihoods. Eventually the government intervened and banned the production of indigo, destroying the trade in Bengal completely.

AROUND RAJSHAHI

SANTAL VILLAGES Several Santal villages dot the countryside around Rajshahi. If you fancy some anthropological explorations contact the modestly staffed office of Adivasi Unnayan Sangastha (*Ranidighi, Rajshahi Court Station Mor, City Bypass Rd; ☎ 770380*). Their activities mostly focus on advocacy for the Adivasi groups surrounding Rajshahi. Santal people possess slightly different facial features from typical Bengalis, and their villages, usually consisting of a few decorated mud houses, are fascinating to visit. In early March, the community holds the Baha Festival or flower festival, and this is an excellent time to pay a visit to see the traditional culture and dress on display.

KUSUMBHA MOSQUE This Jami mosque was constructed during the later sultanate period in 1558, under the reign of Ghiyasuddin Bahadur Shah I. Black basalt stone imported from Rajmahal in Bihar was used in the construction of this mosque, a characteristic shared by many other mosques in the region (eg: Chotta Sona Masjid). Ornately sculpted *mihrabs* depict grape plants, creepers, rosettes and other geometric designs in a style similar to the other mosques of the pre-Mughal period. The mosque is located 42km north of Rajshahi on the Rajshahi–Naogaon–Bogra road. Manda, the town 15km north of here, is accessible by public bus from Rajshahi.

BAGHA MOSQUE This mosque is another creation of Nusrat Shah, who, along with his father, was responsible for consolidating the borders of greater Bengal in the pre-Mughal period. Built in 1523, the mosque nearly fell into total disrepair but some restoration work has been done by the Department of Archaeology. Best of all, this monument is decorated with excellent specimens of terracotta art, depicting rich floral patterns with grapes and rosettes on several wall surfaces, but especially the *mihrab*. The mosque is located at Charghat, which is on the road between Rajshahi and Ishurdi, just under 20km from Rajshahi.

PUTHIA

Visitors to Rajshahi will definitely want to include a stop at Puthia, the home of some magnificent temples that lie just off the Rajshahi–Natore Highway. The town lies just 23km away from Rajshahi (16km from Natore), and so it is easily visited in a half-day trip from either city.

The Puthia estate originates from the early Mughal period when Emperor Jahangir gave the title of Raja to a subordinate named Nilambar during the early 17th century, which included a large area of land that comprises modern-day Puthia. The land was further subdivided among his descendants. Most of the construction visible today occurred under the watch of the Devi family during the 19th century, whose women demonstrated excellent administrative abilities in the management of the estate. Of note are Saratsundari Devi and her daughter-in-law Rani Hemanta Kumari Devi, both of whom were reputed philanthropists. The younger of the two was also responsible for the construction of several public works buildings in Rajshahi. Today, three buildings decorate the main archaeological site at Puthia, and the last, the Tahirpur Palace, is another 18km away.

GETTING THERE AND AROUND Puthia is easily accessible by public bus from Rajshahi's main bus terminal near the train station (Tk20; 30 mins), as the town lies directly on the Dhaka–Rajshahi Highway. Once you get off the bus, most locals will recognise you're here to see the temples and can point the way there. A rickshaw is not really required as the temples are located just a few hundred metres off the main road.

Accommodation options are few; it's simpler to head to Rajshahi (see page 298) for the overnight stay if needed.

WHAT TO SEE

Puthia Palace This dilapidated two-storey *rajbari* is now used as a college. Built in 1895 in Hemanta Kumari Devi, it is an imposing building with 13 dominating columns decorating its frontage. It's not always open to explore but if you ask around a caretaker should be able to open the gate that leads upstairs.

Govinda Temple This Hindu temple thankfully remains in excellent condition, and unlike the Kantajis Temple in Dinajpur, it still has all of its ornamental towers intact. Like the other buildings of the Puthia estate, this temple was also completed by the Devi women in 1895. Numerous terracotta plaques, depicting tableaux from the Hindu epics like the Radha–Krishna, decorate the face of this temple. Thankfully these are also in good shape and make this temple a must-see attraction of Rajshahi.

Siva Temple At the entrance to the estate lies the picturesque Siva Temple, which overlooks a pond of the estate. Constructed by Rani Bhuban Mohini in 1823, this temple differs from the Govinda Temple's terracotta decorations in that plaster was used to finish its face. It stands atop a raised plinth and its beehive-like towers give it an imposing and king-like appearance rarely seen amongst other temples of Bangladesh.

Jagaddhatri and Gopala temples Two more ornately decorated buildings lie 150m east of the Puthia Palace, and both are decorated with some beautiful terracotta designs depicting noteworthy scenes from Hindu epic stories such as the Ramayana. The hut-shaped **Gopala Temple** is small but the restoration work is extremely well done.

NATORE

Natore is located about 75km from Bogra and 40km from Rajshahi, and definitely warrants a stop for those interested in looking into Bangladesh's more recent history. During the British colonial period, this place was known as the Rajshahi Raj, and it served as a central administration point for one of the largest subdivisions under Mughal rule at nearby Murshidabad. Because this Raj was largely successful in its management, it earned the trust of Murshid Quli Khan, the Subhadar of Bengal from 1704–27. Thus it gave rise to the many buildings and *rajbaris* that survive from that period.

GETTING THERE Buses for the north and east leave from the eastern part of Natore (Bogra, 2hrs; Tk70; Pabna, 1.5hrs; Tk40), whereas those for Rajshahi leave from the west (1hr; Tk40). Pabna is also accessible from Natore (1.5hrs; Tk40). Natore is on the Saidpur–Khulna rail line, which means you can get to either place from here.

WHAT TO SEE

Uttara Gono Bhaban (*3km north of Natore Town area; ⌚ 10.00–16.00 Sat–Thu; permission required*) Also known as the Dighapatia Rajbari, this stately building is now one of the official residences for the President of Bangladesh. Its gardens, moat, frontages and furnishings have been kept in immaculate condition and allow visitors a living glimpse of what a *rajbari* lifestyle was like. Picture a Bangladeshi colonial version of *Lifestyles of the Rich and Famous*.

The *rajbari* was constructed by the resourceful Dayaram Roy, who began life as an orphan of unknown origin, but then rose through the ranks of the Natore Raj, eventually becoming its *dewan* (administrator and tax collector). After Dayaram led a small army in support of the nawab of Murshidabad, then capital of Bengal, his victory over an enemy *zamindar* gave him the capital he needed to build the estate. Apparently, this *rajbari* was also the scene of some very glamorous European-style dress-up parties.

At the time of research, permission was required to see the building, and this requires a lengthy process of chasing around paperwork. It should theoretically be possible to get the permission, but the problem is that few people seem to give a firm answer, hence this amazing building has remained hard to see for foreign travellers in the last few years. You may wish to contact a Dhaka tour operator to see what they can arrange. **Green Channel** (*Hse 11, Rd 1/A, Blk J, Banani, Dhaka;* ☎ *02 989 4479, 881 8557;* **m** *01730 012454;* **e** *info@greenchannelbd.com; www.greenchannelbd.org*) is suggested for this purpose. You're best to call at least one week in advance; longer is better.

Natore Rajbari Dating from the mid 1700s, this *rajbari* is actually a set of seven *rajbaris* spread around the former estate of Ramjivan Roy, and four of them remain largely intact. The prolific builder commissioned most of the buildings that make up the *rajbari* complex, and also designed the extensive orchards and gardens that decorate the grounds. Rani Bhabani, a philanthropic *zamindar* of Rajshahi during the colonial era, furthered the development of the complex. Nowadays, some of the buildings are used for Natore's district administration.

Two main blocks make up the complex, the *boro taraf* (big palace) and *chotto taraf* (little palace). The larger of the two has a wide frontage of over 30m, and a central porch supported by a series of Corinthian columns and semicircular arches. At the back another veranda is supported on 20 more pairs of columns, plus a set of stairs leading to the roof where views over the complex are good. *Chotto taraf* is a set of two more *rajbaris*, one of which is very beautiful and overlooks a pond. Inside, there's a unique reception area with high ceilings, crowned by a pyramid roof.

To find the Natore Rajbari, take the Natore–Bogra road, and 1km before reaching Uttara Gono Bhaban, turn left for a further 1.5km on an unmarked paved road that leads west.

Rani Bhawani Gardens Maybe the country's current female politicians could have learned a thing or two from Rani Bhawani (1716–95), the wife of the owner of the Natore Rajbari who came into the management of the estate after her husband died an early death. Rani was best known for her charity work, and with the help of Dayaram, the competent tax collector and administrator, she created many institutions and infrastructure for the greater good of the Rajshahi area. Today a garden in Natore bears her name; many visitors come here to take picnics. To get here, head to the Natore *thana* office (police station), go north and begin asking directions, or ask a rickshaw wallah to take you there.

Chalan Beel Numerous rivers and streams feed this massive inland marsh, making it a rich area for wildlife in Natore. During the monsoon the marsh rapidly expands and covers a massive area, but then during the winter dozens of migratory birds pass through here *en route* to southern destinations. Locals like to take picnics on boats during all seasons.

Getting there To reach the wetland, travel about 12km northward on the Natore–Naogaon Highway. You can take a public bus from the west station, near where the Rajshahi bus departs.

PABNA *Telephone code 0731*

Pabna's history flows much like the major rivers of Bangladesh – its fortunes have changed with the currents of economic trade.

Before the advent of the East India Company in Bengal, Pabna had not yet taken advantage of its location at the confluence of both the Ganges and the Brahmaputra rivers (their modern names in Bangladesh are the Padma and the Jamuna respectively). When the British arrived, they introduced roads and railways that brought the Pabna region into direct contact with industrial centres at Kolkata and the rest of the world. The jute, handloom weaving and hosiery industries did particularly well, and Pabna benefited greatly from the export trade opportunities and exposure to outside commerce, especially during the fading years of British colonial rule.

Bridges have also had a major impact on Pabna's history. The first was the impact of the Harding Bridge, a 1915 rail bridge that brought nearby Ishurdi into direct rail contact with Kolkata on the Kolkata–Assam route. The second bridge to change Pabna's fate was the Jamuna Bridge, completed in 1998. Previously, traffic to Rajshahi travelled through Pabna on its way from the ferry crossing at Nagarbari ghat, but with the construction of the Jamuna Bridge, Pabna is no longer on that route. In 2002, the Lalon Shah Bridge was completed, and runs alongside the Harding Rail Bridge, once again boosting Pabna's position in terms of connections to the rest of Bengal.

Pabna fabrics were particularly well known for their quality of the cotton weaving, and competed with the markets at Tangail in the production of high-quality textiles. But unfortunately these weavers suffered under the heavy import taxes levied on cotton goods from Bengal, as the British sought to sell their industrial-manufactured textiles in Bengal through unfair trade policies. Today some remnants of that industry remain in Pabna, although you'll have to shop hard to find the quality found in the good old days.

Today Pabna is a bustling town of almost half a million people, and it feels quite crowded at its heart. There are a few interesting historical sites here of interest to the slow-going traveller of Bangladesh, but those on a tight schedule will probably not want to veer off the main roads to include Pabna in their itinerary.

GETTING THERE AND AROUND From Dhaka, you can catch Pabna-bound coaches from the Mohona petrol pump near Mirpur 1's Technical Mor; costs are Tk240 for air conditioning and Tk300 for non air-conditioned coaches. The **Pabna Express Company** (m *01711 024088, 01712 834900*) has been recommended.

When departing from or arriving at Pabna during the day, buses are not permitted to come into the central city area. For that purpose you need to go to the new bus terminal near the Pabna Bypass Road. Before 08.00 and after 20.00 buses leave from Abdul Hamid Road in the heart of the city. It takes about 30 minutes to get to the new bus terminal from the centre of town.

Two bus services head to Jessore (Ashirbad; 08.20; 5hrs; Tk170) and Khulna (Mim; 06.45; 6hrs; Tk220) via Kushtia. Buses are also available to Rajshahi and Bogra.

Rickshaws are the primary mode of transport in town, but you may see a horse-driven cart (*ekka gari*) tooling around town.

TOURIST INFORMATION

UBINIG (*5/3 Barabo Mahanpur, Ring Rd, Shyamoli, Dhaka;* ☎ *02 811 1465;* m *01715 021898*) The Arshinagar Centre is in Ishwardi *thana* of Pabna district and promotes organic farming.

WHERE TO STAY

Hotel Shilton (25 rooms) Abdul Hamid Rd; ☎ 62009; m 01712 433249. Straight-up service at this hotel that does the basics right. AC rooms available $$

Prime Guest Hotel (26 rooms) Traffic Mor, Abdul Hamid Rd; ☎ 66901; m 01711 402677. Facilities include car parking & AC rooms. A bit noisy in the area but a reasonably clean place to stay. $$

Hotel Park (50 rooms) Abdul Hamid Rd; ☎ 64096. A little less friendly than its neighbours but also a bit cheaper. AC rooms available. $

WHERE TO EAT

Midnight Moon Chinese Restaurant Abdul Hamid Rd; ☎ 65787. Also offers a range of Bangla-fied Chinese dishes, but the Shagatam seems to get better reviews.

Shagatam Chinese Restaurant Rupkatha Rd; ☎ 64029, 65861. Your best choice for Chinese in Pabna. Has the prerequisite AC darkness. $$$

WHAT TO SEE

Jor Bangla Temple The 'twin-hut' style used at this temple is one of the few remaining specimens in all of Bangladesh. Like many Hindu temples of this period, the monument has a series of restored terracotta plaques decorating its façade, and is topped with twin sloping roofs that are quite pleasing to look at. Braja Mohan Krori, a sub-officer of the nawab of Bengal, started the construction during the mid 18th century, but before it was completed it was defiled and it always remained an abandoned shrine. The temple is located in the Dakshin Raghabpur area.

Arifpur Graveyard This graveyard is revered among local people as a symbol of peaceful co-existence between Muslims and Christians, as people of both religions are buried here. It's also a peaceful and tranquil place, and its headstones are a mixture of folk and Saracenic architecture. Ask a rickshaw wallah to take you to the Arifpur Gobhostan.

Ananda Gobinda Public Library This gleaming new building is a real standout among Pabna buildings. Constructed in 2002, it was built entirely through the donations of the Square Group, one of Bangladesh's largest pharmaceutical companies. The building has a small but interesting collection of English books along with a bigger collection of Bengali titles. The library is a good place to find people who are knowledgeable about Pabna, namely the Pabna.net staff

AROUND PABNA

CHATMOHAR SHAHI MASJID Located in the heart of the Chatmohar Bazaar in Pabna district, this mosque was restored in 1980 by the Department of Archaeology. An ancient Persian inscription, now preserved at the Rajshahi Varendra Research Museum, indicates that the temple was built in 1582 by Khan Muhammad Bin Tuwi Khan Qaqshal. Built entirely of brick, this medium-sized mosque has three domes on its top and three archways on its eastern face.

The mosque was built at exactly the same time as the Kherua Mosque in Sherpur, and using an identical plan. Together they are the earliest existing monuments from the Mughal reign of Bengal. Although it shares a lot of the similarities with the previous sultanate period of Bengal, such as the floral patterns and decorated *mihrabs*, the building's internal arrangement and disposition shows a definite break from earlier designs. In particular, the north Indian Mughal three-domed prayer chamber shares similarities with the Sinheri Mosque at Delhi and the mosques on either side of the Taj Mahal.

Getting there To get there you need to take a Chatmohar-bound public bus from the new bus terminal. Head there by rickshaw first, about 25 minutes away, and then find a bus to get you there.

SHAHJADPUR This district borders Pabna on its northeastern edge, along the road to Sirajganj. A little-known fact is that Rabnidranath Tagore also lived in the area at Kacharibari, now the home of a half-hearted museum to Bengal's most famous poet. The museum, housed in the principal building of Tagore's former estate, contains some memorabilia from his time here, including tubs, hookahs, seals, *khadam* (wooden sandals), a harmonium and rare photographs, among other things. Unfortunately the building and its relics are badly in need of maintenance, but that shouldn't stop cultural visitors from paying homage to the place anyway, in an effort to bring attention to its maintenance needs. Tagore is said to have authored some of his famous works from this estate.

There is also a famous mosque here at Shahjadpur, a 15th-century creation built by Makhdum Shah. It stands on the bank of the river Hurasagar near Dargapara, at the extreme end of Shahjazdpur Town. The most noteworthy feature is its seven-stepped canopied *mimbar* (platform). The stylistic and decorative elements are characteristic of the early sultanate, pre-Mughal architecture of Bengal.

To get there, the Alhamra bus line services Shahjadpur. The bus departs from Dhaka's Kallyanpur bus stand (*Dhaka* m *01721 802032; Shahjadpur* m *01719 734859*) (4hrs; Tk220). Buses depart hourly from 05.30 to 17.30 and take four hours. All Dhaka–Pabna buses pass through here too.

BHARERA MOSQUE About 15km southeast from Pabna, and alongside the Padma riverbank lies the 18th-century Bharera Mosque. A white colour distinguishes this mosque from the others, and some locals say that a Thursday evening prayer brings together Hindus and Muslims under one roof.

SITLAI AND TARAS ESTATE HOUSES These two separate *rajbaris* allude to Pabna's ties to the *zamindar* empire. Although not as grand as their Natore counterparts, they are worth a quick look if you're in the local area. The Taras estate is just a few hundred metres south of Pabna's Zero Point. The Sitlai Palace is east of town on the banks of the Pabna River. Both places are now used as offices.

HARDING BRIDGE In a country with so many rivers, bridges represent real chances for economic progress and have even become tourist destinations among Bangladeshi people. While you might not make a special trip to see the bridges, their history is actually pretty interesting, especially if travelling over them.

The Harding Bridge is one of Bangladesh's oldest, responsible for connecting the Pabna district to the economic opportunities of Kolkata by rail, and completed in 1915. Construction began in 1910, and over 24,400 workers built the 1.8km-long structure. During the Liberation War, the bridge was bombed by the Indian air force on 13 December 1971, in an effort to cut off the Pakistani army retreat from Jessore. The bridge was later reconstructed with help from India and Japan. If you've got your own transport, you might like to stop at the small **Paksey Railway Museum** (🕘 *10.00–17.00; entry free*) on the north bank, where the remains of the shell that hit the bridge in 1971 is on display. The former residence of Sir Robert Gailes, the bridge's chief engineer, is nearby.

The Fokir Lalon Shah Bridge stands next to the Harding Bridge. Completed in 2002, it serves vehicular traffic and cuts the travel time to Kushtia down to six hours. Traffic heading to Jessore and Kushtia still crosses the Jamuna River by the Aricha–Goalando ferry crossing.

CHAPAI NAWABGANJ

While most of the historic Gaur monuments lie on the other side of the Bangladesh–India border, there is another reason to visit this far-flung destination 34km outside Rajshahi. And that's for the most heavenly fruit Bangladesh has to offer: the mightily delicious mangoes.

During the honey month(s) of May and June, Nawabganj and its satellite towns become pulsating veins of market activity, as mangoes of nearly every variety are harvested from the thousands of little orchards located throughout the district. In Chapai Nawabganj, they are sold for as little as Tk30 (US$0.50) per kilo. It's worth organising your own private transport here just for this reason – if you buy 12kg, the merchants will take great care to package your mangoes for their safe passage back home, making giant fruit basket gifts for friends both Bangladeshi or foreign. Lychees also enjoy a short season during May, harvested from here but also from other parts of the division.

The Nawabganj Municipality held a Mango Fair in 2008 and it remains to be seen if they will do it again in future years. Several kinds of mango-related food products were on sale (and of course some delicious mangoes themselves), as well as local *nakshikantha* (embroidered cloths) and *tama kansa* (handmade pots).

A precious few monuments of the historic Kingdom of Gaur also lie on the Bangladeshi side of the border. These are also worth the journey although it's a bit sad to see that this unique archaeological destination is inaccessible to both West Bengal and Rajshahi despite their shared heritage (see *Chotto Sona Masjid*, opposite).

HISTORY During the 13th and 14th centuries, Bengal's rulers fought to maintain a sense of fierce independence from the sultanates of Delhi. Despite repeated attempts to subjugate the inhabitants through force, the area managed to maintain its identity and establish a kingdom here, known to historians as the Ilyas Shah dynasty. In 1420, Gaur was once again named capital and saw its first prosperity under early pre-Mughal rulers. During the late 15th century, Bengal emerged for the first time as an independent entity under the rule of Alauddin Hussain Shah, who ruled Gaur from 1493 to 1519.

Shah's rule represents a seminal event in Bengal's history, as historians acknowledge that he and his son Nusrat Shah were responsible for consolidating Bengal's previously undefined borders, as well as founding the Bengali language. Some even credit them with founding the secular nature of the Bengali people as the liberal ruler demonstrated no discrimination between his Hindu and Muslim subjects, ruling both equally. But after Nusrat's assassination in 1532, his luxury-loving son Mahmud Shah could not continue the achievements of his forefathers and the Shah dynasty ended in 1538, beginning a long process by which the Mughal rulers would eventually take control over Bengal. Gaur never again enjoyed such prominence after the Shah rulers left the scene.

GETTING THERE If using public transport, the journey between Rajshahi and the mosques of Gaur is laborious, and so if you have the time and you're on a budget you may wish to consider staying in Chapai Nawabganj to reduce the amount of bus hopping in one day. Otherwise, Rajshahi definitely has the better hotels for those who can afford to hire private transport (expect to pay Tk1,000–1,500 per day plus petrol costs, depending on the quality of the vehicle).

The distance between Rajshahi and Chapai Nawabganj is about 34km. Two direct buses service this route, the **Gatelock** and **Mohananda** bus lines, although the latter is more popular (1hr; Tk50). From Rajshahi, head to Shaheb Bazaar's Alupotti intersection. Otherwise there should be buses from the new terminal near the train station.

WHERE TO STAY AND EAT

Alauddin Hotel Uddyan Mor. Serves up a regular Bangla feast & there are 3 branches in the town – Uddyan Mor is the best bet.

Changpai Chinese Resturant Lies at Sonar Mor.

Hotel-Al Nahid Shanti Mor. Known as the best residential hotel in Chapai Nawabganj & offers AC rooms & a Chinese restaurant.

WHAT TO SEE

Kansat Mango Market This spectacular mango market is one of the most populated (by mangoes and people) in all of Bangladesh. Every day, heaping baskets of the green gold are taken to the main markets, where they are eventually loaded onto trucks and delivered around the country. Seeing the market at its peak is really a matter of timing. Somewhere between mid-May and mid-July are the best months, but these can of course vary according to the weather. When the mangoes start showing up in bazaars around Bangladesh, it's probably just the right time to consider a journey to Kansat to see the source of it all, as mangoes typically take three to five days to ripen after picking.

To get there, board a Gaud-bound bus for the approximately 28km from Chapai Nawabganj (1hr; Tk30) or considering hiring a *tempo* to do the whole journey from Chapai Nawabganj to Chotto Sona Masjid and then back again via Kansat, which should cost under Tk500, depending on your negotiation skills.

Chotto Sona Masjid Translated, Chotta Sona Masjid means 'Small Golden Mosque'. Although much smaller than its contemporary in West Bengal, the Large Golden Mosque, it is in much better condition. From the outside it's nothing remarkable, but the inside is where the mosque's true beauty comes to life. Look up. All along the mosque's inside domes there are a series of terracotta decorations. The inside walls also contain intricate carvings that have stood the test of time because most of this mosque is made from stone, although its foundation is brick.

The mosque (and the border) is about 38km from Chapai Nawabganj. Once again, it's recommended that you hire a *tempo* to do your sightseeing as the bus service is highly irregular.

Khania Dighi Mosque and Balia Dighi Further along in the village of Chapara lie three more tourist sites: Balia Dighi (*dighi* means tank), Khania Dighi and its associated mosque (also known as Rajbibi Mosque). The mosque here also has a series of terracotta designs, but unlike the Small Golden Mosque, its frontage is primarily brick, although there are a few reliefs that do use stone.

Darasbari Mosque This mosque is the other Jami mosque found on the Bangladeshi side of Gaur. Its architecture is compelling because it resembles the Adina Mosque that lies in nearby Pandua (on the Indian side of the border; with an Indian visa you could cross here, but unfortunately there is no transport available from the other side and the other sights are at least an hour away by car). Unfortunately, this mosque is not in as good a condition as are the more accessible Small Golden Mosque and the Firozpur mosques. A nearby inscription dates the mosque's construction, by Yusuf Shah, to 1479. Like some of the other mosques, this structure also shows indications of a royal gallery on an upper storey which is only accessible from a flight of steps outside. The floral patterns of the *mihrabs* also show a similar pattern to those found at Adina. The name *darasbari* reflects the fact that a *madrasa* was probably attached to this mosque, to which a low mound was discovered in nearby Ghoshpur.

Firozpur mosques Nearby the Small Golden Mosque are a series of buildings dedicated to Shah Niamatullah Wali. There's a three-domed mosque that has been restored to an interesting salmon colour (which may or may not be the original colour), plus Shah's mausoleum. Finally, there's the Takhana Palace, a small building with a flat rooftop that overlooks a pond.

BOGRA *Telephone code 051*

The proximity of Paharpur and Mahasthan make Bogra the ideal base to explore these two archaeological treasures of Bangladesh. Also, trips to the Jamuna River can be mounted from here, a chance to see the scenic *chars* (pronounced 'chors'), shifting river islands on the Jamuna River where millions of people live, vulnerable to the vagaries of yearly flooding.

Certainly the *chars* are not a 'sight' in the tourist sense of the word, but for those who have any knowledge or experience in development work, or an anthropological interest in populations of people who remain totally off the grid (electricity, water or any government infrastructure whatsoever), the *chars* are absolutely fascinating places to see and visit, and allow some escape onto the rivers of Bangladesh. For further information, see box, *Bangladesh's river chars* and *The Char Livelihoods Programme*, page 311.

The town is large but not crowded, except at the Shat Mata (seven roads) intersection, which marks the centre of town.

GETTING THERE AND AROUND Buses are the best option for reaching Bogra as the train schedule is not favourable and the travel time far too long. From Dhaka, you

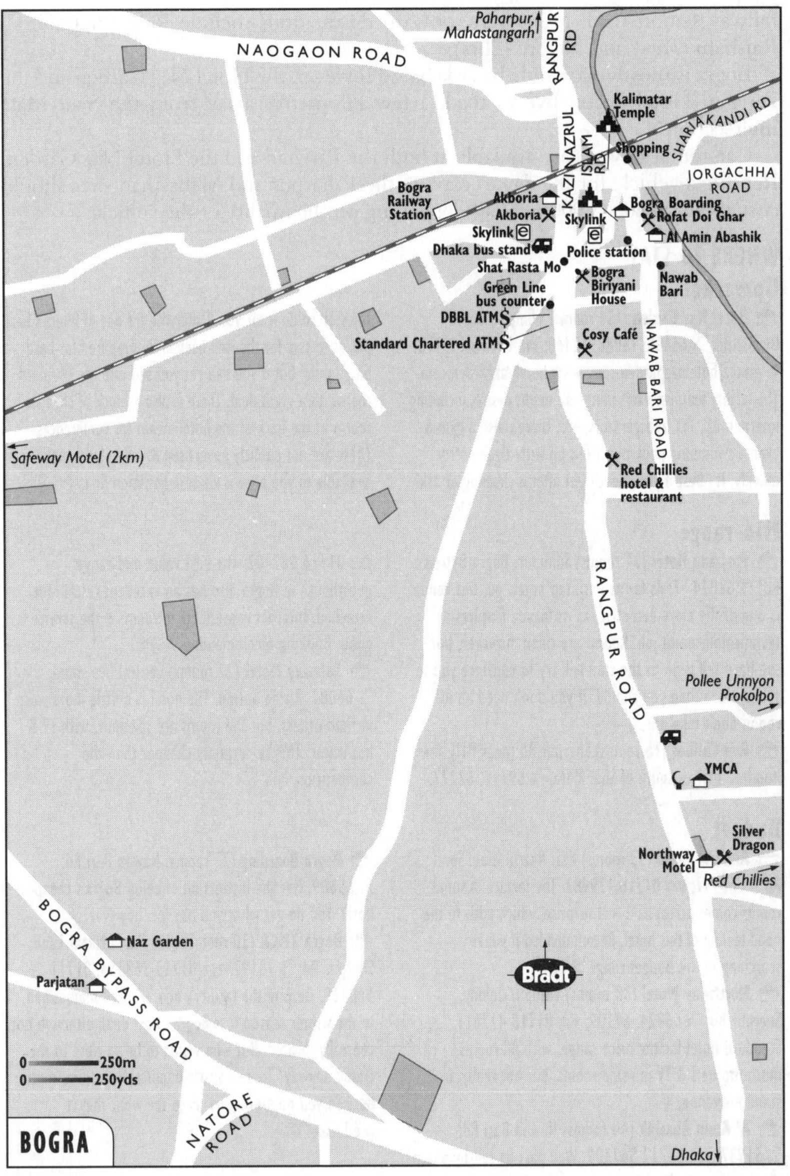

can take **Green Line** buses, which make a stop into Bogra *en route* to Rangpur. Otherwise, the **Modern Enterprise** and **TR Travels** bus companies have chair coaches from Dhaka's Gabtali bus stand, departing through the day. Tickets cost Tk400/220 for air-conditioned/non air-conditioned seats, with the latter available in greater numbers too.

From Bogra, the Green Line bus office is just south of the Shat Mata intersection. Otherwise there are several counters on the road west of Shat Mata, including the BRTC bus stand which has departures in many directions. However, it may be faster to head to the central bus stand 2km west from Shat Mata on the railway station road. From here, onward destinations include Rangpur (2.5hrs), Rajshahi (3hrs) and Natore (2hrs).

Bogra is mostly accessible by rickshaw. However, the Hotel Naz Garden and the Parjatan Hotel lie on bypass road, a few kilometres away from the Shat Mata intersection.

Car-rental services are available at both the Parjatan and the Hotel Naz Garden. Renting a vehicle for the day to explore the Paharpur and Mahasthan sites should cost about Tk800–1,000 per day, depending on the quality of the vehicle.

WHERE TO STAY

Upmarket

Hotel Naz Garden (156 rooms) Silimpur, Bogra Bypass Rd; ☎ 66655, 78088, 62468; m 01715 139773; e gm@hotelnazgarden.com; www.hotelnazgarden.com. The facility features everything you might desire, including internet, AC, TVs, refrigerators, etc. There's also a gym & even a swimming pool, but it fills up with algae pretty quickly. It's best if you use it right after a cleaning or ask the staff to do it for you. Otherwise it's one of Bogra's best places to stay for the well heeled. Be prepared for hard bargaining, but if you can get yourself into the standard rooms it's a great deal. There is also a block of cheaper rooms at the back of the hotel meant for conferences. These are not publicly advertised & will only be made available to you after a lot of negotiation first. $$$$

Mid-range

Parjatan Hotel (34 rooms) Silimpur, Bogra Bypass Rd; ☎ 67024–7; As far as Parjatan hotels go, this venue is one of the more eccentric, as its façade features a technicolour paint job. Rooms are clean, however, but the hard sell is on as the staff will try to convince you to spend more than you should. If you don't need an AC room, don't take one. $$$

Red Chillies (15 rooms) Sherpur Rd (near PTI), few hundred metres south of Shat Mata; ☎ 69777, 62277; m 01716 982402. The best value mid-range guesthouse in Bogra also has an excellent restaurant attached. Internet is available in rooms & the service is good. Booking recommended. $$$

Safeway Motel (22 rooms) Central bus stand; ☎ 66087. A safe option. The hotel is a little more worn in than others, but the rooms are spacious, with TV & hot water. They're certainly cheaper than the competition. $$$

Budget

Akboria Hotel (33 rooms) Kazi Nazrul Islam Sorak Rd; ☎ 66997; m 01716 179982. The terrace in some rooms comes across as a real surprise, which adds to the good feeling of this hotel. Recommended if you're searching in this budget range. $$

Northway Motel (38 rooms) Latifpur Colony, Sherpur Rd; ☎ 66824, 67109; m 01718 412611. Standard hotel for the price range, with AC rooms, mosquito nets & TV in some rooms, but not really a standout venue. $$

Al Amin Abashik (40 rooms) Nawab Bari Rd; ☎ 51937; m 01712 567309. Well past its sell-by date; there are newer & better options in town. $

Bogra Boarding (22 rooms) Nawab Bari Rd; ☎ 65609. Has the distinction of being Bogra's cheapest hotel. You do get what you pay for, however. $

Bogra YMCA (20 rooms) Bhai Pagla Mazar Lane, Sherpur Rd; ☎ 73192; m 01713 368354, 01711 568369. Despite the facility's age, it's well maintained. In the winter season it is Bogra's best deal, although not centrally located. But who wants to be so close to the traffic anyway? There's also a handicraft training centre here so you might inquire as to see what they're producing. $

WHERE TO EAT

Red Chillies Farhad Mansion, Sherpur Rd; ☎ 69777, 62277. Upmarket place with decent service & very good impersonations of authentic Chinese cuisine. $$$

Bogra Biriyani House Shat Mata; m 01725 638717. Sat right on the Shat Mata traffic circle, this *biriyani* house is hard to miss. Also offers *khichuri* if you want something a little different. $$

Cosy Café Saiful Complex, Yakubia Mor; m 01711 310911, 01717 288444. Real coffee & cappuccino, & a nice décor to boot? Can't complain, considering this is Bogra & there isn't a lot of places to choose from when it comes to coffee. Food is awfully slow though, be warned. $$

THE CHAR LIVELIHOODS PROGRAMME

Chars are sandy islands and low-lying flood-prone areas at the river's edge that are deposited, eroded and re-deposited by the Jamuna River. Approximately 3.5 million people inhabit the *chars* in the Char Livelihoods Programme (CLP) intervention areas, with around one million people actually living on island *chars* that are surrounded by water for most of the year. This population comprises the poorest of Bangladesh's poor. It is the households living on these island *chars* who are the main target group of the CLP.

One of the principal causes of poverty in the Jamuna *chars* are the high levels of river erosion, of both its banks and of the island *chars* themselves. Erosion and near-annual flooding force thousands of households to move each year. Some of these households shift five to seven times in a single generation. Furthermore, the *chars* are isolated from major markets with significant amounts of time and money being spent by their residents to reach the mainland. The vast majority of *char* households are not covered by standard government services including health, education and police protection. Interaction between *char* dwellers and the private sector is also weak as transport costs are high and the *chars* are not connected to the electricity grid.

The Chars Livelihoods Programme (CLP) has begun a series of interventions meant to improve the livelihood security of the very poorest people in these areas, and is funded by the UK Department for International Development (DFID). Sponsors include the Ministry of Local Government, Rural Development and Co-operatives of the government of Bangladesh. Their working area includes the riverine districts of Kurigram, Gaibandha, Jamalpur, Bogra and Sirajganj. The programme was originally conceived in 1996 but has since been modified to target the very poorest populations on the river *chars*. Today there are five main components of the programme:

1. Providing infrastructure, primarily in the areas of flood protection, sanitation and clean water supply
2. Asset building and livelihoods interventions aimed at the poorest island *char* dwellers, based around the provision of income-generating assets
3. Encouraging social development, with group interactions and exposure to important topics in health, sanitation, disaster preparedness and social rights and responsibilities
4. Offering social protection, through 'cash-for-work' monthly stipends to the poorest households and the development of community safety nets
5. Promoting enterprise that facilitates growth in agricultural and non-farm sectors and also supports the development of key growth-related services, in particular microfinance and livestock services

With £50 million in grant funding, the CLP is the largest project in the DFID–Bangladesh portfolio of activities. The long-term goal is to address extreme poverty in Bangladesh and contribute to achieving the First Millennium Development Goal.

✕ **Silver Dragon** (38 rooms) Latifpur Colony, Sherpur Rd; ☎ 66824, 67109; m 01718 412611. Multi-cuisine restaurant attached to the Northway Hotel. Has Chinese, Indian & Bangladeshi cuisines on offer. $$

✕ **Akboria Restaurant** Kazi Nazrul Islam Shorok; ☎ 66997; m 01711 902641. The best kebabs & *naans* in town, according to locals. $

✕ **Rofat Doi Ghar** Nawab Bari Rd. One of Bogra's brand-name *mishti doi* (sweet yoghurt) shops. We can't really tell the difference between Rofat's yoghurt & the others, but some locals swear by this stuff. $

SHOPPING

Pollee Unnyon Prokolpo *(Khanik Niloy, Chalklokman;* ☏ *65703;* m *01711 302470;* e *shaidpup@btcl.net.bd; www.catgen.com/pup*) For those interested in the potential of fair-trade handicrafts to bring economic development opportunities to women, the offices of Pollee Unnyon Prokolpo should be a definite stop. Not only can you purchase some well-designed *nakshikanthas* (embroidered fabrics) here, you can also learn about this fairtrade-certified organisation's work.

OTHER PRACTICALITIES

Banks There's a **Standard Chartered** (*Shatani Hse, Sherpur Rd;* ☏ *78907–9;* ⏲ *10.00–15.30*) branch just south of the Shat Mata intersection, plus a few DBBL ATMs in Bogra.

Internet There are cybercafés called **Skylink** (*Kazi Nazrul Islam Rd; Tk20 per hour*) in the large multi-storey shopping complexes near to Shat Mata intersection. Look above the Quality Sweets.

Medical Several hospitals and clinics line Kazi Nazrul Islam Road north of the Shat Mata intersection. But the best nearby facility is the Khwaja Yunus Ali Medical College and Hospital at Sirajganj (for further information, see page 299).

WHAT TO SEE

Nawab Palace grounds (*East of Shat Mata;* ⏲ *10.00–19.30; entry Tk10, museum Tk6, each amusement ride Tk10*) This palatial, aging *rajbari* belongs to a long line of nawabs who lived in the Bogra area, and who have always occupied prominent positions of power in Bengal. Originally the building was an indigo plantation warehouse, until the nawab family purchased it for use as a country home, given its proximity to the Karatuya River. The 200-year-old building now houses a museum, and just outside there is a collection of painted concrete animals as well as an amusement park for the kids. The museum is full of family relics from previous generations, and includes a collection of clothed mannequins reflecting the fashion trends of Bengal's royalty under British colonial power. There is also a volume of old photographs of Muhammad Ali (for more information, see below) with Commonwealth and international leaders like Queen Elizabeth II, John F Kennedy and Jawaharlal Nehru.

The most influential nawab of recent history is Muhammad Ali Bogra, whose political career is outlined on a small monument near the entrance of the Nawab Palace. This prominent politician first served in the government of Bengal and gradually moved up through the ranks to become the Health Minister of Bengal. When Pakistan was created in 1947, Ali served as Ambassador to Burma, High Commissioner to Canada and then eventually as the Ambassador of Pakistan to the United States. In 1953, under the appointment of Pakistan's governor general, he became the country's third prime minister. Within six months, he forwarded a proposal for the constitution of Pakistan that created a formula for sharing power between Pakistan's disparate halves, and while the plan was well received by the masses, Pakistan's early political turmoil meant that the Constitution was never approved by the fledgling parliament when it was dissolved in 1954. Ali then turned his attention to the Kashmir issue instead, but when Governor General Ghulam Muhammad eventually resigned his posting owing to illness, his replacement Iskander Mirza forced Ali to resign, and so he returned to his former posting in the United States, followed by a stint in Japan. Eventually he came home and ran for parliament in 1962, and served as the Foreign Minister until his death in 1963.

Hindu Quarter (*North along Kazi Nazrul Av, first right, then 200m down the road*) Close to Shat Mata, there is small Hindu Quarter that holds a distinctly different flavour from the rest of Bogra. The **Kalimatar Temple** lies on the northern end of the road, and beside that is a Hindu marketplace. During January and early February, there is a Saraswati *puja* (Hindu celebration day) with some festivities here, which is interesting to see if you're in the area. Finally, if you've ever wanted to pick up a pet rat, this is the place to come!

AROUND BOGRA

SARIAKANDI About 20km east of town lies the Sariakandi ghat, one of the main boat terminals servicing several *chars* – river islands – on the Jamuna. From here you can hire a small motorised boat for a few hundred taka per hour and tour the river. Alternatively, you could hop on a boat with a few dozen other villagers and go where they're going, and then figure out if the boat will return to Sariakandi later in the day.

PAHARPUR AND MAHASTHAN: THE BUDDHIST MONUMENTS

Before visiting any Buddhist monument in Bangladesh, it is important to understand the history of Buddhism, its architecture and its evolution in Bengal. In Bangladesh, Buddhism is still practised by half a million people, most of whom live in the plains and hilly regions of Chittagong, Comilla and Dhaka. The once dominant religion has almost completely disappeared from the land of its creation with the exception of Bangladesh – its last stronghold – and so it is difficult to truly appreciate the depth of its belief amongst the people of 15 centuries ago. Although numerous testaments to the period remain in the form of literary accounts (including Chinese pilgrims who came to Bengal between the 5th and 7th centuries), Buddhist architectural practices have totally disappeared, leaving only their ruins in jungle-clad mounds dotted around the countryside.

The exact date of Buddhism's arrival in Bengal is not known, but common belief dictates that the religion was firmly established during the reign of Emperor Asoka, who ruled from 273–232BC. Under his imperial command, Bengal developed Buddhism to new heights. Chinese Monks Fa Xien and Xuen Zhang made their famed visits in the early 5th and the mid 7th centuries respectively. They saw a religion that flourished even in the remote corners of Bengal. In his account, Xuen Zhang described over 20 Buddhist monasteries with over 3,000 monks. In a place he called Po-Shi-Po, he witnessed 700 hermits living near a gigantic Asokan stupa. In Samatata, he witnessed another 30 Buddhist monasteries with several thousand more practitioners of the religion.

The strength of the religion largely came about from the royal patronage of subsequent Buddhist dynasties, namely the Palas, Kadgas, Chandras and the Devas. Under the Palas and the Chandras, Buddhism transformed into its tantric forms known today, symbolised by a complex polytheistic view of Buddhism. This gave rise to the numerous Bodhisattvas, Taras and Sakti, icons that are all present in today's modern form. This style of the religion had a much greater appeal to the local population, whose animistic and paganistic world views reshaped the Buddha's original teachings. Historians theorise that these forces heavily influenced the Mahayana Buddhism practised outside south Asia, especially in Tibet.

ARCHITECTURAL STYLES Buddhist monuments are largely constructed in two styles throughout the world: the stupa (earthen mound) and the monastery, known as a *vihara* in Bangla. The stupa did not become important until the reign of Asoka, who created the idea of a Buddhist fraternity by shipping pieces of the original stupas to the towns and villages of his empire, and specifying that a new stupa be built over each one. Thus the cult of the stupa developed and soon became the primary symbol of Buddhism, whether it had a relic or not. At the Paharpur and Mahasthan sites, no stupas have yet to be unearthed, but this is not the case at Mainamati in Comilla, or among the living Buddhist people of the Chittagong Hill Tracts.

The monasteries served a different purpose in ancient Bengal. Originally these were little more than garden retreats for the monks, who located these places close to the cities where they could collect alms. As the Buddhist traditions matured and began to receive royal patronage, there was distinct change in the architectural plans as these monasteries began to accumulate wealth. Historians theorise that the need for increased security resulted in the quadrangular-shaped, thick-walled brick structures seen at Sompura Vihara (Paharpur), Vasu Bihara (Mahasthan) and Salban Bihara (Comilla). Inside these monasteries, a series of inward-facing monastic cells opened onto a large inner courtyard. Thus the monasteries resembled defensive brick fortresses more so than typical religious establishments.

Several of the stupas and monasteries in Bangladesh largely remain unexcavated and unknown, even by Bangladeshi people. Other Buddhist ruins include the Bharat Vayana in Jessore, the Vikrampuri Vihara in Dhaka, and the Rajasan and Harish Cahndra Rajar Badi in Savar. For all we know there could be a future discovery of some extraordinary archaeological treasures of unknown proportion, but for now a lack of funding means that Bangladesh's archaeological wealth remains largely unearthed.

WHERE TO STAY If you're using public transport or cycling around the Mahasthan or Paharpur sites, it is possible to stay at the **Department of Archaeology Rest Houses** at either place by first contacting the Dhaka office (*Director, Department of Archaeology, Ministry of Cultural Affairs; ↘ 02 812 6817, 811 2715*). If you just show up and be friendly, there's a pretty good chance you'll be allowed to stay and the rates are quite inexpensive (perhaps Tk300–400 per night plus more for food). Both places offer quiet surroundings and a village atmosphere. Food can be prepared with advance warning but it is best if you supplement it with your own supplies.

MAHASTHAN Mahasthan is the oldest known city in Bangladesh. Its ancient brick buildings are spread over the west bank of the Karatoya River within a 12km radius. Over its history it has seen the rise and fall of Buddhist, Hindu and Muslim empires. At Govinda Bhita, archaeologists discovered coins dating to the 3rd and 2nd centuries BC; inside the Mahasthangarh citadel, the remains of a sultanate mosque, dating from the 15th century, have been unearthed with its terracotta designs intact. More often than not these archaeological treasures have been built on top of one another as the dynasties passed over the centuries. Excavation of the massive site is far from complete, and for the moment, Buddhist monuments dating from the 8th to the 11th centuries are the most common.

Getting there and around Mahasthan is easily accessible by bus from Bogra. To get there, catch a bus from Bogra's central bus stand, a few kilometres west of Bogra's railway station for the 12km journey (30mins; Tk10). From there you can take a rickshaw to the museum or walk the 1.7km required to get there. Rickshaws are available to ferry you between the various monuments.

What to see There are plenty of mounds, buildings and monasteries to see at the Mahasthan site, far more than can be listed here. The following sites are included as recommended places to see, but if you're an archaeology buff contact the Department of Archaeology in Dhaka for the full background.

Mahasthan Citadel The massive citadel ruins are the principal attraction from which the entire Mahasthan area takes its name. It's an irregular, oblong brick enclosure measuring 1,500m long by 1,370m wide and in some places the wall rises 15ft over the surrounding paddy fields. The amount of work required to build the site must have been extensive, with archaeological work revealing four building and rebuilding phases taking place over its history. Silver and copper coins, as well as black-polished ceramic work were discovered, indicating the earliest inhabitants of Mahasthangarh were the Sunga people of the 3rd and 2nd centuries BC. The Gupta and Pala periods are represented by the regular walls of tile-sized bricks, with the latter period forming a major portion of the currently exposed remains. Flooding was a problem even then, as many of the exposed walls have either been swept away or found in a heavily damaged state, with thick deposits of river silt covering the eroded tops and sides of these walls. Finally, the discovery of a pre-Mughal mosque inside the citadel indicates the presence of Muslims.

The citadel is also home to the Bairagi Bhita Temple, located in the citadel's northeastern corner, as well as the Khodair Pathar Mound, and the Mankalir Bhita, two mounds which held a Buddhist temple and a mosque underneath. About 200m north of the Mankalir Bhita Mound, a comparatively modern dwelling was discovered, consisting of four separate blocks surrounding a courtyard. Nearby, the famous Jiyat Kunda, or 'Well of Life', was discovered, in which legend says that King Parasurama resuscitated his dead soldiers using the magic water from this well during his battle with Sultan Balkhi. Learning about the well's extraordinary powers, the Muslim saint destroyed the well's magical powers by instructing a kite to drop a piece of beef into it, which allowed him to defeat the Hindu king in battle.

Govinda Bhita Temple During further excavations of a mound situated on a high bank of the nearby Karatuya River, two temples of separate origin were discovered inside the same 2m-thick boundary wall. The western temple was erected in the 6th century, while the eastern one, built partially on the ruins of the western temple, was dated to the 11th century. Although tradition identifies this complex with the temple of Govinda or Vishnu, nothing of Vaishnavite character was ever discovered during excavation. Archaeologists also discovered a series of retainment walls, which were built to protect the temple from the river.

The temple lies to the northeast of the citadel, just a few hundred metres up the road.

Mahasthan site museum (*⌚ Apr–Sep 10.00–13.00 & 14.00–18.00 Sun–Thu, 10.00–12.30 & 14.30–18.00 Fri; Oct–Mar 09.00–13.00 & 14.00–17.00 Sun–Thu, 09.00–12.30 & 14.30–17.00 Fri; entry Tk2*) A visit to the museum will introduce the visitor to a fairly large range of antiquities, ranging from terracotta objects to gold ornaments and coins recovered by archaeologists. Among these is a limestone tablet that carried an imperial decree to release food grains to the suffering citizens of Pudraranagara, the ancient name of Mahasthan. There are also a series of stone sculptures, as well as copper rings, bangles, medallions and weaponry. Finally, the terracotta plaques demonstrating Mahasthan's connection to the 2nd-century Sunga dynasty are on display.

Lakshindarer Medh At the nearby village of Gokul, about 3km away from the Mahasthan Citadel, is the 13m-high brick mound, which was possibly a Shiva temple. The excavated mound reveals a cellular construction laid out in a haphazard fashion. Antiquities retrieved from the site suggest that this was a base for a stupa built in the 6th or 7th century. There was also a human skeleton discovered in one of the cells, probably that of a religious hermit who lived and died here.

Vasu Bihar When Xuen Zhang came to Mahasthan in the 7th century, he described a large monastery situated 9km west of the main citadel, which he called Po-Shi-Po. In his account, he described a grand monastery remarkable for the size and height of its towers and pavilion. It was occupied by no fewer than 700 monks, who studied the Mahayana. Men famous for their learning flocked here from the eastern districts. At a short distance from the monastery there was a stupa built by Asoka on the site where Buddha explained his laws to the Devas. Near this was a spot where the last Buddha had taken exercise and rested, and traces of his footmarks were still to be seen.

Xuen Zhang's account seems to correspond with the current location of Vasu Bihar, from which two medium-sized monasteries and a shrine have been excavated. The building layout resembles the Paharpur and Mainamati *biharas*, except that there is no central temple structure. A large collection of delicate bronze images and a few superbly decorated terracotta plaques, as well as a 2ft stone image of a standing Buddha, are now housed in the museum.

PAHARPUR At first glance you might think that this massive enclosure doesn't quite deserve the title as the most impressive monument in Bangladesh. But with a little knowledge of Paharpur's history and background, it's easier to appreciate why the Buddhist ruins of Paharpur were inscribed on UNESCO's World Heritage List in 1985.

Getting there and around From Bogra, take a Jaipurhat-bound **bus** for the 44km journey (1.5hrs; Tk50). From Jaipurhat, buses leave regularly for the 9km to Paharpur (25mins; Tk10). Finally, a rickshaw will get you the rest of the way. It's best that you do this trip early as transport begins to peter out after 18.00. If you can afford it, a hired vehicle from Bogra is suggested (Tk800–1,000).

What to see

Somapura Bihara Clay seals of the great Pala emperor Dharmapala helped identify this temple as a late 8th-century construction. It's hard to imagine the massive undertaking required to build a temple covering an area as large as this, given that it was constructed over 1,200 years ago in the middle of the jungle – certainly no small feat. Inside the monastery, there are numerous stupas and extensive ancillary buildings.

At the centre of the complex, a colossal temple rises 22m above the surrounding flat fields. The temple is a gigantic square cross, with each receding terrace providing circumambulatory passages around the monument. Access to the first and second terraces was provided by a grand staircase from the north and although the upper part of the temple is missing, archaeologists think that the whole structure was likely crowned by a towering single shrine, and was completed in a single round of construction, unlike other Buddhist temples that were built in successive constructions.

At the temple's base there are a series of stone images that surprisingly belong to the Brahmanical Pantheon, indicating an intersection of Hindu and Buddhist histories, while above those is a row of terracotta plaques that depict the folk art of Bengal. About 2,000 of these plaques remain attached to the temple and a further 800 were removed from the site during excavation. They depict Hindu deities such as Shiva, Brahma, Vishnu, Ganesh and Surya, while others depict Buddhist deities such as Buddha, Bodhisattva, Padmapani, Manjusri and Tara. The depiction of gods from both religions indicates the lineage they both shared here at Paharpur.

The monastery surrounding the temple is also impressively large, known to be the biggest monastery south of the Himalayas. The massive quadrangular monastery comprises almost 80,000m^2 of space, 280m in each direction, with 177 monastic cells laid out around the surrounding courtyard with an elaborate gateway complex flanked on both sides by guard rooms. Five shrines decorate the southeast corner of the complex, including a star-shaped 16-sided structure.

Seen from above, the entire complex resembles the centrepiece displayed in a traditional Tibetan *thanka* (religious painting), which alludes to the beauty that this place must have had in its day. Tibetan monks were also known to have studied here during the 9th to 12th centuries.

Satyapir Bhita About 300m east of the Paharpur Monastery lies this temple complex, although it's now mostly in ruins. The temple's purpose was ascertained by the presence of 50 circular terracotta plaques stamped with the figure of an eight-headed goddess and a Buddhist inscription. The goddess was later identified as one of the forms of Buddhist Taras, dating from the 11th century.

Site museum (*🕘 Apr–Sep 10.00–13.00 & 14.00–18.00 Sun–Thu, 10.00–12.30 & 14.30–18.00 Fri; Oct–Mar 09.00–13.00 & 14.00–17.00 Sun–Thu, 09.00–12.30 & 14.30–17.00 Fri; entry Tk2*) This small museum houses the relics discovered at the Paharpur site, although its most impressive find, an 8ft bronze Buddha, is usually away on tour. The Buddha was probably cast using the 'lost wax' process in which a clay mould is prepared from hand-carved wax and then melted away during the firing process. The mould is then filled with molten brass and then cracked open on cooling to reveal a cast-bronze image.

RANGPUR *Telephone code 0521*

Rangpur is the principal city and base for exploring northwest Bangladesh, an area very different in character and quality from the rest of the country. The region is scenically beautiful and delightfully calm, and boasts the lowest population density of any flatland area of Bangladesh. Travelling here, especially on two wheels, offers visitors a glimpse of one of the least explored regions of the least visited countries of the world. Thankfully there is a lot to see, but most of these destinations definitely do not qualify as 'tourist sites' in the traditional sense, and so a helping of adventurous spirit will really help you enjoy what this region has to offer.

There's also a darker side to the story of the northwest. The reality is that the greater Rangpur–Dinajpur area is also home to the poorest and most marginalised people in Bangladesh. With little industrialisation, the region's economic mainstay remains agriculture, but with sandy soils and low water tables this land is also the least agriculturally productive out of anywhere in Bangladesh. With seasonal drought and severe cold in the winter (there are deaths from cold reported in the newspapers every year), and severe flooding during the summer, the people who live here face some of the most difficult living conditions the country has to offer, and indeed most of Bangladesh's internal migration comes from here. If you ask any rickshaw wallah on the streets of Gulshan where he's from, most of the time it's from somewhere in the northwest.

So while advocating a form of 'poverty tourism' for visitors to the northwest might seem a little strange, it's because the potential for some informative travel experiences is excellent.

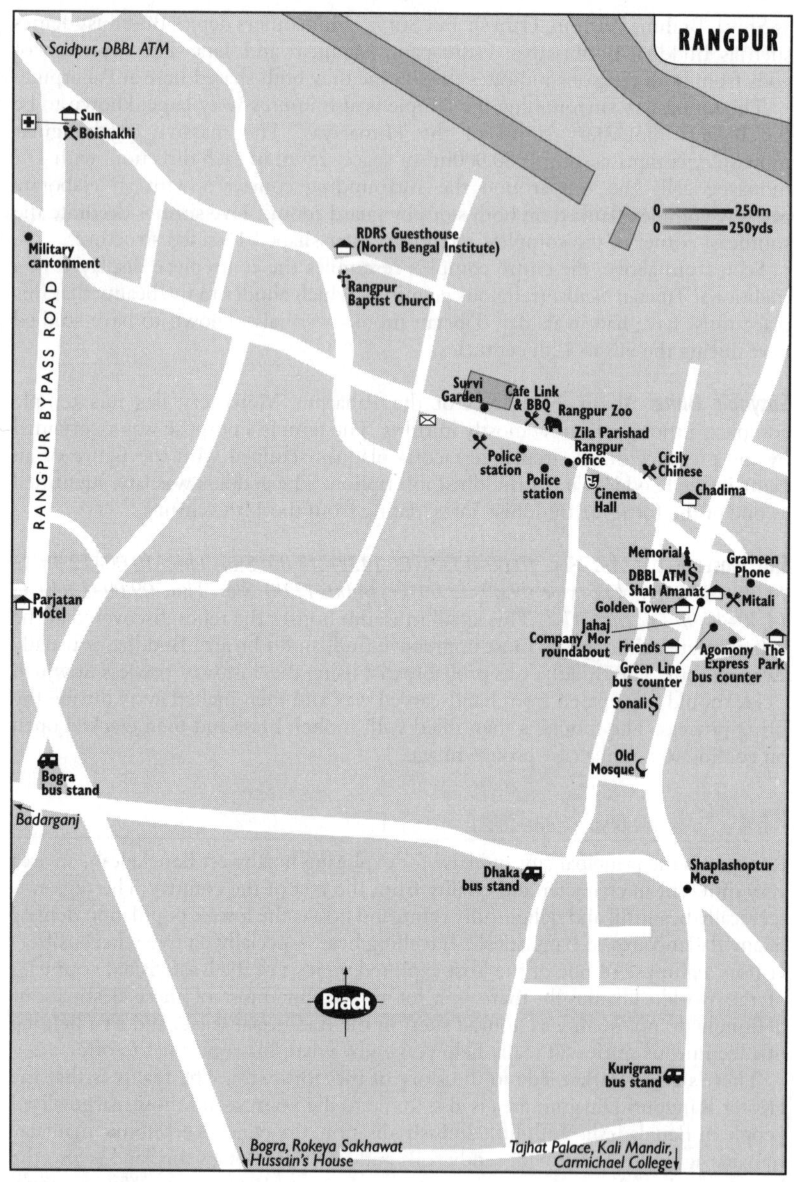

GETTING THERE

By air Sadly all flights to the nearby Saidpur airport have been cancelled.

By bus **Green Line** (*counter at Jahaj Company Mor;* ☎ *66678;* **m** *01730 060041*) and **Agomony Express** (*offices also at Jahaj Company Mor;* ☎ *63313, 51933;* **m** *01712 092123; 01911 416861*) offer a luxury air-conditioned bus service to/from Rangpur. Both companies have three departures a day each way, usually at about 08.00, 15.00 and 23.00. Buying your ticket in advance is highly recommended. Dhaka-bound buses depart from the Kamarpara Dhaka bus stand located in the southern part of the city. Rickshaw wallahs know it and it's a 15-minute ride from the RDRS (see below).

For Bogra (2.5hrs; Tk60), buses depart from the main bus stand on the Rangpur Bypass Road (also known as RK Road). The same stand also has buses for Saidpur (1.5hrs; Tk30). For Dinajpur, you may need to transfer to another bus at Saidpur, which is about 2.5 hours away.

For Kurigram (2hrs; Tk50), Lalmonirhat (3hrs; Tk75) and Burimari (4hrs; Tk100) buses leave from the bus terminal south of the Shapla Chotta Traffic Mor (the traffic circle with the lotus in the middle).

By bicycle A most interesting route for Dhaka-bound cyclists would be to cross the Jamuna River via Kurigram and Chilmari from Rangpur. The journey could be taken entirely in one direction and would get you to the opposite side at Raumari. From there it would be easy to go overland to Jamalpur and then eastward into the Garo areas of Mymensingh, or turn south towards Dhaka.

GETTING AROUND Rangpur is fully manageable by rickshaw or by long walks. Some areas with heavy traffic are not that nice to walk through, however.

TOURIST INFORMATION

Rangpur–Dinajpur Rural Service (*Jail Rd, Dhap;* ☎ *62598, 62863, 62893;* e *nbi@rdrsrangpur.org; www.rdrsbangla.net*) In terms of knowledge and professionalism amongst northwestern NGOs, the Rangpur–Dinajpur Rural Service (RDRS) is one of the best organisations, hands down. In addition to the North Bengal Institute, which is a fountain of knowledge and experience of the issues of northwest Bangladesh, the NGO maintains a network of beautifully maintained guesthouses at Rangpur, Thakurgaon, Lalmonirhat and Kurigram, all of which are far cleaner and more comfortable to stay at than any hotel the northwest has to offer. Journalists, development workers, potential interns and informed travellers should definitely get in touch with this organisation if planning a trip to the northwest as they are keen to improve their international connections.

The NGO is quite large, so do your homework by researching their excellent website first. Truly, RDRS is one of those excellent NGOs that you wish were more common across Bangladesh. Car hire is also available here as well.

WHERE TO STAY

Mid-range

Hotel Shah Amanat (36 rooms) Jahaj Company More, Station Rd; ☎ 65673; m 01724 123434. Oddly, all the toilets are squatters in this place, save for the Tk1,000 rooms. AC sgl would be good value though based on its price. $$$

Parjatan Motel (30 rooms) RK Rd; ☎ 62911, 62091; m 01710 157093. A location not quite in the heart of town, which is maybe what you want while staying in Rangpur. Looks well maintained but not necessarily well managed. The RDRS really does beat it hands down. $$$

RDRS Guesthouse (24 rooms) Jail Rd, Dhap; ☎ 66492–3 ext 102; m 01713 200185; e www.rdrsbangla.net. Beautiful facility in a greened-out campus. Simply one of the best places to stay in all of northern Bangladesh, with excellent management & food. Rooms have hot water, TV, balcony & AC. Downstairs a library, pool table & restaurant are attached. There is also a cabinet containing handicrafts from RDRS projects. It's not the cheapest place to stay, but excellent value if you can afford it. $$$

Budget

Hotel Chandima (18 rooms) Nabobganj Bazaar, Station Rd; ☎ 62026; m 01718 409615. The regular dbls are better value if it's not stinking hot. Tiled rooms & desks provided. $$

Hotel Golden Tower (25 rooms) Jahaj Company Mor, Station Rd; ☎ 65920, 91169; m 01718 409692. Comfy but cave-like; at least it is quiet, clean & tiled. Allah presides over this place. $$

The Park (18 rooms) GL Roy Rd; ☎ 66718; m 01199 381034. Good-value rooms & clean tiled surrounds, although some rooms only have a squat toilet. Check the bathroom first. $$

Friends Hotel (19 rooms) Station Rd; ☎ 51329; m 01728 656217. Just the basic bed & bathroom combo at this place. $

Hotel Sun (15 rooms) Medical Mor, Jail Rd; ☎ 51612; m 01712 685492. A bit dark, but certainly a friendly place to stay, with Western toilets. $

WHERE TO EAT

Cicily Chinese Restaurant Raja Rammohon Club Biponi Bitan; ☎ 63076, 66263. Definitely mark this place as a party hall for big groups of Bengalis. Has a fairly extensive Chinese menu. $$$

Café Link & BBQ Police Community Hall; ☎ 61028. Kebab place in the evening & fast food. Has AC if you need to escape the heat. $$

Boishakhi Medical Mor; ☎ 67666. Evening kebab place that comes recommended from locals; nicer atmosphere than the nearby restaurants. $

Mitali Restaurant GL Roy Rd, to the right side of the Hotel Shah Amanat entrance. Well known to the locals & housed inside a wonderfully old & decaying building, the food is tasty here & very cheap. Recommended. $

OTHER PRACTICALITIES

Banks Rangpur has several DBBL ATMs around town. One is located just north of the Medical Mor in the northwest end of town. Another lies inside Mostafa Supermarket near Jahaj Company Mor.

For exchanging money, there is a Sonali Bank branch near Jahaj Company Mor, situated in an aging yellow colonial building. Consult the map for the exact location.

Internet The RDRS Guesthouse has internet facilities on site.

Medical The northwest corner of town has several hospitals and clinics should you have a medical emergency. Head for Medical Mor.

Post office (*Across from Police Community Hall; ⌚ 10.00–16.00*) Located along near Rangpur's other administrative buildings.

Telephone **Grameen Phone** (*Horin Biri Project Complex, Central Rd, Paira Chattar; ⌚ 11.00–22.00*) is a handy place to get a sim card if you've just arrived in Bangladesh, especially if you want an internet enabled sim for use with a 2.5G/3G mobile.

WHAT TO SEE

Tajhat Palace (*5km south of the Jahaj Company Mor; ⌚ 10.00–17.00; entry to palace and museum Tk50 for foreigners, Tk5 for Bangladeshis*) Distinctly out of place given its Bangladeshi village surroundings, this European-style palace was originally built at the turn of the 20th century by Kumar Gopal Lal Roy, a Hindu *zamindar*. An emigrant from the Punjab, the Hindu *khatari* (merchant) was a jeweller by profession and managed to make his fortune in Rangpur. The frontage is 76m wide, and the building two storeys tall, making this palace an imposing sight on first glance. A large *dighi* (pond) also lies to the left of the palace, where many canoodling couples take refuge from the city.

From 1984, the building was an active high court, but in 1995 its management was turned over to the Department of Archaeology. In 2005, the **Rangpur Museum** was relocated here. The room at the top of the marble stairs houses numerous Sanskrit and Arabic manuscripts. A few black-stone carvings also grace the museum's back rooms.

Vehicles are allowed to enter the compound after paying a vehicle fee of Tk57. It has large grounds, with two large symmetrical ponds on either side of a tree-lined driveway entrance.

Kali Mandir *(entry free)* This decaying Hindu temple is close by the Tajhat Palace and can easily be reached by rickshaw. It's a stout brick structured topped with a Florentine-style dome. Sometimes the gate is locked but if you ask some of the people living around the temple a caretaker will open it for you. See if you can spot the marijuana plants nearby.

Carmichael College This college takes its name from Sir Thomas Gibson Carmichael, who had a five-year stint as the Governor of Bengal from 1912–17. His assignment was made more difficult by the fact that he was the province's first governor after the annulment of the first partition of Bengal, and thus he was tasked in repairing the rift between the colonial government and its citizens. Perhaps his greatest achievements relate to the establishment of education institutions in eastern Bengal (such as this college), which had received less of the government's support during the bulk of the colonial era.

The college building, with its frontage of over 100m, is a pleasing blend of British and Mughal architecture. Its series of Mughal-style archways give it an appearance that is very unique to the area.

North Bengal Institute *(RDRS Bangladesh Complex; Jail Rd; www.rdrsbangla.net)* The resources and information available at the NBI make it a destination in its own right. Even if you're not staying at the RDRS Guesthouse, it is worthwhile to visit here and get plugged into the resources of what feels like a travellers' café but is actually a NGO facility.

Rangpur Zoo *(Across from Police Line School; ⌚ 10.00–17.00; entry Tk5)* This small zoo houses a few animals of Bangladeshi origin and would be an interesting place to take the kids for an hour. Leave your animal rights activist sentiment at your hotel, however.

AROUND RANGPUR

CYCLE TRIPS The RDRS also has a few bicycles you can hire with a Tk500 security deposit. These would be great for exploring some of the neighbourhoods in Rangpur or perhaps the countryside just outside the city. The bicycles are not in great shape but at least they have them.

ROKEYA SAKHAWAT HUSSAIN'S HOUSE *(Pairabond village, Mithapukur Upazilla; 20km south of Rangpur)* Begum Rokeya is widely acknowledged to be one of Bengal's first feminist voices. The writer and activist was a very loud voice against the constraints of purdah (the practice of keeping women veiled and 'secure' from society) and the limitations that Islam placed on the education of women. One of her most well-known writings is a short story entitled *Sultana's Dream*. The story describes an imaginary world where men are tucked away in a *mardana* hidden from view (a parody of the women's *zenana*), and the women occupy positions of power and influence in public society. The story is an absolutely fascinating read given its 1908 publication date – the text can be found on the internet quite easily (see *www.wikipedia.com* for the full story).

Rokeya's life was no less controversial as she is said to have worked tirelessly to improve the lot of women in Bengali India. Her earliest work was to advocate for the education of women. In 1909, she established one of the first Muslim girls' schools in Calcutta; she was said to have gone door-to-door persuading parents to enrol their daughters. In her own words: 'What we want is neither alms nor gift of favour. It is our inborn right. Our claim is not more than Islam gave women 1,300 years ago.'

Each year, 9 December is celebrated as 'Begum Rokeya Day' at the village of Pairabond, Rokeya's place of birth. There's also a NGO operating here and a small memorial in her name. To get there, travel south from Rangpur for 20km until you reach the Mithapukur Upazilla, and from here ask your way to the village.

KURIGRAM *Telephone code 0581*

Tucked as it is into the confluence of the Tista and the Brahmaputra, the town of Kurigram is defined more by its rivers than its land. Boat journeys here reveal a shifting landscape of sandbars and river channels, all of which blend into one another and become indistinguishable at times. During years of heavy monsoonal rains, Kurigram is the first to feel the pain of the ensuing floods in Bangladesh. As a result the development of the region has lagged far behind the mainstream, and the region's infrastructure (roads and electricity) is some of the patchiest in all of Bangladesh.

Despite this, large populations of people persist here, sometimes on the very edge of survival. If you spend enough time in the region you will eventually hear the name 'Monga' used in news stories and NGO press releases about the region. Monga is a seasonal famine that occurs in Kurigram and its surrounding areas when there is a lack of agricultural work. After the post-monsoon planting of August and September, there are no other jobs to be found in this region, causing many of its male inhabitants to migrate temporarily to the cities for work.

GETTING THERE AND AROUND Kurigram can be reached by public bus from Rangpur's southern bus stand (2hrs; Tk50). From here, the town is large enough to require a rickshaw to get around, especially from the bus stand to the NGO offices.

WHERE TO STAY AND EAT

RDRS Kurigram (8 rooms) New Town, Hospital Rd; 61760; e rdrskg@tistaonline.com; www.rdrsbangla.net. The Kurigram guesthouse of the RDRS, with AC or non-AC rooms. Some rooms also have a shared bath & are cheaper. Set meals are served at specific times depending on other guests who are also staying at the facility. Booking ahead at the Rangpur office is highly recommended. $$$

Chinnamukul Bangladesh (9 rooms) Hospital Rd, 61690; e info@chhinnamukul.org, cbk@bttb.net. Another NGO resthouse with good facilities. The head office is in Kurigram. It also has another guesthouse in Chilmari, about 40km south of Kurigram. $$

WHAT TO SEE

***Chars* at Chilmari** If you're not here in a working capacity to view the *chars*, your best option is to head 40km south to the town of Chilmari and catch one of the regular service boats that ferry people to these river islands nearby. Most of these *tolars* depart in the morning and return in the early afternoon. By asking around the local ghat you could plan your journey in this way.

Otherwise, a fascinating travel route would be to cross the Jamuna River entirely by making for Raumari, which lies on the Jamuna's eastern bank. The Char Livelihoods Project (see box, page 311) and the RDRS also maintain modest guesthouse facilities here. Enquire at the Rangpur or Dhaka offices for more information.

LALMONIRHAT DISTRICT *with contributions from Jason Cons*

Unless you're a sociologist, international relations expert, or lover of quirky destinations, there isn't much reason to stop in this backwater district of the north, one of the last outposts of northern Bangladesh. But if you qualify as any of the above, you'll be surprised to learn that this remote district is home to a fascinating tale of India–Bangladesh relations. All along the Indian–Bangladeshi border, there are an estimated 51 chunks of Bangladesh completely surrounded by India, and 111 Indian enclaves inside Bangladesh. The majority of these enclaves are concentrated in and around Lalmonirhat.

Known in Bangla as *chhitmahals*, their residents must illegally cross two borders simply to reach their home countries. Though the *chhitmahals* date from Mughal times, the particular complications for those living within them began with partition and became acute in 1952, with the implementation of a passport/visa system between the two countries. The largest of these enclaves is the Angorpota/Dahagram (AGDH), connected to Bangladesh via a specially agreed-upon 178m by 85m tract of land called the Tin Bigha corridor. The corridor is open just 12 hours a day, and a score of army and border security forces from both countries manage the passage.

As the Indian high commission wrote in a white paper: 'The importance of the Tin Bigha question involves much more than leasing of a particular piece of land. Its resolution symbolises, above all, the will of the people of India and Bangladesh to live together in amity and good neighbourliness. The leasing reflects the shared resolve of the two Governments to eliminate a long-standing and major irritant in bilateral relations, thus setting the stage to bring about a mutually beneficial upgrade of Indo-Bangladesh relations.' If this is so, then the partial fulfilment of the 1974 Treaty and the ongoing difficulties faced by residents of the enclaves are also symbols of the incompleteness of this 'upgrade'. Yet, part of the difficulty faced by enclave residents is the result of seeing the Tin Bigha corridor and the enclaves as 'problems' or 'issues' to be sorted out: territorial oddities that are a feature of the uneven and incomplete border between India and Bangladesh.

Understanding the enclaves not as territorial puzzles but rather as the homes of beleaguered residents helps to reposition the enclaves as absurd and easily remediable impediments to residents' rights as citizens. The official history of the enclaves raise a series of questions: which country do the enclaves belong to? Who should control the Tin Bigha corridor? However, the questions have more immediate answers if instead one asks: how can we ensure the enclave residents' rights as citizens? What does it mean to prevent someone from accessing their home country for 12 hours a day?

Indeed, it is critical to view the *chhitmahals* not as policy puzzles but as places where people live their daily lives in the face of complicated and at times dangerous institutional and political configurations. From this perspective, the various different stumbling blocks in resolving the enclave issue and the Tin Bigha corridor by both India and Bangladesh appear as petty squabbles over small and strategically unimportant pieces of land. As long as both countries continue to view the enclave issue in general from the perspective of territory and sovereignty, as opposed to citizenship and rights, their desire and their long struggle, not to mention two treaties and numerous promises, will remain.

GETTING THERE AND AROUND

By bus If you have time and are concerned about the comfort of your ride, it's best if you first journey to Rangpur (8hrs from Dhaka) to break the journey. Otherwise you can catch the Shyamoli Paribahan Siliguri service that departs Gabtali Bus Station at about 22.00 (☎ *02 836 0241*). It arrives at the Burimari border at about 06.00, so you'll want to disembark slightly earlier at Patgram. Tickets can be purchased from any Shyamoli Paribahan offices but it's probably easiest to meet the bus as it leaves the city from the Gabtali Bus Station. There's also a Shyamoli Paribahan office just north of Asad Gate in Mohammadpur in Dhaka.

Getting to the enclaves From Patgram, you can get a rickshaw to Angorpota/Dahagram. It's about 45 minutes going and one hour returning, and so your best bet is to hire a rickshaw for the day. This should cost you between Tk150 and Tk300. Angorpota/Dahagram (AGDH) is easy to explore by rickshaw. If you get a knowledgeable driver, he can take you to other enclaves as well.

Be aware that you absolutely cannot take pictures of/inside the Tin Bigha corridor. Once you're inside AGDH, however, you can snap away. Indian Border Security Forces don't like you to take pictures of the border, their watchtowers, camps, etc, but in truth, there's not too much they can do about it. The BDR (short for Bangladesh Rifles, the country's border force) folks, however seem to be absolutely great, friendly, and more than happy to have you in for a cup of tea. You don't need your passport to cross into AGDH, but it's not a bad idea to bring it, just in case you run into trouble. Even better, bring a photocopy and keep the passport somewhere safe.

In fact, it's kind of a minor tourist spot for middle-class families in the north. At the time of research, every now and then I'd run into vans full of Bengalis on border sightseeing tours. On the other hand, going as a *bideshi*, not surprisingly, is a bit different. The more exposure and visits the area gets, the harder it will be for India and Bangladesh to keep sweeping the issue under the proverbial rug.

WHERE TO STAY AND EAT You have two choices for staying in Lalmonihat district. You can stay at Lalmonirhat itself, which offers better accommodation at the RDRS, or you can go to Patgram, which is closer to the Tin Bigha corridor. Backpacking anthropologists will probably want to consider the latter because it's cheaper. But those equipped with vehicles would enjoy staying at Lalmonirhat much more.

RDRS Lalmonirhat (6 rooms) Saptibari, Patgram Rd, Lalmonirhat; ☎ 0591 61378; e rdrslal@tistaonline.com; www.rdrsbangla.net. The Lalmonirhat guesthouse of the RDRS. Some rooms have AC. Set meals are served at specific times. Booking ahead at the Rangpur office is highly recommended. $$

Motel Paradise Patgram. It's no paradise, but is reasonably fine & cheap. $

SAIDPUR *Telephone code 0552*

With an airport, railway connections and major roads leading in all directions, Saidpur is mainly a transit junction. During the British colonial period, there was a railway manufacturing yard here which represented the town's largest industry, although today it is in deep decline as the Kolkata–Assam railway no longer transits through Bangladesh. Stopping here is not really recommended as there are better hotels in both Rangpur and Dinajpur, but Saidpur remains a great place to catch onward rail connections.

Interestingly, Saidpur is also the home to the second largest concentration of Bihari people outside Dhaka. The Biharis were previously defined as 'stateless' people because of their affiliation to the pre-Bangladesh Pakistani government. When the Liberation War was lost, nearly half a million people, delineated by the fact they spoke Urdu, remained in Bangladesh. Half of them lived around the Saidpur area.

Today about 70,000 of them remain concentrated in camps scattered around Saidpur and the majority had already been repatriated to Pakistan. In the 2008 election, this population was given the right to vote in the parliamentary elections, effectively making them citizens of Bangladesh. People in the camps remained divided over whether or not they should accept citizenship, as the next question then became one of repayment, as many of the Biharis were forcibly removed from their residences and stripped of their possessions at the close of the Liberation War.

Visiting these camps is possible while in Saidpur, although there is little to distinguish these areas and their people from the surrounding countryside. Ask a rickshaw wallah to see the Bihari people and they'll guide you there.

GETTING THERE

By air With the entrance of a few new airline companies to the Bangladesh market, daily flights to Saidpur had started up but stopped once again due to lack of business. Only time will tell whether or not Saidpur flights become a regular item, but when considering the length of the road journey to northwest Bangladesh, a one-hour flight sounds a lot faster. However, at Tk5,495 for a one-way ticket to Dhaka, this is still considerably more expensive than a bus ticket. You'll need to check the below numbers to see if flights are an option.

✈ **Royal Bengal Airlines** 1st Fl, Shop M8, Saidpur Plaza; m 01841 600109, 01841 600107. Flights were running but had suspended just before going to press. Call for the latest info to see if they've resumed.

✈ **United Airways** 1st Fl, Shop M8, Saidpur Plaza; m 01715 771263; Flights were running but stopped just before publication.

By bus **Hanif Enterprise**, **Babul Enterprise** and **Shyamoli** (m *01734 136604*) have a regular service to Dhaka, leaving every two hours from their bus counters across the street from the Hotel Arafat International, which takes about eight hours. Otherwise, you'll need to catch a rickshaw to the eastern part of town to catch Rangpur- or Bogra-bound buses. The Dinajpur bus stand is on the west part of town.

By train The main long-distance destinations from Saidpur include Dhaka, Rajshahi and Khulna.

WHERE TO STAY

Al Jahara (17 rooms) Dinajpur Rd; m 01731 113186. Attached bathrooms & hot water by the bucket are on offer at Saidpur's newest hotel. Rooms are tiled & the Western loo looks kind of comfortable. AC rooms available. $$

Hotel Arafat International (25 rooms) Zikrul Haque Rd; ☎ 0644 5590054. Previously Saidpur's best option, but now appears a bit well used. AC rooms available. $$

Hotel Prince (18 rooms) Kamal Rd. On first impression, the Prince seems more like a prison, but

TRAIN TIMETABLE

No	Destination	Train name	Off day	Dep time	Arr time
748	Khulna	Simanta Express	None	18.55	04.40
728	Khulna	Rupsha Express	None	07.45	17.50
734	Rajshahi	Titumir Express	None	14.10	21.15
766	Dhaka	Nilsagar Express	Friday	22.00	07.00

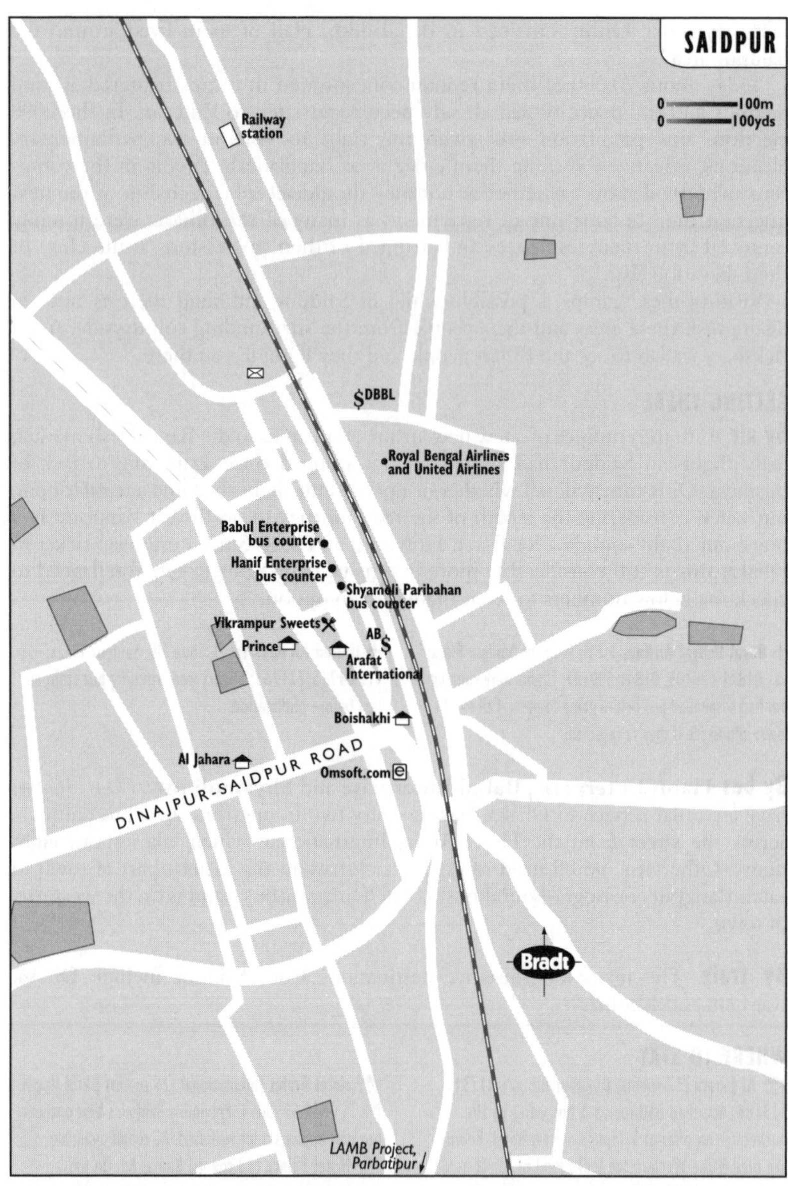

upstairs there are a couple of rooms with linoleum flooring & better furnishings, including a couple of AC rooms. There are also some sgls without bathroom that qualify as Saidpur's cheapest. If you're going for an non-AC room, you're better off somewhere else. $

WHERE TO EAT

Boishakhi Restaurant Zikrul Haque Rd. With hand-painted pictures of chickens on the signs, this upstairs restaurant seems to have a constant stream of customers, making it worth a try. $

Vikrampur Sweets Zikrul Haque Rd. Bangladeshi food served fast & hot, although not with any particular concern for hygiene. Has kebabs at night & serves hot naan bread all day. $

OTHER PRACTICALITIES

Banks Saidpur has an ATM that accepts Plus and Cirrus cards at DBBL, near Saidpur Plaza on the east side of the railway tracks (see map opposite). Money can be changed at the AB Bank (⌚ *11.00–16.00*) in the central bazaar on Zikrul Haque Road.

Internet There's an internet café in the central bazaar on Zikrul Haque Road called Omsoft.com.

AROUND SAIDPUR

LAMB PROJECT (*2km west of Parbatipur, 10km south of Saidpur;* ☎ *05334 74386;* e *inquiries@lambproject.org; www.lambproject.org*) The LAMB Project provides primary healthcare and community development services to what might be some of the poorest regions Bangladesh has to offer. Best known for its 150-bed hospital, the project is located near the main railway junction of Parbatipur. The project accepts short-term and long-term volunteer placements, but these should be arranged with the administration beforehand.

The vision for LAMB began in the early 1950s when a missionary of the American Santal Mission in Dinajpur felt an urgent need for medical work for the hundreds of thousands who had no access to proper healthcare. LAMB thereby has its foundations in providing health services around the communities of the area and has since expanded its activities considerably.

Today, its 500 staff are mostly Bangladeshi, but there are a number of foreign staff who bring additional expertise to the project. The hospital currently treats more than 55,000 out-patients per year – nearly 200 per day – and more than 8,000 in-patients per year for surgery or medical treatment, and focusing only on the potentially difficult births they still deliver more than 4,000 babies per year. Most of these patients would be unable to afford suitable treatment even at the government facilities.

In the community, LAMB has 23 static clinics and safe delivery units, spread over an area of more than 80km in length. The community activities are however much broader, not only with health-related activities, but also covering micro-credit and community development. LAMB has now extended its service into provision of high-quality training for third parties, primarily in the health area, and because of its access to a large archive of health and socio-economic data is increasingly called upon to assist in research programmes.

Despite its growth, LAMB retains its original mission to serve God through serving the poor and underprivileged, particularly women and children. The blend of religions of the patients reflects fairly closely the proportions of the populations of the whole of Bangladesh.

DINAJPUR *Telephone code 0531*

Dinajpur is the largest city of northwest Bangladesh, and possesses a depth of history that pre-dates its own 'mini partition' into modern-day West and East Dinajpur (half of it lies in West Bengal). The area used to be part of the Pundravardhana kingdom, an empire that spanned from Bihar to Dinajpur, and as far south as Pabna and Rajshahi. The principal ruins now lie southeast at Mahasthan, and there isn't much left in the Dinajpur area to signify the region's connection to that ancient past.

What are visible, however, are a few monuments that attest to the Hindu and British histories of Dinajpur, including the famous Kantanagar Temple located

TRAIN TIMETABLE

No	Destination	Train name	Off day	Dep time	Arr time
758	Dhaka	Drutajan Express	Wednesday	08.40	18.15
706	Dhaka	Ekota Express	Monday	20.10	05.30

north of town, and the ruins of the Dinajpur Rajbari located in town. The town's old trading district lies at Maldipotti, where a mishmash of colonial architecture blends with the accoutrements of modern-day shopping – several sari shops now decorate this street.

GETTING THERE AND AWAY

By bus The Dinajpur bus stand is just north of the Cinema Hall along Station Road. There are no air-conditioned bus services to Dhaka, but you'll find plenty of chair coaches ready to take you on the ten-hour journey. **Shyamoli Paribahan** has an office here but your best bet is to head to the bus stand and see which bus looks the least scratched up.

By train Dhaka is accessible by day and overnight train from Dinajpur and vice versa. The ticket prices are Tk855/535 for air-conditioned/non-air-conditioned sleeper, or Tk535/370 for air-conditioned/non-air-conditioned chair. Tk250 will get you to Dhaka in the unreserved section. The train travels southward via Natore and Iswardi before turning east towards Dhaka.

WHERE TO STAY

Mid-range

Parjatan Motel (12 rooms) Housing More; 64718. Luxurious-looking hotel compared with Dinajpur's other options. This newer Parjatan facility has AC rooms located at a building outside town. A stay here would be awfully tempting if it was the hot season. Towels provided, as well as a desk & TV. $$$

Budget

Hotel Diamond (30 rooms) Mouldapoti district; 64629, 65720; m 01718 626674. Newer wing (B Wing, across the street) much nicer but still under construction at the time of research, so it should be completed by the time you read this, but perhaps may be noisy because of other construction work. Older wing looks a bit aged & sandwiched between many old buildings. Some rooms have AC & carpets, others are rock-bottom budget in appearance & quality. $$

CDA Central Training Centre (3 rooms) Blk 1, Hse 51, Upa-Shahar; 64428. Basic but comfortable, & very friendly. $

Hotel Al Rashid (28 rooms) Nimtala district; 65658, 64251. Best-value option, friendly smiling manager, but the place is pretty popular & therefore noisy. Rooms have attached bath & mosquito net. $

New Hotel (16 rooms) Station Rd; 64155. A bit of a dive, pretty old & a bit ratty looking, but offers the absolute cheapest bed in town. $

WHERE TO EAT

Martin Chinese Restaurant Just off Jail Rd, Goneshtola; 64074. Thai, Chinese & Bangla fare, dark but the food is pretty good. $$

Puffin Chinese Restaurant Station Rd, across from the train station; 64672. As usual for Chinese restaurants in Bangladesh, dimly lit, with AC & friendly enough service. The menu has a better selection than the Martin. $$

Pabna Sweets T&T Rd, Bahadur Bazaar; 65411. Famous *mishti* & *doi* (sugary Bengali doughnuts & sweet yoghurt) shop in Dinajpur. The *rosh malai* is very good. $

Purnima Restaurant T&T Rd; m 01719 314453. Tiny little nook with fast food & snacks, where all the cool kids go to flirt. Former UK resident & owner Mr Pulok is very helpful & friendly. $

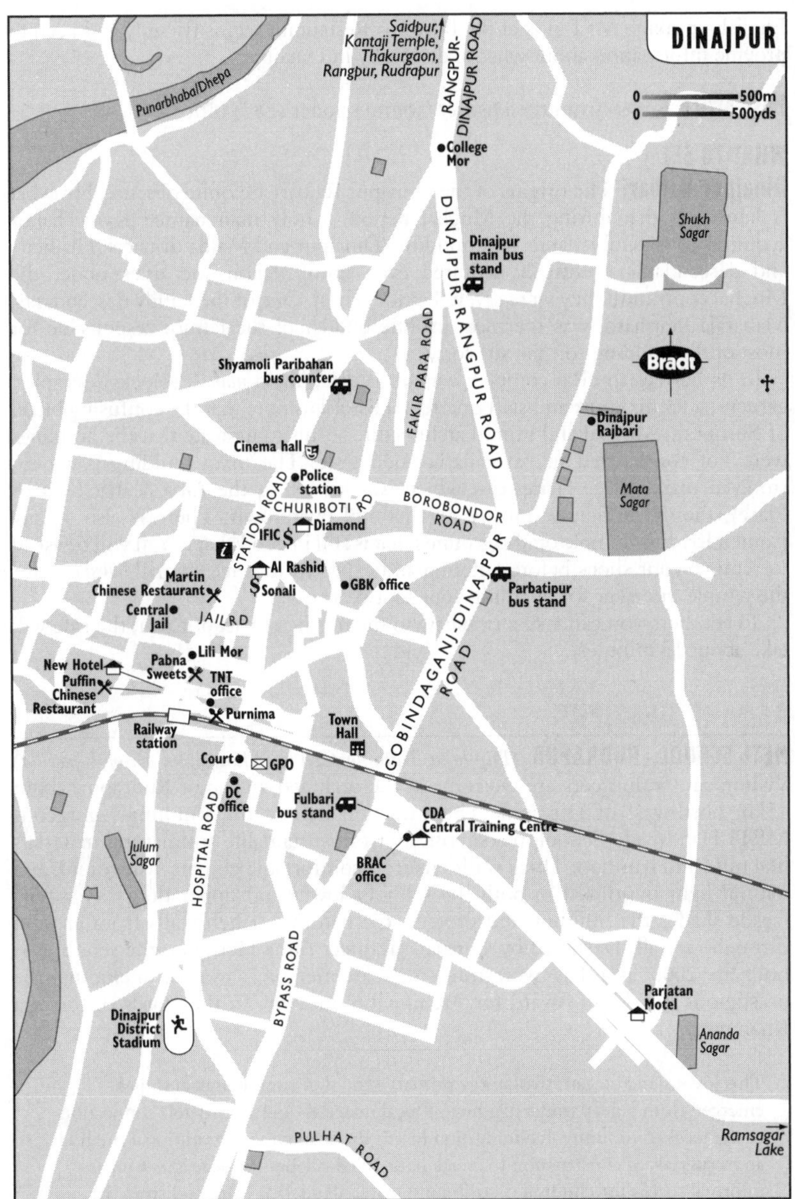

OTHER PRACTICALITIES

Banks There are no DBBL ATMs in Dinajpur and the nearest location is in Rangpur. You can exchange cash at one of the bank branches (try the IFIC Bank or the Sonali Bank indicated on the map) in Maldipotti Bazaar in a pinch, however.

Internet There's a small internet café next to the Martin Chinese Restaurant, along with a few others in the bazaar surrounding the central jail. Otherwise, the

English-speaking Mr Pulok at the Purnima Restaurant seems friendly and keen to provide information about what to do locally in Dinajpur.

Post office Across from the District Commissioner (DC) office.

WHAT TO SEE

Dinajpur Rajbari The origins of the Dinajpur Rajbari are quite obscure, but what is known is that during the Mughal period, a holy man named Kasi Thakur acquired considerable lands in around the Dinajpur and Malda districts. His heirs and descendants eventually acquired even more wealth and titles under the Mughal court until they were given the title of Raj. One of the family descendants, Maharaja Prannath, was the most prolific builder of the family, responsible for most of the buildings on the site today.

In its heyday, the Raj complex contained three main *mahals* (blocks), temples, gardens, a tennis court and staff quarters. Historians note that the confusing blend of European, Mughal and Hindu architecture seems to indicate that the buildings were not constructed in particularly good taste. The main building is a two-storeyed main palace facing east which was known as the Aina Mahal (Mirror Place), though it is now mostly derelict and overgrown. There is also a gaily painted Krishna Temple on the grounds that is still in good shape. You will be asked to remove your shoes before entering and expected to leave a small *baksheesh* for the temple caretaker for guarding your footwear.

To get there you can take a rickshaw to the northeast part of town; the ride will take about 15 minutes.

AROUND DINAJPUR

METI SCHOOL, RUDRAPUR (*Dipshika Training Centre; Mangalpur, Birol Upazilla*) Visitors and volunteers are welcome at the secluded village of Rudrapur, about 15km northwest of Dinajpur. The attraction here is the stunningly gorgeous METI Handmade School, made entirely from sustainable and natural materials like mud and bamboo. Thick walls ensure a comfortable climate year round, and natural light is utilised in both the school's lower and upper floors. A special façade shades the building and protects the natural earthen walls from erosion through rainfall. Designed by German architect Anna Heringer, the school was built in 2005 and has won numerous architectural awards, including the prestigious Aga Khan Award for Architecture in 2008. In the words of the Aga Khan jury:

> This joyous and elegant two-storey primary school in rural Bangladesh has emerged from a deep understanding of local materials and a heart-felt connection to the local community. Its innovation lies in the adaptation of traditional methods and materials of construction to create light-filled celebratory spaces as well as informal spaces for children. Earthbound materials such as loam and straw are combined with lighter elements like bamboo sticks and nylon lashing to shape a built form that addresses sustainability in construction in an exemplary manner. The design solution may not be replicable in other parts of the Islamic world, as local conditions vary, but the approach – which allows new design solutions to emerge from an in-depth knowledge of the local context and ways of building – clearly provides a fresh and hopeful model for sustainable building globally. The final result of this heroic volunteer effort is a building that creates beautiful, meaningful and humane collective spaces for learning, so enriching the lives of the children it serves.

The school is the principal building of the project but there are many other buildings completed or under construction using the techniques acquired while building the school. More information on the school is available from Dipshikha, the NGO working in the village of Rudrapur (*282/5 1st Colony, Mazar Rd, Mirpur 1, Dhaka; ☎ 02 900 0782; e dipshika@agni.com; www.anna-heringer.com, www.meti-school.de which has an English version*).

Getting there From Dhaka's Gabtali (also known as Kallyanpur) bus stand, the Nabil bus company offers a direct bus to Mangalpur but the ride, at 11 hours, is long and laborious. Upon arrival in Mangalpur, you need to take a rickshaw van to the Dipshikha NGO office where the school is located, which is another 30-minute ride away. It's best to make arrangements with Dipshika if you wish to stay at the site, otherwise you can stay back in Dinajpur. Public bus services run frequently from Dinajpur.

KANTANAGAR TEMPLE While Maharaja Prannath may have received some criticism from historians over his architectural experiments at the Dinajpur Rajbari, there is no doubt that he achieved a masterpiece when he commissioned the Kantanagar Temple, completed in 1757. The structure is the best example of the 'Nava-Ratna' or 'nine-towered' Hindu construction style, found in temples all over the country. Of these examples, however, the Kantanagar Temple is the best preserved, although its towers collapsed in the earthquake of 1897.

Nevertheless, the temple is still an impressive sight for the terracotta handiwork that decorates every square inch of its façade. The themes are similar to those found on many other temples of northwest Bangladesh: there are floral and geometric motifs, as well as scenes of lovemaking tucked away in its corners.

The nearby Nayabad Mosque is another 2km from the Kantanagar Temple across some very bumpy dirt roads. You can ask your rickshaw van to pass by here on your way back out. The humble mosque was constructed for the builders of the Hindu temple.

Getting there From Dinajpur, take a Thakurgaon-bound public bus 23km north. About 7km after the turn-off to Saidpur and after a bridge crossing (15km away from Dinajpur), you'll see a village marked with giant green signs indicating the turn-off to the temple. This village is named Rampur. From here you can take a rickshaw van to the site. Some bus drivers may drop you off earlier than Rampur village if you don't ask them, which means you'll need to cross a river to get to the temple.

CDA Central Training Centre (10 rooms) Mokundupur at Rampur bus stop; ☎ 64428 (Dinajpur office). Basic but comfortable enough. Rooms have attached bath & mosquito nets. There's also easy access to Kantaji Mondir, great for spending a night out of the city & taking in the countryside atmosphere. Rickshaw vans provide local transport. $

RAMSAGAR LAKE Earning the distinction as the largest manmade water tank in Bangladesh, Ramsagar Lake is now a national park, and a wildlife refuge to many migratory bird species. The tank was constructed by Raja Ram Nath in the 18th century in an effort to alleviate drought conditions. Today there is a small resthouse on the grounds and it's a popular place for Friday picnickers from Dinajpur.

Getting there You can take a rickshaw for the 10km ride from Dinajpur, or catch a bus along the Pulhat Road. The lake is about 250m off the main road and not visible on the approach, so be clear about where you want to get off.

THAKURGAON AND PANCHAGARH *Telephone code 0561*

These two remote districts constitute the very edge of Bangladesh, with its northwestern tip protruding like a snout towards nearby Sikkim. The border is a mere 20km from Nepal, and less than 100km from the former British hill station at Darjeeling, now a world-famous destination in its own right. This region is rural Bangladesh at its most tranquil, making it perfect for quiet cycle journeys and back-road explorations; it's also incredibly scenic thanks to its numerous picturesque tea gardens. On a clear day some visitors have even reported glimpses of nearby Kangchenjunga Mountain in Sikkim, the third-highest mountain in the world.

While Thakurgaon is more of an overgrown country town, Panchagarh has attained more fame as Bangladesh's third tea-producing region, after the gardens of Sylhet and Chittagong. With its cooler climate, the region is well suited to tea production, and there are seven tea estates spread around the district.

The most well known of these gardens is the Kazi and Kazi Tea Estate, which is producing Bangladesh's first United States Department of Agriculture-certified organic tea under the Teatulia brand name (the name is a take on the nearby town of Tetulia). The company has also highlighted its social responsibility practices in that most of its employees are women (the workers on most tea plantations are women, whose hands are known to pick tea leaves more delicately than those of men), as well as several other community initiatives that benefit what is one of Bangladesh's poorest regions. Without the income from tea picking, most of these women would have no other source of income.

Tea touring aside, the region is a paradise of rural landscapes, and the least densely populated area of northwest Bangladesh. Thus, the area feels quite peaceful and secluded, or at least as secluded as you can get in flatland Bangladesh.

GETTING THERE Public bus services are available to both Thakurgaon and Panchagarh, but from Dhaka these are about the longest bus journeys you can do in the entire country. To Thakurgaon you need at least ten hours, sometimes more, and Panchagarh probably requires 11 hours (catch the bus from the Gabtali bus stand in Dhaka). So if you're in any sort of hurry or the thought of sitting on a bus for that long is off-putting, then your best bet is to fly to Saidpur and take a bus from there. Alternatively, there's an overnight train to Dinajpur and then it's a 55km journey to Thakurgaon (1.75hrs; Tk40) on good roads or a 90km journey onwards to Panchagarh (2.5hrs; Tk80). This is probably the best way to do it without having to spend loads of money. There are overnight trains both ways between Dhaka and Dinajpur (see *Dinajpur*, *Getting there and away*, *By train*, page 328, for more).

In Thakurgaon, the main bus stand is on the Dhaka–Panchagarh Highway. Look for the gaggle of buses and you've found it.

WHERE TO STAY

RDRS Thakurgaon (4 rooms) Jagannathpur; 52395, 52032; e rdrstk@tistaonline.com. The best place to stay in Thakurgaon, although it's located 3km south from the city on the Dinajpur highway. The rooms are frequently booked, so it's best if you call the Rangpur office first. $$$

Hotel Salam International (35 rooms) Chowrasta; 52246. If the RDRS is full you can try this place out. Dbls are good value with tiled bathrooms & TVs. Also has AC rooms, & friendly service. $$

Prime Hotel (32 rooms) Town Plaza, North Circular Rd; 53505. A last resort, if the other places are full. Dark rooms that don't look like they've been cleaned in a while. $$

RDRS Panchagarh (Contact RDRS Rangpur on page 319 for more information) The RDRS also maintains a guesthouse at Panchagarh but the facilities are more basic than the other guesthouses. Booking at Rangpur office is essential. $$$

BANGLABANDHA – WHEN THREE IS A CROWD

If you're looking at the map and wondering how easy it would be to hop over the border to explore Nepal, Darjeeling and Sikkim, you're not alone. For nearly ten years there has been much talk between Nepal and Bangladesh on cross-border trade, but unfortunately India has rarely been at the table.

After several rounds of talks, there was an agreement made 2002 to promote this trade route between Nepal and Bangladesh. Landlocked Nepal had wanted to benefit from the port facilities at Mongla, from which goods could transit through this remote northwestern corner of the country to the mountain kingdom. Bangladesh moved to set up customs and warehousing facilities at Banglabandha, but then India did not hold up their end of the deal (according to the Bangladeshi media reports, at least). The road from Banglabandha to Fulbari remains in poor condition and the borders are only open for two hours per day for vehicles to cross, and so Banglabandha has remained largely unused.

As for travellers, there are no confirmed reports about whether those carrying foreign passports can cross here, and as far as we can tell there are still no immigration facilities at Bangladbandha. With the border's 90km proximity to Darjeeling and 37km to the Nepalese border at Kakarbhitta, these beautiful places seem tantalisingly close but remain inaccessible from here due to a lack of border crossing facilities. Currently public buses take passengers to Siliguri via the Burimari land crossing in the Lalmonirhat District, even though travelling through here would be much more scenic.

Teatulia Kazi & Kazi Tea Estate www.teatulia.com. This international brand of organic tea maintains a guesthouse at its estate near Tetulia, & has hosted foreign interns at the estate before. Contact Teatulia for more information, the company sometimes hosts interns at the estate.

WHERE TO EAT There's some street food stalls in a grassy field at the western end of Thakurgaon's main road. At night, crowds of men stand around and take fried snacks and tea. Some vendors also sell *halim* here, which is a spicy, slow-cooked mutton and *dal* soup.

Spring Garden Chinese Restaurant 2nd Flr, Islam Plaza; 01718 170545. To the west of the *maidan* (central field for festivals/gatherings), this restaurant has recently opened. $$

Shuruchi No 2 Restaurant Bangabandhu Rd, also known as Hospital Rd. Popular with locals, this serves tandoori naan bread all day long. $

Appendix I

LANGUAGE

PRONUNCIATION Spoken Bangla is not too difficult to learn as you'll have plenty of opportunities to interact with local people, all of whom will applaud your effort to learn their language. As Bangla is very much tied to the identity of Bangladeshis you'll find that even English speakers often revert to Bangla when debating issues of the day, despite your presence. This is not meant to be offensive and represents a chance for you to brush up on your Bangla by tuning your ear to its sounds even when you don't understand.

Hundreds of English words have been transliterated into Bangla and so if you're struggling to find a word, offering the English word in its place will probably help you on your way. A few tricky aspects are covered below.

The letter 'a' can be pronounced differently depending on the word. In common words such as *agami-kal* (tomorrow), each 'a' retains the short form, as in the word 'b**a**t' or 'p**a**ss'. But in some words, like 'office', which uses the letter 'a' in its Bangla spelling, the 'a' becomes more of an 'aw' sound, as in 'aw-phish'.

There are three letters to represent the 's' sound but in the majority of cases, these are pronounced using a 'sh' sound.

With time, practice and an open ear, you'll gain a better sense of which words are pronounced in what way. The spellings below use phonetic translations, as opposed to the direct translation system that comes from written Bangla. Serious students of the language will find the following guide largely inaccurate, spelling-wise.

BASIC GRAMMAR The most difficult aspect of sentence construction is learning the 'subject–object–verb' sentence structure, as opposed to the 'subject–verb–object' structure used in English. For example, while you might say 'I drink water' in English, you would say 'I water drink' (*ami pani khay*) in Bangla. When referring to yourself, the subject is often dropped, however (ie: *pani khay*).

Verbs are heavily conjugated in Bangla, which makes them the most difficult aspect of the language to learn. For example, the verb 'eat' has many different forms depending on the person (first, second, third), tense (present, past, future), aspect (simple, perfect, progressive) and honour (intimate, familiar, formal). Taking a class to master grammar is highly suggested for long-term visits.

Particle words such as *ki* or *na* can be added to the end of sentences (with a rising tone) to denote a yes–no question. For example, *eta rasta Dhaka jabe na/ki?* literally translates as 'this road Dhaka go na?' The response should be *ji* for yes, or *na* confirming no.

Asking if something available is easy: add 'ache?' to the end of any noun. For example, *mineral pani ache?* means 'Do you have mineral water?' If the answer is positive, the response is *ache*, and if negative, *ney*.

ALPHABET Like all Sanskritic languages, the alphabet is grouped according to sound in Bangla. Most of the letters can be represented by English spellings but the variation in their pronunciations has to be learned by rote. There is also a system of consonant clusters that makes learning all the letters difficult, even for native speakers. The easiest and most practical approach to learning the language is to get a grasp on the basic consonants and then practise them as you travel around by keeping your eyes open and reading the street signs.

ESSENTIALS

Good morning	*Gud morning*	শুভ সকাল
Hello	*Assalam aleikum* (Muslim)/	আসসালামু আলাইকুম
	Nomoshkar (Hindu)	নমস্কার
See you again	*Dekha hobe*	দখো হবে
God be with you	*Allah hafez* (Islamic)/	
	Khoda hafez (non-denominal)	
My name is…	*Amar nam…*	আমার নাম
I am from…	*Amar desh…*	আমার দশে
How are you?	*Kaemon achen?* or *bhallo achen?*	কমেন আছ
I am fine	*Bhallo achi*	ভাল আছি
		ধন্যবাদ
Thank you	*Dhonnobad*	সমস্যা নাই
No problem	*Shomosha ney*	ঠকি আছে
Is everything OK?	*Thik ache?*	ঠকি আছে
It's OK	*Thik ache*	জি
yes	*ji*	না
no	*na*	বুঝি না
I don't understand	*Bhuji na*	আস্তে বলনে
Please speak more slowly	*Aste aste bolun*	বুজলনে
Do you understand?	*Bhojen?*	

QUESTIONS Questions are sometimes shortened using the word *koy* – often a catch-all phrase to ask 'where', 'how many' or 'what time'.

How?	*Kaemon?*	কমেন
What?	*Ki?*	কি
Where?	*Kothay?* or *koy?*	কোথায়
What is it?	*Eta ki?*	এটা কি
Which?	*Eta?*	এটা
When?	*Kokhon?*	কখন
Why?	*Keno?*	কনে
Who?	*Ke?*	কে
Whose?	*Kar?*	কার
How much?	*Koto?*	কত
How expensive?	*Dam koto?*	দাম কত
How much (taxi fare, rent)?	*Bhara koto?*	ভাড়া কত
How long (time)?	*Koto shomoy lagbe?*	কত সময় লাগবে

NUMBERS Numbers are pesky to learn because there are individual words for every number up to 100. Also, when discussing big numbers you'll learn to think in *lakhs* and *crores*, which are 100,000 and 10,000,000 respectively. For example, Bangladesh has over 15 *crore* population.

1	*ek*	১
2	*dooy*	২
3	*tin*	৩
4	*char*	৪
5	*pach*	৫

6	*choy*	৬
7	*shat*	৭
8	*at*	৮
9	*noi*	৯
10	*dosh*	১০
11	*egaro*	১১
12	*baro*	১২
13	*taro*	১৩
14	*chod-do*	১৪
15	*ponero*	১৫
16	*sho-lo*	১৬
17	*sha-tero*	১৬
18	*at-tero*	১৮
19	*unish*	১৯
20	*bish*	২০
21	*ekush*	২১
30	*tirish*	৩০
40	*chollish*	৪০
50	*ponchash*	৫০
60	*shayt*	৬০
70	*shottor*	৭০
80	*ashi*	৮০
90	*nobboi*	৯০
100	*ek-sho*	১০০
1,000	*ek hazar*	১০০০
2,000	*dooy hazar*	২০০০
10,000	*dosh hazar*	১০০০০
100,000	*ek lakh*	১ লাক
1,000,000	*dosh lakh*	১০ লাক
10,000,000	*crore*	১,০০,০০০,০০০

TIME To put it bluntly, Bangladeshis are not very bothered about precision when it comes to time. If you're making cross-city journeys in Dhaka, double the amount of time you think you'll need, and be prepared for successive delays when travelling owing to excessive traffic or other unforeseen delays. It pays to be patient and go with the flow – there's plenty of street life to see! A good exercise is to practise reading Bengali on signs and licence plates when you're stuck in traffic.

What time is it?	*Koyta baje?*	কয়টা বাজে
It's… am/pm	*Ta shokal/bikal* (eg: *shokal shat ta* is 07.00)	…টা সকাল/ …টা বিকাল
yesterday	*gotokal*	গতকাল
today	*ajke*	আজকে
tomorrow	*agamikal*	আগামী কাল
yesterday/tomorrow	*kalke* (must be determined from context)	কালকে
two days from today	*prosho din*	পরশু দিন
morning	*shokal*	সকাল
noon	*dupur*	দুপুর
afternoon	*bikal*	বিকাল
early evening	*shondha*	সন্ধ্যা
late evening	*rat*	রাত

Days

Sunday	*Robibar*	রবিবার
Monday	*Shombar*	সোমবার
Tuesday	*Mongolbar*	মঙ্গলবার
Wednesday	*Budhbar*	বুধবার
Thursday	*Brioshpoti bar*	বৃস্পতবিার
Friday	*Shukrobar*	শুক্রবার
Saturday	*Shonibar*	শনবিার

Months When using months (*macch* or *mash*) from the Gregorian calendar, transliterations are used. For example, January would be *january mash.*

GETTING AROUND Negotiation is essential when dealing with rickshaw wallahs and taxi/CNG drivers. Most of the time the drivers will be looking for an extra Tk10–20 from you for cross-city journeys. If you're patient you'll be able to find a driver willing to go for less.

I want to go to…	*…jabo*	যাব/ যেতে চাই
I am going to…	*…jachi*	যাচ্ছি
How much?	*Bhara koto?*	ভাড়া কত
When does it leave?	*Kokhon jaben?*	কখন যাবনে
What time is it now?	*Koyta somoy ekhon?*	কত সময় এখন
The train has been…	*train…*	
…delayed	*…deri hobe*	দেড়ি হবে
…cancelled	*…cancel hocche*	ক্যান্সেল হয়েছে
AC sleeper	*AC berth*	
sleeper	*berth*	
first	*first*	
chair seat (reserved)	*seat*	
unreserved seat	*shuvon*	
platform	*platform*	
ticket office	*tee-ket oph-ish*	টেকেট অফিসার
from	*…theke*	থেকে
to	*…jabe*	যাবে
bus station	*bus station*	বাস স্টশেন
bus counter	*bus counter*	বাস কাউন্টার
railway station	*railway station*	রেলওয়ে স্টেশন
airport	*airport*	এয়ারপোর্ট
port	*ghat*	ঘাট
bus	*bus*	বাস
train	*train*	
plane	*plane*	
boat	*nowkha*	নৌকা
overnight ferry	*launch*	লন্চ
car	*gari*	গাড়ি
taxi	*taxi*	টেক্সি
baby taxi	*CNG*	সি এন জি
minibus	*microbus*	মাইক্রোবাস
motorcycle	*honda*	হোন্ডা
bicycle	*cycle*	সাইকলে
here	*ekhane*	এখানে
there	*okhane*	ওখানে

Private transport

Is this the road to…?	*…rasta thik na?*	রাস্তা ঠিক না?
This way to…?	*…eh dike jabo?*	এই দকিে যাব?
Where is the service station?	*Filling station kothay?*	পেট্রল পাম্প কোথায়?
Please fill it up	*Full korun*	ফুল করুন
I'd like… litres	*…litres chay*	লিটার চাই
petrol/octane	*petrol/octane*	
My vehicle has a problem	*Amar gari shomosha ache*	আমার গাড়ির সমস্যা আছে

Directions

Where is…?	*…kothay?*	… কোথায়?
go straight	*shoja jan*	সোজা যান
turn left	*bam dike* or *bam-ey*	বাম দিকে / বামে
turn right	*dan dike* or *dain-ey*	ডান দিকে / ডানে
turn around	*guraguri*	ঘুড়াঘুড়ি
…at the intersection	*mor…*	মোড়
behind	*pichon*	পছিন
in front of	*samne*	সামনে
near	*kache*	কাছে
far	*dure*	দূরে

Street signs

entrance	*prabesh*	প্রবশে
exit	*bahir*	নগিমন
toilet	*toilet*	পায়খানা
men	*purush*	পুরুষ
women	*mohila*	মহিলা

ACCOMMODATION In rural towns and villages, restaurants and accommodation are both called 'hotels'. An *oboshik hotel* designates a 'residential' hotel and has rooms to sleep in.

residential hotel	*hotel (abashik)*	হোটেল (আবাসকি)
Where is a good hotel?	*Bhallo thaka hotel kothay?*	ভাল ঠাকা হোটেল কোথায়
Where is a cheap hotel?	*Com dami thaka hotel kohtay?*	কম দামের ঠাকা হোটেল কোথায়
Could you write the address?	*Theekana likha den?*	ঠিকানা লিখতে ডেন?
Do you have rooms?	*Rooms ache?*	রুম আছে
I'd like…	*…dorkar*	…দরকার
…a single room	*single room…*	সিঙ্গল রুম
…a double room	*double room…*	ডবল রুম
…a room with two beds	*dooy-ta bed room…*	দুইটা বডে আছে
Where is the toilet?	*Toilet kothay?*	টয়লেট কোথায়
Where is the bathroom?	*Paikhana kothay?*	পায়খানা কোথায়
Is there hot water?	*Gorom pani pawa jay?*	গরম পানি পাওয়া যায়
Is there electricity?	*Current pawa jay?*	বিদ্যুত পাওয়া যায়
Is breakfast included?	*Bhara shate ki sokale nasta ache?*	সকাল নাস্তার খরচসহ কি না
I am leaving today	*Ajke checkout korbo*	আজ চলে যাব

USEFUL PHRASES

I am vegetarian	*Ami mangsho khabo na/ Ami shudhu shobji khabo*	আমি মাংশ খাই না
Do you have an English menu?	*Ingrajite menu ache?*	ইংরেজিতে মনেূ্য আছে
I do not eat beef/fish	*Ami gorur mangsho/ Mach khabo na*	আমি মাংশা / মাছ খাব না

I can't eat…	*Ami …khete pari na*	আমি খেতে পারি না
…spicy food	*jhal khabar…*	ঝাল খাবার
…Cilantro	*dunia patta…*	ধনিয়া পাতা
…fish	*mach…*	মাছ
…meat	*mangsho…*	মাংশ
Delicious!	*khub moja!*	খুব মজা
What's in this dish?	*Eta vetore ki ache?*	এটার ভিতরে কি আছে
No more, please	*Aro na, dhonnobad*	আর না ধন্যবাদ
Bill please	*Bill, please*	বিল প্লিজ

HANDY WORDS

rice	*bhat*	ভাত
spoon	*chamoch*	চামচ
knife	*churi*	ছুরি
glass	*glas*	গ্লাস
fork	*kata*	কাটা
lemon	*lebu*	লেবু
salt	*lebon*	লবণ
water	*pani*	পানি
tea	*cha*	চা
less sugar tea	*cha chini com*	চায়ে চিনি কম
sugar-free tea	*cha chini chara*	চা চিনি ছাড়া
bottled water	*mineral/bottle pani*	মিনারেল পানি
bread	*ruti*	রুটি

MENU ITEMS

Breakfast

tandoori naan	*naan*	নান
fried flatbread	*parata*	পরোটা
thick dal	*boot dal*	ঘন ডাল
spicy omelette	*momelette*	মামলেট
fried egg	*dim*	ডিম

Snacks

mashed lentils	*piaju*	পেয়াজু
battered eggplant	*beguni*	বেগুনি
chickpeas	*chana*	চানা
chaat and peanuts	*chanachur*	চানাচুর
chickpea snack with onions, spices	*chatpoti*	চটপটি
potato and chickpea in *puri* shells	*phuchka*	ফুচকা
spicy puffed rice	*jhal muri*	ঝালমুড়ি
rolled flatbread with egg, spices	*mughlai parata*	মোঘলাই পরোটা
deep-fried bread stuffed with *dal*	*puri*	পুরি
steam rice cakes (winter only)	*pita*	পিঠা

Main meals

rice with slow-cooked meat	*biriyani*	বিরিয়ানি
rice with meat and spices	*kachchi biriyani or tehari*	কাচ্চি / তেহারি
rice with lentils and meat	*khichuri*	খিচুরি

lentil soup	*dal*	ডাল
mashed eggplant/potato	*begun/aloo bharta*	বেগুন / আলু ভরতা
double-onion with chicken/egg	*murgi/dim dopiaza*	মুরগী / ডিম দো পয়োজা
beef kebab	*beef shik kebab*	বিফ শিক কাবাব
hilsa curry fish (national fish, bony)	*hilsha mach*	ইলিশ মাছ
rui fish	*rui mach*	রুই মাছ
yoghurt curry	*korma*	কোরমা
meat curry, served with potato	*kalia*	কালিয়া
rice cooked with ghee (butter)	*pulao*	পোলাও
spicy meat curry	*jhal fraizee*	ঝাল ফ্রাই
prawn	*chingri mach*	চিংড়ি মাছ

Dessert

dough balls in milk	*rosh malai*	রস মালাই
dough balls in sweet syrup	*rosh golla*	রসগোল্লা
rice pudding	*payesh/fini*	পায়েশ / ফিরনি
vermicelli in sweet milk	*shemmai*	শেমাই
sweet milk cake	*shondesh*	সন্দেশ
rice molasses pudding	*kheer*	ক্ষীর
vegetable dessert (plain, carrot, etc)	*halua*	হালুয়া
sweet yoghurt	*mishti dui*	

Fruit

banana	*kola*	কলা
jackfruit	*kathal*	কাঠাল
mango	*am*	আম
dates	*kejur*	খেজুর
lychee	*lichu*	লিচু
papaya	*papaya*	পেপে
coconut	*narikel*	নারকেল
guava	*payara*	পেয়ারা
blackberry	*kalajam*	কালজাম
grapefruit	*jambura*	জাম্বুরা
indian apple	*bel*	বেল
wood apple	*kathbel*	কতবেল
custard apple	*ata*	আতা
indian jujube	*boroi*	বড়ই
starfruit	*kamranga*	কামরাঙ্গা
pineapple	*anarosh*	আনারস
watermelon	*tarmuj*	তরমুজ
lemon	*lebu*	লেবু

Vegetables

potato	*aloo*	আলু
eggplant	*begun*	বেগুন
carrot	*gajor*	গাজর
tomato	*tomato*	টমেটো
okra	*dherosh*	ঢেরস
cucumber	*shosha*	শসা
onion	*piaj*	পয়োজ
cauliflower	*phulcopi*	ফুলকপি

spinach (red/green)	*lal/shobuj shak*	লাল/ সবুজ শাক
long beans	*barboti*	বরবটি
pumpkin	*kumra*	কুমড়া

Spices/flavourings

chilli	*lonka*	মরিচ
cinnamon	*darcini*	দারুচিনি
cloves	*lobongo*	লথ লমঙ্গ
garlic	*rosun*	রসুন
ginger	*ada*	আদা
mustard	*sorshe*	শর্ষে
salt	*lebon*	লবণ
sugar	*cini*	চিনি
turmeric	*holud*	হলুদ
cumin	*zira*	জিরা

Dairy

butter	*makhon*	মাখন
cheese	*poneer*	পনির
milk	*dudh*	দুধ
yoghurt	*doy*	দই

SHOPPING

I'd like to buy…	*…kinbo*	কিনবো
I don't like it	*…bhalo lage na*	ভাল লাগে না
I'm just looking	*Dekhi dekhi*	দেখি দেখি
It's too expensive	*Dam beshi*	দাম বেশি
I'll take it	*Kinbo*	কিনবো
Please may I have…?	*…ache?*	আছে
Do you accept…?	*…paren?*	পারনে
credit cards	*credit card*	ক্রেডিট কার্ড
travellers' cheques	*travellers' cheques* (usually at banks or five-star hotels)	
more	*aro den*	আর দেন
less	*com den*	কম দেন
a little bit	*kichu*	কিছু
smaller	*kichu choddo*	কিছু ছোট
bigger	*kichu boro*	কিছু বড়

EMERGENCY

Help!	*Shahajjo korun!*	সাহায্য করুন
Call a doctor!	*Doctor lagbe!*	ডাক্তার লাগবে
There's been an accident	*Gari accident hoyche (vehicle)*	এটা জরুরী
I'm lost	*Ami hata korchi, harano korchi*	আমি হাড়িয়ে গেছি
Go away!	*Jao!*	যাও
police	*pulish*	পুলিশ
fire	*agun*	আগুন
ambulance	*ambulance*	
thief	*chor!*	চোর
hospital	*hosh-pital*	হসপিটাল

HEALTH

diarrhoea	*patla paikhana* ('*diarrhoea*' also common)	ডাইরয়িা
nausea	*bomi bomi lagche*	বমি বমি লাগছে
doctor	*doc-tar*	ডাক্তার
prescription	*prescription*	প্রেস্কিপশন
pharmacy	*oshodh-er dokan*	ফার্মেসি
paracetamol	*paracetamol*	প্যারাসিটামল
painkiller	*betha oshodh*	ব্যাথার অসুধ
antibiotics	*antibiotics*	এন্টিবায়টিক
antiseptic	*bijaborak*	বিজারক
condoms	*condom*	কনডম
I am…	*Amar… achi*	আমার … আছে
…asthmatic	*shash kosto…*	
…epileptic	*mirki rog…*	
…diabetic	*diabetic…*	
I'm allergic to…		
…penicillin	*Penicillin amar shojho hoy na*	
…nuts	*Badam khele amar allergy hoy*	
…bees	*Momachee khamraley amar allergy hoy*	

TRAVEL WITH CHILDREN

Is there a…?	*…ache?*
…baby changing room?	*baccha room…?*
…children's menu?	*baccha khabar maynoo…?*
nappies	*buti*

OTHER Intimate forms are usually reserved for less formal situations like within family or towards children. However these should not be used towards those with superior social status.

I	*ami*	আমি
my/mine	*amar*	আমার
me	*amake* (eg: 'give it to me' is *amake den*)	আমাকে
we	*amra*	আমরা
ours	*amrader*	আমাদরে
you (singular)/you (plural)	*apni/apnara*	আপনি
yours (singular)/yours (plural)	*apnar/apnader*	আপনার/ আপনাদের
to you	*apnake*	আপনাকে
you (intimate)	*tumi*	তুমি
yours (intimate)	*tomar*	তোমার
to you (intimate)	*tomake*	তোমাকে
and	*o* (eg: *dim o ruti* or 'egg and bread')	এবং
some	*kichu*	কিছু
a little bit	*opul*	অল্প
but	*kintu*	কিন্তু
this/that	*eta/ota*	এইটা / এটা
these/those	*egulo/ogulo*	এগুলো / ওগুলো
expensive	*dam beshi*	বেশি দাম
cheap	*dam com*	কম দাম

beautiful/ugly	*shundor/ashundor, bishri*	সুন্‌দর
old/new	*puran/nuton*	পুরাতন / পুরান - নতুন
good/bad	*bhalo/kharap*	ভাল / খারাপ
hot/cold	*gorom/thanda*	গরম / ঠান্‌ডা
easy/hard	*khibabe/koshto*	
boring/interesting	*khub boring/khub interesting*	

Appendix 2

FURTHER INFORMATION

BOOKS

Fiction

Anam, Thamima *The Golden Age* HarperCollins, 2007. Anam's debut novel takes readers directly into a personal story of the Liberation War, told from the view of Rehana Haque. The novel reveals the young widow's attempts at a normal domestic life amidst the chaos and murder of the Liberation War.

Das, Jibananda *Selected Poems with an Introduction, Chronology, and Glossary* (translated by Fakrul Alam) University Press Limited, 1999. Largely acknowledged to be one of the best Bengali poets of the late 20th century, well after his death. Das's poems received more attention because of their post-modernistic qualities, making him a scribe well ahead of his time.

Ghosh, Amitav *The Hungry Tide* HarperCollins, 2005. A novel depicting the natural and human hazards inhabiting the Indian Sundarbans, told through the eyes of a passionate dolphin researcher. A good read for the lazy afternoons spent cruising through the forest.

Nasreen, Taslima *Shame* Penguin Books, 1997. As a fictional account with a factual underpinning, this novel depicts the history surrounding the destruction of Babri Masjid in Uttar Pradesh through the eyes of a Hindu family in Bangladesh. The event had repercussions around south Asia, including the targeting of Hindus inside Bangladesh. The book garnered Nasreen a religious fatwah declaring she should be murdered and she very nearly was on several occasions during speaking engagements. She currently lives in exile in Paris.

Roberts, David Gregory *Shantaram* Scribe Publications, 2003. A hefty chronicle of 'fictional' criminal Lindsay Ford, a heroin addict turned bank robber who escapes from an Australian prison to Mumbai. While no part of the novel takes place in Bangladesh, Ford spends a portion of the novel living in a slum and serving as its doctor, mirroring Roberts's own experiences in India's commercial capital.

Rushdie, Salman *Midnight's Children* Jonathan Cape, 1981. In his typical frenetic voice, Rushdie describes the tumultuous periods following partition through the eyes of its protagonist, Saleem Sinai. The book has a component covering the Liberation War.

Tagore, Rabindranath (author); Radice, William (ed & trans) *Selected Poems* Penguin Classics, 2005. Most of Tagore's work has yet to be translated into English but thanks to the tireless efforts of William Radice, this book of Tagore's poetry can be enjoyed by the English-speaking world.

Tagore, Rabindranath (author); Radice, William (trans & contributor) *Selected Short Stories* Penguin Classics, 2005. An excellent grouping of Tagore's most profound and humanistic short stories, forming part of the work that helped earn him the Nobel Prize in Literature in 1913 (he won it primarily for *Gitanjali*, a book of his most famous poems).

Non-fiction Most of the following titles, save for Dr Mohammad Yunus's books, are hard to find although most are available on Amazon.co.uk. Folk International and Words and Pages maintains the best collection of relevant titles in Gulshan, although the Bookworm, near the old airport, does yield a few gems. If you want to dig deeper, visit the collection of the University Press Limited in Motijheel or the bookstores at New Market.

Baxter, Craig *Bangladesh: From a Nation to State* Westview Press, 1998.

Bornstein, David *The Price of a Dream: The Story of the Grameen Bank* Oxford University Press, USA 2005. Canadian journalist, David Bornstein, takes a critical and balanced look at the Grameen Bank and its operations, including interviews with Dr Yunus, bank employees and, most importantly, the borrowers themselves. Originally published in 1996.

Denzau G & H and Fahrni Mansur E & R *Living with Tides and Tigers*, 2009. A collection of amazing photographs from the Sundarban forest compiled with interesting background information and personal insights. The perfect souvenir.

Fahrni Mansur, Elisabeth & Rubaiyat *Sundarban: A Basic Field Guide*. The only guidebook available for Sundarban – illustrated and user-friendly. Only available at the Guide Tours offices or aboard their vessels.

Gardner, Katy *Songs from the River's Edge* Pluto Press, 1997.

Hartmann, Betsy & Boyce, James K *A Quiet Violence: View from a Bangladesh Village* Food First, 1985. Distinctly hard to find in Bangladesh, but a worthwhile read for its direct insights into village culture in post-war Bangladesh.

Inskipp, Carol, Grimmett, Richard & Inskipp, Tim *Pocket Guide to the Birds of the Indian Subcontinent* Christopher Helm 1998. A useful field guide to local birds.

Novak, James *Reflections on the Water* University Press Limited and Indiana Press Limited, 1993. One of the most passionate accounts written on the history, birth and childhood of Bengal and Bangladesh. Novak was a correspondent based in Dhaka for several years during the 1980s. A must-read for any visitor to Bangladesh.

Sen, Sudeep & Lynch, Tanvir & Kelley *Postcards from Bangladesh* University Press Limited, 2002. A lovingly crafted photography book and one of the best available on Bangladesh.

Van Schendel, William *The Bengal Borderland: Beyond State and Nation in South Asia* Anthem Press, 2005.

Yunus, Mohammad *Banker to the Poor* Grameen Bank, 2003. Dr Yunus's autobiography, including the history behind the founding of Grameen Bank. Available for purchase at Grameen Bank from their library.

Yunus, Mohammad *Creating a World Without Poverty: Social Business and the Future of Capitalism* Grameen Bank, 2008. Dr Yunus's inspirational post-Nobel Prize book, where he details the potential of a new economic model that supports community development.

Language

Radice, William *Teach Yourself Bengali*, 2003. This is the best self-instruction book for speaking, reading and writing Bengali, although it is a little advanced for casual learners and is focused on Kolkata Bangla.

Otherwise, Dhaka bookstores or Bishaud Bangla in Chittagong stock plenty of entry-level guides or you may be able to find an old copy of Lonely Planet's *Bengali Phrasebook* lying about, which is the best practical pocket guide available, although it focuses on Kolkata Bangla as opposed to Bangladeshi Bangla.

Health

Wilson-Howarth, Dr Jane, *Bugs, Bites & Bowels* Cadogan, 2006.

Wilson-Howarth, Dr Jane, & Ellis, Dr Matthew *Your Child Abroad: A Travel Health Guide* Bradt Travel Guides, 2005

FILMS

Apu Trilogy Directed by Satyajit Ray, 1955–59. *The Apu Trilogy* is three films that form one of the most famous works of Calcutta director Satyajit Ray. *Pather Panchali* (Song Of The

Little Road), *Aparajito* (The Unvanquished) and *Apur Sansar* (The World of Apu), trace the life of Apu, a young Bengali, during the early part of the 20th century.

Bostrobalikara: The Garment Girls of Bangladesh Directed by Tanvir Mokammel, 2007. A compelling inside look at two million people – mostly women – powering Bangladesh's burgeoning garment industry.

Concert for Bangladesh Film released 1972. Footage from George Harrison's 1 August 1971 benefit concerts that raised money for the refugees of the Liberation War.

My Architect, A Son's Journey Directed by Nathaniel Khan, 2003. Documentary detailing Nathaniel Khan's search for the soul of his late father, legendary architect Louis Khan. Includes some very rare footage of the inside of Bangladesh's stunning National Assembly Building.

Ganges Created by the BBC Natural History Unit, originally aired 2007. A fantastically filmed documentary on the natural and cultural significance of the Ganges river system, whose third component features footage from the Bangladeshi Sundarban.

Songs of Freedom (Muktir Gaan) Directed by Tareque Masud and Catherine Masud, 1995. A documentary compiling the war footage of American filmmaker, Lear Levin, who followed a musical troupe who sang songs of inspiration during the 1971 Liberation War.

Swamp Tiger: Natural Killers. A 2001 video documentary detailing Mike Herd's difficulties filming tigers in their natural habitat. Excellent tiger footage.

Teardrops of Karnaphuli (Karnaphulir Kanna) Directed by Tanvir Mokammel, 2005. A documentary account of the effects of the Chittagong Hill Tracts' Kaptai Dam. Provides great insight into the guerrilla insurgency that plagued the region until the 1997 peace treaty. (*www.teardropsofkarnaphuli.com*; *www.tanvirmokammel.com*)

The Clay Bird (Matir Moyna) Directed by Tareque Masud, 2002. A film capturing the director's own experiences growing up in a *madrasa* during the turbulent pre-Liberation War period. Highly recommended viewing.

The Journey (Ontarjatra) Directed by Tareque Masud, 2006. A simply filmed homecoming journey taken by a divorced mother and her son to their native Sylhet home to pay their last respects to the husband and father.

Tiger Hounds. BBC documentary investigating the human–tiger conflict and possible solutions.

WEBSITES A continuously updated archive of links is available at the book's sister websites, www.bangladeshtraveller.com. Please head there and check out our links plus a wealth of other resources related to travel in Bangladesh.

www.chapai.net Chapai Nawabganj tourism website run by some industrious web programers. Contact information is available on the site if you need to look up a local tour guide.

www.pabna.net (*Ground Fl, Anando Public Library, Abdul Hamid Rd;* **e** *pabnadotnet@hotmail.com*) Offers one of the most extensively researched destination websites ever discovered in Bangladesh. Browsing the site feels like an online tour of Pabna. Although it's not that easy to navigate it has lots of information.

Bradt Travel Guides

www.bradtguides.com

Africa

Africa Overland £16.99
Algeria £15.99
Benin £14.99
Botswana: Okavango, Chobe, Northern Kalahari £15.99
Burkina Faso £14.99
Cameroon £15.99
Cape Verde Islands £14.99
Congo £15.99
Eritrea £15.99
Ethiopia £16.99
Gambia, The £13.99
Ghana £15.99
Johannesburg £6.99
Madagascar £15.99
Malawi £13.99
Mali £14.99
Mauritius, Rodrigues & Réunion £13.99
Mozambique £13.99
Namibia £15.99
Niger £14.99
Nigeria £17.99
North Africa: Roman Coast £15.99
Rwanda £14.99
São Tomé & Principe £14.99
Seychelles £14.99
Sierra Leone £16.99
Sudan £13.95
Tanzania, Northern £14.99
Tanzania £17.99
Uganda £15.99
Zambia £17.99
Zanzibar £14.99

Britain and Europe

Albania £15.99
Armenia, Nagorno Karabagh £14.99
Azores £13.99
Baltic Cities £14.99
Belarus £14.99
Belgrade £6.99
Bosnia & Herzegovina £13.99
Bratislava £9.99
Budapest £9.99
Bulgaria £13.99
Cork £6.99
Croatia £13.99
Cyprus see North Cyprus
Czech Republic £13.99
Dresden £7.99
Dubrovnik £6.99
Estonia £13.99
Faroe Islands £15.99
Georgia £14.99
Helsinki £7.99
Hungary £14.99
Iceland £14.99
Kosovo £14.99
Lapland £13.99
Latvia £13.99
Lille £6.99
Lithuania £14.99
Ljubljana £7.99
Luxembourg £13.99
Macedonia £14.99
Montenegro £14.99
North Cyprus £12.99
Paris, Lille & Brussels £11.95
Riga £6.99
Serbia £14.99
Slovakia £14.99
Slovenia £13.99
Spitsbergen £16.99
Switzerland Without a Car £14.99
Tallinn £6.99
Transylvania £14.99
Ukraine £14.99
Vilnius £6.99
Zagreb £6.99

Middle East, Asia and Australasia

Borneo £17.99
China: Yunnan Province £13.99
Great Wall of China £13.99
Iran £15.99
Iraq: Then & Now £15.99
Israel £15.99
Kazakhstan £15.99
Kyrgyzstan £15.99
Maldives £15.99
Mongolia £16.99
North Korea £14.99
Oman £13.99
Shangri-La: A Travel Guide to the Himalayan Dream £14.99
Sri Lanka £15.99
Syria £14.99
Tibet £13.99
Turkmenistan £14.99
Yemen £14.99

The Americas and the Caribbean

Amazon, The £14.99
Argentina £15.99
Bolivia £14.99
Cayman Islands £14.99
Chile £16.95
Colombia £16.99
Costa Rica £13.99
Dominica £14.99
Falkland Islands £13.95
Grenada, Carriacou & Petite Martinique £14.99
Guyana £14.99
Panama £13.95
Peru & Bolivia: The Bradt Trekking Guide £12.95
St Helena £14.99
Turks & Caicos Islands £14.99
USA by Rail £14.99

Wildlife

100 Animals to See Before They Die £16.99
Antarctica: Guide to the Wildlife £15.99
Arctic: Guide to the Wildlife £15.99
Central & Eastern European Wildlife £15.99
Chinese Wildlife £16.99
East African Wildlife £19.99
Galápagos Wildlife £15.99
Madagascar Wildlife £16.99
New Zealand Wildlife £14.99
North Atlantic Wildlife £16.99
Peruvian Wildlife £15.99
Southern African Wildlife £18.95
Sri Lankan Wildlife £15.99
Wildlife and Conservation Volunteering: The Complete Guide £13.99

Eccentric Guides

Eccentric Australia £12.99
Eccentric Britain £13.99
Eccentric California £13.99
Eccentric Cambridge £6.99
Eccentric Edinburgh £5.95
Eccentric France £12.95
Eccentric London £13.99

Others

Your Child Abroad: A Travel Health Guide £10.95
Something Different for the Weekend £9.99
Britain from the Rails £17.99

WIN £100 CASH!

READER QUESTIONNAIRE

Send in your completed questionnaire for the chance to win £100 cash in our regular draw

All respondents may order a Bradt guide at half the UK retail price – please complete the order form overleaf.

(Entries may be posted or faxed to us, or scanned and emailed.)

We are interested in getting feedback from our readers to help us plan future Bradt guides. Please answer ALL the questions below and return the form to us in order to qualify for an entry in our regular draw.

Have you used any other Bradt guides? If so, which titles? ....

....

What other publishers' travel guides do you use regularly? ....

....

Where did you buy this guidebook? ....

What was the main purpose of your trip to Bangladesh (or for what other reason did you read our guide)? eg: holiday/business/charity etc. ....

....

What other destinations would you like to see covered by a Bradt guide?

....

Would you like to receive our catalogue/newsletters?

YES / NO (If yes, please complete details on reverse)

If yes – by post or email? ....

Age (circle relevant category) 16–25 26–45 46–60 60+

Male/Female (delete as appropriate)

Home country ....

Please send us any comments about our guide to Bangladesh or other Bradt Travel Guides. ....

....

....

....

Bradt Travel Guides

23 High Street, Chalfont St Peter, Bucks SL9 9QE, UK

+44 (0)1753 893444 **f** +44 (0)1753 892333

e info@bradtguides.com

www.bradtguides.com

CLAIM YOUR HALF-PRICE BRADT GUIDE!

Order Form

To order your half-price copy of a Bradt guide, and to enter our prize draw to win £100 (see overleaf), please fill in the order form below, complete the questionnaire overleaf, and send it to Bradt Travel Guides by post, fax or email.

Please send me one copy of the following guide at half the UK retail price

Title		*Retail price*	*Half price*
...	....	....	....

Please send the following additional guides at full UK retail price

No	*Title*	*Retail price*	*Total*
...	....	....	....
...	....	....	....
...	....	....	....

Sub total ....
Post & packing ....
(£2 per book UK; £4 per book Europe; £6 per book rest of world)
Total ....

Name ....

Address..

Tel .... Email ....

☐ I enclose a cheque for £........ made payable to Bradt Travel Guides Ltd

☐ I would like to pay by credit card. Number: ....

Expiry date: .../... 3-digit security code (on reverse of card) .....

Issue no (debit cards only) .....

☐ Please add my name to your catalogue mailing list.

☐ I would be happy for you to use my name and comments in Bradt marketing material.

Send your order on this form, with the completed questionnaire, to:

Bradt Travel Guides BANG1
23 High Street, Chalfont St Peter, Bucks SL9 9QE
+44 (0)1753 893444 **f** +44 (0)1753 892333
e info@bradtguides.com www.bradtguides.com

Index

Entries in bold indicate main entries; those in *italics* indicate maps